Re-membering
Osir

Aankh Benu

For information contact; address www.Henensu.com

Book and Cover design by Aankh Benu and Tahir RBG

ISBN-13: 978-1512181395
ISBN-10: 1512181390

First Edition: November 2015

Dedication

To nTr (The Creator), the Jertiyu (Ancestors), Hamat Nisut Warit (H.N.W.) Meri Netert Skhrrennut Benu, (H.N.W.) Warit Rekhiyit Benu, Nisu sit (Princess) Khemhlring Benu, Nisu sit Waniset Shukara Benu, my Mother and Father, the Henensu family, Repat Nation, Afrikan People around the world. Let us Re-member!

CONTENTS

Table of Contents

Acknowledgements

I would like to give a special thanks to all of those great scholars, some of whom are now Ancestors, that paved the way for those of us today that are reclaiming the Kemetic Culture, Afrikan Culture, and Black Pride in general. I want to thank Cheik Anta Diop, George G.M. James, John G Jackson, Dr. John Henrik Clarke, Ankh Mi Ra, Yosef Ben-Jochannan, Ashra and Merira Kwesi, Ra Un Nefer Amen I and the Ausar Auset Society International, Muata Ashby, Queen Afua and Baba Heru Semahj Smai Tawi and Shrine of Ptah, Dr. Phil and Nalani Valentine, Dr. Rkhty Amen, Dr. Denise Martin, Dr. Mfundishi Akeweya Nicobi Tirhaka Bey and Priestess Neferu and the Ancient Kemetic Culture Institute. Baba Koleoso Karade, Sa Neter and the House of Konsciousness, PerAnkh Khamniversity, Prof. James Smalls, Mfundishi Jhutyms Ka n Heru Hassan K. Salim, Asar Imhotep, Wudjau Iry-Maat, Kwesi Ra Nehem Pitah Akhan and Afuraka Afruraikait, Ta Nefer Ankh, Olabisi Olakolade and Pa Nkwasum, Ajose Afrikan, Kamali Academy, Black Star Café, Community Book Center, The Nile Garden Bookstore.

Foreword

<u>Subik</u>: *See the book...be ready to be baptized into a new way of thinking...(chuckling) you thought I would say more?(short pause, still chuckling) needless to say, this journey is a much anticipated one.*

<u>Anpu</u>: *I was there at the birthing house; the dawn of the new era. No ways! No ways! Do you know where to look for the markers of you forefathers? Do you? It has been told that centuries ago the people here were lost, never before has it been said otherwise. Drain the water that the treasures might be revealed. Scores of fortune!*

If you take anything away, remember this: we must not forget to claim our heritage. It is the blood, the life force that collects in our bowels; that which I drain in the process of purifying. But it is that which animates the lifeless. Give it (directed at Aankh Benu)!

<u>Tehuti</u>: *It's been a while. I went nowhere... I assume you are in need. Tarry not! There are those who see, and those who ignore. Count yourself as a seer. Listen...listen and you will know it is for the best.*

They tried to forget...to wipe us out. Yet, we are intrinsic. Carry us...carry us

Introduction

Dismember: to cut or tear (a body) into pieces; to separate (something) into smaller parts; to cut off or disjoin the limbs, members, or parts of...

~Merriam Webster's Dictionary~

When contemplating the condition of Afrikan people worldwide (Continental and Diasporian), I can think of no more accurate a term to describe our circumstances and plight, than the above term and it's definition. Due to the history of oppression, slavery, colonialism, neo-colonialism and cultural imperialism, Afrikan people worldwide have been dismembered, in many instances in the most literal and gruesome sense of the word.

Afrikan people, due to the above realities of history and present, have been, and are torn from our roots, heritage, cultural and spiritual traditions, land and language (especially Diasporian Afrikans), worldview, and Afrikan Identity. Because we have been largely cut off, we as Afrikan people have been further dismembered, as a people divided against ourselves, separated by tribe, ethnicity, skin tone, and worst case scenario, the language and religion of the same oppressors that put us into the condition we are in, causing us to see one another as the enemy.

However, maybe even far more grave a consequence, due to our being torn from the greater body of the Afrikan Roots , our being torn away from our spiritual traditions and worldview and subsequent adoption of the slave master's and colonizers religions and perspectives, have lead to our being cut off from our source of power, which for Afrikan people, lies in our connection and harmony with All, Self, our understanding of the order of the universe and our place within it, our reciprocal relationship with the spiritual forces that make up and govern the universe, and our Ancestors. By far the last consequence is the most devastating, as our very sense of being, and by extension agency, the ability to define ourselves and chart the course of our destiny has been lost. We are a dismembered people.

One may say, "Well, if we are dismembered, why don't we just put ourselves back together? Why don't we simply Re-member?" That is an excellent question, and idea. However, if it were that simple we would've done it by now as many Great thinkers, teachers, and leaders have come heralding (correctly) black unity as the order of the day, yet it never seemed to quite catch. Why? Well to address this issue, we as Afrikan people would first have to understand it from an Afrikan perspective, and tackle it with an Afrikan approach.

From an Afrikan perspective, all external circumstances are reflections of internal circumstances, conditions of internal or spiritual realities. Looking at our situation from and Afrikan "angle," we would hold the last consequence mentioned a few paragraphs

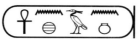

above as the most detrimental of our problem, because it is the deepest, speaking to our internal condition. However, addressing the last issue, the issue of our spirituality, is also the solution for all of the above mentioned issues. For us, everything flows from within, from the spirit and or Spiritual Realm. Therefore, before we as Afrikan people can "Re-member" or Unify and "concentrate our collective power as a people, we must first "Remember," that is recall to memory/mind the ideas that were at the very root of our Afrikan Identity and Wholeness in the first place, while disregarding all other/contrary ideas. We must "Remember," before we can Re-member."

Our great Ancestor and Scholar Dr. Cheik Anta Diop, who was a major advocate of a "Re-membered," or unified Afrika, held the idea that a unified Afrika would become a reality once it is realized that Afrika already shares a unified Afrikan Culture, with Ancient Kmt (Egypt) as its common Ancestor for this Afrikan Culture. In his monumental work **The African Origins of Civilization: Myth or Reality**, Dr. Diop states:

> *Ancient Egypt was a Negro civilization. The history of Black Africa will remain suspended in the air and cannot be written correctly until African historians dare to connect it with the History of Egypt. In particular, the study of languages, institutions, and so forth, cannot be treated properly; in a word, it will be impossible to build African humanities, a body of African human sciences, so long as that relationship does not appear legitimate...The ancient Egyptians were Negroes. The moral fruit of their civilization is to be counted among the assets of the Black world...to become conscious of that fact is perhaps the first step toward a genuine retrieval of himself; without it, intellectual sterility is the general rule, or else the creations bear I know not what imprint of the subhuman.*

In short, Dr. Diop held the view that there is no legitimate Afrikan history (and culture) disconnected from Black Afrikan Kmt or Egypt, and without this connection being made we degenerate to an uncivilized or "subhuman" way of being. I am in complete agreement with Dr. Diop's point, but would also add the following point: It is not enough to simply realize that Egypt was a Black, African nation and hold it as a bragging chip, or trophy of which we can be proud of, as many of our people currently have done, nor is it enough for us to study the history, politics, social structure, etc. We must bring ourselves to understand Kmt, what made her great, the ideas that were the very threads and glue of the society, and elicit the Afrikan genius that went on to build that great civilization. And after any careful study of Kmt, one will quickly realize that the spiritual culture and tradition was that glue, that "thread" that was interwoven throughout every single aspect of the culture and society.

Yes we must bring ourselves to understand Kmt spirituality. But even more so than this, we must reclaim it as our own and live it. We must put it to use as our Ancestors did before us.

We must learn how our Kemetic ancestors viewed the world, the universe, their relationship to and place in it; how they approached life, how they understood the order and organization of reality, the spirit realm, and how to harmonize with it all to create the conditions of harmony and prosperity in their life and land. This is the purpose of this particular work.

The title of this work "Re-membering Osir," is a reference to the story of the great nTr or deity Osir. According to tradition, it was Osir that brought civilization to Kmt. His brother became jealous of him and murdered him, dismembered him, and usurped his throne. As it will be touched on later in this work, the story of Osir bears striking "prophetic" resemblance to the historical happenings of Afrikan peoples as Originators of civilization, that have been struck a cultural and spiritual death blow, dismembered on every level, including geographically (Osir's members were spread across the earth), and those that have played the greatest part placing us in this condition (the Western/European Nations) have usurped the position of power in the world that we once held. However, like in the case of Osir, that is not where the story ends.

We won't go through the entire story here, as there is an entire

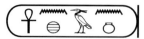

rendering of the story to follow shortly after this introduction. However, like Osir's family, wives and sons put him back together again and reclaimed his throne, we must put our culture back together again, and reclaim our legacy as heirs to this tradition.

In fact just as we are in need to be "Re-membered" So is the the nKmt (Kemetic) tradition. The work of reclaiming and restoring this tradition is one of "reconstruction." However, in order to properly carry out this work, Kemet must be interpreted solely through the eyes of Afrikan people, in the greater context of Afrika and it's spiritual traditions (including modern traditions such as Ifa, Vodou, Akan, which are children of Kmt), and most importantly through the eyes of the nKmt people, as ultimately they are the ultimate authority on their culture and tradition. In order to do this, one must study the language "mdw nTr," and the texts; historical, biographical, political, judicial, and spiritual/sacred. This is most important.

It should be understood that the type of reconstruction that I am speaking of here, is not related to what is called "Kemetic Reconstructionism" today, which has been started by European People (and their descendants), and is a Neo Paganism movement to revive this ancient tradition. Such attempts on their parts are futile as it is wholly impossible for them to comprehend or interpret an Afrikan tradition correctly, let along bear witness to the fact that it was an Afrikan civilization, which they have no connection to outside of the conquering of Kmt by their barbaric ancestors. Therefore they are both intellectually unequipped and spiritually disconnected and therefore unable to reconstruct this tradition.

Just like in anything else, it would be foolish to follow them and their so-called "orthodoxy." Also, all other European misinterpretations of the nKmt spiritual sciences must be discarded, be it western freemasonry, hermeticism, rosicrucianism, kabbalah, etc. We must follow our ancestors!

Also, it should be understood that by reconstruction I am also not referring to the various popular syncretisms that have been attempted as methods of "reconstructing" the tradition. This goes once again for the Kabbalah (and Tree of Life), Taoism, Tantra, Vedic, Hinduism, Yoga etc. While argument can and has been made in regards to the Afrikan Origins of the aforementioned traditions, whether they were Afrikan and or even Kemetic at one time, they are not anymore. We also don't have time to follow behind East Asian people, as they are also placing themselves in position to assume power in the world and viewing Afrika in all it's "vulnerability" as a money pot and resource reservoir from which they can draw from. Also it should be noted that all of the above mentioned traditions are currently practiced by East Asian people for their own edification. We as Afrikan people need and must draw from our own Ancestral traditions. This is not to discredit the work of those Afrikan teachers that have genuinely put together syncratic systems for our people, as I have great respect for some of them, but to disagree with their methodology and present a better solution. Also, this is not to pretend, or be under the illusion, that cultural exchange and syncretism did, and does not happen in Afrikan traditions (including Ancient Kmt historically), but to stress the importance of having a firm foundation in our own traditions before reaching out and adopting aspects of other peoples traditions, if it is necessary at all to do so. However, at no time should our traditions be completely abandoned or overlooked for those of other people.

The purpose of this book is to present the nKmt tradition in it's purest Kemetic, Afrikan context, and to demonstrate the fact that despite the popular misconception about the tradition being a "dead tradition," everything that we need, that makes the tradition complete in its effectiveness and its "Afrikaness" is available to us today, and more "supplemental information" is literally being uncovered daily. In other words, the nKmt tradition is not lost. The ritual information in the latter half of this book is to further demonstrate and solidify these points:

- **The nKmt tradition is a living tradition**

- **The nTrw (deities) are living forces**

- **In following the lead of our ancestors this tradition can work for us in the same manner that it worked for them**.

I have made every effort to "stick to the script," as much as possible to maintain the integrity of the tradition, and what you find in the following pages is an exegesis presented by myself, the author, as a child of Afrika, a student and teacher of Afrikan spirituality in general, and nKmt spirituality in specific, and the way that this tradition is currently being practiced by our community Henensu.

Special care has been made to present the intricacies and unique qualities of the tradition, as well as those things that greatly unite this

tradition with the rest of Afrikan traditions or ATRs (Afrikan Traditional Religions), specifically what I consider to be the pillars:

- **Acknowledgment of One Divine Being**

- **This One Divine Being manifests itself and works through a multiplicity of beings/agencies (so-called deities or lesser gods), all being aspects of the One.**

- **The veneration, approach, becoming acquainted with, and realization/communion with this Divine being is accomplished greatly through his many Agencies**

- **The Acknowledgement, veneration, and interaction with Ancestors, and their interceding in our affairs.**

- **Communion and communication with the spiritual realm through ritual and divination. This includes Deities (nTrw) and Ancestors (Jertiyu, Akhu, etc)**

- **The importance of satisfying and uplifting the**
various agencies of the spirit world through our spiritual/moral cultivation, offerings, and sacrifice, for success in life, and the realization and actualization of one's innate potential.

These points should be kept in mind, and may serve as a guide to understanding and using this book. After reading the book all the way through (taking your time, or a few times) one should have a thorough understanding of the nkmt tradition, the cosmologies, and be able to practice the daily tradition. This book should not be viewed as a guide to "Self Initiation," as there is no such thing.

Initiation is a family and community tradition. This tradition, as an Afrikan tradition is a family and community tradition, so it is encouraged to be studied and practiced as a family and community, and if after reading this you find you have great interest and would like to know more or go deeper into the tradition, potentially get initiated, it is encouraged that your reach out to the Author and the Henensu community. Lastly, this book is for Afrikan People Only! Non-Afrikans be warned.

THE OSIRIAN TRADITION

2

This is the story of the first born son of Nut and Gab (Heaven and Earth), Osir and his family. Osir was born in Nubia, out of the union of Nut and Gab. When Osir came of age he married Auset, and the two of them left home and traveled to Kemet to settle and create something for themselves. When they entered Kemet, they found the land in a state of Chaos. The land was uncultivated; it lacked definition, and there were no borders or channels. There they found the people in a savage state. The people preyed upon one another, robbing and killing the next just for bread, and sometime for sport. Due to the lack of the knowledge of agriculture and land cultivation, the land was impoverished and lacked food, and the people resorted to eating one another. After objectively observing the situation, Osir made an assessment, and knew exactly what to do. "I see potential," Osir said with a smile on his face. Auset's eyes bucked, widened from Osir's response. "Potential for what?" Auset looked quizzically as she turned from the sight of a man biting a chunk out of another man's leg. Osir grabbed her and smiled. "Chaos precedes order my dear. The very existence of Chaos contains within it the seed; the potential of order." said Osir. Osir then walked up to the man that was eating another man and asked him some questions. "Why are you eating this man?" said Osir. "Why does any man eat? I'm hungry, so I have to eat!" the man replied. "Yes that is true, but why are you eating this man?" Osir asked. "Because we've eaten all of the animals so man is all that's left," he replied "What then will you eat when you are the only man left?" Osir asked gently with a smile on his face. The man thought about it for a second as tears fell from his eyes, for he knew that without other men he would surely die. Osir seeing that he has reached the man's conscience, began to teach him. "Surely life is eternal, and the food that perpetuates life, has a root, and contain a seed, that when the leaves and the fruits thereof have been eaten, you will find hidden within it a seed containing the potential of the tree, the leaf, and the fruit, that once planted in fertile soil will yield a harvest that will be Self perpetuating, granting you life for lifetimes..." said Osir. "If you eat the fruit, or the leaf of the tree, or the plant, you will find that they will all live again, however if you eat a man, or an animal, you will not find them Self perpetuating, for they as well as you will eventually die, and you will not

have a seed, nor soil, from whence to sprout again" Osir said. The man then stopped what he was doing and humbled himself before Osir's wisdom, of which he had no doubt was divine in origin. "Would you please teach me how to cultivate the land?" the man asked. Seeing that the man was fully receptive, Osir agreed. Osir then healed and restored the man that was being eaten and taught the two men how to harmonize and work together. In this manner Osir went about establishing Maat (Law and Order) in the land. With the Law being established, Osir and Auset proceeded to teach the people to cultivate the land.

The people were so pleased with Osir and Auset, that they asked them to take up the role of the royal family, King and Queen Mother of Kemet. Osir not being all that concerned with earthly status and wealth did not agree all at once, but took a moment to think about the proposal. "If I am to be King, then nTr (the Divine) must be the fabric that we use to build this civilization." "Spirituality must be the glue that holds this nation together." Hearing these terms the people rejoiced and agreed. Thus Osir became the Divine King of Kemet, and after ten years, he and Auset helped the people transform Kemet into the most prosperous nation on earth. All of this was achieved because of Osir and Auset's teachings of love, unity, harmony, and peace. More important than these, it was Osir's teaching the people that they contained within themselves the seed of nTr. He taught them that within, this seed was their true essence, their true Self, which is nTr its Self, and if carefully nurtured and cultivated, the wisdom and creative power of nTr would burst forth from it and grow until it flowed though their being into the world, and they would produce *fruits* that when eaten would contain within *it* a seed that would perpetuate the ability of the Creator to come into the world through their Being, and those who would partake of their fruits. This was actually the symbolic meaning of the Divine Kingship. The King was considered to be the image of nTr on earth or a nTr incarnate, yet he was more importantly a symbol of the innate potential housed within every man, woman, and child. It was Osir that taught them of this seed, but Auset showed them how to nurture, protect, and cultivate the seed, through devotion, passion and Hesi (ritual work to the nTrw and song chanting).

Meanwhile in Lower Kemet, Osir's brother Sutesh had risen to power. However, his outlook on life was different from his brother Osir. Sutesh felt that survival and Self Preservation should be the chief objective in a man's life. He felt that boundaries and territories were the only way to maintain life. Sutesh also felt that because of survival being the chief motive force in man, fellow men could not be trusted. He felt that preemptive methods must be used to assure that his enemies never gained the upper hand on him and that he must eliminate them before they eliminated him. So for Sutesh life was a competition, like a race, or the survival of the fittest. This being the case, Sutesh's rise to power reflected his outlook on life. He conquered through the might of his hand.

Now Sutesh's wife Nebt-Het, was not like Sutesh. Nebt Het loved harmony, joy, and festivities. But she also liked wealth, which is the reason why she could overlook Sutesh's obsession with power. Sutesh brought her things. This sufficed for a while until Sutesh's obsession and territorial ways entered into their relationship. Sutesh was extremely jealous and possessive, for Nebt Het was renown in the land for her beauty. This made Sutesh very controlling because deep inside he feared losing her to another man for he was convinced that every man wanted her, as well as everything else that he owned. When Nebt Het's freedom of expression was taken from her, she became very unhappy with the relationship. Anyway word came to Sutesh and Nebt Het from Kemet that Osir was preparing to make a very important announcement and address to the nation. He was requesting their attendance. Sutesh did not really want to go after all the event wasn't about him so "how important could it be?" he thought, but Nebt Het begged and with her charm, he reluctantly conceded. So they made way to Kemet for the event.

When they got to Kemet, everyone was gathering for the address. This address took place in the city of Abdu. After a wait of about an hour or so, the royal procession began. Sutesh and Nebt Het being a part of the Royal Family, were also included in the royal procession. As the call to attention sounded everyone stood to their feet to catch a glimpse of the parade. For the event, Sutesh took up the role of the head of Security, and as such he was the first to proceed, he wore a commanding red and black robe and wielded the "Was Scepter," a symbol of power and strength, which was studded with finely polished bloodstones, Garnets, and Rubies. Behind him followed the procession of young women performing Hesi (singing and Chanting) and dwA (Adoration). This was the Queen Mother Auset's Procession. She was accompanied by her sister Nebt Het. Nebt Het wore a beautiful yet intriguing earth tone dress that appeared to be studded lightly with a hint of Black Amber and she wore a belt made of fossilized sand dollars. However, everyone's eyes couldn't help to have been glued to the Queen Mother. Auset wore a stunning turquoise colored gown, with a pearl studded Tyet (Auset's Belt, symbol of fertility). She carried a Silver Ankh in

her right hand and wore the diadem of the Queen Mother, which was a crown with a vulture as its base (symbol of Mut/Motherhood), which above it sat the symbol of her role as the "st" (Throne) which was studded with quartz crystals, Moonstone, and Sapphire. Following the Queen Mother's procession, everyone was awaiting the arrival of the Nisu Bity (King of Kings). Then suddenly out came his vizier and chief adviser Tehuti. He was a very wise man; a sage in fact, and was also the High Priest of Kemet, Osir's second in command. Tehuti had the head of an Ibis, and wore a vest that was adorned with the finest Lapis Lazuli and Amethyst. He carried a staff that had the forms of the twin Serpents Nekhebet and Wajet spiraling around from the base towards the top which ended in a Yatin (Disk of Light). Each Serpent wore a crown, one representing Upper Kemet, the other Lower Kemet. Following Tehuti were Nine Apes that are said to open the Gates to the Great Ba (Soul), and immediately following them was Osir Wan Nefir (Osir the Good Being). The crowd rejoiced at his presence and shouted in unison "inej Hr.k It nTr, nTr nfr, Ankh Udja Seneb," which means "Salutation of Power Divine Father, good nTr, Life Prosperity and Health to you." Osir wore his customary white garments along with the Hejet Crown. He carried in his hands, which were held out in front of him, the crook and the flail. The people loved Osir and Auset so much that the dwA-w (praises) filled the entire arena, and could be heard miles away. Everyone was excited, except for Sutesh of course who was honestly a little annoyed. Anyway as the procession ended, the dignitaries took their seats, and Osir made his way to the front to address the nation. Once everyone became settled, he began.

My fellow Kemityu, through our unity we have been able to transform Kemet into this beautiful land we call Ta-Meri (the cultivated land). It was through our aspirations to unite with nTr that we were able to unite with one another, for in spite of our diversity it is nTr at the core that connects us. This nation is filled with many different types of people. The world is filled with many different types of people. We all have our respective perspectives, talents, and goals. This is the beauty of life. This beauty can be seen once the understanding is attained that nTr manifests itself through diversity and multiplicity. These differences should not be set aside and they are not bad. They are beautiful, good, and they have a place in the "sakhar nTri" (Divine Plan). Each angle is pertinent to the whole, and it is only through causing the varying angles to converge towards a single point, which is Maat, that the true beauty and meaning of life can be known. This my beloved, is the meaning of the "Mer" (Pyramid). This is the knowledge I have been blessed with by nTr, and the Jertiyu (Ancestors) to share with you; and now it is my plan to share this knowledge with the rest of the world. Let it be known, we are not seeking to rule or dominate our fellow man, nor are we looking to impose our culture on others. We simply seek to reason, to enlighten, and to learn and be enlightened. Above all this we seek to establish good relationships, friendships, and a common bond with our fellow man. This can easily be accomplished through our recognition of one another as expressions of nTr, and teaching others to see the same. With that said brothers and sisters, I along with Tehuti, will lead a delegation on a friendship tour around the world. We will depart tomorrow on the New Moon. dwA nTr! dwA Jertiyu! dwA for your attention. Shim m Hetepu (Go in peace!)!

The crowd rejoiced, and many were crying from Osir's beautiful and profound words. The Queen Mother was rejoicing and her heart beat with so much love for Osir, and for her people. Nebt Het sat there in a trance, mesmerized. She had never heard anything like that before, yet she found the words resonated with her spirit. Osir's word's moved her so much, that she began to feel a little awkward. Sutesh on the other hand began to feel a little nauseous. He found Osir's speech sickening, and infuriating. The whole time he was there he couldn't help but think to himself, "what an idiot Osir is. Does he really believe the foolishness he's saying? How could I have let this woman talk me into coming here? How could mother give birth to such a moron!?! All this talk of Peace and Unity and Blah Blah Blah...this kingdom won't last too much longer. If I were King these people would really see what true power and authority looks likes." The more Sutesh thought about it the more his blood began to boil. Suddenly his thoughts were interrupted. While everyone was preparing to leave Bes came to the rostrum to make an announcement. "Everyone please make your way to the hall for the festivities!" All the people needed to hear was party, and they were there.

The energy of the party was very high. The people of Kemet loved life to the fullest. They loved to have a good time. There was such a positive vibe in the room everyone felt elevated. Everyone except "you know who" of course (do I really have to say :-)). There was so much food, piles and piles of food. Every type of fruit, vegetable, and grain you could think of. There were several roasted meats, everything except for boar, and catfish which the people of Kemet saw as unclean. And of course there was all kinds of wine of the finest quality, and plenty of beer, oh yes Kemet was renown throughout the earth for their beer. Everybody ate and drank except for Tehuti, and it wasn't long before most of them became drunk.

Osir usually didn't drink, but he was feeling so much of the spirit of the party that he decided indulge.

At the royal table everyone was laughing and having a good time, except Nebt Het and Sutesh. However, at least Sutesh wasn't in a bad mood, he was just unconscious from eating and drinking so much. He is the "king of overindulgence." Nebt Het was still in her head, in a daze, with all kinds of thoughts and questions running through her mind. "What am I doing with my life?" she thought. "Why am I with Sutesh?" "He's always so angry, and possessive."We don't have any real friends; everybody is nice because they fear him." "Why couldn't he be more like Osir: so wise, compassionate, and dignified?" I just sit around doing nothing, surrounded by material things; I want my life to serve a greater purpose." She began to think how much she admired her sister Auset, how great she became, but she also wished she could experience what it was like to be in her shoes. She then began to imagine herself as Auset, and then her mind moved her towards the images of seeing herself being with Osir. "If only for one night she thought." She quickly became enflamed with passion. As the images rushed like a torrent through her mind, the sound of Auset's voice finally penetrated her senses from without. "Nebt Het!" Sister, are you alright?" Girl I've been calling to you for about fifteen minutes. "I'm fine sis; just have a lot on my mind. This is quite a party" she said.

As the party went along, Osir began to realize that he had a little bit too much to drink. He touched Auset's hand to get her attention. I'm feeling a little tipsy Meri (love); I think I am going to retire to my chambers. "Are you ok?" Auset asked. Would you like me to escort you? No, no, stay and have a good time, I'll be fine." Osir assured her. Nebt Het watched the way Osir touched Auset's hand the way he moved with her, such gentleness. She longed for that experience. As Osir left, Nebt Het's eyes happened to glance over at Sutesh, who was snoring, with his head laying face down in his own vomit. "That's it!" she thought. "I can't do it anymore." She let a few minutes pass, and then she got up to leave. "I'm feeling a little tired, I think I'm going to retire myself," Nebt Het said. "What about Sutesh?" Auset asked. "Umm yea," Nebt Het responded as she quickly walked off.

As she walked towards her quarters, the thoughts and images of her being with Osir revisited her. She became so full of desire for him, that she began to think of a plan. She decided at that moment that she would disguise herself as her sister Auset, after all they were twins. She would have him "if only for a minute" she thought, maybe she could feel alive. She disguised herself and made her way down to Osir's Chambers. The guards let her in assuming that she was the Queen Mother. Once inside she found Osir lying in bed. "Meri" Osir said, thinking she was Auset. Nebt Het lied down beside him and they fell into a sensual embrace. Once Osir had fallen asleep, she got up to leave. Nebt Het felt, that she must have a token to remember him by, so she decided to take the crown of flowers from his head. She then made her way to her chambers.

When the morning came, Osir and the convoy left at once. Auset escorted him to the banks of Hopi (the Nile) and they kissed and embraced for it would be the last time they would see each other for a while. Osir smiled at the Queen Mother and left at once, leaving her in command of the Nation. She, along with many of the common people of Kemet waved in adoration as they watched Osir sail away.

Meanwhile, Nebt Het had not slept very well for her conscience began to haunt her. She realized what that she let her feelings get the best of her. She thought about how great her sister was, how much she loved her and how good Auset was to her. She couldn't bare it. At once she decided to come clean, and tell Auset what she had done. She quickly stormed out of her chambers to go to Auset.

At the same time Sutesh was just waking up, from his slumber in the puddle of puke. He smelled awful. "Whoa what a party!" Sutesh thought to himself. "I have to get the names of all those liquors he said. He got up to go and find Nebt Het. As he was leaving the hall he passed two guards. "That was some party huh Senu (brothers)! The stinking smell coming from his face and breath was too much for them to bear. They covered their faces with their forearms. "Yea ...*cough cough* it was great they said." Sutesh looked at them and thought "they must have colds, let me keep it moving, I don't want to get sick." Sutesh left in a hurry. As he walked off, one of the guards said to the other, "man did you smell that? Niha Hra! (Stinking Face)." And ever since that day Sutesh has been known all over by that name, Niha Hra.

Sutesh found his way to Nebt Het's quarters, only to find that she was not there. "Hmm, she must've gone to see that idiot brother of mine off." Sutesh thought. Oh well! I'll just stay here and nap until she gets back. As Sutesh's head lay upon the pillow, his hands brushed against something underneath it. He pulled it out and there it was; Osir's crown of flowers. Immediately Sutesh's mine raced towards the worst case scenario and

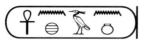

became enraged! He got up and flipped the bed over. Smashing and throwing everything in the room. His breathing was becoming very erratic and very fast that tornadoes began to come from out of his nostrils blowing the door to the room off the hinges. I'm going to kill them! He screamed and rushed to find Nebt Het, and hoping Osir had not left yet. Storming down the hallways all of the commotion alerted the guards. Seeing that he was very irrational they sought to restrain him, but he hurled tornadoes at them injuring them both instantly, as he hurried pass them.

Meanwhile Nebt Het was waiting for Auset to return to her Quarters when she finally arrived. Before Auset could even get a chance to speak Nebt Het fell at her feet confessing what she had done. "Please forgive me my sister." Auset's noticed a very tight feeling in her stomach as if she had just been hit in the gut. However, her heart was made of love and filled with compassion and understanding. She took a deep breath, exhaled, and let it all go. She then pulled Nebt Het up from her feet and embraced her. "It's alright sn-t (Sister); everything is going to be fine. "But what am I going to do?" Nebt Het sobbed. "We will figure it out don't worry," Auset assured her. "Oh my! Sutesh is going to kill..." before she could even finish her statement the door flew open. It was Sutesh and he was very angry, so angry that red smoke was coming out of his nostrils. As soon as he saw Nebt Het he charged towards her. Seeing quickly that things were going to get very bad, Auset chanted Hikau (Words of power), and Sutesh became frozen in place, yet looked as if he was frozen in motion. Auset was a master magician, and as long as she maintained control of her Self, she maintained control over Sutesh. Seeing that Sutesh no longer posed a threat, she alerted her guards, who were the most elite that the military had to offer, and were also trained in Hika. Take Sutesh back to his home, and don't release him until the waning moon. Obeying their orders, the guards quickly carried Sutesh away and did not release him until the moon began to wane.

A few months passed, and Nebt Het and Auset were able to work things out between themselves. Auset listened to Nebt Het, all the things she endured while married to Sutesh. She empathized with her, and her heart was full of compassion. Also Nebt Het was now a few months pregnant which was a major surprise for up until that point she was convinced that she was barren. It turned out that it wasn't Nebt Het that was incapable of procreation, but Sutesh was the one that was sterile. From the union of Osir and Nebt Het Anpu was born.

Though Auset had forgiven Nebt Het for her affair with Osir, Nebt Het had not yet forgiven herself. She was full of shame and guilt, and fell into a deep

16

depression. This was especially the case after her son Anpu was born. She could barely bring herself to look at him. "How could I ever be fit to be your mother," she said to the baby boy. After what I've done, I'm not even fit to live." She thought to herself. At that moment, full of guilt, grief, and sorrow, Nebt Het decided to do the unfathomable. She decided to leave the child abandoned in the wilderness and she herself would ingest poison.

While Net Het was on her way to the wilderness to carry out her dark objective, Auset was back at home tending to her vineyard. While she was nurturing some melons she was growing, a vulture perched on a bush beside her. "Auset, I am the nTrt Mut. I have come to warn you of a terrible thing that is about to take place. Your sister Nebt Het overcome with grief and guilt has decided to take her life, and leave the boy Anpu in the wilderness. You must hurry and stop this before it happens." The vulture said. Auset immediately transformed into a kite and flew straightway to where Nebt Het was headed. Auset, flying high and fast, spotted her sister and nephew and landed immediately. "Nebt Het you must stop!" Nebt Het seemed as though she didn't even hear Auset, nor even aware of her presence. Auset looked at her sister and noticed a darkness around her. She then looked more deeply when she noticed a mit.t, a malevolent deceased woman was shadowing Nebt Het, feeding off of her misery. Auset addressed the dead woman immediately: "I don't know who you are, or why you are here, but I command you to leave...NOW!!!" Auset's eyes became full of light and the dark spirit fled at once, fearing that Auset would destroy her. At that moment Nebt Het became aware of herself and what she was doing, and immediately fell at Auset's feet. "You are not alone sis, I am with you." Auset said to Nebt Het, reassuring her. Auset immediately picked up her sister and child off of the desert ground and brought them back home.

Auset exercised her authority as Queen Mother and Woman of the House, and through an expression of immense love toward her sister, asked Nebt Het to join her family as a Sister Wife to Osir. As a family they would work together and raise their children.

Meanwhile back in Seperemu, Sutesh was livid. There was no way he would let someone take something away from him. And when he got word that Nebt Het had become pregnant and produced a son that was it. This news pushed him to his limit, for he felt his manhood had now come into question for Osir had done what he was unable to do, and that was produce a child. This infuriated Sutesh and he vowed to have revenge. So he set his

eyes toward Kemet. After all, having a wife was ok, sometimes, but what he really wanted was power, and in his mind whoever ruled Kemet controlled the world. Also Sutesh felt that Osir was a fool, with his philosophy of unity, and was unfit to run a Nation like Kemet anyway. However, Sutesh was also aware of the people's adoration for Osir and Auset and he knew that he couldn't just walk in there and take over the throne. He needed a plan. For that he turned to Subik.

Sutesh went down to the delta to seek out Subik. When he got there he found him swimming in the marshes. "Hetep Subik, I need your help." Sutesh said. Subik came unto the land to meet Sutesh. Subik was a very interesting man with the head of a crocodile, and eyes the color of emerald. Once he stepped onto the land he morphed into the form of a normal man. He knew that whatever Sutesh wanted his help for had to be major, for Sutesh usually took what he wanted by force. "Hetep!" Subik said. What is on your mind? He asked. "I want to take over Kemet. Osir is weak and a fool, and lacks the wisdom and power to run such a powerful nation." As Sutesh explained himself, Subik watched his mannerisms, the intensity and passion in which he spoke and deducted from what he observed that Sutesh wanted this badly, badly enough to be extorted. "Yea yea yea ok I hear you; you hate your brother and you want to take his place. Ok how does this fit my interest? What is in it for me?" Subik asked. "I'll give you 30 pieces of gold." Sutesh replied "No, no, no," Subik chuckled, "you are going to need a plan and I will only do it if you make me second in command!". Subik was known throughout the land as a master strategist, yet was a man without that lived on the fringe of the country and had loyalties only to himself. This being the case, as long as what was being done served his interest, Subik was for sale. Sutesh, hesitated, but knew that he would not be able to succeed without Subik's help, he had accepted the deal. "Ok Subik, as you wish." Sutesh said. Subik smirked, and began to speak. "You see Sutesh, what you lack is tact. You are too forceful. This objective will call for you to be deceptive, shrewd, and manipulative. You will have to master your words to influence people, to make them think that you are a friend, and that you come in peace." Sutesh liked what he was hearing so far; he hung on Subik's every words. "I will send a spy into Kemet to see what is going on in the land, and based upon their observation, devise a plan of attack. So Subik sent a spy into Kemet.

After spending about three years in Kemet, Subik's spy came back with news of Osir's return. They saw this as the perfect time for the attack. For the past few years Subik worked diligently to repair Sutesh's image. He

18

wrote letters for him to Osir, and to the Queen mother, feigning as though he was ready to let bygones be bygones, and as a result gave the impression that he wanted to make a mends. So Auset being ever loving and compassionate invited Sutesh to the welcome back party that they planned for Osir. Subik devised the perfect scheme. He knew that the Kemityu were very spiritual people. This being the case every Kemityu aspired to live a life of Maat that they may be found worthy to enjoy the life in the Duat (Spiritual realm) upon their transition. So everyone in Kemet made preparations for their departure while they were still around, so that temples could be constructed for their Khaut (bodies) that the proper rites could be performed on their behalf, and that their family could have a place to come and give offerings to their Ka. So Subik figured he would have a sarcophagus crafted in the form of Osir, made to fit only him precisely. However, to avoid any suspicion he decided to present it in the guise of a game. "We will let everyone try it on with the promise of giving it as a prize to whoever it fits." Subik said. Meanwhile, Sutesh had secured the assistance of foreign mercenaries called Sebiyu to assist in his wicked plan.

The night of the party came and everyone awaited the arrival of the Royal Family. The place was full with visitors from Punt, Kush, and all the surrounding nations. There was every type of food and drink of the exotic type. People were fellowshipping and just having a great time. Sutesh was present, and so was Subik, but Subik was incognito. The call to attention was given for the arrival of the Royal Family. The procession went as before except this time, Nebt Het accompanied Auset as a Sister wife to Osir, and as it was Sutesh that led the way at the previous party, this time it was Anpu that was the opener of the way. Also, this time Tehuti was not present as he was traveling with the Great nTr Ra. It took everything in Sutesh to not react and ruin the plan; Subik was thinking to himself "please don't let this fool ruin the plan."

As everyone took their seat, Osir got up to perform the libations, giving thanks and praises to nTr, the Peseju nTrw, the Jertiyu, and the hierarchy of Kemet. He took time to honor the Queen Mother Auset who had governed the Kingdom flawlessly while he was away. He stressed how family was the foundation of civilization, and that at the very root, Kemet was a family, and now shared a bond with the greater family of man. "Sometimes we make mistakes that bring disorder into the family, into the Kingdom, but because we are family, we must make the effort to restore Maat to the family. For at the very foundation, family is our spiritual way of life." At this moment he became aware of Sutesh's presence and smiled at him. That smile hit

Sutesh at the very core of his being, for he felt Osir was speaking directly to him. As Osir ended his address and took his seat, Sutesh stood to make a toast. "To family, Sutesh said, may we all live in peace with one another." Also, I have a surprise for the family here tonight on this glorious occasion." At that moment, Sutesh unveiled the sarcophagus. Everyone in the party gasped, at the sight of it and marveled at its beauty. It was made of the finest gold, and decked with the finest jewels."This coffin is fit for a King, Sutesh chuckled under his breath. "However, tonight is the lucky night for one of you." Whoever can fit comfortably into this sarcophagus may have it for their burial. The crowd went was very excited, and lined up one by one to try it on.

As the night progressed the festivities continued, the people continued to try out the coffin. Subik waited patiently, observing the people, waiting until they were good and drunk. Alas, Osir's turn came after everyone had tried it out, and was heavily intoxicated. As soon as Osir got into the coffin Sutesh gave an evil grin that served as the signal to go ahead with the plot. At that very moment Subik Chanted a Hika, "BANG!"...that immediately blew all of the lights out in the building, knocked everyone unconscious, and blew the doors of the place wide open. At that moment seventy two of the foreign mercenaries came running out, slamming the coffin door shut, nailing it down tightly and pouring molten lead on it to assure that Osir would not be able to get out. He eventually suffocated and died. Achieving the task, they quickly carried the body off and threw it into Hopi (the Nile River). After regaining consciousness, Auset became aware of what was happening, she woke Nebt Het and called to Anpu, to make an escape. Anpu transformed into a Jackal and led the way out. As everyone else at the party was still unconscious, they made their way out safely.

Away and in a safe place, Auset finally came to the realization of what happened. Her beloved husband, The King, Osir had been killed. Immediately she became distraught and cut a lock of her hair and put on ritual morning clothes, which was customary of Kemet. "I have to find the body" Auset cried. "We have to perform the customary rites on his behalf to help guide him through the doors." Just as she was speaking she came to the unsettling realization that Osir was dead and without an Heir to perform the Opening of the Mouth Ceremony on his behalf, and to inherit the throne. All of this proved unbearable to Auset and she immediately left to begin her search for the body. After a while of searching, she came across some children that told her they saw the conspirators throw the body in the Nile. Hearing this she became very upset, for she thought the body may be lost forever.

Meanwhile the body was actually being carried by the currents to the coast of Palestine. The Shekhem (Power) emanating from this sarcophagus was magnificent that as soon as it hit the banks a Tree immediately sprang up around it encasing it in it's trunk, causing the coffin to become totally concealed. They say this tree grew so large and became so beautiful in a very short period of time that it was thought to be miraculous. The King of Palestine marveled at the majesty of the tree, and had it cut down and set up as the chief pillar of his temple.

When news of this tree reached Auset, in an instant she transformed into a bird and flew to Palestine. When she reached she took a seat next to the Palace. How am I going to gain access to the Palace? She thought. After sitting there for a while she caught a glimpse of one of the Queen's maidens and called to her. "Do you like perfume?" Auset asked the maiden. "Of course," she replied, "what lady doesn't?" "Great I have the finest aromas and oils come let me show you." When the girl came close Auset began to chant Hikau in her mind and as she spoke, the Aroma emanated from her breath. Then she caressed the maiden's hair and the aromatic oils began to pour from her sweat, and not only placing the wonderful scent on her but also her Shekhem. The maiden became enchanted and left to return to the Palace. As she was leaving, Auset went into trance and began to guide the maiden's actions through her Shekhem which was now connected to the Maiden. The aroma quickly filled the queen's chambers and becoming aware of it the Queen inquired about it. "Girl you smell sweet what are you wearing?" Seeing that she made contact, Auset began to speak through the maiden, guiding her words. "Queen Mother there is this lady seated next to the Palace and she is very mysterious, the aroma came from her sweat and her breath! What! Girl, have you lost it? I've seen and heard some crazy things in my day but this takes the cake." The queen began to laugh and started to dismiss what the maiden was saying when suddenly a strong breeze entered the palace through a window that caused the Queen to become engulfed in the Aroma. Now Auset's Shekhem also possessed the Queen. "Bring her to me," said the Queen. Immediately the maiden went to get Auset. Once inside, the Queen questioned Auset. "I hear you have a certain talent, that you can breathe and sweat the finest perfume. Is this true? The Queen asked? "Yes," Auset said. "Show me," the queen asked with a smirk on her face. Auset figured this is her big chance. She then began to breathe the sweetest smell, "Whoa!" The Queen said. Auset then walked up to her and caressed her hair, and oil so fine began to pour from her sweat.

This oil was so fine that it changed the texture of the Queens hair, making it softer, yet healthier. The Queen was so impressed that she made Auset a nurse for her son. However, she thought it better to keep her away from the King!

Auset looked upon the young prince and saw that he was a little anemic. She thought that if he were here son, he would be immortal, and at that very moment she decided to grant him the gift of immortality. So instead of giving him her breast, she gave him her finger that he may feed on her spirit. That night she placed the child in the furnace and began to chant Hikau. After performing her work, she left the child in the furnace that it might burn away his fallible parts, and then she changed into a bird and flew to the part of the palace that contained the pillar that housed Osir's body. She began to circle around the pillar, chanting mournfully. This became a nightly ritual. However, one night while she was placing the prince in the furnace the Queen walked in! She freaked out and snatched the child from Auset, instantly depriving him of Divinity. Auset began to explain to her who she was and what she was doing. "I am the ntrt Auset, Queen Mother of Kemet." She said, with glowing eyes. The Queen of Palestine, immediately fell to the feet of Auset in reverence. "I have come to claim the body of my husband Osir." Auset said. The Queen asked "where is it?" Auset took her into the chamber where the Pillar was and pointed to it. "In there!" Auset said seriously. The Queen ran to get the King and brought him immediately to Auset. Auset then began to explain to them both what happened to her and Osir. "My husband, the Nisu, Osir, Wan Nefir, King of Upper and Lower Kemet, was killed in an insurrection that was carried out at the behest of his brother." "I escaped and was in hiding when word reached me about the whereabouts of his body." He was killed, and there is no heir to make retribution for him. There is no heir to perform the proper funerary rites on his behalf, to guide him through the duat, to enshrine him as an Ancestor, to remove the corruption from him, and to continue his lineage, there is no heir! But I am Auset! Mighty of Hikau, and by my word he will be redeemed and he will have an heir...now give me my husband!" After listening to Auset, and looking into her eyes the King had the body exhumed from the pillar, immediately falling to his face in reverence of it. He ordered a boat be prepared for Auset that she may carry the body back to Kemet. From that day on the people worshiped that tree in secret, yet it no longer contained the body of the nTr.

Auset left with the body of her husband at once. However, there was also a very immature boy that stowed away on the ship, whose curiosity led him to try and steal a glimpse of the body of Osir. One night while Auset was performing Hesi over Osir's body, the boy snuck up on her to steal a glance. Auset's spirit alerted her to his presence and immediately she turned with her eyes full of light. This frightened the boy so badly that he stumbled and fell into the deep abyss of the river and was never seen gain.

Auset knew she could not just walk into Kemet with the body of Osir, for she knew that Sutesh was looking for her with intentions on making her his wife so that he could have legitimate rights to the throne. "Ughh!" She shuttered at the thought. So she figured she would have to sneak the body into Kemet, but how? "Aha!" She exclaimed. "Subik!" That's right, Subik ☺; the same Subik that assisted Sutesh in the murder of Osir. She needed a plan, a scheme. She needed to be shrewd and incognito and there was no one better for the job. She knew what Subik was capable of, and she also knew what he had done, yet that was the nature of Subik. He was always for sell, if the price was right. However, since Sutesh had made him his "Second in Command," the price obviously had gone up. She needed something good. Also there was always the possibility of betrayal. She sat still for a moment while breathing deeply yet gently. As she sat there the image of a man playing a flute, charming a snake flashed in her mind's eye. At that moment she opened her eyes and the path was revealed. "I am going to charm Subik! I will tame him and train him." But I'll have to approach him from a position where he is vulnerable, Ha... I'll have to "trick" the trickster!" A plan like this would have been virtually impossible for anybody but Auset, I mean sure Tehuti could've pulled it off but he was probably off in a cave somewhere totally aloof to it all. Auset was clever enough, and could be manipulative and tricky when she needed to be; After all it is these very traits that allowed her to become the Warit Hikau (Great Woman of Words of Power/Magic). She once tricked Ra into giving up his "Secret Name" to her, which he caused to emanate into her through his Shekhem. And it is that very power that is the one trick Subik did not have up his sleeves.

When she approached the banks she saw Subik ducked off, in his crocodile form, appearing as if asleep, yet surely just seeming that way probably stalking something. Anyway he was always alert and picked up on someones vibe quickly. So when Auset docked with the boat he was right there to meet her, blocking her from passing. "Well, Well, Well, what do we have here?" Subik chuckled. "Oh and you brought lunch how sweet of you" he said licking his teeth as he glanced over at Osir's Sarcophagus. He couldn't stop himself from laughing. "Subik, I need your help. Auset said.

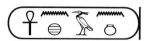

"Oh really? How can I serve you my Queen?" Subik responded condescendingly. I need you to help me sneak Osir's body into Kemet, and assist me in hiding it from Sutesh. Oh that was it, at this point Subik was now rolling around on the floor as if possessed, laughing hysterically. "Subik, Subik, Subikhu!" Auset shouted, this time getting Subik's attention. It had been a long time since he's heard that name. "Why should I help you?" SUBIK inquired in a brief moment of seriousness. "I am already Sutesh's second in command." "Oh yea? And how long do you think that relationship will last?" "How long before Sutesh perceives you as a threat?" "After all, you are sharper than him; it won't be long before he turns on you." She made a very good argument Subik thought. "She's right, Sutesh is no match for my wits, he is very paranoid and jealous, hmm... betrayal is definitely something to look out for with that guy! (Authors Note: the nerve of Subik ☺). Auset seeing that she has made him think, she decided to make her move. "But know what Subik, I can offer you something that Sutesh cannot. "And what might that be Subik asked?" "Respect!" Auset replied, with a slight smirk on her face. "Everywhere you go you will be respected." "As it stands you stay on the fringe of civilization for in some places people love you, in others you are despised and they seek to kill you, but I can make you respected throughout the earth." Subik knew what she said to be true so he asked anxiously "How?" "By getting you access to Ra's court." Subik's eyes widened. "I can get you into Ra's court and once he is made aware of your tremendous skill and intelligence he will no doubt make you an officer in his court." "All you will need is the password, which is Ra's secret name." Subik listened very attentively, this was by far the most receptive he had ever been. Plus he also had heard that Auset knew Ra's Name. "Ok, Ok, Ok, tell me and you've got yourself a deal." Subik agreed. "Ok, I'll have to whisper it to you, I don't want anyone else to hear," Auset said. She approached Subik to whisper into his ear. Subik was fully open to receive the name of Ra, and Auset knew that this was the moment that she waited for, when she reached Subik's ear she began to make Hesi with Ra's name, but in a manner that caused Subik to go in to a trance instantly coming under her command. Subik stood at attention. "inej Hr-k Queen Mother!" He said, standing there like a soldier saluting his superior officer. Auset then begin to chant the Madu nTr alphabet from start to finish and at the sound of each letter Subik changed position at command. "Aye!" She called Subik back to attention. Seeing that he was good and trained, she gave him his orders. "Subik, you will find me a place where I may hide the body of Osir, and you will tell no one of its whereabouts." Without hesitation Subik led her to a place that was safe and secure, at least at the moment. Auset then made her way to meet up with Nebt Het and Anpu at the safe haven they secured.

Meanwhile back in Kemet, Sutesh sat upon the throne, implanting his laws, oppressing the people, and destroying anyone that rose up and spoke out against him. He was so worried about the people conspiring against him that he kept them under tight surveillance. He made the people worship him and the nTr of his choice, Owapep. He threw out the old way of Maat and communalism with a limited domestic market, and instated a system where the majority of people had to compete with one another for crumbs, while he and his chosen few horded all the nations wealth. It wasn't long before he started to enslave the people. Now that he had Kemet under his control, his ego was ridiculously big, so big that he began to refer to himself as "The World, Superpower," "The World Leader," and "the World this" and "the World that." His ego was BIG! He now felt that it was his duty to go around "civilizing" the "savages" of the world. He needed an empire big enough to fit his ego. He went about conquering nation after nation; from the wealthiest to the poorest. If the nation was strong, he would send his agents in to destabilize things by sowing seeds of dissention, exploiting the dissatisfactions of the people, and literally creating problems if there were none. He imposed harsh trade sanctions that began to erode the economy of the nation he was seeking to conquer. Propaganda and religion were his major weapons. He would first destroy the image of the leader to sway the public opinion to think that the leader was corrupt and that they and the world would be much better without them, and then he would come in to overthrow the leader, placing someone he could control in authority. Next to further pacify the people, he would cut off the food supply, and then send in his priest to get the people to worship his image for food, thus making himself to seem as though he is a savior. Once he has infiltrated the nation, he exploits its natural resources, and leaves the people with nothing. This made it easy for him to introduce his philosophy of "planned parenthood," and population control, which in his mind was a way to eliminate the "useless eaters" from the earth, and if that didn't work he had his sorcerers conjure up plagues to unleash upon the people. He then placed a military base in every nation that he conquered, and if a nation did not submit to his will he labeled them as terrorist to create the atmosphere for war. It was really his military power and deceit that made his plans a success.

In spite of all of this, no one could have predicted what would happen next, not even Subik. Subik, at the order of Auset, hid Osir's body in a place that he was sure no one would find it; he hid it in the swamps among the Crocodiles, and hippopotami and Wild Boar. No one hung around there.

Well it just so happened that Sutesh had a little secret that no one knew about, and that was that he loved pork! You had very few people in Kemet that ate the pig and it was mostly the poorest people, however this usually occurred due to a bad harvest or famine that brought the people down to their last. For the most part the animal was considered unclean due to its habits, and was a symbol of great evil. Taking all of this into consideration, who would have guessed that Sutesh, being extremely wealthy, and coming from royal blood, had a swine fetish! So one night Sutesh was down in the swamps hunting wild boar, and as he was running after it, he stumbled over a stump. He had mud all over his face. As he wiped the mud from his eyes he saw something twinkling from the moonlight a few feet away from him. As he approached it he realized what it was. He knew that someone was trying to sneak it back into the country because he had thrown it in the Nile so there was literally no way it could have to found its way to the Delta.

In a rage he ripped open the coffin and began to hack Osir's body into pieces, fourteen pieces to be exact, and then scattered the members of his body all over the land, but the phallus, which was a very important symbol of Creative Power and Resurrection, he took to the river and fed it to a catfish."Now let's see somebody find you now" Sutesh snickered.

That night Auset dreamed that Osir was being tortured and ridiculed in the Duat. He looked at her and appeared to be calling to her, but he did not have the ability to speak, and the spirits of the Duat made mockery of his condition. She woke in tears "What is it sister?" Nebt Het asked. "Something is wrong! I have to go to the body to see what I can do. I believe I can use my Shekhem and Hikau to reanimate his body enough to take his seed and bear an heir." Just as she stood up to leave Anpu came rushing through the door."Queen Mother, Sutesh has found the body!" Auset went into a rage and ran out but Anpu tried to restrain her. "Don't go...don't go Queen Mother, you don't need to see this." He tried his best but he could not restrain her for she was a woman on a mission. However, by the time she reached the center of the town, she wished she would've listened. Sutesh had placed Osir's head on a stake in the middle of the town for everyone to see. His body had been desecrated. Sutesh had done this to lure her out of hiding in hopes that he would capture her. Auset let out a piercing scream and Sutesh knew that she was there. He had his men move in on her but before they could close in she transformed into a bird and flew away, taking the head of her husband with her.

With Sutesh hot on their trail, Auset, Nebt Het, and Anpu searched throughout the land for the missing pieces of Osir. It took, much time but they eventually found every single piece. In each location where she found a member she erected a Temple and Tomb there. This was to rebuild reverence for Osir in the eyes of the people. Sutesh tried his best to suppress it but without Subik's master planning he was quickly running out of ideas.

Auset was ready to perform her Hesi, to attempt to use Hikau to reanimate Osir's Khat, however, she was missing a critical piece, and that was the phallus. Without the Phallus how would she be able to conceive a child? She was almost at her wits end, for she had searched everywhere. So one night she went down to the banks of the Nile to meditate on a solution. As she sat there, and went within, the nTr Hopi, the spirit of the Nile came to her. He informed her that it was a catfish that had eaten the phallus. She came out of trance very distraught but she refused to give up. So she calmed back down, and stilled her thought process. She must've sat there for hours, when suddenly the image of a vulture came to her in her mind's eye. This vulture called her name. "Auset!" then the vulture began to transform into a woman. It was the nTrt Mut, the Divine Mother. She wore the double crown of Kemet, and carried an Ankh in one hand and a papyrus scepter in the other. Seeing that she had Auset's full attention, Mut then began to walk towards her. As she approached, Mut began to say the words "Zefi-per-em-Hes-hri-hapu-jet-f" rhythmically as if projecting it at Auset, repeating again and again as she approached. As she moved closer and closer towards Auset, she began to morph into another form, known as Sekhemet Bast Ra, in which she now possessed the head of woman, with two vultures popping out of her neck. She now had wings for arms, and the claws of a lion. She spread her wings as if to embrace Auset and when she did that she unveiled that she had a phallus. She kept on approaching, until she was totally absorbed into Auset's sphere of awareness. Auset suddenly gasped. Her breathing was very erratic, and was beyond her control. She stood up Eyes full of light and began to walk, against her Will, towards the body of Osir. As she walked towards the body, the words of Mut kept replaying in her ears Zefi-per-em-Hes-hri-hapu-jet-f. In her mind's eye, it was as if she was the nTrt Mut, and as she moved, it was Mut moving. When she reached the body, she spread her arms out, as if spreading her wings, and enshrouded the body of Osir. Her breathing became more and more erratic and with each breath the Shekhem began to build up. Auset's breath, full of Shekhem, began to enter into Osir, causing his body to vibrate and glow. The shekhem began to emanate from Osir's body, and as Auset breathed

she absorbed his essence. A flood of images began to rush through her mind. She saw Mut again, with and erect Phallus, arms out as if waiting to embrace her again, and suddenly it was Osir, standing there, in the same manner. She then saw herself walking into Osir's embrace. At that moment the images began to move so fast that she couldn't make it all out, but the very last thing stood clear. She saw herself, in the bush standing upon a birthing brick, in labor, and at that very moment she heard the cry of a hawk that was so loud, that it immediately brought her back to her regular state. She told no one about that night, she had been through some powerful experiences, but never anything like that. Needless to say, nine months later she gave birth to a son. She called him Heru.

At the very moment of Heru's birth Auset was informed of his Destiny. The nTrw Shai, Meshkhent, and Renenutet were there along with the Seven Het-Heru. Meshkhent, kept track and took notes of the conditions surrounding the birth, and took note of the words from the 7 Het Heru and handed the notes to Shai. Shai proclaimed the notes, instructing Auset on the fate of the child. Renenutet gave Auset the name that would help the child to fulfill his destiny, and reap the harvest of actualized potential. "He will be a very great and powerful man. He has the potential to redeem his father and to claim his birth right in ascending to his father's throne. However, he has a fire burning within him and he must temper it with wisdom or it may consume him. If he is taught well, and makes the right decisions, and lives Maat, he will be successful." Shai said. Auset listened to these nTrw as tears rolled down her face. Then Renenutet stepped forward to speak. "His name shall be called Heru, for he is exalted, and set apart, the face of his father; Heru!"As these three were preparing to leave Tehuti made an appearance to advise Auset. "You, Auset, must be mindful that Sutesh will attempt to destroy this child before he reaches maturity, to prevent the child from challenging him for the throne. So you must take care to hide him, protect him, teach him, that he may reach maturity and if this is done he will be king."

Auset raised Heru, mainly in the south, along with Nebt Het and Anpu. However, they never really stayed in one location very long or they were always on the move to make sure that Sutesh would not be able to track them. They lived the lives of common people, and if you didn't know them you would not be able to tell that they were royalty. No matter how uncomfortable the living situation, it was best. Also traveling with Auset were seven scorpions that surrounded her on all sides. Their names were Tefen, Befen, Mestet, Mestetef, Petet, Thetet, and Maatet. They served as protectors, and guides, and were her eyes and ears. Tefen and Befen walked behind her, Mestet and Metetef walked on her sides, and Petet, Thetet, and Maatet walked in front of her clearing her path. She admonished them not to speak to anyone that she did not know. These scorpions always protected them, and alerted Auset to any potential dangers. It was as though Auset had eyes and ears everywhere.

One day Auset and the family were on the road. They became very tired and stopped in a nearby town to seek shelter. Maatet led the way, being that it was his job to clear the path. He led them to a house that was adorned, and very well kept, and obviously belonged to someone with money. Being that the house was spacious and everyone was hungry, it was as he saw it the best way. "Are you sure about this?" Auset asked Maatet. "He signaled to her that he was sure."Alright", Auset said as she knocked at the door. A woman came to the door. "May I help you?" the lady asked as she looked Auset and Nebt Het up and down with a somewhat disgusted look on her face. "Dear lady, we were passing through town when we all became terribly tired and hungry. Could you please allow us to take up shelter on your floor for the night?" You couldn't help but notice the pungent smell of whatever she was cooking. It smelled so good that Anpu had begun to drool. Auset noticed that the table was full with food. As the lady was about to answer, she suddenly noticed the scorpions. "AHH... I don't have any room or food for you now go away!" she yelled as she quickly slammed the door in Auset's face. "Ooh the audacity!" Auset exclaimed. She was a little flustered. Not only was she upset about the lady slamming the door in her face, but the fact that she lied about having room and food in spite of seeing that they had two young children with them. The more she thought about it the more upset she became. Nice job Maatet! She said. Well we better keep it moving. As they were leaving from the rich woman's home a poor lady called to them. "Hi my name is Taha. I don't have as much room or food as Warit over there, but I notice you have small children with you. You may come into my place and I will share whatever I have. dwA nTr!' Auset said and they all went into Taha's home.

Shortly after entering, the scorpions gathered together and all placed their poison on the Tefen's tail. He then left to go to the rich lady's house. He crawled under the door and took notice that the lady had a young son. He then went over to the child and stung him, releasing all of the poison into the boy. The poison quickly made the boy feverish. Tefen's stinger was so hot from all the power from the venom of the other six, that it caught hold of a curtain and quickly caused it to set a blaze. The fire was burning the

house down, and Useret did not have enough water to put it out. She let out a screeching scream that reached the heavens. She grabbed her son and ran out of the house, running through the streets screaming and crying. Auset took notice of what was happening and her and Nebt Het grabbed hands and began to chant Hikau that caused rain to fall upon Usenet's home. When Useret noticed that the fire was out, she began to calm down, and thanked the creator. She clutched her son, who had been sleeping through all the turmoil and noticed that the little body was very cold, and he was not breathing. She cried out for help but because she was not friendly or helpful with her neighbors people just ignored her, some were even laughing thinking that she had gotten what she deserved. However, the ladies cry penetrated the heart of Auset, for seeing the child in the condition he was in, she couldn't just ignore him. She then went up to the child, and began to make Hesi over his body. She then noticed some small punctures that let her know he had been stung by her scorpions. "I know that this has happened as a part of this ladies shai, and that she may have caused this by her ways, but for the sake of her son, I will revive him to life." Auset said to herself. "Come here!" Auset said to Useret. "I have skills that I have acquired in my travels and I can use them to save your son." She then by the use of Hikau, called forth the poison from the boy. She placed her hands upon his throat to cause him to breathe. Auset then took some barley and made a cake that drove out the poison, and then placed natron on the wounds to absorb it. She also gave him some herbs to get rid of the fever.

After seeing everything Auset had done for her and her son, in spite of the fact that she slammed the door in her face earlier, Useret felt very indebted to Auset and gave her all of her possessions, who in turn rendered them to Taha for taking them in.

Auset was ready to go so she summoned the scorpions to fall into rank. However, she noticed something was a little off. For some reason it seemed like the symmetry in their formation around her was different. She lined them up and then noticed that there was an extra scorpion. "Who are you?" Auset questioned the strange insect. She noticed the odd red stripes on its body. The scorpion's eyes suddenly turned a dark red. "My name is UHOT!" the scorpion said as it lunged in full attack at Auset's feet. JAH-JAH! Auset exclaimed quickly while snapping her finger causing a bolt of light to tear through the scorpion, instantly killing it. "Sutesh must have sent him she thought." It was at that moment that she heard Nebt Het scream. "AHH!!!" Auset hurried but in her heart she knew it must be something terrible, for she had a feeling in her as though she had been stuck in the sides with a knife. When she reached Nebt Het, she found her sobbing over the lifeless Heru. She grabbed him. "Look at me, Look at me! Heru! Don't worry my son; this will not happen to you for you have a destiny to fulfill. Within you is the very essence and power that willed creation into existence. You are not of this world. You proceeded out of Nu, and you are the Great Benu that burst forth from the top of the Persea Tree which sits in the house of the Ancient One of Inu. You are the brother of Abdu fish that guides the boat of Ra and you were nursed by Miwa aA herself, the Great Cat that cuts the head off of Owapepi! The fire of this poison shall not conquer you! You are the son of the Great nTr, Wan Nefir, Grand Son of Gab, Great Grand Son of Ishu and Tufnut, and Great Great Grandson of Ra himself! This poison will not defeat you Heru!"

Auset's cry was so great that it reached all the way to Ra who was traveling in his celestial boat through the heavens. When he heard Auset he immediately sent Tehuti to tend to Heru. When Tehuti arrived, he leaned over the child and performed Hesi over every member of his body. Tehuti as a Sage and Judge made it his point to remain aloof and impartial in matters. He always left out his personal feelings and made decisions based upon reason, and the dictates of the time. He described things the way that they were. With this being the case, he knew that it was not written for Heru to die here by the sting of a scorpion, so he made the choice to restore life to Heru. "I am Tehuti. I have come to revive Heru, and to remove the poison of the scorpion which has spread throughout his body. Your head belongs to you Heru. Your Eye belongs to you, Heru, son of Gab, Lord of the Two Eyes in the midst of the nTrw. Your nose is to you, Heru, you are Heru, the son of Ra, and you shall not inhale the fiery wind. Your arm is to you, Heru; great is your strength to slaughter the enemies of your father. Your two thighs are to you, Heru. You receive the rank and dignity of your father Osir. Pitah has balanced for you your mouth on the day of your birth. Your heart is to you, Heru, and the Yatin makes your protection. Your eye is to you, Heru; your right eye is like Ishu, and your left eye like Tufnut, who are the children of Ra. Your belly is to you, Heru, and the children are the nTrw who are therein, and they shall not receive the essence of the scorpion. Your strength is to you, Heru, and the strength of Sutesh shall not exist against you. Your phallus is to you, Heru, and you are Kamutef, the protector of his father, who makes an answer for his children in the course of every day. Your thighs are to you, Heru, and your strength shall slaughter the enemies of your father. Your calves are to you Heru; the nTr Khnum has built them, and the nTrt Auset has covered them with flesh. The

soles of your feet are to you, Heru, and the nations who fight with the bow fall under your feet. You rule the South, North, West, and East, and you see like Ra. And likewise him that is under the knife."

From these words, Tehuti revived Heru, and placed a protection "spell" over him and his family so that he may grow and go on to fulfill his destiny.

As Heru matured, his mother would take him through various rites of passages. He learned the healing arts from his mother; from her he also learned the art of dream interpretation and other forms of divination. He wore his hair mainly shaven with one braid coming from the center of his head. This was customary for Kemetyu youth. Once Heru finished his rites of passages and initiations, and became a man, the loc would be shaved as well. Growing up he'd always heard so many wonderful things about his father. He heard of how wise and just Osir was, and how much he reminded his family of him. The thoughts that he was the son of such a great man made him very happy. However, when he would see other children with their Itau (fathers) he would become over taken with sadness. He knew that his father was a great man, and that he died before he was born, but he didn't know very much else about him. Because Auset raised him as a commoner he was not aware of his great destiny, or that he was the son of the King of Kemet, and Heir to the throne. Anpu on the other hand knew, but was told to hold it secret until Heru was mature enough to handle that knowledge.

When Heru turned 14 the day came that he finally needed to know. After seeing a young boy playing a game of Senet with his father, and having such a good time, Heru ran to his mother and asked her the question. He came in the house and found Auset braiding Nebt-Het's hair. "Mut I have to ask you something." Heru said. Can't it wait Heru? Nebt Het asked? If I have to sit hear any longer I am going to cry!" Nebt Het said in a slightly irritated manner, for although she loved the way she looked in braids, she hated the long process of getting them done. "Sorry Senet en Mut e (Sister of my Mother/Auntie), But I would like to know about my Ita. And just like that the room became very silent for a few seconds. After a moment, Nebt-Het said "on second thought, why don't I go and let you to talk." Nebt Het looked in Heru's eyes and knew this was "the Big Talk" her and Auset had spoken about, and as much as she loved Heru, she wasn't trying to be there when Auset broke the news. As she tried to get up and leave Auset tightened her grip on the braid in her hands and Nebt-Het knew she better not move. "What is it that you want to know Heru?" Auset asked. I want to

32

know everything about him, but most of all I want to know why he died! "Yea I really think it's better if I go and give you two your privacy' Nebt Het said as she tried to leave a second time. Auset tightened that braid again. "Alright alright!" Nebt Het responded to Auset's grip as she sat down. Auset looked her son in the eyes and told him to have a seat. She let go of Nebt Het's hair just long enough for her to get loose and run out of the room.

"Heru your father, Osir, was the King of Kemet, and you my son are the crown prince." Heru kind of chuckled, but when he saw the seriousness in Auset's face he realized she was not joking. "Before you were born, before your father's death, he and I brought civilization to Ta-Meri, and became the King and Queen Mother of that once great civilization. Your father was so wise, and so compassionate that he wanted to share the prosperity his teachings brought to Kemet with the rest of the world. So he, along with Tehuti, set out and brought civilization to the world. He was so loved wherever he went that the people built monuments and temples in his honor. Also everywhere he went, the people gave him a name of praise in their own language. He brought peace to the earth. However, his brother Sutesh was very envious of him. Although they were brother's they were very different. Osir believed that we all need one another, and that we should help one another, and work together for the benefit of the collective. To him that was Maat. He was a man that felt that reason should always be precedent and war should be the absolute last resort to resolving conflict. Your uncle on the other hand, felt that Osir was soft, and that he was not fit to be King. Sutesh is a man of might and power. He feels that his ability to dominate others is the only way to assure security. Nebt Het was married to Sutesh at one time. "Really? How could she be with such a man?" Heru asked? My son as you grow older and wiser, you too will look back at your life and wonder how you ended up in some of the situations you will encounter. Well as things would happen, your Senet n Mut ek would become very unhappy with Sutesh, and began to fall in love with your Father. Well as fate would have it, on the evening that Osir addressed the Nation prior to the trip around the world, he had too much to drink and he became drunk. Nebt Het, in her desperation saw this as the opportune time to be with him, without Sutesh's knowledge. She disguised herself as me and went to Osir in the night to lay with him, and he was too intoxicated to know the difference. From the union of Nebt Het and Osir, your brother Anpu was born. Anyway, Sutesh eventually found out, and was outraged. This caused a rift in our family. We did our best to try and pick up the pieces, but Sutesh was lost in his pain and anger. So he began to secretly plot to murder your father and usurp the throne. On the night that your

father returned, Sutesh along with 72 co-conspirators killed your father through treachery, and we have been on the run ever since.

As Heru listened to the history of his family, his eyes began to swell with tears. "How could such a fate befall my father, he was such a great man" he thought to himself. Just as he was about get lost in his thoughts, Auset called to him. "Heru, now that you know your family's history, you can understand your present circumstances. Now it is time that I inform you of your future, your destiny." Heru sat there very attentively. "My son, you were born a King, and your destiny is to rule. You must grow into a strong and wise man, and confront your uncle Sutesh to reclaim your Father's throne. In doing so, not only will you redeem your Ancestors, but you will also bring order back into the Kingdom, and actualize your full potential." "But, I don't know anything about being a King, and how will confront Sutesh, when I am so young and small?" Heru replied. "You are the son of Osir and Auset, grandson of Nut and Gab, Great Great Grandson of Ishu and Tufnut, Great Great Great Grandson of Ra Himself, Who is the Son of Nu!" Auset stated emphatically. "You come from a line of Divine Rulership, the same power resides within you my child, it just needs to be nurtured and cultivated, and for this is what we have been doing with your Rites of Passages. Now it is time for your last Rites of Passage, before you enter your first Initiatory Rituals with Tehuti." "Tehuti! I'm going to be taught by Tehuti!" Heru was beyond ecstatic for he had heard all about Tehuti who was known throughout the earth for his tremendous wisdom. "Yes my son, and he will teach you the Rituals of The Ancestors. Make sure you rest up tonight, for you'll begin first thing tomorrow morning." Tiyu Mut, Heru went to bed!

The following morning Auset woke up to find a very eager and energetic Heru sitting at the foot of her bed, face full of anticipation. "Heru, how long have you been up? Auset asked her son." A few hours," He said. "I was so excited I could hardly sleep." What's that smell? Auset asked. "It smells great!" "Well since I was up I figured I might as well go ahead and fix breakfast," Heru said with a big grin on his face. Wow! You are excited aren't you, Auset chuckled. Okay, let us go ahead and eat so that you can get started, Auset suggested. Heru ran into the kitchen.

A few hours later Heru began his final rites of passage before he could begin initiation with Tehuti. Heru wasn't new to rites of passages. From a very young age his mother and aunt began to train him in the traditions of his Ancestors. He was taught from very early how to read and write mdw nTr. He had already learned the proper way to conduct himself, and how to honor his elders, asking them permission to speak, bowing to them when they entered his presence, and opening doors, and giving up his seat to them if there were none available. He was taught that he was not only responsible for himself, but for his family, Ancestors, and also the World. He knew how to properly cleanse himself. He had also learned certain survival skills, such as how to hunt, gather herbs and medicinal plants, collect rain water and make it drinkable, and how to treat and heal wounds and certain illnesses. Auset taught him how to pay attention to his dreams and analyze them for interpretation. He knew how to service the shrines of the Ancestors, as far as keeping them clean, pouring libations, although he didn't really understand it fully. All of these things were common place for a child to learn. This last rites of passage, was for Heru to spend ten days alone in a cave, blind folded, and only given certain foods periodically to sustain him for that duration. When the time came, Heru was guided to the entrance of the cave where he would spend the next week, and found his older brother Anpu at the entrance standing guard. Anpu had already been through his rites of passage, and now stood there to welcome Heru. Auset and Nebt Het at his side, Heru's excitement began to slowly shift toward nervousness. Anpu began to speak to him: "Heru Pa Khrad (Heru the Child), today you enter this rite a boy, but before you can leave this place and enter into the next door of your life, you must answer these questions: Who are you? And why are you here? Up unto this point these questions have been answered for you. Yet you cannot say that you know these things to be true, you only believe what you've been told, what you've been taught. You have been led for you walk in darkness. This is the meaning of the blindfold. It is a symbol of your journey in darkness. Yet though there is darkness all around, and you are unable to see, you must find the light within the darkness. You must find the light within." Heru was then blind folded and was escorted into the cave by Anpu. Anpu holding Heru by the hand, guided him to his destination, seating him. The cave was heavily scented with frankincense and myrrh. Heru sat there very still, for it was too dark for him to see, and he could feel the rocks around him, some of them very sharp, and he didn't want to risk stumbling upon them, for he could not see his way around. "Man what have I gotten myself into; I didn't know it was going to be like this! I have to be in here ten whole days!" Heru thought.

As Heru sat there in the darkness, the doubts and fears began to creep up on him. "Maybe I'm not ready for initiation. Maybe I'm yet just a boy, a child. Maybe I'm not fit to be King, to sit on my father's throne." Thought

after thought began to race through his mind, and feelings of hopelessness and quitting started to come forward. At that very moment, Heru began to feel something crawling on his hands. Quickly he attempted to brush it off, but then he felt something crawling on his neck. Then he began to hear something moving a few feet away from him. Heru could feel himself becoming afraid. His eyes began to fill up with tears and it was at that very moment that the feeling of quitting, of failure, of insignificance became almost unbearable. Thoughts about what had happened to his father...everything it seemed to began to hit him all at once. Just when he was about to scream out for help, the words of his mother Auset began to ring in his mind "You are the son of Osir and Auset, grandson of Nut and Gab, Great Grandson of Ishu and Tufnut, Great Great Grandson of Ra Himself, who is the Son of Nu! You come from a line Divine Rulership, the same power resides within you my child" At that moment Heru began to chant that to himself, over and over again, dwelling on his lineage, and the power within. He remembered what his mother taught him in regards to calming the mind and he became really still and focused on his breathing, breathing lightly and gently, eventually the thoughts began to slow down, and ultimately cease. "The same power lies within….within...within...within… within" kept ringing in is ears, and with every "within" he felt himself going deeper and deeper into the darkness...then he saw Anpu say "Yet though there is darkness all around, and you are unable to see, you must find the light within the darkness. You must find the light within." And at that very moment he blacked out.

Heru then found himself looking at a scene out over the Universe, but there were no stars, no planets. There wasn't anything but this dark watery substance, but it wasn't water. "It's everywhere, but what is it? Heru wondered. Then Heru came to this room that was completely dark except for a light before a great mirror. Heru approached the mirror only to find he had no face! At that moment he heard someone whisper "Who are you?" and he snapped back to. Gasping for air, Heru quickly put his hands to his face. "Whew, it's still there" he said with a sigh of relief. "It's still there but I'm still here," he thought. "Anyway, I have no idea how long I was out of it. I might as well get some sleep." Heru began to feel around, moving some of the rocks aside so that he would have enough room to lie down comfortably. Once he had a descent amount of space cleared, he stretched out and slept.

Heru woke up to the sound of a drum and people chanting, "Nehest Heru, Nehest!" (wake Her, Wake!) He felt his mother's touch, and she began to feed him some type of broth. However, he was still blind folded. With each note, each beat of the drum, Heru began to see various colors manifest in the darkness of his mind. Then the colors began to swirl. Heru could feel his body begin to swirl along with the colors. "Oh no, I think I'm about to go out of it again." He thought. Suddenly he saw a Hawk flying directly at him in his mind's eye. At that very moment a tremendous force overtook his body. He observed his person get up and began to dance, yet he was not in control, nor could he stop it. In his mind's eye he saw a man with the Head of a Hawk, crowned with the Yatin (Sun) enveloped by a Serpent. "It's Ra he thought! As the beat of the drum intensified, so did his dancing. Auset and Nebt Het then began to chant "Damed Dadamej Ra! Ra! Damed Dadamej Ra Ra!" As they made hesi with those words, Anpu began to speak. "Heru do you know the story of your coming into Being? Do you Re-member? As Anpu spoke, in Heru's mind he observed the Serpent upon Ra's Head began to unravel from around the Yatin, and the Yatin itself then transformed into a Serpent of Light. The two began to dance together to in harmony with the chanting, before coming together to form one great Black serpent. This Serpent than began to swirl into several great coils, and as it coiled, Anpu bean to chant, "Kheperi, Kheperu, Kheperi, Kheperu." Heru then began to see his life flash before his eyes. He saw everything, every event that led up to that very moment. He then saw the face of every Ancestor in his bloodline, and the events that set the conditions in their lives for him to descend through their line. All of these things flashed so suddenly and finally he found himself again looking out over that Dark "Ocean" from before. As he stood there however, he heard the name "Osires," though the sound of the name was so subtle, its resonance caused massive ripples in the dark watery substance. With each ripple Heru began to see the image of his Father, Osir, standing in silence. Heru then began to recall Osir and Auset's life together, coming into Kemet, bringing civilization. The events began to speed up to the point where some of the events were difficult to make out, but then there came the very last ripple, a huge ripple that culminated in an explosion. The force and light from this explosion was so great that Heru had to shield his face. As this was taking place, Heru observed more events coming to his mind, and finally there he was, Sutesh. He observed Sutesh and Subik plotting to kill Osir, and before he could blink his Eyes, He was shown the very night that his father died. He saw them trap Osir in the coffin, and just as quickly throw the coffin, with Osir trapped inside, into the Hopi. At this time the heat of the explosion grew in intensity. He then saw his mother, searching tirelessly, as if possessed, throughout the earth to find the body of Osir. He saw all of her trials, and felt all of her pain and insecurities and desperations. He felt the glimpse of

hope when she recovered the body, as well as the initial doubt she felt in regards to the thoughts of conceiving. He then saw the ritual that led to his conception, and experienced the very moment of his conception, the seed and egg that came together. He then experienced his evolution in his mother's womb and finally the very moment of his birth. Right as he was witnessing his being born, a great Yatin began to rise out of the Dark Water Substance, and with every inch that Heru came forward from his mother's womb, the Yatin, rose higher and higher, causing the darkness to recede. At that moment Heru was absolutely speechless, and frozen in shock, and then suddenly he found himself passing out, falling to what felt like the ground. When he came back to, he attempted to sit up, but was unable to move. He then attempted to stretch out his arms, but there was something blocking his efforts. I'm inside of something, some sort of box! At that moment he began to panic. He tried to calm down, but then he heard his mother weeping outside the box, "Osir, o my Osir what have they done to you." She then opens the box and grabs Heru, saying, "Osir, O my Osir!" Before laying him back into the box. Heru realized that the box that he was within was his Father's coffin. At that moment Auset closed the lid, and Heru finally woke up to the sound of Anpu's voice saying "Nehast Heru, Nehast!" Heru was now fully conscious, and Anpu removed the blindfold from over his eyes. To Heru's surprise, he was sitting right in front of his father's coffin, and the cave that he had been in all of this time, was Osir's Tomb.

Immediately Auset, Nebt Het, and Anpu began to debrief Heru as to his experiences during his time in the tomb, and also took the time to share with him the revelations that they had received while participating in the rituals. Finally the time came when Heru was to take the ritual bath, in which he would be cleansed, made of special herbs, and then to be fully submerged into the water, and then brought forward a man. Nebt Het and Auset cleansed Heru, while Anpu made hesi with special words. "Heru," said Anpu. "Today is the first day of the rest of your life, for as Ra rose from the waters of Nu coming forth as a new creation, so you today emerge from these waters, purified, a new creation, a new man." At that very moment Auset cut the braid from Heru's head, to signify that he had successfully gone through his rites of passage and had now entered manhood. They then clothed him in some very nice red and white garments, anointed him with the finest oils, and a great feast was prepared for the occasion. They drummed and sang the entire evening in celebration of Heru's accomplishment.

Heru left that experience with a greater confidence, a greater knowledge of himself, his heritage and ancestry, as well as a strong sense of what his purpose is in life. The events that he experienced were burned into his mind and would serve as a constant reminder to him of his great destiny, and while he didn't fully understand everything that happened, as he went forward, slowly it would all begin to make sense.

The following morning Heru woke up and went to his father's tomb to pour libations to his Ancestors, and to pray before leaving to find Tehuti. After his rites of passage, he had committed his entire lineage to memory. During the libations he would call the name of his Ancestors, and pour water while thanking them for the things that they had done in paving the way for his coming into being. When he was all done he quickly left to find Tehuti. He was told that he could find Tehuti in a place called Khemenu, and it would be an eight day journey to get there. Anpu would assist him as his guide to get there.

After traveling for several hours they decided to stop and rest. From afar they could see a place where there was a tremendous darkness encapsulating it. "Man what is that?" Heru wondered. "That my dear brother is Kemet." Anpu replied. "WHAT!!!" "That's Ta-meri? But it looks so dark and gloomy, like all of the life has gone away from there." Well a lot has changed since Sutesh has been in power. People no longer live Maat, and going against Maat is going against life. Sutesh has everyone except a few, working like slaves, so much so that they barely have time to really learn about life and themselves, let along cultivate themselves. They are so miserable that they just want to make it to the end of the week when they get a break. They have not learned that the true source of joy is within, so they seek joy by way of external and artificial means, overindulging in intoxicants and sex. This is a continuous cycle that has depleted the vitality of the people, and also their intelligence. Kemet once was considered the light of the world, now look how dim she has become." Anpu said rather matter of fact. As he spoke, Heru noticed tears began to well up in his eyes, followed by a burning sensation in his chest. He thought about how great he heard Kemet was, and how she still would be great if Osir was still alive, and how Osir would still be alive if Sutesh hadn't killed him! As those thoughts rang through his mind, that burning sensation grew hotter and hotter spreading throughout his being. "Enough! He cried out. Let us be on our way!" Anpu realized that the conversation really struck something deep in Heru, for he had never seen that side of him before. Okay, Anpu agreed, as they collected themselves and left immediately.

After eight days they finally arrived in Khemenu. They went to Tehuti's home, which was very modest for a man that was considered one of the most powerful and wisest men to ever live. He served as Herald of Ra, and at one time he was the Thaty to Osir, so he was a man of great renown. They knocked on the door but no one answered. Let's go around back Anpu suggested. When they got to the back they found a woman there sitting in grass writing. Ankh Udja Seneb Seshata! Anpu addressed the lady. Anpu! Look at you! I haven't seen you since you were a khrad (child); and you must be Heru, I've heard much about you. It is an honor to meet the son of Osir and Auset. I'm Sesheta, Tehuti's wife. Inej Hr-k Sesheta, said Heru. You have come to see Tehuti, yes, well, he's not here. You must go down to the pond, that's where you'll find him. "Dua!" Said Heru. They went quickly to the pond. The pond was very still and quiet, and there were lotuses everywhere. There they found Tehuti with his back towards them, singing a tune while two serpents danced with one another before him. They stood there very quietly in amazement as they observed what he was doing. As he sang, the snakes would swirl around one another making certain shapes with their bodies in relationship to one another based upon the tone of his voice, the notes he sang. He then pulled out a reed and a Shekhem (Sistrum) and began to play the same tune that he sang, and noticed that the Serpents danced and made the exact same patterns. He stopped and took notes of his observation, and without even turning around he said to the two young men, "If you strive to harmonize you will become enlightened." Come sit with me, Tehuti said calmly. They both bowed before the wise man and sat at his feet. "It is good to see you two again. You both are growing to be strong men. Heru I haven't seen you since you were a mesh (baby). How are Auset and Nebt Het?" Tehuti asked. "They are well and send you and Seshata their blessings." Anpu responded. "That is very good to know." Tehuti said smiling. He was very humble for a man of immense wisdom, very familial. "So, you boys have come to learn the sacred wisdom and traditions of the Ancestors, yes? They nodded anxiously. That is very good. These traditions have been handed down generation after generation since time immemorial. Even before the founding of Ta Meri, these teachings were passed down to our Mwwt n Itw (Mothers and fathers) when they were children sitting at the feet of their Seru (elders), and their parents before that, all the way to the beginning. It is said "How good it is that a son should take from his father that by which he had reached old age. Let a son receive the word from his father, not being heedless of any rule of his. Instruct your son that he may grow old, reach a position of honor and reverence, and pass on the tradition in like manner to his sons and daughters that they become famous in their deeds. Implant truth and justice into the lives of your children that they may grow to become the leaders of tomorrow, full of righteousness." Tehuti's words were very profound, and Anpu and Heru hung on his every word. They would spend the next several years like this, sitting at Tehuti's feet, engaging in questions and answers.

When Tehuti felt that the young men were ready, he began to instruct them in the sacred rituals of the Ancestors. He taught them the deeper meaning of the libations, and how to properly honor each Ancestor. Tehuti, how do I properly, honor our Ita Ra? Heru asked. First know that you cannot honor someone without honoring their Ancestors. Everything that makes a person up at the very foundation of their being, they inherited from their Ancestors. Therefore, to really properly honor Ra, we must first honor Ra's Father and Mother Nu and Nunet. They are the source of Ra and by extension the source of us All. Honor them by remembering that in essence we are all one, connected springing from the same source. Also, Nu being the inert one, or the one who rests, we must honor him by connecting to and maintain our inner peace, and offer peace to others, as it is said, "Hetep is the Offering." From there you have a foundation by which to honor Ra. "Honor Ra by recognizing, acknowledging, and reverencing the Divine light within yourself and everyone else, and protect the light, keep it shining bright." Tehuti responded. "What about Ishu and Tufnut?" asked Anpu. You honor them by respecting the law of duality, form and function, and compliments. This is the foundation of Maat, balance. It is this duality that makes life possible. The greatest example of this that we have is of Man and Woman, and how these two come together to create life. It is as though the two were created with one another in mind yes? It is said that a phenomenon always arises from the interaction between complimentaries, and if you want something, look for the compliment that will elicit it. This we owe to the great Ancestors Ishu and Tufnut. "How do we honor Mut Het Heru?" By living a life of harmony, Tehuti replied. While it is duality, multiplicity that makes life possible, it is harmony and order that allows it to thrive. We see the greatest example of harmony in nature. Nature is a beautiful song, with tremendous rhythms and harmony. We see this in the cycles of the days and seasons, and how all things relate to one another. Het Heru is Cosmic Rhythm, yet, she is much much more. By learning the dance of nTr, you will in turn learn to harmonize with and respect life. Het Heru is life itself, the vehicle that makes it all possible, Ra's Eye, his Yatin in which all creations are made. One more thing about Het-Heru, when you learn to move with her rhythm, you will find that you will come to truly enjoy life

no matter what is happening. It is said that Ra gets depressed every now and then. "Really?" Heru asked. Yes, even Ra as powerful and mighty as he is gets down ever so often. When he is in this mood it is said that only Het-Heru can cheer him up, and if it were not for her, it would be impossible to lift his spirit. Without her, he would just retreat back into the Abyss. Wow! Anpu and Heru exclaimed in unison. Yes, my sons, Het-Heru is very important and must be honored. How do we honor Nut and Gab?" asked Heru. By learning to read, hear, and dance with their rhythms, and recognizing that complimentaries or opposites are really mirror reflections of one another. It is said "As Above, So Below, and vice versa." What happens on earth is directly reflected and correlated to what is happening in the heavens. This is why we built Kemet in the image of heaven, and the spirit world. What happens in the world is an effect, a culmination of the creative processes of the spirit realm and the heavens. For example, it is said in our tradition, that it is the Seven Het-Heru that announces the Fate of every individual at birth. These Seven Het-Heru, are the Seven Planets. The position of these Planets in the Heavens amongst the Stars, and the position of our planet in relationship to them at the time of one's birth, and in truth at any given time, has a direct affect on the events that take place on the earth, the temperament and personalities of the people born during this time, etc. Understanding this, it is important to know that these things are cyclical, and one may thus make certain predictions as to the time and what must be done; and by observing and dancing with the rhythm of the heavens and the rhythms and cycles of the earth, one will find themselves by consequence in tune with the time. Also, we must understand that each person has their own rhythm based upon their destiny and the heavens and earth at the time of their birth, the grand cycles of their incarnations and must learn to recognize and respect it, and move with it. As the Ancestors have always said "Every person must operate within the rhythm of their time, this makes them wise." There is something else to be known about Nut and Gab, and that is for everything that exists, there is a heavenly aspect, as well as an earthly aspect, and these dual components like all dualities must be harmonized. For instance, man consists of multiple spiritual bodies, just as the heavens consist of multiple celestial bodies and the earth consists of multiple bodies of land and water. The heavenly bodies within man, such as the Shekhem, Yakhu, and Ba, must be balanced and harmonized by the mediating bodies, the Zoh, Ib and Khaibit, with the earthly bodies, the Ka, Ren and Khat. Maat, order must be maintained amongst these."We have several bodies? Anpu asked. If this is so why don't we see them? They vary in levels of density vs. subtlety, Tehuti answered. Take water for instance, it goes through three different phases, gas, liquid, and solid. These different expressions of water vary in density, air being the most subtle, and ice being the densest. The variation is caused by the difference in frequency and vibration; the higher the vibration or frequency, the more subtle the form. In contrast, the lower or slower the vibration is, the denser the form. This is a very important lesson that you to must understand. The reason why we began with Shekhem is because it is the foundation. Where have you heard this word, Shekhem, before? "My mother has a rattle that she calls Shekhem" Anpu replied. "Ahh," Tehuti smiled. "Yes the sistrum rattle is called Shekhem. When you hold the Shekhem, and began to move it, it begins to make sounds. It vibrates! This also why it is said that Ra brought all of this into being by speaking the word, and he is called the Exalted Shekhem. The underpinning of all life is Shekhem, power, motion and sound. The form a thing takes varies based upon the sound that brings it into being."

"Another interesting thing is this," Tehuti continued, "because we descend from our Ancestors and Predecessors chemically, we also inherit many of their characteristics and tendencies. Notice how people in a family tend to look alike, and even have places in behavior that reflect the family culture. Someone may say to you, "You know you look just like your father, or you act just like your grandmother, you have your Mother's smile, or you inherited a certain gift or talent from your Ancestor. Sometimes the things we inherit from our Ancestors may be certain inclinations or simply the worldview and perspective on life and tradition. We must observe and study ourselves, and also study our families so that we may see what exactly it is that we have inherited; be they gifts or curses, assets or liabilities."

"From here we can talk about the family." Tehuti taught unceasingly." "Maat must be maintained in the family. As it should be obvious from all that we have talked about thus far that family is our spiritual way of life, it is our religion." Tehuti said. "The family is the foundation of all life. It is the family that serves as the basis of society. When Maat is upheld from the familial level, it then extends into the greater community. We each have a role to play in life. The eldest son has a function to carry out that differs from that of the eldest daughter, or even the middle or youngest son. The father's duty and role, differs from that of the wife in that his duties take him out to work in the fields, or to work with the black smith, while the wife's duties are mostly home oriented, rearing the children, etc. However, both roles are critical to the sustenance of the family unit, and reflect the differences in our nature that make us unique. Form follows function,

always in nature. There is an interconnectedness and interdependence that is exhibited by the family that prepares us for the world at large. In the family there are different roles, and relationships vary based upon those roles. There are also different personalities that have to learn to harmonize and coexist in the same house. This in truth is preparation for the larger society. We must learn about one another so that we can peacefully live together. Due to the close nature of a family it creates the perfect opportunity to grow spiritually and mentally due to the challenges presented from the friction of the closeness. We learn our parent's limits, what angers them, what disturbs their peace; we learn what causes strife between our siblings. We learn to express our love by seeking not to intentionally cross those lines, as to ensure that Maat is maintained in the home. This wisdom should serve as a blueprint on how to walk in our journey through life interacting with the people that we meet. We will meet many different types of people, we must learn how to harmonize and coexist with each one. This is Maat. This same law extends to the various situations we go through. As we move through life we encounter different events, circumstances, situations, that may call on respond or behave in a manner that is different from our normal way of being, yet suits the time and the situation. If we are not able to harmonize with these experiences, we clash with them, we compete with them. It becomes a fight, a struggle. Keep this in mind and you shall walk though life finding that you are always in harmony with Maat."

"How do we Honor our Father and Mother," the young men inquired? "By upholding the traditions and sense of Maat that they've instilled in you, living by them, and passing the tradition on to your children." Tehuti answered. "However" he continued, "due to the dual nature of reality, there will always be things that can be improved upon, some things that become totally corrupt, and some things that become outdated. This is true of traditions, and things that may have been true or proper for the time, yet are no longer appropriate. For these things, we must make corrections where corrections are needed, repair where reparation is due, update and evolve where evolution is necessary, and discard if something needs to be discarded. So our duty to our parents, as well as all of our Jertiyu (Ancestors), is to build upon what they have given us, but also correct some of the mistakes that they have made. In doing so, we actually correct the effects of these things at a constitutional level, purifying the blood. Everything that we do, think, eat, etc, has a biochemical component to it and ultimately trickles down to our blood chemically, and is engrained in our genes. This is why our ancestors say that "preaching Maat to men is pointless, it must be infused in their lineage." When there is isfet (chaos) in the bloodline, the child must work to repair the corruption, through a life of Maat, eating, thinking, and living properly. By doing this we create an avenue for our Ancestors to come back through our seeds at a more evolved state of being. In a way, we are our own Ancestors, just as we are all evolutions of the "One," Ra. We stem from the one source and continue to come back through our own ancestral line. Our life on earth is recorded into our blood, the information is registered. This creates a portal, so to speak, for us to enter back into this plane from the Duat into our family. As it is written, "the Ba goes to the place it knows, and it doesn't stray far from the past."

"In regards to our parents, we must remember that they took care of us when we were unable to take care of ourselves. We must return the favor when the time comes and they need us to do the same for them. We have a responsibility to make sure that we give them a proper burial, and have the rites set in place to maintain the rituals to keep them strong and happy in the Duat. Life doesn't end; it is a continuous journey, similar to the cycles of Ra. The Yatin rises in the east and sets in the west, only to rise again in the east. The east and west represent this realm(earth) and the duat, the beautiful west. Also, our relationship with our Ancestors does not end when they make their transition from this side of life. They are still family, they are still with us, just at a more subtle, higher, yet more powerful state existence. We have a responsibility towards them, and they us. This is what family is about, responsibility, and each member doing their part to see that the whole flourishes, to make sure that everyone is good. There are things that our Ancestors need to survive in the Duat, just as there are things that we need to survive in this world. We spoke earlier about the various spiritual bodies we possess, yes. While our Khat remains here, the other bodies are free to travel, through the Duat. Yet, all of these bodies are made up of energy, and like everything, they need energy to survive. Everything eats, no matter how subtle an energy body it may be. We set up our Ancestral Rites to make sure that our Jertiyu stay fed. It is the Ka that we feed during libations, and through the offering of food, and other articles and sacrifices. The Ka is the body that is the actual Personality, which made them who they were. It also stores the information that we accumulate during our sojourn on earth. Through the constant feeding and remembrance of the Jertiyu, they can be elevated to the level of a nTr, and can become very powerful and effective. To facilitate this process, we

perform what is called the Opening of the Mouth ceremony. In our helping them, they are in a better state to be able to effectively help us. Heru, Anpu, the two of you must now be prepared to perform these rites on behalf of your father Osir." Anpu and Heru hung on this great sage's every word. Time would past so quickly during these sessions. They would sit down and before you knew it hours had past, but the two young men eagerly awaited each lesson. The following morning they would leave to make their way back to Auset and Nebt Het, and Tehuti would accompany them as to prepare them for Osir's ritual.

When they finally reached their destination, Tehuti greeted Auset and Nebt Het and then quickly retired to rest up for the next lesson. The following morning Tehuti began to teach them about the Opening of the Mouth ritual. "Ser (Elder), why is it that we call the ritual the Opening of the Mouth?" Anpu asked. "Great question Anpu," said Tehuti. "Let us examine it and see if we can come to a solution, as our great Jertiyu have said "The answer to a question resides within the nature of the question." Looking at the name of the ritual, we see that its main subject is a mouth. There is this mouth and it needs to be opened. This is obvious; the mouth must be closed if the ritual is called Opening the Mouth. We are speaking to the Mouth of the Ancestor. Why is it that they need an open mouth? What is the purpose and function of the mouth? To eat, Anpu replied. "Ahhh, very good," Tehuti smiled. It is through the mouth that we take in food and drink, to nourish and sustain us. We have already spoken to the fact that our Ancestors need nourishment, they need energy just like we do. They must be fed so they can remain healthy and strong, and happy. So this is one reason why we open the mouth. "What else do we do with our mouths?" Tehuti asked. "We speak with the mouth," Heru answered. "Yes!" Tehuti responded cheerfully. "It is through the mouth that we speak, that we communicate. The Ancestors are still much a part of the family and community, and just as we go to our parents and elders for advice and guidance, or an elder may give you instructions, our Ancestors communicate to us in various ways to give us guidance, instructions, etc. How is this so? Anpu asked? How are they able to communicate seeing that there is no life in the body? The body is but a vehicle to carry the more subtle elements of a man's being. We see a person's Khat, yet all we see is a culmination of various subtle levels and processes that happen beyond the gross physical. What we see is mostly a symbolic representation of a deeper and more subtle reality. When the Khat is no longer available to use for communication, then communication continues on a more subtle level, or a new symbol is used. From this ritual the Ancestors are given a vehicle to use for communication; a tomb, an altar, a shrine, a statue, a coffin that is made in the form of the Khat of the person, and contains within it the preserved Khat of the person. The tomb is actually a temple, and home for the Ancestor, where we go to make offerings, to make sure that they are taken care of, and to ask for assistance when we need it. When we go in the Shrine, there is Hesi that we can perform, going in to a more subtle level of awareness where we are able to communicate with them. The symbol serves as a medium, a doorway so to speak, between this side and the next." "Why do we preserve the Khat?" Anpu asked. "The Khat is the part of a person that is most familiar to them, and carries so much of the person's shekhem with it. We become familiar with our Khat, before we become acquainted with the more subtle bodies, including our own Ren. In preserving the Khat, we preserve much of the semblance of the Ancestor, and enshrining it in a coffin that in truth is a totem or Tut (image) of the person as well, further adding to the familiarity of the ancestor with the shrine. This is also the reason why we place objects that belonged to the Ancestor in the tomb. The very next thing that a person is most familiar with following the Khat is the Ren. A person's Ren is the thing that they will hear more than anything in their life, and the fact that it is spoken to draw the person's attention, which is the highest level of ones being, adds to the effectiveness of the use of it during ritual in invoking the Ancestor's presence. So the name is written throughout the tomb and on the coffin. Also, the Khaibit, the presence and residual shekhem of the person will be present in the shrine, via the Khat, and various belongings. The belongings and everything in the shrine, including the Khat itself serves to paint a picture, and tell a story about who the person was, to serve as a reminder to them, us, and anybody that may visit the tomb. Also in regards to speaking, the "Mouth" is opened, and the person is given offerings of Hikau to enable them to speak and influence things from the Duat, to create in the spirit realm. This is why we write various Hesi on the walls of the tomb, the walls of the coffin, we may even wrap the person's Khat in papyrus containing the Hesi, or even write it on the Khat itself, Hesi that contain the Renu of various nTrw and forces that they may encounter during their traverse through the spirit realm, giving them the ability to move about uninhibited, and to make things happen when they need to make things happen. Now before any of these rituals can take place we must first preserve the Khat. Anpu, this will be one of your duties." Tehuti then showed Anpu how to prepare, embalm, and preserve the Khat of Osir. Their mothers somehow managed to smuggle a coffin made in Osir's image from Behudet, to replace the one that Sutesh had murdered him in. It was made of the finest gold, and decked in the finest jewels and stones. Anpu properly preserved the vital organs, the liver, the

stomach, the intestines, and kidneys, placing them in canopy jars. He bathed the body in fine oils and spices, honey, natron, and salt, and then proceeded to wrap it in clean bandages, all the while making Hesi over it.

Heru, along with Nebt Het began to prepare the tomb of Osir, and also acquired the Ka (Bull) that would serve as the Ritual Sacrifice to Osir's Ka. "Tehuti, why do we sacrifice a Ka?" Heru asked. "My son for every joy to be had there is a price to be paid. Everything makes a sacrifice. In regards to the Ka, we make an exchange, a Ka for a Ka. We perform divination, and make a careful selection on the proper Ka for the ritual. We then offer the Ka to the Ka of the Ancestor, that they may feed on the shekhem of the Ka, thus assimilating the shekhem. This makes the Ancestor very powerful. The Khat of the Ka is then preserved and buried, and its Ka is deified." They then began the ritual. They purified the tomb with a solution made of natron and water. They then began to make circumambulation around the tomb while making hesi, speaking certain words of blessings and vows of protection, soothing to the spirit of Osir. They then began to make circumambulation around the coffin which was now standing upright, while burning incense of frankincense and myrrh as offerings to his Ka. There are special tools made of iron that were used during the ritual to symbolically open the mouth and eyes of Osir, restoring these faculties to life. At this moment there was a sacrifice of a goat and a goose, symbolizing the triumph of Osir over his enemies. Then the first of two bulls were offered. The foreleg and the heart were cut out and placed at the feet of the shrine. There were many offerings during the ritual which consisted of tons of incense, grapes, beer, bread, and fresh water. The final bull was offered in the same manner as before, however, this time the horns were taken to be stripped (left out in nature to have the flesh eaten away, then purified, and later placed upon the shrine.). The statue was then anointed and clothed. A head band adorned with one ostrich plume feather was placed upon the head, and garland of flowers around the neck. Libations were then poured to all the nTrw and Jertiyu. A few more blessings were uttered and then the ritual was complete. The entire process took about 70 days.

That evening Osir appeared to each of them in a dream, giving each one a set of instructions. However, he only instructed Heru to come to his tomb. When Heru entered the shrine, he could feel the presence of Osir. "Whoa, the shekhem in this place is popping." He thought. He went over to his father's shrine and prostrated before it saying, Inej Hr-k Ita. He then began to pour libations of water, offering to Osir's Ka, remembering the words of Tehuti "The soul goes to the place it knows, and comes to those who give it water." He then kneeled before Osir's Statue and began a special Hesi that Tehuti taught him, to call forward the Ka of his father. After chanting it mentally to himself for several minutes, a voice began to speak to him from the statue saying, "Heru, close your eyes." He then closed them as instructed and found himself transported into a hall where there was a council of elders dressed in white seated on each side of the room. In the very center of the hall seated upon a throne, was Osir. He was very regal in his white crown and holding his crook and flail. "He began to speak gently: "Heru, my son." He said. Heru in awe fell upon his face, weeping. This was the first time that he'd been in the presence of his father, seemingly alive, hearing his voice, feeling his presence. "My son, please look up." Osir asked. "How I've longed for the day that I would be able to look upon you, to speak to you.," he said. Osir stood up and raised Heru to his feet, and embraced him. "We have much to discuss, you and I." After relishing in the moment, they both took a seat. Osir then began to speak. "My son you have grown into a fine young man. Your mother has done a magnificent job. The time has come that you must take my will in hand and reclaim my throne and your rightful place as Nisu Bity of Tameri, and in the process restore Maat to the world. Sutesh has become very powerful, and is hungry for more power. He has an insatiable thirst for power, yet it is this same blind ambition that will lead him to his demise. Though he has spread his empire far and wide over the earth, he himself has become more isolated than ever, as it is fear that drives him, and it is fear that prevents people from rising up against him. He has slaughtered many of our people, enslaved others, and others have fled to preserve their lives as best as they can. Kemet is now run and populated by foreigners of a strange persuasion. Our people are oppressed and have lost the knowledge of who they truly are. As a result they are quickly falling away from civilization. It is on you, my son, to liberate them, and show them the way back to mAat. However, know that your task won't be easy, for Sutesh has over time, conditioned our people to embrace their own oppression, and even fight against those that try to extricate them from it, in some cases, even killing those who fight for them. Sutesh is very shrewd." "In these circumstances, how can I defeat Sutesh? How can I separate the people from him if they won't let him go? How can I fight for them if they are willing to fight me? How can I fight Sutesh? I don't know anything about fighting!" Heru interjected, becoming more overwhelmed with anxiety with each question. "If others have tried to fight Sutesh and have been unsuccessful, what makes you think that I will succeed?" Osir smiled at his son, and placed his hand upon the back of his neck in a comforting manner "Because it is your destiny Heru, yours and yours alone..." Osir replied. "Time is on your side, and I am with you."

Heru found comfort in his father's words. Also, he noticed that for a situation so dire, Osir was very calm, very much at peace. Heru found this comforting, but wondered how his father could be so calm when discussing war. Osir without Heru's speaking a word, read Heru's thoughts, and said to him: "Heru let me tell you a story." Heru became very excited, like a little boy, but tried his best not to show it externally, knowing he was supposed to be a man and all now. However, this is something that he had longed for all his life, a chance to sit at his father's feet, to hear his voice, to be taught by him, for him to tell him a story, something he had grown up seeing the other children have. Heru took the moment to catch his breath as to conceal his excitement, but Osir had just read his thoughts, so of course he knew. "Has your mut told you the story of when I traveled around the world, spreading mAat throughout?" Osir asked? "Tiyu!" Heru answered. Osir continued: "you know everywhere we went the people were so excited to see us, so happy, and they embraced us. We brought them the information that would help them to realize the potential they had within, allowing them to raise themselves out of the darkness of ignorance, isfet, and poverty. We didn't force them, didn't threaten them, we offered them a solution; we offered them friendship, true friendship...you see wise men seek friendship, fools seek enemies, and forced friends are no friends. Anyway, everywhere we went the people welcomed us with open arms, throwing festivals in our honor. However, there was one place where this was not the case. There was this nation, to the north of us where the people were afraid to welcome us, out of fear of their "King." This nation was very impoverished, but the king lived as a rich man. He enslaved his people, building up his wealth from their labor. You see the good Shai (Destiny and Fortune) of a Nation is it's Nisu who lives mAat. This so-called king did not live mAat, and therefore was no king at all. He did not allow us entry into the kingdom; in fact he met us at the gates with his military. He had heard about the success we had in the surrounding nations, and how the people were empowered by our teachings, and the last thing he wanted was for his people to be empowered. So not only did he not want us to enter his country, but if he could, we would've killed us all on the spot. I was always a man of peace and taught that war should always be the absolute last resort, but I was also taught that sometimes the price of peace is war, and that chaos precedes order. I attempted to reason with this man, but his bA (Conscience) had deserted him a long time ago. I began to turn our troops away, and at that moment we noticed his people began to congregate, making their way towards us. Seeing this, the king began to slaughter his own people. Once I saw this, I ordered your uncle Heru, whom you are named after to attack. "War," that's what we call your uncle, immediately took the troops into battle. We defeated him, and held a tribunal before his people. Seeing that he was defeated, I was prepared to let him leave. However, he took an act of mercy for weakness. As his bA no longer spoke to him, he was full of darkness, so much so that if given the chance, he would do it all over again. As soon as he was released, he grabbed a sword from one of the guards who was caught unaware and attempted to take my life. However, I felt him, I sensed his heart, and I quickly grabbed my sword and with one fatal swipe, I beheaded him." Heru's eyes grew wide in shock as he listened to his father recount this event in great detail. He had never heard of this side of Osir before, "Osir the Great Warrior." "Ahh see you thought I was soft huh!" Osir said jokingly. Just as there is the spilling of blood at the birth of every child, sometimes great ventures require great sacrifice. While we shouldn't seek war, sometimes it seeks you, and cannot be avoided. It is wisdom that allows you to discern the time, and the appropriate measures. Heru, you're time has come, you must travel to Behudet, there you will find your uncle War working as a Blacksmith. One look at you and he will know who you are and why you have come. This is a time our family has waited for. However, you must not reveal your identity and purpose to anyone before it is time. War will train you, and make you into a great warrior. You will know when you are ready, and remember I am always with you, as your bA, there to advise you. When the time comes, you shall reveal yourself to your people, and when they see the light emanating from you, they will be inspired, and congregate around you. They will fight with you, and I along with all of the ancestors will be there to fight with you." After, giving Heru his instructions, Osir stood up and raised Heru to his feet. "Father if I may, I have one more question for you." Osir knew the question before Heru conceived it. "You want to know how Sutesh got into a position to do what he did." Heru looked at his father in amazement. "The most dangerous enemy is the one within, for he is so close that he may go undetected before it is too late. It was a lack of vigilance on my part. Isfet had entered into the family, however if Sutesh had not done what he did, this weakness would not have been known, and the conditions fit for its correction would not have presented itself. It is those very conditions that resulted in your coming into being my son; you are Heru Nej It.f (Heru the Avenger of your Father). Now arise!" Heru stood tall, full of confidence. Osir embraced him, looked him in his eyes, smiled and said "Shim" (Go)...and at that very moment Heru opened his eyes, finding himself at his father's shrine.

As he exited his father's tomb, he walked with a confidence that had never

been seen in him before, without saying a word, his mother knew that her son's life had been greatly changed, and that he was not the same little boy that she had raised, but was growing into the man that she always knew he would become. He walked up to her and embraced her. He embraced Nebt Het, and instructed Anpu to take care of their mothers. The following day, he and Tehuti made their way to Behudet.

When they arrived in Behudet, they found War hard at work. Heru took a moment to look at this man after whom he had been named. There he stood looking like he had been carved out of a mountain. He stood just under 6 ft, but carried the presence of a 7 footer. As he hammered away at a sword he was fashioning, his biceps and shoulders exploded. Tehuti walked up behind him and said, "you know you're in pretty good shape, for an old man." War smiled, slightly, recognizing Tehuti's voice, and put his hammer down. He grabbed Tehuti hugging him, picking the Sage up in the process. "Tehuti!" War exclaimed! "How have you been my friend? Age has treated you kind!" War said, obviously thrilled to see Tehuti. "Well you know Seshata keeps me on my toes...feeding me good," Tehuti chuckled. "That is great to hear, it's good to see you!" War said. But if you're here it could only mean..., and at that very moment Heru entered into the room. Immediately War recognized him. Heru walked up to him, "Ankh Uja Seneb! Uncle it is great to meet you." War embraced him tightly, but briefly, and then looked at him and said: "I've waited long for this day, and now look my Shai stands before me." War then kneeled before Heru. This greatly affected Heru; even puzzled him. He looked at his uncle and asked: "uncle, what do you mean your Shai stands before you?" War answered without hesitation, "I was born to prepare you for your great work, and now that you stand before me, the time has come for me to fulfill my purpose." He then bowed his head in humility before Heru. Heru was totally speechless. He could not believe that a man as great as War would even speak to him, let along kneel before him; and to deepen matters, this great man believed that his very reason for being was to serve Heru. Heru quickly grabbed his uncle, raising him off the floor (as best he could, War was huge of course) and helping him to a seat, War called to his wife, "Het Heru, come here my love." In walked this gorgeous woman, by far the most beautiful woman Heru had ever seen. Tehuti quickly reminded him that she was his Aunt! When she saw Heru, she also bowed before him, graciously, and then looked to her husband's need. "Honey would you please prepare a great meal for us." She smiled the most beautiful smile, and said "of course," and went right away to get it done. Het Heru loved to cook, for this reason she is called "Lady of Food," among other beautiful names. "Heru, how is your mother? And Nebt Het?" War asked. "They are very well and both send their love." Heru noticed that his response brought much peace to his uncle. They talked for a few hours, awaiting the great meal that Het Heru was working on. When the food was finally ready, they all ate and drank to their hearts desire. Het Heru danced and played the sistrum and sang the most beautiful song. War encouraged Heru to enjoy himself, and rest, for tomorrow their training would begin. Heru took his uncle's advice and relished in the moment.

The following morning War began Heru's training at sunrise. He brought Heru to a room in the back of his workspace that was very dirty, yet full of weapons. "Here," said War, handing Heru a bucket of a natron and water solution and a wash cloth. "What do you want me to do with this?" Heru asked seemingly confused. "Ha ha," War chuckled. If your mother handed you a bucket of natron water and a rag what would you think she wants you to do?" War said with a slight smirk on his face. "Clean?" Heru replied. "Exactly!" I want you to clean this whole room, excluding the weapons. Yes some of them are also very dirty, but I don't want you to clean them just yet...don't touch them. I'll be back to check on you around midday." War began to leave the room. "But I thought I was going to start training today," Heru stated still seemingly befuddled. "You have..." War replied, still walking out of the room, closing the door behind him. "Ok," Heru thought to himself. "I don't get it, but I'm going to follow my uncle's instructions." He promptly got to work. Every now and then, Heru would take a break to rest, and take a glance at his uncle's weapons. There were some of the finest crafted weapons: spears, maces, daggers, sickles, swords, and shields. Heru had never really been around weaponry before, he was curious, but remembered his uncle's words. He refocused himself and finished cleaning. He was unaware of the fact that War was checking on him periodically, evaluating his work ethic, his focus, discipline and obedience. A little before mid day, War came in and found Heru had finished the whole room. It looked very clean. "Come with me," War said. He brought Heru back to his living quarters. "Get cleaned up, and meet me in the kitchen." He instructed him. "Yes Uncle," Heru replied. Heru was a very obedient young man; very respectful. His rites of passages and lessons from Tehuti, along with good genes paid off. After he washed up and got dressed, he hurried to the kitchen to meet up with War. "What took you so long?" War asked, with a slight smirk on his face that largely went unnoticed. I wasn't long at all, Heru thought to himself, but apologized anyway. "Ok," War replied. Heru looked around and noticed that there were dishes sitting around, as though someone had already eaten. After all the work he had done that morning,

he was ready to eat. However, he noticed there didn't appear to be any food left. Almost getting lost in his thoughts, War got his attention. "Here," War said, handing him another bucket of natron and water and a cloth. You want me to clean? "Yes," War said, leaving the kitchen. "I'll be back in a few hours," he said. Heru could feel a little frustration rising within himself, but he remained calm, and followed his uncle's instructions. Heru got to work, trying his best to ignore his hunger pangs. After a few hours of cleaning he was really hungry, and even more frustrated. He thought to himself, "maybe I'll learn to fight after I finish cleaning this kitchen, hopefully I won't be too tired." When War came to get Heru, he found the kitchen very clean. He then instructed Heru to return to his living quarters and get cleaned up. After you are washed up, meet me back at the kitchen. Heru didn't understand. He was hungry, tired, and frustrated. He thought to himself: "every time he wants me to wash up and then clean up, I wash up, and then he wants me to get dirty again." On top of this, I do a great job cleaning, and he doesn't even acknowledge it, no show of gratitude, nothing. He didn't even save me any food!" Heru could feel his temperature rising, this time it was beginning to show a little on his face. War noticed, but he didn't say anything, only smirked slightly. Nonetheless, Heru went on and did as his uncle instructed him to do.

When Heru arrived at the kitchen he found all of the furniture removed. There he found War and Tehuti playing some drums, while Het Heru danced before them. When he walked in the room the music stopped, and War addressed him. "Ahh… good, you are just in time. We are ready to begin your dance lessons." "Dance Lessons!" Heru thought to himself. After all this time…all the work; he was tired, hungry, frustrated, feeling unappreciated, and after all of this he still wasn't learning how to fight. This time he couldn't hold it in any longer. "I don't want to dance; I want to learn how to fight!" Heru stated in frustration. "Is that so?" War said, with that same small smirk on his face. "Ok, I tell you what, if you can dance for five minutes without stepping on your aunt's feet, we will start the combat training immediately." "Ah…easy," Heru thought, with a smirk on his face similar to the one War had been concealing all day. However, War was very keen, and chuckled to himself. "Good!" He said, as he and Tehuti began to play a rhythm. As they would beat the drums, Het Heru would move to the rhythm, almost as if her body was making the beat itself. She smiled, and motioned Heru to join her. He went to her very confidently, and began to dance with her. It wasn't long before he had her feet screaming. "Yow!" Het Heru said, still forcing as cute of a smile as she could. "It's ok, War said, give it another shot." Heru was happy to get another chance, but this time he wasn't as confident as before. After a few steps…same thing, "Yow!" Het Heru yelled! This time Heru could see her smile fade. War and Tehuti were having a great old laugh. "I don't get it!" Heru said. "What does any of this have to do with me learning to fight?" War collected himself, and smiled at his nephew who was obviously frustrated. "Everything Heru," War replied. "You see a warrior must be disciplined. He must be patient, and know how to follow orders. He must be able to work sometimes without eating, and sometimes without rest. He must be clean both internally and externally, making his exterior reflect his interior. He should be cleaned up and disciplined before he learns to take up arms or fight, otherwise he may be corrupt and abuse his power, hurting himself or others in the process. Also, a warrior, in having to sometimes follow someone else's orders, must surrender and move to the beat of another's drum. Furthermore sometimes a warrior may work very hard for very long, without any form of compensation or appreciation. However, if he is truly a warrior, he must learn patience and perseverance, for this will make him great. In dancing, you learn harmony, you learn how to lead, as well as follow various rhythms, and you learn timing, all of which are needed to become a great warrior. Heru hung on his uncles every word, and humbled himself before his wisdom." Heru kneeled before his uncle, smiled and said, "I understand uncle, but you know you sound like Tehuti right?" Heru said, jokingly, War smiled, while Het Heru and Tehuti laughed. Well you know the saying, "The friend of a Wise Man is another Wise Man," Tehuti replied, placing his hands on both War and Heru's shoulders. After this they ate together, and retired for the evening.

Heru would follow the same routine for several months, cleaning his uncle's workplace, the kitchen, and learning how to dance. After while, it all became second nature to him; especially the dancing. He learned to dance very well. Soon War allowed Heru to begin cleaning the weapons. This allowed him time to get acquainted with each weapon, intimately, learning how to handle and maintain them. Heru would follow this routine for several months. After a while War instructed Heru to load the weapons, and bring them to him in his yard. There Heru would watch his uncle train. Carrying the weapons to and from the field helped Heru gain the strength to handle them over time. This task was very strenuous initially, but grew easy, and Heru was able to get it done very quickly eventually.

War was a great warrior, the best. On the battle field only Sutesh rivaled his skill. However after everything that happened with his family, Sutesh usurping the throne, War retired from active combat, and decided to work

as a smith for the military, and a trainer of the warriors. This allowed him to keep his skills sharp, as well as have an arsenal prepared for the day Heru would go forward to challenge Sutesh, without attracting too much attention to himself before then. Besides, Sutesh had moved the capital to Inu, while War settled in Behudet in the south which allowed him to move somewhat freely.

Everyday Heru would watch War work. He would watch him make the weapons, and eventually he himself learned how to make them. He watched War train, watched the way he handled weapons, his footwork, fight hand to hand, wrestle; he observed his rhythm. Heru was very perceptive, and made every effort to reproduce what he saw his uncle doing. He also watched his uncle train some of the warriors. He watched the way War worked with them, spoke to them, commanded their respect, and disciplined them. Heru was always there by War's side, taking notes. This went on for several years.

One day Heru was watching one of War's students that was having trouble with a particular exercise. Heru noticed a flaw in his form, but he dared not say anything to interrupt his uncle. Yet, War noticed Heru's expression and knew that he saw something that he had not seen himself. "Heru, come," War said. "You seem to have something on your mind, what do you see?" War asked, curiously. There is a problem with his form. He is a smaller fighter than some of the others, yet his stance mimics the form of a big man. This is causing him to move about inefficiently, and leaving several points of vulnerability. This is the moment War had been waiting for. Show me, War responded, with that signature smirk of his. Heru stepped up to the Warrior, and quickly demonstrated his points, exposing several weakness and points of attack. The other warriors took notes and were very impressed with Heru. War was also very pleased, and began to call on Heru more and more to assist him, eventually having Heru fall into rank with the men.

Heru quickly climbed up the ranks with his fellow warriors earning their respect in the process. He worked hard and payed his dues. However his greatest quality was his ability to make the men around him better from training with him, helping them realize and actualize a potential that they may not have been aware of. War continued to call on Heru for assistance, and gradually began to defer to him, only stepping in every now and then when his experience needed to take precedence. Over time Heru took charge of training the men. This made War very happy because he got to watch Heru become the great warrior and leader he was destined to be, as well as spend some much longed for time with Het Heru.

Meanwhile, Sutesh's power had grown far beyond measure, and his influence extended even further. Out of fear of his wrath, surrounding nations crafted their policies with his benefit in mind, and people began to place limits upon their own aspirations to avoid being viewed as a problem or threat to him. They turned on their own people to gain his favor, and even groomed their daughters to be wed to him, and their sons to serve him. Needless to say, he had become the most powerful man on the planet. He had up unto a certain point, also conquered, or at least neutralized the duat, as he forbade the people from practicing the Ancient traditions and venerating the spirits of their Ancestors, leaving them without a sense of direction and impotent. Instead he made them look to the sky and worship the sun directly. While the people worshiped the sun in the sky, he secretly enslaved the spirits of their ancestors, forcing them to do his bidding. This made him almost invincible. However, this power was not enough to satisfy his thirst for it. His ambition and appetite for power and competition was insatiable, so much so that conquering the world was not enough for him. Sutesh was bored.

One day Sutesh was sitting down eating roasted hog with extra sauce, one of his favorite meals, while watching two Nubian men fight for a loaf bread. When he was not out hunting or fighting, this was one of the ways he loved to spend his time. Actually he had made it sort of a sport. He would capture two Nubians and place them in a cage together, keeping them starved and exhausted through over saturation of their senses with lots of noise. After a long period of this he would come to the cage and offer a loaf of bread to the man that would defeat the other in a fight. However, if one of the men killed the other, this would increase the probability of his being freed from the cage, and given a position as a servant of Sutesh. Anyway, while watching two Nubians tear each other apart one day Sutesh thought to himself "this is so boring, I'm too great, and way ahead of my time and the world has become too small for me." Becoming increasingly irritated, he opened the cage and killed both of the men. At that moment one of his assistants opened the door, causing the light of the sun to enter into his chambers. At that moment Sutesh had his greatest moment of sadistic inspiration. "AHA! I've got it! I know what I must do." "Lord?" his servant inquired. "I have become too big for this world, I have conquered the entire known world, and yet I still feel incomplete. However, I now realize what I have yet to accomplish; what I have grasp. Everyday Ra travels in his boat,

exploring the heavens, journeying through the dwAt, traversing the land. This boat allows him to reach destinations that I have yet to even behold! Nut! The Cosmos! To have such reach, such access, only the most powerful of men should have possession of such a vessel; and who is more powerful than I?" "Nobody Lord" the servant answered unsolicited in an attempt to stroke his masters ego who didn't mind of course. "I mean look at Ra, he has gotten old, his bones are like silver, his limbs are like gold, and his hair is like lapis lazuli! Look at him his mouth is drooping, he drools...his shrine is empty! He's pathetic!" He went on like this for a while, insulting Ra, while pumping himself up, becoming more and more obsessed with the idea of taking his place. "It's time to put that old man out of his misery and let someone who is truly worthy take command of that ship. Bring the general to me!" Sutesh ordered his servant. "Yes, Lord."

The general arrived with haste. "Your majesty," the general said addressing Sutesh. Sutesh looked him straight in his eyes and said "formulate a plan and prepare all of the men...I am going to kill Ra!" The General's eyes widened in disbelief! He thought to himself that Sutesh was beyond insane, yet he dare not defy him. So he got fast to work on a plan to assassinate the divine father, Ra.

"I am going to kill Ra!" These words echoed in Tehuti's head as he snapped out of meditation. He had been allowed to hear the voice of Sutesh as he declared his wicked aspiration while he was in trance. He immediately recognized the voice. He jumped up and proceeded to leave when Heru stopped him, "where you headed to in such a hurry Tehuti?" Heru asked. "I'm going to pay some old friends a visit." "Oh, you want some company?" Heru asked. "No these friends are not too open to strangers." Tehuti replied. Heru nodded his head as Tehuti left. "Hmm, I wonder what is on the elder's mind. He seemed slightly rattled, just slightly which is very odd for him. I better follow behind just in case he's in trouble." Heru got up and followed Tehuti.

It seemed like he had been following Tehuti for a few hours when he noticed they arrived at some mountains, where Tehuti entered into a cave. Heru approached the mouth of the cave when he heard someone whisper his name behind him. He turned around to see who it was, and to his utter bewilderment it was Tehuti. Heru was taken aback, slightly jumped, just slightly. "What! How? I just saw you enter the cave! How did you do that?" Tehuti chuckled, "Heru I've been following behind you the entire time. You were following my projection." Heru's eyes widened in amazement. "I knew you would try to follow me from the moment I walked out the door." Tehuti said, still chuckling. "Anyway, son, I am serious, do not follow me into this cave. You should not enter unless you are invited, and the only reason I am here showing up unannounced is because we have history." At that moment they hear a woman's voice call out from the cave, "bring the boy along, old man." Tehuti looked at Heru, shook his head and said, "I hope you're ready for this." Heru looked at Tehuti, and thought to himself there is some serious shekhem emanating from this cave. "I haven't felt anything like this since visiting my father's tomb. I don't know what it is, but there is no way I'm letting you go in there alone." Tehuti laughed, again shaking his head, "I knew you'd say that…come on." They both entered into the cave.

The cave appeared to be fire lit, as there was a glow that became brighter the further they progressed. He heard what sounded like wings flapping above him, and serpents hissing and slithering around him. He felt slightly on edge, and was definitely hyper-vigilant, but thought to himself, "Hey if I'm going to fight Sutesh, one day I have to be ready for anything. They continued to walk when finally Heru could see someone. There before them he saw two women, one wearing white, adorned with all kinds of dark stones, Henna tattoos with what looked like sacred writings on her arms, and a vulture sat on her shoulder; the other woman wore red, adorned in like fashion, only her stones were also red, and instead of a vulture, she had a cobra draped around her neck. They were very mysterious, yet they had a certain allure to them. The one in white, her name was Nekhebet, and the one in red, was Wajet. Nekhebet was rather quiet, which made her even more enigmatic, while Wajet, though quiet, spoke with a certain intensity. Together these sisters were two of the most powerful juju women in the world, and had the ability to see far into the past, and far reaching probabilities of the future. They looked to be in their 30's but they were far older than they appeared.

"So this is the boy?" Wajet spoke, referring to Heru. Tehuti nodded. Heru kneeled before them, as he did with all of his elders. "I see you've taught him well." Wajet said. Nekhebet remained quiet; kind of just staring.Tehuti began to speak "Mothers I've come to…" "we know why you've come Tehuti," Wajet interjected, cutting Tehuti off. Heru was blown away, for he had never seen anyone do to Tehuti, what Tehuti always did to him, read his mind that is. "The question is not why you are here, but what do you care? Since when did you concern yourself with the affairs of politics?" Wajet asked. She was right. Tehuti as a sage usually did not get involved in the affairs of kings and warlords, for his only concern was the spiritual

evolution of man, and maintaining balance in the universe. "If you've heard what I've heard you would realize that no petty power struggle could compare to the wickedness or isfet this concern, if proven to be true, could cause." Tehuti replied. "He's right; there is something more to this than simple politics... I can feel it," Nekhebet chimed in, speaking for the first time. "Speak your mind Tehuti," Nekhebet said, encouraging Tehuti to continue. Wajet deferring to Nekhebet's request listened quietly. "While in meditation earlier tonight, I heard the voice of Sutesh declare that he was going to kill Ra." Heru gasped! He couldn't believe it. Would Sutesh really go that far? Tehuti continued. "No man has ever thought to transgress mAat to this degree. This plan if carried out successfully, has the potential to cause Nut and Gab to embrace once again, throwing the entire Universe back into Nu." Wajet seemed a little rattled, while Nekhebet seemed unfazed. Rumor had it that she was so old that she knew Nu personally! "What I need to know, is if what I heard is true, and if so, when is this supposed to happen?" Tehuti said. The sisters got up and walked slowly over to a fire that was lit in the middle of the floor. Nekhebet took a black feather from the vulture that sat upon her shoulder, and Wajet took some venom from the tooth of the cobra that was wrapped around her neck. They then threw these things into the flames. They then walked over to Tehuti, and plucked a hair from his head and threw it into the fire. The women then joined hands and began to sway side to side while chanting some words repetitively, and after doing this for a moment they both spat into the flames, causing the fire to grow in height, while pulsating greatly from Blue to Red. Heru watched intently. He had never seen such Hika (magic) worked before. He knew that his mother and aunt were also very powerful, but they never did the real powerful stuff around him because he was too young. After several minutes of swaying, Wajet said, "we are not able to see it...there is a dark magic so potent that is putting up a block." I am not able to penetrate it. "What can we do?" Tehuti asked. Wajet looked at Nekhebet, who calmly nodded her head. Wajet then called Heru over to the fire. Heru stood up, and walked over cautiously. "It's ok boy, don't worry," Wajet said. Heru looked at Tehuti for reassurance, and Tehuti nodded. This caused Heru to lower his guard somewhat. As soon as he did that Wajet grabbed his hand and cut his palm with a sharp knife, taking some of Heru's blood and throwing it into the fire. Before Heru could even respond, the fire raged so intensely that it totally took his mind off of what just happened. Immediately the two sisters grabbed hands again and began to chant, and as soon as they did so images began to manifest in the fire. There they saw Sutesh killing the two Nubian fighters, and then going on to declare his plan to assassinate Ra. Then in the flames they saw an image of

Heru kneeling on the ground, with one of his Eyes missing. That greatly startled Heru. After that scenes of Ra traveling in his boat with the nTrw appeared, then his boat stood still as there appeared to be armies gathered all around him with Sutesh and the gigantic serpent Owapep prepared to attack, this scene ran right into an image of Ra laying lifeless, then proceeding to turn into dust, and at that very moment everything went black. The ladies sat down, obviously exhausted, as it took great shekhem to get this vision. Tehuti walked over to check on them and then called to Heru. "Heru bring them some water," Tehuti instructed. Heru, still in shock from what he just saw, didn't hear the sage the first time. "Heru!" Tehuti said again, this time getting Heru's attention. Heru quickly went to get them some water. When he returned, he brought them the water. Tehuti looking as though he was deep in thought, thanked the ladies and left some food for them. He and Heru then proceeded to leave. As they walked out of the cave Tehuti heard the voice of Nekhebet in his head call to him and say "Let him go, it is a lesson that he must learn." He knew that she was referring to Heru, but he wasn't sure exactly what was going to happen. He could tell Heru was extremely disturbed by what he saw, but he didn't say anything to him.

Heru was quiet the whole way home, but his mind screamed louder than ever as his thoughts were all over the place. He was afraid, and angry. When he got back to Behudet, he called a secret meeting with some of the guys he had been training, those that were dissatisfied with Sutesh and his rule. "Brothers, I've learned of a heinous plot by Sutesh to murder Ra." The warriors couldn't believe it! "Would he really go that far?" they asked. "Yes," Heru responded, "He must be stopped at all cost." The warriors agreed. "We will leave tonight, the few of us, and secretly travel to Sutesh's domain and take him out before he has a chance to even finish formulating this plan. He is not aware that we know about it, nor is he aware of my presence in the country. Let's take it right to him and catch him sleeping!" The men were fired up and anxious! They thought about the horrible oppression that their people had endured under Sutesh, how many of their people, including children had been slaughtered in the streets. All of these memories added more fuel to the rage that gave them more than enough reason to want to kill Sutesh. They gathered their weapons and left immediately. Also War and Het Heru were away on vacation, so this gave him a chance to carry out this mission without having to run it by his uncle, as he was in charge when War was not around. Though Heru's plan was a secret, Tehuti knew what he had in his heart to do. It was very difficult for him to let Heru go as he had grown very close to him over the years, but he

remembered Nekhebet's words and did not interfere. Tehuti was very wise and far seeing. He knew that Heru was not ready to go up against Sutesh, for even though he had become very skilled as a fighter, there was one lesson he had not yet learned: how to handle defeat. Tehuti realized that this was all in the Divine Plan, and let him go.

It took three days for them to reach Cairo, but not even one day for Sutesh to become aware of their presence. He had spies everywhere. However, he did not want anyone to stop them because it had been a long time since he had a challenge and he was thirsty for blood. He wanted to deal with these guys himself. However, he was not aware of the fact that Heru was one of these men.

They reached Sutesh's palace in the darkness of the early morning. One by one they picked off the soldiers that were on guard. Heru thought to himself this is easy, he was sure he had the upper hand on Sutesh. Eventually they made it to Sutesh's quarters. They kicked the door in and there they found Sutesh sitting on a throne, completely relaxed with a slick grin on his face. It appeared as though he was expecting them. Heru took a moment to take this all in; this was the first time he had set eyes on his uncle, the man who murdered his father. Finally he would have his revenge, he thought. However, Sutesh looked very calm for a man who was about to die. The room was silent for a few moments and then finally, Heru signaled for his men to stand down. He wanted Sutesh all to himself. This really intrigued Sutesh, as well as got his juices pumping. Who could this man be? "Who would dare attempt to fight him man to man?" He thought to himself, "could this be a worthy opponent?" Finally, Sutesh stood up, and when he did it was as if the room shook. His presence was so powerful, yet so dark. Heru stepped forward, and Sutesh did the same. And there they stood about ten feet away from each other. Heru pulled out his machete and sickle, and Sutesh pulled out a sword, decked with red and black jewels. They stood there for a few seconds and sized each other up. Sutesh could tell that there was something different about this man, something special, but he couldn't see who he was for Heru was wearing a face mask. The energy of the silence was intense; Heru's men were on edge as they stood on and watched. Finally, after a few moments of this build up, Heru made his move. He rushed at Sutesh, and Sutesh followed suit and when their blades crossed it let out a spark that could've set the room ablaze. They went at it for a few seconds, going back and forth, neither one getting the upper hand, and then Heru got a clean shot in, slashing Sutesh on the neck, right above the collar bone. Sutesh was stunned, he took a moment and stepped back. He was amazed at the skill of this warrior. The only man he knew with such skill was his brother War, but he could tell that the man lacked the experience of War; by the way he attacked him first. He was impatient, and Sutesh could tell. He took a moment to feel the adrenaline race through his body, the pain from the wound Heru inflicted. He took his hand and tasted the blood. Finally after a few seconds he stood back in fighting position and said, "At last a challenge." The two stared each other down again, and then Sutesh said to him, "why don't you remove the mask, so I may see the man that gave me the best fight I've had in a long time, before I Killed him!" "You want to see my face?" Heru said. Sutesh nodded. Heru removed the mask and said. "I am my father!" Heru exclaimed. Sutesh's eyes widened! He knew exactly who he was. This excited him even more. "Ahh... it's been a long time nephew" he said. His heart was racing. "I'm so glad that I failed at killing you when you were a baby, I would've missed out on this fight. Now your death will mean so much more to me, and after I kill you, I will go back and finish your wretched mothers and that bastard brother of yours!" Sutesh said. His arrogance and words greatly angered Heru, and he immediately moved in to finish him off. They met in the middle of the floor, and this time the room actually did quake! They went back and forth for a few minutes; this time however, Heru was apparently winning. Heru went in for the kill and Sutesh quickly parried him and countered with a blow that knocked Heru's eye from the socket. Heru's went down to his knees, and his men immediately moved in to attack Sutesh. Sutesh yelled, "ENOUGH OF THIS CHILDS PLAY!!!" The torches that lit the room went out, and then they immediately relit with the flames reaching the ceiling. Sutesh's eyes lit a deep red and he flung off his robe. His muscles were pumping, he was as big as War, but being that he was younger, he was even more ripped. His breathing became very erratic and immediately a tornado began to form in the room, throwing Heru's men to and fro. Sutesh then rushed them tearing them limb from limb. Heru watched in horror with his one good eye. Sutesh killed all of his men. Heru tried to approach, but the wind from the tornado was too great, and his hanging eye became detached, and was lost in the storm. He could only get away with his life and made his escape through a back exit. After Sutesh finished with the men, he summoned a lance from the corner of the room and let out a great laugh, and said "whooo I feel like hunting," and immediately went out after Heru. Heru ran out into the woods, and Sutesh was hot on his trail. He could barely see and there was no way he was going to be able to get away in his condition. Finally he gave up and sat up against a tree. He thought to himself "this is it," and for the first time in his life he felt a feeling that he had never felt before, failure.

As he sat there for a moment, he saw a baboon seated on a branch of the tree in front of him. The baboon looked at him, and placed his finger to his lips, as to tell Heru to keep silent. Suddenly the baboon clapped his hands, and Heru found himself sitting under a tree in what appeared to be Behudet. The baboon was there with him, and began to walk towards him. Heru could barely move, as he had lost a lot of blood and was very weak. He just watched, as the Baboon transformed before his eyes. It was Tehuti. Tehuti had saved his life. Heru, didn't say anything, he just began to weep. Tehuti embraced him, saying, "It's ok son." Het Heru walked towards them bringing a gazelle with her. She tied the gazelle to the tree and then began to milk it. She then took the milk into a cup and handed it to Tehuti. Tehuti placed his hand over the cup and began to chant over it. After this he spat in the cup and gave it back to Het Heru who poured the milk in to the socket of Heru's missing eye. She then bandaged it up and sat there for good while, holding and consoling Heru under the tree. After a while they led Heru to his room and laid him down to rest.

Heru rested for a few days, gaining a little of his strength back. Tehuti and Het Heru took care of him. War didn't go to see him during this time for two reasons: one he didn't want to see his nephew in that condition, and two he was furious with Heru, but even more angry with himself. He thought that it was all his fault; he should've been there to stop him. One day Tehuti caught him thinking this and told him that there was nothing he could've done as this was part of Heru's Shai. It did little to comfort War, but he understood.

Heru slept most of the time, but when he was awake he was miserable. He kept reliving the battle in his mind, thinking about what he could've done differently. The death of his men, the loss of his eye, it all replayed in his mind over and over again, and then there it was again, that feeling, this time it was very strong. During this time Heru's thoughts became very dark, and he even thought about taking his own life to make them stop. One day while he was absorbed in his dark thoughts, he heard the voice of his father call to him. "Heru, close your eyes." He did so, and he found himself standing before his father, who had the men who had died in the fight with Sutesh seated in front of him. They didn't say a word, just sat there smiling, apparently glad to see Heru. Heru fell to his knees, hiding his face in shame. Osir, called to him. "Heru, why do you hang your head?" he asked. "Because I failed you father, I am weak, I cannot defeat Sutesh and I am not worthy to be your son." Osir listened to his son, and then smiled. He then rose to his

64

feet and walked over to Heru, lifting him up. "Stand up my son," Osir said. "How can I father? I am afraid. I don't think I could ever beat him, I am a failure." Osir stood him up and lifted up his head, and said to his son "Do not lie down at night in fear of tomorrow: 'Come day, how will tomorrow be? man knows not how tomorrow will be. The nTr is success. The man is ever in his failure. The words men say are one thing, but the deeds of nTr are another. The wrong belongs to nTr. He seals (the verdict) with his finger. There is no perfection before nTr but there is failure before him. If one labors to seek perfection, in a moment he has marred it. Keep firm your mind, and steady your heart. Do not steer with your tongue. If a man's tongue is the boat's rudder, the Lord of All is yet its pilot. It was your Shai Heru! nTr is in control. Each man is created to his Shai by nTr, be trustful and follow him. Failure makes a man humble, and nTr protects the humble. If nTr humbles a man, and if he accepts it and is strong, he will grow from it and become wise. A wise man accepts the correction of nTr, Heru, he listens. But the fool, he does not listen, in which lies the fault of every kind. Those who are steadfast and thoughtful are chosen among the people and those who listen to a correction protect themselves from receiving another. The nTr of wisdom has placed the stick on earth in order to teach the fool by means of it. But he gave the wise a sense of shame in order to avoid all punishment." Heru listened to his father attentively. His father embraced him. "Heru look at your men, do they look as though they see you as a failure? No, they were happy to have known you and to play a role in your evolution, and you in theirs. They were honored to give their life for their people. Your people look to you for guidance. Remember this, as one who guides the multitudes, you must always be gracious, having no defect in your conduct. Next time you will guide them wisely." Heru found comfort in his father's faith in him. Heru lifted his head up, and took a deep breath to calm himself. "Now listen to me carefully Heru, You must take your family and your people and leave Kemet for Sutesh will not rest until he finds you, and he already has received word from his spies that you are in Behudet. You must go deep south, and then west. When you go as far West as you can, you will come to a great ocean. You must cross this ocean, and live for a while in a land far away from your home. After several years, I will come to you with further instructions. While you are away, you must train, and you must train your people, you must prepare them for the day that they must go with you into battle against Sutesh. Do not worry my son; it is your shai to rule. Be patient, and remember, with nTr is success. Walk with nTr." At that moment Heru opened his eyes, and that feeling of darkness was no longer there. Not only that his eyes were completely healed, and he could see clearly, more clear than he ever had before. He felt a great peace come

over him, and found strength in knowing that his father was with him. He sat up on the bed and removed his bandages. At that moment War came rushing into the room. "Heru come quickly, we have to leave Sutesh is on his way." War said. "I know uncle; don't worry, follow me." Heru said, and walked past his uncle. There was a light emanating from him, and War knew that he was being guided. He went out to the center of the town, and the people gathered around him. His light attracted them. He revealed himself to them, his true identity, and shared with them what his father had said to him. They couldn't believe it, the son of Osir was standing before them; he had been in their midst all along; breaking bread with them, training them, struggling with them, laughing with them, and crying with them. The people rejoiced for their true Nisu had returned, and they loved him and would die for him, because he loved them and lived for them. The people did as Heru instructed and followed him, and over time his light lit theirs.

Heru led his people deep south and then west, and then crossed the ocean as his father instructed. It was a very long journey, some died along the way. When they reached they found a great land mass there that was uninhabited. There they found a place and settled. Like his father before him, Heru brought his people back to civilization, teaching them how to work together, and grow their own food, build their own homes, and do business as a collective. He and War trained their people in how to protect themselves and police their own community. He and his family gave the people back their Ancestral Spiritual Tradition, and the people venerated their Ancestors once again. Heru was very successful in all of his affairs. They spent many years in this new place, and many people died there. Monuments, temples, and tombs were built there in their honor, in the same manner that they had been built in Kemet. Heru spent many years training himself, as well, physically and spiritually. He and War trained tirelessly. War would not rest until Heru had mastered the Art of War. He and Heru trained day in and day out for hours on in.

One day Heru and War were sparring and it seemed like they had been going back and forth forever. These matches usually ended with War coming out on top, however, this time it appeared as though Heru had learned War's every move. He matched War, blow for blow, pound for pound. Then suddenly Heru had the idea to try something different. He knew that War knew his every move, for it was War that taught him everything he knew. He knew that if he was going to come out on top, he had to switch things up. He decided to feign a strike over the top, which

War immediately prepped to counter, in which Heru then immediately followed up from beneath with his short sickle. He stopped just short of destroying War's practice shield. War stood up and looked Heru in the eyes with a big smile on his face, and said "very good, now defend this!" Immediately war's Eyes began to glow a bright orange. He stuck his arms out and shot straight up into the air like a ball of fire; like the yatin (sun). It was as though he had wings, he flew so high in to the sky. There were rays that emitted from him like fiery serpents. The heat was so intense, it was unbearable. Heru noticed his thoughts becoming very erratic. It felt as though he was losing his mind. He was not prepared for this attack, as War had taken the battle to a plane that Heru had not yet learned to fight on. He went down to one knee, signaling to War that he had- had enough. When War descended back down to the land, he raised Heru up, and said to him. "Today Heru, you have mastered the science of fighting with your body. Now you must learn to fight with your kA!" Heru listened very carefully. War's attack reminded him of Sutesh's ability to weaponize the weather through creating storms. He knew that if he wanted to defeat Sutesh, he would have to be able to fight on a higher level. "I have taught you all that I can teach you," War said, "now you must learn the Higher Arts from your mothers." Heru's eyes widened and his jaws dropped. He knew that his mother and aunt knew something, but he didn't know it was on that level. The following day he started his training immediately.

Heru trained with Auset and Nebt Het for several years. They taught him how to focus his mind, focus on his breath and move his subtle shekhem. They taught him how to activate the kA of the plants and animals around him, to release their shekhem and direct it towards his objectives with his mind. He also learned from them the ability to channel, possess, carry, and wield the Shekhem of the nTrw; how to command and direct them through song. He also learned how to purify and protect himself form psychic attacks from dark sorcerers and malevolent spirits. Overtime Heru was deeply initiated into his Ancestral Traditions, and became a keeper of them. Auset and Nebt Het taught him everything they knew, and he absorbed it all. Then one day his mother walked up to him and said, "Heru, there is one more thing that you must learn." Heru listened, but he had learned so much, he wondered what else could there be? She said to him "You have learned how to possess and carry the nTrw. Now you must learn how to relinquish control, and allow the nTr to possess and carry you." Heru listened to every word, but he didn't quite understand. "How do I do that mut?" He asked. Auset looked him straight in the eyes and said "You must die." Heru was startled. He thought to himself, "what does she mean I must

die? That doesn't make any sense," he thought.

As time passed he thought very deeply about his mother's words, still seeking understanding. He knew she couldn't be talking about a literal death, as how could he defeat Sutesh and become Nisu Bity if he was dead? He said to himself, "Well at least I don't have to worry about that." He was pretty certain about this. Then one day, the community was gathered watching a play some of the children put on. The play was about Heru's life, and his great destiny. They did this to honor their Nisu. He was really enjoying the play, until one scene came up, in which there was a re-enactment of his battle with Sutesh. The child that was playing the role of Sutesh looked at the one that was in character as Heru and said in a way that sounded very matter of fact, at least to Heru, "You're going to die!" There was something about the way those words hit his ears that deeply affected him. However, he stayed and watched the remainder of the play, which ended with him defeating Sutesh and ascending the throne of Kemet. After it was over he retired to his home.

That night he dreamed about various people dying, some he knew, some he didn't, and some he was close to, some he was even related to. He woke up in the middle of the night, a little disturbed from the subject matter. He took time to calm himself, and went back to sleep. Eventually he started to dream again, this time of what looked like his own funeral! He laid there in a coffin, and there were people all around him dressed in white. Then there was a gigantic black cobra that was wrapped around his body and appeared as though it was ready to strike at anyone that approached the coffin. The serpent moved back and forth hissing, and then it moved toward his sphere of awareness which immediately caused him to wake up again. "What is going on?" He thought. "Why am I having all of these dreams about death? Maybe someone is about to make their transition? Who could it be? One thing for sure, it couldn't be me." This is what he told himself, but he was definitely not as confident as before. Heru was rattled. He tried to get himself back to sleep one more time. This time he was so tired that he immediately fell asleep, and as soon as his head hit the pillow, he was dreaming again. This time he was on his way back from training. He was feeling real good because he had accomplished all that he set out for that day. He reached his home and opened the door to enter, just as he was about to walk in he noticed this huge serpent, much larger than the one in the previous dream, waiting in his house. Heru immediately ran, and the serpent appeared to follow behind him. This serpent was so large that it caused an earthquake as it moved. Heru was in his dream, running for his life. He found a spot and hid as the snake passed him by. He was at a loss for words. He just made his way back to his home. When he reached he noticed that the snake had shed its skin in his bed. At that moment Heru woke up.

After all that he experienced the previous night, he decided that he needed to perform some divination for further insight. Normally he would go to Tehuti for such matters, but Tehuti did not travel to west with them, but instead went to Ra, to inform him, and prepare him for Sutesh's plan. However, Heru had spent many years training with Tehuti, so he learned how to divine for himself. He pulled out some shells and threw them to the floor as he concentrated on his question. "What is the significance of all these death omens I'm seeing?" As the shells fell he would receive his reading from the pattern they made. From the reading, there was only one word he could make out: "Surrender." "Surrender?" He said. "I don't understand. Well. Anyway, I'm getting hungry. I think I will go and see what has been prepared." He walked out of his divination shrine, and every where he looked, he saw death. People were talking about death; he saw the images of skulls everywhere, tattoos, jewelry. The further he walked, the more he saw, until it seemed as though he was completely surrounded by death. However, he noticed that no one seemed to be aware of these things. They could not see what he saw. At that moment the words of Auset replayed in his mind: "You must die." Heru came to realize that these omens were meant for him and with the reality that he was staring death in the face. He also came to accept the fact that as he was totally surrounded by death, there was nothing he could do about it, there was no escape, and he was afraid. As he stood there motionless, he took the time to look his fear in the face. He questioned it. "Why am I afraid?" he asked. After a minute of further contemplation of his predicament the answer came to him: "Because you are not in control." He fell to his knees and accepted the fact that there was nothing he could do and he said to himself "Well if you are going to go, do you want to afraid, or do you want to go free?" I want to be free, he declared, and at that moment he let his hands fall down to his side in a posture symbolizing surrender. Heru surrendered. As he did this, suddenly there was a deep thick darkness that surrounded him. Its presence was so intense, so powerful. It appeared as though this darkness was examining him. Then he saw a face manifest in the darkness. It was his face, and it was staring him in the face. Heru stayed completely still, completely relaxed, he looked it in the face, and he let go. Immediately the darkness entered into him, and he found himself standing in a boat, sailing down a river. The boat had at one end the head of gazelle, and in the center

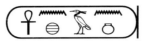

of the boat was a great black mound that had the head of a hawk seated on top. Then suddenly it seemed as though Heru became the boat and it was Osir standing in his place. Heru looked to his left, and he saw himself, seated upon his father's throne within a shrine in the dwAt, in his father's clothes, and the name Sukari written upon the shrine. Then he looked to his right and he saw himself as his father, leading an army of Ancestors and nTrw from the dwAt, in to battle. After this Heru heard his father's voice say to him "Walk with nTr," and at that moment he opened his eyes, and realized that death was no longer all around him, but was within him; it was him, and he would carry his Ancestors into battle with him. Through his learning to accept his Shai in complete surrender, Heru was given the power to command and carry the spirits of the Dead; ancestors and malevolent spirits, in to battle with him. He was now as one well equipped. Also, something interesting had happened to his eyes, for it seemed as though the various planes of existence, PT (Heaven) tA (earth) and dwAt (spirit realm) were now merged, and the line between man, nTr, and Ancestor no longer existed, it was all One. When he looked at people, he could see the spiritual force, nTr or Ancestor that was moving them. When something happened, he could see the spiritual force and significance of it. When someone spoke to him, he could hear the message of the nTr and Ancestor speaking through. Heru had become as an nTr, a fully enlightened being.

Heru spent the next several years teaching his people through his new eyes of wisdom. His teachings spread gradually throughout the earth, and even reached Kemet without his being there. When the people heard his teachings, and learned that the true king, Heru son of Auset and Osir lived, one by one they woke up and began to pass the word along, organizing amongst themselves. Sutesh caught wind of it, but by then it was too late and there was nothing he could do about it. It was apparent that he was losing the control he once held over the people as more and more of them began to rebel. They threw away the religion that Sutesh had imposed on them and reconnected with their roots. Sutesh tried everything he could to stop Heru. He killed some of his people; he sent spies and assassins, both alive and dead, but to no avail. Anybody that got even remotely close to Heru either lost their minds or their life because the shekhem surrounding him and his community was to strong. Over time Heru's people had become a well trained and organized force.

A lot of time had passed, and Heru was not the young teenage boy any more. He was now a middle aged man, full of wisdom and power. There once was a time when he was always anxious to achieve his Shai, to defeat Sutesh and reclaim his father's throne. It was all he would think about. However, now he had learned patience, and how to be fully present in the moment, recognizing that he did not have to go out to look for his purpose, just keep walking and it would find him, and finally, it did. A day came that found Heru sitting in a chair teaching, while children sat at his feet. He heard the voice of his father whisper in his ear. "It is time my son, go with nTr. Immediately Heru stood to his feet and signaled to the guard to sound the alarm. The people knew the call and gathered their things and met in the center of the city in preparation to leave. They said their goodbyes to those that would not be going back home with them, for some had grown accustomed to living in the west, and chose to stay there, and others stayed to keep the shrines of their Ancestors that had transitioned and been buried there. The rest of the people followed Heru, and they crossed the ocean once again, making their way back to Kemet.

All in all, the journey took about five months for them to get there. At each country they passed, they were joined by the people that had heard Heru's teachings. By the time they made it to Upper Kemet, it was the summer solstice, and they had amassed a great army. Summer solstice was the time of the year that Ra took his time traveling through the country, enjoying the sights, and greeting the people, the perfect time for Sutesh to carry out his plot. Heru and his people stopped in Nubia to perform a pre war ritual, to ensure that the spirit world was on their side. There Auset and Nebt Het began the chant, Anpu led the precession, and War and the warriors began the warrior's dance, which involved great acrobatics, dancing with heavy metal chains, blades, and spears. They offered a sacrifice of a long horned Red Bull, and a Black Boar to the Ancestors. Each fighter took a dab of the blood with their fingers and painted an ankh on their heart as a symbol of their allegiance to Heru, their Ancestors, and their people, and that they would fight, and if need be give their lives to reclaim their land and remove Sutesh from power. They took some more of the blood from the sacrifice and smeared it on the drums, as they beat the rhythm of battle. Heru went around along with Auset and energized the drummers, and energized the warriors, blessing them. Then the time came for Heru to make a speech. "The time is finally upon us family... the time that we have long waited for... (Looking at his mother) the time that many of us have prayed for... (Turns to look at War) that many of us have lived for... (He turns to look at his people) that many of us have died for, have sacrificed for. The day has finally come for us to come face to face with Shai, take back our beloved land, and avenge our Ancestors! Some of us may die out here today, some

of us will survive...but for those of you who give your life today for our freedom, I swear to you that your Shrine will be taken care of, your Ka will be well fed, you will traverse the dwAt freely as one in command of themselves and well equipped with HikAw and when you rise again in the east as Khepri you will find the Kemet of our mothers and fathers waiting here for you!!! The people were in an uproar, some were laughing, others crying, others completely silent and focused. Heru then gave the order to move out. The women and children stayed behind, many setting up medical camps for their warriors. Some of the priesthood also stayed behind to perform rituals. Heru had an army that was both seen and unseen. The warriors wore sandals with the image of Sutesh drawn on the soles, so that every step that they took, they were sympathetically trampling him. They were ready, but were also out numbered.

Sutesh's army was huge as he appeared to have help from all of the pale skin nations of the north with him. This of course made him feel extra confident, but he was not prepared for what was in store for him. He spotted Ra in the valley at Behudet, in a part of town called Jeba, and gave the order to his general to start the attack. Just before the general could give the order, they saw at the other side of the valley Heru's army approaching. Sutesh signaled to his General to wait a moment so that he could get a good look at the competition to see if it would be worth the fight. When he saw that his army greatly outnumbered Heru and that they were still a good distance away, he figured it was a waste of time and decided to proceed with his attack on Ra's caravan. However, Tehuti was with Ra, and he saw Sutesh preparing for attack and signaled to Heru by lighting a fire. Immediately spotting Tehuti's signal, Heru gave the command to War to attack. As soon as Sutesh's men began their approach War shot up in to the air and took the form of a Winged Sun, in the same manner that he did when training with Heru, however, since this was an actual battle. The heat he emitted was much greater. Immediately Sutesh's men, the first regimen became affected, some falling fatally ill, others losing the ability to see and hear, and other's loss their minds. The men one by one began to turn on each other and slayed one another, leaving not one person of the first regimen alive. After this War descended back to the earth and took the form of a lion and began to trample Sutesh's men, creating a major hole in their ranks, he was followed by his elite guard of ten men with spears, chains, machetes, mace, and sickles. This greatly angered Sutesh who began to try and counter this by creating a storm.

The land began to get very dark, there was thunder and lightning, and tornados began to form. Some of Heru's people became afraid, but he assured them not to worry. Sutesh then unleashed the storms, causing only those that did not listen to Heru and ran in fear, to lose their lives. Sutesh then took on the form of a Great Hippoatamus and began to charge, leading the remainder of his men into battle. However, he found this strategy very difficult as War's men also had the ability to transform into lions, baboons, and bulls. Five of them took these forms and dealt with Sutesh's men, while the other five went after Sutesh with their harpoons. They were able to wound Sutesh and weakened him, but they couldn't stop his attack and got injured in the process. Sutesh continued to rage forward; this time he assumed the form of a great black boar. He raged through goring several of Heru's men, killing quite a few. At this point he caught a glimpse of Heru, who appeared to be totally unaffected with what's going on. This angered Sutesh even more. He kept approaching until he found himself completely vulnerable. Heru then stepped down from his horse and placed his right hand in front of him in the posture of invocation, and at that moment things became very interesting for Sutesh. As he gazed upon Heru and his army he could have sworn he saw Osir and the millions of Souls he had murdered in their place, and this kept happening, he would see Heru and then it wasn't Heru but Osir; he would see the army, and then it was the Ancestors. He didn't know what to do. His dark magicians were at their wits end, for none of their rituals had any affect. At this point Sutesh didn't know what to do, as he watched Heru's army of men, both living and dead tear through his army. He became livid and completely lost it. He assumed his true form and rushed straight towards Heru, or was it Osir?

Sutesh came at Heru with everything he had, every stance, every weapon, every type of blow and fighting style, every animal form, from crocodile, hippo to pig, he tried it all! Yet, Heru was able to block all of this and had yet to even throw one blow. Sutesh became greatly exhausted and out of desperation invoked the Great serpent Owapep, a move that could destroy everyone, including himself if he were not able to control the snake. Because he was on the verge of defeat, he had literally become suicidal!

The Great Serpent began to move forward, straight towards Heru causing a great earthquake. This was all too familiar to Heru, as if he had been here before, and he had. His dreams during his time in the west, where he was looking death in the face, all of it came back to him, and in that moment he realized that nTr had already prepared him for that very moment. Heru stood there in complete peace as the great monster rushed towards him, looking it square in the eyes, and then all of a sudden Owapep began to

slow down ultimately coming to a complete stop right at Heru's feet. Sutesh couldn't believe it; neither could anyone else, every one stopped fighting and looked on in astonishment. Heru quelled Owapep. Realizing that victory had slipped his grasp, Sutesh tried with one last attack to catch Heru slipping while everyone was distracted by his mastering of Owapep. He quickly rushed at Heru and swung his sword directly at Heru's head. Heru easily side stepped him, but returned a counter attack across the front of Sutesh's body, castrating him in the process. AHHH! Sutesh let out a great scream, as he fell down to the floor into a fetal position. Realizing that he had rendered Sutesh powerless, he signaled for his guards to bind Sutesh's hands and feet behind his back and they placed him at the feet of the Divine Father Ra so that he might do with him as he saw fit. The rule of Sutesh was over. There was a great festival that day; everyone came from near and far to witness the return of the Nisu Bity, the son of Osir and Auset. There was a great procession led by Anpu, who opened the way for the Nisu, who was known from that day as the Good nTr. War and his elite guard served as the personal security for Heru, and they accompanied him in making a secure formation around him as he walked. Heru however, was fully relishing the moment; the reality of what was happening was just sinking in. He looked around at all of his people, the joy and relief in their faces. He looked up ahead of him and there stood Auset and Nebt Het along with Tehuti by the throne, when he reached, he took an oath to live his life for his people, to take care of the spirit realm to ensure the continuous prosperity of Kemet, to protect his people from all enemies wherever they may be, and to be a protector and preserver of Maat. After giving his word, Auset placed the Shekhmti, the Red and White Double Crown of Upper and Lower Kemet upon his head. Like his father before him, his crowning took place at Henensu. He took a moment to look out at the great crowd that gathered, he took a deep breath and then released it, and at that moment he heard the voice of his father say, "well done my son, well done." Heru fulfilled his purpose, and now he has a new one.

Kemetic Spirituality

3

From the tradition surrounding Osir, Auset, and Heru, there is one thing that can be known about the spiritual tradition of Kemet, and is that it is different. If we were to say that this is just a story, a myth, a fairytale, then one may say to themselves "oh, ok that makes sense. However, when we say that this is not just a story, but a cosmology, a spiritual story, a story about the Divine, then the first thing that one may find themselves thinking, is "oh that's different." Indeed different is a good place to start. As a spiritual tradition, a religion, Kemetic Spirituality is different. It's unique and is distinguished in its expression from what most people are familiar with what religion and spirituality is supposed to be. Just take into consideration the fact that Osir is considered nTr (God), and take note of what happened to him according to the story. Now compare this to what most people consider God to be. When comparing the Idea of Osir to let's say Allah, or YHVH, and holding the latter as somewhat of a standard as to what a Divine Being is supposed to be, one would quickly dismiss the notion all together, that this Osir character could be anything more than just a flawed human conceptualization. I mean, come on, how could a man that is tricked, and murdered be Divine? How could someone that needs so much help and assistance; saving even; be considered God? Because most of us consider God to be above all, Omnipotent, and Omniscient, then we would quickly dismiss the traditions of Ancient Kemet to be nothing more than mythology at best, or the failed attempt of a primitive people to understand and conceptualize the Divine. However, before we jump to these conclusions let us consider the following. Have the religious traditions that we hold as authority today ever correctly articulated, or defined clearly, what they mean by God, and if so, how did these Idea's come to hold the authoritative positions in the minds of the masses of people? Well, that's neither here nor there as it relates to this particular book. My purpose is not to debate, or contrast Kemetic Spirituality and

Western Religion, but to present the Kemetic traditions and the concepts that undergird them in a way that has yet to be brought to light. My wish is to focus solely on the Kemetic Tradition, bringing to light what makes it unique and beautiful, and present it in a way that it may be understood and applied in ones daily life. All of the above being stated, allow me to elucidate what I believe to be the most unique thing about the Kemetic Spiritual Tradition.

While most traditions center on the idea of man aspiring to salvation and redemption by seeking the Divine, the Kemet Tradition centers around the antithesis. To the ancient Kemetyu, it is not the Divine, or God, that must save man, but it is man that must seek and save the Divine. Thus I have rendered this ideology "Nehem nTr" or "Saving nTr." Now before you throw this book away, or burn it, and run and grab your prayer beads and holy water :-), let's take a moment to clarify some things. Before we can come to a judgment on this Tradition, it is important to take into account what exactly the Kemetyu understood by nTr. What was their understanding and experience of the Divine? To do this we would have to look deeper into the things that they wrote about the Divine. For these purposes, the cosmologies are the perfect place to begin.

While I know adherents to the "Big Three" religions may quickly take issue with the Idea of Nehem nTr, they may not be the only ones. There have been many to write, teach, and expound upon the teachings and cosmologies of Ancient Kemet that have not approached, or viewed it in this manner, and thus may have some reservations about things thus far. However, the best evidence and support of Nehem nTr, is within the cosmologies and traditions of Ancient Kemet itself, and I feel it is not necessary to use any other traditions or works to substantiate this claim. Truth is, whether we are speaking of Osir, or Ra, we will find that these nTrw were said to need protection, preserving, rescuing, salvaging, healing, nourishing, etc. Ra, who is considered to be the Creator, is said to need help from his children. As he ages, he is upheld by his son Ishu. When he is poisoned, it is his great granddaughter Auset that heals him (she also was the one who actually poisoned him!). When he is being threatened by Owapep, it is his children that must bind Owapep, overthrow him, to allow Ra to triumph over him. When Osir is killed and dismembered, it is his family, wife and children that carry out the role of restoring him and elevating him to life and power in the spirit realm. As Ra travels through the spirit realm there are several spiritual beings that he must pass by that lead him, and in many cases protect him from his enemies. As he passes through the earth, it is Heru Behudet that keeps his enemies at bay.

These examples are just a few of many that alone give ample proof that the Kemetyu understanding of the Divine Reality is profoundly unique and gives an authentic historical basis for Nehem nTr. In fact, the Divine, in all of its manifestations, were understood to need things just as we need things. Just as we eat, the nTrw needed to be fed. Just as we need to be cleaned, the nTrw needed to be cleansed. Just as we needed to be sheltered, the nTrw were provided with shelter. These needs were met by the priesthood on a daily and consistent basis, and the view was held that if these needs were not met, then our life would fall into chaos, and the entire universe even, would fall out of order. Thus not only was Nehem nTr held as a necessity for the Divine at it's highest and most authoritative expression, but also for all of the nTrw; the specific expressions of nTr.

Now that we have provided evidence for Nehem nTr, the only questions, are why, and how? Why does nTr need saving, and how can we save it? In actuality, to answer these questions to the best of our ability, we must first delve into the understanding of whom and what nTr is. What is nTr, and why does it need saving? We will deal with the stories and cosmologies but, what does it all mean? These are the some of the questions we seek to answer as we proceed in this work.

Who; What is nTr?   4

The Cosmologies

nTr is a term from *Madu nTr* language that has been rendered by those that have attempted to translate the language historically, as God. However, the way that God has been understood by western man can easily lead to a misunderstanding of what the Kemetyu meant by *nTr*. Many understand God in the western connotation to be a Supreme Being that exist above, apart, independent from its creation, and manages it, and is above man having no special need of them yet expects man's devotion, love, and obedience. This is far different from the meaning of nTr. nTr as understood by the Kemetyu, comes into being as its creation. nTr is Self created, comes into being, and goes through an evolutionary process as creation, the universe, the world, the plant life, animals, and Man. Whereas Western man may view God as a separate superior being that has created many inferior beings, the Kemetyu understood nTr as the only Being in existence; and all things are simply expressions, manifestations, emanations, limbs, cells of nTr. This is demonstrated clearly in the *Book of Knowing the Evolutions of Ra and of the Overthrowing of Owapep.*

In order to really gain an understanding of the Kemetyu concept of Divinity, it is important that we examine the things that they wrote and said about nTr. To serve these purposes, the best help that we have are the cosmologies that they left for us. While there are many such cosmologies that give an account of the creation, foremost among them are the "Annunian Cosmology," which is fully laid out in *the Book of Knowing the Evolutions of Ra and Overthrowing Owapep*, The Cosmology/Tradition of

Khemenu, and the so-called Memphite Theology. These three are some of the most well defined accounts, and while they vary somewhat in description, they tell the exact same story, in different ways.

The Tradition of Khemenu centers on Tehuti and a group of eight nTrw that have come to be known as the Ogdoad. *Khemenu* is a term in Madu nTr that actually means "eight", and it is from these eight nTrw that the tradition derives its name. According to this tradition, these eight forces existed in a state of perfect balance to one another in four pairs. Each pair consisted of a masculine and feminine force. The nTrw who make up the four pairs are *Nu* and *Nut* (*Nun* and *Nunet*), *Heh* and *Hehit*, *Kek* and *Keket*, and *Amun* and *Amunet*.

These nTrw are considered the oldest of nTrw. They represent and describe the nature and condition of the Universe prior to creation, and the potential for its opposite condition (change). **Nun** corresponds to a state of rest or inertia. **Heh** speaks to a state of infinity or that which is undefined. **Kek** is a term in Madu nTr that means "darkness," and thus corresponds to this attribute of the universe prior to creation. *Amun*, means hidden, or concealed, and is held as an attribute of the Pre-Creation universe. For clarity purposes, it is necessary to state that all of these principles can be classified under the nTr, and term "**Nu**." Nu corresponds to what many scientists, and ancient philosophers refer to as the "Primordial Waters of Chaos," or the "Abyss," and "cosmic ocean." These "Waters" of chaos, speak to the state of energy/matter prior to creation, in an undifferentiated, formless, and indefinite state, a state of No-thingness (no separate/plural things). It can be said that all of the Khmenu nTrw describe the nature of Nu, which is pure Being or existence itself (the word in Madu nTr for Existence or Being is "Un," Nu in reverse).

Nu, this primordial Matter, was Nun; in a state of inertia. The vast "ocean" of inert energy/matter was *Heh*; infinite and undefined. Nu, in this inert, infinite, and undefined state, was also, undifferentiated, or in a state of Chaos (lack of Order, due to lack of separate things.) and was thus *Kek*, in a state of complete darkness. This darkness is not simply a substantive darkness but an absolute darkness. To better explain Kek, we must give an example, an exercise of some sort. As you read this, I would like for you, the reader (yes you ☺) to close your eyes. As you close your eyes, I would like for you to just focus in; peer into the darkness, and after a moment reopen your eyes. Everyone that does this exercise will say that they saw

darkness. However, this is as close as we will ever get to understand the nature of Kek. In this state of Nu, this primordial, infinite, and undifferentiated matter was Kek itself. The intelligence, the consciousness that was this state of Being could not even observe this Darkness for it, itself, was the Darkness. There was no one, nothing else to describe the darkness, all that was, was Nu, this Darkness. This being the case Nu, being Nun, and Heh, and Kek, was thus Amun; hidden, or unobservable.

The four male nTrw, Nun, Heh, Kek, and Amun, are represented by frogs, and the four female nTrwt are represented as serpents; both aquatic creatures (remember Nu is likened to an ocean.) There are a few reasons for these depictions. The male forces are depicted as frogs because of the association of frogs with a heightened state of fertility, and at times can be seen in abundance (frogs and tadpoles). Men in general, as long as they are healthy, will produce an infinite amount of sperm cells, which are very interestingly similar in form to tadpoles. Also, frogs in form are very compact, yet at any moment can explode into a leap, just like a spring that is compacted and then released (Potential Energy). This compactness is analogous to the state of the Nu as Nun, Inertia. Now to understand this a little more clearly, it is important to know that Inertia does not mean "no motion," but a movement at a constant rate. According to the laws of Physics, it is said that an object that is motion will stay in motion unless acted upon by another force, and the same goes for an object at rest. However, rest is not speaking to a state of "no motion" for everything moves, but a constant state of motion, revolving around self, or motion in place. This last explanation is perfect to understand Nun, as constant motion revolving around the Self. In fact the symbol for Nun, is a Double "N'

or 〰. The 〰 in Madu nTr is the symbol for the "N" sound, but is also Nu, the symbol for the Primordial Waters. But looking at this symbol, which is a "wave," we also have a breakdown as to the nature of Nu as well, being "motion" and "sound "which travels in waves, and speaks to Motion and

Sound as the foundation/underpinning of creation. When 〰 is rendered

〰, we are speaking of *Nu* as *Nun*, motion around the Self or inertia. In fact, Nun literally means "The Inert One." This sound and concept is similar to the Eastern Vedic concept of Nada Bindu "*ng*" (seed/sound of No-thingness) which corresponds to the state of "Nir-Vana' (No-Motion or Inertia). From the study of Nu and Nun, we come to find that the people of

Ancient Kemet had a very profound and in depth understanding as to the origins and nature of the Universe. Anyway, not to digress, the inert state of the Nu, as it revolved around itself, was in a state of contraction, and yet had the potential to explode/expand at any moment, just like a frog (The Big Crunch/Big Bang Cycles?). The feminine counterparts are depicted as serpents as to represent the ability to actualize that potential, and bring forth the opposite condition, represented by their masculine counterparts. The serpent is a symbol for change and transformation for the way that it sheds its skin, leaving the old part behind going forward renewed. Also the serpent is a symbol for energy and actual motion (Kinetic Energy). The manner in which a serpent moves is almost identical to the way everything moves, as science has learned recently that nothing moves in a straight line, but in an undulating manner. The manner in which a snake coils its body is similar to the spiraling of the universe, and its celestial bodies. The serpent is also a symbol of cycles. Everything about it, from shedding of the skin, to the way that it moves, is cyclical, and is analogous to the Woman.

While her male counterpart has the capacity to produce an infinite amount of sperm, and when aroused at any time can inseminate a woman, The Woman, has a finite number of eggs that she releases periodically, or in cycles. It is somewhere in the midpoint of this cycle, that a woman can be impregnated. To clarify further, it can be said that the four masculine forces represent seeds, potential, and intelligence, while the feminine forces represent the capacity to nourish and give substance to the seed, actualize it's potential, and the power to make the intelligence manifest. Just as a man's seed display's intelligence, it is worthless without the egg of the woman, which provide the matrix for its evolution; and the bulk of the genetic material that will go on to become the offspring. The four nTrwt provide, structure, boundaries, order, and limits, which allow creation to take place. The chief symbol for all nTrwt ("goddess") is actually an aroused serpent wearing a crown of horns and Yatin (sun). This "serpent power" is another striking similarity between Kemet and India, with the Indian concept of the Mother Goddess Shakti (meaning Power), who is also known as the Great serpent Kundalini, and Kali among other names; And just as the Shiva (Intelligence/Consciousness) and Shakti are in essence one[1], The four nTrw and four nTrwt are in essence one, undifferentiated Power and Intelligence. The use of terms that speak to duality and differentiation is simply to describe the nature and qualities of this state of

---

[1] Kundalini in it's most subtle and undifferentiated state is pure consciousness

81

being, for in reality there is no duality to this state of being; no male, no female, and no differentiation between the Innate Intelligence (masculine) and Power (Feminine) or energy/matter, they are one and the same, dwelling within one another, as one another.

Thus we can say that the eight Primordial forces of Khemenu are Inertia, and the potential for Motion, Infinity, and the potential for limitation and definition, Darkness, and the potential for light, and the Hidden or Unobservable, and the potential for the manifest and observation, and all of them can be summed as Nu, Infinite Potential. Together, these forces are considered the "BAw," or souls of Tehuti, the chief nTr of Khemenu, and the Creator in one variation of the cosmology that can be found there.

Tehuti represents the Divine Mind, or Mind in general. It is from Tehuti that the Greeks came up with the name Thoth. According to some traditions, Tehuti is said to be the originator of all sciences, and the "Lord of Madu nTr, that is, "Divine Words", which is also the name of the language of Kemet. In some cases Tehuti was considered the Divine Word itself, what some scholars and theologians today refer to as the **Logos**. In general, Tehuti is considered to be the nTr of Wisdom, or Wisdom itself. We will dedicate an entire section to Tehuti a little later on in this work, however, for now, let's look at what we know thus far in regards to the cosmology.

If we are saying that the nTrw Khemenu constitute Tehuti, and that Tehuti is the Divine Mind, then we are in essence saying, that universe itself is Mental. If the eight forces of Nu, which represents infinite potential and substance, and they also constitute Tehuti, then we are saying that All is Mental, and this mind exists as the basis of everything. This idea is actually the foundation of the Western Occult science known as "Hermetics," which is adopted from and based upon the Ancient Kemetic teachings of the nTr Tehuti. Anyway, taking these ideas into account, we come to understand that the Cosmology of Khemenu depicts nTr, as a Great Infinite Mind.

Now there are a few versions of the story. In all accounts, the eight primordial forces are said to have been in perfect balance with one another. However, when these forces began to interact with one another, the conditions became volatile and led to a great explosion. This great explosion led to the formation of a great mound. Now following the explosion and formation of the mound, is where we have varying renditions. In one account it is said that a goose by the name of Gengen War (Great Cackler or Honker) laid an egg upon the mound, out of which hatched Ra. In another version, it is said that Tehuti, in the form of an Ibis (his main form/sacred animal) laid the egg upon the mound. Yet, another version states that the explosion from the interaction of the eight forces led to the emerging of a lotus bud from the Primordial Waters, which slowly blossomed, revealing within it Khepri , the "Dung Beetle," a symbol of the process of creation, evolution, Becoming, and Change. Khepri eventually transformed into a young boy , who is said to be Ra, which began to weep, his tears eventually led to the creation of Man.

Now some may look at this cosmology and its variations, and come to the conclusion that it is full of contradictions. However, this is far from the case. In actuality, each version tells the same story, just in different ways, and when all are taken into account, we receive a more holistic understanding of what is being conveyed. For example, each begins with the interaction of the eight which leads to an explosion. Following this explosion, there is the emergence of a phenomenon out of Nu. The Phenomenon in one instance is a mound, in another a lotus. In the case of the mound , a Cosmic bird, be it goose or Ibis, lays an egg upon the mound, out of which is hatched Ra, and in the case of the lotus, from it blossoms Khepri (the young Ra), who becomes a weeping boy. When taken as a whole, we can say that according to this tradition, nTr is a Great, Infinite, and Substantive Mind. This is symbolized by the eight forces of Nu, and the fact that they are said to be the very constitution of Tehuti. The interactions between these forces lead to an explosion. Now this interaction is speaking to motion or action. It must be remembered that prior to this interaction, this state of being, Nu is in a state of Inertia or Nun. So this Inter-action speaks to motion. This motion causes an explosion, which is usually known by expansion, a tremendous sound, and an eruption. The motion and eruption is symbolized by both the rising of the mound, and the emergence of the lotus. The sound or word in every instance is the creative agency, which is symbolized by Tehuti as the Great Word or Madu nTr, Gengen War as the Great Honker, and Khepri who transforms into Ra as a weeping boy. Also, in every version it is Ra that comes forth and carries out the act of creation.

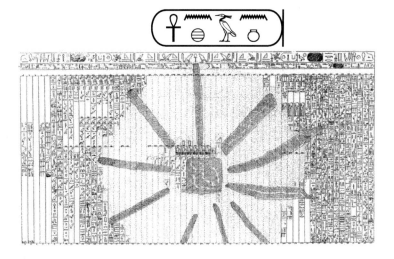

The Cosmology of Mennefer

The Cosmology of Mennefer is largely derived from what has come to be known as the Shabaka stone, which is accredited to the King Shabaka of the 25th dynasty. This cosmology is very special as it marks a restoration of the traditions of the Ancestors after the Libyan conquest of Kemet. This tradition centers on the nTr Pitah, in the role of the Creator. In ancient times, Pitah was long associated with craftsmen, architects, and blacksmiths. In this cosmology we find that it is Pitah that is associated with Nu/Nun, and it is he that produces the Itum (Ra) and the nTrw that come from him. In the text we find Pitah being referred to by names such as **"Pitah Nu/Nun," Pitah- Tathenen (**the primeval mound), and he is said to have carried out the work of creation by first conceiving of it in his heart (mind/will) and declaring what was conceived in the heart with his tongue, which brought the thing into being. As Pitah-thenen, all creation takes place within him, forms coming forth from his substance. We also find that Pitah's "Hati" (heart) is associated with Heru, and his "Nisit" or tongue is associated with Tehuti. He is also called **"PtH Wr HAt nst PsDw nTrw"**, that is "Pitah the Great heart and tongue of the nine nTrw."

According to the cosmology of Menefer, it all begins with Pitah in his name of Ta thenen, the primeval mound, and it is in this form that he makes his decrees, carrying out the work of creation. Pitah is the source of and power behind everything, existing within all things. The name "PtH wr Hat Nst PsDw nTrw," speaks to Pitah's existence within all of the divine forces as "heart and tongue," or Intelligence and Vibration, and indeed it is through these divine faculties, *HAti* (heart), and *Ns* (tongue) that this great work of creation is carried out.

His first act of creation would be to bring Itum (Ra) into being:

xpr m hAti ns m tit tm

Manifesting in the heart, manifesting through the tongue, the image of Itum.

wr aA PtH sbS anx nTrw nbw kAw-sn s ek

Great Great (So great or twice Great) is Pitah, giving life to all of the nTrw and their kAw.

m hAt pn m ns pn

Through this heart, and through this tongue.

Here we have a description of events that are overall similar to the cosmology of Khemnu, in that creation begins within the Mind, and is carried out through the word or sound. In fact Tehuti actually makes an appearance as he is said to be tongue of Pitah, and Heru the heart.

xpr n Hrw im-f xpr n DHwty im-f PtH

 Heru comes into being within him; Tehuti comes into being within him, as Pitah

xpr-n Sxm hAti ns m at.w xft.

Power manifest as heart and tongue and limbs according to

SbA wn.t-f xnt Xt nbw m xnt r

The teachings that reveal: it is within every body and within

Nb-n nTrw nbw rmT nbw awt nbw HAft
Every mouth, all nTrw, all men, all flock, every creeping thing,

anx-t Hr kAAt Hr wD mdw xt nbw mrrt-f

And everything that lives. Commanding through thought, and commanding through words whatever he desires.

From the above we come to understand that Pitah is the essence of all things, exists in all things as the power (energy), intelligence, and the very vibration or sound that gives each thing its form and function (definition). In this sense, we come to understand nTr, as Pitah; as a Grand Designer, an artist, and in the same way that an artist may first conceive of their work in the mind, prior to the actual creation of the project, the same is being said here of Pitah on the cosmic scale, and in actuality, this quality within man, is the nTr Pitah within our being.

The cosmology of Mennefer goes on further, to describe the creation of the other divine forces, the nTrw, and their relationship to Pitah, and their function and role in the creation.

PsDt nTrw-f m mt-f m ib Hw nD Htw
His Nine nTrw are before him as heart, authoritative utterance, teeth,

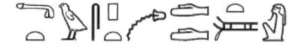

Mtw Spt Drti tm
Seed, lips, and hands of Itum.

IpA xpr n nA PsDwt nTrw Itum m Mtw-f
These Nine nTrw came into being from Itum's Seed

m Dbaw- f
and his fingers

psDwt nTrw Hm pw nDHwt spt m r
Indeed these nine nTrw are the teeth and lips in the mouth

pn mAth rnn xt nbt pr n Sw
Proclaiming the name of every thing, from which came forth
Ishu

tfnwt im-f ms-n PsDwt nTrw
and Tufnut as him, and giving birth to the nine nTrw.

mAA irty sDm MsDrw ssnwt fnD nf
The vision of the eyes, hearing of the ears, breathing of air through the
nose

S-ar-n sxr ib-n tf di pr arqy nbw

relays the plans of the heart, bringing forth every decision

I ns wHm KAAt HAti sw
Indeed the tongue repeats the thoughts of the heart

ms nTrw nbw
It gives birth to all the nTrw

tm psDwt nTrw-f
His nine nTrw were complete

Sk xpr-n is mdw nTr nbw m KAAt HAti wDtw Ns
Behold every Divine Word came into existence, by the thoughts of the heart and commands of the tongue.

Based upon the above, we come to understand that nTr, as Pitah, manifest through the nTrw, and the nTrw are the various faculties of his being. The description of the nTrw as his heart, tongue (utterance), teeth, lips, fingers, hands, and seed, speak to these forces as the form of Pitah, the agencies through which he carries out creation; bringing definition (articulation) and order to the universe. If it is through thought and the tongue or Word that all came into being, then the nTrw are the teeth, tongue and lips, giving variance, distinction, and definition to each Word. They are his hands and his fingers, through which Pitah, as Grand Architect and Master Craftsmen, shapes and molds the universe; the seeds through which he impregnates the Mind/Spirit to give birth to the aspirations of the his Will. Thus nTr as Pitah exist on all levels, first as Pitah Nun/Nunet, then coming forth as the primordial mound Pitah Thenen, then coming forth as Itum and from here manifesting as all of the nTrw. The interesting thing in all of this, is that based on the description of the forms and functions of the nTrw, one comes to the understanding that their coming into being, brings

Pitah form and definition. In other words, as the nTrw come into Being, it is actually Pitah coming into being, in a more defined, and ordered state.

Another interesting thing about all of this is that all of this takes place via the thought and Word/sound. Pitah thinks all of this into being, and then decrees what he is thinking. In a way one could say that Pitah is in a state of deep concentration or meditation. In fact, the statement *"the seeing of the eyes, hearing of the ears, and breathing of air into the nose, relays the plan of the heart, bringing forth every decision,"* is a direct reference to mediation and its primary use in creation during ritual.

This is quite profound as we come to find that Kemetic cosmologies and traditions have relevance on multiple levels, have multiple dimensions to them, and have multiple purposes. Not only do these cosmologies give and account of the origins of the universe, but also serve the purpose of spiritual instruction, and socio-political organization within the society. Later, we will also come to find that their relevance evolves along with the time and the people that adhere to them, and are even prophetic in scope.

Similar to the cosmology of Pitah, the cosmologies pertaining to the nTr Khnum offer another account of Creation at the hands of nTr as a Divine Artist, a potter to be exact. Khnum is said to have given form to all created things from his potter's wheel. Like all of the previous traditions, Khnum is said to have brought forth creation from Nu/Nun, he being the personification of Nu itself. This association with the Primordial waters of Nu was also described in an analogous way, in associating Khnum with the Hopi (Nile), being the nTr responsible for the annual flood that would continually bring life and prosperity to the region.

As **"Khnum nHp** (Khnum of the Potter's Wheel) is said *"to join in secret, and build soundly, providing the breath and waters of life,...fashioning nTrw and Men, flocks and herds, birds and fish, bulls and cows, etc."* What's special about the cosmologies pertaining to Khnum, is that his is one of the only ones that give a detailed description of the creation of Man. According to the **"Great Hymn to Khnum-Ra"** found in the Temple at Esna, Khnum is said to have designed man, right down to the finest detail, providing the form and function of every aspect of his physical being, even the relationship between the male and female genitalia. Khnum gives form and life to the child in the womb of her mother, and causes the womb to release the child by his Will. He is said to be responsible for the rise of the great egg from which hatched Ra, and is in some instances

associated with Tehuti. Whereas Khnum carries out the actual designing of man, Tehuti provides him with the schematics.

Khnum's work of creation is very personal. Not only does he bring all life into being, but he personally sustains it. There is a story about a terrible famine that took place in Kemet, which lasted for seven years. The King nTr khat (Djoser) went to his TAty (Prime Minister), the wise sage Imhotep to seek counsel. He asked Imhotep where was the origin of the Hopi and who was the nTr that governed it. Imhotep told the King that the origin of Hopi was at "Yebu" and Khnum is the nTr that resides there. He then informed the Nisu of all the other nTrw that had a shrine in the temple, and what offerings he should bring to Khnum. The King made his way to "Yebu" where he found a temple and shrine dedicated to Khnum in shambles. He made offerings and sacrifices to Khnum and then proceeded to ask for his assistance. Khnum after a while appeared to Djozer as saying:

> *"I Am Khnum, your Creator. My hands are upon you, to keep together your body and to maintain your limbs; I gave you your Ib. Yet in spite of all of the abundance of materials surrounding this place, they go unused, and the temples and shrines are unkept, and have been for the longest!"*

After this Khnum then tells the King that he will return prosperity to Ta Meri, greatly detailing all of the blessings he shall bestow. After hearing this, the King made a decree to ensure that Khnum's Temple and the surrounding areas were rebuilt and well Kept.

There is much wisdom to be drawn from this story, some of which we will deal with a little later in this work. However, my reason for bringing it up at this point was to show how Khnum's relationship with man is very personal, in that he not only creates/designs the universe, he is constantly in charge of its evolution. He shapes and forms man, molding our body and spirits on his potter's wheel, he is the force that gathers all of the elements that makes us up and holds us together, he evolves us in the womb, and is present from birth, throughout the entirety of one's life. The reason for this will be understood, once we come to understand Khnum as the Great Ba.

Khnum was depicted as man with the head of a Ram, which in the language of Madu nTr is the word "Ba." Interestingly enough, this word Ba, is a homophone of the term that has been translated as "Soul." The Ba is the aspect of the Spirit that houses Consciousness, and is the unifying factor of our personal being with the rest of existence and source of creation, Nu. For this reason, the Ba came to be known as the "universal soul," or the "World Soul." The Ba is the aspect of the individual that continues its existence after the death of the physical body, reincarnating into another vehicle. It is the aspect of man's being that is directly responsible for moving man toward his or her personal evolution.

Khnum was said to be the "*Ba Ra,*" or "*the Ba of Ra*," "*Ba Ishu*," or "*the Ba of Ishu,*" "*Ba Gab*" or "*the Ba of Gab*," and "*Ba Osir*," or "the *Ba of Osir*." These names for Khnum, is not simply because he is depicted as a "Ba," but because he is the Ba, par excellence. As the Ba of these four great nTrw. It is being stated that Khnum exist as the Ba on every level of existence, every stage of evolution and the coming into being of creation; guiding the evolution from one phase to the next. In this form, he is depicted as a man, or ram with four "Ba heads," and is called "*Shefit HAt*," or "*Heri-Shef*" at Henensu.

Just as in all of the previous cosmologies, Khnum begins as "Khnum Nu," The Originating Chaos, and from there he brings his own Self into being as Khnum Tathenen, or Pitah Thenen, the "mound" that rose from Nu bringing the first point of definition/differentiation into being. From here he is Khnum Ra, and comes into being as his own creation transforming himself into the various nTrw as he comes into being, and brings all things into being.

Cosmology of Inu

The cosmology of Inu centers on Ra, and describes his coming into being, out of Nu, as his own creation. One the main texts that gives an account of this tradition is known as "**mDAt nty Rx xprw Nw Ra sxr aApp**," or "**The Book of Knowing the Evolutions of Ra and the Overthrowing of Owapep**." This text is one of the best defined of the

cosmologies of Kmt, and in it one can see the source of where other well known creation stories (I won't call any names) drew from. However, this cosmology differs from the other aforementioned in that it describes Ra's coming into being, and the Peseju nTrw that came into being from him. This cosmology describes in great detail Ra's evolution, coming into being as creation, evolving through the various kingdoms, as well as the creation of man. The terminology and choice of words that are used in this text are quite profound and add to the immense richness of the tradition.

Dd mdw Nb r Dr Dd-f m-xt xpr-f
Words of Nebertcher after his coming into being

Nwk pw xpr m xpri xpr-n xpr xprw
I Am that which came into being as the Creator. I came into being and brought into being the various manifestations

From the very beginning it is stated that Ra came into being as the Creator. This is very deep because here it is being conveyed that "The Creator" had a "beginning," and as Ra came into being, creation came into being, for they are one. For there to be a creator, there must be a creation and vice versa.

xpr xprw nb m-xt xpr aSt xprw
Bringing into being all that came into being. After I came into being, many things formed

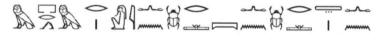

m pr m r nn xpr pt nn xpr tA nn
coming forth from my mouth. The heavens did not exist, neither did the earth exist. Nothing

Here it is being said, as it will be expounded on further in the text, that Ra "spoke" creation into existence. A reference once again to the Word as creative force.

92

QmAm sAt tA Ddft m bt pwy

Had been created on the earth, not even the creeping things in that place

Prior to Ra's coming into being, No-things existed. The matter of the universe was in a formless and indefinite state.

Tz-n.i im.sn Nw m Nwn.

I raised them from Nu, a state of Inertia

Nu is the formless, indefinite state of matter that we're referring to. Prior to Ra's coming into being there was only Nu, and Nu was Nun, or in a state of inertia, thus the bringing of forms in described as a motion; Ra "raising" them out of Nu. "Raising" is the same as the "Speaking" as motion and vibration are intricately woven together. Everything moves, thus everything makes a sound. Also this Nu; this substance, is the source of all existence, and creation actually takes place within Nu. Thus the "raising out of Nu, is analogous to an icecap raising, solidifying within the sea. The ordered universe forms and exists within Nu.

nn gmi-n.i bt aHa.n.i imi xwt-n.i m ib

I didn't find a place that I could stand there in. I worked incantation with my heart.

"I could not find a place to stand" is another reference to this formless state of Nu. In Nu there is absolutely no definition, no "place." There was No up, down, left, or right. All that existed was the "inner."We'll touch on that a little later.

znty –n.i m mAa iri –n.i irw nbt wa.kwi nn

I laid a foundation with the Law, and I made every form. I was alone, I had not

iSS-n.i m Sw nn tf-n.i m tfnwt nn xpr
Spit out Ishu, neither had I spat out Tufnut, not existed

ky iri-n.f Hna-i znty-n.i m ib-i Dz xpr aSt
Another who worked with me. I laid a foundation with my heart ,
my Self, and came into being the multitude

The past few lines provide enough evidence to debunk any argument that the people of Ancient Kemet were polytheist. Ra, the Creator states that he was alone when carrying out this work. Also, coming from a state of chaos where there was "no place to stand" the very first thing that needed to be done, was the laying of a foundation. There needed to be a place to stand, to build upon. So Ra laid a foundation in "MAa," which I have rendered as law, however this term also means order. So from Chaos, Ra laid a foundation in law and order, and thus made every form. This took place through an act of the "Heart" or Will.

xprw nw msw-sn inwk pw hAt-i m xfa-i
Of things which came into being, many things that had been born.
I had union with my clenched hand

Once the "Law" was laid down and "things" came into being, the interaction or "intercourse" between these things went on to produce more and more things.

TAtAit-n.i m Swt-I xr-n.i m r-i Ds-i
I joined myself in an embrace with my shadow; I poured my seed into my own mouth

iSS-n.i m Sw tf-n.i m tfnwt nn it-i
and emitted Ishu, and spat out Tufnut. Says my father

Here the picture is being painted through the use of metaphor and analogy. Ra's sexual embrace with his shadow is another monotheistic reference, and so is the reference to masturbation which is a singular act. However, there is something that is quite profound being conveyed. Ra says that he poured his seed into his mouth, and spat out ishu and Tufnut. This pouring of seed into his mouth and spitting out creation is poetry. It's a reference to the Creative Potential of the Word. Interesting to note, is that the term for the Word of nTr is Madu nTr, however the term Madu (Word), is a homophone of another word Metu, which means seminal emission or seed, and is symbolzed by an erect phallus emitting seed. So through analogy there is an equating of the Word of nTr, with the Seed of nTr. We have this same concept handed down today in the term "Seminary," of which the root is semen or seminal, and is a place where one goes to study the "Word of God." Aint nothing new under the Yatin ☺.

Nw sAtt-sn mAAt-i m-sA-sn Dr Hnti
Nu: "they weekend my eye when they proceeded from me, because for two periods of time

wAw-sn r-i m-xt xpr-i m nTr-wa nTr xmt
they proceeded from me, after I became from one nTr, three nTrw

pw -r-i xpr-n.i m tA Haa irf pn Sw Tfnwt m nwn
that is, from out of myself I came into being as this earth. I raised Ishu and Tufnut from the state of Inertia

Nu saying "they weekend my eye, or diminished my eye, is a reference to the fact that all of this creation is happening of Nu's substance, drawing from Nu. However, there is a subtle message about the coming into being of "duality" which in reality is an illusion, for in essence it is all one, it is all Nu. So he says I became from one nTr, three nTrw, Ishu and Tufnut bring duality into being, the illusion and perception of separateness, thus "weakening Nu's eye." Disallowing him to see clearly or see reality (Self).

wn-sn imi-f in-sn-n.i mAAt-i m-xt-sn m-xt

They existed within him. They brought to me my eye following behind them. After

Ra says they, ishu and Tufnut, brought to him his eye. We talked about Duality coming into being and weakening Nu's "Eye." However there is something that must be understood. Nu representing an undefined state, in Nu there were no-things to perceive, no form. Nu was all that was. So the bringing of duality (form and definition) i.e. ishu and Tufnut, automatically brings Ra's eye with them, for it brings "things" and thus the ability to see/perceive, "something" to look at. Also, the term translated as "eye" in this case is maat. This word *mAAt* has its root in the term *mAA* meaing "to see." However, the actual word for eye in Madu nTr is normally ir or ir-t "meaning "eye." This is not just a coincidental selection of terms or an innocent mistake; they are using "mAAt" here, to subtly call to mind a similar term MAat (pronounced Maat) meaning Law, Order, or Truth. This is due to the fact once again that without ishu and Tufnut, duality, there is Chaos, no definition, formlessness, no order, and nothing to perceive. So Ishu and Tufnut bring the maat (awareness), and MAat (order).

Irf sm-n.i at.w-i rm-n.i Hr-sn xpr rmT-i pw m rmw

I then united my limbs, I wept over them and mankind came into being from the tears

The form that Ra takes when creating man is a nTr called Rem or Remi, the weeping nTr. The deep significance of this is too much to expound upon at this time, but will be dealt with later on in this work. However, the fact that man is said to have come into being from Ra's tears, is a poetic way of speaking to man being of the substance of Ra's "eye" (Consciousness). Also, in saying that he united all his limbs, which is a reference to the nTrw (divine forces of Nature,) and then weeping over them and which caused man to come into being, is to say that Man is the unification of all of the nTrw forces (limbs) and consciousness (tears) of nTr.

pr m mAAt-i Xa rw-s r-i m-xt ii-s gmy-s

coming out of my eye and it was angry with me after it came and

found

𓂋𓄿𓈖𓏏𓄿𓉐𓏏𓄿𓈖𓈖𓏏𓎛𓏏𓊨𓈖𓂻𓄿𓊃𓐍𓈖𓏏𓂋𓆑𓊨𓏏𓊃𓅓

iri-n.i kt m st-s Tbi-s m xwt irw-n.i s-xnti irf st-s m

I created another in it's place. I endowed it with the light I created. Then it approached its place in

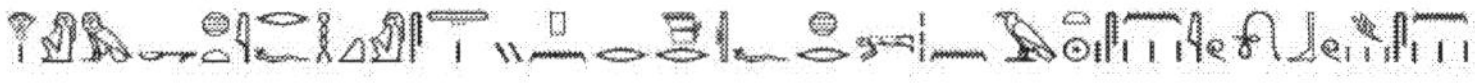

𓁷𓂋𓂻𓅓𓐍𓏏𓂋𓆑𓎛𓈎𓊃𓏏𓄿𓊪𓈖𓂋𓇥𓂋𓆑𓐍𓂋𓈖𓇯𓊃𓈖𓇋𓅱�wꜣbw𓊃𓈖

Hr-i m-xt irf Hq-s tA pn r Dr-f xr n At-sn iw wAbw-sn

my face, afterwards it therefore ruled this earth in its entirety. The seasons fall upon their plants

Ra's Eye is a reference to the Yatin. The Yatin on one level represents the Sun, and on a deeper level represents the entire physical universe. The Yatin is the vehicle through which Ra manifest itself through his various forms. It is the nTr.t Arat, who is also known as Het-Heru. Ra's eye becoming angry with him after the evolution of Man represents the conflict between man and nature, due to the incorrect use of man's personal will in his spiritual ignorance (represented in the tradition as Ra's other Eye). Once Ra endows it with the light he created (enlightenment) it took its proper place and everything fell into order (the regulation of the seasons.)

Tbwi-n.i Tt-s imi-s pr-n.i m wAbw Ddft

I endowed it with what it contained inside. I came forth as the plants and

nbt xpr nbt im-sn msw in Sw Tfnwt Gbb Nwt

Every creeping thing and all that came into being within them. ishu and Tufnut gave birth to Gab and Nut

The past few lines speak to Ra's evolution through the various kingdoms, coming forth as the plants, and animals, man, insects, etc. This is one of the most critical teachings in Kemetic Spirituality, as it firmly establishes that for the Kemetyu, Ra, nTr, The Creator, is not separate from its creation, but comes into being as creation itself. This being the case, every single aspect of existence is nTr, is Divine.

Msw in Gbb Nwt wsir Hrw xnti nn MAA stS Ast Nbt Hwt

Gab and Nut gave birth to Osir, Heru Khenti in Maa, Sutesh, Auset, and Nebt-Het

m Xt wa m-sA wa im-sn msw.sn aSt-sn m tA pn

one after the other coming forth from the womb. They give birth and multiply in this earth.

These lines speak to the birth of the Children of Ra: Ishu, Tufnut, Nut, Gab, Osir, Heru Khenti in Maa/Heru War, Sutesh, Auset, and Nebt-Het. As these forces come into being, they are responsible for the maintenance of order in the world, and the various manifestations and qualities of each thing that comes into being.

The cosmology of Inu consist of two parts, two versions so to speak, both of which are very important and must be included. I will include, for now, what I see to be critical aspects of part B at this time:

Part B.

Dd mdw Nb r Dr Dd-f xpr-I xprw xpr-kwi

Words of Nebertcher. He says: I came into being as the creator of all that manifested. I came into being

m xprw n xpri m zp tpy xpr-kwi m xprw n

as the evolutions of khepri, coming into being in the first time. I came into being as the evolutions of

xpri xpr-i xpr xprw pw n pA-n.i iw

Khepri. I became the creator of forms, that is to say, I produced myself from

pAwtt irw-n.i pA-n.i m pawtt pA

the primordial matter I produced myself from the primordial matter.

Here Ra is making it known that He himself is his own Creation. He created himself from Nu, the primordial matter. Nu is considered the Father of Ra; however, in actuality Nu is Ra in an inert/inactive state of Being. So Nu represents pure Being/Existence, Ra represents living, motion and activity.

rn-i iwsirs pAwtt pAwtit iri mrtw-i

my name is Osirez (Osir) the Primordial Matter of Primordial Matter. I have done my will

This is a very important line, for it gives a complete understanding into the very nature of nTr. The statement "My name is Yusirez (Osir), the Primordial Matter of Primordial Matter," lets the student know that in nature Ra and Osir are one. So as the saying goes "***Osir Hetepit m Ra, Ra pu hetepit m Osir***," That is, "***Osir rests within Ra, and This Ra rests within Osir***." As will be demonstrated later on in this work, Osir in his highest sense represents Consciousness/Awareness, thus his main symbol is the eye and the Throne. This Yusirez (Osirez) represents consciousness that is the very essence of all energy/matter (Nu), whereas Osir represents consciousness within the ordered realm, each things "is-ir" (As-ir) or "place of Awareness." Ra declaring his name as Osir, lets us know that not only is Ra Consciousness, but also that consciousness is substantive (primordial matter of primordial matter). It lets us know that matter at its most finest, subtle, and undifferentiated state is pure consciousness, and consciousness is power.

nbt tA pn wsxt-n.i im-f Tz-n.i Drt-i

all in this earth. I've spread within it. I lifted up my own hand

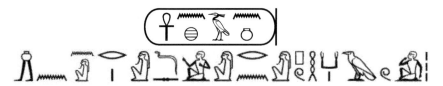

in-n.i r-i Dz rn pw HkAw

I brought my own name into my mouth as a word of power

inwk pw xpr-n.i m xprw xpr-kwi m xprw n

I, even I, came into being in the form of what manifested, and I came into being in the form of

Here is another reference to the Word as the creative force. Ra says he spoke himself into existence by speaking his own name as "Hika," which in this case means a word of power. This concept of *Ren* as Hika, you will find is one of the most important aspects of Spirituality, period. These names, as Hikau, represent the unique sound/vibration that causes each and every single thing to manifest in its unique form and quality.

xpri xpr-n.i m pAwti xpr aSt xprw m tp-a

Khepri. I came into being from the Primordial Matter, manifesting as the multitude of forms from the beginning.

Ir-i xprw imi m BA pwi Tz-n.i imi

I made forms within by means of my Ba that I raised within

M Nw m Nwn nn gmi –n.i bt aHa-n.i

From Nu, from a state of inertia. I couldn't find a place to stand

The Ba is considered the "soul" or universal soul. It is the unifying element within all things, moving each thing towards its evolution. This evolutionary motion is in this case, the first motion in the creation in the universe, the "raising out of Nu."

Imi xwt-n.i m ib-i znty-n.i m Hr-i iri-n.i iri-w nbt waw-kw

in there. I used my heart and laid a foundation before me. I made all that was made. I was alone

Znti-n.i m ib-i

I laid a foundation with my heart.

The Ib or Heart, is a symbol for the Will and the Mind. It is the element of being through which one makes their choices. Here Ra is saying once again that he initiated the creative evolutionary process through the application of his will.

Snwt-sn rn-i s-xr xftiw-sn qmAm-sn

They (Ra's children) invoke my name to overthrow their enemies. They create

HkAw n s-xr aApp iw-f Ar sAw Hr awy

Words of power to overthrow owapep, who is to be restrained by the hands

n Akr nn wn awy-f nn wn rdwy-f zAtt-f

of Aker. His hands shall not belong to him; his legs shall not belong to him. May he be shackled

n st wa mi Hw Ra sDw wd-n.f iw s-xr-tw.f Hr sAti-f

to one place as Ra inflicts the blows which he has ordained for him. He is overthrown on that wicked back

Pwi dw znpw Hr-f Hr iri-n.f mni sw iw sAti-f pwi dw

His face is slit open for what he has done, and he remains on his evil back.

In the **mDAt nt Rx xprw nw Ra Sxr aApp** or **Book of Evolutions of Ra and Overthrowing Owapep**, we find a very detailed description about the Creator, in this case Ra, and his coming into being as his own creation, literally going through process of evolution. Like all of the previous cosmologies, the creation begins with Nu or Chaos, from which Ra rises from within. After coming forth from his "Father" Nu, Ra goes forth to bring more and more definition to himself. The wording of this text is so profound, that if one were not a student of the language of Madu nTr, much would go past the reader without notice.

What makes this cosmology so important is the fact that it is centered on Ra, who is featured as the form that the creator takes in all of the previously mentioned creation accounts. In other words, no matter whether it is Pitah, Khnum, Tehuti, etc, each of them come forth as Ra, to begin the act of creation. Why is this so? What is so special about Ra?

As stated earlier all creation begins with Nu. Nu is the source. recalling that Nu represents not only the Primordial Water of Chaos, or the undifferentiated energy/matter that existed prior to creation, but the very source of all matter itself, sound/vibration. Physicists have been on a mission for a long time trying to come up with a "Theory of Everything." Today, they have actually struck gold, with the "String Theory," which speaks to subtle vibrating, oscillating particles of "coils" of matter that are the very underpinning of the universe. Well I would like to take this time to congratulate the Quantum Physicists for this achievement, in spite of the fact that they arrived very late. The understanding that sound is the foundation of it all is something that the ancients knew very well. Ancient Kemet knew this all too well and really applied this knowledge to the utmost. If Nu is the "Primordial Matter" that is in a state of inertia, yet is subtly vibrating, Then Ra is the "Mouth" that gives definition to the sound and vibrations, causing them to manifest as the "Word." This is actually demonstrated by the fact that the open mouth is the very symbol/alphabet that makes up Ra's name. As was the case with the cosmology of Khemnu and Mennefer, the act of creation took place via the word. Ra spoke creation into existence. In fact, the word as the creative agency is evidenced in the description of the act, through analogy.

The act of Ra pouring "seed" into his mouth, and then speaking out creation, the nTrw, is a symbol of the Creative potential of the Word. Like a seed once it takes root in the soil, or fertilizes an egg, it activates and quickens a new creation. Likewise, when the Word takes root in the mind and spirit of an individual, that word quickens and activates the individual to manifest the power and meaning of that word. The Word, in a sense, goes on to create who and what that person is, as the thoughts, ideas, and beliefs that define the person. In this same sense, the Word on a Macrocosmic as well as microcosmic scale, has a shaping affect on matter. This Creative Potential of the Word is symbolized as Ra's Seed. When he spits or speaks out the nTrw, Creation then comes into being. Also, as mentioned earlier, there is an interesting love of pun or the play of words present in the Kemetic Language. The Words Madu and Metu are considered homophones. *Madu* generally means "**word**," and *Metu*, generally means "**semen**." The phrase *Madu nTr* can mean "**words of nTr**," or "**nTr words**," Whereas "*Metu nTr*" means **Seeds of nTr**, or **nTr Seeds**. However, when properly understood, these terms actually mean the exact same thing. Being that the Source/Underpinning of all existence is Nu, and Nu at the very core is Vibration/Sound, then it should be understood that in essence, at the very core, the nTrw are sounds/vibrations. If Nu, as the infinite, primordial matter that is the very substance of which all creation is constituted, then the nTrw are the specific sounds that bring definition to Nu. In other words, the nTrw are Words/Sounds. This is why they are spoken into existence in every cosmology. Understanding this fact, it is further elucidated that nTr's word is its seed, and its seed is It's Word. So we return to the question "What makes Ra so important? In a way, when looking at nTr as a Whole, (Including all forms, nTrw, etc) as pure Being/Existence, one could say that Ra, is Its "mouth," (ra also means mouth) which from a creative standpoint is the agency of the Creative Power.

Another thing that distinguishes this cosmology from the others, is the fact that the Cosmology of Inu gives a detailed account of the Creation, whereas the Cosmologies of Menefer, Khemnu, are in a since "Pre-Creation) accounts that speak more to the Cause of Creation, and the nature of nTr, rather than the actual creative process. This is evidenced by the fact that both of the aforementioned cosmologies go on to describe Ra's coming into being, which ultimately leads to the creation of the Peseju nTrw (Nine nTrw), which are the forces that are the creative processes of the ordered universe. It is this common thread that actually unites all creation accounts as one grand detailed account.

The Cosmology of Waset

The Cosmology of Waset centers on Imun. Imun, next to Ra, just may be the most well known of the nTrw of Ancient Kemet. Evidence of Imun's existence in the traditions of Kemet date back far into the formative periods of the Kemetic civilization. Over time this aspect of nTr, would come to be regarded as the highest. This being the case, many have come to see Imun as the "**King of the nTrw**." Some scholars that are ignorant of Kemetic Cosmology speak to a supposed conflict or competition between the priest of Imun and other priesthoods. This is very inaccurate. The error on the part of these would be scholars, is in thinking that Imun was in a popularity contest of some sort, where he was raised from obscurity to ultimately become the most important of all the nTrw. However, once again, this is not the case. To say that Imun rose out of obscurity goes against the very nature of Imun (the name itself implies obscurity). Also, Imun is present in every single cosmology, whether it is stated explicitly or not. When we look for example, at the cosmology of Khemnu, we find that Imun is listed as one of the Eight Primordial nTrw. However, just as I stated earlier in the section pertaining to the cosmology of Khemnu; that all the Eight could be summed up as Nu, likewise all of the Khemenu can be summed up, or classified as Imun. I'll explain further.

Imun is a term that has been translated as "hidden, or concealed." However, this term while it can be accepted to mean "hidden or concealed," when we delve into the language and study the pun, we gain a clearer understanding of the meaning of Imun. When we observe the term Imun, we are observing another wonderful example of the genius of the Madu nTr language. The term Imun is written thus 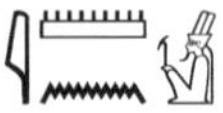 in Madu nTr. This word actually consists of two words, shrewdly woven together. However, before I touch on this point, it must be understood that within the Madu nTr language there are symbols called "Biliterals." ***"A Biliteral is a symbol that represents one syllable consisting of two sounds in a certain order.***[2]***"*** Within the word "Imun," There is the biliteral 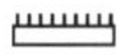 , which represents the "**mn**" sound. However, if we were to write Imun out alphabetically and phonetically, it would be rendered so  , or **imn**. Now looking at the letters that form this word, we can see two words

[2] Amen, Rkhty Medu Neter pg 36

within it. First there is 𓇋𓅓 or **im**, which means "within," and lastly there is 𓅓𓈖 or **mn**, which means "firm, stable, or secure." Taking all of this into consideration, we can understand that Imun does not simply mean "hidden,", but "that which is hidden inside, and is secure." So when we say that Imun is hidden, or concealed, it is due to the fact that Imun refers to the innermost recess and secure place of all, the Self. In other words, Imun" is hidden away" securely within the holies of holies of Self, that sees all yet no-thing can see Imun, for it is that which does the seeing within that which sees!

The Khemnu nTrw can be summed up or classified as Imun for the fact that the pre-creation state of the universe that they represent; the Chaos, was/is an infinite substantive consciousness (Ausirez), yet because it is a state of existence that lacks definition, in spite of it also being pure substantive consciousness, it has absolutely nothing to be conscious of, including Self. Imun is formless, and thus cannot be seen. This is the reason why Imun is mostly depicted Blue, in the same manner as Nu, being that they both represent the "Primordial Waters," and as Hopi who is the "nTr of the Nile River." Now some say that Imun is depicted as blue in association with air being that air is invisible. I'm not saying that this is incorrect because there are examples of nTrw depicted as blue, in association with the air or sky, as we see such an example in Sutesh in the temple of Hibis (Sutesh is the nTr of Wind, and weather, especially storms,) however, I don't see this as the sole or chief reason for Imun being depicted thus, for if it were the case, then we should see examples of ishu depicted as blue, being that most Egyptologist consider him the "air god" par excellence. However, the fact that the Khemnu nTrw as a collective can be summed up or classified as "Imun" is evident from a hymn to Imun that states:

xmnwy xprw-k tpy-k
The Eight were your first form

Km-k nniw-k wati
Until you completed these, you were one.

zStAw Dt-k m wrw

Hidden was your body among the Elders (the Khemnu)

Imn n tw Imn m HAt nTrw

You kept yourself secure within as Imun at the head of the nTrw.

The Khemnu are here described as Imun's first form. This is very interesting, because the Khemnu nTrw are considered the oldest of all nTrw, and represent Chaos or "formlessness." All of them together are the body of Imun, and as it is said here, Imun is the head among the elders, and is one. Now I've translated the last line as "you kept yourself "secure within, "but it can also be rendered "hidden." The reason why Imun is hidden among the "Elders," is because they are his "body," while "he" is the inner most essence of it. And while these Khemnu nTrw are the source and substance from which all things are made, Imun is the "Inner" most essence of it all. This aspect of nTr came to be considered the "highest" or "transcendental," that is "unknowable," unconditional, and indestructible. Imun just "is." However, consequently, Imun is "unknowable" in this aspect, even unto itself, for Imun is the "Knower." This aspect of existence, in actuality pure "existence/being," is acknowledged by Quantum Physicists today. The world renowned and illustrious Physicist Stephen Hawking states the following in regards to the origins of the universe:

> *...Rewind far enough and everything gets closer together. All galaxies, in fact, every single thing converges to a single point, The Start of Everything, 13.7 billion years ago...the universe burst into existence, an event called the Big Bang...At the very beginning the Big Bang, actually happened in total darkness because light didn't even exist yet... to see it we would've needed some kind of cosmic night vision...But even this, a view from the outside is impossible...Again it sounds strange but space didn't even exist then either, so there was no outside.*

The only place there was - was INSIDE[3]. (Emphasis mine)

As we have stated numerous times, that prior to the creation of the ordered universe, there was a state of chaos, an undefined, undifferentiated state of Matter, represented as the Khemnu nTrw, Nu/Nun, etc. This fact is conveyed by Mr. Hawking's statement of a "closeness" that ends in a "convergence to a single point." However what Mr. Hawking does not relay, is the fact that this "point" is "totality." Anyway this indefinite state where there was no "outside," no space, no time...etc, all that exited was the "Inner" which we know in the language of Madu nTr as Imun. Imun, the "inner, concealed, secure" always existed, and our Ancestors knew that. Funny to note, that Mr. Hawking constantly makes the statement that "our" Ancestors were clueless to this fact, and "we know more about the universe than "our ancestors have for the last 200,000 years." Tsk tsk! Speak for yourself Mr. Hawking, speak for yourself. Nevertheless, it is nice to see these guys finally starting to catch up☺.

Imun, just as all of the aforementioned cosmologies, comes forth as Ra, when he begins the act of creation, first by causing the rise from Nu, of the primordial mound, Ta-thenen, just as every other cosmology teaches us. When he comes forth as the Creator, he is Imun-Ra. In fact, of Imun it is said that he is:

> *"Ta-thenen who first formed himself as Pitah..."*
> *"appearing as Ra from Nun..." ..."As Itum (Ra), Sneezing from his mouth producing ishu and Tufnut...""He honked by voice as Gengen Ur, coming into a land he created for himself..."*

All of these descriptions of Imun unite all of the previous cosmologies and further demonstrates that the Kemetiyu were never polytheist, that there was One Being that manifested as the Creative force. In other words, Imun is Pitah, Ra, Tehuti, Gengen Ur, Khnum, and every other nTr; he is simply the hidden essence within each and every one of them. This is further demonstrated by the fact that in many of the temples, no matter

---

[3] "The Story of Everything," Into the Universe With Stephen Hawking, 2010

which nTr you were making offerings to, you were making offerings to Imun-Ra[4]. nTr is one that manifest through/as the nTrw (many).

Imun as the innermost consciousness is spoken to in his relationship with the eye. It is said of Imun that he conceals himself within the eye. The eye of course has always been a chief symbol for consciousness/awareness. Imun is called "*nb xprw aSA inw hap sw wADt r msw-f*" that is, "**Lord of manifestations, plenty of colors, who conceals himself within the Wujat (eye) from his children**" and "*htp-f m wADt-f Imn sw m-Xnw DfD-s*" that is "*just as he rests himself within the Wujat, so does he hide himself in the Iris*, "*ntf imn sw m-xnw DfD n wADt*, "*he conceals himself within the iris of the Wujat*." This wADt is the "Yoriyit," Het-Heru/Sekhmet, the "mAAt n Ra," or "the eye of Ra," and is also referred to as the Yatin.

This is a wonderful time to shift gears so to speak, and bring up the nTrt. Where is the feminine aspect of the Creator in these cosmologies? We've talked about Tehuti, and Ra, and Khnum, and Pitah! What about the nTrwt? Where is she? The Answer is "Present!" The nTrwt is the material essence and medium/vehicle of the nTr. She is the vehicle, and the material through which creation is carried out and manifested; and just as it is with all of nature, Creation takes place within her. This is clearly demonstrated by the fact that Imun is said to exist within his "eye."

The *MAAt, ir-t*, or *wADt* of the nTr is the nTrwt Het-Heru. This is a well attested and established fact. In the story of the "Destruction of Mankind," Ra sends his "eye," Het- Heru, into the earth to deal with the men and women that had been disrespectful to him. Het-Heru went in the form of Sekhmet, and began the bloodshed according to the tradition, in Henensu. In a hymn to Het -Heru found in her temple at Yunut (Dendera), it is said of Het Heru, also called Rait (the feminine counterpart to Ra), that "*Hbs-s nb-s m s-Sp-s imn-s sw m-xnw DfD-s*,"" *she clothes her Lord with her light, she hides him inside her iris*."Again, In a litany to Sekhmet it is said "*I sxmt Hbs nb-s m sSp-s imn sw m-xnw DfD-s*" *O Sekhmet, she clothes her lord with her light, hides him within her iris*." We also find other nTrwt such as Auset, Nebt-Het, to name a few referred to as the "eye" of various nTrw. This eye is the Yatin, the so called "sun disk."

---

[4] Sabban, S., Temple Festival Calendars of Ancient Egypt, Liverpool Monographs in Archaeology &Oriental Studies, 2000

Figure 1: Ra seated with the Yatin with Yuriyit upon his head.

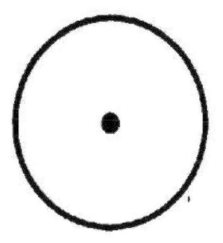

Figure 2: The Yatin, a chief symbol for Ra

The Yatin is one of the most special and profound symbols in the

Kemetic tradition, due to the depth of wisdom that can be acquired from the philosophical study of it. For our purposes, we shall discuss a few of its associated meanings. The outer circle represents the "All," the infinite, existence in totality. If we remove the inner circle or dot from the center, we would have a nice symbol that represents the state of the universe prior to creation. There is nothing outside of this circle; the circle is all that is. Within this circle there is no differentiation, no definition. There is consciousness, there is substance, but due to its undefined and formless state, it has absolutely nothing to conscious of; including Self. This outer circle alone is what we call Imun, Nu/Nun, and the Khemnu nTrw. The first differentiation within the circle comes with the rising of the inner circle or dot. This "Dot" is Ra. This dot is also referred to as the "Benben," Ta-thenen," the "Primordial mound" upon which the cosmic egg was hatched, the foundation Ra laid. This differentiation, Ra's coming into being (the inner dot) automatically brings Duality into being, symbolized by Ishu and Tufnut, and of course Ra's "mAAt," or "Eye" follows behind them, bringing with them the ability for consciousness to be conscious of. As such the Yatin also resembles an Eye. Once this dot is present within the outer circle, the Yatin is created and is also a symbol for the physical, ordered universe ("mAAt" n ra, catch the pun). It is within the "dot" that all creation takes place, as is demonstrated from the fourth invocation of the "Praising Ra in the West"

Hknw.n-k Ra qwA Sxm

Praise to you Ra exalted Shekhem

z-mAA tA s-HD imnti

Looker on the The Earth, Brightner of Imenti

Pn nty irw-f xpr-f ir-f xprw-f m itn aA

Whose forms are his creations; you make all of your creations within your Great Yatin.

The Yatin, as seen in Figure 1, is usually coupled with the Yuriyit, the "serpent of light," which is actually a part of the Yatin. The Yuriyit is one of the chief determinatives designating the feminine Divine force, depicted following the name as ![glyph] or ![glyph] . With the second example we see the Yuriyit adorned with the cow horns and Yatin, just as Het-Heru is usually adorned (The cow horns and Yatin is Het-Heru's main headdress). Also, if one recalls the pre-creation nTrw, the Khemnu, it will be remembered that all of the nTrwt are depicted as serpents as well. And as the four masculine nTrw of the Khmenu represent the inner/hidden, infinite, chaos, darkness, the feminine represent the opposite conditions, the outer/manifest, finite (cyclical) order, and light. Also as serpents travel in waves, so does light, which is the length of a wave or "wavelength."

The nTrwt is always present, as the Kemetyu are very rational people, and understood that it was through both the masculine and the feminine principles that life takes place. Even in instances such as the Book of Knowing the Evolutions of Ra, when Ra makes the statement, "I was alone...I embraced my shadow..." the shadow is a reference to the nTr.t Yasuiset, a cosmic form of Het-Heru (Rait, Arat), the Mother of Ishu and Tufnut, the "son and daughter" of Ra. The Mwt nTr (Divine Mother) is the vehicle and substance of existence, and creation. She is the fabric.

I was asked once by someone "why isn't Het- Heru" Present on "Tree of Inu," My response was "because Het-Heru IS the Tree of Inu" (Tree is a reference to the Tree of Life, associated with the Pesju nTrw by modern Kemetic "Syncretist"). In actuality *pA PsDw nTrw*, or *"The Nine nTrw,"* is one of the renu or names of Het Heru. Also, the horns with the Yatin within it, is a symbol of the womb full of its fruit. Those horns are the Het (House) of Heru (nTr), symbolized as the Yatin, as it is said, on the day that Auset conceived Heru; he took up residence within her womb. Her womb became the "Het-Heru." This is also why Auset, the Archetypal mother shares this crown with Het-Heru.

It is interesting to note that both the words "Mother" and "Matter" share a common root in the Latin "mater/materia" and the Greek "meter," meaning the substance from which something is made, source, origin, etc. Even more interesting is the similarity of these words to the terms for "mother" in several seemingly unrelated languages, and also the term in Madu nTr "Mut," meaning "mother." Mut of course if also the name of the wife of Imun, and is in reality his materiality.

Taking this point further we can look at another symbol that is used

when writing the ren (name) of a nTrwt, and that is an ⃝ "egg," which is usually present with the Yuriyit, and the seated nTrwt, or Flag of nTr. The suhet or egg, is said to be used as a method of expressing filiation or line of descent, and may be derived from the sign for a clod of earth[5]. Both of the preceding explanations convey the essence of the nTrwt. Though the seed of a man is analogous to the Intelligence/Will of Being, it provides the Creative spark that quickens the Egg. The egg goes further to become its vehicle, providing the bulk of the Genetic Material that will come forth as the new life. It is the egg that provides the substance, nourishment, protection, and the means to make the "intelligence/Will" manifest. Creation/Evolution takes place within the egg, and it is out of the egg that things "Kheper," that is "come into being." In fact, whenever nTr is spoken of as "Bringing into being" or "Khepri" this is a feminine form of nTr. While Kheper can simply be rendered as "change," or "transformation," which is transitive and neutral, the act of bringing into Being or birthing is maternal. This is evidenced in **chapter 30 in the Ra Nw Prt m Hrw (Chapters of Coming Forth by Day)**, which can also be considered a Hymn/Prayer to Khepri, in which the hymn begins *"Ib-i n mwt-i, ib-i n mwt-i HAti-i n xprw-I"* That is *"my heart, my mother, my heart, my mother, my heart as I come into being."* This hymn is recited while meditating over a green model of Kheperi (green dung beetle). It must also be noted that the egg is also associated with Khepri as a symbol of "coming into being" as the Kheper lays its eggs within a mound of Dung, and as the eggs hatch it is analogous to the rising out of the primeval mound.

Looking back at our earlier examples of Imun residing within the Eye, we come to understand that Imun conceals himself within the nTrt, the dense material universe, the nTrwt of Light. An interesting paradox! We come to understand that everything that we can see and feel, everything in essence is a manifestation of light, and this light enables us to see. However, it is this very same light that conceals Imun, the Self. Imun hides within light, and not darkness, and in a way Imun is the darkness. This paradox is evidenced in inscriptions from the coffin of the High Priestess Ankh Nis Nefer ib Ra *"iw mAA-n-I n dbn-f n.i inD irw-f m Hr-I sqD m-xnw ir-ti-f hbs-n Axw irw-f mAa"* *"I see by means of his circuit, his visible form did not shrink from my face, the one who sails within his eyes his*

---

[5] Gardiner, Alan. Egyptian Grammar, 3rd edition, pg 474, 1957

radiance/light clothed his true form." At this point it should be clear that it is within his eye, the nTrwt, that the nTr resides.

As it relates to the Divine in totality, the family, usually symbolized as a trinity, represents the various aspects to nTr and the creative process. As we have related, the nTr represents the subtle, intelligence/mind/Will, while the nTrt, represents the substantive, tangible, material and power, that serves as the vehicle to give form and expression to the nTr. This expression is symbolized as the third member of the triune, the "Khrad nTr" (Divine Child). This child is the Creator, coming into being through the Creatress, manifesting as creation. The Child in the various trinities, represents the universe, birth of nTr, and the realization of nTr. Allow me to say it another way. If the nTr is the Word, or the Idea, the nTrt is the medium and means to give form and expression to the idea; the ability to convey it, ultimately leading to its birth or realization; the Khrad nTr. On another level, as we shall demonstrate later in this work, these trinities represent our spiritual makeup, and journey.

The "Father" is the Self, the Intelligence/Will, the Mother, is the e-motive element, the vehicle that gives the Father form, our "Persons," and the Child is our ultimate goal, the realization of Self, symbolized by Auset's journey to re-member Osir, conceive and give birth to Heru who is Osir in the flesh. However in essence all three are one. Sounds awkwardly familiar don't it ☺.

The science of the triune nature of nTr, is laid down in a Hymn to Imun, in which it is stated that "*xmpt nTrw nbt Imn Ra PtH nn snw-sn imn rn-f m Imn ntf Ra m Hr Dt-f PtH*," that is "*All nTrw are three, Imun, Ra, Pitah without their second. His name/identity is hidden as Imun, Ra is his Face, and Pitah is his person.*" Imun occupies the natural position of the Father and represents the hidden/unseen essence. Ra is the vehicle of creation, as is stated in all cosmologies that nTr takes the form of Ra when carrying out the Creative/Evolutionary process. Ra is also associated the light of creation (the sun), and occupies the natural place of the Mother. Pitah is the nTr that is the Divine Craftsmen and Architect, and is the principle of definition or form. Pitah is Imun Manifest, and occupies the natural position of the child. From the standpoint of natural Law, the trinity represents the Cause (father), the evolutionary process (mother), and the effect (the child). This same hymn goes further to demonstrate this Law, in stating that "*a message is sent from heaven (Imun), it is heard in Inu (residence of Ra), and is repeated in Het-Ka Nefer Hri (Het-Ka-*

Pitah/Mennefer), and is made a decree by Tehuti." The Original Word/Decree from Imun, is heard by Ra in Inu, but it is repeated or spoken again by Pitah, I.e. the Word becomes Flesh.

The Family, as we will speak on a little further, is the vehicle through which nTr continues to "Kheper Jes-f," that is "bring himself into being." It is the Maat of the family that perpetuates life. This is one of the most important concepts of Traditional Afrikan Spirituality, and in essence the foundation of it all. The importance of the family is evident, due to the fact that a nTrw were considered to be a family.

OSIR WAN NEFIR 5

SYMBOL OF NEB ER JER

"THE GREAT BA"

We cannot leave the subject of creation and cosmology without talking about the Osirian Tradition, and its cosmological implications. In the Cosmology of Inu, Book of Knowing the Evolutions of Ra and overthrowing Owapep, Ra says "ren-i yusirez (Osir), The Pautit n Pautet." With this statement, Ra is Identifying himself as Osir, and also Osir as Nu (Pautit n Pautit, Primordial Matter of Primordial Matter). However, this is not an isolated event. There are several examples of Osir being identified as Ra, or the Creator. One such example is from the Tomb of Queen Mother Nefertari, Royal Wife of Nisu Ra Mesis II.

In the above illustration we have Nebt-Het and Auset, with Ra/Osir

standing between them. The inscription reads, "weir Htpt m Ra pw Htpt m wsir" that is "Osir rests within Ra, this Ra rests within Osir;" which speaks to the unity of the two. We also find it written of Osir that he is called "Nsw HH...nswt nswwt nb nbw Hq Hqw..." Eternal King... King of Kings, Lord of Lords, ruler of rulers." It is further written that "wAD.n.k tAwi m mAa-xrw m-bAH a nb-r-Dr," that is "the earth becomes green in mAa kheru by the hand of Lord of uttermost limits (all). In his form of Sukari (Lord of the Duat), he is called "sA smsw nw pAwt tpy," the "eldest son of Primeval Matter." Osir is the "di-k anx m hAt," that is "giver of life from the beginning."

From all of the above descriptions we can see that Osir is associated with nTr as the Creator, Ra, who first came forth from Nu and brought life into being. In fact Osir is the "Ba Ra" that is "Soul of Ra." Also as "Yusirez" he is associated with Nu, the Pautit n Pautit (Primordial Matter of Primordial matter) or the very crust/foundation of Nu. This also relates him with Imun and Pitah in their forms of Nu. We will demonstrate this further as we proceed; however, taking all of this into consideration, we must now take a look at the Osirian Tradition in the light of a Creation account.

It is said that Osir and Auset brought civilization to Kemet. They found the land in "Chaos," and it was mostly swamps and marshes. It is also said that the people in Kemet were engaged in cannibalism...i.e. eating themselves. This is a reflection on the origins of the cosmos, beginning in a state of Chaos; a water like material which of course is Nu. The cannibalism is a reference to Nun. As you will recall, we spoke of Nun as the state of Inertia and Contraction Nu was in...i.e. "consuming itself." From here the very first thing Osir did was teach the people how to cultivate the soil, the science of husbandry, and established Maat (Law) in the land. Afterwards Osir went forward to expand civilization. This is a reference to the creation of order, and expansion that takes place in the universes coming into being. After this Osir has intercourse with Nebt-Het. If you will recall, Nebt-Het was barren. Nebt-Het is a reference to the inert matter, in a state of "being-ness," but "life-less." It is said that Osir was inebriated, and mistook Nebt-Het for Auset, as she was disguised as her sister. The intercourse of Osir and Nebt-Het produced Anpu. This part of the story is quite profound. Osir's inebriation, and Nebt-Het's disguise, represents the nTr getting lost in the illusion of the physical world, the "Matrix" if you will, which leads to nTr's coming into being as Anpu. Anpu is a nTr that is depicted as a jackal.

He is earthbound, learns through observation and investigation, has a strong sense of hearing, but cannot see clearly (dogs cannot see the full color spectrum and see much better at night). As it will be demonstrated later, Anpu represents the intellect and discriminative faculty, and is detail oriented, which is the reason he is depicted up close to the scales of "judgment" to check the "details," but cannot see the "big picture" as Tehuti who stands off and away. This represents nTr's mode of awareness, learning, being "trained" mostly by hearing, following its appetite, and detail oriented perspective (discrimination). It is Osir's intercourse with Nebt-Het that led to Sutesh's murdering of him, first by encasing him in a coffin made in his image, and then pouring lead within it. This coffin represents matter and the lead represents the densest expression of it, and the imposition of limits on the "infinite." The coffin made in Osir's image is also the Khat (human body). Anyway, this coffin is then thrown into the Nile, and is carried along by the currents to Palestine where it becomes encased in a "Tree." Auset travels to Palestine to reclaim the body from the Tree, out of which a pillar had been made to serve as the chief pillar of the Kings Temple. The throwing of the body of Osir into the Hopi, represents nTr in a state where It must surrender to the flow of the creative process, that is the Cosmic Laws, and forces of Destiny. Early in its evolution it is not "free" but is bound by these laws. The tree represents the "Tree of Life," which we know was taken from the Peseju nTrw. (The 9 nTrw)

The Tree of Life was popularized by the "Jews," but is without a doubt Kemetic in origin, at least in principle. The Tree of Life represents the paths, emanations, and differentiations the Divine went through in bringing order to its chaos, coming into being from a singular to a plurality, as its own creation while ultimately maintaining its unity through the working relationships, laws, and harmony of the various spheres. In the story, Osir's body is encased in a Willow tree. However, this is not the only case of a tree in the Kemetic tradition. Het-Heru, Nut, and Auset are all associated with trees. Yasuiset, a cosmic form of Het-Heru, is considered the "Grandmother" of the nTrw. It is said that she in the form of a tree, gave birth to the first nTrw. Heru was said to have been born from his mother Auset, who assumed the form of the acacia tree. The Benu, which is associated with both Osir and Ra, is said to renew itself in the branches of the Willow. One of the names of Het Heru is "Pa Pesjut nTrw," which relates that she is the entire peseju nTrw herself. The tree is a symbol of the Duat, which is the dwelling place of the nTrw and Spirits of the Deceased. It is also analogous to the womb, as it is the place from which all things are born, and where all things return to be born again. Also it is the place

where the initiate plants "seeds" in order for the fruits to born into this realm. In actuality if one were to look at the outline of the tree as a whole it makes the shape of the womb. Interesting enough, the word Duat resembles a "slang" word for the female genitialia in English. According to tradition, it is Het Heru that stands at the door to greet those that enter with an embrace. Anyway the "Tree" has been, used as a classification system for the nTrw and the working with them for ones spiritual evolution by modern Kemetic Syncretist, however, the information contained in the various dwAt text and cosmologies provides us with the actual Kemetic system of organization of the spirit realm, as laid down by our ancestors, which we will find far more enriching and meaningful, as well as more profound than the Kabalistic Tree of Life. It is my argument that the Jewish Kabbalah was literally taken from the Kemetic Concept of Khepri (also pronounced Khepera). In other words, if one truly studies the Kemetic Tradition, they will find no need for the Hebraic Tree of Life, Kabbalah, Hebrew Angels, etc... Remember, Auset went to Palestine and found the body of Osir encased in a tree. She took the body, and left the tree. We should do the same.

The Differentiation of nTr, depicted by the "Tree" is symbolized in the story, with the dismemberment of Osir by his brother Sutesh. It may come as a surprise to most, but in this particular aspect of the story, Sutesh represents the "Creative Force," the "Big Bang," so to speak, and that is responsible for the differentiation of the Primordial Matter, "Nu, or Yuzirez." There is a passage in the "Festival Songs of Auset and Nebt-Het" that speak to this aspect of Osir, and by extension Sutesh. The passage states " wn-n anx m ga-k." This translates in English something like, "life rises up from your loss of it." Also the term, un-n, is a clever pun, and homophone of the term "wn-n" meaning "to exist, to be, being." So by extension we could also translate this passage as "life exists by your loss of it." It is the loss, diminishment of the Primordial Matter, Nu, Yusirez, and Osir in this case. Osir's dismemberment by Sutesh makes creation possible. It is also written of Sukari-Osir, that "ga pi.f xpr m zp tpy," that is to say, "this calamity happened to you in the first time" (a reference to Nu/Pre Creation). In other words, Osir's death and dismemberment on the highest level represents the actual creation of life. Osir had to "die" from the primordial state of "Being," in order for "living" to begin. It is this same "destruction" that begets life, that causes Osir to be associated with the Benu, which is the prototype of the phoenix; a bird which consumes itself in flames, and is reborn from its remains or ashes, renewed. For this reason, Osir is the nTr of the "resurrection" par excellence, whether it is the spiritual life, or cycles of life, spiritual and physical such as the seasons of the year.

The "Creation" by Sutesh in this story bears a very interesting similarity to something called "Sethian Gnosticism," which follows it thousands of years later. In Sethian Gnosticism, it is taught that the physical universe was created by an "evil god" called "Yaldabaoth." Just as interesting, is the fact that "Seth," though in this case referencing Seth the son of the biblical Adam, is also the Greek rendering of the name of the Kemetic Sutesh. Interesting indeed.

The dismemberment of Osir as the creative process is further symbolized, by the fact that each "member" of Osir's body is said to represent one of the nTrw. In the 32nd chapter of the Prt M Hru each body part of Osir is identified as a nTr. Osir declares "Sni-i m Nw. Hr-i m Ra. MAA-i m Hwt-Hrw. Mesjer-i m ipuwat. Fnd-i m xnti Sps. sptw-i m inpw." That is "my hair is Nu. My face is Ra my eyes are Het-Heru. My ears are Wapuwat. My nose is Khenti Sheps. My lips are Anpu..." and the text continues to name more and more nTrw. Earlier in the same chapter Osir declares "Nwk Ra mn hswt..." "I Am Ra, securer of those who praise me." This is important because it is also found in the teachings regarding Ra, that all of the nTrw are also considered his "members" or "limbs," as demonstrated in the book "Praising Ra in the West," in which seventy-five forms of Ra are spoken of in seventy-five invocations, and each passage declares the nTr to be the "body" of Ra. Also, in the "Am Duat," Ra declares at the very beginning of the book "I've come to avenge the blood of those of my members that have risen against me." This same teaching of the nTrw as the members or limbs of nTr is also present, if you will recall, with Pitah in the cosmology of Mennefer. The nTrw as limbs of nTr, the distinctions between each, provides nTr with form and definition. As this relates with Osir, his dismemberment is the creation of the nTrw, the forces that come as creation, and serve as the spiritual laws that underpin it. The Re-membering of Osir by Auset represents the (re)establishing of law and order, Maat, causing all of the forces and the universe to function as a complete "body" or whole, in spite of the diversity and multiplicity through which it manifests.

From this point on in the story, follows the Re-membering of Osir's body by Auset, the conception and birth of Heru, and his growing and going to battle with Sutesh to reclaim his father's throne, all of which represents

man's spiritual journey and evolution. This is the journey that we must now delve into as we proceed.

NEHEM NTR

One of most fascinating and profound things about the cosmologies is the idea of coming to the rescue of Osir. nTr, as Osir, must be saved and protected. This is spoken of in the Cosmology of Menefer where it is said "owing to the fact that Osir was drowned in his water. Auset and Nebt Het looked out, beheld him, and attended to him. Heru quickly commanded Auset and Nebt Het to grasp Osir and prevent his drowning. They heeded in time and brought him to land." In the "Great Hymn to Khnum" it is said that Khunum:

"changes his form to Khenti Seh nTr (Anpu), to wrap Osir in the place of Embalmment, he models all things between his hands, to guard Osir on his right, save him from the water..."

From these examples, and of course the Osirian Tradition itself, it should be clear that though Osir, the Creator incarnate is nTr, he needs assistance. He needs protection, preserving, and ultimately resurrection and elevation to the throne in the Duat.

We also find this same understanding of saving nTr in regards to Ra. If you will, recall the very end of the Book of Knowing the Evolutions of Ra and Overthrowing Owapep it reads "my children invoke my name to overthrow their enemies, and they make words of power to overthrow Owapep...may he be restrained while Ra inflicts the blows decreed for him." This demonstrates that it is the children of Ra that protect him from Owapep; his enemy. This is also evident in the Am Duat and the Book of Gates, in which it is the nTrw and Ancestors within the Duat that protect Ra from his enemies, and allows him to pass through safely.

This common thread of the need of salvation between Osir and Ra should not be surprising as we have already established that in essence Ra

and Osir are one and same nTr, as Ra declares in one instance "My name is Osir (Yusirez)" and Osir proclaims in another "I Am Ra." This however, unites all of the "creators" and their cosmologies, as it is once again Ra that each and every one of them comes forth as in their form of the Creator. So by extension, each and every nTr, be it Pitah, Tehuti, Khnum, Imun, etc through Ra comes forth as Osir. This is to say that nTr, regardless of which cosmology one prefers, needs to be saved...but saved from whom?

From the cosmologies it is clear that nTr comes into being, evolving as its own creation. So in Kemetic spirituality, the very essence of it is the fact that nTr alone exist. All is nTr. If this is true, what, who is it that nTr needs saving from? Who are the "enemies of nTr? Also if nTr or "God" is everything, then why is there so much darkness in the world; So much inhumanity? To answer these questions, we must look back at the nature of nTr once more.

In every cosmology nTr comes forth as Ra to begin the Creation of the Universe. Ra makes the statement "I became from one nTr, three nTrw." This is another reference to a triune nature of nTr, similar to what we find in the teachings of Imun. However with the Cosmology of Inu, in Ra's case we find something quite elucidating in regards to his nature. Ra says "I became from one nTr, three nTrw, that is to say, from out of myself." This statement is a reference to Ra's bringing forth Ishu and Tufnut from out of his being. Ishu and Tufnut as we have discussed, have been symbolized as "Air/light" and Water, and the Akeru, the twin lions of the horizon. The main correspondence of their symbolism, however, is that of duality. When Ra rises out of Nu, he brings forth Duality, coming forth from the "Chaos," or undifferentiated state of Being. Another, point to add is the fact that Ishu is male, and Tufnut is female, another reference to Duality. Prior to their creation there is no explicit reference to duality or male and female distinction. When Ra brings them forth he becomes from one nTr, three nTrw, becoming a Trinity in which he himself, occupies the neutral position. Ra Brings forth Duality but He is One, and from the One come the Two and Three. However, the Two and Three are simply the Dual aspects, opposite poles of the One. So Ra comes forth as Ishu and Tufnut, bringing forth Duality, leaving a state of Being, and entering into a state of Living, of experiencing.

This Duality exists within all things, and applies to all things considered opposites, and it is this Duality that makes life possible. Understanding this, one comes to understand that there is no "light" without "darkness," for how would we know one without the other? How would we know up, or front, if we did not have down, and back to contrast it with. Without this Law of Duality, everything would be Chaos.

Let it be known however that as nTr manifest as this duality, it maintains its neutrality as its Self. In other words, nTr is both male and female, and neither, positive and negative, and neither. This Law also applies to what we consider to be "Good and Evil," "Positive and Negative," etc. It is Ra coming forth as Ishu and Tufnut, and his "eye," MAAt (Law/Order) follows behind them. Ra, nTr alone exists in reality, yet manifest through/as duality. Looking back at the above question, "what does Ra need saving from? Who are his Enemies?" The answer is "Itself," the negative aspects of its own being.

The "enemies" of nTr have various names in the tradition. They are called sebiyu, smaiyu, Owapep, Isfet, and Sutesh to name a few. However, remembering that only nTr exist, and comes forth as its own creation, then is should be understood that all of these forces are just the "negative" aspects of nTr. So Ra and his enemy Owapep are one. Osir or Heru and his enemy, Sutesh, are in essence one. This is the reason why we find images of the heads of Heru and Sutesh joined on one body, or images of them "tying the knot" representing the Unity of the "Two Lands." It is because they are one; just opposite aspects of the Self that need to be harmonized and brought into order and agreement. This should be a simple principle to understand as we can see this duality manifest within our own beings; the "war" between the positive and negative characteristics and behaviors, positive and negative thoughts; the fact that when we focus on accomplishing something the opposing or contradicting thought, doubt rears its face. This experience within our being of the battle with the "other," is the expressions of these forces we're speaking of, the "enemies" of nTr, and at anytime we can give Heru, or Ra expression, or we can give "Sutesh", or "Owapep" expression.

It has been stated that the nature of nTr is intelligence and power, which science calls energy. This intelligence and power, or energy is the very fabric of the universe and everything in it. It is this intelligence and power that we use throughout our daily lives and its various activities. It is what I am using to write this book as we speak. However, this very same intelligence and power can be used to destroy, build a nuclear weapon, kill innocent people, etc. Regardless of what it is used for, it is still nature; it is still nTr. This is to say that nTr, this intelligence and power, is in essence

123

infinite potential (Nu), period. It is the potential for anything. nTr, the Creator, is creation and creativity. In actuality, creation is all that the Creator can do, creation is all that can happen, period, regardless of what is being created. Whenever we give this intelligence and power positive expression, we are manifesting the nTrw. However, whenever we give this intelligence and power negative expressions, we are manifesting the enemies of nTr, but in essence it is the same intelligence and power, simply expressed in different ways.

This speaking of nTr as Nature, as Intelligence, as Power indicates that nTr is more of a function, ability, a potentiality, rather than an overlord that is in control of everything. This ability is at our disposal, our mercy. It is this understanding of the Divine that sets apart Kemetic Spirituality from the "Religions" of the West. The Priesthood of Ancient Kemet understood the teachings of Nehem nTr very well. They knew that they had a responsibility to nTr, and if they did not fulfill this duty it could potentially throw everything, even the universe, ultimately, into Chaos. This is the meaning of the Ancestors feeding, clothing, protecting the nTrw of the Temple, and the reason why they can be seen offering "Maat" (Law/Order) to the nTrw. Without Maat, these forces, the nTrw, nTr could manifest the negative and destructive aspects of their nature. This is to say that it is man's responsibility to maintain order/law in their regards.

So in answer to the question of "Why is there so much darkness, so much inhumanity, so much evil?" It is because we are ignorant to the Nature of nTr and as a result, ignorant to the Nature of Self. So when one asks the question "if God exists, why does he allow this to happen?," it is because we allow it to happen. We have not fulfilled our duties in regards to nTr and the nTrw. We have become ignorant of our responsibility because we now "believe that "God" is here to save us. We believe that we need "God," and it is not the other way around, or reciprocal. We believe that God is out there somewhere in control of everything, when in reality THAT "God" does not exist. The truth is nTr is right here, right now, waiting for us as Heru to take the throne (Command), and if we are not aware of that, than more than likely nTr is in trouble.

Man (male and female) is the Savior, the Redeemer, and Avenger of nTr, not the other way around. This fact is clearly demonstrated in the "Book of Praising Ra in the West." In this text in the 21st invocation, it states "*hknw.n.k Ra qA sxm nDt Nw pr m imi.t.f Twt is XAt Rmi*," That is, **"Praise be to You Ra, Exalted Shekhem. Avenger (or Protector) of Nu**

124

coming forth from what is within him, indeed you are the body of Remi." Remi is the form that Ra takes as he "weeps," man coming into being from his tears. In this passage, it is indicated that the nTr that "Weeps," and creates man is the Avenger and Protector, savior of Nu. This is profound on so many levels.

Firstly we must ask why it is that nTr is "weeping?" What does that mean? Also, why is it that "Nu" is the one being avenged, and what does man have to do with all of this? First let's deal with Nu. Nu as we know is the Primordial Waters of Chaos, the infinite and undifferentiated state of Being that preceded the creation of the ordered universe. Nu is infinite potential. This state of being lacks any form and definition. It is said that Nu became "weak" once creation came into being. Also as we have demonstrated before, Osir's murder on the highest level represents creation, and in essence Osir, Yusirez is Nu. Anyway, Ra is said to have "united all of his limbs, the nTrw, and wept over them, causing men and women came into being from the tears." As stated earlier, this "is a poetic way of speaking to man being of the substance of Ra's "eye" (Consciousness). Also, in saying that he united all his limbs, which is a reference to the nTrw (divine forces of Nature,) and then weeping over them, which caused man to come into being, is to say that Man is the unification of all of the nTrw forces (limbs) and consciousness (tears) of nTr." Also the idea of uniting or "re-membering" the limbs is a very important part of Kemetic spiritually tradition and is present throughout every aspect of the tradition. The idea is to ensure that one has a form, a vehicle, a body, in order to experience life. This is part of the significance of the "mummification" process, though it is grossly misunderstood. As this relates to nTr, this unification of the limbs, and weeping over them, speaks to man providing nTr with a "complete" form and vehicle. These limbs are also the nTrw. Now each and every nTr has a specific role and function, part to play that is unique to its individual being. This is part of the symbolism of the "limbs and members," in that each body part, organ, etc has a unique and specific function. The hands and feet serve different purposes, the heart and the lungs have different purposes, the brain and the buttocks serve different purposes, and each of these has a unique form to facilitate the successful carrying out of its function. However, each of these together make the body complete. Applied to the nTrw, all of them together make up the body of nTr. However, what type of form would it take to give them all, expression, together?

When we look at the way the Ancestors depicted the nTrw, we find

125

some with animal heads of various kinds. We also see some depicted as men and women and some even trees. Each of the nTrw has a specific temperament. Some are cool, some are fiery, some are maternal and nurturing; some are aggressive and warrior types; some are logical and analytical; some are emotional and empathetic. Now like the nTrw individually, animals are limited in their functions and expression as well as in form. The same goes for trees. They are bound by the laws of their nature. Some animals and trees/plants are docile; some are aggressive, or hostile. Only man has the potential to be all of these. In fact within man we find the unification of all of the Kingdoms and Domains of Biology. We can also see this union present in the evolution of man's brain. In fact it is understood that everything, every element that is found in the universe, man consists of. This is to say that man provides nTr with a form efficient enough for it to experience and explore itself in the fullest capacity possible. Understand that nTr is Infinite Potential, and man is the only creature that is able to express this reality.

Man is constantly redefining himself, and what is considered "possible." We are constantly evolving, transcending the so called impossible. We have found our way into the air, though we are not birds, and we don't have wings. We have found our way into the water, though we are not fish, and we don't have gills. We find our way into earth though we are not insects or rodents. So, though we are physically what one would consider terrestrial creatures, we constantly transcend the boundaries, exploring the infinite possibilities that we are.

What is being said here is understand that Nu is infinite and limitless potential, and in its original state lacks definition. When nTr comes into being, it goes through an evolutionary process, constantly transforming and adapting until it reaches a form suitable for it to express and explore Self. So it started as the elements of life, then lower life forms, aquatic life, each form limited in its own way. This is only natural as it is through the imposition of limits on its self, that creation was possible. However, nTr kept evolving until it attained a form that allowed it to come as close as possible to expressing the fullness of it's Being, which is infinite. Man is the edge.

Let's say it another way: nTr as infinite potential, inert matter was pure being. It simply was, but what was it? There was no life, no experience, no knowledge, not even the knowledge of Self. So nTr's coming into being as creation allows all of these things to happen, providing nTr with an opportunity to answer that burning question, who am I? What am I? Why am I here? Creation allows the Creator to search for purpose, for meaning, and once it comes into being as man, it now has a vehicle that will fully facilitate that journey. Man is the definition nTr; and by this I mean definition as in providing boundaries and structure, form, as well as the way that we use the word in terminology, as in "meaning or purpose". Man is the definition of nTr.

nTr's weeping also represents (poetically) a longing, an inner urge, a want, frustration. Those limbs individually did not suffice, in form; nTr's getting to know Self in its fullest capacity. So the unification of all the limbs, and the weeping over them brought man into being to answer this longing, to provide the right form. Man provides just the right amount of "limits" that will allow nTr to explore the depths of its limitlessness, and we are still evolving, still pushing the envelope ☺.

This is the reason why Remi, the creator of Man, is called the "Avenger of Nu," and one of the terms for man in Madu nTr is "RmT." This is the essence of nhm nTr. To give nTr, form, expression, purpose, definition; to let the infinite potential that we are flow. To liberate the nTr within, this is also the meaning of Osir being trapped in a coffin and suffocating, or drowning (inability to move or breathe). We can either be nTr's vehicle (Heru Henu or Heru the Boat) or we can be its coffin! Both are potentialities.

The Seed (potential) of nTr rest at the very core of our Being. It is the Self and is infinite potential, infinite possibilities. We must make our very reason for living its cultivation and realization. Potential unrealized and not actualized begins to ferment and decay; it breeds corruption and corrodes away at the Inner Essence. When this happens, Osir him Self becomes the very demon that haunts the temple. This is why we Nehem nTr. Open the Sarcophagus; free the nTr.

Misunderstanding the Divine has been the major stumbling block to the spiritual growth and evolution of man. We've been waiting on someone, something else to come here, step in and do what it is that we were born to do. We have relinquished our responsibility, and by consequence we have also relinquished our birthright; our Divinity. We should not be waiting on the return of nTr, nTr is waiting on us! This is to say, we are what, who we have been waiting for. We are nTr; we must re-member this.

Duality is somewhat of a paradox, a contradiction. While it is necessary in order for life to be possible, it creates the illusion that there is something "other" than Self, and that we are separate. It confuses us. This confusion causes us to believe that we are separate from nTr, and that nTr is some "big daddy" that exists out there somewhere. We have forgotten that from the "One" all came, and that all are simply expressions of the one. We have forgotten who we are, and have gotten lost, and nTr awaits our return, our return to Self.

There is a story in the Kemetic tradition that portrays this beautifully. It is called the "The Distant nTr.t." The Distant nTr.t is a reference to Het-Heru, the Eye of Ra. If you will recall, when Ra came into being he brought forth Ishu and Tufnut, out of himself, and his "eye" followed behind them. Following behind "them" his eye got lost in creation, and Ra was lost without his eye. It is said in some traditions that the Eye traveled "south" (leaving from a higher or elevated state, to a lower). Ra was so lost and powerless without his eye that he had to send Tehuti after it to bring her back. However, Tehuti would not have an easy task. The Eye had taken the form of Shekhemet and was on a war path of destruction. It is said that Tehuti disguised himself, and used stories to calm her and finally got her to come back home. Some say she still had to get into the river to cool off because she was so angry, and she was so hot that the water turned red. But when she returned she was greeted with joyous festivities. Another version of the story says that she left because she became angry with Ra. When she followed Ishu and Tufnut, she came back and found Ra had created "another" Eye in her place! Of course Het-Heru won't have any of that (You will become acquainted with Het-Heru...snap snap ☺). Angry, she took off and got lost in creation as Shekhemet. It is said that through song and dance, and getting her drunk, that she was able to return to her normal joyous self as Het-Heru. Both traditions end with Het-Heru being greeted with joy and festivities, and Ra placed her as a Yurayit in his forehead/crown. It is also said that her return to Ra brought the inundation, which brought life and prosperity back to Kmt.

These stories represent nTr's eye, representing his vehicle, his consciousness, himself getting lost in creation. It represents getting lost in the world of "duality," to the point where you lose yourself, your oneness. This is symbolized by the eye following Ishu and Tufnut, as well as the eye finding "another" in her place. The "other" eye is the lunar eye. In this case, when we think of the moon and its nature, it is a physical sphere, earth, that reflects the light of the sun, but is not the light itself. This is symbolic of the illusion of duality, the false light, the reflection. Though this world, this physical reality appears to consist of many apparent separate things, this is not the true light; although it appears real, it is only a reflection. Tehuti's stories represent the truth, the Divine Word, wisdom that causes us to come to our senses, to wake up, to get in the river and clean ourselves up, and the song, dance, and drunkenness in the other version represent the use of spiritual ritual and trance.

So Het Heru's return to Ra represents us as nTr; our return to self, and to our senses. It is another great symbol of our epic journey through life, on the path to remember; to realize Self, and once we return, once we re-member, the party truly begins, and the flood that brings life and abundance, prosperity, follows us wherever we go.

Without this return we will remain lost and confused, angry, and suffering. This return is nTr's salvation, our salvation. We must Nehem nTr to Nehem Jes (Self!). We must do away with the erroneous concept of a vicarious "God" that is separate from us, that is not us, but not only has interest in , and control over our affairs, but also commands us to worship it as though it needs it's ego stroked, and get's jealous, and will damn us to "hell" if we do not comply. If anything, we must save nTr from the WHACKNESS that is taught about it!

When we talk about nTr, we are talking about Being, we are talking about Life! We are talking about a nTr that lives, evolves, that is learning; learning about itself, exploring itself, in and as the universe. Us, we, our bodies, our minds, are the vehicles of this exploration. Our duty is to keep the vehicle running smoothly, to enhance it, and enjoy the ride. As we evolve, it is nTr that is evolving! As we learn, it is nTr that is learning. When we "know," it is nTr who knows. And when we enjoy ourselves, it is nTr who enjoys itself. This is nTr. This is Divine. This is Kemetic Spirituality.

It should be understood, that when we talk about saving nTr, we are talking about re-membering, realizing, and actualizing the Divine Potential within ourselves. We are talking about returning to our senses, returning to Self; re-membering who we are. Once we've returned, once we've re-membered all of our divine limbs, we are the walking embodiment of nTr, and the nTrw, the Divine Forces, and we will be able to wield them as we would our limbs. Our lives become full of joy, abundance, and wisdom and power flows through, and emanates from us. We are nTr, the Creator, and

we sit upon the throne of creation, our lives, and now have the capacity to bring what we will into being. This is our Divine Potential, Our Divine Destiny, but we must first, Re-member, we must Nehem nTr.

The journey towards remembrance is what you will find in the pages and chapters that follow. We explore various aspects of Kemetic spirituality, re-membering them, and utilize them as a vehicle to facilitate our journey. The following pages shall consists of ideas, information, hymns, invocations, and rituals, all of which are meant to converge and come together to form the body of Kemetic Spirituality, the re-membering of the Wisdom Corpus of our Ancestors.

THE ANATOMY OF BEING

In practicing Kemetic spirituality, it is important that we get a a view of the universe and reality through the eyes of the Ancestors. The rekhi Ikat (Knower of Things/sages) of Kemet did a wonderful job in mapping out a detailed description of the Physical and Spiritual universe, and the various components that make it up. These descriptions can be found in various texts, such as the Am Duat, Book of Gates, Book of Nut, Book of the Day, Book of the Night, Book of Caverns, Book of Hours, Book of the Heavenly Cow, The Pyramid and Coffin Texts and the Prt M Hrw. These texts provide insight into the nature of the Spirit, the cycles of life and creation, and the identification and classification of the numerous forces that make up and govern reality. Also, from these texts as well as others, we can gain insight into the nature of Man, our spiritual make up, and the various components that make us up. All of this we shall refer to as **The Anatomy of Being**.

In referring to "Being" we are referring to that which is, that is to say, that which exists. So in referring to Being, in this particular instance we are referring to everything that exists. For the Kemetic people, as well as many Afrikan and Indigenous people worldwide, there is only One Being in existence, period, and everything that exists is simply a manifestation of that one being. This Being we refer to as nTr, or Neb r jer.

In approaching this subject it is important that we do so free of the Western concept of God. Neb r jer is not "God" in the way that western man tends to think about the Divine, that is as an Independent, All Powerful, All Knowing, Omnipresent overlord. Instead we must understand Neb r jer in its Afrikan context. The reason why we must understand Neb r Jer in its Afrikan context, is because it is in Traditional Afrikan Spirituality that we find cognates with the Kemetic Neb r jer. When we look at many Afrikan

traditions, we find that there is one Being that is considered the "Supreme Being," or more correctly the Source of Life. However, this Being does not interact with the universe and world directly, but through various forces that emanate from it. Likewise, this Being is not served, or worshipped directly, but known through the various spiritual forces through which it operates. The reason for this is not just that this Being doesn't care about creation and is aloof, but it is that this Being is <u>Pure Being</u>, that is to say that "<u>it just is</u>."

In the Kemetic Tradition, one of the names of this being is Nu/Nun. As discussed earlier, Nun refers to the Infinite Undifferentiated matter that made up the universe prior to creation. This substance/Being was also inert. Also there was no locality or definition in this state of being that is to say that it was **All.** This is actually a very good way to describe and understand this Being; It is **All.** How does one quantify all? How does one Know All? How can one Worship All? What is all? Can it be defined? Sure as an indefinite, indefinable something, that is everything! All is Abstract, and it is for this reason that many Afrikan traditions recognize that the All exists, but is unapproachable. The All is Chaos, Oblivion! When some say "no man see's the face of "God" and lives," there is a good chance that they are speaking to The **All**, Neb r Jer. However, referring to Neb r Jer as God is incorrect and causes much confusion.

Neb r Jer is Pure Being, Existence itself, <u>It simply is, and always has been</u>. However in it's original undifferentiated and undefined state there is no knowledge, no perception, no experience, no Living. There isn't even the knowledge of Self. All of these things exist simply as an unknown potentiality. For this very reason instead of describing Neb r jer as All Knowing and All Powerful, it would be more correct to describe it as All Power, and All Knowledge, or "All THAT CAN BE POTENTIALLY KNOWN." As described in earlier chapters, it is when this Being creates definition and order within itself that life, experience, knowledge, etc, take place. <u>Life is this Being moving from an Inert to an Active state</u>. Even with that being said, **Life in Reality is truly this Being learning about, interacting with, and experiencing itself.**

This is a very important concept that shall serve as the ruling "law" if you will, throughout ones journey on the path; the fact that all life in reality is nTr. At the very foundation of all "beings," in reality is One Being, nTr. Every man, woman, child, animal, plant, mineral, etc, everything is nTr. All life is Divine. Also, in understanding that all life is One Being, nTr, we then come to understand that all life is one. This oneness is to be worked at consciously, until it is ultimately realized. It begins with looking for nTr all around you, but most importantly and firstly within you. It is for this reason that the Kemetic Ancestors used life, Nature, to depict the Divine. They recognized that nTr was the common denominator, the root of it all, regardless of how a thing may be individually expressed. However, they also understood that it was through the Many that we become acquainted with the One, which in reality, again, is a reflection of the one becoming acquainted with Self through the Many. As above, so below.

The All, the Infinite had to create definitions, boundaries, limits, and distinctions within its Self. These distinctions we have come to somewhat know as the ordered universe. However, it is important to remember that the ordered universe is only made up of a small portion of the All, and not the totality. In fact it is impossible for Order to truly come to the All as once again the All cannot be weighed, calculated, measured, grasped, or observed. Only a portion was used. However, this portion is still nTr, and is analogous to an Ice cap solidifying within a portion of the Sea. In reality it is all the sea, in reality it is all nTr.

Once definition is created within the All, order comes into being, the Universe comes into being, and life begins. This is represented by Ra rising from Nu/Nun, which automatically brings into being Duality, which is definition and differentiation, represented by ishu and Tufnut. It is ishu that represents a force of expansion, which is responsible for the separation of Nut and Gab, Heaven and Earth which represents bringing Order from Chaos, and the formation of the Universe. Also the four pillars of ishu, which also represent the four "sons" of Heru, represent the four cardinal directions, which speak to definition, locality, the creation of time and space. For this reason ishu wears the feather of Maat upon his head. Once there is Order, life and experience begins, which in many traditions is spoken of as a Journey. In this case, we are speaking to life as the Journey of Ra.

Ra is the Creative Force. No matter which cosmology we are dealing with, all of them ultimately display Ra in the Role of Creator. More importantly, however, is the fact that Ra is not simply the Creator, but also Creation, as he comes in to being, transforming, evolving, and coming forth as his own creation. This is another important key to grasp in attempting to understand the cosmologies of Kemetic spirituality. Everything is Ra, as Ra is the creative force, the energy that makes it all happen. If we understand

Ra as Energy, then we shall come to understand another key part of the traditions. This key, is the Law of Conservation of Energy, which states that Energy is Neither Created, nor Destroyed, but is constantly Transforming. Energy is constantly on the move. Thus we understand Ra's journey, not only of energy in constant motion, but also a journey of constant Becoming. We'll touch more on this point in a moment.

The universe in Kemetic Worldview consists of three "planes," so to speak. These three planes are "*Pet*" or **Heaven/Sky**, "*Duat*" which is the **spirit realm** or "**underworld**," and *Ta,* which is the **earth**. Ra's journey consists of a continuous cycle through these planes. This journey represents the cycles of life, the process of "becoming."

Pet, which many scholars translate to mean sky, in reality refers to the Universe, both created and uncreated. In other words, when speaking to Pet, one must clarify whether one is referring to "Nut," the Ordered Universe, or Nu, the Chaos. This is to say that to translate Pet simply as "sky" is to do a great disservice to the wisdom being conveyed. There are two levels to Pet, the Chaos, or Nu, and the Ordered Universe. This is clearly laid out in the **Book of Nut**.

According to the **Book of Nut,** the uppermost part or furthest region of Pet is "Uniform Darkness." According to the text:

The upper side of this sky exists in uniform darkness, the southern, northern, western, and eastern limits of which are unknown, these having been fixed in NU, in NUN. There is no light of the Ram there: he does not appear there, (a place) whose south, north, west, and east land is unknown by the nTrw or Yakhu, there being no brightness there. And as for every place void of sky and void of land, that is the entire Duat. ..."

The above passage couldn't be any clearer in describing the uppermost part of the sky or "Heaven." In speaking of it as a state of complete darkness, which is completely void, indefinite, and has no locale, we are to speak of the uncreated aspect of the universe that is called the Chaos, or Primordial Waters of Nu. This is a place in which there is no light, thus there is no perception, which is spoken to by the fact that it is unknown to the nTrw and the Ancestors. The fact that it is void of Sky, Land, and Duat is to show that is a state that lacks any type of definition. This state is also Nun, or Inert, and therefore it just is. This we can label as "Upper Pet."This aspect of Being is the Source of all life, and all existence, all life takes place within it, and consists of it. After "Upper Pet" we have the actual Created Universe, the Ordered Realm, which is personified by the nTr.t Nut.

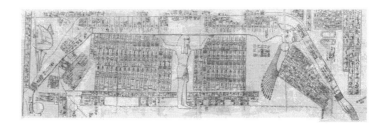

Nut represents the ordered physical universe. According to the texts, the body of Nut, especially the limbs, represents the cardinal Directions. Her right arm represents the Northwest; her left arm represents the northeast. Her head represents the western horizon, her mouth represents the West. Her crotch is said to represent the East, from which Ra is born. In his cycle, Ra is said to enter into the Duat, through the mouth of Nut, and journey through the Duat which is "Within." Once this journey through the internal body of Nut is complete, Ra is born from her womb in the east. Interesting to note, is that the text states that the entrance to the Duat is in the "North," which is also a reference to uppermost Pet, which is the Chaos or Nu. The texts states:

> *"The uniform darkness, fount of the nTrw, the place from which birds come: this is from her (i.e. Nut's) northwestern side up to her northeastern side, open to the Duat that is on her northern side, with her rear in the east and her head in the west."*

There is something very important being conveyed here, and that is the fact that Duat is said to be on her northern side, which is to say that it is in proximity to Nu, the Upper Pet. Ra enters into the Duat and exits through the womb in the east. However, there is also an "entrance" to the Duat in

the west. Is this a contradiction? No, there is an entrance into the Duat in both the North and the West.

The Northern Entrance to the Duat is the gate that connects the realm of Order to the All. It is the entrance through which Ra entered in his coming into being in the "*Zep tupi*" (The "first time"). This is also the Entrance or Exit rather, through which all shall return to the Chaos. However, this is not the entrance through which Ra enters into the Duat in his cycles from moment to moment. That entrance is the one in the West. The Western entrance is also the one through which the spirits of the Deceased enter into the spirit realm. To make this clearer, the Northern entrance leads to Nu, which means obliteration for anything that passes through it, be it nTr or Yakhu, similar to a Black Hole. This Northern entrance serves three purposes: to initiate the act of creation, to maintain a connection to the rest of Creation and influence it to return to nTr, and to bring an end to the ordered universe, a return to the Original state of Being.

The fact that the Duat is said to be within the body of Nut, which represents the Physical universe, is to say that the Duat represents the Inner Plane. This elucidates much in regards to the Duat, and helps to liberate us from much of the fallacies that have been taught in the misinterpretation of it. We can say that the Duat is the Inner Plane, meaning that it is the spiritual reality that exists within this physical plane, or we can refer to it as the "Underworld," in that it is the "world" that exists under or beneath the surface of this "reality."However, it is not a "place" that exists in the sky, or under the ground of the earth, but is, literally, the insides of reality.

To truly understand the Duat, we must take some time to clear up a few misconceptions. First things first, we must do away with this whole, "afterlife" or Kemetic Heaven and Hell jargon. The Kemetic people did not and do not believe in an "Afterlife." They believed in life, period. The Duat, though it is a place where the spirits of the Deceased depart to, it is more of a place of transition, and not an "eternal" abode. The Duat is a transitional state in the journey of life, which one travels in between incarnations. While it is possible for one to remain there for a certain period of time, it is only temporary. For this reason the Duat is always depicted, and spoken of as a "Highway" so to speak, through which Ra journeys in between the east and the west. Also the Duat is a place in which interaction between "there" and "here" is not only a possibility, but it is a reality. Spirits that are in the Duat have the ability to journey into the earth, and people in the earth have the ability to journey to the Duat.

When we read the various Duat texts, we see that there are nTrw and Yakhu that exist there within shrines in the Duat. These shrines are portals that connect that realm to this realm. Likewise, the shrines that we erect on this plane, serve as gateways to the Duat. Another interesting thing that we find in the Duat texts, is the fact that many of the rituals contained within them make statements like "if these things be known or performed by one on earth..." giving instructions in the use and result of the ritual, not only for those that live in the Duat, but also those that live in the earth. This is to say that access to the powers of the Duat, the nTr and forces within it, was also available to those that live in the "east."This conceptualization of the Duat cancels out the idea that this is "heaven" or "hell," or that this is a land that is exclusively for the Deceased.

Secondly in understanding the Duat as a transitional state, or a state in between, we must also place it in its proper order and context in relationship to the other planes of reality. When we understand that the Duat is a place that exists in between the East, which represents the Day, the light, and the Physical Plane and world, and the West, a place that represents the Night, the Darkness, and the Spiritual world, we should further understand that we are dealing with the cycles of life, and not look at it in a linear manner. To view this from a linear perspective is to say that "okay, life comes into being from Pet, we live in Ta, and when we die, we exist in Duat." This perspective creates the illusion that the Duat is the "afterlife" and it is the point at the end of a finite line. However, in understanding it from a cyclical perspective, we realize that the Duat in reality is in the Middle. So the proper Order would be Pet, Duat, and Ta, understanding that the Duat has an eastern and western horizon.

When we revisit the Book of Nut, and we think about this from a standpoint of Creation, It begins with Ra rising from Nu. From here Ra enters into the Duat from the North, and journeys through the Body of Nut. This journey continues until Ra is born from her womb in the east, in which his course is Ta. This is from a standpoint of Creation. However from a day to day, moment to moment perspective, Ra rises in the east (exiting the Duat) and sets in the West (entering the Duat), only to journey through the Duat again ultimately to be reborn in the East. In both cases the Duat represents the transition, or more accurately the "process" that leads to

Creation, Ra's manifestion, or Becoming. In order to better understand this we first have to deal with the significance of Ra, and what he represents, and also the significance of this journey.

We must remember that according to the cosmologies regarding Ra, once he comes into being from Nu, he comes into being as his own creation, going through several evolutions and transformations. Ra is Creation itself, and everything that exists is ultimately a transformation or manifestation of Ra. This is to say that Ra is not simply "The Sun," though the sun is a major source of Ra. Ra is Energy. He is Life, and his journey is living.

Based on the cosmology of Inu, we see that Ra comes forth as the nTrw, he comes forth as the Heavens and the Earth, he comes forth as the things that exist within the earth, the plants, and things that creep in the earth. He comes forth as man, etc. Ultimately all things are simply expressions of Ra. This adds further to the understanding that ultimately there is only one being in existence. However, Creation is a constant happening. It does not solely relate to the creation of the Universe at the "beginning of time," but creation on a constant basis. Creation is constant. Ra as Creator, can only create, this is to say that Creation is all the Creator can do. Even in destruction there is creation. Every single event is tied to the Laws of Cause and Effect, Mathematics, and every cause is an effect and every effect a cause, and in between the two is the creative process that takes place within the Duat.

Creation happens within the moment, from moment to moment. It is cyclical. However these are cycles within cycles within cycles, and the same principles are operating at every level, and Ra's coming into being, or **Prt M Hrw** (Coming forth by day) in reality deals with the Creation of the Moment, and all that it entails. Following this principle, we must delve deeper in to Ra, in regards to what I call the "Four Phases of Ra."

Four Phases of Ra

Ra goes through four different phases in his cycle and journey. In his coming into being he is Khepri. This is symbolized as the "Morning Sun" or Sunrise. At noon he is Ra, symbolized by the "Midday Sun." In the Evening he is Itum, which is symbolized by the "Setting Sun," and this form of Ra is usually depicted as an Old man leaning on a walking stick. After this phase, Ra becomes "iwf," the "dead" Ra, or the flesh of Ra that sojourns through the Duat. He continues as iwf, ultimately emerging from the Duat in the east as Khepri, and repeating the cycle. Each phase is significant as it pertains to the Moment.

The first phase, Khepri, represents the emergence of the moment. The word Khepri can be translated to mean, "becoming," transformation, or simply change. In a way, Ra's entire journey can be summed up in this word (Khepri). Khepri (change) is constant, and as Ra moves he is changing, evolving, transforming from one phase to the next. The second Phase, Ra, represents the moment, the situation, a thing, reaching a state of maturity, its fullness. At this moment it is at its brightest, it's fullest, and it's most potent stage of existence. The first two phases correspond to the birth of a thing, its maturation, and peak. The Third Phase, Itum, represents the moment and time of decline that follows the peak of the moment. It is the passing of the Moment. The fourth and final phase iwf represents the Death, or End of the moment, and the time of transition into the next moment; the next phase, the new time. These latter two phases correspond to the aging and decline of a thing, its death, and its subsequent transformation and renewal. Everything that exists goes through this cycle, all the way down to a moment, and a thought.

Once Ra comes into being, he exits the Duat, and enters into Ta, the earth. This means that whatever has been ordained within Pet, has gone through its evolutionary process in the Duat, and has manifested in the physical realm or Ta. Taking this into to consideration, it should be understood that everything that happens in Ta, in the physical realm, has its origins in the two Higher Planes. Also, Ra's coming into being represents the everlasting process of Change. This is to say that as he manifests, how he manifests shall depend upon the moment and what it calls for, what is in harmony with the cycles of time. How he manifests, or what happens on earth, depends upon what has been decreed within the Duat.

According to the text known as the Book of Gates; another work that pertains to the Duat, it is said:

"This great nTr (Ra) hath decreed the plans or designs, having made them to spring up in the earth which he created."

In the Second Gate it is said:

"This god is drawn by the nTrw of the Duat in order to make divisions or, distinctions in the earth and to work out his designs

therein..."

This is to make it known that what takes place in the earth, is a result of the decrees and plans of Ra in the Duat. As Ra travels, he gives decrees and orders to the nTrw and Spirits that exist within the Duat, and they carry out the orders causing the effects to manifest on earth.

Within the Duat exist nTrw, which are forces of Nature, and the spirits of those that have transitioned from the earth, the so-called deceased. As anything that manifests on earth is a result of the inner workings of the Duat, it is these spiritual agencies that are responsible for what manifests in life, and the qualities and unique expressions of each situation. Each of these forces are *"transformations of Ra,"* or *Ra's limbs/members.* When Ra is born in the east, he comes forth expressing himself as at least one of these forces, determining not only the manner in which the situation happens, but also what the situation calls for. For example, if Ra manifests as Auset, then the situation will be a sensitive situation that requires one to be nurturing, nourishing, maternal, empathetic, patient, etc. If Ra comes forth as Heru Behudet, then it will require one to be assertive, vigilante, aggressive, courageous, bold, militant, firm, forceful, etc. Also in any given moment when Ra manifests in this way, these are examples of what people will actually encounter in the situation. A good exercise to verify this science is to familiarize oneself with the Cycles of the planetary hours. Each day at sunrise the Planet that rules the Day governs the energy of the day overall, and initiates the cycle through the planets for that day. For example, Sunday, is ruled by the Sun. This means that the overall energy that governs the day is the Sun. However, in spite of the energy that is the main influence during the day, there is still a cycle through the other planets that takes place throughout the day and continues until the next sunrise. At the hour of sunrise on Sunday morning, the day begins with the Sun Planetary energy, which influences the events that take place during that hour. Following the sun will be Venus, which will put her spin on things, which is then followed by Mercury., etc In each "hour" if one is consciously paying attention to the cycle, one will notice that everything from what one thinks about, talks about, does, feels, watches on TV., listens to on the radio, the people that one encounters and their personalities, all of this will be an expression of the planetary energy that is ruling the hour. It happens like clockwork, literally! What I've personally noticed, is that my friends that are more "mercurial," i.e. chatty, brainy, witty, comedic, etc,

140

will call during the hour of mercury, or if I get into an argument with the misses, it'll take place during the hour of Mars, and when we "kiss" and makeup, it'll be during the hour of Venus. If there is a delay many times it'll take place during Saturn's hour, and sometimes one will find themselves sleepy or drowsy during the hour of the Moon. Interesting to note, is the fact that the nTrwt of the Hours, plays a very prominent role in the Duat books. This also brings up an interesting philosophical point in regards to destiny and "free will." However, let us table that discussion for the time being. The forces and laws that operate through the planetary hours are the same as those that are in effect in Astrology, Numerology, etc. It is the nTrw that are at work.

Much has been said already in regards to the association of the Duat with the Womb. To verify further according to the tradition, we find it written in the Pyramid Texts 1527a "*iwr n sw pt msi n sw dwAt,*" That is "*Pet (Heaven/Sky) has conceived him; Duat has given birth to him.*" This passage makes it clear that the Duat is associated with the Womb. Ultimately the Duat is the place from which all things are born. However, like the womb, the Duat is not a one way road, but a place of "intercourse."

The Duat not only gives birth to what manifests in Ta, but it also receives the "seeds" of things from the earth, to be nurtured and nourished in its womb, ultimately to be born in the earth. This is one of the main reasons why Gab, the nTr of the Earth is personified as a man in the Kemetic tradition, whereas almost every other tradition personifies the earth as feminine. We are born from the womb of the universe, spiritually and physically, and the bulk of the organic material that makes us up, we receive from Nut, just as the bulk of the genetic material that makes us up we receive from our mother. Even though we, in this body, may physically come up from the earth, the earth itself is born out of the universe. For this reason one will notice that Gab lies within the Arch of Nut's body, for the earth exists within the Universe.

Gab as the nTr of the earth, is the place in which we live and experience. It should be known that Gab is not simply the "Earth" as in this planet, but the Earth as in this plane, and all that is "earthly." As such he represents physical existence. However, Gab corresponds to the active aspect of physical existence that "fertilizes," seeds, and activates the divine potential that is housed within our spirits/mind (Nut.) Nut represents the Spiritual/Mental plane, and the Mind. The mind, as the Duat, is a place of intercourse, and it is through intercourse with the physical plane, i.e. Experience, that all the divine powers and geniuses within us are activated. The mind takes in the seed of experience and processes it, nurtures it, ultimately bearing fruit in our actions, back into the physical plane. For this reason Gab, though considered to be the grandson of Ra, in some cases is the father of Ra. As Ra is said to be born from the womb of Nut daily, it can also be held that Gab is his father, as he and Nut conceive him daily, and it is from Gab that he enters into Nut. Gab as the father of Ra can also be seen and confirmed by the form of Gab as the creator, **Gengen War**, or **Negeg War**, i.e. the **Great Honker** or The **Great Cackler**, in which he is said to have laid the egg from which Ra hatched, or Made the sound that initiated the creative process, knocking the universe out of inertia (Nun). Also it is held in one tradition, that Nut and Gab were in a perpetual "sensual embrace," until Ra ordered ishu to separate them. Nut and Gab's embrace represents the undifferentiated state of Being, the chaos that preceded the coming into being of the ordered universe. In this way Gab and Nut are associated with Nu/Nun and Nut/Nunit, the nTrw of the Chaos, the mother and father of Ra.

The intercourse between Gab and Nut, that is the Duat and the Earth, can also be seen in ritual. Through rituals on earth one is able to influence

142

and activate powers within the Duat, causing them to come to expression in the earth. It is for this reason that ritual is performed, offerings and sacrifices are made, etc. It is the idea that we can activate, influence, nourish, and empower creative powers within the Duat that is reflected in the offering of food and drinks at shrines, and also rituals to cultivate spiritual power. This same principle is at play in learning of any kind, in which our interface with and actions in the earth, help to enrich the mind and spirit. "Feeding" the nTrw is reflective of the cultivation and empowerment of that force that will enable them to perform tasks for us and operate at an optimal level, in the same way that we take in nutrients through feeding the body. For this reason the nTrw are associated with Limbs and members of the Body. If the Body is weak it cannot perform its tasks. It needs the energy. Likewise the nTrw must be "fed" or cultivated, so that they have the power to perform the work that they are meant to. More on this point later.

Finally to add on to the point of Gab as the "Father of Ra," and his intercourse and seeding of Nut, the Duat, there is the fact that the life that one encounters within the Duat is a direct reflection of the life that they lived on earth. The Earth, ones experience with Gab, "fathers" their journey and life in Nut. This also applies on a moment to moment scale, in that it is our experience in Gab that goes on to create our mental landscape, or at least plant the seeds that enter into the mind for us to process and work out, which produces the fruits of our actions in creating the next moment. In other words it is the moment that creates the moment, and our intercourse with our experiences that create our "future experiences." Even the content of our dreams, which are a nightly journey through the Duat, is a reflection of, in many cases, our experiences in Gab. In other words, it is Nut's intercourse with Gab, the process of our mind and spirit with our earthly experiences, which ultimately leads to the birth of Ra, all that manifests in life.

One more important point that must be fleshed out at this time is the Peseju nTrw as the forces of the Duat, and Itum/Ra as the "Alpha and Omega." In the cosmology of Inu, it is Ra in the form of Itum that comes into being, and he brings ishu and Tufnut into being from himself. However, there is a subtle reference to the Duat being made here. *Itum* means **"complete," "finish,"** and **"totality."** As "totality," he corresponds to Neb r jer as "The All." From here he brings ishu and tufnut into being, which deals with him creating Duality within himself. This means that he became from One nTr (Itum), Three nTr (Itum, Ishu, and Tufnut), himself remaining the

neutral unifying principle of the Dual Aspects of Being. This Duality further manifests in the separation of Nut and Gab, their coming into being. However, once this Duality comes into Being, a "rift" is created. This "rift" is a "door" or portal, if you will, which is the entrance to the Duat. For this reason, ishu and Tufnut are associated with the Akeru, the Twin Lions that are the nTrw that Guard the entrance to the Duat. Interesting to note, is that this is the origin of the custom of having twin lion statues at entrances. Anyway, after ishu and Tufnut, Ra enters into the Duat and makes his "decrees and distinctions" which cause things to "spring up in the earth." As a testament to this, we have the fact that it is Itum that Initiates Creation, bringing ishu and Tufnut into Being from Nu/Nun, and you will recall that it is also Itum that enters into the Duat in the West. This is to say that Itum is the "beginning and the end," and the process in between is the journey through the Duat. Understanding ishu and Tufnut as Akeru lets us know that the nTrw that follow them, Nut, Gab, Osir, Auset, Sutesh, Nebt Het, Heru War, and all other nTrw correspond to the forces of the Duat. This means that as Ra transforms into the various things, the various nTrw, this is a spiritual happening that takes place in the Duat, and ultimately manifests in the world that we see.

Ta is the physical plane. It is the densest aspect of Reality. Everything that can be observed, either with the naked eye, as well as those things that are so subtle that one would need a microscope to see them, all of these exist within Ta. In actuality, lower Pet, that is the Physical Universe, is included in Ta as well. Ta being the plane of earthly experience, the things that are encountered in Ta can be proven, weighed, calculated, and measured, far more easily than it's more subtle counterparts. However the other two plane's existence can be deducted from what one encounters in Ta, as once again everything that happens in Ta is an effect, an end result, a reaction to processes that transcend mundane reality. In a way Ta is illusory, in that it creates the illusion for the uninitiated and unenlightened, that there is no greater reality beyond this, and that what one "sees" is as real as it gets, when in reality, nothing could be further from the truth.

The truth is, the higher we climb in the planes, the more subtle the matter gets; and the more subtle things get, the less differentiation exists, ultimately leading to a reality that transcends time and space, where separate things are nonexistent. If one were to contemplate existence and it's nature and essence from this point of view, one would realize that in reality, Upper Pet, The Highest Plane, is the Only and Ultimate Reality, and in actuality the physical world with all of its illusion of separateness and all

144

of the concern that it creates, is the furthest thing from "Real." We'll clarify this point in a moment.

The next most subtle plane after Upper Pet is the Duat. The Duat is less dense than Lower Pet, and Ta, but more Dense than Upper Pet. It is a world of the abstract, whereas Ta is the world of the concrete. There is definition within the Duat, though more subtle than those in Ta, which creates spheres, gates, etc, of influence. This being the case, the forces within the Duat control or govern things that may seem totally unrelated in Ta. For example, Heru Behudet, is a nTr of war, protection, and Male Sexuality, just to name a few of his correspondences. However, how this manifests in the world transcends the boundaries of concrete differences, applying its laws on the level of relationships between things through abstract analogy. For example, as a nTr of War and Protection, Heru Behudet manifests not only on the battle field, but he also governs policeman, fireman, soldiers, warriors, athletes etc. Taking it a step further, in the body he governs the epidermis, the immune system, and white blood cells which serve the purpose of protection and defense for the body. In the same way that the white blood cells go to war against free radicals in the body to maintain the security and integrity of the body's health, a military will go to war to defend its territory from "enemies" both domestic and abroad. Though on a concrete level these seem to be two totally unrelated subjects, on an abstract level it is the exact same force at work. However, in Ta someone who deals with the health of the body, the immune system, may not deal with skin at all, let along be skilled and knowledgeable in the science and art of warfare. This is to say that things in Ta, due to the individuation of forms, the sphere of influence of a thing is limited in capacity. Thus the sayings, "I only have two hands", "I'm just one man," "I can't do it all by myself," "I don't have eyes in the back of my head," etc. These limitations are not as concrete in the Duat. For example, using the same example of Heru Behudet, if there is a problem with that particular force, it may manifest as problems within every aspect of an individual's life, or a society, that is governed by Heru Behudet. If Heru Behudet is two weak in a person's life, then they may find themselves having problems with their defense system, not able to defend themselves from attacks from germs/disease, malefic forces/spirits, or people intent on harming them. This is the exact same problem manifesting on multiple levels. In addressing the root of the problem, working with Heru Behudet, one could in essence correct all of these issues, all at once, whereas if one were to address the issue solely from the Perspective of Ta, one would spend time trying to fix each issue separately. It's the difference between holistic and

western medicine. One addresses the issue in a system, the other addresses a symptom while never eradicating the root of the disease.

These three planes make up the whole of existence. Each of them is real in their own way, and vary in there levels of density verses subtlety. It is not correct to dismiss the physical world as "unreal" or "illusion." As far as life and experience goes, it all takes place within Ta. The highest plane, Upper Pet, is Chaos, and Pure Being, and not living. Its existence cannot be experienced, only sensed through a deep feeling of inner peace and bliss. However, at this level one ceases to exist as an individual being. Though this is the "Ultimate Reality," it is not one that can be experienced or "Known." One could "philosophize" that this is the reason for life. nTr brought itself into being to learn about itself, experience itself. However, in order to do that, it created Ta, the "illusion" of something other than itself, to serve the purpose of interaction with itself, and thus becoming better acquainted with Self. The Duat, though more "real" than Ta, is still a part of the "illusion." However, these two planes are the only ones that can truly be known, experienced. It is a "real illusion," a paradox. We are presented with the "Illusion of Reality," and the "reality of the illusion."

The working out of this Paradox is the ultimate goal of an Initiate. As all three of these "planes" in essence are aspects of One Being, nTr, the goal of the initiate is to Realize Self as this One Being, ultimately experiencing all levels of Being at once. The goal is for the lines between these planes to be eradicated without one "losing their minds," so to speak. The more one becomes aware of self and synchronized with nTr/Nature through the living of Maat, one will ultimately experience reality on earth, that is to say, one will experience all as Self. One will experience the world in such synchronicity, where the World, the universe even, becomes one's mind, the people and things within it one's thoughts, etc. Also, the line between Man and nTrw, no longer exist. So when one is interacting with "Mr. Tchass," one will be conscious of the fact that one is interacting with not only Mr. Tchaas, but Tehuti, nTr, Self. This experience of reality brings a peace, joy, and harmony that is not tied to things, or people, but is eternal and unshakable. This state of being is spoken of in chapter 175 of the "Prt M Hrw," in a conversation between Osir and Itum. In this conversation Osir is inquiring as to why and how he has come to be in a place that is "without water, air, is doubly deep and dark, and is doubly infinite, or nowhere." This place in which Osir is describing is the Chaos. However, Osir's experience is not one of oblivion, which cannot be experienced, but one of peace and bliss. Itum answers Osir saying "Live there with peace of Heart.

He states that it is not a place of "sexual pleasure," and one is given "light" instead of water, air, and sexual pleasure. He goes further to state that he is given a "peaceful heart instead of bread and beer." It is this experience that the spiritual aspirant seeks, a state of peace and harmony, and enlightenment that transcends all mundane concerns. This takes place through, according to the conversation, the union of Osir with Itum, that is to say, ones realization of Self as Itum, complete, and total, that is to say "The All" experiencing all levels of Being as One.

It has been stated that all life is Ra, and in essence the difference between Nu and Ra is a state of Being vs. a state of Living. Nu is Inert, whereas Ra is in constant motion. As Ra journeys, he is accompanied by a few nTrw in his boat. The main nTrw that we would like to examine are Sia, Hu, Hika, and Tehuti. In many cases we find Sia and Hu together, as is portrayed in Am Duat texts, then in some instances Sia is accompanied by Hika, as is portrayed in the "Book of Gates." In both cases Hika and Hu are representing the same reality, and Tehuti, when he accompanies Ra is a unification of all these principles. Sia is the nTr of Consciousness, awareness, perception, intelligence, etc. Hu is the nTr of "Sound," vibration, etc, spoken of in terms of the "tongue," and "authoritative utterances." Hika is the nTr of Creative Power, that is to say, the ability to "Will" things into being, especially through the use of the "Word." For this Hika and Hu, are interchangeable. Tehuti is the nTr of wisdom, knowledge, representing the Divine mind/intelligence, and he is also the "Neb Madu nTr" or "Lord of Madu nTr." He is considered to be in some instances the heart, or tongue of Ra, the Tongue of Pitah in his role of Creator, etc. In this way Tehuti unites all three of the aforementioned nTrw (Sia, Hu, and Hika) within himself as he journeys with Ra. As they journey in Ra's boat they represent the "faculties," of his being, or even more accurately the nature of his being. Ra as energy, manifest as light and sound. Everything that exist, as mentioned in earlier chapters are ultimately manifestations of these phenomenon. Ra is energy. He is light, and within this energy and light, is consciousness/intelligence, and sound vibrations that create variances in how this energy and light manifests and projects itself. Once again Ra being all things, this means that ultimately all things consist of these properties. Light and Sound, Will and Word, Consciousness or Intelligence and Power is the nature of all existence, and everything manifests and expresses these qualities in varying degrees, no matter how small or insignificant a thing's existence may seem.

These Aspects of Ra interact with one another according to a chain of

command, a hierarchy of being so to speak. It is their responsibility to direct the motion of Ra's boat. Sia and Hu/Hika, or Tehuti in directing Ra's motion, are actually representative of the relationship between the Divine Intelligence and Word, the creative affect that it has on Energy, Ra. Sia is the Awareness of Ra. He is Ra's ability to observe, focus, pay attention to, and ignore. After Sia, Hu/Hika represents the Word manifested as thought, or Mind going on to create effects, symbolized as directing the motion of Ra's boat. Together, Sia and Hu, in that order go on to determine how Ra moves or "e-motes," ultimately determining his destiny (destination) in becoming. To simplify this, wherever ones attention goes their energy follows, and that energy goes on to create affects in the world. Also this speaks to the fact that there is an Intelligence that permeates throughout all things that is responsible for guiding energy and its workings. However for the initiate, the goal is that one gain mastery over these faculties. For this reason the "oarsman," in the boat of Ra, according to the Am Duat, is called "Khurp," meaning "Master." If one wishes to master the Self, one must first master these faculties, beginning with their attention!

This Hierarchy of Being is present in every single situation. Our experience begins with our awareness, followed by our thoughts, then our feelings, and reactions. For example, if one gets into an argument, let's say someone says or does something that one dislikes, first things first you become aware of the person and what they have done. You observe it. After they have entered into your sphere of Awareness, you then begin to interpret what it is that you are observing. This interpretation depends upon the words that make up your "worldview." These words "Authoritatively Utter," or dictate to you what it is that you are seeing. These words go on to give form and direction to your energy, manifesting in the emotions as how you feel about what you are observing. From here the physical reaction manifests automatically. If you are upset it may manifest in a change in your breath rate, an increase in body temperature, sweating, trembling, or maybe you'll fly through those and go straight to choking the life out of them ☺. Regardless of the reaction, it all began with Sia, you becoming aware of the situation. Once again, all experiences follow this scheme.

As an Initiate, the goal is to take control over Sia and Hu/Hika, and in that order. By taking control of Sia, one becomes the commander of their attention. One of the chief hindrances to one's spiritual evolution is their inability to control their attention. The most important thing that the

148

Initiate must do/learn is to distinguish between Self as Pure Awareness/Consciousness (Sia), and his/her Mind. The Self is that which perceives the inner workings and contents of the Mind but is not the mind. This being understood, we must objectively observe, and weigh our thoughts on the scales of Maat. Not all thoughts are legitimate, and just because a thought surfaces or comes into our sphere of awareness does not mean that we should pay attention to it. There is a difference between Thought Drift (Thoughts that flow freely without being willed) and Thinking (Willed thoughts). Some thoughts simply arise from external triggers and are related to previous experiences; others arise and cycle freely due to programming and conditioning of the mind and Spirit. Other thoughts we choose to think about. In any case both types of thoughts must be placed on the scales of Maat to see how they add up compared to Divine Law or Truth. Thoughts that cycle freely, do so based upon laws of momentum, regardless of whether they were initially Willed or not. Everything is energy, including thoughts, regardless of how subtle they may be, and just as all energy does, thoughts operate upon the Laws of Cycles and Momentum. It is our attention that either increases the momentum and frequency of the repetition and cycle of the thought, or slows it down. When we withdraw our attention from the thought, ignore it, it causes the thought/mental scheme to lose momentum, and one will notice that the cycle of the thought will slow down, and if continued, will eventually come to somewhat of a stand still where reversal of the mental processes can take place. The Master Key in all of this is Our Attention, which is the Self, Who and what we are. This chain of command beginning with our Attention, followed by the Mind, Emotions (Energy) and ultimately the Concrete Physical plane, must be maintained. Consciousness must reign supreme. Sometimes the mind will get to rambling and may really be saying a bunch of nothing, yet it seems to be going to work on us ⯑. Re-member the Self and do one of two things: either place them on the Scales (Question them!) or Ignore them. Question the legitimacy of the thoughts, where do they come from? Do they reflect Maat, your Divinity? If not, ignore them. Starve them of attention and energy and slowly they will die out. If one wishes to Master the Self, they must Master their Attention!

After gaining mastery of Sia, one must next master Hu/Hika, the "Word." While on the highest level, Hu/Hika correspond to the actual sound or vibration that underpins and constitutes all physical phenomenon, giving each thing it's unique form, structure, and laws that govern its functioning. On a more mundane level, Hu and Hika represent the "Words" that we allow to define us and shape our perception of reality.

As mentioned earlier in this work, the "Word" Sound/Vibration, has a shaping affect on matter, and the nature of the sound or word will go on to shape our lives. Everything else that follows behind the Word is determined by the Word, and the Word is the window through which we perceive the world. In order to properly direct Ra, we must have dominion over our "Word," our Vibration; otherwise we run the risk of having another shape our reality. The Word, as thought, as mentioned earlier, has the ability to be slowed down, brought to a standstill, reversed, or changed completely. Yes you can change your mind!

Mastery over Sia and Hu can be represented by Tehuti, who is the master of time and change. As pictured above, he sometimes wears the Yatin and iaH (**Kiya**) (Sun and Moon) upon his head as a crown. The Yatin and Moon were utilized by the Kemetyu as well as other cultures to keep track of time. Tehuti as the nTr of Wisdom represents the master of Change as wisdom is about being aware of the time, and what must be done or not done.

Timing is very important as we move into the next phase of dealing with Ra and his journey, as his journey is actually a symbol of the cycle of time itself. The four phases of Ra on an annual scale correspond to the seasons of the year, Khepri (Spring), Ra (Summer), Itum (Fall), iwf (Winter). Spring is the time in which things "come into being." Summer takes place about midyear, and it is the point in which the Sun reaches its peak, along with the temperature. Fall, just as Itum, represents a point in the year where things are on the decline, along with the Sun, the life that came into being in the spring begins to change, most evident in nature with the plants and trees. Winter comes, and much vegetation dies, creatures slow down or migrate, others hibernate, ultimately to return refreshed and renewed in the spring, just as iwf journeys through the Duat ultimately to rise in the east. This cycle also corresponds to the circadian rhythm of the body. As the sun rises, naturally we rise. Our bodies begin to heat up, and produce serotonin to induce wakefulness. This increase in temperature continues throughout the day as Ra continues to rise, ultimately reaching its peak at about between 12pm and 3pm. Once evening comes, and the Sun begins to set, our body temperature begins to decrease, we begin to slow down, and the body prepares us for sleep, producing Melatonin, etc. As we sleep the body makes its repairs, and we wake up refreshed and renewed in the morning. This is at least the ideal if we are following in harmony the Journey of Ra (rhythm of the time). When we wake up we are with Khepri. As we go throughout our day we are with Ra, at evening when we begin to wind down we are with Itum, and when we are asleep and dreaming we are with iwf, journeying through the Duat. Each phase of Ra has it's time appropriate activities, and in order to keep Ra moving along smoothly we must be in harmony with his movements.

When the sun is rising (spring/Khepri) we begin to rise and start our day. The earth begins to heat up (In our hemisphere) and so does our body. At the midpoint of our day (summer/Ra), between noon and 3:00pm the heat of the day reaches its peak. Our body temperature does the exact same thing. It is at these times when we have the most energy available to carry out our strenuous activities (mentally and physically). This is the best time to work, exercise, and eat our largest meals of the day. Once the evening comes around 5:00-6:30pm (fall/Itum), the sun begins to make its decline and the earth begins to cool off. Our body begins to cool off as well. Because of this our activities should begin to decrease in quantity, as well as intensity. I don't recommend large meals after this time for the energy needed to break it down, digest it, and disseminate nutrients is on the decline. Dessert on the other hand is perfect for this time. Strenuous work and exercise at this time also goes against this natural rhythm. Once night comes (winter/iwf) it is time to sleep. The sun is gone and the earth is cool. Our body cools down as well, and the energy that we have is needed to make the repairs from the events of the day. It is not recommended that much be done at this time other than sleeping. Activities that have and

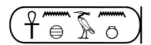

excitatory affect, and cause the body to heat up are damaging to the central nervous system. Meditation is perfect right before bed. Other than sleep and meditation, the other activity that it ok at this time is, well you know (smile). But take it easy okay 😊. When planning activities during the seasons of the year, one should also keep this rhythm in mind and follow it as much as possible. Failure to live in harmony with Ra creates disease and disharmony, and discontinuity in our energy system, our bodies, which can also lead to disharmony in the spirit and mind. This leads to Ra being over taken by Isfet/Owapep, chaos and disorder in the ones being, and the inability for one to function at an optimal level and perform efficiently ones objectives; and achieve ones goals and aspirations. Living in harmony with these laws and cycles is Maat, which is the food and drink of Ra. It is good to live Maat; Ra's health depends on it! All of the powers and faculties of Ra, their proper functioning, is also dependent upon the maintenance of harmony, and the continuity of his journey.

There are more aspects of Ra's Being that are of special mention, specifically those known as the Seven BAw, and the Fourteen KAw of Ra. The Seven BAw and The fourteen KAw are as follows:

7 BAw of Ra
1) bA WAb Itw -Pure Seed
2) bA wDA iwf -Strong Flesh
3) bA xw wDA -Strong Light, Intelligence
4) bA HkA - Creative Power/Activate the Ka
5) bA irw - Manifestation, Form
6) bA TAi -Man, Male
7) bA znk-Ejaculation. To copulate/beget, the Ability to Reproduce

14 KAw of Ra
1) Hw -Sustenance, Food
2) DfA -Provisions, Supplies, Blessings
3) Sps -Honor, Nobility, "Holiness"
4) Smsw -Service, Assistance, Help
5) Iri KAw - Ability to Create more provisions
6) wAD -Health, Prosperity, Freshness
7) Thn -to Shine
8) Nxt -Strength, Force
9) wsr- Power, Wealth
10) wbn - To Rise
11) Psd - Backbone, Spine

12) wAS -Praise, Adoration

13) spd - Readiness, Prepared

14) HkA -Creative Power, the ability to wield the forces of Nature

In some instances the "nTrw of the senses" are added to the list of the fourteen, *Sia, Hu, MAA, Sejem*; that is **Awareness** (The Master Sense), **Authoritative Utterance** (Power of the Tongue/Word), **Sight** (Includes the sight of the Mind's Eye), and **Hearing** (Includes the Inner Ears).

The **Seven BAw** speaks to Ra's manifestation or coming into being. They correspond to his coming into being from light, manifesting in the flesh via the seed of the father at conception. The **Fourteen KAw** represent the qualities, structure, support, and maintenance of his existence via the egg of the mother. Being that Ra is our Life Energy and power, these are things that we can expect to manifest in our lives as we walk the path; our potentialities. We can expect to have our needs met (**Hw, DfAw**), to receive assistance when needed (**Sms**), to have good health (**wAD**), to be prosperous (**wsr**), to manifest strength and power (**Nxt**), to be loved (**wAS**) and to be prepared (**spd**) for whatever comes our way because we have spiritual power (**HkA**), and to become well respected and venerated in life and in the Duat (**Sps**). As long as Ra'a journey is harmonious and his movment is uninhibited, these Qualities will manifest themselves. This is to say that it is the Spirit that is responsible for what takes place in our lives. If we are living Maat then we are in harmony with the Cycles of Ra, and therefore our spirits will attract to us everything that we need. It's all about harmony. It is said that when Ra is upset Only Het-Heru can lift his spirits, and without her he is powerless. Once again, Harmony is the Key!

Nine Spiritual Bodies

Just as Existence consists of several layers or realms that vary in terms of density vs. subtlety, likewise there are layers to our existence on a personal level that vary in consistency also. Our Being, our existence, is not limited solely to this gross physical body, but spreads across several dimensions. We are multidimensional beings, and I mean this in the literal sense. Our true selves as nTr, is not limited by space nor time, and exists in multiple dimensions, time zones, galaxies, universes, planes, etc, all at once. This is something that the Kemetyu understood very well. To demonstrate this understanding, they were able to describe some of the main components that make up a things existence, and this includes the existence of Man. One such example of this is what many have called the Nine "Divisions" of the Spirit, or the Nine Spiritual Bodies.

Each one of these bodies vary in terms of the levels of density, and vibrate at different frequencies. Each one has a specific purpose in relationship to the whole being, but some of them have the ability to carry on an "independent" existence. **The Nine Bodies** are as follows:

1) Shekhem
2) Yahku
3) Ba
4) Sahu
5) Ib
6) Ka
7) Ren
8) Khaibit
9) Khat

The Shekhem corresponds to the Life energy and matter that constitutes the existence of a thing. The term Shekhem, is a word that means "Power," in the language and is symbolized by a staff. This same term and symbol, is also used to refer to the sistrum, a musical rattle that one moves in a shaking or waving manner. This instrument is used for ritual purposes, to invoke and please the nTrw. There is a connection between this notion of power, and vibration. As the highest Spiritual Body, Shekhem is the most subtle of all of the bodies that follow it, actually serving as the source of their existence. All of the spiritual bodies consist of Shekhem. This particular body corresponds to Nu/Nun. As mentioned earlier in this work, the underpinning of all life is Shekhem, power, motion and sound. The form that a thing takes varies according to the sound that brings it into being. This word, shekhem, has also been translated "form." As this body begins to "vibrate" it generates power which manifests as light. This light brings awareness into being, and is the body known as Yakhu.

Yakhu is the Body of Light, Intelligence, Awareness, Consciousness etc. As mentioned earlier, Yakhu comes into being based upon the workings Shekhem. This aspect of our Being corresponds to Ra. Together the Shekhem, and Yakhu, or Power and Intelligence, constitute everything in existence. Shekhem and Yakhu are said to both exist in Pet (Heaven), and together go on to form the next lowest body in density, the Ba.

The Ba is a concept that has been rendered by many as the equivalent to the western concept of the Soul. The Ba is the aspect of our Being that links us as individuals to the All, and consist of Shekhem and Yakhu. However, it is a things own individuated portion of Shekhem and Yakhu within the All, similar to the manifestation of an Ice cap within a portion of a vast ocean. The Ba is the part of us that is directly connected to the source, and thus connects us on a deep and subtle level to one another. As it is connected to the Source, which is Nu/Nun, it pulls on us to "return" so to speak. The Ba pulls us towards the living of Maat. When we are in conflict with this "pull," our Ba lets us know it. We experience guilt, which causes us to experience a lack of peace. When we heed the words of our conscience, we are in harmony with the motion of the pull, and it leads us to the Nun/Inertia, which we experience as Peace. This aspect of our Being is the force within us that is responsible for our spiritual evolution and ultimate return to our Divine State of Being. It has been referred to as "the voice within," "The Higher Self," The "God" within, etc. The Ba is the house of the highest aspects of our Being. It is the seat of the Self. This part of our Being can be conversed with, as many have had experiences in which they felt as though they were in battle or conflict with themselves, or they say "I should have followed my first mind," or "something told me so and so was no good." This is guidance from ones Ba. Failure to take heed to this "voice," can lead one to commit errors that may prove to be very detrimental in their life, and also ruin ones relationship with their Ba.

According to the tradition, one of the worst things that can happen to someone was for their Ba to stop "speaking" to them. This is the subject of the text referred to as the "Discourse between a man and his Ba." A man that is disenchanted with life is engaged in a debate with his Ba as he contemplates suicide. He is distraught that his Ba no longer speaks to him nor guides him. His Ba attempts to reason with him, and change his outlook on life, and suggests to him to enjoy life and be content. The story is a beautiful example of the function of the Ba, and the type of relationship that one can have with it.

The Ba is in essence the manifestation or incarnation of Divine Power and Intelligence, nTr, within an individuated cell of the body of Neb r Jer. This body is immortal (potentially), and it is the aspect of ones being that "wHm anx" (Repeat's life or re-incarnates) into another body when the time comes. It is said to unite with or exist within the Ka, which we will touch upon in a few moments. Also, in regards to the manifestation or Osir

incarnation aspects of the Ba, it has been spoken of as the Divine Presence when the nTr makes itself known or shows its hand in a situation. This is called bAw. When a person manifests the Wisdom and Power of the Divine Self their Ba is in effect.

The bA according to tradition incarnates into an individual's father through the crown of the head and is then transmitted through the father's seed. This is alluded to in the 7 bAw of Ra which speaks to how Ra incarnates, one of which "Pure Seed," another being "Male," the very last being "Ejaculation." The transmission of the bA through the seed of the father is also alluded to in the story of si-Osir, in which he battles with a Nubian magician.

The Ba is the part of the spirit that houses all of the Bodies that follow behind it; all of the elements that go on to make someone an Individual. It is in a sense one's own personal sphere or universe. Just as a universe may consist of several stars, planets, galaxies etc, the Ba has the ability to contain within itself (or existing at the core of them), several of the lower bodies: saH, Ka, Khaibit, accumulated across several incarnations, or also consisting of what is known as "Soul Groups," several "individuals, that incarnate together to play a pivotal role in the evolution of that Ba. The Ba also houses the records of all a person's incarnations, and the lesson that they are to learn in the present incarnation. As the Ba is the first element that manifests in the formation of the individual, the next body that forms as a result of the working of the Ba is the Sahu.

The Sahu is the mental body, it contains the bodies that serve as the vehicles of experience in the Ta (Physical World). According to the tradition the Sahu forms after the unification of the Ba and the Ka, that is the Incarnation of the "Self" or so-called soul, and the "personality, or the person that lives/lived." This body houses the accumulated information and experience from an incarnation, and is related to memory. The Sahu can take on the actual form of the individual in the spiritual realm, as a mental projection, serving the same purpose that the Khat (physical body) served on earth, but in the Duat. This aspect of the spirit is somewhat like a spiritual computer, in that it's all about the input, and downloading information. As it is a body that is built up of one's experience, its strength or effectiveness is dependent upon what one puts into it. However, like a computer, the Sahu contains certain elements that are "Hardwired," into its being. The Hardware is the nTrw and Ancestors, the Archetypes that exist within the Duat, the spirit or the so-called "subconscious mind." One of the

156

greatest aspirations that one held was to "receive" a Sahu after their transition from the physical plane and body. To possess a Sahu that was "worth something" allowed one to move about the spiritual realm, the earth, and the heavens freely. The Sahu has the capacity to be immortal and live forever with ones Ba. It is from this relationship that one is able to gain access to information from ones previous incarnations. This body is the Body of the Duat, and as the Duat is associated with the womb, this body corresponds to the nTrt Auset, and other maternal nTrwt, .i.e. Het Heru, Nut, Mut, etc.

Following behind the Sahu is the Ib, the "Heart." The Ib corresponds to the Will, and ones "Conscious Mind." It is the Mental Body through which one manages their attention, their thoughts and their decisions. This body serves as the "heart" or middle point, and mediator between the higher four bodies and the lower four bodies. As all of the bodies coming into being are based upon a condensation from the bodies that precede them, the Ib comes into being from the Sahu, and thus consists of and expresses some of the qualities of it. One of the main aspects inherited from the Sahu is the quality of Memory. As the Ib is the part of us that we utilize to govern our lives, make choices, it is the part that houses the imprints and impacts of our decisions. For this reason, the Ib is depicted in the Usekhet n Maati in the "Weighing of the Heart" scene. In this scene, the Ib is weighed against the feather of Maat, which represents the measurement of our Thoughts and actions, against the Divine Law, or what is "right." Did we "do the right thing?" If we did, then our heart is declared light, and we are declared mAa Xrw. However, if we did not do the right thing, then the memories of those events causes the Ib to be heavy with Guilt.

As the Ib is the part of our Being that gives us the capacity to actively think, determine and manage our thought process, and make our choices, it is one of the key elements that speaks to our divinity and separates us from the rest of Nature, as far as creatures go. The freedom to choose is something that most animals do not possess. They are compelled by their nature to follow its laws and dictates. However man, though ill advised, has the absolute freedom and capability to ignore her nature, violate the laws of nature, and choose to attempt to become something other than Self. This aspect of our being plays the central point in establishing our individuality, and can either lead us to Maat, or lead us on the path towards egoism.

The Ib itself was considered in some instances, to be a nTr. According to an inscription of Neb nTrw "...*the Ib is a nTr, the stomach is its shrine*."

This is implying that there is a connection between the Ib and ones appetite and desires. In order to "appease" the Ib, just like any other nTr, it must be fed. However, the feeding of the Ib is not simply nutrition, but the fulfillment of its Will, desires, and aspirations. The great Rekhi ikat (Sage) Pitah Hotep teaches:

"Sms ib.k tr n wnn.k m ir HAw Hr mddwt m xb tr n Sms ib bwt kA pw HDt At.f...xpr xt Sms ib nn km n xt iw sfA.f,"

that is

"Follow your heart as long as you exist. Do not shorten the time of following your heart. Trimming it's moment is bwt (evil, taboo, abhorent) to the Ka...As things happen follow your heart. Things are of no benefit if it (your heart) is smothered."

This is to say that the role of the heart is to lead us toward a life of fulfillment, and to "Sms ib.k" or "follow your heart" is to do what you love, what makes you happy.

While it is suggested that one follows their Ib, or does what makes them happy, it is important that one does not become a slave to their desires, appetites, and emotions. Though the "stomach" may be the shrine of the Ib, we are also reminded by Pitah Hotep that:

"iw sDm Xt.f nsw xfty," that is "He who obeys (literally listens to) his belly is ruled by his enemy." With this in mind we must remember that Maat, balance is the key and we must avoid excesses. Also it should be remembered that the Ib is the nTr and the "stomach" the shrine, and not the other way around. Therefore we must maintain the proper perspective in the relationship, and make sure that the servant does not become the master.

There is a relationship between the Ib, desire, and emotions, as evidenced in the language of Madu nTr. Many words that relate to emotions contain the word ib within them. The following terms are examples of such:

1) awt.ib - Happiness, joy, elation, gladness (literally to swell the heart)

2) nDm.ib - joy, happiness (literally a sweet or pleasant heart)

3) snm.ib -grief, sorrow

4) snd.ib - fear

5) Sxm.ib - courage, boldness

6) sDw.ibw - (broken hearts (broken spirit)

7) twt.ib- to "get the mind right"

8) dd.ib - will, desire (what the heart gives)

9) xrt.ib -the heart's desire

10) HD.ib- to be disheartened

11) Htp.ib - peace of mind, content, satisfied heart

12) aA.ib - Great of Heart (pride, arrogance)

13) am.ib -guilt, regret (literally to eat the heart)

These terms demonstrate clearly that the Ib is associated with emotion. The emotions are not simply the result of things achieved, loss, and longed for, but the vehicle through which things are sought out. In other words emotions "e-mote," motivate us. They move us. These are the beats/rhythms of the hearts. The heart being the aspect of our being that we utilize to choose, and to initiate action, then these emotions are what determines the manner in which these actions manifest. It must be understood that these two realities, heart and emotion are inseparable, however, just as is the case with the stomach, the proper perspective must be maintained, and the proper relationship established.

To not fulfill the aspirations or desires of the heart was dangerous as one could be said to have "am.ib" or "eaten their heart," that is to say have a heavy heart due to guilt or regret, which violates one of the 42 oaths. At the weighing of the heart, if ones heart was found to be heavier than the feather of Maat, then the ib could be fed to the ommomyit, the "devourer of hearts." This according to many represents annihilation; however, this is not the only possible consequence of a heavy heart. If one's heart was found to be heavy, then they could be "held prisoner" by Gab, that is to say confined to the earth. This represents individuals who no longer possess their "ib," or "will," and are slaves to their unfulfilled desires and ambitions. As a result they "roam" the earth still seeking to scratch that "unscratchable" itch. These are spirits that are not at rest, and can become parasitic and malefic if they are not uplifted.

On the other hand if ones Ib was found light and equal to Maat, then they were allowed to enter into the inner sanctuary, that is, unite with..i.e. become Osir. This means that they unite with and become an empowered Ancestor. In order to attain this level one must have possession over their

Ib, and must not have anything of the earth and yesterday weighing them down. Simply put, in order to "Prt m Hrw," or Come forth by day, one must be free from the shackles of their past, and exist beyond their desires. Speaking to this, we have one of the Renu (Names) of Osir, "wrd.ib," "still of heart" or "he whose heart no longer beats."

The Ib, or Heart has been the subject of much research as of late that has been confirming much of the information that has been handed down by the Ancients regarding the Heart and its function. According to some scholars, the Ib has been found to have somewhat of a "brain" of its own, consisting of over 40,000 neurons, a nervous system, and the ability to engage in a two way conversation with the Brain in the head. This information from the heart enters into the brain through nerve pathways and continues into the brain centers, ultimately affecting ones awareness, cognition, and choices[6]. This "Brain in the Heart" enables the heart to learn, and retain information, intuit, sense, and feel. The mental functions of the Heart have also been found to function independently of the brain. Also the Ib has been found to generate an electromagnetic field that is greater than any other part of the body, and extends several feet outside the body encapsulating the person completely. Through this electromagnetic field, a person's heart is able to communicate with the heart and brain of those around them.

The Ib is the first organ to form after ones conception. It is my contention that one day scientist will discover that a child's heart beat from this earliest stage plays a role in the formation and development of the rest of the child's being. Also the resonance and rhythm of the heart, communicates the commands and programs of the higher bodies during this early period, assisting in the development of the child's natal constitution, which helps to facilitate its being equipped to carry out its destiny. According to the Kemetyu, the Ib, like the Ba, has the ability to "speak." This "Ib Beat," is the voice of the Ib. In the 30th chapter of the Prt M Hrw it reads regarding the Ib:

> My heart, my mother, my heart my mother, my heart
> as I live in the earth. Let there be no resistance to me
> in judgment. Let not the Divine Chiefs be repulsed

---

[6] **Armour J. A**, Cardiac neuronal hierarchy in health and disease, American journal of physiology, regulatory, integrative and comparative physiology. . (2004)

by me. Don't you leave from me in the presence of the Keeper of the Scales (nTr OF TRIALS/ANPU). You are my kA within my body, forming and making my limbs strong. May you come forth and advance to a place of happiness. May not my name be made to stink Shenit who causes men to be in stability…

Another version of this chapter states:

My heart of my mother, my heart of my mother, my heart of my earthly being. Do not stand against me as witness beside the lords of the ritual. Do not say against me, he did do it, about my actions. Do not make a case against me beside the great nTr. Hail my heart, Hail my heart, Hail my entrails, Hail those nTrw at the fore, tressed, resting upon their scepters. Tell my goodness to Ra, hand me to Nehebkau. See him, uniting the earth at the great one within. May I endure on earth, not die in the west, and be a blessed spirit there.

This chapter speaks to the role that the Ib plays in not only the judgment after ones transition from this physical earth, but one's judgment in general, on a daily basis, from moment to moment. In this hymn, one appeals to their Ib not to lead them astray, not to do something that will make their name "stink," that is ruin their reputation while they are alive on the earth as well. For this reason, the appendix to this chapter speaks of the benefits of the recitation of this chapter by a man on earth or in the Duat "it makes him triumph on earth and in nTr gertet (Duat). He'll perform works and live upon the things of the nTrw." Also, one is asking the Ib not to betray him by speaking of the negative things he's done, but to speak of the good things instead. This is to show that the Ib had a knowledge of, and remembrance of these actions. Also, the statement "*My Heart, My mother, My Heart as I come into being,*" speaks to the heart as the first organ to manifest as one evolves in the womb of their mother.

The ib as a source of man's thoughts and emotions; the initiator of one's actions; is an aspect of one's being that must be mastered. To not only possess the ib, but to "shekhem-ib," or master it (have power over it) allows one to have dominion over their total being. According to the **26th chapter of the Prt M Hrw** it is said:

> *"I have gained power over my heart, I have gained power over my two arms, I have gained power over my feet, I have gained the power to do what pleases my Ka."*

This is to say that mastery or power over ones ib grants them total freedom or "sovereignty" over themselves. Power over ones "limbs," is not simply a reference to the actual hands and feet, but also a reference to the nTrw, in that as one is identified with Ra or Osir, the limbs or members of Ra/Osir are the nTrw. Thus Shekhem, power, or mastery over ones Ib, meant power over their limbs, which meant power and mastery over the nTrw. As testaments to this fact we have chapter **29 of the Prt M Hrw**, called "**not allowing to be taken away the heart of a person in nTr Gert**," in which the "Osir," states to the nTrw:

"you shall not be given my heart which lives. The nTrw advance making offerings to me, they fall upon their faces, all of them, upon the ground themselves."

Also, in **chapter 29B** called a "**Heart of Carnelian**," the Ib is identified with the Benu, and is said to be the Ba of Ra, the "*guide of the nTrw to the Duat, coming forth to do the Will of it's Ka.*" This body corresponds to the nTr, Heru sa Osir Auset (Heru the Son of Osir and Auset), as he is associated with the Ib in the cosmology of Pitah, and in the Prt m Hrw he is called Heru "*imi Ibw hri.ib imi XAt*," that is "**Heru who dwells within the Heart's within the middle of the Body.**" As the Ib is the Mediator between the upper four bodies and the lower four bodies, it is in the place of rulership over the "Two Lands," just as Heru is the Nisu Bity.

From the Ib emanates the Ka, which in actuality is the expression of the forces that are hardwired into the Sahu. The Ka is the body that makes each and everything unique as an individual. It is each things unique persona and quality. This extends to not only people, but animals, plants, minerals, elements, the weather, events, planets, thoughts, feelings/emotions, etc. Everything in existence can be said to have a Ka. However in actuality it is the Ka that is responsible for the way in which a thing manifests and expresses itself, and the thing itself, is simply a medium utilized to give form and expression to the Ka. To demonstrate this we find it written in **chapter 30** of the **Prt m hrw**, **"You are my Ka within my Khat, forming and making my limbs strong**."

As everything is in essence a manifestation of Shekhem and Yakhu, that is Sound and light, Power (Energy) and intelligence, the Ka is what creates the variances in the ways in which this intelligence and power expresses itself. It is what distinguishes between an apple and an orange, a cat and a dog (and differences between types of cats and types of dogs), a pepper and a plum, etc. Within people, it is what creates differences such as an assertive personality versus a passive persona, a free and adventurous spirit vs. an introvert, etc; each thing different, yet each thing providing a unique use, a unique perspective, etc.

What are responsible for these expressions are the forces known as the nTrw. It is from the Sahu, via the Ib, that the nTrw come forth as the Ka. These are responsible not only for the differences within things, but also the commonalities as well. When we see similarities in people and things that transcend national, continental, and even racial boundaries, what we are witnessing is in fact a testimony to the existence of the nTrw, forces that exists deep within us, that unite us with the rest of the natural world. For example, the warrior type is a person that can be found all over the world, throughout history no matter where one may look. So is the maternal, empathetic, nurturing type; the creative artsy, romantic type; the witty, comedic type; the rebellious type; the authoritative, dominant, leader type; the wise one, etc. All of these types of individuals exist, in spite of differences in national origin, language, experiences, etc. One must ask the question "How is this possible?" If who and what we are is based solely upon our conditionings from birth in our environment, the way that we are raised, etc, then how is it that someone that is totally unrelated, comes from different environments, with different backgrounds and experiences can have the same or similar personalities? This is because deep within the spirit or psyche of man live forces that find expression through the individual. This is what Carl Jung called the Archetypes that exist within the "Universal Unconscious." However, the existence of these forces has been known from time immemorial, and has been called by many names by different cultures and people. So that Warrior type called Ogun by the

Yoruba, is called Heru Behudet/Heru War by the Kemetyu, Nana Adade Kofi among the Akan, Gu in Dahomey/Benin, Mangala in Hinduism, Ares amongst the Greek, Buluc Chabtan among the Maya, etc; the force of Love, beauty, harmony and sex called Het-Heru in Kemet, is known as Osun among the Yoruba, Erzulu in Haiti and New Orleans, Aphrodite among the Greek, Tripurasundarī in the Mahavidya Tradition of Tantra, Rati in Hinduism, etc; Whatever the name, whatever the location and expression, these abstract personality types can be found, and it is these forces that manifest through the Ka within each thing. For instance, An animal, let's say, a Bull, or A Lion, can express a warrior type of persona, violent and domineering, just as some plants are considered dangerous, poisonous, carnivorous, or are said to "grow aggressively," as they don't "play well with others." Some plants are prickly and thorny, and are able to puncture ones skin and flesh, just as the teeth and claws of a Lion, or the horns of a bull can. How about those wasps, bees, and hornets, aren't they just a peaceful bunch? I don't think so! Each of these, although seemingly unrelated as they belong to different kingdoms, species, etc, can all be said to manifest the "warrior Ka," which in the Kemetic tradition is known as Heru Behudet, Inhur, Munthu, etc. This as mentioned in the section pertaining to the Duat, also means that the same force governs all of these things, and they are thus related on a more subtle level, as they share the same Ka.

The Ka however, is not limited to simply the way in which a person expresses themselves, or their personality type, but it is also a body that can be said to be the actual person, within the body. The Ka in some instances has been called "The Double," and it is said to be the "twin," of the person's Khat or body. According to the tradition, the Ka was created by Khnum on his potter's wheel along with the Khat (Physical Body)

<u>This is the body that is responsible for the person that we know, and are familiar with; all of their expressions and ways of thinking and doing things</u>. This body survives after the death of the physical body, and has the potential to become immortal, and very powerful. This happens as a result of all of the experience that the person accumulates, all of the knowledge and abilities that they learn; all of this becomes stored in the Ka. Combine this experience with the offerings that it receives via it's **kAri** (Shrine) and this body has the capacity to become very "effective." **It is this body that the shrines and statues are dedicated to, and offerings and sacrifices are given to**. As this is the actual "person" that exists within the Khat, once the Ka leaves the physical body, it has the ability to take up residence in another medium. The purpose of the shrines, statues, and tombs, is to serve as the new "Khat" of the Ka, so that one could come and make offerings to them, and also receive assistance from them. It is for this reason that the statues in the temples doubled as "oracles." Because these shrines and statues housed the Ka of the person or persona (in the case of a nTr), the priest or one that was skilled in meditation and ritual, has the ability to engage in a two way conversation with the Ka of the person or nTr via the shrine. Also, it is this same body, the Ka, which has the ability to

take up residence in another person's body during ritual, which is known as ritual possession. When this occurs on will notice that the individual's voice, mannerisms, disposition, and personality will change, matching the personality of the Ka that possesses them. This being the case, it should be understood that when one engages in communication with Ancestors and nTrw during rituals be they via a shrine, "human medium," or an oracle, it is the Ka of that person (Ancestor) or nTr that one is communicating with.

The Ka is a body that is both Mental and Emotional, and as such it plays a role in manifesting our thoughts and our feelings. As stated earlier, the Ka is what emanates from the Ib. As the Ib is a source of our thoughts, feelings, and the decisions that lead to our actions, the Ka is what gives the specific expression and qualities to these emanations. This is to say that, as we demonstrated how the Ka of the nTrw manifests in nature, likewise our thoughts, emotions, and actions will also reflect the Ka that is responsible for its expression. For example, our thoughts may be aggressive, hostile, protective, combative, or they may be empathetic, compassionate, and caring. Our actions may follow the manner in which our thoughts and emotions are expressed. These thoughts and emotions become actions, which go on to create effects in the physical world, which have consequences. This means that the kA is a creative body, in that it has the capacity to create effects and change in the world.

We see the relationship between the Ka and thought in the language. For example, in Madu nTr there is Ka or Kai meaning "*to think, devise, to plan*," which can be found written out with the monograms for K and A, or with the determinative for the Bilateral "Ka," or the raised Arms. Then there is also the term "**KAAt**," meaning thought, as in **Kaat.ib**, or **Kaat.hat**, meaning the *"thought of the heart*."All of these terms demonstrate the relationship between the Ka and thought. Then there is the association of the Ka with creative power or energy, which is present in the relationship to its homophone "**Ka**," which is the word for "**Bull**." This term, similar to Ba, is also written with the erect phallus, which is in some instances ejaculating, to demonstrate its ability to reproduce or create.

166

The Ka of a person is shaped by a number of things, such as their genetics, their astrological alignment at birth, their "karma" in regards to previous incarnations and the current stage of their spiritual growth and development; their environment and culture, upbringing, and the Ren or Name that they are given at birth. All of these things have a shaping affect on the Ka of a person from birth, and when they make their transition from this realm, all of the experiences that they have accumulated in life are contained within it. As mentioned before, it is this body and all of the knowledge and power within it, which unites with the Ba and goes on to create the "Sahu" body.

The kA is received by an individual from their mother, and is formed along with the Khat or physical body in the mother's womb. It is the "feminine" counterpart to the bA. The kA has been mistaken by scholars to be handed down from "father to son," due to a misunderstanding of certain passages in the "Pyramid Text," that speak to Osir being the kA of Heru. In actuality Osir in this instance, does not represent the "father," but the Ancestors. Also, it should be clear, that anything that Heru receives from Osir, he does so through his mother Auset who represents the Ancestral Lineage and the medium of inheritance being that **Kemet was a matrilineal society**. The kA collects and houses the qualities of one's ancestors; the spiritual powers and wisdom handed down through the generations. The kA is quickened, nourished/fertilized, and influenced by the bA, but it is the kA that gives the bA all of the unique qualities of form and expression. For more clarity, please refer back to the 7 bAw of Ra, and the 14 kAw of Ra. While the physical counterpart of the bA is the seed of the male, the physical counterpart of the kA is the egg, blood, and womb of the female. The latter is demonstrated in the mdw nTr language by the term kAit, meaning "womb' or "uterus." Also the bilateral/determinative of kA being two open arms to signify "embrace," speaks to it as a receptive body that receives its program/laws of its function from the nTr, nTrw, and Ancestors via the bA, and also the celestial bodies and earthly experience. Also, speaking to the relationship between the kA and the woman's womb is the depiction of the open arms, representing the kA

on top of an individual's head in a manner that alludes to and resembles the cow horns of Het Heru, which represent's as mentioned earlier in this text, the woman's womb.

The body that follows the Ka is the Ren. <u>The Ren corresponds to the name that a person receives when they are born.</u> It is only when one receives a Ren, that they can truly be declared alive, or a person. **The Ren or name of a thing originally described its qualities, its function and purpose.** Traditionally, names were not given arbitrarily or simply because one liked the name or thought that it was "cute." The name of a person was given in many cases by a priest after divination was performed. This divination would be performed to gain insight into who the child is, why they have come, and what they are here to accomplish. In some cases this information would be given by the nTr that governs the child's life/Shai (destiny), an ancestor, or even the spirit of the child speaking through the parent or a medium. Also, sometimes one may receive a child's name in a dream. In any case, once this information is received, **the Ren that the child receives should reflect that information, serving as a reminder to the child and the community as to what this person's purpose is, and also to serve as a "Hika," or word of power that actually invokes the meaning of the Ren within the child's spirit.**

The Ren is a very important body and is very powerful. **By calling a person's name, you get their attention, which corresponds to one of the highest bodies and aspect of their being, the Yakhu, their consciousness.** From hear all of the other energy bodies fall in line, as it is said "<u>Wherever your attention goes your energy follows</u>. It is also for this reason that it is the name of a "deity" that is stressed in many religious and spiritual traditions. **The name contains the very power of a thing**, as the true Ren, once again is the very vibration that constitutes its existence. In essence, the Ren is the vibration of the Ka, and this relationship between Ren and Ka is the reason why it is through calling the Ren of a nTr, that one invokes the nTr and its Power. In a sense, Ren and Ka are one. Speaking on this E.A. Wallis Budge in his work "**Egyptian Magic** states:

168

"The Egyptians, like most Oriental nations, attached very great importance to the knowledge of names, and the knowledge of how to use and to make mention of names which possessed magical powers was a necessity both for the living and the dead. It was believed that if a man knew the name of a god or a devil, and addressed him by it, he was bound to answer him and to do whatever he wished...all the "gods" of Egypt were merely personifications of the NAMES Of Râ, and that each god was one of his members, and that a name of a god was the god himself."

The Kemetyu understood that the Ren was extremely important, and went through great effort to protect and preserve it. This is the reason why some names can be found written within the Shenu or Cartouche; a symbol of protection and eternity, to ensure that the person's Ren lived forever. **If the ren of a person was forever, then the person was forever**. However if the reverse was the case, and the Ren of the person was forgotten or destroyed, then the person ceased to be. This is why the striking of one's name from the historical or ancestral records was one of the worst punishments that could be exacted upon them.

One also preserved and protected their name by living Maat, which ensured that they maintained a good reputation, which would precede them in the Duat. This is the reason why the written records, biographies, the temples, and the funerary texts written on ones behalf, stressed that they lived a life of righteousness. It was to ensure that their reputation was known and good. Khun Anpu states:

"Surely, righteousness is for eternity. It goes to the grave with those who do it. When they are buried and the earth envelops them, their name is not erased from the face of the earth. They are remembered because of their goodness."

However, if ones reputation was not good, it was said that their "**sXr rn**" or "name stinked." Thus we find advice such as from the Ancestor **Phebhor:**

"Youth who are not corrupted by base desires are not blamed and those who control their sexual appetite, their name does not send forth an unpleasant odor,"

and

"Do not be greedy lest your name send forth an offensive odor."

The Ancestor **Ani** advises:

"Do not leave when the chiefs enter, Lest your name stink."

To avoid a "sXr rn," or a "foul name," one had to live their life in a way that their reputation would precede them favorably. It is for this reason that in chapter 30 of the Prt M Hrw one appealed to their Ib not to **"cause my name to stink**."

The importance of the Ren is also expressed in the Ancestral libations of various cultures. **To remember and call; literally invoke the name of one's Ancestors was to make them live again**. We find in an inscription form **Pt Osir**, the High Priest of Tehuti at Khemnu:

> *I built this tomb in this necropolis,*
> *Beside the great souls who are there,*
> *In order that my father's name be pronounced,*
> *And that of my elder brother,*
> *A man is revived when his name is pronounced*

When one calls the name of their Ancestors they are feeding energy and life to their Ka. The calling of the name along with the pouring of water, the offering of light and food, hymns etc; all of these things serve to make the Ren, the Ka, and ultimately the Ancestor strong and effective.

To call ones name is to invoke them. From a spiritual perspective, to call ones name is to "bring them into being." This principle is present in the cosmology of Inu, in which Ra states "*I brought my own name into my mouth as Hikau, and I came into being...*"We also find it written in the so called "**Sermon of Aesculapius**," which is a book about the advice of the great Ancestor and Rekhi ikat (Sage) **Imhotep:**

"For that it's very quality of sound, the very power of the Egyptian names, have in themselves the bringing into act of what is said."

This passage speaks volumes about the power of the name, as well as the power of the Mdw nTr, but we will touch more on that a little later. However, it is for this reason **the arbitrary assigning of a name can be dangerous, as the Word has a shaping affect on the Ka of the individual, which will go on to influence how they express themselves**. In other words, if one has a name that does not suit them, resonate with their Shai or destiny, then the name can lead them down the wrong path, and invoke qualities in them that will lead them to fail in life. This is the reason why from an Afrikan perspective, the naming procedure can be a very tedious and meticulous event that can take days, and involves several rituals.

The body that follows behind the Ren is the **Khaibit** or the **Swt**, which is referred to as the "shade" or the "shadow." **The Shadow corresponds to the body that is the electromagnetic body, the life force that powers the Khat**. It is symbolized by a sunshade or umbrella, and is depicted like the actual Shadow of a person as it would appear on the wall behind them or on the ground. This body has been called the "Aura," the "astral body," the "animal spirit," among other names. During our life on earth this body powers the Khat, receives information, and attracts things, as well as sends off Information and repels things. It is the part of our being that gives off "vibes," as well as picks up on them. At the end of one's life on earth, the Khaibit separates form the Khat and has the

capacity to stay near it or travel.

The shut or Khaibit is represented as a shadow for a few reasons. On one hand just as light when projected upon an object will cast a shadow behind that object, it is the light of our Yakhu projected upon the "objective plane" that sends out energy. Also, when we go places, touch things, be they objects or people, anything, we leave behind our Shadow, as a vibrational imprint or residual energy, just as a finger print or DNA. This is the reason why a room or a home in some cases takes on the qualities or personality of the people that live there. In some instances entering into the room of a person that has died there, or handling a possession of theirs can cause someone that is sensitive to "feel" their presence, or even in some cases pick up on things about them and their life. This is the science behind how priests, psychics, or mediums are able to "read" or connect with someone, even the deceased, through some object that belonged to them, or in many cases if someone is performing negative juju, they will in many cases need something that belongs to the target of their ritual, be it a possession, some hair, clothing, etc. It is the Khaibit or Swt of the person that they are utilizing for these purposes.

How the "shadow" is cast, depends upon what the "Light" (Attention) of the person is focused on. What thoughts and emotions is the light filtered through, the Ka that is being expressed? All of this will go on to determine the way in which the Khaibit manifests and the quality or temperament of it. For instance, a home that has a lot of violent activity in it: arguing, or worst case scenario, a violent death, or suicide, the Khaibit from those people will project into the home, and the type of emotion and energy that is being expressed will become the "Ka" of the home. When this happens, many times the person that lives there after the previous owner will begin to unknowingly pick up on the qualities of the previous owner. One may find himself more frustrated, angry, and depressed; couples may find themselves arguing and at one another's throat, almost, apparently, for no reason. **Meanwhile all of this is happening; they have no clue that it is not them, but the environment that they are in that is the cause.** The same thing goes for "second hand" objects that are handed down or purchased from yard sales, thrift stores, or wherever. If it is used it has some of the shadow of the previous owner on it. **This is the reason that one that is in the knowledge makes every effort to "purify" a home or whatever used items they may acquire, to disperse any negative vibes it may carry.**

After all of this, the next reason why the Khaibit or Swt is called shadow is because this is the body that is responsible for what many people worldwide have experienced as a "Haunting." In many cases some people actually report seeing an actual Shadow, or a form that they can't quite make out. In these instances, it is the Khaibit of an individual that one is encountering. Depending on whom the person was, and where they were spiritually and mentally, this will determine whether the Khaibit is malefic of benign.

This body, the Khaibit is also the body that is being utilized in the numerous cases of "outer body" experiences or "astral projection." This is to say that the utilization of this body is not restricted to the death of the Khat, but has been experienced by many unknowingly, and also utilized by trained initiates at will. This is something that is common knowledge among practitioners of Traditional Afrikan Spiritual systems.

Following behind the Khaibit/Swt is the well known **Khat**, the physical body. **The Khat corresponds to the gross physical body, and the densest level of Matter in the material world.** This is the body that we can actually see, touch, feel, etc. This body serves as the vehicle for all of the Higher Bodies that make up the being of man, and anything else that exists physically. Its main responsibility is to provide a medium through which one can experience the physical world. This body, unlike the others, does not have the potential for immortality and is able to decay. It is powered by the Khaibit/Swt, and corresponds to the **nTrw Gab and Nebt Het.**

The Khat was in some cases preserved or "mummified," though many scholars and historians misunderstand the purpose and reasoning for this practice. The preservation of the Khat, was for it to maintain the

173

resemblance of the Ka that once occupied it so that it could serve as a "totem," so to speak, or more accurately, a honing devise. It should be understood that tombs in Kemet also served the purpose of shrines for those to whom the tomb belonged. The reason everything that was placed in the tomb; from images of the Ancestor, the Ren of the Ancestor being written everywhere, personal belongings; everything there, was to add to the familiarity of the environment so that the Ka could recognize this place as its home. Even **the coffin of the Ancestor is made in their likeness for this reason**. Secondly, as mentioned in regards to the Khaibit or Swt, it is upon the Khat of a thing that the shadow leaves its deepest imprint. Thus everything within a tomb, the Khat, etc, carries the Khaibit of the Ancestor, which not only adds on to the familiarity of the environment, but also adds on to the concentration of Shekhem or power within the place. Thus we the words of Nisu Kheti III "*The Ba comes to the place it knows, and it will not overstep the ways of the past.*" There are invocations that are contained within the Prt M Hrw to cause the spirit of the Ancestor to return to "its home on earth." This home is its tomb/shrine, and everything within it is meant to make it feel more like home.

All of these bodies come together to make up the totality of a things existence, and in reality are integral parts of one whole; one body. A good analogy is that of a stone being cast into a pond causing several ripples to emanate from the point of contact. All of these bodies emanate from a single point. The Shekhem is the total Energy/Matter that makes up a things existence, therefore, every other energy body that follows behind it, exists within it and is made up of it. It is the Vibration that constitutes its existence and goes on to create the laws that shall govern its being. The yakhu is the body of Light, consciousness, and intelligence that permeates throughout its being. In actuality, Shekhem and Yakhu are two aspects of the same reality, as **there is no such thing as a "bodiless consciousness" or a consciousness that is non-energy, non matter.** The Yakhu is the intelligence that exists within and as the energy/matter that is the Shekhem. The difference is one is passive (Shekhem), the other is active (Yakhu). **The Light of the Yakhu is projected and then differentiates into the lower seven bodies.** This

174

should be understood as everything that exists is a manifestation of light. Therefore, **all of the bodies that follow behind the Yakhu, are in reality varying expressions of the Yakhu**, just as a light differentiates as it passes through a prism. Each body exists within the preceding body, each coming into being and existing as an effect of the other. Also, there is a relationship of cause and effect that exists within and between these bodies. Events that take place within the body have an effect on the mind and vice versa.

The Goal of the initiate is to achieve harmony within all of their "bodies," and maintain continuity within the system. The preservation of one's "wholeness" was very important as there are hymns and rituals present within the literature to protect the ib, the ba, the khaibit, the Sahu, the Ka, etc. Also, the dismemberment of Osir is analogous to the dismemberment of ones being, as dismemberment was one of the consequences of not living a life of Maat. Thus we find the "**Devourer of Hearts**," the "**Devourer of Shadows**," nTrw who "hack up" Khaibit within the Duat, who Hack up the Yakhu, the striking out of the name, etc. All of these are aspects of a teaching that related to the maintenance of wholeness, and is reflected in the preservation of the Khat, and the re-membering of Osir.

While living one preserves the Khat through a proper lifestyle, healthy diet and proper exercise and rest. The Ren is preserved through living Maat, which will lead one to have a "good name," or reputation. One also empowers their Ren by fulfilling their purpose and living up to their name. The Ka is a body that can be worked on through mental and emotional introspection, weighing the pros and cons of one's personality, and making improvements and corrections where needed. Also, the Ka maintains its health by expressing itself. The Ib as the "master body," carries out most of the work. One Masters and preserves this body by learning to master their attention. Also the Ib is preserved by following ones aspirations in Maat. The Sahu is worked through meditation, especially of the regressive type. This type of work, deals with entering into the so-called sub-conscious, and dealing with issues at their root. This work also includes working with the nTrw within ones being, cultivating their qualities within one's self. The Ba is preserved and protected through paying attention to and following the advice of one's conscience. The more

the Voice of the Ba is sought out and listened to, the louder it will become and the easier it will be to hear. These Highest Two Bodies correspond to our Identity. The Yakhu corresponds to the Self Awareness, Intelligence/Consciousness. It is the Body that shines light on and perceives the World through the "window of the soul," the Ba. Shekhem is the Source, and it relates to our nature as infinite Being; infinite potential. These two Bodies are invulnerable (especially the Shekhem; the Yakhu is vulnerable only to the Shekhem).

MAAT

8

Maat is the Divine Law of the Universe. It is the evolutionary force that keeps all things in order. Maat has been conceptualized as the principles of truth, justice, and righteousness, and extends to include balance, order, harmony, and reciprocity. She is conceptualized as a nTrt, which is to say that this force is feminine.

It has been stated that in order for life to exist, creation takes place through a process of division. It is nTr's coming into being from a singularity, into a plurality, that makes life, experience, and perception possible. In a universe that consists of multiple objects, there must be some form of order set in place to ensure that things don't converge, and infringe upon another. There must be some "code of law" that prevents chaos from taking over. Also, in order for there to be life and experience, the multiple objects must interact with one another. So in a way there is "unity" in the midst of plurality or diversity. This is to say, that all of the various things work together in a system based upon interdependent relationships. In the same way that all of the multiple cells, organs, limbs come together, work together in a system to make up our body, ensure that everything is functioning properly, likewise each and everything that exists must work together to ensure that the "body of nTr" is whole, and functioning properly. In spite of the apparent separateness of the various things that exist in the universe, Maat is the force that holds everything together. This manifests as harmony, order, and the interconnectedness between all things.

Maat is said to be the daughter of Ra, and as such she is associated with several nTrwt, specifically Tufnut, Het Heru, and Auset. In the so called "Coffin Text," Tufnut is referred to as Maat. Itum (Ra) in referring to

Tufnut declares "Tufnut is my living daughter: she will exist with her brother Ishu. Life is his identity, Maat is her identity." In the **Litany to Ra** it is said of Tufnut, that she is the "*Sby Ra r znTytw*," "*Guide of Ra to his limbs*." This is to say that Tufnut is the force that pulls on Ra to reconnect with his limbs, the various differentiations through which he manifests, i.e. the nTrw. Another way to say this is that Tufnut pulls on Ra to "Re-member." This means that Tufnut is a unifying force.

Ishu and Tufnut as has been explained in previous chapters, represent the principle of duality, which is the foundation of all law (Maat). One such example of this law is Electricity and Magnetism. Ishu corresponds to electricity, Tufnut to magnetism. Ishu is the positive, active, masculine force within the universe; Tufnut is the negative, passive, feminine force within the universe. Ishu is a force that differentiates, as demonstrated by the fact that he is the one that separates Nut and Gab who were said to be in an eternal sensual embrace. This sensual embrace between Nut and Gab is a symbol of the Primordial Chaos. In doing this, Ishu is a force of Maat/Order. This is the reason why Maat and Ishu both share the feather as a symbol. They are twins, in that Maat is Tufnut. Ishu separates, Tufnut gathers, and together they are the forces that keep the universe and life in order. Interesting to note is the similarity between Ishu and Tufnut, and what physics refers to as Dark Energy and Dark Matter. It is said that dark energy is responsible for the apparent expansion of the universe, whereas Dark Matter has a magnetic or gravitational pull effect on visible matter. In this way the universe is both expanding and contracting. This is so that things on one level remain differentiated, which is a necessity for life to exist, and on another level it causes things to function as a collective, in harmony. Ishu is responsible for the former, Tufnut the latter. The interesting thing about both Dark Energy and Dark Matter is that they can only be observed by their effects on visible phenomenon, but these forces themselves cannot be seen. If we look back at the cosmology of Inu, we see that Ishu and Tufnut precede the coming in to being (cosmologically) of Nut and Gab. This is to say that they are before the "Heavens and the Earths" or Ordered Universe, but being that they are the mother and father of Nut and Gab, and Ishu is responsible for separating them, Ishu and Tufnut are the forces that are behind the formation of the universe. To further demonstrate this point, we will look back upon this same chapter of the "Coffin Text," in which Ra declares "Life is his (Ishu) identity, Maat is her (Tufnut) identity. I shall live with my twins, my fledglings, while I am in their midst, one of them at my back, one of them at my belly (in front). Life will lie with my daughter Maat, one of them inside me, one of them around me." The one in the front or "at the belly," is Ishu, and the one in the back Tufnut. Ishu is also the one within, and Tufnut is the one around him. This is to say that Ishu is in front "leading" or pushing, and Tufnut is behind pulling. Also, Ishu being the one inside and Tufnut around is a reference to the Yitin.

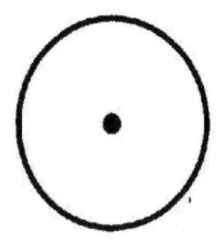

Tufnut is the outer circle, a symbol for the all, the source. Ishu on the other hand is the inner circle, the first differentiation within the All. The inner circle or dot represents the rising out of Nu of Ra. The outer circle represents being, the inner circle represents living. As you will recall Ishu's identity, or name according to this passage is "Ankh" or "Life," and it is within the inner circle that all life takes place. The outer circle representing the source has a magnetic pull upon the inner circle, pulling on it to return. She holds things together. Ishu pushes towards the extension of life, Tufnut pulls for a return to being. Tufnut as a symbol of the source, represents the darkness, Ishu on the other hand is the light. Another interesting thing to note is that between Dark Energy and Dark Matter, dark matter is said to make up the bulk of the universe, some say around 70 percent. Indeed just as the Yitin portrays, the physical universe, visible matter literally sits within this Dark Matter (the outer circle). Funny thing is physicist tend to think that the Universe will keep expanding until it cools so much that it results in a "Big Freeze," meaning it will just stop (really?). Looking at the Yatin, let's just say good luck Ishu ☺.

Another profound meaning of this passage, deals with the creation of order and definition. This is symbolized by the statement "one at my belly, one behind me, one within me, one around me (outside)." The imagery of front and back, within and around, speak to direction, location, definition.

Prior to the coming into being of Ishu and Tufnut, and Ishu's separation of Nut and Gab, there was no definition, no direction, and no location. All of these come into being along with Ishu and Tufnut. This is also symbolized by the four supports or pillars of Heaven (HHw). Our Ancestors were deep!

This Law of Duality is also represented in the forces called the "Maati nTrwt." The Maati nTrwt are the twin sisters Auset and Nebt Het. These two together generally are associated with protecting the body of their husband Osir, and also aiding in the rituals that led to his awakening and resurrection. It is said that when Osir was dismembered by Sutesh, it was Auset with the aid of Nebt-Het that went about the work of collecting his members. It was also Auset and Nebt Het that raised the boys Heru and Anpu. Once they find the body, together they take on the roles of the ritual mourners/songstress that enliven the "dead body" of Osir, invoking his spirit. In this role they can be seen together with Osir, one on each side of him, either while he's standing in between them, or one on each side of his funerary bed. They vow to protect his limbs for eternity.

Auset and Nebt-Het play roles in the most critical events in Osir's life, namely his death and resurrection/rebirth. It is his intercourse with Nebt-Het that initiates the events that culminated in his death, and it is his intercourse with Auset, that led to his rebirth as Heru. Because of this, Nebt-Het generally came to be associated with Death, or at least the process of death and dying, and Auset came to be associated with birth and life. However, these associations are not as concrete or cut and dry as they may seem. Like Ishu and Tufnut, Auset and Nebt-Het are twins. So when we look at their roles, we should keep this fact in mind.

Osir is the nTr of the resurrection, par excellence, and Auset and Nebt-Het are the forces that make sure that he is protected for eternity. This is a symbol of the everlasting flux of change, the cycles of life and death that are ever present in every moment, and the role that they play in the continuity of life through the process of resurrection. Death begets life, and life begets death. Osir's intercourse with Nebt-Het, led to his death from the uncreated realm, which eventually led to his being born in the world. In a way his birth in this realm, is his death in the other. This is important to understand. It is said that Nebt-Het is there to greet the deceased, when they enter into the Iment-t, the West (Duat). This entrance into the Duat, which is considered the death in the earth, is a subsequent birth into the spiritual realm, where our journey in life continues. Once this journey through the Duat is complete, we are then reborn into the earth, in the east.

This birth in the east is a death in the west. We die in the Duat. In many ways, the Duat is a symbol for the womb, and we will touch on this point more a little later. But when we're born in the east, we are exiting out of the womb of Auset, entering the next phase of life, exiting the last. In other words, entrance into the west, into the Duat is intercourse with Nebt-Het, exit from the Duat, and entrance into the world is intercourse with Auset, being born from her womb. These roles are also mirrors to one another, in that the exit of one is the entrance of the other, simply distinguished by planes of existence. In other words, when we are born into the earth we exit the Duat, through the womb of Nebt-Het, and when we leave the earth, the physical realm we are leaving through Nebt-Het, entering into Auset. This is to say that Auset is the spiritual; Nebt-Het is the physical. To enter into one we must leave the other.

This everlasting cycle of life and death is present at every moment. As time passes, each moment passes, dies, and gives birth to the next. This is the motion of life, Change, everlasting change! It is this cycle that maintains the continuity of life, and order, in that it sees that each thing is given it place in space and time, and once that time has passed, it moves on to another phase, it transforms, dies, and begets new life. This is Maat as Evolution, and its twin Extinction. They go hand and hand.

Auset alone also represents Maat as evolution. It is Auset that carries out the bulk of the work of Nehem nTr. She journeys to re-member Osir. If you will recall, it is said that Tufnut "guides Ra to his Limbs." Likewise in the Osirian Tradition, it is Auset that "Re-members" Osir. This is the same principle being demonstrated. In the "Litany to Ra," Auset is said to be the *"Lord(ess) of Journeys moving towards (or within) his Head."* This is to say she is the force that advances, and brings things to a head." She is the evolver. This can really be ascertained from the images of her nursing the baby Heru at her breast. Her breast, her milk, is the food of Heru, it is Maat. Just as it is from the milk that the child shall grow and develop (evolve), in this way we should understand that Auset is the force of evolution, and every aspect of her life represents this fact. So as a force that seeks to re-member, to unite life she is *xnmtt*, and as the Divine Nurse she is *xnmtt*; the evolver. Auset, in her name of Meri, is Love. Love is Maat, it is synergy, it is agreement; it is everything converging towards a common apex (head). Love is when each component of a unit plays its respective part for the best interest of the whole. Love is also Justice.

It is important to understand that Justice is an aspect of love. Love is

not some sappy emotion or display of affection, and it is certainly not just sex. Love is the force that moves things towards convergence, evolution, and oneness. However, if there is a cell that has become a free radical, or a member that has become cancerous, if it comes down to it, Love will eradicate that cell, it will destroy that member, to make sure that the overall collective body survives. In this way, Justice is a force of correction. It restores the balance and homeostasis to the overall organism. There is a story in the tradition that speaks of Auset cutting Heru's hand off. Sutesh had just attempted to rape him and Heru quickly maneuvered his hand and caught Sutesh's seed with it. Heru ran to his mother crying *"look what has been done to me look what has happened to me*!" Auset freaked out and immediately cut Heru's hand off. She then, through the power of her spirit and juju, caused a new hand to grow in its place. The fact that Sutesh tried to force Heru into an act of Homosexuality, is an example of things becoming "unbalanced." Sutesh's seed in Heru's hand corrupted it (there is a homophone of *mtw* meaning seed, and *mtwt* meaning *poison*). So as a result, Auset cut the hand off, quickly, so that the corruption/poison would not take root and spread. This is an example of the force of Justice that comes to correct things, restore order and balance, and will not hesitate if something needs to be cut off or eradicated to ensure that the whole thrives. So in this way it should be understood that Love is not simply an expression of emotion and affection, but can also be a fierce force, even be deadly, if the death of a part will lead to the survival and evolution of the whole. It's all about the "Greater Good."

This same force and principle manifests itself in nature. When the rhythm of nature is thrown out of balance, sometimes by error on our part, there is a natural mechanism that manifests to correct things. This force is the nTrt Shekhemet. Shekhemet is really the fierce form of the nTrt Het-Heru. However, she is Het-Heru when Het-Heru gets upset. In her form of Shekhemet she is quite deadly and destructive, and has the capacity to destroy any and everything that is in the path of her rage. This is symbolic of when Mother Nature lashes out, in order to bring herself back to balance. This may manifests through natural disasters, plagues and pestilence, and also drought and famine. Whatever the case may be, this is nature's way of detoxifying or correcting itself. In actuality, Shekhemet is a healing force, but she is like the healing/purifying power of fire. Fire has the ability to purify and destroy disease, but it also has the capacity to destroy everything else if allowed to rage in excess. This principle is also present in our body as the immune system, white blood cells etc. When there is an agent that threatens the homeostasis of the body, these aspects come to the defense, attacking the agent. However, in all of this the overall objective is healing.

It is the intercourse and interaction of these two forces, Duality that is responsible for life and order. Also, Order is maintained through the balancing and harmonizing of these forces. This intercourse, interaction, and harmony, manifest as the nTrt Het-Heru.

Het Heru is the nTrt of sexual energy, love, joy/festivities, and music. As the nTrt of sexual energy, she is the Creative Power of the universe. All creation takes place through the coupling, intercourse of these dual forces of Ishu and Tufnut, the masculine and feminine energies in all of their various expressions. The interaction, intercourse, results in the production of life on every level. Also, as the nTrt of Music, she is responsible for maintaining the harmony, and rhythm in the world and cosmos. Indeed Het-Heru is the nTrt of the Divine Dance. Her song is life itself. When we observe the various cycles within nature and life, we are observing the Rhythm of Het-Heru. Just as in a song there are several components, keys, notes, patterns, etc, that function together in harmony to make a song, Het Heru causes all of the various things that exist to interact, harmonize together, to make the one song we call the "Uni-Verse." As the daughter of Ra par excellence, Het- Heru is the aspect of Maat that is responsible for keeping everything in tune, order, and in proper balance and rotation. She is also the Yatin (physical universe/manifested light) in totality, the Eye of Ra.

Renenutet is the force within all things that is responsible for its form and function. Her name is said to mean, on one hand, "nourishment snake" as "*rnn*" means *nurse* or *nourishment*, and *utet* means *snake*, and on the other hand her name could mean "*she gives or begets the ren*," as "Ren" means name. As such she is considered the nTrt of nourishment, wealth, and the harvest, and also the innate purpose within each thing. The two interpretations of her name are actually related. As the "she who gives the name," she is the vibration that is responsible for giving each thing its function, and the form that will allow it to carry it out. In this way it is the name of a thing that ultimately houses the potential for the actualization of its purpose, or its harvest. This is not simply the name as we know it to be, but the very vibration that is responsible for the laws that underpin its existence, its constitution. This is the "True Name." Traditionally a name was given based upon the Shai, or destiny of an individual. This Shai was

the individual's purpose. The Ren (Name) that was given was to serve the purpose of not only reminding the individual of their purpose, as to live up to the name, but to literally evoke the innate vibration and power of the name, causing the coming forth of the harvest, i.e. the fulfillment of the purpose, and actualization of the innate potential. In other words the realization of one's "Name" was also the "reaping of the harvest," or fulfilling ones purpose. However, Renenutet is also the nTrt of the Harvest and Wealth in a literal sense. She is the force of Abundance. As she relates to Maat, she is the force of synergy, interconnectedness, and interdependence, causing each thing to "nourish," the next. When all things are working together for the benefit of the whole, it results in the manifestation of Abundance and Wealth which may manifest in resources, or synergy and synchronicity, everything working towards one's favor. This Abundance and Wealth for Renenutet, was symbolized by the Annual Flooding of Hopi, and the Harvest that resulted.

So things are interconnected and interdependent, complimenting one another according to respective forms, functions, and purposes. They work together in a way that is synergistic, where each plays their individual part in the overall sustenance and thriving of the whole. This is the force of Maat, the Cosmic and Universal Law, and all of the "Laws and forces" that fit into it.

This understanding of Divine Law is not the same as one would usually think of as in religious admonishments, or commandments, but the very laws of nature and life itself. The example given above in regards to the workings of the body, the laws of biochemistry, physics, thermodynamics, etc, these are examples of Maat. The various cycles of nature, the energy chain, all of the various systems that are crucial to the continuity of life, these are examples of Maat. Maat is evident. We don't have to demand that we breathe. We don't have to demand that the trees and plant life give us oxygen, nor do they have to demand that we give them carbon dioxide. It is an interdependent relationship that exists, without our making it happen. It is mathematics.

Some have taken the liberty to refer to the entire "Kemetic Tradition" as Maat. This is very acceptable if properly understood. However, if one interprets Maat as a doctrine or ideology, they have gravely misunderstood what Maat is. While certain written codes, laws, and ideals may be reflections or derivatives of Maat, they themselves are not Maat. Maat is a way of life, or more correctly **The Way of/to Life.**

Maat as "The Way of Life," is the natural laws that mean to affirm life. It is the natural way in which the forces of life, affirms itself. We see this manifest in various interrelationships of things, manifesting in form and function. A prime example of this is the Law of Duality, as it manifests in Man and Woman. Maat causes an interrelationship between man and woman that manifests in the physical anatomy (form) of our being. We are literally diametrically opposed. Yet, the way that we are made, we come together like a glove. The intercourse between a man and a woman, as long as everything is functioning properly and the time is right, will result in the production of life. It is a natural life affirming Law. This same principle is present throughout nature in the various interdependent relationships, at every level of living organisms, no matter how small. Each living thing has a part to play in the overall sustenance of the whole. So this goes on to say, that although life happens through apparent separate things, these separate things must function as one system, in order, harmonizing, and reciprocating for life to continue.

Our Kemetic Ancestors made the conscious effort to live Maat, to live a life that was life affirming. In fact, every single aspect of their spiritual tradition was life affirming. They celebrated life and held it as the most precious and sacred thing. Even so-called death, they held as simply another phase of life. In fact it would be totally incorrect to say that they believed in an "afterlife." They believed in life, and the Duat is simply the "other side of life (the Westside)." This contradicts what many scholars have written and stated, inaccurately designating the Kemetic Tradition a "death cult." The Kemetyu simply loved life, and sought to live their life on earth in a way that ensured that they could continue to live and enjoy their lives even when they transcend their physical bodies (khat).

Consciously living in a life affirming manner creates a condition where each thing has the ability to thrive, flourish, and evolve. This was reflected in the way that they spoke, the way that they dressed, hygiene, and the service that they paid to the spirit realm (the Ancestors and nTrw). It is reflected in the way that they held nature sacred, and found things such as the unlawful mistreatment of animals, and the defiling of fresh water as abominable acts (bwt). They understood the part that animals play in the ecosystem, and how important water, air, and light, the earth, were to life, and made every effort not to betray this knowledge. This is the reason why when we look at what has come to be known as the "Declarations of Innocence" or "42 Laws of Maat," we find that they are mainly statements

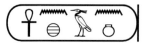

of respecting Nature, and that includes our nature, and others.

Maat is considered the "food of the nTrw." It is said that Ra lived off of Maat. This is symbolized in the images from the temples that depict the priests and priestesses, or the King and Queen offering "Maat" to the nTrw. However, the significance of this, as with much of the tradition, is layers deep. We will delve into a few of them. On one hand, this is to say that it is Maat that sustains nTr, and the nTrw, just as it is Maat that sustains us. Maat as order and harmony, maintains life, and prevents nTr from returning back into the chaos. So it could be said that Maat keeps nTr alive. Maat in regards to the nTrw, not only sustains them, but maintains order in them, ensuring they are fulfilling their respective roles and functions, and are not becoming chaotic at the detriment to the whole system. To understand this one must realize that everything "eats." Everything needs energy, and life is the constant exchange of energy. The nTrw, though they are spiritual forces, need to eat. In actuality the reference to them as limbs of nTr, is quite appropriate in this regard.

In order to ensure that our limbs and organs, our body and minds are functioning properly and efficiently, we need energy. We receive this energy through nutrition. If we are not eating, or taking in energy, along with getting proper rest, we find ourselves over taxing our organism, our limbs and organs, and sooner or later, illness (chaos) will manifest. We have to reciprocate. It is an interdependent and reciprocal relationship. Our limbs and organs serve us, and in exchange we serve them, that we may continue to live and everything runs smoothly. If one understands this, then they will understand the purpose of ritual offerings, sacrifice, etc. It is not that we "worship" the nTrw and Ancestors, but we understand that they need energy just as we need energy. So we invest energy in them, that they may in turn re-invest energy in us. This is the great reciprocal and interdependent relationship between this realm and the spirit realm. Our ancestors understood that to ensure that the spirit realm, the nTrw and Ancestors were good, was to ensure that we and our lives were good, in the same way that we take care of our insides. In a way, the spiritual realm is the internal organs of life. We'll expound on this point a little later.

Another meaning to offering Maat to the nTrw is to regulate them, to make sure that they stay in order. This is the underlying theme of the Osirian Tradition. Everything is out of order. Sutesh is a militaristic force of defense, and is meant for the maintenance of security. However, Sutesh wants to rule in spite the fact that ruling is the proper place of his brother

Osir. Nebt Het desires to be with Osir, yet that is the proper place of her sister Auset, and her place is with Sutesh. Osir sleeps with Nebt-Het, confusing her with Auset. All of these forces are out of order, and this leads to Sutesh taking the throne (Chaos ruling). This is why Heru's job is to restore and maintain Maat, as he is the avenger of Osir. Each and every person is Heru and our duty is to maintain Maat, offering Maat to these forces.

These forces are responsible for every single aspect of life. On a personal level they are our thoughts, our emotions; they govern various aspects of our bodies and their functioning. They govern various temperaments, and various aspects of Nature. When they are out of order it manifest in life. If we experience negativity, it is the negative expression of one of the nTrw. They each have a proper way to function, and roles to fulfill, and our duty is to live Maat, and to offer them Maat, that they may carry out their duties. This is why most of the hymns and inscriptions of the nTrw not only describe their forms and functions, but also describe what it is that you want them to do for you, written in a way that makes it seem as though they are declaring their purpose, and what it is that they will do for you, as though it is the nTr speaking. This is not to be interpreted in the same way that one would with scriptures that claim to be the "word of god," but from a "priestly" perspective, these hymns are written by priests and they are meant to be recited in a way in which one is giving the nTr their Maat, the law of their being. In doing so, order should be maintained in this family of spiritual forces.

FAMILY

9

THE OLDEST RELIGION IN THE WORLD

When we refer to Maat, and the Kemetic Spiritual tradition, or any African Traditional Religion, we are really talking about family. When it all boils down to it, family is what it's all about. We've talked about how the world exists through the working of multiple forces, objects, etc, working together as a collective body. In this body, each thing has a respective role to play; they have a specific function and duty to carry out, and they have a proper place in relationship to others and the whole. In traditional societies the family was also modeled according to this understanding.

As a man, there is a role that one is expected to play that was an extension and testimony to the very nature of one's being. Likewise it was the same for the woman. In other words, these societal and familial roles were reflections of what it was that made us a man or woman functional, and how these traits could be utilized within the family and the community, in the best interest of the collective. Naturally there are things that distinguish us constitutionally, that make us fit for some things, and unfit for others. These things become the foundations of what are referred to as "gender roles." Further as we grow, and evolve in relation to the collective, we become aware of our talents, and more aware of how we fit within the collective scheme. Fulfilling these roles serves to maintain order in the family, the community, the society, the nation, etc. This is to say that everything has a proper place in space and time.

This is a reflection of the very forces that make up creation, and are responsible for the various expressions that manifest through us. Indeed these forces work as a "family," and are responsible for all traits, characteristics, and talents. These forces are the nTrw. Their functioning, interaction, and intercourse together in order and harmony as a family so to speak, keeps the universe in tune with Maat.

In the Kemetic Tradition, like many African traditions, the Divine is spoken of in terms of familial relationships. We have Ra, who is considered to be the father of all the nTrw. Het-Heru in some forms is considered to be mother of all the nTrw and the nTrw are spoken of in terms of kinship and Ancestry. So Nu/Nunet are the father and mother of Ra and Rait/Arat/Yasuiset/Het-Heru, Ra and Het-Heru are the father and mother of Ishu and Tufnut. Ishu and Tufnut are the father and mother of Nut and Gab. Nut and Gab are the father and mother of Osir, Auset, Sutesh, Nebt-Het, Heru War, and these are the fathers and mothers of Anpu, Heru, and all of the nTrw, nature, men and women, etc.

If we were to take a careful look at the Kemetic Tradition, we will come to find that the stories speak of how this family of forces, fell into chaos and disorder. Roles became confused, and lines got crossed. Osir was the King, Auset was the Queen, Sutesh was the General of the Military, and Nebt-Het was his spouse. Each one had a role and place, and function unique to themselves, yet all critical and important to the overall success of the society. It was when Nebt Het wanted to be in Auset's place, Sutesh wanted to be in Osir's place, Osir mistook Nebt-Het for Auset, that the "stuff" hit the fan. This led to the entire kingdom (the whole) being overtaken by Isfet. Heru comes as the redeemer, to restore Maat into the family and the Kingdom. He comes to put things back into order.

Maintaining order and harmony in the family and community is one of the chief purposes of African Spirituality. Kemetic Spirituality as an African Tradition holds this also as its main purpose. The focus on the cultivation of the individual was to ensure that they actualized their innate potential and in doing so, would function at an optimal level for the betterment of the family and the society at large. This was to ensure the smooth continuity of life.

Before Maat can be established in the "external family," she must first be established in the "internal family," which would lead ultimately to her being established in the "outside world." This internal family, the nTrw, are

responsible for everything that takes place inside and outside in life. Internally, each one of these forces has a specific role and mode of expression, governing various faculties of our being, bodily organs and functions, emotions and psychological traits, and temperaments. Certain nTrw are meant to be subservient to others at certain times, and there is a hierarchy amongst them that should be maintained. Heru sa Osir sa Auset for example, is the nTr that corresponds to the Ib, the heart, mind, and Will of an individual. He is the Nisu Bity, or "King of the Two Lands" that is to say, Ruler of the higher and lower aspects of our beings. He is sovereign and is meant to decree, decide, etc, and not follow, or be compelled into action by those of lower rank. However as a vehicle (literally a symbol/avatar) of his father it is his responsibility to ensure that his father's will is done. He is responsible for maintaining order in the world (The Collective). Sutesh however, in his proper place, is in charge of the preservation of life, security. He governs the basic animal instinct of fight and flight response, and is associated with the breath. His purpose is survival. Nebt-Het is originally the wife of Sutesh, his complement, and corresponds to the physical life and body. Thus she is "*Nebt-Khat*," that is, "*lady of the body*." Her name Nebt-Het or Lady of the house, speaks to her role as that which "houses." She is the body as the "house" of the "higher" forces or more subtle aspects of reality/being, and corresponds to physical existence, and the "external world." Also as "lady of the house" according to the tradition she was brought into the family by Auset as a "sister wife" or second wife to Osir. In this role she is "subservient" to Auset the first royal wife, and she is portrayed in many ways as an assistant to Auset. This is speaking to the receptive, passive, and subservient place of the body. The body is a submissive and reactionary organism. It is meant to do the bidding of the mind and spirit, and the creative intelligence, as well as serve as a vehicle through which the Divine can manifest and enter into the world. As such it is said that "Auset conceived and Nebt-Het gave birth, which is to say the seed/cause took root in the spirit, and then manifested (being born) into the physical world." So Nebt-Het is portrayed following Auset wherever she goes, assisting her in whatever she needs. Auset on the other hand, is the first Royal Wife of Osir; she is the Queen Mother, the Throne. It is through her that the Nisu ascends to power. As the throne, she is the power, the e-motive aspect of our being, the medium between the Self and the world, and the ability for it's (the Self) aspirations/will to manifest. She is spiritual, emotional and mental, the vehicle of the Self. It is said of Osir that his throne is "Within" Auset. So in this way she is the Duat (Osir sits upon the throne in the Duat), the mind, especially the so-called subconscious mind. She is the internal, spiritual reality. It is said of Auset that she "follows Osir wherever he goes, and this is clearly demonstrated through the stories and the literature. When Osir's body floated up to Palestine, Auset made her way to Palestine. When Osir was taken into the palace in Palestine in the form of a pillar, Auset made her way into the palace and proceeded to revolve around the pillar (circumambulation). When the body was dismembered and spread around the land she then followed/sought out every member, also in her form of Sopedet, she follows Osir (SaH/Orion) saying "I am behind you and I shall not leave from you." This is to say that she follows and supports Osir, the Self, Consciousness; the Intelligence within us. So it should be understood that there is a proper order in which these forces are meant to relate and operate.

If this order is not maintained, then chaos will enter into one's life, internally first, then spilling over into the outside world. If one's own survival or personal will takes precedence over the Divine will and what's in the best interest of the collective, or if one's emotions, or bodily urges become chief, there is bound to be trouble. In other words, if these forces are not in Maat, it will manifest as internal conflict, or corruption, that will in turn manifest in ones external life. Once these forces are in order within the individual, harmony and prosperity will sub-sequentially manifest within that person's life, causing them to be a blessing and light to their surroundings.

The family is the foundation of civilization, and is critical to its continuity. It is a microcosm of the community and society at large. Likewise the community, society, etc, is a macrocosm of the family. The condition of one is a testament and reflection of the condition of the other. This is to say that if the family is in poor condition, then the society is in a poor condition, and vice versa. The condition of the family is dependent upon the state of the individuals that make it up. The value of an individual is relative and predicated upon the affect that they have on their surroundings, the purpose they serve in relationship to others (things and people). If the individual is not functioning at an optimal level, is not fulfilling their purpose, then by consequence it will have an ill affect on the other components that make up the "system." This is the nature of the world. It is a web of interdependent relationships, a family.

This is something that our Ancestors knew very well. They understood that family was the basis of it all, and for this reason the cosmologies and stories that served to teach us of the nature of life was relayed in symbolism that

reflected this understanding. When we look at the condition that the world is in, we see the condition of the family, of the individual. What we are witnessing is the result of the fact that we have put the family, the collective to the back burner, and have accepted the ways of those that lack understanding. We are now walking the path of Sutesh, the path of the individual, egoism. We have drunken the "kool-aid" of individualism, being served to us under the guise of "freedom and independence." We no longer realize that we are a part of a greater collective, and contemplate our lives in relationship to it; instead we have become "self serving," and have taken on the role of free radical cells, cancers within the body of nTr. We have forgotten about family, and though many of us are returning to the ways of our Ancestors, we still have a long way to go. We no longer have real families because Osir is dismembered. The members of the body are scattered here and there, doing their "own thing." This is not Maat, but isfet.

The very essence of Kemetic Spirituality is the "re-membering" and preservation of nTr. Some say that the ultimate goal is to Self Realization/Actualization. However, this realization and actualization of one's divinity is not simply for an individual to become "wise" and "powerful" so that they can better serve themselves, but to serve the purpose of allowing them to function at an optimal level to be of better service to the collective. It is for them to use the wisdom and power of nTr to be a blessing to their family and society, creating conditions to further enable them to evolve, and by doing so they improve the quality of life for everyone, and further ensure the perpetuation of life, constantly improving the quality of it. Once again it must be understood that Maat all boils down to life and that which perpetuates and optimizes it.

The purpose of Life is Life, and Maat is that which perpetuates and optimizes it. Family perpetuates life and is therefore an expression of Maat. Traditionally there were rites of passages and initiations that were a part of the family and community that ensured that the values that preserve the integrity of the family and society were maintained and handed down generation after generation. These institutions were a critical piece of our culture. They taught us the importance of family and community, and prepared us as individuals to better ourselves that we may play our part in bettering the collective. The spiritual traditions are also included amongst these institutions, in many cases being the foundation of them. The priests and the elders played a pivotal role in guiding the community to stay in harmony with the divine order of things. There were conditions consciously created in the community, a "culture of cultivation" so to speak, that would automatically lead to an individual's evolution, simply by being born and raised into the culture of the community. It happened for the most part, automatically. When one was born, there was a curriculum waiting for them already; a program. This was a critical key to the maintenance of the integrity and Maat of the community.

Now some take issue with the idea of being "programmed," but this issue is due to a misunderstanding of the nature of life and man's being, or just ignorance of it. Physical life and existence is all about conditions, limits, definition. This is what makes life possible. As soon as we are conceived (and actually before that), we are being conditioned and programmed; we are being shaped and molded, influenced. We are conditioned by the stellar bodies at the time of our birth. We are conditioned by the blood and chemicals that we inherit from our parents and ancestors; they go on to become our natal constitution, determining much of our destiny and potentialities. When we are born and as we grow and live, we learn, we are programmed, influenced, conditioned by our environment and the people that make it up. Whatever the culture is that we come up in, it plays a major role in shaping who and what we become. This is a natural fact of life. All of these things play a major role in "who" it is that we are to become in the world. The issue is not with the fact that we are programmed, but with the program with which we are programmed. What is the culture that we are cultivated in? Who is the author of this said culture? What and who has it led us to become? Traditionally the answer to these questions would have been nTr via our ancestral heritage and the community. Now the answer for the most part is Sutesh via those who have been our oppressors, colonizers and slave masters.

For most of us, Afrikan People, the answer to this question is not our Ancestors, but the European through the imposition of their "Sutanic" culture of isfet. Western culture as the dominant world culture has led to the abandonment of our Ancestral ways of Maat, and the deterioration of the Afrikan family, as well as the family of every other people that have been influenced by the white supremacist power structure and their culture of egoism. In truth even if those that we have been influenced by on the surface are physically Afrikan, the mindset, and program by which they are operating is as European as the European. In this sense it is our attempting to be other than our Afrikan selves that have been our downfall.

Afrikan people historically have been mainly a familial/communal people.

We are inherently "Maatic," being that we are naturally inclined towards being family and community oriented. This truth is still evident in Black culture in spite of the poor condition of it. We are still family and community oriented. We still recognize the kinship in our Blackness, even if this recognition is subconscious and subtle. Yet it is our coming up in a foreign culture that has been, and still is our undoing. It is when we try to operate on the principles of individualism, capitalism, etc, that we see our demise. Sure we see certain examples of so-called successful individuals, but what is the standard of this so-called success? What is the cost of this so-called success? Can the success of the individual at the expense of the collective truly be deemed a success? If one is filthy rich yet the masses of their people, the family, the nation is poor and struggling, are they really successful? From an Afrikan, "Maatic" perspective they are a failure, no matter how (in)famous or "rich" they have become. In truth and spirit they are poor, and this system, which is not a true system, cannot sustain itself. The current economic conditions of the world at large, Afrikan and Non Afrikan, is a testament to this fact. How can 1 percent of a population own almost half of the nation's wealth, or 20 percent own close to 95 percent, leaving 80 percent of the population to fight over the remaining 5 percent? How does that make sense? (Where they do that at???). Imagine if one of the organs in your body decided to absorb all of the energy and nutrients the body takes in. Sooner or later the rest of the body will lash out at you. The system will shut down. Even if it were the brain, the "head of the operation" consuming all of the energy, as important as the brain is, the body will not allow this to continue for long. When a cell operates in this manner we call it cancer. If one understands this then they will understand why the current system is on the fast track towards oblivion, and why the current individualistic order is inherently flawed. It is not based upon Maat and therefore it is not self sustainable and life perpetuating.

Traditionally for Afrikan people this type of social structure would be unheard of, neither would it be tolerated. Even royalty would not dare to take it this far. In fact many people in looking at all the gold and the jewels of our ancestors misinterpret this to mean that they were living lavish, when in fact, in places like Kemet, these things were used for sacred/talismanic purposes first, and adornment and aesthetic second, and not as much as a significator of status and wealth as many believe. In fact in Kemet, and in many places in Afrika, and the east, a good name is still worth more than gold. Even when the Nisu exemplified wealth and status, majority of the time is was to honor their Ancestors and the nTrw, as offerings to their temples. Even when Nisu erected monuments adorned

194

with images of themselves, their name plastered all over the temple, it was more about being in good graces with the nTrw, and for the elevation of their name. One only need to examine the numerous temples and the dedicatory inscriptions carved throughout testifying that this illustrious and lavish temple was built as a dedication to this nTr, or to ones Ancestor, a chief example being the temple of Nisu Seti I at Ibdu (Abydos). In fact, in the few examples of the abuse of power and wealth, the individual was in many cases disposed of. This is because the Nisu was a priest first, and his main responsibility was to ensure that the nTrw were taken care of in turn ensuring that the entire nation was flourishing. And if by chance he was not fulfilling his purpose, and was living fat while his people struggled, it was within the right of his people to kill him as it is they who lift him up and empower him. All of this is to say that the Nisu is a servant to the people and his responsibility was to the collective, including the Divine. His heart had to be weighed against the feather of Maat, just like the commoner, and he had to stand before Osir and his Ancestors just as everyone else, and he was not found Maa-Kheru, his heart was fed to the ommomyit. This is evidenced by how a Ruler that was not deemed Maa-Kheru, in many cases his name would be struck from the Ancestral/historical record, signifying that he is dead/ceases to exist. "Akh n Yatin" (Akhenaton) is a prime example of this type of ruler.

Some hold Akh n Yatin to be of a high spiritual level of attainment, but to the Ancestors this was not the case. Not only did he attempt to destroy the tradition of the Ancestors, but in his imposition of his religious dogma, he brought instability to the nation. While his literature is considered beautiful and unique and he lived the life of a hermit chasing his spiritual aspirations, the nation fell into disarray due to the neglect and lack of leadership. So even though he was pursuing what he perceived to be a noble spiritual pursuit, in actuality because his individual ambitions outweighed the collective welfare he was deemed unspiritual, and not maa-kheru, and his name was struck from the books. Simply put, true spirituality, true religion is about the collective, and the divinization of the individual to aid in the growth and development, prosperity of the collective.

From a Maatic stand point ones value is relative to the role they fulfill in relationship to the collective. Are they fulfilling their purpose, their function in elevating the family and community, the legacy of the Ancestors? The nTrw? This is the chief standard by which we measure success, not by the gold spinning rims on ones chariot, or how "religious"

one appears to be. In fact, when we look at texts such as the "Immortality of the Writer," we find that the work of the scribe, the sages are heralded and found to be of more importance than the gold and silver monuments, the illustrious tombs, the grand estates etc. The Rekhi ikat (Sages) of Kemet were remembered and championed because of the sacrifice of themselves to their work, and the role their writings played in the elevation of the generations that followed them, and it is through their work that their name shall live forever.

Afrikan People must return to the way of family, the way of Maat. The current way is on its way out, and those that seek to hold on to it will face the destruction that it leads to. We are heading into a time that will demand our return to being collective minded. We will be forced to function as a collective, as we will find it increasingly impossible to survive following the path of the ego/individual. We have to get back to the community, collective resources and collective effort. Our power is in our unity. If you want to know how we built the pyramids, the answer is in the pyramid itself.

When most people think about Ancient Kemet, the very first thing that comes to their minds is pyramids. These monuments are so awe inspiring in their complex architecture that they are considered among the wonders of the world. Reason for the amazement lies in the fact that no one really knows how these so-called primitive people could have the mathematical expertise (expertise that has yet to be mimicked by "modern man") to build something like that. Some of the stones literally weigh several tons, yet these people, without what we would consider as advanced technology, and the fancy gadgets got it done. What we have to look at in the pyramids, is a monument that has literally stood the test of time, a testament of immortality, genius, and the immense capabilities of Man (unless you want to claim that "Aliens" built them). However, what exactly do we see when we look at a pyramid, and what lessons can we extract from it?

What is a pyramid? By definition, it is a polyhedron, having a polygonal base and triangular sides with a common vertex or pinnacle. It is a massive monument with a square base and four triangular sides. Now that is the technical definition, which is actually pretty good. In fact we can extract some jewels from it. Notice that although the pyramid has multiple sides and angles, all of them nonetheless converge towards a single point. This is profound on multiple levels.

As it relates to the family, community and nation, it is when all of the different personalities, perspectives, talents, and individual dreams are harmonized toward the common good of what's in the best interest of the collective. It is everyone bringing their gifts to the table and making them converge toward a common purpose and goal. It is Collective effort at its finest. That is how Kemet built the pyramid, as well as why they were a successful civilization for several thousands of years. As a wise man once said," our unity alone is more powerful than a hydrogen or atomic bomb." Together we can and will move mountains. Together we can get more accomplished than we ever could as individuals. Our unity is the Spiritual Power, Omnipotence of nTr It Self. We must be able to come together, and sacrifice all selfish intent and vision for the benefit of the collective. There is no mine, only ours, and there is no I, only we. Following this state of mind, we will build a nation that will stand the test of time, just as the pyramid. In this way the pyramid is a wonderful demonstration of Maat.

Maat must be the perspective through which we perceive the world, and the determining factor in our idea of success. In fact, Maat is the ultimate success path. In the text of Khun-Anpu (The So-called Eloquent Peasant) it is said:

"ir ha shi n MAat sqd.k im.f maow nn kf ndbyt hta.k nn ihm dpt.l nniwt iyt m xt.k nn saw sgrg.w.k nn sxm.k haoo.k hr tan n it tw nwt nn dp.k Dwt nt itrw nn mA.k hr. snd iw n.k rm.w Snay.w pH.k m Apd.w Dda"

"If you go to the Lake of Maat, you shall sail in it with a breeze, Bunting will not strip away your sail, Your boats will not lag. Mishap will not come to your mast. Your yards will not break, You will not founder nor touch on land. The water will not take you. You will not experience the evil, of the river. You will not see the face of fear. There come to you the darting fishes, you attain like fat birds."

This is to say that if he lives and journeys the path of Maat, he will be

successful. The text goes on to give examples of what living Maat looks like. He says:

> *"For you are the father of the orphan, the husband of the widow, the brother of the desolate, the garment of the motherless. Let me place your name in this land higher than all good laws: you guide without avarice, you great one free from meanness, who destroys deceit, who creates truthfulness."*

This is to say that much of the living of Maat is predicated upon how one lives in relationship to others, helping to elevate them. He states further that "*mr wAH mi Dd Taw pw n fn dirt mAat,*" "*Desire to live long, it is said "Doing Maat is breath to the nostrils*." Osir Kheti III in his instructions to his son Merikara says "Do Maat and you will endure on earth." Osir Pitah-Hotep says:

> *"wr Maat wAH spdt n xnn.tw.s Dr rk wsir iw xsf.tw n swA Hr hpw swat pw m Hr n awn.ib in nDyt iTt a Haw n pA Dayt mni sp.s iw.f Dd.d sxt.i r.i Ds.i n Dd n.f sxt.i Hr Hnt.i..."*

> *Maat is great and it's sharpness is enduring. It has not been overturned since the time of Osir The one who overlooks the laws is punished, that is what is overlooked in the sight of the greedy. It is the small minded that seize riches, but crime never managed to land it's rewards. Whosoever says "I snare for myself" does not say "I snare for my needs…"*

He also says :

"wAH.s aqA.f mAat Sm r nmtt.f""

198

that is:

"the man endures whose guideline is Maat, who proceeds according to his paces."

In cosmology of Mennefer it is stated that "Life is given to the peaceful, and death to the criminal." In all of the above passages it should be clear that a life of Maat is the key to a successful life and it is a life that takes into considerations ones actions in relationship to the collective. However, how exactly do we determine whether or not our actions are in the best interest of the whole, and what exactly does that mean? Also, suppose one is in a corrupt society with unjust laws, would one still seek to live in a way that is for the best interest of the collective? Does one have to wait to take counsel with the community before doing any little thing? Those are some very important questions, the misunderstanding of which can lead to some gross errors, as well as stagnation in one's life. So it is obvious that some things need to be clarified.

How do we move about in life with the collective best interest in mind? First of all, we have to make it clear what is meant by the "collective," and all that entails. By the collective, it is meant the best interest of the whole, and this includes nTr, nTrw, Jertiyu (Ancestors), Shai (One's Destiny), and how all of these relate to the collective society. This list is also the hierarchy through which we should pay acknowledgement and consideration when making plans and taking action. Also, this hierarchy is interconnected and interdependent, meaning that one cannot be in harmony with a few and be out of sync with the others. Understanding this, if we are in harmony with nTr, nTrw, then we are in harmony with our Jertiyu. If we are in harmony with our Ancestors, then we are in sync with our Destiny, as it will be demonstrated in the following chapter that a person's destiny is influenced by their Ancestors. If one is in harmony with their Shai, then the way is open for their success, and that of the community at large. This is to say that the mundane collective (physical community) is dependent upon the spiritual community, the nTrw and Ancestors, Shai (the flow of Time) etc. Understanding this, one should first contemplate the Divine, and determine the "Will" of the nTr/nTrw, and make the effort to fall in to harmony with it. From there all success is assured. Even if that success appears to be out of sync with the collective norm, and way of doing things, ultimately it should be understood that nTr is the true Collective. Determining the "Will of nTr" is accomplished by

learning which one of the nTrw are moving and operating, governing a particular situation or undertaking. We'll touch more on this in later chapters.

The hierarchy mentioned above represents the structure upon which a "Maatic" community/society is ordered. "Maatic" societies seek to pattern and govern itself based upon the Divine Law and rhythm of the Cosmos. In this way, much of the actual structure of the society, as far as hierarchy and government, and even the layout of the community, actually reflect the hierarchy of the nTrw, and also the rhythm of the time as displayed through natural phenomena; seasonal and cosmic cycles. Even on a smaller scale, the buildings, homes and temples, especially the temples, were made to be a universe within itself, being designed "cosmologically." The geometrical patterns, symbols, directional orientation, etc were intricately detailed to reflect various aspects of the spiritual tradition. The names of the cities in Ancient Kemet for example, carried spiritual and cosmological significance as opposed to just being named arbitrarily. These places were held to be the residence of certain nTrw, and reflected the expression of energy in that particular locale. For example, Inu (Heliopolis) is the residence of Ra/Itum, Menefer (Memphis) is the residence of Pitah, as evidenced by its other name Het-Ka Pitah, or House of the Ka of Pitah. Behudet (Jeba) was the domain of Heru Behudet, also called Meshen. Ibdu (Abydos) is the residence of Osir, Yinut (Dendera) is the residence of Het-Heru. There are several other examples as every location had a nTr that lived there. The significance of these locations and their names were both spiritual and physical (in reality there is no difference), but the significance transcended the physical location. A prime example of this is Hopi (The Nile), which is also the name of the nTr that lives there. Hopi came to be held as not only a river, but a source of wealth, spiritually and physically, and ultimately the highway of life in ones journey from the "east" to the "west" and back again. In these examples it should be evident that the entire nation was set up cosmologically, so much so to there were even 42 "nomes," speaking to the nations being in harmony with the 42 "Laws" of Maat. Today we find similar examples of this in traditions such as Yoruba (Ifa), as well as Vodun. The name of locations in Yoruba land are also the names of spiritual places within their cosmology, and various Orishas are held to reside in these places. Haitian Vodun being a diasporic tradition that developed due to slavery, and the mixing of several different groups of Afrikans, the names of locations in their tradition have taken on almost a purely spiritual significance, in spite of the fact that there are actual earthly locations with those names. We even see remnants of this ancient science among modern societies such as the Nation of Gods and Earths in which cities are referred to in a way that reflects their culture and tradition i.e. Harlem is "Mecca," Chicago is "C-Medina," etc.

The governmental structure in Kemet was organized according to the hierarchy of the nTrw, and the role that these forces play in relationship to one another; the way that they express themselves. The living Nisu (so called King) was held to be an incarnation of Heru and the "Queen" was held to be an incarnation Het-Heru. By incarnation it is meant that they personify these particular forces. These were the spiritual and political leaders of the nation. However they cannot govern the nation alone, or fulfill every responsibility themselves. From here there are two roles that are reflective upon the nature of the **Nisu/Nisut**, namely the **TAty** and the **Hm nTr tpy**, that is **Vizier/Prime Minister and the High Priest(s).** These two fulfilled there roles on behalf of and in the stead of the Royal Family. It should be known however, that this dichotomy of spiritual and political was not cut and dry as many times the people were both. Once again there is no separation between the secular and the sacred. These people trained others to fulfill the same roles, but on a smaller and more concentrated or focused scale.

The hierarchy mostly reflected the cosmology of Inu. The "Duality" of the spiritual and physical and their role in the functioning of the society are represented in the children of Nut and Gab (Heaven and Earth), and actually the entire Peseju of that tradition. Osir represents the Ancestors, the "deceased" Nisu, and as such the standard and legacy that is to be upheld. Auset is the mother of the living Nisu, and is the "seat" of power itself. She is a symbol of the nation as a whole, and also the matrilineal structure of the society, the lineage, and the culture that "nurtures" each individual from birth to come up in the ways of the Ancestors (Osir). Sutesh is reflected in the military of the nation that is responsible for maintaining the security of the society. Nebt-Het represents the actual society, and the domestic responsibility of each to work to ensure the community thrives. Heru, once again, represents the living Nisu, and is responsible for leading, managing, correcting, and maintaining Maat in the society, and Anpu is included with Heru. Tehuti and Maat represent the spiritual traditions, laws (spiritual and land), and education. Het-Heru is the harmony that causes all of these various components of the society to work together as a collective body, harmonious relationships, and the social activities, festivals, "holidays," rituals, etc, that strengthen the national bonds and communal ties. All of these are critical parts of a community/nation that

must be set in place and maintained, in order for Maat to flourish. As a system, if any one of these are "off," it will consequently weaken the entire community. This organization should also be present in every household, in every family, in regards to individual roles, and also skills that should be cultivated and present internally.

Osir Khenti Imentiyu 10

It has been stated several times already, that Afrikan Spirituality is about family, and is ancestral in essence. Kemetic Spirituality being an Afrikan Tradition also holds this to be the case. There has been much written about Osir as the "Self" and "Consciousness," etc, but there is something that, for the most part, has been glanced over, totally missed, or completely ignored when it comes to Osir, and that is his relationship to the Ancestors. The reason for this, as I see it, has been the attempt to look at, and interpret Kemetic Spirituality through the lens of Western and Eastern traditions, and not purely through the eyes of the Kemetic people first, and then from a greater Afrikan context. This being the case, that which has been presented thus far as Kemetic Spirituality has been a syncretism, or hodgepodge of various traditions; be it Kabbalah, Daoism, Yoga, Tantra, etc, and very little Vodun, Ifa, Dogon, dawning a Kemetic name and uniform. Whatever the reason for this, much has been missed out on in regards to the richness of the Kemetic tradition itself. In fact, when we look at the Kemetic tradition, its symbolism and literature, we find that there is so much more in common with traditions such as Vodun, Ifa, and other Traditional Afrikan spiritual systems in both philosophy and aesthetic, than anywhere or anything else. Afrikan Traditions are highly community, family, and Ancestry oriented, and this is demonstrated strongly and clearly in the tradition of Osir.

In fact, Osir is a symbol of the Ancestors, and his tradition is one of Ancestral elevation and veneration. In his ren of Khenti Imentiyu (Foremost of the Westerners), he is the nTr that sits upon the throne in the "West," a symbol of the Duat or spiritual realm. He is called "foremost," or in some cases "chief of the westerners," to demonstrate that he stands over and is elevated above those that are not elevated.

203

"Imentiyu" or "Westerners," is a term used to refer to the so called "deceased;" those that live in the Duat. Not everyone that lives in the Duat is elevated, mAa-xrw, "good," etc. Some have not "come forth by day," meaning looking forward, existing in the here and now. Some are stuck in the past, trying to satisfy old desires and addictions. An "Osir" is one that has been elevated and is being elevated, either by their own efforts in life, or through being "fed" by those that are in the "east," their descendants and survivors that are keeping their shrine. When we look at the texts that speak to the Osirian tradition, such as the "prt m hrw" for example, we find that the deceased was identified with Osir, and the books consist of various rituals that were geared towards the enshrinement and empowerment of the Ancestor, elevating them to a position of power and influence. This elevation was to ensure that they would be able to continue their journey in life, and also play an active and beneficial role in the lives of their families and the nation. This, brothers and sisters, is as Afrikan as it gets!

Osir as a symbol of the Ancestors is clearly demonstrated from his story. He is killed, and buried. Rituals are performed on his behalf to awaken his spirit. Once his spirit is awakened he takes the throne in the West. Somewhere in there, his wife Auset takes his seed and conceives, and gives birth to a son, Heru. Heru goes on to defeat Sutesh and reclaim his father's throne, and becomes Nisu Bity in the "East,".i.e. on earth. According to the tradition, Osir spoke to Heru from the Duat and encouraged him to go to war with Sutesh. In the story of the "Contendings of Heru and Sutesh," Osir speaks to Ra and Peseju nTrw from the Duat on behalf of Heru, and when they were not cooperative, initially, he threatens to unleash the forces within the Duat upon them. This is to say once again, that Osir is in the position of power within the Duat. To further demonstrate this truth, we have the fact that the living Nisu Bity was seen as the personification of Heru, and his father, the preceding deceased Nisu Bity becomes identified with Osir. When the living Nisu makes his journey towards the "Beautiful West," he also becomes Osir.

The goal of the deceased, was to "unite" with Osir, and become Osir, that is to say unite with his or her Ancestors, and become an Ancestor herself. This was true for both men and women. There are several examples of women being referred to as "Osir," one of the most famous examples is in the case of "Osir" Nefertari, the Great Royal Wife of Ra Mesis II. This is because in function, Osir is a title speaking to one's role as elevated, in fact, deified Ancestor, and has nothing to do with gender. Also, as is demonstrated by the Prt m hrw of the Ancestor Ani, among many others, being Osir is also not restricted or reserved solely for the royalty or the so-called elite. Ani was a scribe, not a Nisu Bity in the literal sense, yet in his Prt M Hrw, the most famous of all Prt M Hrw, he is referred to as the "Osir Ani." Thus Osir was a state of being that all, regardless of class or gender, could attain. Understanding Osir as the Ancestors grants us another perspective on the Osirian tradition and cosmology.

When we speak of Afrikan Spirituality as "Ancestral," in essence we are speaking to the heavy emphasis on familial ties, lineage, the passing on of essential knowledge down the line, and Ancestral veneration. One is taught to honor their predecessors, uphold the family legacy, and maintain the integrity of the traditions and the family name. When we look at the tradition of Osir, we find that the essence of the story revolves around the redemption of Osir by his son Heru. For this reason Heru is called *nDt it.f* "or *Avenger of his Father*." He restores his father's legacy.

When Osir and Auset came in to Kemet, if you will recall, the very first thing they did was teach Maat to the people. They laid down the law. This Law is the tradition, it's the family way. Each family has their own way of doing things, their own culture so to speak. Maat was the culture that Osir brought to his people. As it has already been touched upon, Maat is about order and harmony, roles and places, timing. The Peseju nTrw are meant to relate to one another in accordance with Maat. There are proper places and roles. Adherence to these laws keeps chaos at bay. Well we all know what happened. Osir and Nebt Het! Osir is married to Auset, and Nebt Het to Sutesh. These are the proper places. This is the Law. Once this law was broken, chaos entered into the family. Sutesh

usurped the throne, and with Sutesh upon the throne, Maat goes out the window. Osir is killed, without an heir, and Auset is on the run for her life. It is not until Heru comes through the Ancestral line that Osir is redeemed and Maat is re-established in the family.

One of the most profound aspects of the Kemetic spiritual tradition, is the understanding that nTr comes into the world as its own Creation. For these Afrikan people, Creator and Creation are one. In this way the very essence' of everything that exists is nTr, and in reality nTr alone exists. This means that everything that makes us up, the very energy and intelligence that we consist of, is nTr. The same holds true for the Osirian tradition. Osir dies, yet he is reborn through his seed, Heru. Osir is Heru and Heru is Osir. This is the idea that we are our own Ancestors come back, and that when we leave this plane of existence, we are reborn through our Ancestral Bloodline. This is the Afrikan equivalent of the eastern concept of reincarnation, which in our tradition is called *waham Ankh* or *"repeating life.".* We find this concept present amongst the Chewa People in Kenya, the BaManianga people of the Kongo, the Yoruba people of Nigeria and their concept of Atunwa, and the Akan people of Ghana to name a few.

In the same way that the very essence of our being is nTr, and everything that makes us up is nTr, likewise everything that we consist of physically, we inherit from our Ancestors. Just as Heru is the culmination of Osir and Auset coming together, so each and every person is a culmination of their parents coming together, and what they were made of at the time of their conception. In fact, Heru is a product of the conditions surrounding his conception. He exists because of what happened to his father, what his mother went through.

Everything that our parents ate, thought, did, etc, trickled down to the chemical level. It registered in their blood; in their genes. We came forth through, and by way of that blood, those genes. This inheritance plays a major role in determining our natal constitution, physically, and goes on to determine much of our capacity. This is the reason why doctors ask their patients if there is a history of a particular type of disease or illness in their family, including mental illnesses. What we inherit can create predispositions and inclinations within us from day one. We inherit the good things; talents, genius, but we also inherit their issues, their scars, their demons. Just as physical diseases can be handed down genetically, also spiritual, emotional, psychological diseases and imbalances can be passed on.

This is an important point to understand. Everything ultimately translates or distills down into the physical, even something as subtle as our thinking. Even our thoughts have a biochemical dynamic to them, they translate physically and mentally. This is why stress and emotions, though they may start out as pure ideation, we see the effects of them in our bodies. Likewise, in the reverse, things that we do physically, things that we ingest, can have an effect on our minds. Also, the way that we think, our thought process, after a while can actually become "hardwired" in our brains as actual brain tissue...i.e. the "word" literally "becomes flesh." These things translate into the blood and goes on to shape our seeds, chemically.

If Osir represents the Ancestors, then Heru represents the living descendent of the Ancestors. Once again this goes for both male and female. Each and every person that is born into the physical plane is Heru, yet each and every person that is born is their own Ancestor, Osir, come back. In a way Heru is actually the vehicle and avatar of Osir. He is Osir's "face."

There has been much debate over the meaning of the name Heru. Some people have incorrectly translated Heru to mean "Hawk," since that is one of his main symbols. However, just because Heru is depicted often as a Hawk, or a man with the head of a Hawk, does not automatically denote that Heru means hawk. In actuality the word for "hawk" in mdw nTr is "*bik*," and not Hrw or Hr. Also, though the hawk is one of his main symbols, Heru is also associated with the lion, bull, and is also depicted fully as a man. One does not say that his name is "Ka," or "Rumuth", or "Miyu" or "Ru" because of these associations. Likewise, we cannot simply settle on "hawk" as the meaning of Heru. Many

scholars, understanding this, have taken the name to mean "that which is above," or that which is "far off or removed," and is usually associated with the high flight of the Hawk. Because many of these scholars interpret Heru as a "sky god," they settle on this etymology for his name. However, though this is much better than hawk, there is not sufficient evidence text wise to support this meaning either. To discern the meaning of Heru's name we have to delve into the Mdw nTr language.

When we look at the glyphs that make up name of Heru we have Hr,

and ▭ Hr. The latter symbol is usually written along with the former as the latter can be vocalized either Hr, or Pt. So we can say here

that the main bilateral for the Hr sound is ☺ . Hr or ☺ literally means face. However, this sound and symbol is associated with words such as "above" (as our heads rest above our bodies), "far away/removed," "upon" (as in to rest upon the sur-face of something), chief/authority (the "head" of a group or clan), etc. Some of the simpler terms associated with this sound have meanings of conveyance such as "with," "by way of," and causality as in "because of." All of these are connected to the personage of Heru in the literature through the use of "Paronymy." However, the clearest meaning is in the glyph itself, which is a head or face. From here we can deduct other interpretations and meanings, such as the surface, above, top, high, etc.

When we look at Heru conceptually, we come to understand that he is the face of Osir, the façade. He is the earthly personification of his Father. He is what we see, the face, the surface. He is that which is "above," while Osir, exist within, below or beneath the surface in the Duat or so called "under-world." Heru, in his association with the so-called "Kingship" we see that he is the "Head" and "Face" of the Nation. When one looked at the Nisu Bity, one was looking at the Nation; one was looking at the Ancestors. The same holds true for the Divine

Kingships that still exist within the Afrikan Continent today. The Nisu is a symbol, an Avatar, the conveyor or vehicle of the Divine and the Ancestors. He is their face. Even in his association with the "sky" the focus tends to be on his "eyes." Heru is said to have two "eyes" one solar and one lunar. The "Eye of Heru" is offered to the nTrw and Ancestors during rituals. However, the focus on the symbolism of eyes adds even more weight to Heru as the head or face, in that anything that has eyes, those eyes exist within the head or face.

In relationship to conveyance, we find Heru as a vehicle or medium of Osir. If we take a look at the so-called Pyramid Texts, we find many examples of Heru as a vehicle of Osir. In several places in the Pyramid Texts Heru is referred to as "Henu." The Henu is the boat that carries the nTr Sukari from the "East" to the "West" and back again. Sukari is the form that Osir takes when he is awakened and elevated in the Duat as ruler of the Duat. In the "Litany to Sukari" Sukari is called "the living Ba of Osir," "Wsir m nTr Grtt" that is "Osir in the Duat." Interesting to note, as it will be expounded upon in a moment, is the fact that the zoo-type for Sukari is also a hawk.

As "Heru Henu," Heru carries Sukari. In "Utterance 347:620 b,c, it is said that:

"Heru has set you up in his name of Henu, he carries you in your name of Sukari."

In Utterance 645:1824 a-g it is said that:

> *"Heru carries you in the Henu, he carries you as a nTr in your name of Sukari, as he carries his father. Osir, he unites himself with you. You shall be powerful over Upper Kemet as Heru, over whom you have power. You shall be powerful over Lower Kemet as Heru, over whom you have power. You shall be powerful; you shall be protected in your body from*

your enemy."

The same notion is expressed in Utterance 647. Thus we see that Heru is the Henu, that is the Ship that carries his father Osir/Sukari from the East to the West, and from the West to the East; yet Heru exist in the East i.e. the "land of the living." It is also expressed here that Osir-Sukari shall have power over Upper and Lower Kemet as Heru, to further demonstrate that Heru is a vehicle and medium of Osir, his Ancestor, and also a conveyor of his Will. Again in Utterance 347 it is declared that "Heru has equipped you (Osir) with his eye...he opened the eye so you may see with it. Heru is not far from you, you are his Ka." This speaks volumes to the nature of the relationship between Osir and Heru, in that it is through the eyes of his living descendent, Heru, that he sees, and it even goes as far to state that Osir is the Ka of Heru. The Ka has been translated as Spirit, but extends to mean genius, personality, Double, etc. The Ka is born along with the Khat of each person. It is the hidden essence that makes a person or thing who and what they are. It is this aspect of the spirit that takes up residence in shrines or statues dedicated to the Ancestor/Deity, and also possess mediums, allowing us to interface and communicate with them. To state that Osir is Heru's Ka, it to make the statement that after the physical vessel, the Khat that is Heru is gone, it is Osir that remains, or beyond the Khat, the twin essence that gives life and unique expression to it, the real person, the Ka is Osir. This same statement speaks to the essence of Kemetic Spirituality, in that regardless of what the physical vessel may look like, the essence of a thing, a person is nTr. When we look at someone, we see the face of their Ancestors.

When we look at a thing, we are looking at a culminating point, an effect. We are looking at the birth; a process that has come to a head. In truth this is another way to understand the trinities in the Kemetic Cosmology; as the law of cause and effect. As it relates to the Osirian Triune, Osir is the hidden Cause, Auset is the e-motional (movement); the evolutionary process in between, and Heru is the Effect, the result. A child comes in to being from the coming together of his mother and father. His coming into being physically was initiated by his father's impregnation of his mother. The Father is the cause. However, from here, the entire evolutionary process, the nurturing, the nourishing, the bulk of the genetic and physical matter that will become this child, develops in the womb of the mother. From the mother, after the process is complete, the child is born from her womb. The child is the effect. He is what comes after the equal sign in the equation. It was stated in an earlier chapter that Auset is the force that "brings things to a head," this being so, Heru is that "head," the culmination.

We are a culminating point in a long line of people, and events that came before us, and all of the information that was taken in; all of the experiences. All of this was registered in our DNA. This DNA, this blood, is our lineage. It is our "Tree of Life," or "Family Tree." From an Afrikan perspective, we are because of what our Ancestors are/were, and we are not only responsible to and for ourselves, but also to our Ancestors. As we journey in life, we should keep in mind that we are a vessel of our Ancestors, we are their face, and our actions should reflect and elevate (glorify) them. This should be reflected in our thoughts, as well as our lifestyle, including who it is that we marry and mate with.

Sexual reproduction is in essence the exchange of Ancestral Information, and the joining together of bloodlines. Just as with anything else, we should be mindful of what we are taking in; what we are ingesting. We should be careful of who we are mixing chemicals with. Who are their Ancestors? What is their mindset? What is their lifestyle? What is their diet like? All of these questions should be taken into consideration because our actions not only affect us, but also our Ancestors, our children who are in essence our Ancestors come back. When we marry someone, we actually marry their Ancestors as well, and they marry ours. It's a collective/communal thing. In Henensu, we marry before the Ancestral Shrines, and we make oaths to the Ancestors and to the community that we shall elevate them as we elevate ourselves and one another. This is the great circle of life. Everything that we do, mentally or physically, is going to translate chemically, and will go on to either elevate the Ancestors, our Bloodline, or add more corruption to it. As

Heru it is our job to avenge Osir; to remove corruption and establish Maat. With that in mind, once again, we must be mindful of whom we're mixing chemicals with.

I recall once in my early stages on the path, that I was paid a visit from my Ancestors. I was still rather young, so as a young, single man full of fire, I had a very high sexual appetite. Anyway I was studying the art and importance of retaining the seed, during sexual intercourse. I was learning how constantly spilling your seed, or ejaculating, over time depleted the life energy and health, and sooner or later "Smack!" right into that brick wall of exhaustion. Now though I was studying this, I had not as of yet mastered this science. Anyway, one day after spilling my seed, I laid down and closed my eyes. As soon as I closed my eyes I saw all of these Ancestors standing around the bed. This experience along with a few more dreams and divination, made the message clear, that although this seed comes through me, it does not solely belong to me. It is sacred. It is a vehicle through which I assist my Ancestors to come into the world. In fact, it is a vehicle that carries my Ancestors, and all of the information and experiences accumulated over eons of time. This recalls to mind the story of Heru's seed asking the question "shall I spill out onto the ground, even though I am Divine Seed?"

It is through our "seeds;" our children that the Ancestors come back into the world. In the Pyramid Texts, utterance 364-370, it is said that Heru:

> *"gives his children to you (Osir) that they may carry you."*

It also states that:

> *"Heru has accustomed himself to his children, you have united yourself with those of his body (his children)."*

212

These statements add on to the previous statements, in that not only does Heru carry Osir, but the children of Heru also carry Osir, being united with him. In other words, not only do we carry Osir, our Ancestors, but our children carry them as well. They are Osir, but when they are born, they are Heru, and they carry Osir, those Ancestors which have not yet reincarnated. It is a cycle that can go on for eternity, which is one of the reasons why Osir is called "Traverser of Millions of Years." He exists, potentially, eternally within his lineage, constantly coming into being through cycles of deaths and rebirths, through his Ancestral line. This is the great secret of how nTr continues and perpetuates its existence. Every time that a child is born, nTr is born.

Another important aspect of the teaching of Osir as the Ancestors is his relationship, physically to the seed/semen. Osir corresponds to the sperm/semen that conveys the Ancestors physically. This is part of the reason why he is depicted in all white garbs, and the symbolism behind the shape of his crown which is called "Hejet" (White). The crown itself is made to resemble the phallus, but the head of the crown itself, is made to resemble a sperm cell. The Sperm Cell/Semen is the sex cell of the male, and it is this cell that makes him "it" or father. To add weight to this we see that in the 42nd chapter of the Prt M hru (Ani), in which Osir is describing various parts of his body identifying them with a particular nTr, when he gets to his phallus he states "*iw Hnn n Wsir m Wsir*," that is, "*The Phallus of Osir is Osir*." So while his face is Ra, his eyes are Het Heru, lips Anpu, ears Wapuwat, etc, when it comes to the phallus, he himself is the phallus. Once again, the phallus is the vehicle of semen/sperm, and it is this organ that gives us the capacity to be father. One should also keep in mind that Osir is also considered a nTr of Husbandry, which is the science of agriculture or seeding.

Further we find that in the book of "Am Duat," "Traversing the Duat," in the 5th hour, Osir is present in his form as Sukari, and Auset is present before him in the form of an egg. Auset's Head sits atop the "Egg of Sukari." This egg is considered the place where the solar union of Ra and Osir take place, it is the place of "Solar recreation," regeneration, rebirth,

and bodily renewal within the Duat. This egg is also surrounded by Nun. The egg is referred to as the "**sSTA n wsir**" or "**Mystery of Osir**." In this egg, Ra unites with Osir, and his body is renewed. From here he continues to make his journey towards the East. This Egg is also the egg that Ra emerged from to begin creation, and is associated with the Yatin. The fact that Auset, the chief maternal nTrt's head adorns the top of the egg gives insight into it's meaning. This is her egg, the "egg of the Mother," and in a way it is being stated that she is the egg herself. As it has been touched upon earlier, Auset is said to have given birth to creation. Osir/Sukari/Ra's transformation takes place once they enter into the egg, and it is from the egg that they are born. Once Osir, the seed, enters into Auset, the egg, new life can emerge.

As mentioned earlier, there is a relationship between the Duat and the womb. The Duat is the place from which life is born into the physical plane, and it is the place where life returns to ultimately be born again. Physically speaking, the Duat is the womb, it is Auset. Within the Duat, the union of Osir/Sukari, the seed, and Auset, the egg, takes place. Interesting enough, this union takes place almost midway in the journey through the Duat, which is a cyclical journey.

Ra represents Life, and Osir/Sukari represents the Ancestor. Once they unite within the egg, the journey continues until they emerge from the Duat, being born in the east as Khepri, and also Heru Pa Khrad. For this reason, Sukari, in his litany, is also called "Sedenu per m khat," that is "Prince who comes forth from the womb," making the link between him and Heru Pa Khrad even more solidified.

Finally, to bring this point home, we also have the teaching regarding the sounds that are associated with the "mysteries of Osir," which are the sounds of" women wailing and mourning," and the sound of a male bull experiencing "sexual pleasure," or an orgasm. These two sounds are polar opposites. However, they capture fully, the mystery and secret of the Osirian Ancestral Tradition.

The Wailing is a part of the funerary ritual. It is associated with the

214

burial of the deceased and their enshrinement as an Ancestor. In many traditions, mourning was a very important part of the funerary ritual, and in many cases there was an elaborate set of rituals that were carried out over an extended period of time. The purpose of the mourning was to assist in the awakening of the Ancestor, and the empowering of their Ka, causing them to become "effective." The power in the mourning came from the intense focused emotions on the Ancestor, which fed energy to their Ka, and assisted in creating a strong link and ritual presence in the minds of their descendants. This being the case, mourning was a very elaborate ritual that could last for several months, and in some cultures as many as three years. It all went to create a powerful link between the Ancestor and the community.

The sound of a bull experiencing an orgasm represents the moment that houses the potential for that very same Ancestor from the funeral to be reborn again; the moment when the male ejaculates and impregnates the woman. Bulls were considered creatures of high virility. As a testament to this fact, the word for "bull" in Madu nTr is "Ka," Which is written with an erect phallus, which in some cases the phallus is also emitting seed. When we examine a name such as Kamut.f, which means "Bull of his Mother," we find that this name is used to refer to several male nTrw that are considered "Self Begotten" or "Self Created." Osir is among these nTrw that are associated with the bull as he is called "kA Imntt," or "Bull of the West," and he is also associated with the "Bull of Heaven that mates with the "even Sacred Cows."It is also interesting to note that during the Opening of the Mouth Ceremony, which is the name of one of the main funerary rituals; there are two bulls that are sacrificed to the Ka of the Ancestor. Once the bull is slaughtered, the heart is offered to the Ancestor as a symbolic gesture for the offering of Heru's heart, or that of the descendant to the Ancestor as a symbol of offering one's self as their vessel.

Another name for Osir that speaks to his association with sexual potency and virility is "**Osir wtt**," that is "**Osir the Begetter**." Sexual potency and fertility is a very important part of African culture and spiritual traditions. The Kemetic people were very practical people, and they

understood clearly that life takes place through the sexual intercourse between a man and a woman. And being that Maat is about life and that which perpetuates it, sex is considered a sacred part of life that is full of creative power. Sex is considered so sacred that creation is spoken of taking place through the intercourse of masculine and feminine principles. For this reason, practices such as celibacy and homosexuality are relatively unheard of, or shunned in Kemetic culture, just as is the case with most Afrikan societies. Taking all of this into account, it should be clear that there is a connection between Osir and the actual semen of a man.

When we look at DNA cosmologically, we find many correlations to aspects of the Kemetic Tradition, and also concepts of Astro and Quantum Physics. For instance, the primordial waters from which one rises and comes into being is one's DNA; one's Blood. The Genes that code, and their specific configurations, are reflected also in the coming into being of specific nTrw, and also one's astrological configuration at birth. Also we find that what scientist refer to as "non-coding DNA or" or so-called "Junk" DNA, has a very interesting resemblance to Dark Matter of Astro-Physics. According to physicist, Dark Matter is matter that does not emit photons, which means that it cannot be detected directly. Also, because it does not emit photons, this also allows it to pass through physical phenomenon undetected. The main reason why its existence is substantiated is due to the fact that its presence can be deducted and ascertained through the effect that it has on what we can see, somewhat of a magnetic or gravitational type of affect. Be that as it may, scientists are convinced that the bulk of the universe consist of this substance, literally sitting within it. Similarly, Non-Coding DNA is reference to the bulk of genetic material that does not code. This material makes up approximately Ninety-Eight percent of our genetic material. However, though these Gene's themselves do not code, they have an effect on the Genes that do code. It has also been noted that when certain conditions are present, some of these genes may become activated. These Genes are our Ancestors within us, and are responsible for much of who we are, how we look, etc. Their "coding" is another way to speak to their "incarnating."

216

Recent research has found that genetics has the strongest influence on a person's psychological traits and well-being. This research also concluded that genetics has a major impact on how one views themselves and the world, sense of purpose, how they interact with others, and their capacity to continue learning and evolving. All of this went on to determine their general capacity for success in life. This is something that the Ancients understood very well. From here it can be ascertained that one's Ancestors plays a major role in determining one's destiny, at the least from a constitutional level; chemically.

Some scholars have made the error of stating that the Kemetyu did not have a concept of Re-incarnation. However, with the careful examination of the kemetic literature it can be clearly seen that they saw life as a continuous circle, spanning across several incarnations. This concept can be derived from the various Duat texts, such as Am Duat, and the "Book of Gates," in regards to Ra/Osir's journey into the Duat, and back into the land of living, reborn. Also, there are concrete examples of "reincarnation" in other texts as well. One such text is the story of the "Magician" Si Osir.

According to the Story, a Kushite Magician came to Kemet to challenge the magicians of the Nisu, to prove that the "juju" of Kush was more powerful than that of Kemet. To do so he brought a sealed scroll and challenged all of the Kemetic Magicians/Priests to tell him the contents of the scroll without opening it. The Nisu entrusted Setna, whom he deemed to be worthiest of the challenge, with the task. Setna went home and was pretty much distraught because he knew that he was unable to read the scroll. However, in hearing of his father's situation, Si-Osir laughed and told his father not to worry for he would take up the Kushite's challenge. Now Si-Osir was just a little boy and his father had no idea just how powerful this young man was. So to test him, Setna sealed one of his personal letters and asked Si-Osir to read it, and to his astonishment, Si-Osir read the letter flawlessly. When the time came for Setna to face off with the Kushite, he presented Si-Osir to him, stating "My little son will deal with this guy." Si-Osir then began to read the

contents of the scroll. It told the story of events that took place 1500 years in the past (at that time), in which some Kushite's used juju to get the upper hand on, and embarrass the Nisu Bity of Kemet. As a result, the Nisu sanctioned his best Magician at that time and had him return the favor, and then bind the Kushite Magician by oath that he would never try this again. After Si-Osir finished reading, the Kushite in amazement confessed that what Si-Osir read was in fact the truth. However, before they released the Kushite, Si-Osir admonished them from doing so by revealing that the Kushite that stood before them was in fact the same Kushite from the story, from 1500 years ago. Further, Si-Osir then revealed to everyone, including his father, that he was in fact the Magician that stopped him then, and that when he heard that this guy had left the Duat with the intention of trying to dishonor Kemet, he begged Osir to allow him to come back to stop him once and for all. In doing so he incarnated as Si-Osir (which means "Gift of Osir"), the son of Setna.

Getting back to the Osirian Tradition, as Sutesh took the throne, Isfet, chaos entered into the family. In actuality, even before Sutesh's taking of the throne, it was actually Osir's lack of vigilance and intercourse with Nebt-Het, stepping out of his proper place that began the process of decay in the family. Corruption entered into the blood. It is up to Heru to correct the errors of his predecessors.

So Heru represents the living descendent, who is the redeemer of his Ancestors bad "Karma," and he liberates them from the shackles of the past. His actions are as a cleansing of his Ancestral blood line, re-establishing Maat in the family. This is the role of each and every person that is born. We are here to correct the errors of our Ancestors, remove corruption from the blood, lift them up, and raise them to a higher stage of evolution. We are to remove Sutesh from the throne in our family, in our blood. If this is not done, then our line may continue to degenerate as we'll be dealing with the same issues for years to come. This is the essence of "generational curses." It is corruption, decay; Isfet in the family and blood that has become a perpetual cycle. Heru's job is to break the cycle, and liberate his Ancestors from this "Hell." This is the

218

essence of Nehem nTr as it relates to the Ancestors.

An interesting show that comes on the T.V. is "Who do you think you are." The show is about celebrities that with the assistance of Ancestry.com, are tracing their lineage, and are also researching and learning about their Ancestors. One interesting episode focused on this one Actor, which grew up without knowledge of his paternal Grandfather. His father never knew his father, and his grandfather never knew his father either. So the actor began to conduct his research, and he found that his grandfather was a "bigamist," and left his (the actor's) father and family to live with another family. He also found that his Grandfather's father had done the same, because he grew up without his father who died when he was very young. So what we saw was in essence, a cycle of corruption that needed to be broken. The line needed to be healed. It wasn't until the Actor's father came through the line, that things were set straight in this regard. In this way, his father was the "Heru" of their family. If this cycle wasn't broken by his father, who knows how long it would have continued.

Even though everyone that is born is Heru, sometimes conditions can be so corrupt that the Ancestors must send one through that makes a huge impact in establishing order in the blood. Sometimes this person can establish Maat in the entire family, sometimes this person may become so evolved within themselves, that they serve as a new root, to become a new tree that will create a "new species," so to speak, allowing their Ancestors to come through their specific line at a higher state of existence, consciousness, and culture. These people are "The Heru" of their family. It is said that every family has at least one that is consciously Re-membering their Ancestors, and is actually "sent" here to fulfill the mission of restoring Maat, re-establishing the "Kingdom of Osir." All one has to do is just think about how many people they know personally, that is venerating their Ancestors, feeding their kAw, pouring libations, lifting up their name, elevating their consciousness? Don't be surprised if you find yourself on a very small list, if not alone.

For Afrikan people this is a shame. While it is important that everyone,

regardless of their race or ethnicity, understand their connection and relationship with their Ancestors, and consciously lift them up, for Afrikan people, this is something that we did as a collective for countless thousands of years. We should know better, but we've forgotten, we've forgotten Osir. So for the most part, the journey spiritually for Afrikan people worldwide is for us to Re-member.

We have to Re-member Osir, our Ancestors, and our responsibility to them, and them to us. It's a reciprocal thing. They still play an active role in our lives and the lives of the family and the community, even though they are not "physically" here. We forgot that, and because we've forgotten them, we've ceased to lift them up, and have neglected their shrine. This is something that is a reality for Afrikan people worldwide, including those on the continent. We've neglected our Ancestors following behind "strange gods." We venerate everyone else's Ancestors but neglect our own. We shun and look down upon our ancient ways and practices because those that have been the slave masters and colonizers of our people do so. But the truth of the matter is, while we are neglecting our spiritual culture and sciences, Europeans are picking them up!

I cannot tell you how many times I turn around and see a Caucasian claiming to be "an Authentic Voodoo Priest," a "Houngan," a Babalawo, the "Nisu Bity," etc. While we sit around afraid to even look at our traditions, they are picking them up and rocking them! Meanwhile we are practicing the so-called religions that they gave, and imposed upon us. However, we fail to realize that we are still practicing Ancestral Veneration, just not the veneration of our Ancestors, but those of our oppressors. The Western traditions are bastardized and whitewashed versions of our great Ancestral Traditions. When we give our attention, energy, and sacrifices to them, we are venerating/worshiping their ancestors, and they take that energy and direct it towards furthering their national agendas.

These so-called religions, are nothing more than poor copy's of the original; a cheap bootleg. They've taken from our sciences, flipped them, and sold it back to us, while demonizing the original. So we fail to realize that "worshiping" or venerating "Jesus," conceptually is Ancestral Worship. "How?" you say. Well, he lived (allegedly) he died (allegedly) he was buried, and then was elevated to a position of power and authority in the spirit realm or heaven. Not only that, by calling upon this "living dead man" He will come to your aid or rescue...i.e. save you. How in the world is this not Ancestral Veneration by another name; in another skin? Whenever we venerate their prophets, saints, deities, etc, we are venerating their Ancestors. Meanwhile, our Ancestors are starving, and the ones that we are worshiping are kicking our behinds!

We once understood the interconnectedness and interdependence between this realm and the spirit realm. For Afrikan people, our community consists of the living and the Ancestors, and also future generations, and all are taken into consideration in our daily affairs. For us, the Ancestors are very much a reality, and play an active role in the lives of those that are still physically here. The success of the family, and the community, are dependent upon the maintenance of this relationship. If this relationship is established and strong, then "the way is open" for us to receive guidance and assistance from them, through ritual, divination, communication via dreams, and their actual intervention in our affairs. For this to take place, their kA(w) must be strong.

The Ka, as we've mentioned in this work, Is the part of a thing that gives it its personality and uniqueness. It is the "Spiritual Person" that exists beyond the physical body. For this reason it has also been translated as "double," to speak to the fact that it is somewhat of a spiritual "twin" of the physical person that lives. This part of the individual survives the death of the body or Khat. Along with the Ka survives the person's talents and capabilities, and whatever mental characteristics and genius they may have possessed. Depending upon the level of consciousness to which person has attained, the Ka of that individual may be weak, or very powerful and "effective." If the Ka is not already powerful by the efforts of the individual in their physical life and experience, then it may become powerful in the spirit realm through rituals, offerings, and

221

sacrifices performed on their behalf. This is to say, that just because one may "die" on a certain level, does not mean that their evolution stops. Their journey continues in the Duat, and through time and effort on their part, and on the part of those that are keeping their shrines, they may become very powerful. Also, it should be known that the Ka is a spiritual body that must be "fed." All of the various bodies that make up a thing must be fed as it is all energy and everything that is energy must consume energy in some form. Everything eats. If these spiritual/mental bodies are not "fed" they cannot develop and may degenerate. Just as a person that is physically alive will scrounge for food, and eat anything edible if they find themselves in a starved and malnourished state; or may steal for food, likewise kAw, XAbytw will also become starved and malnourished and eat whatever they can get. They may become parasitic, and feed off of the energy of the living and other spiritual bodies. This is the true essence of many so-called haunting and possessions. These are in many cases starved KAw. Many of them are not bad or evil, just hungry. Because they are not in a state of Hetep (peace and satisfaction), they go on to create dissonance and dissatisfaction in their environment, which includes the physical plane, and many times this is unintentional. Most of these KAw need to be elevated and fed, and there are rituals that can be done for those purposes.

When we look at the state of our people worldwide, we are looking at a tree that has been cut at the roots. The disconnection in those roots is between us and our Ancestors. Afrikan people worldwide have abandoned our traditions and are no longer feeding the KAw of our Ancestors. As a result, most of our Ancestors are in a diseased and miserable state, and our condition is a direct reflection of that. Many of us have even become disrespectful in regards to our Ancestors, which is to place a curse upon ourselves. If we disrespect our Ancestors, then we disrespect the very blood within our veins, and our blood becomes a curse to us. Isn't it interesting that the major diseases and epidemics that are wiping our people out by the millions are diseases of the blood?

If our Ancestors were fed and happy, then we would be fed and happy, and flourishing. We would be able to receive insight from them for they are able to see things that most are unable to see, and can affect things on a level that many could not fathom. This is something that the Kemetyu understood very well, and it is the reason why great importance was placed upon the Ancestral traditions. Even though the Inner Sanctuaries of the temples were reserved for the initiated priesthood, and the general populous of the uninitiated were not allowed into the temples; were not permitted to work directly with the shrines of the nTrw, everyone was expected to work with and keep the shrines of their Ancestors. One simply has to look at the examples of the letters that were written to one's Ancestors as proof that they understood the importance of keeping their shrines, and the fact that the Ancestors were expected to play an active role in the lives of their families and communities.

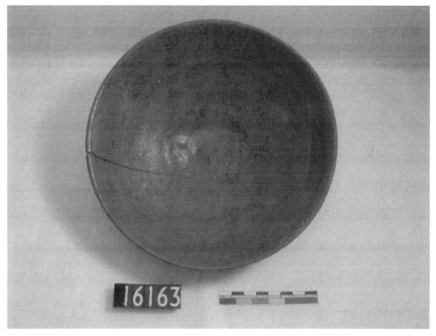

Figure 1:Letter to the Deceased Parent of Shepsi, at Qau Petrie Museum of Egyptian Archaeology, University College, London

Many of the letters were written in bowls, in which offerings may have been placed. The subject matter tends to range from asking assistance of the Ancestor in regards to legal cases, protection, settling family

disputes, and also combating one's enemies. One example of such a letter is the letter of Shepsi to his parents. The letter reads as follows:

Inside:

Shepsi speaks to his father Iinekhenmut.

This is a reminder of your journey to the dungeon (?), to the place where Sen's son Hetepu was, when you brought the foreleg of an ox*, and when this your son came with Newaef, and when you said, Welcome, both of you. Sit and eat meat! Am I to be injured in your presence, without this your son having done or said anything, by my brother? (And yet) I was the one who buried him, I brought him from the dungeon (?), I placed him among his desert tomb-dwellers, even though thirty measures of refined barley were due from him by a loan, and one bundle of garments, six measures of fine barley, one ball (?) of flax, and a cup- even though I did for him what did not (need) to be done. He has done this against this your son evilly, evilly - but you had said to this your son, 'All my property is vested in my son Shepsi along with my fields'. Now Sher's son Henu has been taken. See, he is with you in the same city. You have to go to judgment with him now, since your scribes are with (you) in the same city. Can a man be joyful, when his spears are used [against his own son (??)] ?

Outside:

Shepsi speaks to his mother Iy.

This is a reminder of the time that you said to this your son 'Bring me quails for me to eat', and when this your son brought to you seven quails for you to eat. Am I to be injured in your presence, so that the children are badly discontent with this your son? Who then will pour out water for you? If only you would judge between me and Sobekhotep! I brought him from another town, and placed him in his town among his male and female dead, and gave him burial cloth. Why then is he acting against this your son, when I have said and done nothing, evilly, evilly? Evil-doing is painful for the gods!

Another example is the letter of Merti to her Ancestor, who in this case is her son Mereri:

O Mereri, Son of Merti. The nTr Osir Khenti Imentiyu assures that you shall live for millions of years, by providing for the breath in your nose and by placing bread and beer by the side of Het-Heru, lady of the Horizon. Your condition is like one who lives millions of times by the order of the nTrw who are in heaven and on earth. You make obstacles to enemies who have evil characteristics and who are against your house, against your brother, and your mother who loves her excellent son Mereri. You were excellent on earth and you are beneficent in the land of the Ancestors. Invocations and offerings are made for you. The Haker Festival is celebrated for you. Bread and beer are placed upon the altar of the nTr Khenti Imentiyu. You sailed downstream in the night bark; you sailed upstream in the day bark. You are justified in front of every nTr. Make yourself my

favorite Ancestor. You know that he said to me, "I shall report against you and your children." You report against it. You are in the place of justification.

The following example demonstrates that appeals were made in some cases, on behalf of the entire family:

This is a reminder of the fact that I told you regarding myself, "You know that Idu said regarding his son, 'as for what may be in store in the beyond, I won't let him suffer from any affliction.' Please do the like thereof for me."Now I have brought this jar stand over which your mother should institute litigation. May it be agreeable for you to support her. Moreover, let a healthy son be born to me, for you are an able spirit. Now as for those two maid-servants, Nefertjentet and Itjai, who have caused Seny to be afllicted, confound them! And banish for me whatever afllictions are directed against my wife, whom you know I have need of. Banish them completely! As you live for me, may the Great One favor you and the face of the Great God be kindly disposed toward you and he give you pure bread from his two hands. Furthermore, it is for your daughter that I am begging a second healthy son.

However, there are also examples of letters in which the surviving member suspects that the Ancestor may be unhappy and as a result is either causing or allowing misfortune to fall upon the house and family:

An offering which the king gives to Osir and Anpu who is upon his mountain, that voice offerings may be made to the revered . . . tjat. It was without any discontentment on your part against me that you were brought here to the city of eternity. If it is the case that these injuries are being inflicted with your knowledge, see, the house is held by your children, and yet misery is renewed. If it is the case that they are being inflicted against your will, your deceased father remains influential [in] the necropolis. If there is a reproach in your heart, forget it for the sake of your children. Be gracious; be gracious that all the nTrw of the Thinite nome might be gracious to you.

To the able spirit Ankhiry:

What have I done against you wrongfully for you to get into this evil disposition in which you are? What have I done against you? As for what you have done, it is your laying hands on me even though I committed no wrong against you. From the time that I was living with you as a husband until today, what have I done against you that I should have to conceal it? What [have I done] against you?' As for what you have done, it is the reason for my laying a plaint against you, although what have I done against you? I shall contend at law with you in the presence with the words of my mouth, that is, in the presence of the ennead of the West, and it shall be decided between you and [me through] this letter because a dispute with you is what I've written about. What have I done against you? I took you for a wife when I was a youth so that I was with [you] while I was functioning in every office and you were

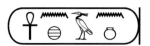

with me. I did not divorce [you], nor did I cause you to be vexed. Now, I took you (for a wife) when I was a youth, and I functioned in every important office for Nisu Bity, l.p.h., without my divorcing [you], saying, "She has got to be with [me] ," so I would say. And when any visitors(?) came to me in your presence, did I not receive them out of consideration for you, saying, "I will do according to your desire"? Now look, you aren't letting my mind be at ease. I shall litigate with you, and right shall be distinguished from wrong. Now look, when I was instructing officers for Nisu Bity's infantry and his chariotry, I [had] them come and prostrate themselves before you, bringing every sort of fine thing to set before [you]. I concealed nothing at all from you during your lifetime. I did not let you suffer discomfort [in] anything I did with you after the manner of a lord, nor did you find me cheating on you after the manner of a field hand, entering a strange house. I did not let an upbraider find fault with me [in] anything I did with you. And when I was assigned to the post in which I now am, I became unable to go out as had been my habit. I got to doing what someone who is in the same situation as I does when he is [at] home [regarding] "your oil, your bread, and your clothes; and they would be brought to you. I didn't direct them elsewhere, but said, "The woman is still with me(?)," so I would say and not cheat on you. Now look, you are disregarding how well I have treated you. I'm writing [you] to make you aware of the things you are doing. When you became ill with the disease which you contracted, I [sent for] a chief physician, and he treated you and did what you told him to do. Now when I went accompanying Nisu Bity, l.p.h., in journeying south, this condition (i.e., death) befell you, and I spent these several months without eating or drinking like a normal person. When I arrived in Memphis, I begged leave of Nisu Bity, l.p.h., and [came] to where you were. And I and my people wept sorely for you before [you] (i.e., your body) in my quarter(?). I donated clothing of fine linen to wrap you up in and had many clothes made. I overlooked nothing good so as not to have it done for you. Now look, I've spent these last three years without entering (another) house although it is not proper that one who is in the same situation as I be made to do this. Now look, I've done this out of consideration for you. Now look, you don't differentiate good from evil. One will judge between you and me. Now look, as for those sisters in the household, I have not entered into a one of them (sexually).

These letters and several more show that the Ancestors had power to affect various aspects of life, from protection, conception and child birth, assisting in matters of justice, and also healing illnesses. All of the above examples clearly demonstrate that not only were the Ancestors considered alive in the Duat, but also they were still considered active parts of the family and community, and their intervention in the resolution of matters was expected and sought. Also, it should be clear that not only was it important that they were taken care of, that they might be happy and helpful, but also that if by chance they were unhappy, they might cause some trouble for their family as well. This is a concept that can be found throughout Afrika and the Diaspora as it relates to our spiritual traditions.

Perhaps the greatest example of the consequences of Ancestral neglect is the story of Khnum and the Seven Year Famine. The bulk of this story was told in the chapter on the cosmologies; however, for our purposes

here, we shall revisit some of the key points to bring another important principle to light.

According to the tradition, Kmt had been in famine for seven years. The people were greatly impoverished, for there wasn't any food. Many people left, many people died. The people of Kmt began to rob and steal from one another. Men lacked the strength to walk, children cried, the elderly were crushed in despair, and rubbed themselves in great pain. Shrines were unkept and dirty. It is said that the Nisu Bity, Djoser, "turned his heart towards the past," and sought counsel with Imhotep, his vizier. He asked Imhotep "In which place is Hopi (The Nile) born?," "What town?," "Which nTr lives there?." Imhotep went to the temple to retrieve the information for his Nisu. Upon his return, he informed Djoser of regarding the origins of the Hopi, his ancestors, and that Khnum was the nTr there. He then informed him of all of the nTrw that had shrines in the temple there, and what items he needed to bring as offerings. Djoser quickly made his way there. Once he arrived he found the temple there in complete shambles. It is said that he purified himself and performed a ritual along with offerings and sacrifices to Khnum of "bread, beer, geese, cattle, and all the good things…," and shortly after fell asleep before the shrine. While sleeping, Khnum appeared to the Nisu, and informed him about himself (Khnum), all of the things he had done, and informed the Nisu as to the reason for Kmt being in the condition that it is in. Khnum said:

> "I am Khnum, your creator. My arms are around you, to steady your body, to protect your limbs…I bestowed on your ore and precious stones from antiquity, and they were not used to build temples, rebuild ruins, sculpt shrines for his master (Khnum)…It is up to me let loose the well (Hopi)…"

Because of Djoser's offerings and repair of Khnum's temple, life, prosperity, and health returned to Kmt.

The meaning of this story is quite profound. The Nisu's focusing his heart (mind/attention) on the past, and then inquired in to the birth place of the Hopi, symbolizes the fact that he had lost the Knowledge of Self, and forgotten where he came from. While the place named in the story as the birth place if the Nile was Yebu (so-called Elephantine), the actual origins of Nile, in central east Afrika, is the birth place of the Ancestors of Kmt. This is why Imhotep informs him also regarding his ancestors. Djoser had forgotten. This is why he did not know the town, or the names of the Ancestors or nTrw that live there. In fact, from the story we can conclude that this was the general state of Kmt, as even Imhotep had to go and find the answers, and returned with the information later. It should also be noted that the Hopi, not only corresponds to the actual Nile, but symbolically represents the blood, lineage, and the flow of blessings from the spiritual realm. The fact that Khnum is the nTr that lived there further solidifies this point, as he symbolizes the Ba, which as mentioned, is the inner Ancestral Spirit within man. At this point it shouldn't have come as a surprise that the temple and shrines of the nTrw and Ancestors were in complete shambles, as they had not only been neglected, but totally forgotten, and as Khnum informed the Nisu, this was the reason why Kmt was in the condition it was in, seven years of famine, as ultimately all things that come into the world emerge from the Duat, and must first pass through the Ancestors. Afrikan people worldwide should reflect on this story, and contemplate it with regards to our present state as a people; it not only gives great insight into the reason for our predicament, and also the solution that will elevate us from it.

Communion with the Ancestors is very important as they have eyes for things that we are unable to see, and they are able to inform us into things we might have missed, as well as things to come. Also, as it has been stated earlier in this work, when we seek success in life, we must do so with the collective in mind and that includes our Ancestors. There is a reason for our incarnation that is related to the grand scheme of things, and affects our collective destiny. That being said, it is good to get their input, see what they think about our goals. However, if we are on our jobs spiritually and are keeping the lines of communication clear and open, then they often will make their intentions and will known.

Communication with the Ancestors may take place via meditation, dreams, visions, ritual possession via yourself or a medium, oracles, or omens. How they come depends upon how awake/aware we are. The more distracted we are, the more difficult it is for us to hear and see the words and movements of the Spirit. However, when we intentionally seek to communicate with the Ancestors they will make sure that we get the message.

Another important part of Ancestral Veneration is the "Libations," in which the Ren (Name) of the Ancestors are invoked. This is a very important ritual as it has been said "to speak a person's name is to make them to live again." Also the pouring of water while calling the name is very important as water is the essence of life and all living things need it. Water is also symbolic of the spirit. The Osir (Ancestor) Ani instructs us to "Libate for your father and mother, who are resting in the valley; when the nTrw witness your action, they will say: "Accepted." Do not forget the one outside; your son will act for you likewise." Osir (Ancestor) Kheti III says "the soul goes to the place it knows… and it reaches those who give it Water."The Ancestral Libations is almost a universal element in Traditional Afrikan Spirituality and is a very important part of Kemetic Spirituality.

nTrw 11

The nTrw are the forces of nature that underlie, and are responsible for everything that we experience in life. They are the manifold expressions of life. As it has been pointed out in previous chapters, it is through the nTrw, that nTr comes into being, and as nTr comes into being as Creation, the nTrw are the forces of Creation itself.

The act of creation has been defined, as nTr coming into being, from an infinite, undefined, undifferentiated state of pure being; to the defined state of being we call living. This "definition" of nTr is described within the literature as the "limbs" or "members" of nTr, which is a reference first to the nTrw, and more generally all of creation. However, in regards to the nTrw, we recall to mind the cosmology of Men Nefer in which Pitah refers to the nTrw as different aspects of his body ex. *"his heart, his tongue, his teeth, his lips, his seed, his hands,"* etc. We also find it in the **42nd chapter of the Prt M Hru**, in which the various parts of the body of Osir are each described as a nTr, and the statement is made **"nn at im.i Swt m nTr,"** **"Not a member/limb, within me is without an nTr."** We also have the example of the "Litany to Ra," in which there are Seventy-Five nTrw that are declared to be the "**of the body of Ra.**" All of these examples serve to express the understanding that the nTrw are parts of, or aspects of nTr, and it is through the nTrw that nTr lives and expresses itself. It is through the nTrw, that nTr "acts," and experiences itself. It is our body that facilitates our journey through life. It carries us; allows us to express our selves. Our limbs allow us to

do things; create, work, as well as communicate; the nTrw, as limbs or "members" of nTr, serve the same purposes in creation. They are members or limbs of his body, and together they constitute "the oneness of nTr."

This idea has been described as "*The Many and the One*," in which it is understood that **there is one Divine Being**, that manifests itself **through a plurality of forces** (the Many), yet **maintains it's essential Oneness**. This is a concept that is present in many Afrikan traditions, and allows Afrikans, if they so choose, to define their spiritual traditions and worldview as "Monotheistic." However, such a description is not, in my opinion, adequate enough. To describe Afrikan spirituality as "Monotheistic," is to imply that it is monotonous, and causes much of the richness of Afrikan spirituality and culture to become lost in translation. Afrikan Spirituality is "Polyrhythmic." It recognizes the oneness of all things, yet also recognizes that in life this oneness is expressed through order, and the harmony between various things. While the "One" is acknowledged in Afrikan spiritual traditions, it is understood that it is through "the Many" that "the One" is known. It is actually quite poetic, in that it is through the Many that the One comes to "know Self," and in reverse it is through the Many, that we come to know the One (Self), meaning that the "Journey of nTr" and the "Journey of Man" are one and the same journey. How can the "One" be known? Who is there to experience it if there is only the One? "The One" is also "the All," which cannot be defined. It is an Abstract, and it is for this reason that while the One (the All) is a recognized reality, it is normally depicted as a being "aloof," for it is Pure Being/Existence, but in its essential state of Being, it has no defined qualities, no experiences, no needs, no relationships, etc, which makes it impossible for man to relate to. For this reason, the nTrw, the many, are the ones that are considered directly approachable, and are usually the ones engaged through ritual, and depicted in art, crafts etc. Anyway, life happens through variety, and since Afrikan spirituality is about the honor and appreciation of life, the nTrw, the many, are recognized as being just as important as the One, and there is no conflict. At the end of the day the understanding is that ultimately all is nTr. All is one remains the strong foundation, yet

234

the richness and beauty of the experience of the nTrw; the Many, is relished in and appreciated. Both the One and the Many (to even say "both" runs the risk of causing a psychological slip for some), make up the totality of reality, and you cannot have life without these dual aspects.

The nTrw provide avenues for the nTr to know, and be known. However, in the Kemetic tradition, the recognition of both aspects of reality has been expressed in depictions, hymns, etc. Because our people are a people of rhythm and are very imaginative, we have even created stories, and made depictions that allow us to describe the indescribable, fathom the unfathomable, and perceive the unperceivable. This being the case, we find even the All; the One, is "personified" as Imun, Nu/Nun, Niyit, etc, and described in concepts and theories that give Astro and Quantum Physicist nightmares, yet can be grasped even by our children!

In the same way that western science has been able to observe and classify the elements of life, and the various particles and sub atomic particles of matter, our Ancestors were able to observe and classify the various forces that exist in the universe. These forces are referred to as the Peseju nTrw, which has been translated to mean "Company of nTrw" or "Cycle of nTrw." These nTrw were seen to be the motivating forces in operation behind all of the events that take place in the world. Like the classical elements of the Periodic Table of chemistry, the nTrw also serve as the "elements" that constitute all life and matter. This also includes aspects of life not fully understood by the "Physical Sciences," such as the mind and emotions. Life, and everything that it entails; every aspect of it is constituted of these natural forces called nTrw. However, whereas in western science there are several "fields" that are established to deal with the so-called "different" aspects of life and the universe, the Peseju nTrw, provide the ability to unite all sciences under one system. In this way Biology, Astronomy, Physics, Chemistry, Health and Medicine, Psychology, Sociology, Political Science, Philosophy, "theology," etc, are all seen as integral parts of one whole, as at the root of all of them are the same forces, the nTrw that are in operation,

expressing themselves in ways that appear different on a concrete level, but are united on an abstract level. This allows us to gain insight into any area of life, to grasp an understanding of any subject, through an understanding of the forces that are expressing themselves in that particular area. However, instead of utilizing a chart and complicated equations to understand the relationship between certain elements, the Kemetic people, did what Afrikan people have always done, taught about these forces through stories, songs, dances, rhythms, plays, symbols, hymns, litanies, etc, allowing us to not only understand the qualities of these forces individually, but also their deep principles, and how they relate to one another, and in a way, allowing us to learn all of the above subjects and sciences at once.

Another key difference from western science and their understanding and teaching of the classical elements, is while they recognize that these elements serve as a basis of life in their culmination in coming together, they are not necessarily considered "alive." *The nTrw on the other hand, are living forces, meaning, they not only constitute life, but are themselves also alive.* For example, while gold is considered by Western scientist to "exist" or have "Being," it is not considered "alive," as to them it (gold) has no experience, no ability to know, and be aware, or consciously interact with the world (This is what determines whether a thing simply exists or lives). This knowledge and perspective goes further to add to the depth of understanding in regards to these forces because they are understood to be alive, and are experienced as living forces that can be engaged and interfaced with, asked questions and **give coherent answers**, teach, influence, prognosticate, and evolve right along with the world. This is a fact that can be, and has been experienced by Afrikan peoples through Traditional Afrikan Spirituality.

nTrw: Forces of Nature, Principles, or both?

There is much confusion floating around the "Kemetic Community," as to the nature of the nTrw. Are they principles, symbols, etc, or are they forces or deities? With contradicting answers floating around, varying depending on whether or not the person considers themselves to be a scholar, or a spiritualist, the confusion has led to a great stagnation in the aspirant's or seekers growth on the path.

In answering this question truthfully, one must have the integrity to deal with the Kemetic Tradition as they find it; as historically attested, without adding their personal bias to it, or attempting to reinterpret it into what they want it to be. With that being said, the answer to the above questions is "all of the above," that is to say, that the nTrw are forces/deities, principles, and symbols. However, there is an order in which this answer should be understood.

First and foremost, it should be understood that the nTrw are LIVING forces of nature, that are intrinsic to, constitute, and permeate all existence. As Man (Male and Female) exist within and as part of Nature, these forces are also intrinsic to, constitute, and permeate man's Being. Understanding the nTrw as LIVING forces is a precursor to understanding the Kemetic Tradition as a LIVING tradition.

Next, it should be understood that it is from our Ancestor's observation of these forces, their qualities, the natural laws by which they operate, and how they relate to one another and the whole, that principles were derived. In other words, the principles are derived from the observation of the forces at play, and not the other way around. Based on this observation, cosmologies were developed, and the society, social order, culture, and institutions were developed and organized.

Another important question that needs to be addressed is whether or not our Ancestors "worshipped" the nTrw. This question has two "parents." One parent is the misconceived notion that the nTrw are just principles or symbols as mentioned above. The other parent is the

different schools that profess to teach "Knowledge of Self." The argument from these schools is that man is "God," and therefore does not (should not) worship anything outside self. While the rationale behind this argument is fundamentally correct, it is not completely understood from an Afrikan context.

It is true that man (Male and Female) is nTr, but the same can be said of all other things, as nTr alone exists. However, what this means for man, is not truly understood in all its implications, until the oneness, sameness, or intrinsic relationship with nTr is realized, experienced, and lived. In other words, it is not enough to simply say that you are "God" or "Divine," nor is it enough to think or believe it. Believing that you are God, and not completely understanding what it means or actually experiencing this reality, is no different than any other belief. It is in Afrikan traditions and their initiation systems, that this "theory" is determined to be truth. Afrikan Traditions, the wisdom, the ritual science/system, provides one with a closed system and controlled environment to test one's "Godhood."

However, even if actual knowledge and experience of Self/nTr takes place, it does not change the fact that all is nTr. With that said, there is still the acknowledgment, reverence, and adoration of nTr in others. There is the recognition of our essential "oneness," and our responsibility to one another. This last point really applies when we understand our relationship to the nTrw.

From the various texts, temple inscriptions, etc, it is obvious that our Ancestors considered the nTrw actual living forces; real, and they could engage them in different ways. One of the most obvious ways was the temple ritual, and the shrine. One only needs to visit Kemet once to see the shrines, and the depictions of what took place in them, all around the temple walls, to know for a fact that our Ancestors held these forces in very high regard. There are depictions of offerings of libations, beer, wine, food, and animal sacrifices. This alone informs us that they revered these forces. However, we also find images of our Ancestors in a posture called *"dwA"* meaning *"praise," "worship," "adoration,"* etc.

238

We also find this term used in the phrase *"dwA nTr"* meaning *"praise nTr,"* or *"thanks be to nTr."* We find an example of this on the Stela of Muntuhotep:

> *Rx xm Hr mriwt.i*
>
> *Bw nb dwA nTr.n.i*
>
> *The wise and the ignorant loved me*
>
> *Everyone praised (thanked) nTr for me...*

The above Stela demonstrates the fact that the Ancestors gave "praise" or "thanks" to nTr for the good things in life. This in a way is similar to the modern expression "Thank God," or "Praise God," or "Thank you Lord." However, the understanding behind it is different in that nTr is understood to ultimately be the source of all things, is present in/as all things, and is ultimately responsible for all things, including us.

Another phrase that we have to demonstrate how our Ancestors perceived the nTrw and approached them is the phrase *"Sn tA,"* meaning *"Kiss the Ground,"* which speaks to the act of prostration.

"Sn tA" or prostration is an obvious act of reverence or obeisance. It could be interpreted as an act of worship or surrender, or simply an act of honor, as it is still to this day a custom in various parts of Afrika to prostrate before Elders or Royalty. However, this should not be interpreted in a way that gives the impression that one "kisses the earth" before the nTrw out of fear or compulsion. Speaking to this point we have the Stela of Semti in which it is stated:

> *Xnm.n.i nTr m mAat wn.i. im bA.kwi Ax.kwi m zmyt*
>
> *HqA.t nHH iri.i Hmw HAi.i r nSmt sn.i tA n wp-wAt*
>
> *I made nTr happy with Maat, that I may exist*

239

therein as a Ba and effective in the necropolis

Mistress of Eternity, that I may act as an oar when I board the nSmt, and <u>so that I may kiss the earth before Wapuwat</u>

The above passage expresses the sentiment that "Sn tA" was something to be cherished, a privilege, or honor for the individual performing it as an offering to the nTr.

Traditionally, our relationship with the nTrw was one based on acknowledgement, respect, and responsibility, all of which are aspects of Maat or love. We acknowledged their existence, their function in the universe and our lives, and how they were the motivating forces in operation behind everything we experienced. We respected them. However, we also understood our responsibility to them, and they to us. We gave them what they needed to remain in order (Maat) in our lives and in the universe, and they in turn reciprocated, giving us the things that we needed. Also in understanding that these forces actually make up our being, in taking care of them it is analogous to taking care of our health, our organs. Our giving praise and thanks for them is an expression of gratitude for their carrying out of their functions for us, which helps to facilitate our capacity to live and experience. We should show gratitude and appreciation for the nTrw in the same way that we should for our body.

The question of whether or not we worshipped the nTrw will be dealt with further in the Hika chapter. However, for now we can say that our ancestors had no problem reconciling their oneness/sameness with nTr and nTrw, and their adoration and veneration of them. In essence the adoration of the nTrw is the adoration of life, the forces that constitute it and make it possible, and the expression of gratitude for the experience and the goodness that it/they bring(s).

From this understanding of the nTrw and Kemetic spirituality, we are able to look at, and approach it as a **<u>Living Tradition</u>** in every sense of the word, and this Living Tradition should evolve as we evolve. We adapt our traditions to our current ecology. Also, while our Ancestors laid down an immense wealth of information and wisdom in regards to the knowledge and science of the nTrw, **their work is ultimately to serve as a solid foundation for us to build upon**. This means that as we go forward with our living and experience of the tradition and the nTrw, **it is our duty to add on**.

It should be understood that the nTrw are the forces of Life, and that they express themselves in every aspect of life. Therefore, things such as offerings to the nTrw, an area of life that falls under the influence of a particular nTr, can and should be expanded as our understanding and experience expands. In accordance with this understanding, one will notice that included in this section pertaining to the nTrw, will be the traditional offerings that were made by the Kemetyu, as well as things that can be offered today. In this way the tradition will live forever.

In the following sections pertaining to the nTrw, there will be included some of the many elements of the Kemetic Tradition that served to inform one in regards to the nature of the nTrw, how they express themselves, and how they are approached through ritual. This will include Hymns, Pictures, Litanies, their Renu (names), stories, offerings, and much more. I will that it will serve as a firm foundation for us to walk upon and build upon, as we re-establish and reaffirm our relationship with the nTrw and this tradition.

Figure 2:Ra Mesu II with Imun and Mut.Turin Museum, Egypt

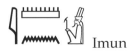 Imun

As pointed out in the chapter pertaining to the cosmology of Waset, Imun represents the Highest level of Being, as well as the innermost essence of existence. His name means "the Inner and Secure." He and his feminine counterpart Mwt, Imunt, correspond to the aspect of the universe and existence that we can refer to as the "source," or the "All," and is related to other conceptual nTrw such as Nu(n) and Nut/Nunet. As such, all life takes place within Imun/Imunt, as they in their highest significance, represent the primordial waters. For this reason, Imun is sometimes depicted with Blue skin. This aspect of being cannot be "experienced" in its totality, as there is no experience within it. However, its existence can be sensed through an experience of what the name implies; an inner sense of security, manifested as Hetep or peace.

Hymns to Imun

StA xprw THn irw

244

nTr biAyti aSA xprw
nTr nb ab.sn im.f
r SaA.sn m nfrw.f mi nTri.f

Ra Ds.f zmAw m Dt.f
ntf pA wr imi Iwnw
iw Dd.tw TA-tn ir.f
Imn priw m Nnw sSm.f Hrw

Secret of manifestations and sparkling of shape.
Marvelous nTr, rich in forms.
All nTrw boast of Him,
to magnify themselves in His beauty, to the extent of His Divinity.
Ra himself is united with His body.
He is the great one in Iwnw.
He is called Tatenen.
Amun, who comes out of the Nun,
to guide the peoples

kii xprw.f m xmnw
pAwti pAwtiw msiw Raw

Another of His forms are the Eight,
primeval one of the primeval ones, begetter of Ra.

tm.f sw m Itmw Haw wa Hna.f
ntf Nb r Dr SAa wnnt

He completed himself as Atum,
being of one body with him.
He is the Universal Lord,
who initiated that which exists.

bA.f pw xr.tw pA nti m Hrt
ntf pA nti m dwAt xnti iAbtt

bA.f m pt Dt.f m imntt
Xnti.f m Iwnw Smaw Hr wTz
Haw.f

His bA, they say, is the one who is in the sky.
He is the one who is in the dwAt,
foremost of the East.
His Soul is in the sky, His body in the West.
His statue is in southern Heliopolis, elevating His body.

wa Imn imnw.sw ir.sn
sHApw.sw r nTrw
bw rH.tw iwn.f
wAiw.sw r Hrt
mDw.sw r dwAt

One is Amun,
who keeps Himself concealed from them,
who hides Himself from the nTrw,
no one knowing His nature.
He is more remote than the heavens,
He is deeper than the dwAt

bw rx nTrw nbw qi.f mAa
nn sSm.f prxw Hr zSw
nn mtr.tw ir.f Driiwt

None of the nTrw knows His true form.
His image is not unfolded in the papyrus rolls.
Nothing certain is testified about Him.

sw StA r kfA Sfiit.f
sw aA r dDdD.f
wsr r rx.f

He is too secretive

246

for His Majesty to be revealed,
He is too great to be enquired after,
too powerful to be known.

xr Hr-a m mwt n Hr-n-Hr
n wD rn.f StA xmw rxw
nn nTr rx nis sw im.f
bAii imn rn.f mi StA.f

People immediately fall face to face into death
when His Name is uttered
knowingly or unknowingly.
There is no god able to invoke Him by it.
He is Soul-like, hidden of name, like His Secrecy.

Renu n Imun (Names of Imun)
Imun
Imun Ra
Imun Ra Pitah
Imun Ra Neb NIst Taui
Imun Men Men Mut.f
Imun Ka Mut.f
Imun Minu
Imun Ra Nisu nTrw
Imun Khnum Heh
Imun Qwa Ist

Major Festival-
 Opet 19th Day of Menkhet

Offerings
None/All (Animal- Goat)

Bwt (Taboo)

Sheep/Ram/Crocodile

Mut/Imun.t/Nun.t

Mut is the wife of Imun and is a "Supreme" nTrt."Even more correctly, she is all of the nTrwt combined, the ultimate Feminine expression of the Divine. Her ren means "Mother," and as such she is considered the "Mother of All," but she herself has no mother, for Mut is considered to have always existed. In this way she is associated with Imunt, and Nun.t, as the feminine counterpart of the "Pre-Creation" universe, and the "Primordial Waters of Chaos." Though there in reality is no differentiation or duality in this state of Being. As a symbol, she represents the actual "Waters," the "Ocean of Matter" from which all things came to be, while her male counterpart Imun represents the intelligence aspect of this matter. Together, Imun and Mut represent the totality of the Chaos (just as Nun and Nun.t). From the union of Imun and Mut comes Khonsu, which represents the coming into being of motion, and time (Khonsu's name means "Traveler").

As a symbol of the Divine feminine, Mut is also associated with the nTrt Auset, and Het-Heru/Sekhmet, which are some of the other important maternal nTrwt. This relationship is evident, especially in the case of Auset, in which the foundation of Auset's crown is the vulture, which is the sacred animal of Mut. As in the case with Imun, Mut represents the "All," and as such should not be seen as a "separate" nTrt than the other nTrwt, but as the culmination of them all. In other words, Mut is Het-Heru, as Well as Auset, Sekhmet, and Nut. This is evident from the fact that some of the "forms" of Mut contain the renu of these nTrwt, as in the case with the form of Mut called Shekhemet Bast Ra.

Hymn to Mut

aAt iAxw sHDt-tA-tm-m-mAwt.s

great of splendor who illuminates the entire land with her rays

iw.s m MAAt.f rdit-tA-wDA Axt-nt-Hr-Axty

she is his Eye who causes the land to prosper, the glorious eye of Heru Khuti

HqAt n unnt nbw wrt wsrt

Queen of All that exists, Great and Powerful, Life being in her hand

wrt wsrt sHDt mAAt.s m Axt

Great and Powerful one, her eye illuminates the horizon.

r psDt awt.ib n.s

the Peseju (nTrw) hearts swell (with joy) for her

HqAt rS.nw m ren.s pn n pt

Queen of their joy in this her name of Pet

Prt m iAxw im.s n.s

The Yakhu go forth within it because of her

sanxt-tAw-m-stwt.s wbnt m pt

Who lets the two lands live by her rays when she rises in the heavens

Prt m.s msi rnpwt nfr nbw

When she comes forth all good plants are born

Nhpt wnnt aSt irw

Early morning existing in many forms

mnt-m-xnmt

who lasts as the nurse

Htp-imn-n-mAA.s

Imun is satisfied from the sight of her

Haa-Hr-nb-mAA.sn-nfrw.s

All rejoice when they see her beauty

Wat iwtt-sn-nwt.s

The only one who is second to none.

<u>Renu</u>

Mwt

mwt-nTr-nt-pAwty-tpy (The Mother of the Gods of the first Primal Ones)

mwt-nTr-nt-nTrw-nTrwt (The Mother of the Gods and Goddesses)

mwt-nTr-nt-xnsw-pa-xrd

(The Mother of Khonsu, the Child)

mwt-nt-qmA-sy

(The mother of him who created it)

mnxt-sxrw-n-sn.s

(She with excellent plans for her brother)

mst-pAwty

(Who gives birth to the primal/primeval ones)

mst-ra

(Who gives birth to Ra)

mst-snwy

(Who gives birth to her two brothers)

nDtyt-mnxt-nt-it.s-ra

(The excellent protector of her father, Ra)

rpatt-wrt-nt-it.s-ra

(The great princess of her father, Ra)

papat-Hry-tA-m-wDH

(Who brings the Foremost of the earth to the world as a child)

mwt-irt-sAt

(The mother, who appears as a daughter)

mwt-nt-it.s

(The mother of her father)

Major Festivals

Opet

Offerings

Women's Perfume, Jewelry

Shares offerings with Auset and Het Heru

Bwt (Taboo)

Vulture, Cat (Felines), Ram/Sheep, Cobra, cow (these are sacred animals and should not be offered)

Khonsu

Khonsu is the son of Imun and Mut, and in other traditions he is the son of Subik and Het Heru. His name means "*Traveler*." As the son of Imun and Mut, on a cosmic level, Khonsu represents the "Traveling," or "motion" that led to the creation of the ordered universe, and the coming into being of time and space. As such he has always been considered the nTr of time par excellence, and a nTr of "Destiny," that came to be associated with the moon. His association with the moon deals with the Kemetyu use of the moon to keep time, and its effects on the fertility or sterility of the crops, animals, as well as people on the

earth. In regards to his association with "Time," although he is normally associated with the moon (by scholars), he wears both the sun and crescent moon upon his head. The sun and moon were the main sources of time keeping, as the Kemetyu utilized both Solar and Lunar Calendars.

Khonsu is a very powerful force and is both beneficent and malefic. As a nTr of time, he can work for us or against us, as time has been known to do. He is also a nTr of healing, especially of the mind and spirit, and is known for his ability to exorcise "demons," and "dark forces." He can be terrifying and has the ability to scare these forces off. As the nTr of time, these forces, along with everything else, are made either stronger or weaker by him. As the nTr of the moon, specifically, these forces gain strength during the waxing phase of the moon, and become weaker during the waning phase as he, in similar fashion to Ra, is said to be a strong "Bull" during the waxing phase of the lunar month, and a weak, "old ox" during the waning phase. Understanding this, it should be noted that the most efficient time to perform purifications of homes, and exorcisms, etc, is during the waning moon, and if possible, should be held off until then, especially if one is not fully competent in dealing with such matters.

Khonsu as the moon can also be malefic, in that if one is not living Maat, and not constantly purifying and refining themselves, any negativity, can be magnified by the power of Khonsu, and can lead to psychic disturbances, madness, obsession, etc. In this way, he is said to "Live off of Hearts," and "live off of heads," indicating that he has the ability to cause someone to lose their mental faculties and Will. This power of the moon has been known by the ancients for a very long time and is the origin of such terms as "Luna-tic," and stories of "werewolves... i.e. a person that becomes a beast in conjuction with the full moon.

Khonsu, in his role as the nTr of time, was said to be responsible for writing a person's destiny. He governs the cycles of life, and on a cosmic scale, he represents the point in which all things shall return to the "Chaos," represented by his mother and father Imun and Mut. In this role, he is said to assist the "Nisu" in the killing and eating of the nTrw. This is of course a reference to the Pyramid Texts of Unas, the so-called "Cannibal Hymn." This hymn has been greatly misunderstood and misrepresented as a "testament" that the Kemetyu engaged in cannibalism, however, this is not the case. The text is a metaphor, speaking to the Nisu, in this case the Osir Unas, and his identification with the Chaos (Imun/Nun). It is a declaration that he has attained a level "higher" than the nTrw, realizing himself as the "nTr whose name is hidden," or Imun. As Khonsu is considered the son of Imun, it is only natural that he would play a role in the return of creation, which includes the nTrw, back to Imun; the Inner; the Chaos. This is to say that he completes the cycle (Remember all "Trinities" represent cycles of Causes and Effect), and it is through Khonsu that all things return to Imun, first by being dissolved into Mut, undifferentiated Matter, and ultimately contracting to the state where only Imun, the Inner, exists.

Khonsu is also associated with learning and wisdom, and is in some cases identified with Tehuti. He can be seen playing a game of senet with Tehuti, as it is said that Khonsu loves games. According to the tradition, Tehuti played Khonsu in a game of Senet after Ra placed an infertility curse upon Nut, basically preventing her from becoming pregnant or giving birth during any day of the year, which at that time consisted of 360 days. Nut confided in Tehuti and he decided that he would challenge Khonsu to a game of Senet, for some of Khonsu's light. Tehuti and Khonsu played and played, with Tehuti repeatedly coming out on top. Once he received about five days of light from Khonsu, he used the light to add five days to the end of the calendar. From here the calendar was now 365 days. During these last five days Nut gave birth to Osir, Heru War, Sutesh, Auset, and Nebt Het, respectively.

The story represents the relationship between wisdom, the wise man or Rekhi ikat (Sage) and Time. Being wise is knowing what time it is, what the time calls for, and how to act or not act accordingly. The light that Tehuti wins from Khonsu represents the knowledge of the Time, and also the wisdom that comes with time (experience). However, Khonsu in his own right is a nTr of learning and knowledge, and represents the

wise man as the Master of Time, as well as the "Wandering Sage."

Spiritual work with Khonsu should be performed for gaining knowledge of one's Shai (Destiny), and also falling into harmony with it, and finding one's path or way in life. He is also very powerful as a protector, and is utilized in purification rituals, healing rituals, and also exorcisms. Finally, Khonsu can assist in making one receptive, flexible, and less dogmatic, allowing them to learn from different perspectives, schools of thought, etc.

Invocation of Khonsu for Healing (Physical, Mental, and Spiritual)

inD Hri.k Xnsw m wAst nfr Htp, nb nfr iri.i nm m.bAH.k Hr (Name of person)

Show your face, Khonsu m Waset Nefer Hotep Good Lord, I perform in your presence for (Name)

pA nb Nfr iw ir da.k Hr.k r xnsw pA iri sxr nTr aA z.Hr SmAw rdi shi.f r (Name)

good Lord turn your face upon Khonsu the maker of destinies, the Great nTr who repulses "demons" and grant that he may go to (name)

Ma zA.k Hna.f rdi shi m Hm.f r (Name) nHm (name)

Let your saving power be wth him and let me send his Majesty to (Name) deliver (name).

Renu of Khonsu

Khonsu

Xnsw Nfr Htp m WAst (Supreme Form of Khonsu, contains all forms)

Xnsw pA iri sxr z.Hri SmAw (Purifies, Heals, Repulses and Destroys Demons, also has the ability to elevate disturbed deceased beings)

Xnsw pA Iri sxr (Creator of Destinies)

Xnsw Hsb aHa (Decider of Life Spans/Fate)

Xnsw DHwty (nTr of Wisdom, especially as it relates to Timing)

Xnsw pA XrAd (nTr of Joy, Healing, Fertility)

Day

Wednesday – (Xnsw pA iri sxr z.Hri SmAw)

Saturday -(Xnsw pA Iri sxr & Xnsw Hsb aHa)

Major Festival

Opet

Colors

Blue and Gold, Silver

Stones

Emerald, Jet

Number

14

Totem

Ankh, Djed, Uas, Crook, Flail

Pitah

Pitah is the aspect of nTr that brought forth the universe through the power of thought and speech. In some instances, he is identified with Nun and corresponds to the pre creation Universe. Pitah is the innate, hidden intelligence; the consciousness that permeates throughout all existence, and is responsible for the "Grand Scheme" and "Design" of this thing we call life. He is a Master Craftsmen; the Grand Architect of the universe. His ren literally means "to open, to engrave, and to create." His Ren also contains within in it the terms Pt (Heaven/Sky) and Ta (Earth), indicating (through pun) his being, in a way, a symbol of the universe in totality; Neb r Jer. This role of Pitah is expressed in some of his other renu, such as Pitah Sukari Osir, Pitah Sukari Itum, and Pitah Nun, indicating that he exists on every plane, including the pre-creation level of Nu/Nun.

Pitah corresponds to the force within us that grants us the capacity to create our lives, first through inspiration (thought), and then through actualization (work/deed). He is our ability to define ourselves, and chart our own destinies. He is also Neb Maat, the Lord of Maat, which speaks to his ability to master the Law, and also create the law. This is to say that, what we think about will go on to create the laws that will govern our existence, and further extend to determine what happens in our lives. This is reflected in the cosmology of Men Nefer in which Pitah brings the universe into being, first by "defining himself," and in actuality, creating the universe/world through this act. This means that the world is a reflection and extension of the Self.

He is called the "Listening Ear," and "He who answers prayers," which speak to the law that practices such as prayer and meditation invoke; the idea that there is an aspect of our being that hears our thoughts; our needs on a deeper level, and works to answer/manifest them for us. He is the "Inner Ear" that resides within our own inner sanctuary. What is brought to him is granted if one is living Maat. However, he does not like lies, and there are stories of Pitah coming down hard upon one who took a dishonest oath upon his (Pitah's) name. As a result, he, the transgressor, was met with great misfortune. This happened by way of his own consciousness, his conscience, as Pitah is our own Self, our own Inner Eyes and Ears, and while the person we may lie to, or cheat, may not be aware of our dishonesty, Pitah knows.

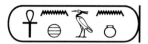

Pitah is the nTr of Craftsmen, especially smiths and masons, but is also associated with artisans such as sculptors and painters. He is considered to be the aspect of nTr that brought forth creation, first by conceiving of it in his mind, while speaking it into being. He is the power to conceive an idea, map out the plan/blueprint for its implementation, and the hard work to see it through to its fruition. This is represented in his family; his association with Shekhemet and Nefertum. While Pitah represents our ability to be inspired, to conceive of an idea within the mind, Shekhemet is the Fire, the Power, the passion, and the relentlessness/determination that nurtures and converts the idea to a project, ultimately bringing it to a "Beautiful Completion," or "Perfection," represented by Nefertum.

In his name of Pitah Sukari Osir, he is the nTr of Generation, degeneration, and regeneration, or Life, death, and resurrection, as Pitah is a creator nTr par excellence, Sukari is the nTr of death, and Osir is the nTr of resurrection/regeneration par excellence. Speaking to this sentiment, we have the **82nd chapter of the prt m hrw** called **"For assuming the form of Ptah, that is eating bread, drinking beer, excreting from the anus, and existing alive in Iwnw."** The idea being conveyed here, is the understanding of Pitah as a force that nourishes and sustains (eating bread and drinking beer) breaks down, decays, and discards the non - essential (excreting from the anus), and finally regeneration, associated in this case with his existing alive in Iwnw, the site where Ra rose from Nu.

258

Pitah-Sukari Osir is sometimes depicted as a dwarf, and as such is called **"PtH sDm pA nmw,"** that is *"Pitah who listens, The Dwarf."* It is important to differentiate between Pitah as a dwarf, and Bisu (Besu) as a "pygmy" or Batwa person. While the Batwa, as well as other "pygmy" groups are simply people who are considerably short collectively, dwarfism on the other hand is caused by a mutation or disease. For this reason, Pitah Sukari Osir or ptH sDm pA nmw, can be seen not only short, but with a swollen stomach, bowed legs, clubbed foot, flat head, etc. his children were called Patakoi (Patakos), and were adopted by the Phoenician, and also the Greeks as Hephaestus. As such, he is a nTr of diseases, deformities, plague, etc, and governs the disabled. His amulets were worn and used for protection purposes, and also healing of all types of diseases. He also, in this form, assisted in childbirth, and removing the poison from snake bites, etc. His amulets were of popular use in medical treatments of all kinds, to the point where he almost became completely connected to the field.

His association with pestilence and plagues are nowhere more evident, than in the account of the story with the Nisu Bity Taharqa and his defeat of the Assyrians in battle. According to the account by Herodotus, the Nisu Bity Taharqa, who was a Kushite Nisu, either didn't respect the Kemetic warrior class, or felt as though he had no need for them, and took away the provisions that were normally provided for them. After

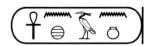

this happened, the Assyrian army at the behest of their King, marched against Kmt. Because of the way in which the Nisu dealt with the warrior class of the nKmt people, they refused to fight for him. When this happened, the Nisu sought refuge in the Inner Sanctuary of Ptah, as he was also a priest of Pitah, and called out to the nTr regarding the impending threat. He cried out to the nTr until he fell asleep, and Ptah came to him in a vision. Ptah assured him that he would protect him, and that he should go out to meet the Assyrians in battle, and not to worry for he would send helpers with him.

Taking comfort in and trusting the words of his nTr, he went out to battle with the Assyrians, taking only the few nkmt people that were willing to fight with him; none of them from the warrior class, just artisans and merchants. Upon their arrival, night time fell, and with it an army of mice descended upon their enemies, the Assyrian army. The mice chewed through their bows and quivers, and also the handles of their shields. Because of this, the following day the Assyrians retreated, because they had no defense, and many died. And according to Herodotus, at the time when he was writing his account, there stood within the temple of Pitah a statue of the Nisu Bity holding a rat in his hands, with the inscription stating "Let him who looks upon me learn to revere the nTrw." Now the interesting thing about this story is that it is corroborated by an account from the Biblical book (yes biblical ☺) of **II Kings chapter 19**, in context, which references Taharqa by name, and specifically verse 35 which speaks to death of 185,000 Assyrians "at the hand of The Lord." Most biblical scholars and historians agree that this mass killing happened by way of a plague. There are also the accounts of Josephus, who quotes a Babylonian historian by the name of Berossus, who stated that it was a disease that befell the Assyrian army, causing them to lose 185,000 men. There is even the account of the Assyrian King that, though it contradicts the other accounts (he lies and says he defeated Kmt and Kush); it still informs us that this battle did actually take place. It has been held since time immemorial, that rats are considered symbols, and creatures of disease and pestilence. The account of Herodotus speaks in symbolic language, in which the mice "chewing through the bows and shields, causing them to lose their

260

defense," represents a "plague" (also the termto refer to a group of rats) or disease eating through the immune systems of the Assyrians and a mass number of them perishing as a result. This same symbolic language is echoed in the biblical text in the preceding verse, in which it is stated that the "Lord" says..."he will not enter this city or shoot an arrow here. He will not come before it with a shield..." In fact, the entire 19th chapter of II Kings, specifically regarding the war with the Assyrians sounds interestingly similar to Herodotus' account of Taharqa's actions (though it allegedly follows by at least 100 years). It should be noted, once again, that the biblical text mentions Taharqa by name as the King, yet this particular text is dated at best c.550.bce, whereas the reign of Taharqa is dated at c.690 bce – 664 bce. In other words, the biblical account was likely written at least 114 years after the death of Taharqa. In fact, according to biblical chronology, this event took place about ten years before Taharqa came to power, yet it mentions him by name, as the King?

Anyway, this story should make Pitah's association with disease clear. His presence in the medical field should be understood as follows: since he is a nTr that causes life, he also has the power to take life; since he is a nTr of generation, he also has the power of degeneration and decay, and also regeneration, since he is a nTr that causes disease and pestilence, he also has the power to cure them.

Also, tying Pitah to disease and healing/medicine, is his familial relationship with his wife Shekhmet, who brings pestilence and plagues, and his son Nefertum who cures them. Shekhemet, as we will see shortly, was associated with annual plagues, and Nefertum as the tradition holds, was a nTr of pharmacology, and was considered to be Ra's personal physician. The formula is as follows, Pitah (Divine Intelligence, force of generative/degenerative power) + Shekhemet

(Divine Power, Purging force of correction, disease and pestilence) = Nefertum (the science and field of medicine and pharmacology).

When consulting the oracle, we (Henensu) were informed that Pitah was the nTr that Afrikan people needed to work with in order to elevate out of the position that we currently find ourselves in as a people. To better understand the implications of this reading, we must take a look at Pitah on a functional level, in relationship to our present condition.

When we look at the cosmology of Pitah, we are faced with a nTr that created, designed, and defined himself out of the undefined, inert state of the chaos. He defined and organized himself, made his place in the world/universe. It is said of him:

"Builds his own limbs himself… When the heavens, earth were not yet created, before the Waters of Nu burst forth… You knit together the ear, you gathered your members, you united your limbs… You found yourself as one who made your throne (or place), nTr who fashions the Two Lands…"

Afrikan people worldwide are currently in a state of chaos, and confusion. We are inert. This is caused mainly by the lost and lack of Knowledge of Self and identity. We have not defined ourselves, and have either been defined by, or accepted the definition of those who do not serve our best interest. We are divided amongst ourselves, which adds further to our impotence. So we must like Pitah define ourselves, design ourselves, and unite with a renewed sense of purpose. Once we do this we will then be able to go forward and find or create our throne/place in the world, individually, and as a nation(s).

It is further stated of Pitah:

> *"You had no father to beget you in your coming into being… You had no mother to give birth to you. You*

fashioned yourself... you lift up the work you've made (i.e. himself)... you support yourself with your own back... you raise yourself up by the vigor of your two hands... the upper part of you is pet, the lower part of you is Duat."

Afrikan people have been disconnected from our roots, from our origin in the world and life; our culture. This has taken place either by these roots being severed, or through our own rejection and neglect of our Ancestors and our heritage. So like Pitah, it is as though we were without mother and father, i.e. a foundation to build upon. So we have as a consequence, spent the greater part of our recent history on a search for identity. This is especially true of Afrikans of the Diaspora, but also includes continental Afrikans who have been colonized and have greatly shunned their traditional ways. As a result of this we are in a state of disarray. We are confused and disorganized, in many cases grasping to any piece of Traditional Afrikan Identity we can find. However, it is out of this undifferentiated (disorganized) ocean of Afrikan Identity and thought that we gather the elements that we need to create and define ourselves. It is from this melting pot of Afrikan fragments that we find our own aesthetic. Like Pitah we gather and unite our limbs, we fashion ourselves. We must in a sense, start from scratch, as we have greatly degenerated on all levels. Also, we must realize that this is something that we must ultimately do for Self. We cannot wait on or expect anyone else to fix our situation. No one is coming to our rescue. We must rebuild ourselves step by step, limb by limb, no matter how long it takes. Like Pitah, we lift up ourselves by the vigor and work of our own two hands.

Also it should be understood the level that Pitah is functional on, so that we can fully understand the nature of our work. In the statement "the upper part of you is pet; the lower part of you is Duat." It indicates to use that the bulk of Pitah's work is in Pet, and Duat. It is said of Pitah "The vision of the eyes, hearing of the ears, breathing of air through the nose, relays the plans of the heart, bringing forth every decision." Pitah's

264

work begins with "vision," with inspiration. Afrikan people need a far reaching vision, a revolutionary, inspirational, and determined idea that defines us, that unites us, that gives us a sense of belonging and purpose. This vision must conjure an image so pristine and beautiful; a vision of our own realized and actualized potential; a vision of who we want to be and what we want to see in and for our lives and world. This vision must be so potent, that to relish in the thought causes a smile to form in the faces of the people. We must be able to describe, articulate, see, in words and images our aspirations, with the same amount of detail or more as we can our pain. We must envision and describe, in full vivid detail, our bliss to the same degree in which we can describe our misery. We must follow our bliss and allow it to lead us to our purpose. We must take this vision deep into our spirit, we must articulate it within the Duat, so that it may organize and mobilize the forces there that it may manifest in the earth. This is the bulk of our work with Pitah. We must have a far-reaching inspirational idea, and then plant the seed of it deep within the Duat and organize the Duat (our minds and spirits) around it. This must be understood: We have for one reason or another neglected the spiritual realm, ancestors and nTrw, and have followed our oppressors in matters of the spirit. We, in many cases, now worship the oppressors, their Ancestors, and their corrupt and greatly imaginary concepts of deity, while neglecting and shunning our own Ancestors and spiritual forces. In other words, not only have the oppressors colonized and enslaved Afrikan people physically, but they have also colonized and enslaved our Duat. As a result, we are completely out of sync with the Ancestors and nTrw, which create the sense that these forces that should be working for us, are working against us. Afrikan people must cease worshiping the Ancestors and machinations of the imagination of their oppressors, and venerate and elevate the kA of their own Ancestors. Whether we know it or not, OUR LIVES DEPEND ON IT!!! So like Pitah, the Bulk of our work is becoming inspired, and then organizing and working with the spiritual realm and its forces, to ultimately bring forth the plans and decisions of our hearts, our "mrwt" or "mrwt.ib," that is our desires, or what our heart loves.

The last point is extremely important as it pertains to Pitah, and what he teaches us in regards to the science of creation; the power of the spirit. First there is in my opinion, the blatant reference to the science of meditation and its role in ritual; the visualization, the chanting, the correct breathing (through the nostrils), and the role of the breath in mobilizing the shekhem, and transmitting the focus of the will via the spiritual bodies that play the role in attracting to us the things that take place in our lives. The ancestors were deep! However, there is also perhaps a more subtle, yet most critical key given here, and that is the role of love or joy in creation.

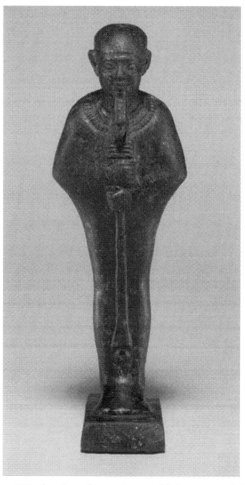

It is said regarding Pitah, that he exists within everything as "heart and tongue," (Thought/Intelligence and Word/Sound) "commanding through thought, and commanding through words, whatever he desires (or loves)." This is once again, a critical teaching to comprehend. It is very difficult to find an image of Pitah in which he is not smiling. Pitah is always smiling, for this reason he is called "nfr Hr," that is "Beautiful Face." The reason Pitah is smiling is because of the vision he has, and how it reflects what he loves or desires, and his ability to make it manifest. The idea of nTr creating "mrrt.f" or "mrrwt.ib.f," that is, "what he or she desires," or "what their heart loves," is a very common motif in nkmt cosmology. However, it is a motif that must not be underplayed or overlooked. We are naturally attracted and drawn to things that bring us joy and happiness, and are naturally repulsed by things that bring pain and misery. However, the mind, especially when focused and emotionally charged, will work to bring into being whatever thoughts

267

are occupying it, regardless of whether they bring joy or pain. So Pitah being ever so wise, only focuses on what brings him joy, what he desires, what his heart loves, and never his bwt (i.e., Taboo or what he hates). He is smiling because he's not worried about anything, for he has conceived the beginning, and seen the end; all reflecting the life he desires, for only a fool would create a life that they don't want to experience. This is also said to be the reason why the images of the various Nisu Bity, always depict the Ancestor with a slight smile. He creates what his heart loves, for the fortune of his people.

Hymn to Pitah

InD Hr.k PtH tA-Tnn nTr aA Imn sm.f

Show your face! Pitah, Tatenen, Great nTr whose form is Imun

wn bA.k rs.k m Htp

You open your Ba, you Awaken in Peace

It it.yw nTrw nbw

Father of fathers of all the nTrw

itn n Pt

Sun of Heaven

n MAAti s.HD tAwi m mAwt.f m Htp

you illuminate the Two Lands with your two eyes and your rays in peace

rdi Sxm.n.k Hr tA m nn.f

you're given power over the land as "he who is inert"

sbk.n.f r.f m.kt iw.k m irw.k tA Tnn

You collect (concentrate) after in your form of Ta Thenen

M xpr.k n dmd m tAwi m wtt r.k qmA n awy.k

As you form the Two Lands are joined, begotten from your mouth and created with your two hands

wtt rmTw, iri anx.sn

Begetter of mankind, maker of their lives

QmA n nTrw

Creator of the nTrw

sbi HH DtA

He who journeys through eternity and everlastingness

nt QmA Irw

Of Many creations and forms

sDm zpr.n.f rmT

Hearer of the petitions men make to him

iqd Ha.f Ds.f

Builds his own limbs himself

Nn xprr pt nn xpr tA nn bsi Nw

When the heavens, earth were not yet created, before the Waters burst forth.

Tz.n.k tA dmd.n.k iwf.k Ha.k Hpt n.k at.k

You knit together the earth, you gathered your members, you united your limbs

gmA n.k m wa ir st.f nTr nbi tAwi

You found yourself as one who made your throne (or place), nTr who fashions the Two Lands

Nn it.k wtt m xpr.k

You had no father to beget you in your coming into being

Nn mwt.k mswt Xnm.k Ds.k

You had no mother to give birth to you. You fashioned yourself

Spd pr spd

Equipped! You came forth fully equipped!

Rd.k Hr tA

Your feet are upon the earth

tp.k m Hrt m xprw.k m IMI dwAti

your head is above (in the heavens) in your manifestation of Imi Duati

iw.k Tz.k KAt ir.n.k

you lift up the work you've made

rhn.k.tw m pHt.k Ds.k

you support yourself with your own back

s.Tz.k tw m rwd awy.k

you raise yourself up by the vigor of your two arms

pt m Hr.k dwAt gr.k

the upper part of you is pet, the lower part of you is Duat.

Renu of Pitah

PtH

PtH Nw/Nwn (Primordial Form)

PtH Tnn (First to form)

PtH aA rsw inb.f (Pitah the great South of his Wall)

PtH nb anx (Lord of life)

PtH wr HAti Ns PsDw nTrw (Great heart and tongue of the nTrw)

PtH nb Qidwt (Lord of the Outline/Dezign)

PtH nfr Hr (Beautiful Face)

PtH Ra (Pitah Ra)

PtH s-mn MAat (Establisher of Maat)

PtH skri (Pitah Sukari)

PtH skri wsir

PtH skri Itm

PtH Dd

PtH QmA Hmwt

PtH xrp Hmw (Master of Craftsmen)

MsDr sDmw (Listening Ear)

sDm zpr.n.f rmT (Hears the prayers of men)

Pth sDm pA nmw (Pitah who listens, The Dwarf)

Day

Saturday (Creative/Cosmic forms)

Friday (Artistic forms)

Colors

White, Dark Blue, Green

Number

22

Herbs

Myrrh, Moringa

Offerings

Shares offerings with Osir and Sukari

Psychological Traits

Genius, Deep Concentration, Profound Thought, Meditation, understanding (the ability see how things relate and work on the deepest levels), organization and planning, Focused (One Pointedness). Inspirational, Creative/Artsy

Emotional Traits

Calm, Peaceful, Determined, thorough (Perfectionist), overwork, overly occupied with perfection

Totems

An Ear, Ankh, Djed and Uas, Potters Wheel

Figure 3: Sekhmet Statue at Turin Museum Italy

Shekhemet (See Het-Heru)

Shekhmet is one of the most important and most powerful nTrw in the Kemetic tradition. While she has many forms, she is most known for her violent and destructive side. This aspect of Shekhmet is known from stories such as the so-called "**Destruction of Mankind**," and the so-called "**Wandering nTrt**." In the Destruction of Mankind, the nTrt Het-Heru takes on the form of Shekhmet after Ra sends her to slaughter

272

mankind due to their rebellion and plotting against him. He is advised by the Tribunal of nTrw to send his "Eye," Het-Heru/Shekhmet to deal with them. She began the slaughter, and then it is said that after while Ra had a change of heart, or at least felt that she had done enough. He told her to come back home, but she replied that she "felt alive, and having power over man was sweet to her heart." Then it is said that she "waded in their blood." The only way Ra was able to stop her and the slaughter was to appease her with beer (i.e. get her drunk).

The next story that speaks to Shekhmet is the so-called "Wandering nTrt." This is the story of Het Heru getting lost in creation following behind Ishu and Tufnut. When she returned she found that Ra had created another "eye" in her place. This angered Shekhmet, and caused her to lash out at Ra, and leave him. As a result, Ra was left powerless and depressed. It wasn't until Tehuti went and convinced her to return, that she came back to her senses.

These stories speak to the nature of Shekhmet, her temperament, personality, etc. She is protective, and fierce. As the Eye of Ra, she is the Physical Counterpart of Ra, and is associated with Het-Heru, in that she is the fierce form of Het-Heru. As Het-Heru is the physical Universe, and the order and harmony that keeps life going, Shekhmet is the destructive side of Nature that takes place when there is disharmony and things become unbalanced. She is a force of correction, justice, and healing.

Speaking to Shekhmet as a force of healing, is her is association with plagues and pestilence/disease. Disease properly understood, is a result of the body becoming unbalanced, and its homeostasis being thrown off. When this takes place, there are mechanisms within the body that will begin the process of reversing the situation, and restoring balance and harmony to the body. In this way Shekhmet though seen as the Lady of Pestilence, is also the great healer of disease. She is the fire of purification that destroys all impurities, and is also related to the body's defense and immune system, which manifest as heat (fire), whereas sickness tends to manifest through "cold" symptoms, etc. She governs

surgery, and aggressive (emergency) healing measures such as radiation and chemotherapy.

According to the tradition, Shekhemet has followers called "*xAyty,*" or "Murderers," "*wpwty,*" or "messengers" and "*SmAyw,*" or "wanderers." All of these collectively are known as the "**Arrows of Shekhmet**," and are particularly associated with the "plague of the year," but also misfortune of every kind. At the beginning of every year rituals and sacrifices were made to Shekhmet to ward off these forces, with the intention to ward off the pestilence and misfortune they bring. These forces "shoot forth" from Shekhmet in her form as the Eye of Ra. Attesting to this is the text called the "Book of the Last Day of the Year," which is dedicated solely to placating "Shekhmet's wrath," from the forthcoming year.

On a deeper level, these forces, to the uninitiated considered "demons," are "messengers of Shekhmet:" to the initiated. They are the forces that signal to us that we are off course. They manifest when we are out of balance and alignment with Maat and nTr, and manifest as disease. They are the forces of the disharmony, disease, and dissonance. Like any symptom, or pain, their purpose is to alert us to the fact that there is something wrong so that we can do something about it. Bring peace to the situation/ So that we can begin the efforts in healing. The purpose of pain and symptoms of disease is to warn us. However, if the warning is not heeded, and we continue in our errors, then the situation may worsen or become fatal.

Shekhmet as a great purifier manifest as the destructive power of nature. She is pestilence, plague, and natural disasters. It is appears to be natures ability to lash out at life on the planet, but in actuality is a natural mechanism that exists to restore order and harmony in the world. It is Shekhmet that brings things to extinction, the removal of organisms that have become obstacles or threats to the evolution of the collective, and or redundant.

Also in association with purification, Shekhmet is the nTr.t that governs the woman's menstrual cycle, which in which the term for it in mdw nTr is "Hsmn," meaning "Purification." To understand this connection, we must contemplate the story of the wandering, nTrt, in association with the annual flooding of the Nile, and how this cyclical event is analogous to the woman's cycle.

First look us back at the story. Shekhemet begins as Het Heru, the nTr.t of love, music, fertility, and sex. Het Heru is said to have wandered off into the world, and upon her return, she discovered that Ra had created another in her place. She then transformed into Shekhmet, lashes out at Ra, and left. As she left Ra he became impotent, and life left Kmt. This part of the story represents on one hand the cycles of the seasons, particularly the summer and its solstice, in which the Sun and heat reaches its peak, as Shekhmet is associated with the intense, scorching heat of the sun. The summer, called "*Smw*," in mdw nTr, was the season of the harvest, and also the dry season in Kmt. As such, this was not the season for planting. This is the season which precedes the season of Inundation, called "*Axt*." It is during the season of "coming forth," called "*Prt*," in which the waters from the flood would recede, revealing the fertile black silt of the land. This was the period of planting.

Continuing with our story, as Shekhemet goes forth, life leaves Kmt. As "water" is the essence of life, this represents the land drying up, and the loss of fertility. It is said that Shekhmet left blood in her wake, and that she waded in blood. In fact, one of her names, *dSrt*, meaning "**Red**," is also, a term for "**blood**," as well as the term for "**desert land**," (desert comes from dSrt). Anyway, this aspect of the story corresponds to the period of menstruation, which is the time during a woman's monthly cycle of fertility wherein an unfertilized egg is being released as a result of the absence of pregnancy. Shekhmet's wading in blood, represents menstrual blood. During this time, it is highly unlikely that a woman will conceive.

Shekhemet's leaving Ra, in a sense, going into isolation during this time symbolized the way in which many women in traditional cultures spent this time; in seclusion. In Kmt many women would spend time in seclusion, or stay in their homes. There was a place called "*st Hmwt*"

("**the place of women**") which was on the outskirts of the town, that was reserved for menstruating women, some in synchrony. This particular place is attested in locations such as Deir El-Madina. According to one account, there was an incident that took place, apparently some sort of crime, as one lady was leaving from the "Place of Women." It is said that this lady was one of "eight menstruating women," in this location. Places of this type are present historically across cultures, perhaps the most similar type being the "Menstrual Huts." Even in cases where the woman did not spend her "period," in these places on the outskirts of the town, there was a place in reserved in the home called "*XrXr.t*" among other terms, referring to the "woman's space." While, it is not known what exactly took place within these places, following the cosmology, it is my proposition that time was spent performing rituals, meditations, purifications, etc, as it was Tehuti in the story that goes to Shekhmet and charms her with music and stories. These things represent rituals. There is at least one example of a "shrine" in a room beneath the stairs, in which stela which shows a lady leading a young girl before the nTrt Taweret, were found within a room beneath a staircase in a house in Amarna[7]. This more than likely depicts a girl's "coming of age," and rites of passage into womanhood, as she is brought before Taweret, the nTrt of fertility, and pregnancy, the protector of women and children. This would demonstrate that there were rituals set in place for women during this time, though the specifics are greatly unknown, more than likely because of their secrecy. Even today in Henensu, no man knows the happenings of the sister's circle, or what their rituals consist of, including the author.

However, after Tehuti brings her brings her back, it is said that she had to bathe in the Nile because she was so angry. As she bathed, the water turned red, yet she began to cool off and transform back into Het Heru. This represents the ritual bath that the women took at the culmination of their Menstrual Cycle and its respective rites, which was the precursor for their entrance back into everyday life, and reunion with their

[7] Szpakowska, Kasia "Daily Life In Ancient Egypt" Wiley-Blackwell 1997

husbands if they were married. This ritual bath is also observed in several traditions to this very day.

Finally upon her return to Ra and Kmt, she was met with great festivities and celebration. Her return signaled the return of the flood waters and by extension, the return of Life to Kmt. This represented the cessation of a woman's menstrual cycle, and the return of her "water's" of life, and the time of fertility in which she could be impregnated. This is demonstrated by the fact that, during the festivals that commemorated this story in conjunction with the annual flood, women, especially married women and also virgins, marched along with the procession singing, dancing, and presenting offerings to Het Heru in hopes that she would increase their fertility and give them children. An example of this can be seen in the temple at Medinat Habu, in which it is written concerning the Festival "May your wives celebrate for Het Heru Lady of the West, so that she allows them to bear for you men and women (i.e. boys and girls).[8]" What this passage informs us of, is the fact that the time following the flood was not only the time of seeding the fertile earth, but also the time of seeding the fertile Afrikan woman. In fact, the "life giving" waters of the Nile are associated with the life giving waters of the womb as we are told by Auset in the so called "Ebers Papyrus" that there is a "Nile between my thighs." It should also be considered that Auset, just like most of the feminine nTrwt, regardless of their respective local cosmologies and traditions, are identified with Shekhmet and Het Heru in a relationship to the annual flood of the Nile, and how this event is observed and celebrated in their town. Auset's association with the menstrual cycle will be further elaborated on in her section in this chapter.

Shekhmet shares the ren **Pa Pesejit nTrw** with Het Heru. In this form she contains within herself all of the nTrw. On one hand while it can be said that she is their power; their essence, on the other hand, whereas Het-Heru can be said to embody all of the nTrw in their harmonious state, while Shekhmet embodies the nTrw in the state where they are not

---

[8] . Daressy, Notes et remarques, in: RdT 20, 1898, 74 (no. 151).

in "Hetep" and must be "satisfied." This is evident in the fact that Shekhmet is the one that must be "satisfied(appeased) when she rages." She is considered to be the most powerful of all the nTrw because she contains all of them within her, and she herself is their power source. It is also said that "all of the nTrw fear her" (except for Tehuti). Shekhemt has the potential to destroy the nTrw. This aspect of Shekmet speaks to the ability of dissonance to deplete the energy of the nTrw, inhibiting them from functioning at their optimal capacity, as well as the potential for them to degenerate.

In her role as the Eye of Ra, she is not only his protector, but also his power and capacity to do. She is also called the "Hand of Ra." This once again is spoken to in the story of the Wandering nTrt. Shekhmet is the Power that exist within the universe, as well as the source of light. Many people have interpreted Ra as the Sun, but in actuality it is Shekhmet/Het Heru, that is the actual sun/light, as she is said to "Clothe her lord within her light, and conceal him within her eye." The Sun and serpent on top of Ra's Head, should be interpreted as one symbol which represents his "eye" his "Yarayit," the nTrt Shekhmt/Het-Heru. As a nTrt of light, she enlightens, or brings knowledge and wisdom. This is attested in the "prt m hrw" in the chapter "Making a Transformation Into the nTr Who Gives Light In the Darkness," in which the ancestor is to declare that "Nuk Ham sshep kekiyu," that is "I am the woman who lightened up the darkness."

It should be understood that although Shekemet manifest what some can consider to be malefic qualities, in actuality, everything that she does is based upon the laws of cause and effect. She is a nTrt of Justice, and what may seem like her "chastisement," is in reality the result of one's own actions, especially those that live other than Maat. She is maternal in that she is protective and defends those that have been wronged, and sternly corrects those that do wrong. For this reason it is said that she loves Maat, but Hates evil, and devours thieves for her satisfaction.

Shekhemet is force that can be worked with for protection, healing,

278

justice, courage, and determination. She is relentless, and is a help in situations where one needs to eliminate obstructions from ones path, even if those obstructions are mental such as distractions. However, she is a force that is not meant to be carried for an extended period of time as she is a force that is meant to correct and protect. Her Shrine should not be placed in the home, but outside.

Hymns to Shekhmet

I sxmt, irt Ra aA nsrt nbt nrw ha ir.s

O Sekhmet, Eye of Ra, Great of Flame, Lordess of Terror surrounding her creator

I sxmt s.HDt tAwi m nsrt mAA-Hr-nb-m-sSp.s

O Sekhmet illuminator of the two lands with her flame, because of her everyone sees (has sight)

I sxmt nbt nsrt nsrt wrt aAt nrw nrw.s-pxr-m-tAwy

O Sekhmet, lady of fire, great of flame, great of terror, fear of her is spread across the Two Lands

dSrt ib r.f prt.s ian.s xft s.nmH.f.s

Red of Heart (Angry) towards him from whom she issues forth, she returns after he begs her.

I Sxmt Hryt-tp-m-tp-ir-sy imn sw m nsrt.s

O Sekhmet Cobra upon the head of him who created her, she hides him with her flame

I Sxmt iri mAA irt nbw nn mAA

O Sekhmet who makes all eyes to see, none are blind

I Sxmt wbn.t m xnti sSp iab.t ii m kk

O Sekhmet when you rise the light shines, when you return (go back) the darkness comes

I Sxmt Hbs-s nb-s m sSp.s imn-s sw m-xnw DfD.s

O Sekhmet who clothes her lord in her light, she hides him within the pupil of her eye

I Sxmt wrt-Sfyt m RmT wbnt nsrt

O Sekhmet Great of Reputation amongst Mankind, rising flame

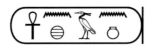

Hymn for Protection

Sxm irt.f im.tn

His eye has power over you

im.s tn

she devours you

swnw.s tn m rn.s pwi n imi wnmyt

She punishes you in this name of hers unumiyit (Devouring Flame)

sxm.s n im.tn m rn.s pwi n sxmt

her power is over you in her name of Sekhmet

xr.tn n hh.s

You fall because of her blast

Renu of Sekhmet

sxmt

Irt Ra (Eye of Ra)

Hr.t DAHDAH Nb.s (Upon the Head of Her Lord)- Psychic Protection

Hebs neb.s m shesp.s (Shrouds her Lord within her light) - Allows one to contemplate the Self

dSrt (Blood)

Nsrt (Flame)

Nbt Nru (Lady of Terror)

Wawty (The One) -Builds Confidence, Courage, Indepedence

PDt Ibw (Spreader of Hearts)

Nbt xryw (Lady of Enemies) -Defeats Enemies

Nbt SmAyw (Lady of Demons)- Exorcises Negative Spirits

Nbt iAdt (Lady of Pestilence) - Cures Diseases

Day

Tuesday

Colors

Red (Blood)

Stones

280

Cats Eye, Tigers Eye, Fire Agate

Herbs
Peppers (Cayenne, Guenie. Etc), Asafoetida (Exorcisms),

Offerings
Blood, Red Wine, Beer mixed with Red Ochre (Iron/Red Dirt)
Raw Meat

4 goats 4 geese, and 7 jars of blended honey and grape juice/red wine, beer. This is a variation of a Traditional Offering to appease Shekhmet (traditionally oryx was offered, however Shekhmet will accept goat instead) and receive protection. If you think need to make this offering and for more details contact a <u>High Priest of Henensu.</u>

Bwt (Taboo)
Felines, Cow

Totem
Felines (especially Lioness)

Number -55

Nefertum

Nefertum is the son of Pitah and Shekhmet. His name means "Beautiful Completion" or "Perfection." According to the tradition, he burst forth from a lotus which rose from the Primordial waters (Nu). In this way he represents an aspect of Khepri, who represents the new creation. He is often depicted as a child seated upon a lotus, or as a man with a lotus upon his head. Yet, in many cases Nefertum, himself, is considered to be the lotus that burst forth from the primordial waters.

Nefertum is a force of renewal, which is demonstrated in his association the Khepri, the chief symbol of creation beginning anew. It is said that Nefertum is "born every morning," renewing himself daily." However, this renewal is not limited to "morning," but like Khepri as it relates to the phases of Ra, takes place from moment to moment.

Like all of the child nTrw, Nefertum represents the birth and renewal of creation, and also the Divine experience, and enlightenment. This is expressed in his ren, meaning "Beautiful Completion" or "Perfection." He brings the awareness and experience that everything is as it should be, Beautiful and complete, in that he only sees the beauty of the ever present and ongoing divine process of creation (Kheperu); the realization that each moment is as it should be, it is complete, it lacks nothing, and is therefore all "Nefer." He represents living in the moment, and accepting and experiencing each moment as new, in the same way that a child does.

As a constant force of renewal, he is a force that keeps the universe moving, working towards perfection, or better yet, "wholeness." He keeps things on the constant path of perfecting, evolving; each step in the process complete within itself, yet constantly revealing the beauty, the newness, and the perfection within imperfection, and the constant strive towards the reconciliation of the two.

As his mother and father, Shekhmet and Pitah are both associated with disease, Nefertum as a nTr of constant renewal, he is the force that brings healing and restoration. His relationship in regards to his family can be viewed and understood a few ways. First, one can understand Pitah as the force that is constantly building, constantly creating, while Shekhmet is the constant force of "destruction." However, as with all life, we know that nothing is actually ever really destroyed, and thus Nefertum is the force of regeneration, renewal, transformation, and transmutation. Another way of looking at his family is Pitah = Creativity +

Shekhmet=Power/Passion/Determination/relentlessness=   Nefertum, one's plan or will being brought to a beautiful completion (fulfillment).

There is another important meaning to be taken from Nefertum's significance in relationship to his family, and that is the lesson of humility. Pitah and Shekhmet bring difficulty and affliction, oppression,

and these things if properly interpreted and assimilated, strengthens, as well as humbles the person that goes through it. It is the result of suffering, as some traditions teach, in that as the body is afflicted, the spirit is enriched. Pitah and Shekhmet reminds us that though we are Divine Beings, nTr in person, we are persons nonetheless, immortal beings, having a mortal experience. They remind us of our humanity, of our mortality, our "imperfection," and it is in these experiences that empathy, compassion, and understanding are evoked. They remind us that we are imperfect, and the application of these lessons goes on to reveal the true beauty and perfection that lies in our incompleteness; our imperfection. This aspect of their family is evidenced in the traditions in which Shekhmet is unleashed upon mankind. In every instance it is due to man's arrogance, that they encounter the wrath of Shekhmet. Nefertum is the result of successfully going through it, the healing, the renewal, the humility, and the acceptance of our incompleteness and imperfection, that we might surrender to nTr and allow ourselves to be made Nefertum (Perfect and Complete) by the Master Craftsmen; the Architect of the Universe. He is the beautiful work of art that has been shaped and molded by the hands of Pitah and forged by the fire of Shekhmet. Nefertum makes things divine, or more accurately reveals the Divine within all things like the young nTr is revealed from the blossom of the lotus.

Nefertum as the revealer of the nTr within the lotus is perhaps nowhere more pronounced than in his role as the nTr of medicine. He is the nTr of Plants, herbs, oils, and incense. He is a healer, and is considered to be the personal physician to Ra. According to the tradition, when Ra was in pain due to his age and failing health, Nefertum held a Blue Lotus up to his nose that the aromatic-therapeutic properties may soothe him. In this way he is an herbalist, and the nTr of "Pharmacology," as he reveals the vital principles within the herbs, in the same way that he reveals the nTr within the lotus. Over time he became associated with Imhotep, the great Sage, who came to be considered his brother.

As the nTr of Plants, he is their Ba. This is to say that all plant life is an incarnation of Nefertum, although there are some flowers that are particularly special to him, such as the lotus (especially the Blue Lotus). In this role, Nefertum is a universal nTr, and is present in almost every ritual in some form, as every ritual involves the use of herbs as incense, oils, etc, and no ritual can be considered complete without it, regardless of which nTr the ritual is focused upon. In this way Nefertum can grant the knowledge of plants, their use in the various healing arts, as well as their ritual use in regards to their effects and which nTrw they personify.

Nefertum is a wonderful force to work with as it pertains to arts and aesthetic as he is associated with all things that are considered beautiful. Also, he helps to cultivate confidence, grace, charm, and feelings of completeness in bringing one to the realization that they lack nothing, yet at the same time, he cultivates humility and acceptance of the "Divine Plan," understanding of the reason for our trials and tribulations, and the transitory nature of life, allowing us to see the beauty in it all.

Hymn to Nefertum
(Name) pi nw n sSsS wbn m tA
(Name) is the flower that rose from the earth
Wab Ssp (name) in ir ist.f
The hand of (name) is cleansed by him who has made his seat
(name) pi ir Srt sxm wr
It is (name) who is at the nose of the Great Powerful One
i.n. (name) m iw nsisi
(name) comes out of the isle of flame
d.n. (name) mAat im.f m ist isft
(Name) has placed mAat in the place of isfet
(name) pi ir sSrw sAA iarwt grH pw n Agbi wr pr m wrt
(name) is the keeper of laundry, protector of the uraeus, in the night of the great flood that comes forth from the great one.
xa (name) m nfr-tm m sSSn r Srt Ra
(name) appears as Nefertum, as the lotus at the nose of Ra
pr.f m Axt ra nb wabw nTrw n mA.f
As he comes forth from the horizon daily, the nTrw are purified when they see him.

Number

36

Color

Blue/Gold

Day

Friday

Herbs

Lotus (Especially Blue Lotus), All Plant life

Stones

Lapis Lazuli

Offerings

Lotus

Sacred Animal

Lion

Khunm

The nTr Khunm is a creator nTr who is well known for his role as the "Divine Potter." According to the tradition, it is Khnum who forms both nTrw and RmT upon his potter's wheel. He is specifically responsible for the creation of the Ka and the Khat of each and every individual. However, this is not the limit of his role in creation, as it is held that he also personally maintains his creations.

Khnum is depicted as a man with the head of a ram, which the term in Madu nTr for Ram is Ba. Portraying Khnum as a Ba, or Ram is to associate him with the "Ba" spiritual Body. This speaks to the role that Khnum plays in creation as a personal "evolver" of his creations, which is one of the chief functions of the Ba. Of all the creator nTrw, Khnum's cosmology speaks to his playing a more personal and hands on role in creation. Thus we find in the so called "Famine Stele" Khnum declaring to Nisu Djoser "I am Khnum, your maker! My arms are around you, to steady your body, to safeguard your limbs," We also find the statement in the chapter "Not letting the heart of Osir be driven away from him in nTr Gertet," in the **prt m hrw**, *"You are my Ka within my Khat which Khnum strengthed, my limbs*." Also, as the Ba he is said to hold together the limbs of his creation, which speaks to him as a unifying force, joining the "higher bodies" to the "lower bodies," and serving as the personal link

within the world between the Uncreated Universe; Nun or Upper Pet, and the realm of Creation and Order. This function is also demonstrated by his name, which literally means "to join."

As the Ba, Khnum corresponds to the conscience and plays the role of a guide and counselor. This function is spoken to in an **Inscription of Djed Khonsu-f Ankh**: "*Khnum fashioned me as one effective, an adviser of excellent counsel. He made my character superior to others, he steered my tongue to excellence.*" He is in some instances, considered the messenger of nTr and the nTrw, bringing forth their words and counsel. As such, he is called "*sbb mdw nTrw n Ra,*" that is "**who sends the words of the nTrw to Ra**," and is called "*wpwty mAat,*" or "**Messenger of Maat**." Khnum, in this form "reports the message to their Lord (Ra)." He is also associated with nTrw such as Imun, Pitah, Tehuti and Osir, in some cases actually being identified with the latter. Khnum is a force of Maat, of love and compassion. According to the **Instructions of Imun M Opet (Amenmope),** Khnum is said to "*knead the Heart of the Hot Headed Man.*"

Khnum is also a nTr of fertility and wealth, and is associated with the development of the child in the womb, the "Waters of Life," represented by Nun, and also the annual flood of Hopi (The Nile River) which leads to the return of planting season. Fertility rituals were performed on his behalf, particularly by women who aspired to conceive children. This is evidenced by the ritual of the "**Installation of the Potter's Wheel**," in which Priestesses carried a potter's wheel into the temple and stood it before the shrine of Khnum so that he could begin his work of creation; the potter's wheel itself and its being "erected," representing a phallic symbol. This was a ritual that was for women only. As the nTr of the Ba, Khnum himself represents the seed of man that transmits the Ba into the womb of the woman, fertilizes the egg, and fashions/forms both the kA and the khat within her womb.

In relationship to the annual inundation, Khnum is said to be responsible for releasing the waters onto the land. This is spoken to in the "Famine Text," in which Khnum declares to the Nisu "Bsi n.k Hapi!" That is "I will make the Nile Burst for you." He goes further in the text, to assure the Nisu that prosperity will return to Kemet.

Figure 4: Khnum performing his work, moulding the body of the Nisu on his potter's wheel. This is from the Temple of Auset in Aswan, Egypt (Island of Philae)

Khunm has several wives, varying according to tradition. In the city of Yebu, he was married to Satit and Onqit (Anqet), the latter sometimes being considered his daughter. These two nTrwt represented the two phases of the inundation: the period in which the flood waters "shoot forth," corresponding to Satit, and the period in which the waters recede, revealing the fertile soil which ultimately leads to the abundance of the harvest, corresponding to Onqit. However, as the daughter of Khnum and Satit, Onqit represents the culmination/realization of the harvest itself. While these descriptions represent the literal motions of Hopi, on a spiritual/cosmic force level, Satit and Onqit represent the motions, the "ebb and flow" of life, which is represented in other traditions as the Akeru, Ishu and Tufnut, Auset and Nebt Het, i.e. the "Duality of Life." This motion is also present in the act of creation that takes place on Khnum's potter's wheel as his hands motion forwards

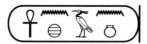

and backwards molding the clay. In a way these two nTrwt are analogous to Khnum's hands, the powers that his creation manifest.

Both Satit and Onqit are protective, and were said to defend the borders of Kemet. In the so-called **"Coffin Texts" passage 313**, speaking of Satit, it states:

> *"Those who shall come against you from the South shall be driven off by Satit, Nebt Yibu, who will shoot at them with her arrows, which are painful and sharp against them."*

The same is held to be true of Onqit.

These nTrwt are also healing forces, especially as it pertains to issues related to the "Waters of Life, "bodily fluids such as blood, semen, breast milk, etc. For instance, women that are having difficulties with their menstrual cycle can work with Satit or Onqit to regulate it. I've had experience, and success working with sisters in this regard. One such instance that comes to mind was when I received a call from a friend, asking that I do some work for a sister he knew and was close to, that was dealing with some very bad hemorrhaging. After performing divination on the situation, I asked for a picture of the sister, along with her name, and began to work with Onqit on her behalf. While performing this ritual, Onqit revealed to me that the issue the sister was going through was a result of her "living too fast," and the depletion and rushing, "bursting forth" of her blood was a reflection of the wasting away of her life force, and that I was to relay that message to her. When I spoke again with the brother, I informed him of what Onqit said and he laughed and said "that's deep," because he knew it to be accurate based on his knowledge of her. Later on that week he called to let me know that she was getting better and the hemorrhaging had stopped. As Onqit corresponds to the receding of the Hopi, she was the force that fit this particular situation. However, in the case of Breastfeeding, she can assist in weaning or stopping the flow of milk, yet she also has the ability to increase the flow and production as she was considered to be the "Nurse" of the Nisu.

Together, the trinity of Khnum, Satit, and Onqit, can also on the highest levels represent "Spiritual Mastery" in regards to controlling the flow of one's emotions and actions, represented by the waters of life, Satit and Onqit, and the realization and actualization of one's Self (Khnum) as the creator of everything that happens in one's life, and as a result, being very conscious and careful in ones actions, that once one does act, the action is very well thought out and precise (Satit) and yields the exact harvest that one set out to achieve (Onqit).

In Isna, Khnum is a part of the family with Menhiyit as his wife and Hika as their son. Menhiyit is a nTrt that plays a very similar role to Khnum, as Shekhmet to Pitah. She is a fiery and aggressive force that is known for her love of slaughter and bloodshed. According to the tradition, Menhiyit was said to travel ahead of the military, cutting down the enemies in their path. This is a reference to her role as a spiritual protector, specifically in regards to the Psychic defense system of the spirit. This part of the spirit gives us the ability to project and influence things from a distance. This is symbolized by the use of "arrows" and the "long bow" by Menhiyit, which is utilized to take out one's adversaries from a distance. In other traditions, Menhiyit's husband is Inhur, whom we will touch on in the section pertaining to Heru Behudet. Inhur is known as the "Harpooner," another weapon utilized in distance attacks. These symbols represent the use of spiritual science, as it relates to "Psychic Defense" and "Psychic Attacks." This is a part of military science that has been lost or slept on in regards to our people and our struggle towards liberation. Traditionally there was a spiritual dynamic to warfare, in which there were rituals performed before, during, and after the war. A perfect example of this is the Haitian Revolution, which was initiated by Vodun Priest and Priestesses, by performing rituals to Ogun, the "Orisa/Lwa" of War. During the ritual there was a blood sacrifice of a pig, given as an offering to the Lwa, followed by a pact to overthrow of their slave masters. This is a very

ancient (and very powerful) practice that is also found in Ancient Kemet, especially in the spiritual warrior traditions. Menhiyit represents the slaughter, and the offering of blood that precedes the physical war, that leads to the "activation of the Ka," personified in her son, Hika. The meaning of her name is a testament to her correspondence to the science of ritual sacrifice/slaughter, as her name literally means "Butcher, Sacrificer, or Slaughterer, and is akin to terms such as "Menhu," meaning "sacrifice, to offer up an animal, sacrificial priest, slaughterer, butcher, slayer, executioner, and "Menhu/Menhi," the name of a nTr that sacrificed animals and foes of the nTr[9]. Also, it is said that she "could only be pacified with streams of blood, roasted limbs of enemies, speared animals, etc[10]."

In a way, the family of Khnum, Menhiyit, and Hika represent the creation of life through the science of ritual sacrifice. As Khnum is the "creator whom fashions the Ka and the Khat on his potter's wheel," he is the father that initiates the creative process. Menhiyit on the other hand, represents the sacrifice of the mother, and the spilling of blood that is present with any birth. This is a principle that applies to all maternal nTrw. Their life, their story represents in some way, the science of sacrifice. Also, almost all of them are associated with the Eye of Ra, and in this way, are related to the nTrt of the slaughter, called by different names depending upon the tradition. Careful study of the traditions will reveal that many of the nTrw are the same force represented differently, varying according to the traditions of the people of the city. In other words, Menhiyit, is identified with Sekhmet, Khnum with Pitah, etc. Anyway, not to stray too far from the subject, the role of being a mother and the act of giving birth is one of sacrifice. The mother sacrifices her body, her energy, her vital essence, her time to this new life that is coming into being through her. The bulk of the genetic material that goes on to become that child comes from the mother as she is the

---

[9] E.A. Wallis Budge "Egyptian Hieroglyphic Dictionary," pg 303

[10] Hallof, Jochen. (2011). Esna. UCLA Encyclopedia of Egyptology, 1(1). nelc_uee_7984. Retrieved from: http://escholarship.org/uc/item/6k78t4w9

"Mater" (Mother/Matter). Sure the father gives up the seed, which contains his vital essence, but after that the total evolution and birth of the child is the result of the mother's sacrifice, and there is nothing to compare it to. The family of Khnum, Menhiyit, and Hika, teaches the science of ritual through creative imagination, and sacrifice as a vital part of creation via the spirit, and the ancient understanding of reciprocity, or the exchange of life for life, and the importance of this in the practice of Hika. While not every sacrifice requires blood, there is always a sacrifice, even if it is just one's time, energy, and attention, or the sacrifice or death of a particular way of thinking and doing things. There is another, higher, aspect to this family, but it must be reserved for the time being.

Prayer to Khnum
mi.n i, mi.n I pA twt n HH n HH
Come to me, come to me, the image of the infinite of infinity
pA Xnmw sA wa
The Khnum, the sole son
pA iwr m sf msw n hrw
the one begotten yesterday, born today
pA nty tw.i rx.kwi rn.f
the one whose name I know
pA nty (77) n irt m-di.f (77) msDr m-di.f
the one with seventy seven eyes and seventy seven ears
mi.n.i di.k sDm .tw xrw.i ngg-wr m grHt
come to me, allow my voice to be heard as ngg-wr (the Great Cackler) in that night
ink baH wr
I am the great flood
ink baH wr
I am the great flood

Renu
Khnum
Khnum Imun
Khnum Ra

Khnum War

Khnum Osir

Khnum Pitah

Khnum Pitah Ta Thenen

War bAw (Great of Baw)

Imn rn.f r msw.f (Whose name is hidden from his children)

Pr m Nt (Proceeded from Niyit)

Ba War Ankh (Great Living Ba)

Ba ankh n Ra (Living Ba of Ra)

nTr nHp (nTr of the Potter's Wheel)

s.mn tA m kAt awy.f (He who established the earth with the work of his two hands)

ir xrt n qmA n.f nb (makes what he has created for the needs of all)

ir xrt n TA m Abdw mD (makes the needs of the nestling in Ten Months)

sbb mdw nTrw n Ra (who sends the words of the nTrw to Ra)

wpwty mAat (Messenger of Maat)

khnum m sheta (who joins in secret)

ir qbHw (maker of the libations)

Day

Friday

Number

77

Color

Blue, Red, White

Herbs

Alkanna tinctoria, Blue Lotus

Sacred Animals

Ram, Crocodile

Totem

Potter's Wheel, Libations Vessel, Clay

Stone

Aquamarine, Sapphire

Figure 5:Niyit at the Temple of Luxor

Niyit

Any claim that women did not hold high status in Ancient Kemet, or the claim that the nTrwt were of lesser importance and only existed as the female counterpart to the male nTr is easily dismissed once one encounters the nTrt Niyit. Niyit is one of the most important, as well as the most powerful of all the nTrw, and is considered to be the feminine expression of "the All;" "Nebt r jer." She is the Great mother of all the nTrw and is in some cosmologies held to be Supreme. In her highest

295

form, she is identified with the Primordial Waters (Nu/Nun), the substance from which the universe, and all that exists within it, consists of. According to a hymn from Esna, Niyit is said to:

> *"give form to the world in her form of nTrt who reaches to the limits of the universe, in her material form of the liquid surface, in her name of unlimited duration...the extension of the water which makes eternity the stream which fashions everlastingness,"*

As such Niyit represents **existence in totality**; "Being "itself, which is spoken to in her name of *"wat"* (**The One**).

The supremacy of Niyit is also evidenced by the role that she plays in the tradition of the "Contendings of Heru and Sutesh." According to the tradition, Ra and the council of nTrw were in the process of determining who should rule Kemet, Heru or Sutesh. It is said that even after 80 years of arguing, they still could not come to a consensus. So they sought counsel with Niyit, and decided that she should make the call. Niyit responded to them saying:

> *"Award the office of Osir to his son Heru. Don't commit such blatant acts of inequity, which are illegal, or I shall become so furious that the sky will touch the ground."*

The fact that the nTrw, including Ra, were willing to defer the decision to Niyit, declaring that "whatever she said to do they would do," is a testament to her position in relationship to them. Also, the fact that she had the power to reinforce her command with a threat, speaks to her power and supreme position over them. Finally, the idea of causing the sky (Nut) to touch the Earth (Gab) is a threat of returning all to the

Nu/Nun (Chaos); the undifferentiated state of the universe prior to creation, in which Nut and Gab were said to be in an "infinite sensual embrace." She was able to threaten them with a return to the "Chaos" because in that state, all forms would cease to be, including the nTrw, and all that would remain would be Her (Niyit) and Subik who "endures forever." This is to say that Niyit and her son/husband Subik correspond to the Chaos itself, and as such exist outside of space and time, whereas all of the other nTrw exist within its parameters. Credence is added to this final point, when we examine that during the whole ordeal, all three planes of existence are engaged, Niyit, corresponding to the Chaos, or Upper Pet, and Osir corresponding to the Duat, while the rest of the nTrw, Heru and Sutesh, are operating within the ordered universe.

Niyit is called "**Niyit the Great who gave birth to Ra, and initiated birth when birth had not yet existed,**" "*Nt iht ms Ra,*" that is, "**Niyit the cow who gave birth to Ra**." However, it is said that <u>she herself was never born</u>. Also, it is said that Niyit gave birth to creation without the aid of a man, so she is called "**One without a second.**" She is a very ancient nTrt, and as such represents the universe itself, and may on some levels represent the very first person, which more than likely was an Afrikan Woman, who brought forth life through parthenogenesis. In this way Niyit is sometimes considered to be "androgynous," containing both masculine and feminine within herself.

Niyit gives us the ability to realize that all is born out of the Self, from within, and we have the ability to conceive within ourselves, and give birth to our aspirations in our lives. Also, the realization that all things ultimately stem from within, provides us with the enlightened perspective, that we are the creator of what takes place in our lives, and any external causes, or apparent "vicarious" fault or blame, is simply an illusion. In truth you as Niyit, are "*Wat,*" (One) and you alone exist.

Niyit is the ultimate reality that exists beyond the ordered and observable universe. She is herself the "Great Mystery" that hides behind the illusion of the physical, objective existence, the realm of plurality.

This aspect of Niyit has come to be known as the "Veil of Niyit (also Auset i.e. the so-called veil of Isis)." The "veil" is the material/objective world that hides the reality of Being. This Veil also played a role in the temples of Kemet, in that before one could enter into the Sacred Shrine of the nTr, they had to first remove the veil from the door, break the "clay seal" over the lock, remove the bolt from the socket of the door, and only then could they enter into the shrine and "see" the face of the nTr, and behold it in its "True Form." The veil represents the illusion of the physical world, and the breaking of the clay seal upon the door represents becoming free of its "fettering." The removing of the bolt from the socket of the door is said to represent the removal of the finger of Sutesh from the "Eye of Heru." Once the "finger" has been removed from the "Eye," one could then "see" the nTr in its "true form," or "behold its face." The Kemetic Science is pure poetry :-)!

This veil was one that was woven by Niyit herself. As such her name is related to terms *ntt*, meaning **"to weave."** She is the "cosmic weaver," who created the "veil" we know as the ordered universe, which is in many traditions considered to be an illusion. This "illusion" formed from the weaving aspect of Niyit, ultimately produces the nTr Subik, who fulfills the role of a "trickster," using confusion and chaos to challenge us to "pierce the veil," and find the light. This is the nature of the earth, and our purpose and goal in it.

The one that Niyit allowed to "unveil her," was one that had realized the Self, and had attained the highest degree of knowledge. As a testament to this fact, the High Priest of Niyit was called *"War Sunu,"* or **"Great one who has recognized."**

Renu of Niyit
Niyit
Wrt (The Great)
Wati (One)
Nt Imntt

Imnt Ra

Nt Wrt Mwt Mst Ra (Great Mother who gave birth to Ra)

Nt Wrt mwt nTr s-HDt Hr tpy anx snb rnpi (Great Divine Mother who enlightens the top of the head causing life, wellness, and freshness)

mwt nTr (Divine Mother)

Iht Wrt (Great Cow)

mwt n Ra (Mother of Ra)

Hnwt anx (Mistress of Life)

Hnwt anx rdi.t Da

Hrrt ant (Beautiful Flower)

Nhm.t Hati

Nt Nbt Hapi (Lady of the Nile)

HqA Dt (Ruler of Everlastingness or Everlasting Ruler)

Hymn to Niyit

I mwt wr

O Great Mother

nn sfx msw.s

your birth has not been unveiled.

i nTrt aAt m xnti dwAt StAt sp.snw

O great nTrt within the duaut which is doubly hidden

itt rx.s

unknown one

I nTri wrt

O you divine one

Nn sfx.tw qrs.s

Not has been unloosed your garment (linen wrap)

I sfx znHw.s

O unloose your fetters

I HApt nn rdi.tw wAt.i n aq r.s

O hidden one, not is given my path of entrance to her

Mait Sspt bA n (your Ren)

Come, receive the Ba of (your Name)

xwy.s m xn.n awy.s

Protect it within your two hands.

Number

0, 7

Day

None, All, Wednesday, Monday, Friday

Totem

Loom, Yarn, Crocodile, Perch, Cow, Vulture Arrows, Shield, veil, Deshert (Red Crown)

Food

Pomeganates,

Sacred Animals

Cow, Crocodile, Perch, quail, vulture, cobra

*Shares offerings with Auset

Figure 6: Stela of Subik receiving offering at the Subik Museum in Nubiyit (Kom Ombo)

Subik

Subik is one of the most misunderstood and yet obscure nTrw that one will encounter in the nKmt tradition. He has been interpreted by some as an evil force, and in some extreme cases, the "devil himself." However, much of the misunderstanding of Subik stems from the complex and obscure nature of the nTr himself.

Unlike many of the other nTrw, Subik cannot be easily classified. In one instance you may find him assisting in helping Auset collect the body parts of Osir, and in another moment he may be seen as a force usurping the throne, or stealing another man's wife ☺. For this reason, many people seem to have a problem "grasping" Subik, and find him to be a rather slippery fellow, changing like night and day.

The reason for Subik's elusive nature is due to the fact he is a creature of Chaos, and is not relegated to one specific mode of expression or being. Of him it is said, "*nn siA irw.f*" that is, "**None know (or perceive) his form,**"*sm StA*, "**hidden image,**" and *iwty rx.f*, "**Knowledge of him does**

not exist." From these epithets, it should be clear that the obscurity surrounding Subik is no accident.

Subik is considered to be the son of Niyit, and as such he is associated Ra. However, this is an aspect of Subik (Ra) many are not well acquainted with. According to the tradition, Subik's rising from the waters of the Hopi and laying eggs upon the shore, were analogous to Ra in the form of Subik, rising from the waters of Nun, in this particular case, the waters being identified with his mother Niyit, or the waters of Hopi. With Subik's rising, time, space, and perception come into being. In this form he is said to have *"nbi m.SAa"* that is he **"fashioned what was at the beginning,** *"qmA wnnt,* **"create that which exists,"** and *"ii m hAt sia n.f pHwy* **"came at the beginning and he has perceived the end.**

Not much is known of Subik's father. According to some accounts his father is Sutesh. However, according to other accounts, his father is called *"Senui"*, of which little is known (according to most scholars). **Senui** literally means **"Two Brothers."** The "two brothers" motif is akin to the *rHwy*, or **"two men**," or as some have put it **"the combatants."** These two brothers are none other than Heru and Sutesh, and represent the principle of Duality or opposites. Therefore, by stating that *"Senui,"* or the "Two Brothers" is the father of Subik, it is being stated that "Duality or opposites" is his father; the understanding of which will provide a key to elucidating much of the mysterious nature of Subik.

Figure 7:Stela of Subik from the Subik Museum in Nubiyit (Kom Ombo) Egypt

Subik being "born of Duality," sheds light onto his "dual nature." He is both a force "light" and "darkness," and can be considered both "positive" and "negative," or "good" and "bad." In fact, it is the duality of Subik, as "*Sia n Neb Jer*," or the "**perception of "Lord of All**," that gives us the ability to not only perceive "light and dark," "good and bad," etc, but also allows us to distinguish between the two, as he is called "*wpi snwi Hr psS.sn*" "**Who segregates the two brothers by dividing them**." However, this particular function of Subik, though a necessity, can also cause us to get caught up in the perception of duality, and never catch a glimpse of the essential oneness of All, ultimately leading one to miss out on the realization of the "Great Mystery" of Self Knowledge represented by his mother Niyit.

Subik as the nTr of the "Realm of Duality," is also "Master of Illusions" and confusion. He is a trickster nTr, and can be very unpredictable. For instance, in his name "*Nb pHwy*," or "**Lord of the Back, behind, or end**," he represents the unpredictable outcome, the hidden opportunity cost that is present in every single decision. He is also a great teacher,

303

especially through trial and error. He meets us at the end of our actions in which the "ends justify the means." He humbles the arrogant, and those who take themselves too seriously. He is a trickster, in fact a comedian, and he loves playing jokes on the high and mighty. However, his comedian side is one of his greatest forms as those who come to learn the ultimate truth to his greatest joke and riddle, i.e. life itself.

Subik is also identified with the nTr Seb (Gab) and is therefore the nTr of the earth. This is his realm, the realm of "illusion," yet at the same time it is the realm in which we've come to learn the truth of reality. This realm, the earth, is the realm of "symbols," and Subik is the nTr of symbols (protector of symbols) in his name of "*ab Sa*," or "*abS.*" The symbols are meant to serve as indicators, pointing us toward a reality that is beyond, however many of us very easily get caught up in the "net" of symbolism, and become confused, mistaking the symbol for the actual reality or truth. A good example of this is the religious dogmatist that fails to realize that at the very foundation of all religions are core principles that unite them beyond the trivial differences in language and symbolism. However, those who are able to see the symbols as doorways will be able to remove the veil from the door, or remove the "sheath" from the eye of Subik, and see through the darkness.

Subik as "*Nb pHww*," is "**Lord of the Swamps/marshlands**," a symbol for the deep abyss, the so called "sub conscious mind." He represents the ability of thoughts to enter into our sphere of awareness, just as a crocodile, snares its prey, seemingly emerging out of the abyss of the water. The swamp however, is significant of that part of the mind that houses all of our deepest, beliefs and fears, our "demons." Fear is definitely one of his chief characteristics as he is called Subik or "*msH hr.ib nrw.f*," that is "**Subik or the Crocodile who dwells within his Terror.**" On one hand this particular form is similar to Shekhmet, in that he is not only the source of fear or terror, but he is also the dispeller of it. He is not only the "guardian of demons" but he also exorcises them in his name *Nb WAbw* "**Lord of Purifications**," and "**Imi Mw**" "Dweller in Water," which annihilates isfet (chaos).

The unpredictable nature of Subik, as well as his "trickery" is meant to

304

keep us perceptive, sharp, and fresh. He means to keep us on our toes. He tests us, challenges us. He manifests as calamity, destruction, chaos, and confusion, as well as the transitory nature of the material world, causing the loss of things, as well as the unexpected "turn of events," or "flipping of the script." In this light, he is considered the "Rebel" amongst the nTrw, playing the part of knocking things out of stagnation by disrupting the current order, to elicit evolution and growth. This "Rebel" form of Subik is especially related to the contradictory thoughts, ideas, and feelings that climb up from the shadowy abyss of the mind, which can be deterrents, or agents that undermine our Will. Overall, the objective is for one to pass these tests.

Subik also somewhat plays the role of a garbage man. He can help one to clean out the clutter of the mind, and also negative energy in one's environment. For instance, in Henensu, Subik is the very first nTr that we bring forth during rituals. This is to clear out any negativity, be it energy in the people present, or any malefic forces that may be present in the space. After this we bring through Anpu to open the way. However, Subik can also be used to end a ritual as well, to remove anything that is left behind. When bwt (taboo) has been committed, offerings are made to him to purify. Subik also assists us in doing away with that which is no longer useful, or serves our spiritual progress.

Number
3
Sacred Animals
Crocodile, Alligators, Lizards
Colors
Red and Black, Orange, Black and Gold, Green
Day
Wednesday
Stones
Carnelian, Emerald
Herb
Tobacco (Cigars), Lavender, Asafoetida (Exorcisms)
Drink

Coffee, Coffee Liquor, Rum, Milk, Palm Wine

Food

Popcorn, Candy, Smoked Fish, Cereal, Kola Nut, Red Palm Oil

Offerings

Two Chickens (Saffron colored)

Sacred Domains

Crossroads, Swamps, Canals, Ditches, Outskirts or end of town, street, neighborhood, etc, Backdoors.

Bwt

Crocodile, Alligator, Lizard, Goose, Ram

Mental traits

Analytical, Vigilante, worrisome, witty, critical, deceptive, erratic

Emotional Traits

Cold, relaxed, comedic, intense/wired,

Hymn to Subik

Nwk msH hr.ib nrw.f

I am the crocodile who dwells within his terror

Nwk msH ini m wAy

I am the crocodile, I bring destruction (the end)

Nwk Rmw aA m xm wr

I am the "Big Fish" in khem war

Nwk Nb Ksnw m sxm

I am the lord of prostrations in Shekhem

Subik Nb Ksnw m sxm

Subik is Lord of Prostrations in Shekhem

Hesi

Imi Mu...Neb Wobu (Chant on rhythm of 123...123)

Remi war Owar...Subik Neb Pehuu

Renu

Subik

Subik Ra

Subik sA Nt (Subik son of Niyit)

Imi mw (Dweller in water)

siA n Nb r Dr (Perception of the Lord of All)

Subik sbiw (Subik the Jester/Comedian)

Nb wAbw (Lord of Purifications)

Figure 8:Shrine of Anpu at Temple of Hatshepsut

Figure 9:Shrine of Anpu at Temple of Hatshepsut

Anpu/Wapuwat

Anpu is another nTr that is of the utmost importance, as he plays a role that transcends the diversity of the various local traditions. Anpu is the mediator between man, the nTrw, and the spirit realm. He is a "psychopompic" nTr, in that he serves as a gatekeeper and guide of the "deceased"/Initiate, through the Duat. However, these are just a few of

309

his functions, as he is also a teacher of the higher spiritual sciences, and a great protector and healer.

Anpu is the son of Nebt Het and Osir, though in some traditions he is considered the son of Osir and Auset, and at other times he is the son of Ra. However, the former parentage is considered general (or the rule), while the other cases are considered contextual. As the son of Osir and Nebt-Het, Anpu is the product of Divine Intelligence (Osir) having intercourse with "Matter" (Nebt Het), leading to the Divine intelligence's incarnating as "Earthly intelligence." He is the concrete, analytical, and investigative intelligence, the force that moves us to learn, and "sniff" and search out the truth. However, the highest function of Anpu in this particular role is to motivate us to learn about, better yet "remember," Osir, the Divine Self. This is portrayed in the tradition as Anpu assisting Auset with finding the missing pieces of Osir's body after his dismemberment by Sutesh. His effort to put the pieces back together again represents the years of research and study, especially Self study that one must partake in, gathering pieces of information bit by bit, and then ultimately applying that information, and utilizing it to elevate and resurrect

Osir, the Divine Within. However, it should be known that as Anpu represents the analytical mind, his journey is one of vigilance, and he does not simply accept or "digest" any and everything he hears or smells. He is our faculty of discrimination.

Anpu's nature is one of Duality, which is reflected much in his parentage. He plays critical roles on every plane of existence, especially in regards to the Duat and Ta. He in is the "Gate Keeper," the "Opener of the Way," who is called "Wapuwat" in Madu nTr. While Wapuwat has been considered by some to be a unique individual nTr in his own right, through time their traditions have been intricately connected to one another, and in many cases even being identified with one another, and in other cases each having a shrine dedicated to the other in their own respective temples. Both were depicted in the forms of Jackals, though Wapuwat is considered to be a ""wolf" (actually both are today considered to be a form of a wolf). However, we should keep in mind

310

that syncretism was not something considered foreign nor taboo in ancient Kmt, and even today it is as Afrikan as fufu ☺.

Both Anpu and Wapuwat are considered to be "Opener of the Way." However, it should be known that this name or epithet is more functionary, and is even shared with the nTrt Niyit, who is called "Wapuwat." In some instances, where Anpu is said to be present at the scales during the "Weighing of the Heart," at other times it is said that Wapuwat is the one that is present. Sometimes Anpu is said to be the guardian of the body of Osir, at other times it is Wapuwat that is guardian. Both are in some instances identified with Heru, and are called "sons of Auset," and both hold the ren *Khenti Imentiyu* (Foremost of the Westerners). It is my position that the differences are of a functionary nature, and not absolute.

Wapuwat is said to open the way for the Nisu in battle, and as such he led the royal procession. He is a force that removes obstacles from one's path. For this reason, some people have proposed that Wapuwat is a nTr of Ta, and is closer to man than Anpu, whom according to these sources, is relegated to funerary traditions. However, this is not true. Anpu is called "Neb Pet Ta," or Lord of Heaven and Earth, and *"Nb aAwy,"* or "**Lord of the Two Doors** (Entrances to both planes of reality)." While he is called "*Pr aA n dwAt*" (**Pharoah of the Duat**) and *Neb Duat* (**Lord of the Duat**), he is also called "*Neb ta*" (**Lord of the Earth**) and *Tupy Ta* (**He who is on the Earth**). Taking all of this into consideration, we can ascertain that Anpu is a nTr who is present and functional on every plane of existence, Pt, Ta, and Duat, and not simply relegated to the Duat or funerary roles and functions. Anpu is liminal, in that he exists on the edge, beyond, not belonging to any one sphere but able to operate on all of them. He is a force of "Change," as spoken to in the "Litany of Ra," in which Khepri is said to be his "hidden support."He is a force of change, transformation, and is associated with Life, death, and rebirth, playing a key role in each. He is called the "**Great Breath and Birth**," and *sqr tbn m pr mnat*," that is, "**he who beats the drum in the House of Birth**"and "*khenti Hwt papa*," that is, "**foremost in the birthing house**," "opening the way" for the child at birth, leading the procession of the

child from the womb, and opens the throat for the child's first breath. This "birth" however, is not simply speaking to literal birth, but also spiritual and mental birth. Before something can be born, Anpu must "Wapuwat," open the way. This is speaking to Anpu as a force that must be "satisfied," before one can seek to accomplish anything. "As "Lord of offerings," not only does he represent the act of offering and sacrifice, but it is also being stated that in a way, all offerings belong to him, or at least he shares in all offerings. Before one can offer to another nTr or approach them, they must first s.Htp (Satisfy) Anpu. Before one can "invoke" a nTr, Anpu/Wapuwat must first be invoked. This is reason why Anpu is known by historical accounts, to lead the procession of the nTrw during the festivals, though the documenters never truly understood this. This very same principle is present and active today in the various traditions of Afrika such as Ifa, Vodou, and all of its many expressions in the Diaspora; in the Orisa known as Esu (Elegba/Legba in the West). During rituals, Esu is the first Orisa or Lwa, who is offered to and invoked before any other. He has a place in every shrine, and it is he that ultimately brings offerings to the Orisa (Deities) and Olodumare (The Supreme). This very same principle is present in the Kemetic tradition in Anpu, in that he is called *"Khenti Hwt nTr"* **"Foremost** (literally "at the front") **of the House of nTr** (Temple/Shrine), *mniyu*, **"of the Shrine,"** or possibly the shrine itself, and *m.xnty sH nTr* (**Foremost of the Divine Booth/Shrine**), etc, and has a place in every shrine. In fact, Anpu is identified with the nTr ishu (Shu)[11], and as it will be demonstrated, the nTr ishu and the Orisa/Lwa Esu are one and the same. Also, he is the nTr that presents the offerings to the nTrw. He is called *DbA psDw* (**He who clothes the nTrw**); *DbA it.f Osir m WAbt* **"He who clothes his father Osir in the Purification House (Embalmment House)."** These last two names are reflective upon Anpu as the patron of the priesthood, especially the High Priesthood, the *Sem Priest*, and the *Kheri Hebt*.

---

[11] Leitz, Christian "Lexikon der Agyptischen Gotter und Gotterbezeichnungen" Vol.7 pg.35. 2002

Traditionally, only the High Priest could approach the nTr directly, and one of his main duties was to take care of the shrine of the nTr: cleanse it, clothe it, feed it, as well as offer "voice offerings" via Hesi (chants, hymns, etc). The priest would shroud the body of the nTr (the statue) with strips of colorful linen; this was a part of the daily temple ritual. The wrapping/clothing of the nTr with colorful strips of cloth, parallels, and is reflective upon the funerary ritual, and the act of wrapping, shrouding, and clothing the body of the Ancestor during the mummification process. The entering into "Inner Sanctuary" and beholding the form of the nTr is reflective of entering the "Body" of nTr (Osir/the Ancestor) and beholding the "secrets/mysteries." Both of these duties are carried out by the High Priesthood, of which Anpu is the Patron and Archetype. For this reason, we find examples of the High Priests performing these duties while wearing masks of Anpu.

Figure 10: Priest wearing Anpu Mask

Figure 11: Priests wearing masks of Anpu and Heru while in the
Henu (Jubilation) Posture

Figure 12: Priest wearing Anpu mask while performing mummification.

Figure 13: Priest wearing Anpu mask while performing the Opening of the Mouth ritual.

Figure 14: Anpu Mask

Figure 15: Anpu Mask

Figure 16: Anpu mask

The relationship between Anpu and the priesthood is further evidenced by renu (names) such *as xry Hb tpy* (**Chief Kheri Heb**), *xry Hb tpy st StAt* (*Chief Kheri Heb of the Secret Place*) and *sm,* all of which speak to his being the "Archetypal" force manifesting through them (The High Priesthood) as they fulfill their duties that are, according to tradition,

317

fulfilled by Anpu, which include: taking care of and the serving the nTr, oracular consultation (communicating with nTrw and Ancestors), embalmment, and guiding initiates through the Duat.

Going back to the point regarding Anpu as a nTr of birth; it was stated that before anything can be born in any plane, Anpu must first open the way. Mentally speaking, this pertains to Anpu as the nTr that manifests as our faculty of discrimination, the "Gate keeper" of our minds and spirits. Whenever we are listening to suggestions, attempting to learn new things, choosing one thing over another, etc, it is Anpu, our discriminative faculty that determines whether or not we are receptive enough to learn, to listen, etc. This faculty is strongly connected to our beliefs and opinions, which can in many cases "tip the scales" in our decision making. Sometimes these beliefs and opinions will prevent us from being able to learn new things or accept advice. Also, faulty logic, erroneous beliefs, and being stanch in our opinions can lead us to much difficulty when we encounter situations that require us to step "outside of our box." When this is the case, we must be like Osir and lay upon the embalmment bed so that Anpu can "remove' the corruption from within us. As the guide through the Duat, he also leads the initiate into the deeper aspects of Self, revealing the hidden motivating factors that ultimately serve as the true causes behind what we believe and what we do. Once these "mysteries" have been revealed the embalmment and healing process can begin.

In regards to spiritual birth, the same holds true. If we are looking to seed our spirits with new ideas, or manifest something through ritual and the power of our spirits, it is Anpu, our discriminative faculty that will determine whether or not that seed takes root and conception takes place. Ultimately it is our own beliefs, especially what we believe about ourselves that will go on to determine whether or not we are successful in our ritual; creative endeavors. It does not matter if one "knows" what they are doing, if they don't "believe" in themselves and their capabilities, if they pay more attention to thoughts of doubt than they do images and affirmations of their success, ultimately they will fail; foiled by their own beliefs and thoughts.

As the nTr that protects and preserves the body of Osir, he is the intellect and discriminative faculty that is purified by ideas that are based upon Maat, which serve as a protector of our awareness (Osir). Ideas, opinion's, beliefs, should not go unchecked and unscrutinized. They, along with our very own thoughts, must be thoroughly investigated, analyzed. Anpu must place them upon the scales of Maat to see if they equate. He is *Iri mxAt* (**Keeper of the scales/balance**). As the keeper of the scales he is also "Master of the Usekhet n Maati," the hall of Two Truths, which is the nkmt Equivalent of the "Crossroads." As our ib (Heart/decisions) is weighed on the scales, how Anpu analyzes/rationalizes the situation will determine whether or not we are allowed to pass through to Osir (our goal, the path of light, nTr) or whether Anpu will deliver our Ib to the Omomyit (our animal passions/ego, the path of Darkness). This is another testament to the Dual Nature of Anpu. As the sekhet n Maati is in fact a symbol of the mind, it speaks to how our own thinking can lead us to the right path, or we can rationalize things in a way to make the wrong thing seem right. Anpu is the Guide, but to which path will he guide? Will he lead us to truth, or will he deceive us? This principle is part of the reason Anpu is depicted as a Jackal or Dog. While a dog can be trained, and can be a loyal companion, excellent guardian and guide, they can also be deceptive and opportunistic, and are known to bite the hand that feeds them. This is the nature of the mind. Train him well! This is also the reason why Anpu is referred to and depicted as the "Black and Gold nTr," symbolizing the Duality of his nature as both light and dark, nTr of both Duat and Ta, etc.

There is a story about Anpu and Sutesh. One day Sutesh was attempting to sneak into Osir's tomb and desecrate his body. However, Sutesh was unaware of the fact that Anpu was there "laying in the cut," and keeping watch. As soon as Sutesh made his move Anpu snatched him up. He (Anpu) then took a hot poker from the furnace and proceeded to poke Sutesh repeatedly. After this, Anpu took a knife and flayed; literally skinned Sutesh. He then took Sutesh's skin and wore it, and from that day on the Sem Priest wore leopard skin to commemorate

Anpu's triumph over Sutesh. Interesting to note, this is the nKmt story of how the Cheetah, or Leopard, got its spots.

The above story speaks to Anpu's role as the guardian and protector of body of the nTr, which in the ritual sense represents the shrine, and spiritually the mind/spirit, and the mysteries contained therein. Beginning with the ritual significance, it is Anpu's job to prevent "bwt," "taboo" and that which is "impure," from entering the shrine of the nTr. This is why all offerings go through Anpu first, and then he in turn gives them to the nTr. He must first inspect the offerings. This is also symbolized in the "weighing of the heart," in which Anpu inspects the heart of the individual seeking to gain access to the shrine of the nTr. Anpu must ensure that they have not committed "bwt" and that they are pure. In this story, Sutesh represent's that which is bwt (he is called "bwt wr" or "The Great Bwt"), attempting to access the shrine of the nTr, or that which is impure trying to approach the "Divine," which is pure. What happens to Sutesh in the story, represents, symbolically, the consequences of offering bwt, or being in a state of bwt when making offerings to the nTrw or Ancestors, or when performing rituals of any kind. The offender gets "burned,' or "zapped," which can result in spiritual or psychological imbalance or worse.

Spiritually, the story represents our ability to defend our minds and spirits, and prevent impure thoughts or ideas from entering in. When our internal Anpu is strong, we are sharp and vigilante, and able to easily "poke holes" in whatever it is, be it negative thoughts, bad ideas, or faulty logic.

Renu of Anpu
Anpu (General Form)
Wapuwat (Opener of the Way)
Iri mXAt (Master of the Scales/Balance)
ZAb wr (Great Judge)
tpy dw.f (He who is upon his mountain)
Km nbw nTr (Black and Gold nTr)
Imi wt (He who is within his "Booth")

320

xnty imntyw (Foremost of the Westeners)

xnty sH nTr (Foremost in the Divine Shrine)

Iri aA mtr n dwAt (Great Gatekeeper of the Duat)

Wpty aA n dwAt (Great messenger of the Duat)

Pr aA n dwAt (Great "House"/ Pharoah of the Duat)

Rs n dwAt (He who is Awake/ Watcher of the Duat)

Ip ib/ip ibw (Counter of Hearts)

Ip ibw xx m wsxt MAati (Counter of Hearts who owns the Usekhet Maati)

Imy.r mXAt (Overseer of the Balance)

Iry mXAt nt nTr aA (Great nTr who owns the Balance)

xnty Hwt nTr (Foremost of the Divine House/Temple/Shrine)

Dr stS m niwt nbt (He who expels Sutesh from every city)

Stp stS m sa.f (He who butchers Sutesh with his knife).

Hymn to Anpu (For Protection)

Rs.k

You who are awake

Rs tpy dw.f

He who is upon his mountain is Awake (Watching)

At.k xsf.ti

Your moment is repelled

iw xsf.n.i at.k Adw

I have repelled your rage

iw.i m zA

I (Anpu) am the protector of (your name)

Hesi

Prt M Anpu

Come forth Anpu

Zeshmi m Maat

Lead me to Maat

Prt m Anpu

Come Forth Anpu

dwA n Wapuwat

Thanks for opening the Way

Day
Wednesday

Colors
Black & Gold (Main), Saffron and White, Red and Black

Number
3
Herb
Clover

Incense
Lavender, Tobacco (Cigar)

Drink
Palm Wine, Milk, Coffee, Coffee Liquor, Rum

Food
Popcorn, Candy, Dry Cereal, Trail Mix, Carrot Sticks, Celery Sticks

Sacred Animals
Jackal, Wolf, Dogs

Totem
Dogs, Jackal, Wolf, Keys, Doorways, Scales

Stones
Emerald, Carnelian, Aventurine

Sacred Domains
Strongholds, Doors, Gates, Walls, Crossroads, Cemetery, Mountain tops, Hill Tops, Every Shrine

Psychological Traits

Sharp Intellect, Analytical, Studious, Quick witted, Mathematical/Calculative, Keen, Vigilant, investigative

Emotional

Dry, Serious

Psychic

Clairaudience, Clairlience, Articulation

Tehuti

Tehuti is one of the most important nTrw, and plays pivotal roles in many cosmologies and traditions. In fact, according to the tradition, it is Tehuti that is responsible for bringing Madu nTr to the world, language (spoken and written), as well as the sacred writings and teachings. He is also the source and inspiration for the "Western Magic Tradition" of "Hermetics," which in truth, is the foundation of all Western Occult Teachings and Secret Societies. He is the nTr of wisdom, knowledge, learning, high spiritual sciences, divination, Hika, scribes, teachers, priests, judges, etc.

As with many of the other major nTrw, Tehuti has many forms. In his highest expression, he is the "mental nature/essence" of the universe,

324

and gives rise to the conceptualization of the universe as a "Great Infinite Mind (This is the essence of Hermetics)." This particular form of Tehuti is spoken to in his cosmology of Khmnu, which we've touched on in the chapter pertaining to the cosmologies. In this tradition the Khmnu nTrw are considered to be the "*bAw of Tehuti*." Also he is said to have laid an egg upon the primeval mound, from which Ra hatched and began the process of creating the ordered/physical universe. Tehuti shares this aspect (in his cosmology) with other nTrw such as Pitah, Imun, Khnum, Osir, Niyit, etc, in that he represents the Primordial Waters, The Source, but in this instance the source as infinite intelligence.

In a lesser capacity, but still highly important, Tehuti is one of the chief creative elements of the "other" Creator nTrw in their cosmologies. For instance, in the Cosmology of Pitah, Tehuti is considered to be Pitah's tongue, which he utilized to create the universe and everything in it, including the nTrw and people. We also find in relationship to Ra, Tehuti is considered to be both the "heart" and "tongue" of Ra through which he brought forth creation. The significance of the "heart and tongue," corresponds to the intelligence and sound/vibrations that constitute existence, and are ultimately responsible for the laws that undergird, govern, and maintain creation. As the "*Ib n Ra,*" or **Heart of Ra,**" specifically, it is being stated that Tehuti is both the "mind" and "Will" of Ra, or in other words "Divine Mind/Will."

As the "Tongue" of nTr, he is the very vibration that constitutes the existence and functionality/purpose of a thing. It is said of Tehuti that he "establishes the throne, rank, shrine, and offerings of the nTrw," and he is also said to have "Crafted the Great Peseju nTrw." As all is a manifestation of nTr, Tehuti existing within all nTrw as their "Tongue," as their ib. He is their ability to "speak" their wisdom. He is the "Will and Word" of nTr, the Madu nTr. This reality is the essence of Oracular consultation and divination, which allows one to communicate with the nTrw, and receive guidance, insight, prophecy, etc. In Ancient Kmt there were many Oracles, and many nTrw and Ancestors were consulted by the people. It is the Tehuti within the nTrw that one is communicating

with during divination.

Tehuti's role as the nTr of wisdom is present in many traditions. He is called "*wp rHwy*," **Judge of the Two Fighters**" i.e. Heru and Sutesh, which represents the ability of wisdom to reconcile conflict, opposing decisions, opposing perspectives, and the ability to distinguish between right and wrong based upon what is relevant to the situation in question, and what the time calls for. This role is also spoken to in names such as "*tx aqA Hr.ib mxAt*," and "*tx ab mxAt*," that is "**precise plummet in the middle of the balance/scales**," and "**plummet which unites the scales**." As mentioned earlier, the usekhet Maati and the scales represent the mind and the "judgment;" the decision making process. As the "Plummet in the middle of the scales," Tehuti provides a non biased perspective that allows one to see clearly into a situation, so that one can make the clearest and most correct judgment possible.

Tehuti plays a few more critical roles in the tradition. He is the nTr that heals Heru's Eye, which had been injured by Sutesh. According to one tradition, Sutesh gouged Heru's eye out in the midst of a battle, and in another tradition Sutesh takes on the form of a "Black Pig" that created a storm in Heru's eyes when he looked upon it. In both of these instances, it is Tehuti that is credited with healing and restoring Heru's eye.

In the coffin text, Tehuti states:

> *"I have come that I may seek out the Eye of Heru, I have brought and examined it, and I have found it complete, fully numbered and intact."*

This is very important as the Eye of Heru is a major offering to nTr. Tehuti healing the Eye of Heru, relates to the role that wisdom plays in changing one's perspective, allowing them to see more clearly (completely) Maat; the truth.

Tehuti is also called "*s.Htp Ra*," "*s.Htp nTrw*," "*s.Htp nsrt nSn.t.s*," that is "**he who satisfies Ra**," "**Satisfies the nTrw**," and "**he who satisfies the fiery one when she rages (Shekhmet)**." This word "s.Htp" meaning "*to satisfy,*" also means "*to offer,*" *to appease,*" and "*to bring to peace.*" These names speak to the role Tehuti plays in restoring, or offering Maat to the nTrw, bringing balance and order back to these forces, and by extension life when things are in a state of isfet. This is done by shedding light on to what a person has done, and needs to correct in their thinking and behavior, as well as any offerings that must be made to the nTrw in order to remedy or supplement (optimize) any situation. This is another aspect of Tehuti that is in operation during the process of divination. (See the chapters on Hika and divination).

Tehuti is also a nTr of Time, or more specific "Timing," and as such came to be associated with the moon, which the nKmt Ancestors utilized as a means to keep track of time, and based their "spiritual" calendar off of. It is said of Tehuti, that he is responsible for the 365-day calendar that we have. Originally there were only 360 days, and Tehuti won the other five days from the nTr Khonsu in a game of Senet, in which moonlight was the wager. During these five extra days, the five children of Nut and Gab were born. Tehuti being victorious over Khonsu represents the ability of wisdom to successfully move in accordance with the time as Khonsu represents time itself. Wisdom is knowing what time it is, and how to act or not act in accordance with it. Also, Tehuti winning "light" represents the wisdom and illumination that is gained from one successfully moving with the flow of time, Shai (Destiny,) etc.

In association with the moon, Tehuti is also considered to be the "lunar eye" of Ra (the left eye). As the moon is associated with the night time, sunset, etc, it is further associated with the "West" or Duat, and the "Inner Eye" or the "Mind's Eye." This eye allows us access to inner vision, or insight, intuition, wisdom, and the ability to look into the darkness of the Duat (Spirit Realm, "Sub-conscious"). This association is also evident in Tehuti's role as a guide or navigator on behalf of Ra, as he journeys with Ra in the night time Bark, as Ra traverses through the Duat. As we look within and encounter the nTrw and "demons," we begin to bring order to them through the commands of Ra via Tehuti, the Madu nTr.

However, it should be known that Tehuti is also the "Guide and Navigator" of Ra in the "Daytime" bark as well. This is evident from stories like **"Ra Herukhuti and Heru Behudet."** According to the Story, Ra was journeying through the land and Tehuti noticed that the enemies of Ra were plotting to attack him. At the behest of Ra, Tehuti commanded Heru Behudet to deal with the enemies of Ra. Every time Tehuti would see an enemy, he pointed Heru Behudet in that direction, and then proceeded to name the location based upon the way that Heru Behudet dealt with his enemies there. As stated before, these enemies represent the forces of chaos, and their attempt to inhibit the harmony and continuity of Ra's journey, which represents the flow, order, and cycles of life itself. This being the case, Tehuti represents the peace, harmony, order, and divine protection, which happens as a consequence of moving according to wisdom.

As Tehuti is called "**Neb Madu nTr**," not only is this talking about the actual language of Kmt, and nature, but this, as we've touched on a little earlier, also represents divination, which some people refer to as the "Word of nTr," or the "Word of God." Looking at the role that Tehuti plays as a guide and navigator, what we have is a precedent and one of the earliest accounts of the idea of the "Word of God," and its function as a guide in one's life. Tehuti as this "Guide" via the "Divine Word," can come from within (Intuition), *bAw n Ra* (omens), the nTrw via oracular consultation, or the Ancestors through any of the aforementioned means. This is once again, spoken to by the association of Tehuti with the "Tongue of the Divine," in which all nTrw are variations of, as well as his role as a "spokesman" or "messenger" of Ra, and Osir, the symbol of the Ancestors. Following the guidance of Tehuti via the Madu nTr in its various expressions will lead one to not only have a successful and harmonious life, it will lead them to actualize their divine potential as a nTr, in this realm and the next. In this regard the **Pyramid Texts 577** states:

> **Htp tm it nTrw**
> Itum, Father of the nTrw is Satisfied
> **Htp Sw Hna tfnt**

ishu and Tufnut are satisfied

Htp Gbb Hna Nwt

Gab and Nut are satisfied

Htp Osir Hna Ast

Osir and Auset are satisfied

Htp stS Hna Nt (or Nebt-Het)

Sutesh and Niyit (or Nebt Het) are satisfied

Htp nTrw nb imi pt

All nTrw in Heaven are satisfied

Htp nTrw nb imi tA m tAw

All nTrw in earth and lands are satified

Htp nTrw nb rsy mHty

All southern and northern nTrw are satisfied

Htp nTtrw nb imntt iAbtt

All western and eastern nTrw are satisfied

Htp nTrw Nb spAtw

All nTrw of the States/Nomes are satisfied

Htp nTrw Nb niwwt

All nTrw of the cities are satified

Hr mdw pn wr aA pr m r n DHwty n Osir

By the great and mighty words coming forth from the mouth of Tehuti regarding Osir

s.DAw anx xtm nTrw

the seal of life and seal of the nTrw

inpw ip ibw ip.f Osir (Name of Initiate/Ancestor) ma nTrw irw tA n nTrw imi pt

Anpu the counter of hearts separates Osir (Name) from the nTrw from the earth to the nTrw in Heaven

The Above passage from the pyramid texts is speaking to the fact that it is by the Word of Tehuti that the nTrw are satisfied with a person, and it is by Tehuti's word that one is declared to be a nTr on earth, as well as in the heavens. This point is also expressed in the Usekhet n Maati, in which it is Tehuti that makes final judgment in regards to a person, and whether they will be allowed to pass through the Hall and Unite with Osir, a symbol of Becoming a nTr and Elevated Ancestor.

Tehuti is also considered the *Nb MAat*, or **Lord of Maat**, as well as the Father/Husband of Maat. He is the progenitor of the Law, in that it is his word, once again, that regulates the nTrw, which in turn regulate the universe. Through following the guidance of Tehuti one can place themselves into harmony and oneness with all, and thus ultimately realize and actualize their Divinity.

Hesi
Tehuti Neb Hu sia…Tehuti Om Taui

Hymn
I iaH Dhwty
O Moon, Tehuti
kA xmnw Imi Hsrt
Bull of Khmnu, Dweller within Hesert
Iri wAt m nTrw
Who makes a path for the nTrw
Rx.f sStA
He Knows the Secrets
smnn r.sn
records their speech
Tnw smi r kii
distinguishes one speech from another
wp n nbw
Judge of All
SsA Hr m wiA n HH inn Hnmmt
Sharp Faced in boat of millions of years
Rx si.wati ma ra.f
Knows a man by his speech
s.wnn iri.t r iriw
causes the deed to rise against the doer
s.Htp Ra
Appeases Ra
nDnD nb wati
advises the Sole Lord
rdi.nb rx xprt nb

lets him know all that happens

HD tA is.f m pt

At dawn he summons in heaven

nn mhy.n.f Hr smi n sf

does not forget yesterdays report

i.nw DHwty

let us Praise Tehuti

tx aqA Hr.ib makAit

straight plummet in the scales

wni isft

repulses isfet (chaos)

Sspti tm rmn r irt iw

Accepts him who leans not on crime

TAti wDa mdwt

Vizier who settles cases

sSrr Xnnw m Htp

who reduces turmoil to peace

sS n tmA s.mn arq

scribe of the mat who keeps the scroll

hAd aDA

punishes criminals

Sspti gri

Accepts the silent

wDA rmn

sound of Shoulder

arq m Xnw psDt nTrw

wise within the peseju nTrw

wTz nb smx

raises all that's forgotten

SsA Hr nti tnm

Wise regarding the errant

sXAw At Hnti

remembers the passing moment

smi wnwt wxt

reports the hour of the night

Ddt.f mn.r Dt

Whose words endure forever

aq r dwAt rx imi.s

enters the Duat, knows what's in it

s.nhi.sn r imi rn.f

records them into the list

<u>Renu</u>

Tehuti

DHwty Nb Hw siA

DHwty Neb Madu nTr (Tehuti Lord of Madu nTr)

DHwty am TAwi (Tehuti Understanding the Two Lands)

DHwty n pr mDAt (Tehuti in the House of Books)

DHwty s.Htp nTrw (Tehuti appeaser of the nTrw)

DHwty s.Htp nsrt m snmt (Tehuti appeaser of the Fiery One win she mourns)

iaH (Moon)

Ib n Ra (Heart of Ra)

Ipi ib nTr (nTr who reckons the heart)

kA mAat (Bull of Maat)

Ns n ptH (Tongue of Pitah)

Ipwti n rmTw (judge of men)

Rx.f sStA (He knows the secrets)

hb hb StAw (traverses the mysteries)

wp n nbw (judge of all)

<u>Day</u>

Thursday

<u>Number</u>

8

<u>Stone</u>

Lapis, Amethyst

<u>Herb</u>

Lotus, thuja, papyrus

Colors
Blue & White, Violet

Totem
Oracle, Scales, **Pen and Pad (Blank Pages)**, Open Book (blank Pages)

Sacred Animal
Ibis, Baboon

Food
Almonds, Dates, Cashews, Lotus, **Figs and Honey (A traditional offering to Tehuti for revelation of truth and justice, also offered for fertility, wealth, and abundance).**

Fresh baked White Bread cut into a "cone" or "triangle" offered with the point up. Offer to be mAa-xrw in Judgment

Drink
Lotus Tea

Psychological
Higher Reasoning, Rational, Observant, Mathematical, Non-Biased/Objective, Intuitive, Sage

Emotional
None

Psychic
Intuitive, Prophetic (Able to perceive the "Seeds" of Events)

Figure 17: Het Heru giving life and protection to Seti I via the Menit

Het Heru

Het Heru is one of the most important of all the nTrw, as well as one of the most popular. She is the nTrt of love, joy, music, dance, Young Women, sexuality, fertility, and Creation. Similar to Mwt, Het Heru can be considered the Divine Feminine par excellence, every other nTrt being considered a manifestation of her. Like many other nTrw, she also has a supreme form, in which she can be interpreted, and worked with, as both the source of creation, and creation itself.

In her Supreme form, Het Heru is the mother of Ra, and by extension, the mother of all the nTrw. This makes her the "mother of all the living." In this role she is a symbol of the Pre-creation universe, and as such she is associated with Nun/Nun.t, Niyit, Imun.t, Yasuaset, and Mehit Warit. In this expression she is "Existence" or "Being" itself. For instance, in the Coffin Text, in the chapter *"Xpr m Hwt Hrw,"* or **"Becoming Het Heru,"** she is called *"Hwt Hrw pAwtit Nbt r Dr,"* that is **"Het Heru, the Primordial Matter, Lordess of All."** "Nebt r Jer" is a reference to the Source, the substantive universe in totality, the All, in its feminine expression. Of her, it is said:

"nn Dr n Hr.i...nn Snw awy.i...iw nTr.nb r wiA.f sw tp-a.i...nwk iart anx.t m mAat s.Ts.t Hr n nTr.nbw...iw nTr.nb gr rdw.i"

that is,

"There is no limit to my face (sight), none can encircle my arms. Every nTr, he is removed from before me. I am the Yoriyit who lives off Maat, who raises the face of every nTr, and every nTr is beneath my feet."

These passages convey the fact that in her highest expression or correspondence, Het Heru is Supreme, and nothing exists outside of her. She is called the "Grandmother" of the nTrw. However, she is not limited to a pre creation role.

As the wife and sometimes daughter of Ra, she is actually the physical manifestation, and vehicle through which he creates the world. Even in cases where Ra is portrayed as alone in the act of creation, Het Heru is present. For instance, in the **"Book of Knowing the Evolutions of Ra and Overthrowing Owapep,"** Ra (Itum) is said to have "embraced his shadow," during the creative act. This shadow is said to have actually been the nTr.t Het Heru in the form of Yasuaset. In another instance he

is said to have ejaculated into his "hand" (masturbation). His hand is in this case, none other than Het Heru, who is called "*Drt nTr nt Ra*," or "**The Divine Hand of Ra**." Yet again we have another instance, in which Ra is said to have wept, and mankind came into being from his tears. Who is the eye of Ra that these tears are flowing from? You guessed it, none other than the nTr.t Het Heru, who in that particular text is referred to as *MAAt n Ra* (**Eye of Ra**). The purpose here was not to hide the participation of the Divine Feminine in the act of creation, but to demonstrate the inseparability (literally indivisible in nature) between Ra and Het Heru, and to also demonstrate that she is critical to each step and there is no creation without her. She is the body of Ra, and thus creation itself.

As all is considered to be a manifestation of Ra, and he comes into being as Creation itself, Het Heru as his physical counterpart is actually the "physical ordered universe," or physical creation. In the same chapter of the Coffin Text, she states "*nwk Hwt Hr init Hr.s, Hwt Hr.s,*" that is "*I am Het Heru who brings forth her Heru, Proclaiming her Heru.* Also "*wnnt wTst nfr.f iabt xw.f,*" *I am she who displays his beauty and concentrates (unites) his powers.*" This aspect of Het Heru, as expressed in the preceding passages, speaks to her serving as the physical vehicle of her nTr Ra (Heru), and the power that causes his power and will to come into expression. In this form she is called "Rayit and Arat," the feminine counterpart of Ra. In the same text it is stated "*nwk irt.tw nt Hr wptyt nb wa,*" that is "*I am the Eye of Heru, the messenger of the One Lord.*" As we know, "messenger of Ra," is a position normally held for Tehuti (or ishu), however, in this particular case Het Heru as "*Ir.t Hrw/Ra,*" that is "**Eye of Heru or Ra**" is the "messenger" in that she is the force that makes the "word," which in the creative sense corresponds to their Will, manifest (She brings forth their "Word/will"). She brings forth their creation. This idea is further demonstrated by the relationship between the word used for "Eye," in this particular case "*ir.t,*" which is also a homophone to the term that means "to do, to cause, to make, to create, etc." This same principle holds true for all nTrw pairs (Husband and Wife) and Trinities (Father, Mother, and Child), in that the Paternal Masculine force represents the creative potential, the Will, and Creative intelligence, whereas the Maternal Feminine force represents the evolutionary process, the capacity to nurture, develop, and ultimately actualize the creative potential, realize the aspirations of the will, the Creative Power, and the child representing the actualization/realization that is "born" from the intercourse of the two parents. This aspect of Het Heru is associated with the nTr.t wADt, the Yorayit, and the Yatin (Aten).

It should also be known that Het Heru as the "physical" universe and cosmos, she is associated with the nTrt Niyit. This is to say, as the physical counterpart and actual vehicle of Ra (Ra exists within His "Eye,") in which all creation is considered an evolution and expression, or manifestation of Him. In actuality, all of creation is Het Heru manifest. She is the creation that we "see," in all its beauty and glory. As the Yatin and Yorayit upon his head, She is the actual light, and sun that is responsible for everything that we "sense (this is really what is meant by her being the nTrt of Sensuality)" and Ra exists within her light (remember she clothes him within her light). She is literally, *Mwt nTr* or **"Mother Nature."** Furthermore, she is the *"MAat"* that is responsible for maintaining and sustaining the universe through Cosmic Order, Harmony, and Rhythm (The Law of Cycles), which is reflected in the rhythm and motion of the cosmos, nature, its seasons, various laws and systems, including how these may express themselves within our own bodies. These cycles also manifest themselves in our lives through our Shai (Destiny) and all of its various expressions. This particular aspect of Het Heru is expressed in her role as the nTrt of Music and Dance. As such she is also a nTrt of wisdom, as it pertains to having an intuitive sense of timing, which in turn allows one to know how to move and act in harmony with the time and their environment. This is something that Het Heru grants to her devotees.

Another manifestation of Het Heru as the nTrt of Creation, Music, and Cycles, is reflected in her ren, *pA PsDwt nTrw*, that is "**The Nine nTrw,**" or "**The Cycle of nTrw**". This particular name is speaking to the fact that as ultimately all creation is a manifestation of nTr, and

the nTrw are the various expressions through which it manifests, or comes into being, ultimately all nTrw are in fact constituents of Het Heru. As she "lifts of the face of every nTr," she is responsible for giving each of them form and expression. The term "*Peseju*," (psDw) or cycle, speaks to the manner in which these forces manifest themselves and operate within the universe and life. Each nTr has a proper place, and role, in space and time. This once again is a reflection of the order, harmony, rhythm, and cycles, expressed in Het Heru. To signify this, a garland (necklace) of nine lotus flowers (or roses) is offered, each symbolizing one of Peseju nTrw. As mentioned before, Het Heru "displays his beauty and concentrates (unites) his powers." These "powers," being the Powers of Ra/Heru, are none other than the nTrw. Therefore, we come to understand that Het Heru is the unification and culmination of the nTrw, and also the law (MAat) that keeps them in order in respect to one another.

Another symbol of Het Heru as a nTr.t of rhythm and cycles is present in her story as the "Wandering nTrt," in which she as the "eye" of Ra gets lost in creation, following behind Ishu and Tufnut. While she was away, Ra had created another "eye" in her place. When Het Heru returned and discovered that another had taken her place, she became enraged, and lashed out at Ra, transforming into Shekhmet and went away from him again. While she was away, Ra was very depressed, impotent, and could not get anything accomplished. He decided to send Tehuti after her to try and bring her back to her senses, her true form (Het Heru) so that she could return to Ra, and life could, as a result, return to the land. Tehuti was successful, and through the use of stories, songs and dances, he was able to bring Het Heru back to Ra. With Het Heru, life and prosperity returned to Kemet, symbolized by the annual inundation of the Hopi (Nile). In honor of her return, Ra decreed that a great festival should be performed annually in her honor. This story has various layers of meaning, but in this instance, for our purposes we should recognize its significance as it pertains to cycles.

While this story depicts a singular event, it is important to understand that it is an ongoing reality. Just as the flood of the Hopi returns, annually, Het Heru always leaves, and always comes back. This is realized in the cycles of life, the seasons, but most importantly, this must be understood as it relates to the things that we "lose" in life. All possessions, positions, etc, are eventually lost, just like Het Heru's place with Ra; just like Het Heru when she left from him. Yet, if we understood that life is about cycles and rhythm, and approached it wisely (Tehuti), we would understand that eventually, that which was lost, in principle, shall always return. And while we await "the return;" our "change to come," we must be like Tehuti with his stories, songs and dances (symbols of Ritual), using them to persuade (attract) Het Heru back into our lives. Ra does not go chasing after Het Heru, and Tehuti does not attempt to force her to come back; after all she had transformed into Shekhmet, and any such attempts would have been met with grave results. Instead, Ra sent Tehuti, the Sage and Master of Time, to influence her to return.

Tehuti took his time and carefully brought her back. There is much wisdom in this story. This is how we must begin to understand life and approach it. When things don't go our way, when we lose something, instead of chasing after whatever it is, or

attempting to force it, we should go to Tehuti, i.e. look at things from a wise perspective, seek counsel from wise ones, receive divination, and after that patiently follow the advice, perform whatever rituals that were prescribed (if any), and allow Het Heru, the thing that we are waiting for to make its way back to us.

As a nTr.t of love, joy, harmony, and peace, Het Heru is, in fact, what life is supposed to be. When we are able to harmonize with life and dance through our journey in love, we are able to live a life of greater joy, peace, and fulfillment. We are also able to meet life, accommodate it, becoming whatever, and however we need to be to meet the situations at hand. This supreme harmony not only leads to peace and joy, but also wisdom, good health and fertility. However, the inability to harmonize with life and its myriad expressions causes one to clash with it; bringing the experience of cosmic dissonance, which is personified as the nTr.t

Shekhmet, the fierce side of Het Heru. Shekhmet represents the absence of Het Heru from Ra (Life), which causes depression, anger, disease, impotence, and infertility.

If there is such a thing as a Kemetic concept of "Heaven," or "Paradise," Het Heru is it. In her ren of *"Nbt Imntt"* or **Lady of the West**," she is, according to the **Prt M Hrw**, *"ist Htp n iri mAat m xnnwt n Hsiw,"* that is, *"Seat or Place of peace for those who do Maat, in the ferry of those who are praised (Ancestors and nTrw)."* This passage makes it clear that being within Het Heru was the reward for those who lived Maat. As mentioned earlier in this work, Het Heru herself is the Duat, just as it is the case with Nut, (whom Het Heru is also identified with) in that the Duat exist within her. Just as Het Heru represents all of the good things in earthly life, likewise she represents all of the goodness, and sweetness, of life in the spirit realm. In other words, whether we are speaking to life on the "Eastside" or "Westside" (tA or Duat), Het Heru is what that life is supposed to be like.

Het Heru is held to be the wife of many nTrw, varying according to tradition. However, in each case, the nTr that she is coupled with represents the "Nisu," and is held to be an expression of Ra or Heru. Het Heru is the nTrt of the "Divine Queenship," the "Great Royal Wife" of the Nisu Bity. Most notably, she is the wife of Heru Behudet (Heru of Behudet). These two together, represent the unification of the masculine and feminine forces of nTr (Nature), and by extension, all duality. Heru Behudet is the nTr of Manhood, Male Sexuality; he governs the physical act of sexual intercourse, while Het Heru is the nTrt of womanhood, young women and girls, female sexuality, the spiritual and sensual side of sex, and romance. Together they produce children, Ihy, the nTr of music, and rhythm, who is also associated with the sistrum, and the "Uniter of the Two Lands. Ihy is depicted as a child, and is associated with your gametes (sex cells) and sexual emissions. On the highest level he is the "Union" and harmony that is realized from the Union of masculine and feminine forces, and the experience of eternal youthfulness, and creative potency and harvest. On another level he represents the literal birth of a child that takes place from the intercourse

340

of the opposite sexes. Ihy also represents the enlightened individual who becomes the musician of the nTrw as he is associated with the sistrum, and is said to play the sistrum for his mother. He is called *"Ihy wr sA Hwt Hr,"* that is, **"the Great Ihy, Son of Het Heru"** and is said to:

"ir sSSt n mwt.f xrt hrw xn n Ka.s r-mrrt.s,

that is

"who plays the sistrum for his mother daily, who plays the sistrum to her Ka as much as she desires."

For Het Heru, Ihy says:

"ir.n.i n sSSt m Hr.t nfr s.Htp.i ib.t m mrt.t xn n.i Hm.t rwi Spt xn.i n kA.t Htp ib.t,"

that is,

"I play the sistrum for your beautiful face, I appease your heart with what you love, I play music to your majesty to drive away anger, I play music to your Ka so that your heart is pleased."

The realization of Ihy, through the union of Heru Behudet and Het Heru, causes one to vibrate in harmony with the cosmos (Ihy Nwn) and causes them to also vibrate in a way in which their life, thoughts, and actions become as a song of praise to nTr, blessing the world.

Just as every Nisu, who is identified with Heru is eventually to become an Osir (deified Nisu Bity/Ancestor), likewise Het Heru, who is the archetype of every Queen/Royal wife, young women and girls, will eventually become Auset, the nTrt of Motherhood, lineage (matrilineal rule of Nisu), and Women. This takes place once the Queen becomes a "Mother." When this happens, she then becomes a "Queen Mother," Auset, giving birth to Heru, the royal heir. As mentioned earlier in this

work, it is held that at the conception of Heru, he takes up residence in his mother, Auset's womb. At this moment, her womb becomes the "Het Heru" or "House of Heru." So in this instance, she becomes the womb that houses, protects, and nurtures the new life. Physically, Het Heru is the womb, especially in her ren of "*Nbt Htpt*" (**lady of the vulva**); and the fact that Het Heru, whose sacred animal and zoo-type is a "*idt/idyt*," or "cow," in which the term "idt/idyt" is also a homophone for a term meaning "vulva." As the nTr of the "womb/vulva" Het Heru can be worked with for increasing fertility (physical and mental/spiritual), as well as healing illnesses of the reproductive system, especially that of women.

Working with the nTrt Het Heru brings, joy, peace, love, harmony, contentment, increases one's intuitive sense of rhythm and timing, allows one to better harmonize and get along with others and their environment, and increases one's attractive power. She also increases creativity and fertility. She helps to maintain and restore harmony in one's life and relationships, and can also maintain and rekindle the fire in one's romantic life. Het Heru can be very maternal and protective, and she provides for her devotees. She is especially a protector of women and girls. She loves the good life, good times, festivities and parties, nature, freedom, food, wine, and beer.

Hymn to Het Heru
dwA! nwbt
Praise Golden One

Nbt iwnt
Lady of Yunut (Dendera)

Spst wrt m pr-Spst
Great Noble One in the Palace of Nobles

Axwt nwb m Hwt Ssst
Shining like gold in the House of the Sistrum

itnt m tA tm
Yitin in the land of Itum

dwA.i Hm.t m mrrt ib.t

I adore your majesty with the desire of your heart

Ns.i sSmt.t m mDt nTr

I invoke your Image with the sacred book

s.qAi.i kA.t m qAi n pt

I exalt your Ka to the Heights of Heaven

snsy.i sSmt.t r Dr n stwt itn

I worship your Image to the limits of the Yiten (Sun) rays

ity m Htp

Come in peace

prt m hi

come forth in Joy

iw s.nDm ib.t m sDm sSA

your heart is sweetened by hearing prayers

Hwt Hr wrt

Het Heru the Great

Nbt iwnt

Lady of Yunut (Dendera)

Irt Ra nbt Pt

Eye of Ra, Lady of Heaven

ityt n nTrw nbw

Sovereign of all nTrw

Hr.tp wrt

Great Hri.Tep (Yorayit)

Hnwt n pr-aA

Mistress of the Great Palace

iw s.Htp Hr.t nfrt m mrr.t sA(t).t

Your beautiful face is appeased by your beloved son (daughter)

Nsw Bty

Nisu of Upper and Lower Kmt

sxm tAwi n.HH

Master of the Two Lands eternally.

<u>Renu</u>

Hwt Hrw

Hwt Hrw PAwtit Nbt r Dr (Het Heru the Primordial, Lordess of

All)

> **PA-PsDt nTrw** (The Nine nTrw)
> **mwt mwwt (**Mother of Mothers)
> **Nwbt** (Golden One)
> **Irt Ra, WADt Ra, MAat n Ra** (Eye of Ra)
> **Nbt** (Lady)
> **Mri** (Love)
> **Nbt tx** (Lady of Drunkeness)
> **Nbt Hsi (**Lady of music/song)
> **Nbt ibA** (Lady of Dance)
> **Nbt Hi** (Lady of joy)
> **Nbt Hai** (lady of rejoicing)
> **Nbt Xn** (Lady of Music)
> **Hnwt iAbwi (**Lady of Desire)
> **Nbt idbw** (lady of the banks/beach)
> **Rxyt** (Wise woman)

Day
Friday

Number
5, 9 (Supreme)

Stones
Zircon, Diamond, Rose Quartz, Turquoise, Green Malachite, Emerald

Metal
Copper, Gold

Herb
Myrrh, Lotus, Papyrus, Rose, Honeysuckle, Parsley, Cinnamon, Sycamore

Colors

Gold (Yellow) and Green, Pink and Green, Turquoise,

Totem
Cosmetics (Makeup, Lipstick, etc), Hand Mirror, Sistrum, Rattle, Tambourine, Cowry Shells, Cow, Cat (Domestic)

Sacred Animal
Cow, Cat (Domestic), Hippopotamus, Female Hawk, Black Kite, Green and Gold Serpent (Renenutet)

Food
Dates, Figs, Sweet Cakes, Desserts, Mango, Peach, Strawberry, Chocolate, Honey.

tA war (Great Bread) fresh baked multi-grain bread of honey and raisins. Offer fresh and hot. This a traditional offering.

Beverage
Beer, Wine, Milk, Honey Wine, Honey Liquor, Peach Schnapps,

Mulled Wine (Heated Red Wine with cinnamon, cloves, allspice, and nutmeg, raisins, dates, orange peel, apple, and then strained) This is a traditional drink.

Homemade Beer made with ground almonds, the spices from the mulled wine above, dates, honey, and myrrh and red ochre or grenadine. This is based on a traditional offering which brings joy.

Sacred Domain
Beach, River Banks, Shorelines

Psychological Traits
Abstract, Imaginative, Synthesis, Romantic

Emotional

Love, Sensual, Affectionate, Sexual, Nurturing, Playful, Maternal, Free Spirited, Joyful (Bliss), Desire

Psychic

Clairvoyance, Creative Visualization, Magnetism, Healing

Ishu & Tufnut

Ishu and Tufnut are the first born children of Ra and Het Heru. According to the tradition, they were the first to come into being upon Ra's coming into being, his rising from Nu(n). After their coming into being, they gave birth to Nut and Gab, "Heaven and Earth," respectively, and all other nTrw and beings proceeded from them. Ishu has been considered the personification of "air" and "light," or "dryness," and Tufnut has been considered the personification of "water" or "moisture." However, these things are not simply to be taken literally.

Ishu's name on one hand is said to mean "void," and on the other hand it has been said to mean "to raise." However, he is connected, through pun, to terms that refer to sunlight, as well as dryness and heat. He is associated with air and space. The significance of his associations and symbolism is that they represent him as the masculine force in nature. For instance, Ra is said to have "projected" or emitted Ishu, which is a quality of both air and light. Light projects; it shines; it emits. Air rises, and expands. All of these qualities demonstrate that ishu is the masculine force in the dual forces and principles that make up the primary laws of the cosmos. Light also differentiates. This is the role that Ishu plays in the cosmologies. He is the projective, masculine side of nTr. As this relates to the cosmologies, as Ra "rises" from Nu (Chaos) he is Ishu. This rise creates the first differentiation in the universe. With this "differention," duality comes into being (Ishu and Tufnut), and "Order"

346

is created from the Chaos. It is for this reason that Ishu wears the "Feather of Maat" upon his head, for he is a force and principle of order. Along with this differentiation, time, space (void), and locality comes into being. It is for this reason that the four cardinal directions are called the "*s.Tzw Sw*," or "Pillars of Ishu." These pillars not only represent the four cardinal directions, but they also assist Ishu in holding up Nut, separating her from Gab. Without Ishu, Nut (heaven) and Gab (earth) would collide, which would cause the universe to return to the Chaos. So Ishu can be seen in between Nut and Gab, representing "the void" or space. This void once again is a result of the "duality" caused by Ra's rising from Nu. It must be understood that Ra's rising automatically brings into being Ishu and Tufnut, or duality, which automatically brings light and perception (Ra's Eye follows behind Ishu and Tufnut), time and space, and the formation of Heaven and Earth. All of these are results of Ishu, a principle of Maat or Order. Ishu "Opens" the heavens (he is also associated with the Opening of the Mouth). In the universe, Ishu is the force that is responsible for the expansion of the universe, and corresponds to Centrifugal force and Dark Energy.

Tufnut's name is said to be related to the term "*tf*", or "*tfn*," meaning "*to spit*," or "*to pour*." Her name is written with the determinative depicting "fluid" issuing forth from a pair of lips. However, it should be noted that though the fluid is "projecting from the mouth, it is curving, and "falling" towards the floor. This is a good demonstration of the contrast between Ishu and Tufnut. Where Ishu is associated with air, light, heat, and dryness, Tufnut is a nTrt that is associated with water, "darkness, coolness, moisture, and death. Unlike light and air which projects, rises, and expands, Water falls and contracts. Whereas Air and Light seeks to "flee," water seeks to return (ever tried to spit and it just then work out right…aww man let me hurry up and wipe my clothes ☺). Tufnut is the feminine force of nature, the feminine force in the dual forces and principles that make up the primary laws of the cosmos. Water seeks to collect itself. In the universe Tufnut is the force that is responsible for the contraction, and containment (order, harmony, etc) of the universe, and corresponds to Centripetal force, and Dark Matter.

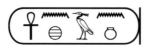

Ishu and Tufnut are considered to be the son and daughter of Ra, but in actuality, they are the dual aspects that make up his Being. Ishu is the masculine aspect of Ra, while Tufnut is the feminine aspect. It must be remembered that Ra is Life, which is energy and motion. All movement happens in a cyclical, undulating manner. Ishu and Tufnut, together, represent the movement and expression of Ra. A passage from the Pyramid Texts, expresses the ultimate unity of Ra, Ishu, and Tufnut. In utterance 301 the passage reads:

> *"tm Hna rwti irw nTr.ti.sn Dt.sn Ds.sn Sw Hna tfnwt ir.ti nTrw wtt.ti nTrw smn.t nTrw"*

> *that is,*

> *"Itum together with Ruti (The Two Lions, i.e. Ishu and Tufnut) who created their divinity, their persons, their selves. Ishu together with Tufnut, created the nTrw, begot the nTrw, established the nTrw."*

What is interesting about this passage is the fact that though Ra (Itum) is considered to be the "Father," or "Creator" of Ishu and Tufnut, in this particular instance it is being stated that both Ishu and Tufnut existed with Ra, and created themselves. This same sentiment is expressed when Tufnut is referred to by the term "*tfn*," meaning "**Orphan**," suggesting that she has no parentage. We also find Tufnut, like Het Heru, being referred to as "mwt n mwwt," or Mother of Mothers, all of this hinting at the fact that she is "Self created." So the question arises, "Is there a contradiction here?" Are Ishu and Tufnut, "Self Created," or did Ra create them? The answer is no, there is no contradiction here.

In order to understand what is being conveyed here, we have to take a deeper look at Ishu and Tufnut, especially in the context of the above passage. In the text they are called "*Rwty*," or the "**Two Lions**" who is also called "Aker," the twin lions of the Horizon.

Figure 18: Aker/Ruti. These are the twin lions Ishu and Tufnut

These two lions correspond to the dual horizon; East and West, Sunrise and Sunset, respectively. As Akeru, they represent the "entrance" and "exit" of the world, from Ta, to Duat, and back again. The eastern horizon is associated with day, sunrise, life on earth (external world), "*dawa*" or "**tomorrow**" (future), and corresponds to Ishu. The Western horizon is associated with night, sunrise, death (life in the spirit world/internal world), "*sif*"or "**yesterday**" (past) and corresponds to Tufnut. This association is evidenced by passage 606 in the "Pyramid Text," which states of Ishu and Tufnut "*di.n.sn n.k Sw m.k iAbt tfnwt m.k imnt*" that is, "*Ishu is placed at your left (or east) and tufnut at your right (or west)*." We also find in **Coffin Text passage 80,** that Ishu is called "*nHH*" or "**eternal**," and Tufnut is called "*Dt*" or "**Everlasting**."

Furthermore, we find in the **17th chapter of the Prt m hrw**: "*ir nHH pw hrw ir Dt pw grH*," that is, "**Eternity is the Day, Everlasting is the night,**" once again speaking to Ishu and Tufnut as opposites (complimentaries); Ishu (Eternity) corresponding to" Day," and Everlasting (Tufnut) the "night." However, there is something else being stated in all of this that is quite fascinating, and that is the understanding of the difference between the "Eternal," and "The Everlasting."

To the average lay person, these two terms are thought to mean the same thing, i.e. "something without end." However, scholars were

correct in translating these terms as such. The term "Eternal," actually does not mean "without end," or "forever," but actually something that last for an age or time, having its roots in the Latin term *"Aeternus,"* meaning "**of the age**," which is a contraction of the term *"aeviternus,"* meaning "**Great Age**," which is ultimately rooted in "aevum," meaning "age." This is appropriate in that the term "nHH" literally means "of a great number," or "of a million years." Essentially "nHH" is eternal, in that it is a long period or cycle of time. However, this does not mean that it has no end.

"Everlasting" on the other hand, literally means "to last forever," or "exist forever," or to "ever be the end (last) or limit." In other words, Ishu as "nHH" is eternal, in that he lasts for a very long period of time, whereas Tufnut as "Dt" is everlasting, in that she endures forever. Understanding this point will open the way to understanding what is meant by the "Self creation" of Ishu and Tufnut.

Ishu is the force that lifts Ra from Nu, whereas Tufnut is the force that keeps Ra connected to Nu, and ultimately causes him to return. It should be noted that Ra travels in the *"wiA n.HH,"* or "**Boat of Eternity/Million Years**." Yet, ultimately his journey shall come to an end and he shall return to Nu, even if only for a brief moment. Tufnut is that return. To put it another way, as Ishu and Tufnut are the Dual aspects of Ra's being, Ishu is Life, whereas Tufnut is Being. Another way: Ishu=Ra=Living, Tufnut=Nu/Nunt=Being.

The tradition, in teaching us that Ra shall return to Nu, is by extension teaching us that Ishu shall be removed from his position between Nut and Gab, for the only way Ra can return is if Ishu is out of the way, causing Nut and Gab to come together again, no longer differentiating between "Heaven and Earth," and thus returning to the "Original Chaos." However, after his return to Nu, Ishu will lift him (Ra) up again, bringing life and order; the universe into being once more. This is the great cycle of Ra.

To further understand the principle that is being conveyed here we have

350

to take a look at the picture of Aker or Ruti once more. When we look at this image we see Ruti; two lions facing in opposite directions. Above the lion on the left, or facing east is written "dawa," meaning "tomorrow," and above the lion facing right or west is written "sif," meaning "yesterday." In between both lions, is an image of Ra in the "Akhet," or "Horizon." Ra in the middle, represents the "present," "today;" the midlle point or common axis in the continuum of time. The term *Ra*, can literally mean "**day**", or "**time**." In other words, Ra is the point that unites "Yesterday and Tomorrow," the present, and he is ultimately "Time" itself. Above all three is the symbol (biliteral) "pt," "heaven or sky." Notice how the limit of "pt" comes to an end at the head of each lion. This is to indicate that these forces make up the universe, in totality, or the "limits" of the Universe. The Term "*Ruti*," also means "**Two Gates**," and this is reflective upon "Aker/Ruti" as the "Gate Keeper" and "two doors" of the Duat.

As Ra journeys through "the East," beginning at sunrise, he travels through the earth. His journey continues until he reaches his extreme point, and then he "sets" in "the West," entering into the Duat. He continues forward through the Duat, until he reaches the limits of it, ultimately exiting, or emerging from the Duat, in the east at sunrise. The point here, is that once Ra's journey reaches its "limit" in either direction, the "direction" transforms, or leads to its opposite. The "limits" of the East becomes the West, and the "limits" of the West becomes the East. In other words, once Ishu reaches his extreme limit, he transforms into Tufnut, and once Tufnut reaches her extreme limit, she transforms into Ishu. This is the reason why the image above depicts Ruti as "Twin Lions," as Ishu and Tufnut are twins. They are reflections of one another, and where one "ends" the other "begins." This continues, perpetually, as a never ending cycle. As this relates back to the universe and creation, Scientists agree that the universe is expanding, and they also agree that it began at a single, undifferentiated point (Nu/Amun). What they are unclear on is how the universe will "end.'" Two theories have been posited: the "Big Crunch:" the universe will reach a limit in its expansion and will ultimately begin to contract back into its starting point, the Chaos, and the "Big Freeze:" the Universe will continue to expand getting further and more scattered

until ultimately it will freeze or come to a standstill. There is another theory that has recently surfaced over the past few years called the "Loop Quantum Cosmology," which proposes the idea that the Universe began not with a "Bang' but with a bounce, and that the end of the Universe will simply be the beginning of another. Could this be Ruti?

The idea that Ishu and Tufnut are "Self Created," is hinted at in the manner in which they are said to have "come forth" from Itum/Ra. According to the tradition, Ra is said to have "sneezed" out Ishu, and "coughed up" or "vomited" Tufnut. The fascinating thing here is that both "coughing" and "sneezing" are involuntary actions, which are not "willed," but happen automatically. What is it that caused Ra (Itum) to sneeze and cough?

These two "involuntary responses," are in actuality, an allusion to another involuntary action: the sexual orgasm. According to the Pyramid Texts 685, it is stated:

> " ii mw anx imiw pt ii mw anx imiw tA nbi n.k pt
> sdA n.k tA tp-a mswt nTr wpi Dwti xpr nTr sxm nTr
> m Dt.f wpi Dwti xpr...sxm...pn m Dt.f mki..pn I sn.ti
> rdw.f in mw wabw wnnw xr tm ir Hnn Sw s-xpr kAt
> tfnwt ii.w n.sn inw.sn n.k mw wabw xr it.sn

that is,

> "come the living waters within heaven, come the living water within earth. Heaven burns for you, earth quakes for you before the birth of the nTr. The two mountains divide, a nTr comes into being. The nTr has power over his body. The two mountains divide (name) comes into being. (Name) has power

352

over his body. Behold this (name), his feet shall be kissed by the pure waters, which come into being through Itum, which the Phallus of ishu makes, which the womb of Tufnut brings into being."

The two mountains spoken of here are Ishu and Tufnut or Ruti, and the waters being spoken of are the "Waters of Nu(n)," as well as the "seed" that came forth from Itum during the process of creation, after he clenched his "phallus" and embraced his "shadow." Here it is being stated that it is the "phallus of ishu" and the "womb of Tufnut" that created these" waters" or "seed." If you will recall, according to the tradition, Itum (Ra) is said to have taken his "seed" and poured it into his mouth, and then "sneezed out" Ishu, "coughed up" Tufnut, and became "from one nTr, three nTrw." If we look at this carefully, it is being stated here that Ishu and Tufnut are responsible, in a way, for the "orgasm" that led to their "coming into being," or to be even more precise, Ra's "coming into being" as "three nTrw." We find the same idea being expressed in **Cofin Texts 77**, in which it is stated:

"nwk.i bA Sw tp nbi hh stt n tm m Drit.f ir.f nDmmt stp xr m r.f ISS n.f Sw Hna tfnwt..."

that is,

"I am the Ba of Ishu, which is in the flame of the fiery blast which Itum, kindled with his own hand. He made orgasm, and saliva fell from his mouth and he emitted Ishu together with Tufnut."

Here in this passage, Ishu is being associated with the "seed" of Itum, through which he and Tufnut would ultimately come into being. Once more we find in the Cosmology of Mennefer (Memphite Theology):

"IpA xpr n na PsDjt nTrw itm m Mtw- f M Dbaw- f PsDt nTrw Hm pw nDHtw spt m r pn mAth rn-n xt

nebt pr n Sw tfnwt im-f Ms-n PsDt nTrw,

that is

"These Peseju nTrw came into being from Itum's semen and his fingers. Indeed, these nine nTrw are the teeth and lips in the mouth proclaiming the name of every thing, from which came forth Ishu and Tufnut as him, and giving birth to the nine nTrw."

Here again the exact same idea is conveyed, that Ishu and Tufnut, as "Seed" and "Fingers," and are ultimately responsible for their own coming into being. Ishu is associated with the Phallus and Seed of Itum (Ra), and Tufnut as is the case with other nTr.t such as Het Heru, is associated with his hand. Also, it should be noted that Ishu and Tufnut come into being as "him" (Itum). What we can take from these passages, is the idea that Ishu and Tufnut existed in some way, prior to their "coming into being." When we consider once more, the words of Itum, "they proceeded from me, I became from One nTr, Three nTrw... that is to say, from out of my Self...I raised Ishu and Tufnut from Nun..." we come to understand that Ishu and Tufnut, existed in Nun, in a state of inertia, and also they existed within Itum, prior to "coming forth." Together, they comprise the dual aspects of Itum's Being, and it was the intercourse of these two forces within Itum that caused him to come forth, rising from Nu, and also the externalization of these dual forces.

We must also take into account the fact that Ishu and Tufnut, gave birth to the Peseju nTrw, and that the Peseju come from them as seed and fingers (Hand)," meaning that all of the Peseju nTrw are ultimately expressions of the fundamental qualities of Itum's being, Ishu and Tufnut. The description of Peseju nTrw as the "teeth and lips in the mouth, proclaiming the name of everything from which came forth Ishu and Tufnut as him, giving birth to the Peseju nTrw..." represent the fact that they are the forces that bring, distinction, variance and articulation on Ishu and Tufnut, as this is the role that the Teeth and the lips play in

354

speech (of course along with the tongue). In other words, All Peseju nTrw are variations of Ishu and Tufnut as the essential qualities of Itum's being, the masculine and feminine principles in nature, bringing greater articulation to their being.

Ishu corresponds to the Consciousness, Will of nTr, and Tufnut represents the Power and Body of nTr. They are interdependent and interconnected realities. Also a portion of each exists within the other, just as there is "water" within air, and there is "air" within water. This is also evident in the symbolism of a sneeze and spittle. Everyone has noticed how a sneeze is comprised mainly of air, but there is a certain degree of moisture within the sneeze. Likewise, I'm sure we all have noticed the little "bubbles" present within the spit, even though the consistency of spit is mainly water (saliva). Once again we also find instances where Ishu is associated with water (providing water to certain individuals, and cooling them with his water), and Tufnut is associated with heat, fire, and light, as she is also, like other nTr.t, associated with the 'Eye' of Ra.

If you are noticing a similarity here between the concept of Ruti/Aker and the eastern Daoist concept and symbolism of "Yin/Yang" you are very perceptive and apt to understand Ruti in some regard. However, one should not make the mistake in thinking that Ruti/Aker is based upon or derived from the Daoist concept in any way. The Daoist concept of Yin and Yang has been dated back c. 300 B.C.E., whereas the Ruti/Aker can be found in the 5th Dynasty Pyramid Texts dating back aprox. 2500 B.C.E.. So though there is great similarity between these concepts, there is absolutely no comparison in regards to age. However, we have to wonder, could it be that Ruti/Aker are the great great great Grandparents of Yin and Yang? Things that make you go "Hmmm?" ☺

Ishu and Tufnut are inseparable, and are incomplete without one another. Ishu is Creative inspiration and aspiration, while Tufnut is Creative realization, actualization and manifestation, Ishu initiates, Tufnut accomplishes and completes. Ishu leads, Tufnut follows. Ishu forces, Tufnut accommodates. Ishu is assertive and aggressive; Tufnut is

receptive, passive and gentle. Ishu is electric and projecting, Tufnut is magnetic, attractive, and welcoming. Ishu is firm and enduring, Tufnut is soft and flowing. Ishu is strict, protective and combative; Tufnut is relaxed, nourishing, and nurturing. Ishu is the individual, and Tufnut is the collective.

Ishu and Tufnut are abstract universal forces that are reflected in everything, in every moment. For this reason, there was not many temples dedicated to these two forces individually, but they did have shrines in a few places, such as Innu and Leontanopolis. This may be in part due to their abstract nature. Any work with these forces would be very general and broad. For example, one may work with Ishu to be more firm, focused, direct, assertive, lucid, dynamic, bold, strengthening individuality, strong will, etc. On the other hand, one could work with Tufnut to increase coolness, calm, introspective capacity, attractiveness (magnetism), amiability, nurturing, healing, Psychic abilities, empathy towards the collective, receptivity, ability to follow and be guided, patience, humility, etc. Generally, rituals related to Fire and Air, and any of the mental and physical characteristics that these correspond to, can be performed with Ishu, and any rituals related to water and earth, and any mental and physical characteristics reflective of these qualities can be performed with Tufnut. However, when the goal that one has in mind is more specific, then it may be preferred to work with some of the other children of these two nTrw. Generally, as it relates to spirituality, Ishu represents the path of Will/Action, whereas Tufnut represents the path of Total surrender and acceptance.

Ishu as he stands between Niut and Gab, represent the ability for us to be conscious, and experience, and the ability to increase our awareness, consciousness, and lucidity through the breath, especially the long deep meditative and methodical (enduring) breathing that takes the air from the heights of the Heavens (Head) all the way down to the depths of the earth (the stomach/lower abdomen.). Without Ishu, Nut and Gab would collide, and we would lose consciousness!

If Ishu is consciousness, Tufnut is the experience. She is our ability to

356

learn, grow and evolve. She is our capacity to acquire the knowledge of Self, the urge for us to "Re-member." She like Het Heru is also called the "Great PsDwt," ultimately all nTrw being expressions of her, meaning she embodies them all, and gives them form. She is our capacity to be spiritual, and to acquire spiritual knowledge, to be initiated. She is also our capacity to create, and attract what it is we want in our lives, and to create and mold ourselves into whatever we Will (Ishu) to be.

Both of these forces are associated with Maat, Law and Order. Ishu brings order by creating differentiation, without which we would not be conscious, and would not have the capacity to experience life. So Ishu individuates. Tufnut on the other hand maintains order by gathering the elements that Ishu individuates, pulling on each to work together in harmony as one system, and collective, without which all the individuated elements would scatter and still lose the capacity to experience, interact, and be aware of, ultimately losing awareness of Self. If either side dominated, or ceased to be (if at all possible), the end result would be the same, Chaos, total unawareness of Self, no life, and no experience. Both of these forces are essential and critical to the overall order and stability of the cosmos and ultimately Maat is about living in a way in which the equilibrium of Ishu and Tufnut is maintained.

Hymn to Ishu

Nwk.i bA Sw nTr xpr Ds.f

I Am the Ba of Ishu the Self created nTr

Xpr n.i m Ha nTr xpr Ds.f

I have come into being from the flesh of the Self created nTr

Nwk.i bA Sw nTr sfg irw

I am the Ba of Ishu nTr of invisible Form

Xpr.n.i m Ha n nTr xpr Ds.f

I have come into being from the flesh of the Self created nTr

Nwk.i imi Drw nTr

I am within the side of the nTr

Xpr n.i im.f

I have become as him

Nwk.i sgr n.f pt

I am he who calmed the heavens

Nwk.i sid n.f tAwi

I am he who makes powerless the two lands

Wsr Dnd.kw r psDw nbw

I am more powerful and raging than all the nTrw

Nwk.i sr sw pr.f m Axt

I am he who fortells his coming forth from the horizon

Nwk.i rdi nrw.f n Dar rn.f

I am he who gives fear to him who seeks his name

Nwk.i imi.m HHw

I am he who is in the midst of the "Chaos nTr'

sDm mdw HHw

and hears the words of the "Chaos nTrw"

nwk.i sbi mdw xpr Ds.f n aStw

I am he who dispatches the words the Self Created to the multitudes

nwk.i srr wiA aprw

I am captain of the boat and its crew

wsr.kw Dnd.kw r psDw nbw

I am more powerful, I am more raging than all the nTrw

iw wHm.n.i mdw nTrw imiw bAH xprw r sA.i

I have repeated the words of the nTrw, Ancestors, and those who came into being after me.

nD.sn xpr.i ma nw

the enquire about my coming into being from Nu

mAA.sn.wi wsr.kw Dnd.kw m wiA sqddt xpr Ds.f

They see me. I am powerful, I am raging in the boat which is navigated by the Self Created

aHa.n.i m m.sn

I have stood there among them

rdi fAw xft xpr.i

I cause my splendor in accordance with my being

Dd.i gr psDw idt nTrw

I speak and the nTrw are silent and smote

Dd.i.n.tn xpr.i m irw Ds.i m nD xpr.i ma nw

I speak to you about my coming into being in my own form. Do not ask me about my coming into being from Nu

mAA.n.wi nw xpr.kw

Nw saw me as I came into being

Rx.n.i. rn.f rx.n.i bw xpr.n.i im

I know his name I know the place where I came into being therein

Nn Maa.f xpr.i m Hr.f

He did not see my coming into being with his own face.

Xpr.n.i. m Ha nTr xpr Ds.f

I came into being from the flesh of the nTr who created himself

qmA.n.f wi m ib.f

he created me with his heart

ir.n.f wi m xwt.f

he has made me with his might

nwk.i nfA irw qmA.n.i. nTr.pn Sps

I am exhaled from his nostril, my shape is formed by this Noble nTr

wpt pt m nfr.f

he scatters the heavens with his beauty

nn tw rx nTrw rn.f

whose name the nTrw don't know

Smsw Hnmmt

Who the Sun People serve

Rwd.n.i rdw.f

I have grown at his feet

Xpr.n.i m awy.f

I am formed by his two hands

Sw.n.i m at.f

I am raised by his limbs

qmA.n.f.wi m ib.f

he has created me with his heart

ir.n.f wi m xwt.f nn mst.i nn mst

he made me with his power when I had yet to be born

irt.n.i smw m sxt sTt

herbage has been made for me in the fields of Asia

nwk.i ir pAwt nTrw

I am the one who made the bread of the nTrw

nwk.i Hr.ib dbn.f

I am within his circle,

nb sxt wADt m dwAt

lord of the green field within the Duat

I Ra tm nw

O Ra-Itum-Nu

Nwk.i s.Htp DfAw

I am the one who offers provisions

s.wAD Hw n wsir

who replenishes the food of Osir

Hr xpr.i m HA n nTr.pn Sps xpr Ds.f

Because I have come into being from the flesh of this noble nTr who created himself

Wpi pt m nfr.f

Who scatters the heavens with his beauty

Dmd irw nTrw

and assembles the forms of the nTrw

Nb mAat xtm awAw

Lord of Righteousness who locks away robbers

dmd.f irw

he assembles shapes

nwk.i nfA irw

I am he whose form was exhaled

nn msnt.f wi m xfa.f

he did not fashion me with his grasp

nn iwr.f.wi m xfa.f

he did not conceive me with his with his grasp

nfA.n.f wi m Srt.f

he exhaled me from his nostrils

ir.n.f. wi m Hr.ib nfr.f

he made me in the midst of his goodness

Haa imi.w StAw isT mAA.sn sSp.f

Those dwell within the hidden place are made to rejoice

Nwk.i nfA irw xnt sxt.f wDa m.xt imntt imi Hwt sisw

I am he whose form is exhaled at the front of his field, whose commands are followed in the secrets matters within the Mansion of Six

360

qmA.n.i bA.i hA.i

I have fashioned my Ba which is behind me

nn ns.f Hr xat

his flame is not over my body

nn sAw bA.i in ir at wsir

my Ba is not restrained by the guardians of the members of Osir

iw.i sTt.i iw bA sTt.f

I beget, my Ba begets

sTt bA.i m rmT imiw iw nsrsr

my Ba begets the people within the Isle of Fire

sTt.i Ds.i m nTrw.t

I impregnate the nTrwt myself

fAi.n.i mAAt nms.f n imi TpHt

I am lifted and his Royal Head Cloth is seen by the dweller within the cavern

Imi TpHt.f fAi.n.i nms.i

He who dwells within his cavern lifts up my Royal Head Cloth for me.

In imi irw.f saH wi fAA saH.i

It is he who is within his form who raises me to dignity

nHm.n.i saH imiw TpHt.sn

I carry away the dignity of them that dwell within their caverns

nn sDm.n.i n HkA xpr.n.i tp-a

I do not listen to any magic, for I existed before it

pr.n.i xnt nTr xpr Ds.f

I came forth in front of the nTr who created himself

xpr wa iAw r nTrw

who came into being alone, who is older than the nTrw

nwk.i dm.n.f qAAw pt

I am the one who has pierced the height of the sky

nwk.i inw.n.f xw.f

I am the one who fetches for himself his power

nwk.i iab.n.f HH.f n kA rdi m.sA wnDwt.f

I am the one that has united for himself the millions of Ka placed behind his associates.

axm.n.i sDt

I have extinguished the flre

sqbb.n.i bA wpst

I have calmed the burning bA

sgr.n.i Hr.ib.t dSr.s wAwAt

I have quieted her in the midst of her rage

nwk.i nbi ns n sDt nn tA nhh.n r.s r wi

I am he who the flame of her fire burns, but the fiery blast of her mouth is not against me

sqdi bA wpst

I convey her burning bA

ir mr ns n Hr.ib dSr.s

I create the pain of the flame of her in the midst of her rage.

wAwAt wDat sAmt nTrw

the fiery one who cuts the hair of the nTrw

iw Dd.n.i HAt.Tn nTrw nn prt m r.Tn

your hearts have spoken to me, nTrw, nothing came forth from your mouths

ntt xpr.n is ma.i irt mi r Dr

because there has come into being through me the doing of everything

Hr prt m r n Sps

Because of what came forth from the mouth of the August one

Xpr Ds.f

The Self Created

Nn wDb.n.f Hr Dd.t.n.f

Who never goes back on what he has said

Hr ntt nwk.i is ir Dr xt.f wD.t.n.f

Because I am he who does everything in accordance with what was commanded to him

Tri.n.i rw.w

I have given respect to the lions

snd.n.i HA kAr

those who are about the shrine fear me

aHa.n.i Snwt Hat

those who are around the shrine stand up because of me

aq.i r pr.i r.i m kAr xpr Ds.f

I enter in and come forth from the shrine of He Who Created Himself

Ssp.n.i nt.i m tp.i

362

I have received my crown of nt on my head

Haat dSrt mAA.s

The Red Crown rejoices in seeing the nt crown

Iw nt.i m tp

My Nt Crown is on my head

Iw dSrt m tp.n xpr Ds.f

And the Red crown is on the head of the Self Created One.

Ha nt mAA n.s dSrt

The Nt Crown rejoices in seeing the Red Crown.

Xrw.sn nTrw sDm xrw.s

So says the nTrw when they hear its voice.

Snsn.s nTr r nTr xpr m Ha.f

The nTr is brotherly towards the nTr who came into being from his flesh.

mAA.n.sn sw

when they see him

ki.n.i naw m hni

the naw serpent cried out to me in praise

ir.sn.n.i wAt nfrt

they have made a good path for me

mAA.sn pr.i m kAr

when they see me come forth from the shrine

wDa.i Snwt Hat kAr

I judge those who surround the shrine

wHa.i wHay.i

I release who I should release

s.anx.i s.anxy.i

I nourish who I should nourish

dr.i sDb dr sDb.i

I remove restraints from the one who needs restraints removed

wHa.i sDb.i

I release my own restraints

bwt.i pw dSr

my taboo is blood

wnn.i Hna nb anx

I will exist with the Lord of Life

nwk.i ab.n.f HHw

I am he who unites millions

Nwk.i Ts.n.f Snwt

I am he who knits together the entourage for him

nwk.i smn HA kAr.f xt.f wDt.n.f.n.i

I am he who establishes those that are around his shrine according to what he has commanded me

iw qmA.n.f wi bA.i HA.i

He has created me, and behind me (afterwards) my Ba

r rdi.t rx.f rxt.n.i

to allow him to know what I know

isk wi xt pt nb

for I pervade all the heavens

sxn.n.i tAw.nbw

I travel through all the lands

iw ir.n.i wDt.n.f.n.i

I have done what he has commanded me to do

nn ns.n bA.i Hr XAt.f

My Ba is not foul, so there is no flame upon it.

nn sA nt bA.i n ir at wsir

my Ba shall not be locked up by the guardian of the limbs of Osir

bA sxm.k.n.k

you possess you Ba and your Shekhem

I in xpr Ds.f r.i

As told to be by the He Who Created Himself

Nn Drt bA.i in bik

My Ba will not be grabbed by Hawks

Nn Amm bA.i in Saw

My Ba will not be gripped by pigs

Nn xfa bA.i in Akrw

My Ba shall not be seized by the Akeru

Nn Amm bA.i in HkA

My Ba will not be possessed by Hika (Juju)

swAi bA.i m sgr Hr r.sn r aq.f r kAr

My Ba shall pass quietly by them until he enters the shrine

iTi.n.f xrt.i n xpr.n.i xnt.f

it has taken possession of what belongs to me because I came into being before him

rdi.f sxm.i m xfti.i

He gives me power over my enemies

iw dr.n.i.sn m is.sn

and I have driven them from their chambers

iw hn.n.i.sn m Hwwt.sn

I have overthrown them in their mansions

dr.n.i ntyw im Hr stw.sn

I have expelled those that are yonder from their seats

s.sni.n.i saH.sn

I have caused their dignity to pass away

HDi.i HkA.sn

I have destroyed their Hika

bHn.i xwt.sn

I have cut off their power

sip.i.sn nDt swn

I have assigned them to be traded as serfs

mi wDwt.n xpr Ds.f

like that which He Who Created Himself commanded

irt r xftyw.i

to be done to my enemies

m mt m anxw

whether dead or alive

imiw pt tA

in heaven and earth

siAt.sn sm.i m Axt

to them that encroach upon my pastures or fields

tmt.sn s.qAw.i

who does not lift me up

nnwt sr.sn.n.i wAt

and they don't show me the way

r hny wiA

to the bark of praise

nwk.i sfg irw

I m invisible of shape
iw.i m Drw Axw
I am merged in the light.

Litany to Tufnut
inD Hr.t Tfnwt
Show your Face Tufnut
mwt mwwt
Mother of Mothers
pAwtyt aAt
Great Primordial One (Ancient One)
DttA
Everlasting
nn kt xr Hat.s
No other is before her

nn Dt nt qmA.sy
Nobody created Her
mwt s.anxt m Xt
Mother who causes life in the womb
s.xprt mw wabw m XAt.s
who causes the pure waters to come into being from her womb
s.xprt xt nbt
who causes all things to come into being
I tfnwt
O Tufnut
anx.t sAt Ra
Living Daughter of Ra
mAat wrt
MAat the Great

mwt nTr msi.t nTrw
Divine Mother who gave birth to the nTrw
irt Ra
Eye of Ra
nbt pt

Lady of Heaven

Hnwt nTrw nbw

Mistress of All the nTrw

Sps.t

Noble One

Wsrt

Mighty One

Nfrt Hr

Beautiful of Face

Xnmt wrt

Great Unifier

sby Ra r znTywt

Guide of Ra to his limbs

s.anx.t ib.n.Ra

Who causes the heart of Ra to live

Hryt-tp nt Ra

Yorayit upon the head of Ra

Nsrt sbiw nw it.s Ra

Burns the fiends of her father Ra

sxrt xftyw.s

Overthrows her enemies

Wbdt aApp m hh m rA.s

Burns Owapep with the heat from her mouth

tfnwt ipt ipt in DttA

Tufnut allots what is to be allotted by eternity

iAw.Tn.s tpaw mw imiw.s

You all shall adore her upon the waters which are within her

Nut & Gab

The nTr.t Nwt is the Great Grand Daughter of Nw and Nwn.t, Grand-daughter of Ra and Rayt, daughter of Ishu and Tufnut, and Wife of Gab (though sometimes she is wedded to Nwn in her Pre creation/Creator form) and mother of Osir, Auset, Nebt Het, Sutesh, and Heru War. She is the nTr.t of the ordered universe or cosmos, the sky/heaven, Mind, and Memory.

Gab is the Great Grandson of Nw and Nwn.t, Grandson of Ra and Rayt, Son of ishu and Tufnut, and husband of Nut. He is the father of Osir, Auset, Sutesh, Nebt Het, and Heru War. He is the nTr of the earth (and "earthly plane"), earthly experience, manifestation, and the physical body.

According to the tradition, Gab and Nut were in an eternal sensual embrace prior to being separated by Ishu at the Behest of Ra. This embrace is symbolic of the original undifferentiated state of the universe, Nw/Nwn. Once the separation of Nut and Gab takes place, the ordered universe, life, and experience comes into being. On one level, this particular story relates to the creation of the universe, and on another level it speaks to the distinction being made between mind

368

(Nut) and matter (Gab). Just as all life in the universe ultimately evolved as a result of the separation, likewise, conscious experience, thought, and life becomes possible.

Many scholars have not been able to understand just why the Kemetyu would personify the "Earth' as masculine, and Heaven or Sky as feminine. However, it is in the understanding of Nut as Mind and Gab as Matter that one may begin to understand this tradition. For instance, Ra's rising from Nu is a description of nTr as the Universe coming into consciousness of itself, creating definition within itself, as well as the creation and perception of time and space, essentially coming from a state of inert existence or Being, into a state of Active existence or Living. In other words, Ra is life, and everything that makes it possible, such as awareness, time, experience, etc. This in truth is what his journey represents. His cyclical journey from sunrise to sunset represents life in the earth. It represents earthly experience. As mentioned in regards to the **Book of Nut**, the Duat resides within Nut's body, and Ra enters into the Duat through her mouth, and exits from the Duat through her womb. This represents the taking in, and recording of experiences into the so-called subconscious mind, becoming memory; and the thoughts that have entered into the mind, becoming memory, ultimately emerging from the Duat, entering back into the Earth (Gab) as Actions and new experiences. Nut's role as memory is spoken to in the "Book of Praying to the Unified One in the West," in which it is stated:

> *"Hknw.n.k Ra qwA sxm aA s.ipw m imi.t.f Twt is XAt Nwt,"*

That is,

> *"Praise be to you Ra, Exalted Shekhem, Great, Who keeps count of that which is within him, you are indeed the Body of Nut."*

The relationship of Nut to memory is described by the act of "Keeping count" of what is "Within." Further evidence of the association of Nut

with the mind or memory, is the association of the Duat with "Sef" or "yesterday." This is further demonstrated by the fact that the Duat, which is within the body of Nut, is the domain of the "westerners," which is a term used to refer to those who live in the Duat, the "deceased,' the "Foremost of the Westerners" being Osir Khenti Imenityu and those in his following, the "*Drtyw*" or **Ancestors**. Of course the relationship between the Ancestors and yesterday is obvious, when we recall the statement regarding Ra and Osir, in which it was said that "Osir is Yesterday, Ra is Tomorrow." Once again Osir's throne is within the Duat, Nut's body. As Ra travels, his journey represents the cycles of Life, all the way down to the coming into being and passing of the moment. As soon as the moment passes, it becomes the past, i.e. "yesterday" and enters into the Duat, the "body of Nut," and becomes a memory. However, as it has been dealt with in previous chapters, and will be dealt with specifically regarding Nut in a moment, the Duat is also associated with the womb. Understanding this, as Ra enters into the Duat as "iwf," though he is "dead/past," he is also a seed from Gab (Earthly Existence/experience) into the body of Nut, which will ultimately be reborn in the east, back into the earth as a new thought, action, moment, etc, and the cycle continues.

In this regard, Gab is the Father of Ra, and Nut is his mother. The reason why Gab, the Earth is depicted as a male is due to the relationship and effects that "physical existence" and experience has upon the mind. Though our minds may have preconditions and certain inclinations due to genetics, spiritual and astrological influences, and Shai (Destiny based upon previous incarnations, all of which are "offerings of Gab,") most of what shapes our minds, nourishes it, enlightens it, .i.e. "seeds" it, is our experiences within Gab. The mind, or Nut, takes in these 'seeds" (experiences) and nourishes them, protects them, and if or when they take root, "conception" takes place. This "conception" is a "thought" being conceived, which may ultimately grow until it becomes an action, a fruit being born from the womb of Nut into the earth. In other words, it is our life experiences that become implanted within our minds as memories, that go on to shape and become the very thoughts that give rise to our actions and new experiences; new memories. This is a perpetual cycle. It is for this reason Gab is understood and described as a male nTr.

In understanding Nut as the mind, we can further breakdown the aspects of the mind in regards to her body. The surface of Nut's body corresponds to the conscious mind, and the stars that cover it represent those thoughts that we are aware of. The stars and "Beings inside of her body, the Duat corresponds to the subconscious mind, and memories. The back of Nut's body which is Nu/Nun, corresponds to Unconsciousness. The term for star in mdw nTr is sbA. This term can mean to lead, to guide, to teach, etc. The connection with these terms and Stars, relate to the role that stars played in the ancient world as Guides (for travelers) and objects that assisted us in staying aware of the time. They showed us which way to go. Also, the light that they gave off dispersed the darkness, just as the light of knowledge transmitted from a teacher casts out the darkness of ignorance. These are the same roles that the mind and its thoughts play in our lives. Our mind and thoughts are meant to guide our actions. Through contemplation and meditation, we can analyze our thoughts, sort them out, and work out solutions to "problems," so that we know which way to go. Also, the thoughts that arise in our minds (especially in meditation) casts a light upon that which exists within the darkness of the deep portions of our mind, within the Duat. We must also take note of the fact that when one wishes to write the term "dwAt" in mdw nTr, the triliteral for dwA is the star. As it relates to the "dark portion" of the mind, we can also understand Ra's entrance into the Duat, as taking the "light" of our awareness into the darkness or hidden portions of the mind/spirit, revealing to us that which lies within, influencing our thoughts and actions. As Ra passes through the Duat ordering and giving commands, healing and destroying, it in essence represents the spiritual work that one does when traversing the deeper aspects of their being.

It is interesting to note that within the Duat there exist several types of Beings. Some of these "forces' are benefic, some are malefic. There are nTrw, Drtyw (Ancestors), Mtw (Disturbed Dead), and several types of what can be considered "demons." All of these things, while very real, as

it pertains to the Duat as the "spiritual realm, or "mental plane," have mental correlations and correspondances. In fact, it has been described by many; including renowned psychologist, that the "deities" of the Ancients represents "Archetypes" within the mind or "Universal Unconscious" (ala Carl Jung). Also, many people use the terminology "ghosts" and "demons," when referring to one's deep rooted issues and negative memories. Furthermore, little study of Traditional African Spirituality or Religions will elucidate the importance of "Remembering" the Ancestors, and their relationship to memory on multiple levels, including genetic.

In the tradition we find Nut playing the role of a Protective Mother. For example, in the "Songs of Auset and Nebt Het" It is said:

> *"come to your mother Nut so that she may spread herself over you when you come to her, that she may guard your flesh from all evil...that she may drive off all evil which appertains to your flesh..."*

We also find in a Hymn to Nut from the Pyramid Texts in which it is asked of Nut:

> *"spread yourself over your son Osir, hide him from Sutesh, Protect him, Nut. You have come that you might hide your son, come now protect this Great One."*

These two passages have significance on multiple levels; however, there are two aspects that we would like to bring to light here. First is the role that Nut plays in protecting the flesh, or body. Just as Nut is arched over Gab, in which some can say, protecting him from Nu (Chaos), her four limbs representing the cardinal points, which are also symbolic of the four sons of Heru and the four Supports of Ishu which help maintain order, the mind is in essence, the keeper of the body. It is the mind that influences the body both consciously and subconsciously. It is the mind, at the deepest levels, that controls the automatic functions of the body, sending messages via the nervous system to keep the body functioning properly, keeping us alive. Also, it is the mind that guides the body to perform its duties, make its repairs, heal, etc, even while we are asleep. It is the mind that registers the "alarms" we know as pain in the body, giving us a warning that there is something wrong. All of these are examples of the role the mind plays in protecting the body physically. As the mind is, or at least should be, the guide of one's actions, if there is trouble with the mind, chaos, then there will be trouble with one's actions, and one's actions will be chaotic, going on to create chaos in the world. Isfet, or chaos in the mind, "*shA*," or **confusion**, not only creates confused actions which add to confusion in the world, but can also create confusion in the body, stress, disease, etc.

On a spiritual and psychic level, ultimately everything that takes place in our lives is a result of our thinking; both consciously and subconsciously. Just as whatever manifests on earth must first come forth from the Duat i.e. the womb of Nut (All things are "transformations of Ra," who is constantly born from the womb of Nut,) ultimately all manifestations in life are effects of the workings of the mind. It is a universally held fact amongst spiritual and occult traditions trans-culturally, that we "attract" whatever happens in our lives, based upon how we manage our attention, our thoughts and our emotions. Therefore, in the end it is the mind that is responsible for protecting us from "evil." It must be understood that thoughts are actions. This truth is demonstrated in the mdw nTr language in the terms "*kAi*," meaning "**to Think, devise;**" "*kAt*," meaning "**thought,**" and "*kAt*," meaning "**work**," "construction," etc. In these terms, our Ancestors sought to demonstrate the connection between thoughts and actions. Again, for further demonstration of this point, one need only to recall the cosmology of Mennefer, in which it is explained that Pitah brings forth all things through the "kAt" (thoughts) and "Mdw" (Words) which repeat the "kAt of the Ib" (Heart). This is to show not only do thoughts guide our physical actions, but also the thoughts themselves are actions

that go on to create effects in the world. This is a very important principle to understand.

In regards to Nut protecting Osir specifically, this is speaking to the mediating role that the mind plays between our consciousness, Ba or "conscience" and the external world. The world (Gab) is constantly seeking to impregnate the mind (Nut). When we take in the seeds of experience it is up to our minds to sort them out. We have to think about what's happening, analyze it, and then decide whether or not to accept or reject it. If we indiscriminately allow experiences to go unchecked, we run the ever present risk of allowing bad seeds to be sown. This, over time can be damaging to our BA, which can become silenced due to the minds preoccupation with bad thoughts, or the voice of the Ba can become distorted, as it has to pass through all of the garbage that we've taken in. Therefore, it is up to the mind, and its various faculties, to discern and determine what it will allow to pass through our sphere of awareness, i.e., allow to pass through to Osir, what it will "feed" him.

Nut, as is the case with many of the nTrw.t, is also associated with the womb. In the case of Nut, she is associated with the vulva, and this also connects her to Het Heru. Her role in the womb, is similar to that of Khnum, in that she evolves or develops the child. In the Songs of Auset and Nebt Het, it is said:

> *"Your mother Nut comes to you in peace, she builds*
> *you up with the life in her body. Become a Ba, a Ba!*
> *Be stable, stable! May you have a Ba! O male, lord*
> *of women..."*

This passage follows a passage that speaks to the "cow" "weeping" for Osir because of the 'love and desire of him." In earlier passages in the same text, Osir is asked to "place life upon the forehead of the cow." The term for cow is *"idyt,"* which is also the term for vulva. Life placed upon the forehead of the "cow" is symbolic of life in the womb, which is represented by the yatin (sun) within the horns of the cow. This head adornment is one of the main symbols of Het Heru. We must recall that once Auset (the mother) conceives, Heru takes up residence in her womb. Her womb becomes the "Het Heru" (literally House of Heru). Nut in this aspect plays the same role as a Het Heru, in that she protects the child in the womb and further develops it. It is said of her in the same text that:

> *"she protects you from him who would do harm against you, she makes strong (healthy) for you your flesh on your bones. She knits for you your nose to your head, she gathers together for you your bones, you are complete!"*

From this passage, we can understand that Nut as mind, as womb, and even the intelligence of the womb, "intelligently designs" the child, developing the baby until it is complete.

In understanding experiences as the "seeds of Gab," we can also understand that though the mind plays a major role in maintaining and protecting the body and physical experience, the physical body, just as physical experiences, have an effect on the mind. For instance, many psychologists have linked the phenomenon of dreaming to communication between the body and the mind, and that in many cases, what is encountered in the dreams, the characters, etc, are parts of the body, its workings, and its issues personified or symbolized. Also, one only needs to reflect upon times of illness or fatigue, and the affect it had on the efficacy of one's capacity to think or focus. Sleep deprivation has been shown to create hallucinations. Also, when certain things are ingested, such as foods with aphrodisiac qualities and properties, or narcotics taken in through the body, they have an effect on the mind. Therefore, it should be understood that the relationship between Nut and Gab is one of reciprocity, it is rhythmic and cyclical.

Gab as physical existence, in partnership with Nut, affords us the ability

to experience, to live. He gives us concrete existence. In this way he allows us a chance to fulfill the very purpose of life, which is life itself; experience, learning, acquiring the knowledge of Self, etc. An alternative way of referring to Gab is Sab. This is the same term, or at least a homophone, of the term mentioned earlier for star, teacher, learn, instruction, and also school. Sab (Gab) as the earth, is where life takes place. He is the school, the lesson, and the teacher. As such he is intrinsically connected to Shai, the nTr of destiny. Destiny is not only the allotted time that we have been given on earth, but also the "*sbAyt*," or "**lesson**" we have come here to learn. As such Shai can sometimes be seen at the feet of Gab, in a manner similar to that of the Omomyit in the "wsxt n mAati." Just as the hearts of those who have not lived Maat are surrendered to the Omomyit, when one enters into the earth, they are surrendered to Shai, their fate/destiny, which is based upon the momentum or "Karma" from their "*wHm anx*," or "**Repeating Life**."

Gab, as Sab, is also associated with a school, for nTr comes into the world to learn about itself. Both the earthly plane, and the earth itself, help to facilitate that. Gab as the physical body provides a vehicle to convey the higher and subtler elements and aspects of the spirit. Without the body we would be unable to have experience in the concrete world, and any experience that we did have would be limited, and vicarious, through the manipulation of other physical concrete things. In this regard the body is a gift of Gab that carries us on our journey through tA (Earth).

It is stated in the "**Prt m hrw chapter 85**" that one "**hAi.i r tA Gbb dr.i Dwt.i**," that is, "*I descend to the land of Gab to drive out my evil (uncleanliness).*" This statement speaks to the reason for earthly life, i.e. a means to "purge" one's self of "evil" or uncleanliness. This is important to understand in relationship to the ultimate purpose of life, which is the realization and actualization of Self as nTr, which as it will be demonstrated later in this work, is accomplished through attaining spiritual/ritual purity. This passage also further affirms the understanding of Gab (Earth) as a place that we come in order to learn lessons critical to the evolution of our Ba. It is the lessons taught to us by earthly life that assist in the "purification" process or the expulsion of Evil from one's being. This point will be expounded on further, in the chapter pertaining to Sutesh, and his relationship to Shai.

Gab as the earth, not only provides us with a body, but also food to sustain it. He is also a nTr that judges us based upon the way that we use these earthly resources. He is quintessential to the continuity of life. Ultimately Gab is the source of all 'offerings" for both men and nTrw, and it is by his "command" that they (offerings) spring up. Although Gab is the "earth," his "gifts," or "offerings" are meant to be transmuted, and channeled towards the heights of the Heavens. These offerings are symbolized as the Eye of Heru. In the **Pyramid Text passage 524,** it reads *"may Gab allow (n) to fly up to heaven that he may take the Eye of Heru to himself!"* In another passage, it is said that the Eye was given to Heru in the presence of Gab. The Eye of Heru is not only a symbol of physical offerings to the nTrw, but literally the offering of one's own life and cognitive faculties, that the nTr might live and experience through it. When Gab allows us to take the Eye to Heaven, he in turn divinizes us. It is Gab that declares us a nTr in both the earth and the Duat. In regards to the becoming a nTr in the earth, symbolized by Heru's ascension to the throne, it is said:

> *"aHa (n) iTi imAx m-bAH.k mi iTi Hrw pr n it.f ma sn it.f stS m-bAH Gbb,"*

that is,

> *"(n) stands, and has taken possession of his honor in your presence, like Heru took possession of his father's house (inheritance) from his father's brother Sutesh, before the presence of Gab."*

Indeed, the Nisw Bity, who is identified with Heru is called **"iwaw Hr nst Gbb'** or "**Heir to the throne of Gab.**" In regards to being a nTr in the Duat, in **Pyramid Text passage 483** it is stated:

"tA sDm nnt Dd n Gbb I s.Ax.f wsir m nTr,"

that is,

"Earth, listen to these words of Gab regarding his spiritualizing (enlightening) Osir as a nTr."

In this same passage he goes further to declare that the "Doors of the Duat" are open to him, and that his words are able to reach Anpu, and that his dignity is in the mouth of Anpu (i.e. Anpu vouches for him), his words are "**Heru Chief of his Stations**." This is speaking to Gab offering Osir dominion over the Duat, and freedom to move about.

Gab sits as judge at the head of a tribunal of 81 nTrw. If his judgments are in one's favor, he opens the earth, or causes the earth to speak for them. However, if his judgment is against one, he will not open his "jaws," he will not allow the earth to speak. This represents on one hand, not allowing "offerings" to come forth, and on the other hand the binding of unworthy or unenlightened souls to earth. As this relates to the "gifts" of one's physical existence, in modern days and times this is called the "Law of Use," or as it is said "use it or lose it." However, as his offerings ultimately are meant to be transmuted and channeled towards the highest good, misuse would also lead one to "lose" their gifts or cause Gab to "close his mouth." This especially holds true for the way that we treat or mistreat our bodies.

Gab is a nTr of resources, health, prosperity, harvest, etc. As this relates to the physical body, he is especially interested in our maintaining good health. He is known to appear in dreams, and meditations, as a sign that one should pay attention to their health, get rest, provide nourishment, exercise, etc. From my experiences, when he appears in the form of a man, he has reddish brown skin, and long gold hair, and has somewhat of a golden aura. However, his appearance can also be a sign that one should take action, or of a coming harvest (or positive results of one's

378

actions), etc.

Hymn to Nut

Nwt pS.Tn Hr sA.T (name)

Nut spread yourself over your son (or sAt/daughter)

s.dgA.T sw ma stS Xnm sw nwt

Hide him from Sutesh, join (embrace to protect) him Nut

ii.w n.T s.dgA.T sA.T ii.n.T is Xnm.T wr pn

you come to hide your son, you come to join this Great One

nwt ixr Hr sA.T (name)

Nut, fall upon your son (or daughter) (name)

Xnm sw Xnmt wrt wr.pn imi ms.T

Embrace him, Great Embracer, this Great One among your children

Dd in Gbb Nwt Axw.n.T

Words spoken by Gab: Nut you are Mighty (Effective/ Spiritual Power)

Sxm.n.T m Xt mwt.T tfnwt nn mst.T

You were Powerful in the womb of your mother Tufnut before you were born.

Xnm.T (name) m anx wAs nn mt.f

You join (name) with life and strength that he does not die

Dd mdw sxm ib.T

Words to say: your heart was powerful

Wn wn .n.T m Xt mwt.T m rn.T.n Nwt

When you existed in your mother's womb in your name of Nut

Dd mdw Twt sAt sxmt m mwt.s xa.t m bity

Words to speak: You are the daughter who has power over her mother, appeared as (or like) bity

s.Axw.T (name) pn m Xnw.T nn mt.f

make this (name) powerful within you, he shall not die

Dd mdw: aAt xprt m pt n sxm.n.T

Words to speak: Great One, who came forth as Heaven, you became powerful

n.imim.n.T mH.n.T bw nb nfr.T

you are therein. You fill every place with your beauty

tA xr.T r Dr f iTi.n.T sw

the entire earth is under you, you have taken possession of him

SnT.n.T tA xt nb m Xnw a.T

You encircle the earth; all things are within your arms

Rdi.t.n.T (name) this m ixm-sk imi.T

May you place (name) within you as indestructible

Dd mdw n pnD.n.T mm Gbb m rn.T n pt

Words to speak: you are fertilized by Gab in your name of Heaven

smA n.n.T tA r Dr f m bw nb

I have united to you the entire earth in every place

Dd mdw Hrt r tA n.T tp it.T Sw sxmt im.f

Words to speak: High one over the earth, you are above your father Ishu

Mr.n.f Tw rdi.n.f sw xr.T xt nb is.T

He loves you, he has placed himself under you, All things belong to you

iTi.n.T nTr nb xr.T Xr HbA.f

You have taken all nTrw to yourself, in his sailboat

SbA.T.sn m Xa bA.s

You teach them as She of A Thousand Baw

Im nn.sn Hmi r.T m sbAW

They will not flee from you like the stars

Im nn.T rdi Hr (name) r.T m rn.T Hrt

Therefore, don't allow (name) to leave from you in your name of High One (Far off One)

Dd mdw nwk Nwt ms.n.T Snwt isk rn (name)

Words to Speak: I Am Nut, born to you, the Granary, I Proclaim the name of (name)

N Hrw mry tAwi nsw bity

Namely Heru Beloved of the Two Lands, Nisw Bity

Nb.ti mry Xt Hrw nbw

Dual Lord, Beloved of the People (masses) Golden Hrw

Iwaw Gbb mr.f nTrw nbw mry

Heir of Gab, his Beloved, beloved of all the nTrw

Rdi anx Dd wAs snb Awt.ib mi Ra anx.ti DttA

Given Life, Stability, and Strength, Health, and Joy like Ra, Everlasting

Life.

Litany to Gab
inD Hr.k Gbb
Show your face Gab
rpat nTrw
Hereditary Prince of the nTrw
nTr aA
Great nTr
it nTrw
Father of the nTrw
nTr Sps
Noble nTr
iri xt nb
Maker of All Offerings
it nsww tA Hr ndb
Father of all Nisww (Kings) the earth over
wnn.t. nb.t Hr sA.f
Everything exists upon your back
HqA
Ruler
Xnti nTrw
Foremost of the nTrw
sxm aA pri m Ra
Great Power coming forth from Ra
wr diw wtT.nf diw
Great one of Five who produced five
pXr sxt.f
surrounds his field
kA n Nwt
Bull of Nut
wAD wr
Great Green
gngn wr
Great Cackler
kA kAw

Bull of Bulls

nb msDr

Lord of the Ear

dwA nTr Gbb di.f.n.i xaw.i

Thanks to nTr, Gab, he has given to me my crown

it.i Gbb m sA.i

My father Gab is my protection

iw wD.n.i it.i Gbb iwa.f nb

My father Gab has paid me all of his inheritance

Offerings to Nut

Food

Honey Filled Cakes glazed with honey

Drink

Milk

Offerings to Gab

Produce of the season

Figure 19: Osir from the tomb of Queen Nefertari

Osir

Osir is the great great grandson of Nu and Nun.t, great grandson of Ra and Rayit, grandson of Ishu and Tufnut, and first born son of Nut and Gab. He is the husband of Auset and Nebt Het, brother of Sutesh and Heru War, and father of Babi, Anpu, and Heru sa Auset sa Osir. He is the nTr of Ancestry, Divine Lineage, the continuity of life, the bA within, the nTr within, Inner Ancestral Spirit, or Divine Self, and Sphere of Awareness. He is the Nisw of the Duat.

The Osirian tradition is a tradition Ancestral elevation and veneration. However, in order to understand it properly, one must understand Kemetic cosmologies and worldview. From the Kemetic perspective, nTr, the Creator, comes into being as its own creation or Creation itself. Therefore, ultimately all things in existence exist as manifestations,

383

aspects, or expressions of that Being. To say it another way, nTr alone exists. However, when we look at the cosmologies, such as the cosmology of Inu, we see that nTr comes into being by reproducing itself through its children. So what is being described in that cosmology is not only the Divine lineage of nTr, but also the evolutionary and creative process through which nTr came into being as its own creation.

For Afrikan people, and this is especially true of the spiritual tradition of Kemet, we trace our lineage all the way back to nTr, through our blood relatives, and through the nTrw. This being understood, not only are our blood relatives considered Ancestors, but also the nTrw, and nTr is considered the first Ancestor. However, once again, for us this lineage is also our very own evolutionary process, as nTr. Understanding this, we are now in a better position to discuss the tradition of Osir.

Once Ra reaches the stage of his creative process where he evolves and comes forth as Osir, we are seeing him reach a higher stage in his own evolutionary process, coming into being as man (men and women). We are talking the evolution of Divine Intelligence. Prior to this, he came forth as the earth; and before that the ordered universe; and before that the matter that formed as a result of the cooling process that the gasses that made up the early universe went through (Gab, Nut, Tufnut and Ishu respectively). As he evolves through these various forms, his scope of activity, experience, and expression, is limited by each, yet expanding as he unfolds himself. In Osir, we are seeing the Divine Intelligence manifest as the "Soul' or "Ba," and his spiritual tradition revolves around its evolution, continuity, and refinement.

This evolution is represented in the tradition, by the "Three Sons of Osir:" Babi, Anpu, and Heru. Babi represents this "Soul" or intelligence in its earliest and most primitive stages. Babi is portrayed as a baboon, and is a nTr of sexual potency, virility, raw vitality. He is highly sexual and violent. He is usually depicted with an erect phallus. He is also said to feed upon the entrails of elders who did not live Maat. He is considered to be ancient, and represents the early Ancestors of Modern Man. As such he is primarily a nTr of the dwAt. Anpu represents the transitional phase between Babi and Heru, in which the latter represents the evolved and enlightened individual. As we have already covered Anpu in detail, to avoid redundancy we will not revisit him here, and Heru will have a section dedicated to him alone. However, as it relates to Osir as the bA, these nTrw represent the evolutionary scheme, stages of growth, and the dangers and potential of degeneration. The ultimate goal of man is to become a Heru on earth through living a life of Maat. However, if one does not live Maat, and goes the way of their animal instincts, then there is the possibility of them falling victim to their own animalism, represented by Babi. Babi, though a nTr of sexual potency, is said to also lead to impotence. His sexual potency is needed in order to perpetuate life and existence. He is the impetus to survive. However, he is also associated with degeneration and impotency. In life this represents reaching a point of stagnation in one's spiritual and mental growth, and is also the potential for regression, and senility.

Osir's name and its meaning has been the subject of much speculation. However, if we examine the symbols that make up his name we can come to an understanding of what the Kemetyu meant when they rendered it. His name consists of two symbols, the "eye" and the "throne." The term for the eye in madu nTr is "*ir,*" which means "**eye,**" and is a homophone of a word meaning "**to do,**" or "**to make,**" and the throne is "*st'* or "*is(t).*" which means "**seat/throne,**" or "**place.**" Taking these two terms into consideration, we can literally understand Osir to mean "the place or seat of the eye (awareness), or "to make a seat/throne." Both meanings are actually applicable to Osir. As the "place/seat of the eye," Osir is the seat or sphere of awareness within all things. He is the center of consciousness. This is a part of the reason for his being the "King of the Duat," as he is also called *xnti Imntt*. In this instance the "Duat" or Imenti, which is also called *Shetati* (**The Hidden Two Lands**) is a reference to the mind and its dual components, the so-called "conscious," and "sub conscious" minds. Osir sits upon the Throne of the mind, as it is Consciousness that oversees it all, the contents of our minds (thoughts), emotions, the things taking place in the world "outside," and throughout the body, as well as also the contents of our dreams. No matter the changes taking place within the mind, emotions,

or bodily changes, consciousness is the universal constant. However, there is a time when we sleep and are not dreaming, and are not aware that we are asleep. This period is associated with Nu/n which is the inert matter that is pure consciousness without being "conscious of" (unconsciousness). In any case, this Awareness is present within everything to some degree; even plants, trees, animals; all the way down to the fundamental elements of life. Yet it is within man that we can really see "xnti imntt."

Osir Wan Nefir is the Ba within man. It is at once the seat of the self, or nTr within, the inner Ancestral Spirit, as well as the conscience. As mentioned in earlier chapters, it is this aspect of man that must be awakened. According to the tradition, it is Osir who spoke to Heru from the Duat, and instructed him to go to war with Sutesh for his throne. This is a very significant aspect of the story that has application on multiple levels. Firstly, as it relates to Osir Wan Nefer as the conscience, it is symbolic of the role that the conscience plays in influencing us to battle Sutesh, the lower aspects of our being, and that which is isfet. The conscience makes suggestions to us, speaks to us, and motivates us to "do Maat," to evolve. This aspect of Osir must be awakened, nourished, and protected. To better understand the role of the Ba in our lives, we must look at the life of Osir, the various phases of the story, and how it applies to the role of the Ba at different phases of our lives and spiritual development.

Osir is the "Judge" within the Duat. He is Osir "*Wan Nefir*," or the "**Good Being**." Initially Osir Wan Nefir is simply a faint voice crying out from the Duat. We have to learn as we grow, to hear and listen to the voice. This "voice," the "conscience," is the "Wan Nefir" or "the Good Being," the "Ba" or "soul" that pulls on us to do "good" or Maat, and evolve. The Ba, as we have demonstrated in the chapter on the "Anatomy of Being," is the aspect of our Being that links us as individuals to the All. It is the part of us that is directly connected to the source, and thus connects us on a deep and subtle level to one another. As it is connected to the Source, which is Nu/Nun, it pulls on us to return so to speak. When we are in conflict with this "pull," our Ba, Osir Wan Nefer lets us know it.

We experience guilt, which causes us to experience a lack of peace. When we heed the words of our conscience, it places us in harmony with the motion of the pull, and it leads us to Nun/Inertia, which we experience as peace. This aspect of our Being, Osir Wan Nefer is the force within us that is responsible for our spiritual evolution and ultimate return to our Divine State of Being.

As this evolutionary force, Osir is also the "seat maker." The idea of "Making a Seat," deals with Osir ascending to the throne. He is the aspect of our being that is constantly "ascending the throne," constantly evolving, as he is the nTr of the "Resurrection." Taking the throne is symbolic of overcoming, ascending to a higher level in life. It is a symbol that suggests that the very thing that appears as our greatest adversity/adversary becomes the very throne upon which we ascend to and sit upon. This is demonstrated in the Pyramid Text of Nisu Teti in which it is written:

> *"Ha wsir...ir s irk r di n Hrw in.t n.k DHwty xfti.k d nf.k w hr sa.f im nn.f Xa iw.k u ir st.k hr.r.f pr. Hm.s hr.r.f m nn nhp.f m a.k"*

That is,

> *"Hail Osir...wake up! Heru causes Tehuti to bring your enemy to you, he sits you upon his back, he shall not defile you. Make your seat upon him. Come forth! Sit upon him, he shall not rape you."*

In the same text it is said:

> *"they set your enemy beneath you, they say to him "you carry one greater than yourself...support one who is greater than yourself."*

The enemy in this case is Sutesh, the murderer of Osir. Though Sutesh "killed" Osir, he is also inadvertently responsible for his resurrection. If Sutesh had not killed Osir, there would not be any resurrection. This is a symbol of the great cycle of life, and how we are constantly "dying and resurrecting." We die from one stage and are reborn to another. It is the "past" (death) that begets the "present/future" (resurrection). We ascend to a higher level, seated upon the back of that which we have died from. It is once again the "death that begets life." Also, it is the adversary/adversity that serves as the very force that moves us toward resurrection, our evolution. As we overcome, the adversity becomes the very throne upon which we ascend. It is very interesting to note, that though the Seat is the chief symbol and component in Auset's name, and she is as we shall see, the "throne" upon which Heru as the Nisu or King sits, we find "st" in this case being associated with "St" of Sut (Sutesh). Another example, as I see it, of the genius of our Ancestors usage of the language and wordplay.

Osir's role in bringing order to the earth (establishing Maat) is related to the role that the Ba, as the vehicle of consciousness, plays in the formation of a life after conception, its development and its autonomous functioning. His journey leaving Kmt, to travel the world is analogous to the birth in the physical world, leaving from the interior, into the exterior. His "death," speaks to the dormant state of the Ba as the conscience at the early stages of an individual's life. As the individual grows, the Ba begins to speak to, guide, and encourage them. Taking heed of this voice strengthens it, allowing one to hear this voice more clearly. However, failure to take heed to the voice of one's Ba, increases the difficulty in hearing and receiving its guidance and influence, increasing the likely hood of erring or confusion. This science (the science of giving attention to the Ba) is symbolized in the tradition by the offering of the "Wadjet Heru" (Eye of Heru).

It is the "Wadjet Heru" that is one of the chief offerings used to awaken/resurrect Osir. Indeed, it is the Wadjet Heru that is used to "Open the Mouth" of Osir. This "eye," to put it in its simplest association, represents one's attention, awareness, and cognitive faculties. Central to the Osirian Tradition, is the possession and well being of the Eye. There is another story, which will be explored in the section pertaining to Heru Sa Auset Sa Osir, which pertains to injuries done to the Eye at the hands of Sutesh. However, for now it should be understood that the Eye will either be given to Osir by Heru, or it will be gouged out by Sutesh.

The offering of the eye represents the giving of the attention. It has been stated that "wherever the attention goes, the energy follows," and that energy will go on to reinforce, and create effects in our world. When we give our attention to Osir, the Ba, we feed it, we awaken him, it becomes powerful, and it is able to speak, and exercise influence in our lives. This is symbolized by Osir's ability to speak to Heru from the Duat. Once awakened and empowered, he was no longer relegated to the Duat, but his influence extended out into the earth. However, when the eye goes to Sutesh, we as Heru become blind to truth and reality; deaf to the voice of the Ba, and we limit its influence in our lives. This is symbolized by Sutesh gouging out the eye of Heru, or by Heru looking upon Sutesh in the form of a "pig," causing a "storm" to manifest in his Eye. Another analogy is that when we give the Eye to Sutesh, we become Sutesh, and our bodies become Osir's coffin, and we reinforce his captivity and suffocate the Ba. It is our attention that is the key to whether Osir lives, or dies (remains "dead"), we must use it wisely.

In our spiritual infancy we are only Osir's coffin. Although we are "conscious," we are not aware of reality of Self, consciousness, and the correct role that it is to play in our lives. So at this stage Consciousness is just conscious, but is not in a position of authority. This being the case, we simply allow anything to come into our sphere of awareness. The chief purpose of consciousness is experience; it fulfills this purpose by default. However, in our spiritual ignorance we take in things that defile the body of Osir. We have not yet learned the power of consciousness; Osir has not yet been resurrected. Also, our awareness is "dismembered. We cannot "see," the "Oneness of all life."" We cannot "see" the whole, and how all of the things that we experience are related in our lives. We fail to understand the "big picture," and the deeper meaning behind it

all. For now, it's all just an endless stream of unrelated events that fluctuate in the sensations that they cause. Our awareness is so fragmented that it disallows us from seeing that every single thing, event, person, animal, etc, is a cell in the body of nTr; a component in a system wherein each component has a specific role and function to fulfill in the overall thriving and evolution of the whole. We cannot see how everything that we experience is ultimately geared towards our own personal evolution. We cannot see! It is not until Osir is resurrected that we begin to see clearly.

The Fully Awakened Ba, in the Osirian tradition, is symbolized by the nTr Sukari. Sukari is the form that Osir assumes once he has been fully awakened and empowered (symbolized by both the Opening of the Mouth, as well as union with Ra in the Duat), and has ascended the throne as Nisu of the Duat. When Osir becomes Sukari, he has complete sovereignty over himself, and the forces within the Duat. He also now has dominion over the earth, as Heru becomes the "Henu" (Boat) that carries him. For this reason, Osir is said to "drag the earth in his name of Sukari." The "earth" here, on one hand, is his son Heru. Let's explore this point a little further.

Sukari is the nTr of death, or to be more accurate "Death" itself. However, Sukari can be considered the "Death that begets life," as it is in Sukari's domain where the "resurrection" of Osir/Ra takes place. As the living individual is identified with Heru, the experience of "death" through Sukari, is the experience of the death of the "ego," or the death of the "sense of separateness" from one's inner nTr. When this takes place, Sukari is Heru and Heru is Sukari. In the tradition of Sukari, there are a few symbols that speak to this science. First, there is the offering of the Wadjet Heru to Osir to awaken/Open his mouth, and secondly, there is the offering of one's "Head," symbolized by a man literally beheading himself as he stands before a woman that acts as the "guardian" of Sukari's path. Both examples represent one completely surrendering to the nTr within, Sukari, the Living Ba, by giving one's Self to it. Once this takes place, Heru becomes the "face" of Sukari, his vehicle in the earth. In Pyramid text 364, it is said that:

390

"...Heru loves you, he has equipped you with his eye, he has joined to you his...that you may see with it...that you may be strong...Heru has completely filled (restored/refreshed) you with his eye..."

In chapter **42 of the Prt m Hrw** it is said by Osir:

"I feel, I perceive...I am in the Wadjet (Eye)...I sit in the Wadjet...I am Heru traversing eternity..."

In utterance 645:1824 a-g it is said that:

" Heru carries you in the Henu, he carries you as a nTr in your name of Sukri, as he carries his father Osir, he unites himself with you. You shall be powerful over Upper Kemet as Heru, over whom you have power. You shall be powerful over Lower Kemet as Heru, over whom you have power. You shall be powerful, you shall be protected in your body from your enemy."

The above aforementioned passages describe clearly the union that takes place between Sukari and Heru, as a result of Heru's sacrifice.

Heru offering his eye to his father, is symbolic of him offering himself. This offering is the ultimate sacrifice, the highest that an individual can make. Heru completely surrenders to Sukari, and he is thus granted power over the earth, as Heru. Heru gives himself over to "death," so that his father can live through him. This represents the extension of the Ba's influence into the external world, regulating and harmonizing an individual's life, effecting their world and experience, forcing them to evolve. One's desire becomes the fulfillment of the Shai nTri (Divine

Plan), and the plans of one's Ancestors. Sukari also brings the experience of synchronicity and oneness with all things, and the awareness of, and communion with the bAw (presence/glory) of the nTrw. Sukari, as King of the Duat, also gives one a special ability to work with the Ancestors, having them more readily at one's disposal. One becomes the vessel that carries their Ancestors, in the same way that Heru, as the Henu carries Sukari. As Heru surrenders to Sukari, Sukari becomes his identity, and his thoughts, emotions, and actions, are transmissions of the nTr. The relationship between Sukari and Heru is a symbol of the experience of the "spiritual master" as a vessel of nTr and the Ancestors.

In the text known as "**nt-a n inn skr r wAt StAy**" (**Ritual of bringing Sukari to the Hidden Path**), Sukari is called forth as:

"**I bA anx.n wsir Xaa.f n iaH,**"
O Living Ba of Osir, crowned with the Moon,"
I nTri imn wsir m nTr Xrtt,
O Hidden nTr, Osir in the City of the DEAD (cemetery),
"**I nA bA iqr nty m nTr Xrtt,**"
O These Perfect bAw which dwell in the City of the Dead,"
" **I bA n Ra m wiA HH,**"
O Ba of Ra in the boat of a million years,"
i pA nbt Hnw rnpi tw m StAyt,"
"O The Lord of Henu, you become young in the Secret Place,

These passages strongly attest to Sukari's identification with the "Living Ba of Osir," as well as Ra who unites with Osir, in Sukari's domain in the Duat.

Sukari on a personal level, corresponds to the fully awakened Ba of the individual, and on a collective level, he is the "World Ba" that pulls on "All" to evolve collectively. It is through Sukari that bAw (Souls) return to the earth to continue their souls journey and mission to evolve.

As mentioned earlier in this text, the Osirian Tradition is a tradition of Ancestral Veneration. In Henensu, the collective Ancestors are

392

venerated as the nTr Osir Khenti Imentiyu. It is important to remember that while Osir, like many of the nTrw, has various correspondences and levels of application (and influence), one of the chief among them is his correspondence to the elevation (resurrection) of the "deceased" to a position of power and influence in the Duat (Spirit realm), symbolized by Osir ascending the throne of the Duat. Many of the text considered "Funerary Texts," are actually rituals that involve the restoration of the cognitive faculties of the "deceased," and "*prt-xrw*" or **voice offerings**" that are meant to empower their spirits, so they might have power over their own beings, and the ability to move about freely. The most important of these rituals is called the "**r wn r.n wsir** " "**Opening the Mouth of Wsir**," and "**ir wpt r n twt n (name) m Hwt nbw** " "**Performing the Opening of the Mouth of the Statue of (name) in the House of Gold**." This ritual text was traditionally used to enshrine a new Ancestor, and empower him or her. The "mouth" of the Ancestor was not only speaking of their actual "mouth" (spiritually), but also the medium through which they would from there on speak and be fed; the shrine. This chapter, especially the version found in the prt m hrw, should be used, along with the chapter of '**Giving a Mouth to Wsir**, ' to dedicate, and activate a shrine. More on this point later.

In Henensu, individual Ancestors are given the title "Osir," having it affixed to their Ren. Since the tradition is one of Ancestral Elevation as well, we venerate all of our personal Ancestors, regardless of whether or not we see them as "good" or 'bad" people or enlightened or not. It is not a part of the tradition of Henensu to only honor "enlightened" Ancestors, or "High" Ancestors. All of our people need love, light and nourishment. As Heru, it is the responsibility of the living to elevate the spirit of Osir, period. Some of our Ancestors need to be purified and uplifted. This can be likened to the mummification of Osir, prior to his elevation. Anpu purifies the body of his father. He removes the corruption from him, and then after he has done this he preserves the body and protects it, keeping watch over it. This is our responsibility to our Ancestors, including those that may not have lived a life that we would deem "righteous." We must find something to honor, even if it's just the fact that they are an expression of nTr on their own personal

journey to evolve. Do this regardless of your personal feelings towards them. This will bring healing to them and you as well. Remember that it was a "mistake" on Osir's part; a lack of vigilance (awareness), that led to his downfall. We all make mistakes. We all are here to learn. All of the Ancestors that we know of should be included in the list of names for Ancestral Libations, and venerated collectively as Osir Khenti Imentiyu. Hymns to Osir are appropriate to use for Ancestral Libations.

The Osirian Tradition is the path where nTr, the Self, and Ancestors, meet. Osir as the Ba is at once the seat of the divine Self, sphere of awareness, conscience, the nTr within, and also the inner Ancestral Spirit. All of these are one and the same. The Ba of an individual enters into the head of their father and is transmitted to the mother through the semen. From there it plays the role in guiding the formation of the child in the womb. This same force goes on to develop and form the various faculties that will make up an individual's being. As time goes on, this Ba will begin to speak to them, encouraging them to live Maat, combat their lower natures, just as it was Osir who spoke to Heru from the Duat, commanding him to go to war with Sutesh. Just as the Ba guided their formation in their mother's womb, the goal is for it to further guide their evolution in life. As one becomes more and more victorious over Sutesh within themselves, Osir, their Ba, is vindicated, and begins to have greater influence in their lives, extending into the external world, affecting their external environment. They become, and experience the bAw (the manifestation, presence, and power of nTr) in their life.

The Osirian tradition is the crux of nKmt spirituality, as it is the tradition of "nHm nTr," the Salvation of the "Soul;" the vehicle and seat of nTr within man that must be awakened and liberated, to be given expression and influence in an individual's life. Essentially, a person's very existence is for its evolution, enlightenment, redemption, and liberation. The awakening of this nTr is the awakening and liberation of our own divinity.

Hymn to Osir
dwA wsir wn-nfr

Praise Osir Wan Nefir

nTr aA Hr.ib ibdw

Great nTr within Ibdw (Abydos)

nsw HH

Eternal King

nb DttA

Everlasting Lord

sbbi HH m aHa.f

who traverses millions of years in his lifetime

sA tp n Xt Nwt

First born of the womb of Nut

wtt n Gbb rpat

Begotten by Gab the Prince

nb wrrt

Lord of the Warret (crown)

qA HDt

exalted of Hejet (white crown)

iTy nTrw rmT

Sovereign of nTrw and man

sSp n.f Hq Xw iawt it.w.f

he has received crook, the flail, and the dignity of his fathers (Ancestors)

aw- ib.k nty m st sA.k Hrw mn Hr nst.k

your heart swells (with happiness) in st (imntt...i.e. "the west") because your son Heru is established upon your throne

iw.k Xaa.Ti m nb dd.w m Hq imi ibdw

you are crowned as Lord of DdDdw as Ruler of ibdw

wAD.n.k tAwi m mAa.Xrw mbAH a nb r Dr

you have greened (replenished/given life to) the Two Lands in triumph before the hand of the Lord of All

stA.n.f nty nn xpr m rn.f tA.Hr.stA n.f

he leads in his following, that which already exists, and that which has not yet come into being in his name tA Hr stA n.f

sk.n.f tAwi m mAa.Xrw m rn.f pwi n skr

He drags the Two Lands in triumph in his name of Sukari

wsr.f aw aA snd m rn.f pwi n Wsir

he is exceedingly powerful and greatly terrifying in his name of Osir

wntt.f Hnti HH m rn.f n Wn Nfr

You exist at the Two Sides (Beginning and End) of Time for millions of years in your name of Wan Nefir

inD Hr.k nsw nsw.w

Salute to your face King of Kings

nb nbw

Lord of Lords

Hq Hq.w

Ruler of Rulers

Tt tAwi m Xt Nwt

possessor of the Two Lands from the womb of Nut

Hq.n.f tAw.w igrt

You rule the lands and igrt (spirit realm)

Dmw Hat

With limbs of Fine Gold

Xsbd tp mfkt Hr.tp awy.f

Head of Lapis Lazuli, arms of turquoise

In.n HH

Pillar of millions of years

Wsxt Snbt

With a broad chest

Nfr Hr imi tA srt

Beautiful of Face in tA srt

Rdi.k xw m pt

You give light in heaven

Wsr m tA

Power in the earth

mAa.Xrw m nTr Xrt

victory in nTr xrt (spirit world)

xd r dd.w m bA anx

sailing down to DdDdw as a living Ba

xntiyti r ibdw m Bnw

sailing up to ibdw as the Benu

aq pr nn Sna.tw Hr sbA nb.w n dwAt

coming and going without hindrance at all the doors of the Duat

iw rdi.n.k tAw m pr qbH

may you be given bread in the house of libations

Htpw m inw

Offerings in Inw

Sxt mn m sxt irw bdt im.f

an enduring field in the Field of Reeds

n.kA n Wsir xnti Imntt

to the Ka of Osir Khenti Imentiyu (Foremost of the Westerners)

<u>Renu</u>

Wsir Khenti Imenti (Foremost of the West)

Wsir Nu (Osir Nu)

Wsir Tum (Osir Itum)

Wsir Pesjut War (Osir the Great Pesejut)

Wsir Neb Warret (Osir Great Lord)

Wsir Neb Ankh (Osir Lord of Life)

Ra Hrw-Axty (Ra-Herukhuti)

Wsir Nb r Dr (Osir Lord of All)

Wsir xnty Nb Wa (Osir, foremost of the the One Lord)

Wsir saH (Osir Orion)

Wsir Saa (Osir the Seer)

Wsir Nb DttA (Osir Lord Everlasting)

Wsir skri (Osir Sukari)

Skri (Sukari)

skri m Shetait (Sukari in the Two Hidden Lands)

skri nb r-StAw (Sukari Lord of the Grave)

skri Hr Sa.f (Sukari he who is upon his sand)

<u>Day</u>

Friday

Saturday (Sukari)

<u>Color</u>

White (Osir)

White, Dark Blue, Black (Sukari)

<u>Number</u>

10 (Osir Un Nefir)

11 (Osir Khenti Imentiyu)

13 (Sukari)

Food

White Rice, Grains, Corn, Seeds, Grits, Coconut (Osir)

Potato, Eggplant, Mushroom, Black Sesame, Black Rice, Onions (Sukari)

Dates. This offering was made to Osir traditionally for rejuvenation and progeny.

Fresh baked White Bread cut into a "cone" or "triangle" offered with the point up. This is offered to Osir Khenti Imentiyu (The Ancestors)

All Good Things (Osir Khenti Imentiyu)

Drink

Beer, Wine, Coconut Water, Coconut Milk, Fresh Water.

Milk (give milk every 10 days) This is a traditional offering

Stones

Amethyst (Osir Wan Nefir)

Malachite (Osir Khenti Imentiyu)

Onyx (Sukari)

Plant

Palm (should be grown/kept on Osir Khenti Imentiyu Kari, or the family cemetary) This is a traditional offering. It is offered to invoke the Ancestors, receive their protection and to purify negative energy. It grants power and victory.

Sacred Animals

Bull

Bwt

398

Fish (especially catfish), pig, rat,

<u>Animal Offering</u>
Ram (Osir Khenti Imentiyu)
Bull (Red)
Ox (Sukari)

Figure 20: Offerings being presented to Auset in her shrine/inner sanctuary at the Temple of Auset in Aswan

Auset

Auset is the Great Great Grand-daughter of Nu and Nun.t, Great Granddaughter of Ra and Rayit, Granddaughter of Ishu and Tufnut, daughter of Nut and Gab. She is the Wife of Osir, sister of Sutesh, Nebt Het, and Heru War. Auset is the nTr.t of Women, Motherhood, Healing/Medicine (especially spiritual healing/juju), Hika, Rivers (Freshwater) "Queen-mothership," ritual, etc. Though these things listed may seem like plenty, they don't even scratch the surface of this powerful nTr.t.

As a part of the Osirian tradition, she plays central and critical roles in the resurrection of Osir. She is also renowned for conceiving, through the power of the "Spirit," the child Heru; the nTr of the "Divine Kingship." For this reason, among others, she is called "*Mwt nTr*" **Divine Mother** or "**Mother of nTr**." However, perhaps most important is the significance of her traditions to the spiritual journey of Man, the continuity and maintenance of the family and community, lineage, ancestry, and legacy.

Auset's love and devotion in remembering Osir, is symbolic of the deep longing for spirituality in man; the longing for union with nTr; a longing that leads one to seek the nTr, and devotion to the path as an Initiate/devotee. She motivates man to transcend the mundane carnal life, to strive towards something higher, their greatest good, their inner nTr (Osir), and to manifest or give it expression in the world (Heru). Her journey, is the spiritual journey of man, the journey of the "Person."

In her supreme form, Auset is "Nebt r Jer." She is the Creator that gave birth to all; the universal mother. In this regard she is associated with the nTr.t Niyit. She is called "**nbt Pt tA dwAt Hr s.xpr.sn n kAt.n ib.s m ir.t.n awy.s**," that is, "**Lady of Heaven , Earth, and Duat, Having brought them into existence through what her heart conceived and her hands made.**" She is also called "**Nbt Pt tA dwAt mw Dww nwn mi qd,**" that is, "**Lady of Heaven , Earth, Duat, Water, Mountains, and the entire Nwn.**" These names demonstrate that in her supreme form, Auset is the "All," manifested at every level, including the Nun. In her highest form, she also came to be known as "She of a thousand names," ultimately all things being an expression of her. This form's popularity expanded far beyond Kemet, even up into Europe.

In her role as a "Co Creator" with her masculine counterpart, be it Osir in his creative aspect, or Ra, she is identified with Rayit, and Het Heru. Corresponding to the "Creative Power," and agent of "Divine Action," she is called "*Drt nTr*," that is, the "**Divine Hand**," or "**Hand of nTr**." As we have demonstrated in the previous sections regarding the "Drt nTr,"

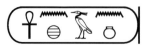

this hand is analogous to the womb, and is thus the power that births things into the physical world, from the spiritual. Auset, in many ways, is the Divine Spirit.

This association of Auset with the Divine Spirit is also evident in the fact that her family, the triune of herself, Osir, and Heru, came to be the prototype of the Christian concept of the "Trinity," Originally held as the Father, Mother, and Son, and over time the Mother being apparently "replaced." However, the truth that can be realized by careful study, will show that what has been called the "Holy Spirit' in that particular tradition, has always been considered feminine.

Within man, Auset corresponds to the Ka, which is the aspect of an individual that is responsible for giving one their unique qualities in expression of intelligence and power (talents and gifts), personality, and is inherited through the mother. It is the feminine counterpart of the Ba, which is received from the father and is associated with Osir. Testament to this fact is in the chapter of "**Not Letting a Man's Heart Be Driven from Him in nTr Xrtt**," in which the relationship between the mother, ib (heart), and kA, are made clear; in which the ib is declared at once to be the "mother" of one's coming into being, as well as the "kA within the body, forming and making strong the limbs." This "kA" once again is the unique vital essence and power within each thing. It is the spiritual "double" of a thing. It is the twin to the physical body. In the nKmt tradition, this is symbolized by the relationship between Auset, and her twin sister, Nebt Het, the former corresponding to the kA, and the latter corresponding to the Khat or physical body. In the Yoruba tradition Auset, (also written Aset), the kA, became *Ase'*, the "*very force which is life and brings things into being in the universe[12].*" Auset as the chief mother principle is the force that brings things into being from the Higher Planes, "birthing" them into the Physical Plane. This relationship is also demonstrated once again in the language, kA, being the vital essence, spirit, genius, personality, etc, "kAA," or "kAi" meaning to "think," and

---

[12] **Imhotep, Asar** "Understanding Ase and It's Relation to Esu Among the Yoruba And Aset In Ancient Egypt" 2012

"kAAt" or "kAt", meaning to "work, create, build," etc. Auset is the force that brings forth the kA as kAi, and then ultimately manifesting it in the world as kAAt.

Looking further into the relationship between Auset and the kA, is her role as a nTr.t that is *"Warit Hikau"* (wrt HkA), or **"Mighty in HikA"** ("so-called magic"). "Hika" is the science of acting upon the Ka of a thing, causing its creative elements to come forth, in order to create effects or change in the world. This once again demonstrates the process and power through which "things" are "born" or manifested into the world. According to the tradition, it is Auset that is responsible for bringing Osir, who sits upon the throne of the spirit world, back into the world through his seed, his son Heru, again speaking to the same principle.

Auset according to one tradition is Omnipotent. She became so by acquiring knowledge of Ra's secret name. By gaining knowledge of this name, she in turn gained power over him. As we have come to understand Ra as Life, and all life as his expressions or evolutions (limbs, body, etc), power over Ra is power over the forces that constitute life itself, the nTrw. The nTrw, by all their various names and paths (epithets) are the "secret names" of Ra. It is these names that are used in ritual incantations and "Hesi" or chants, and hymns. This knowledge gives Auset the power to command and direct the nTrw. She is described in words, as **"Iri mdw m-xnw psDw sSm-tw gr st-r.s,"** that is **"She makes commands among the Nine nTrw, they being lead according to her authority."**

According to the same story, Ra caused his "True Name" or "Secret Name" to pass into Auset. His name also represent's his identity. As Auset represents the spirit of Man, Ra's "name" entering into her represents the fact that it is within the spirit of man, that the "True Name" of nTr can be found. This being the case, it is Auset that houses the greatest mystery and the highest spiritual truth. This is spoken to in **Passage 312 of the Coffin Text**, in which it is stated:

"I have come forth from it to the House of Auset, to the secret mysteries; I have been conducted to her hidden secrets, for she caused me to see the birth of the great nTr."

It is within Auset, the spirit of man that the deepest knowledge; the knowledge of nTr, resides, and her journey is one that represents the path of the Initiate to discover it.

As a nTr.t, Auset is very maternal. She is nurturing, compassionate, sensitive, empathetic, and protective. She is nourishing, and is associated with the nourishing and sustaining waters of life. In this regards, she is called *"Diyit Ankh,"* that is **"Giver of Life," "Lady of Streams of Fresh Water,"** *"nts Sti Hapy,"* that is, **"She is the one who floods the Hopi (Nile),"** *igp.t wAxy Axt m s.xd.s,* **"rain cloud that makes green the fields when it descends."** Her home is said to be *"hr.ib itrw,"* **"In the midst of the River,"** and she is said to **"call out from the river[13]."** Her cool and watery nature gives her tremendous healing powers, and psychic and magical abilities. She is the nTr.t of healing par excellence. This is evidenced by the fact that many of her stories portray her in circumstances where she must heal, or restore someone, be it Osir, Heru, Ra, etc. Also, one of the most important nKmt medical texts, the so-called **"Ebers Papyrus,"** opens up with two invocations addressed to Auset, that are said to have the power to overcome all illnesses, physical and spiritual.

Her watery nature also gives her a very strong magnetism and receptivity, once again lending to her magical and psychic potential. However, this cool and moist nature also makes her very humble, and accommodating. This is demonstrated once again, by the fact that she "follows" Osir wherever he goes, and in her words "will never leave

---

[13] Ritual of Bringing in Sukari

from you." Her life is a life of complete devotion, service, and sacrifice. Almost every time that Auset is depicted it is always in regards to her being of assistance. She is even depicted showing mercy, and attempting to help Sutesh, who murdered her husband, just on the strength that he is family. She is very compassionate.

Auset's power lies in her emotions and passion, which are also associated with her "waters." She is considered one of the "mourners," whose songs, chants, tears, and cries, help to revive Osir. Her cries are so powerful that they are said to be able to literally stop the boat of Ra in its tracks. This is demonstrated in the story of Auset traveling with her family (Nebt Het, Heru, Anpu) and the seven scorpions that were given to her for protection and guidance by Tehuti, in which one of Sutesh's scorpions infiltrated Auset's ranks and stung and poisoned the child Heru. Her cries caused Ra to stop his boat and send Tehuti and Zerqet to answer her and relieve her of her sorrows. This is symbolic of her ability to accomplish anything, any idea that she is passionate about. This is further evidenced by her insatiable passion for attaining the highest knowledge and HikA abilities, which led her to stop at nothing in acquiring Ra's name. The Passions of Auset house the power of life and death. She can give birth to anything that she is passionate about. This is Auset as she who activates the kA during ritual.

Auset became very popular with the masses due to her infinite mercy and compassion. She is the mother that will take care of her child, regardless of how old they get. Her love is a deep unconditional love. Her devotees surrender to her like the child Heru, and she carries them in her arms, nurturing, and nourishing them. She is also very protective of her children, and can be very fierce in defense of them. As a great protector, she is called *Auset Nejit*, that is, **Auset the Protector/Avenger**.

Auset is also a nTr.t of wisdom. She was called Auset *Rekhiyet*, that is Auset **"The Knower."** In this form, she is a nTr.t of learning, and governs *Rekhiyu* (**Wise Ones**) or *"Rekhi iket"* (**Knower of Things**). While Tehuti is the nTr of wisdom and is the sage amongst the nTrw, Auset is the "force," that compels them to share their wisdom with the world; the

force of love and compassion. This is an important teaching in regards to Auset; Compassion.

Let us recall the story of Auset on her journey, hiding and on the run for her life, along with the baby Heru. She stops in a town to take refuge for a while. Traveling along with her, are seven scorpions. Three scorpions walk in front of her, one on each side of her, and two walk behind her. When she came to the town, she stopped by the house of a rich woman to seek refuge. The lady came to the door, but did not recognize Auset. She saw the scorpions with Auset and became frightened, and slammed the door in Auset's face. Very tired, Auset prepared to keep walking. A poor woman then came to Auset and offered to share her small meal with her. Meanwhile, two of the scorpions decided to get even with the rich woman. So they loaded all of their poison into one stinger and went to the house of the rich woman. The scorpion crawled under the door and stung the child of the rich woman. The child fell fatally ill and the woman sought help but could not find any. Auset hearing the woman's sorrows, felt compassion for her, and decided to heal her son, in spite of the way the lady treated her earlier. When Auset saw the lady's child, he reminded her of her own son Heru. Auset looked upon them with compassion. This is the way the Sage interacts with the world, and this is the way that the spiritually evolved view the masses.

Auset causes us to re-member who we were, and the condition we were once in, in our spiritual infancy. In too many instances, people get a little bit of knowledge, and that little bit is allowed to inflate their ego, causing them to look down upon those who are less informed. However, being informed does not equate to knowing, and neither does it equate to being wise. Wisdom, through Auset, causes one to have empathy and compassion, because they remember when their own Heru was a baby. They remember yesterday.

Each and every person carries that seed of nTr, and is therefore nTr incarnate. That seed is the innate Divine Potential that must be cultivated and actualized, in order for one to grow into the full maturity of their nTr-hood. Like Auset, we must hold that baby Heru, holding that seed, re-membering who it's "Father" is, and remember who "He"

406

is, remembering "his" potential. We must hold one another as sacred, and we must see one another as nTr. We must view the earth and everything on it through the eyes of Auset, and nurture and protect it as if it is our own sweet baby. We must remember that each person is Divine, no matter how they may be currently behaving. Potentially they are nTr, but must grow into their nTr-hood. Most people are in their spiritual infancy. This is the chief reason for their transgression of the law, and egoism. They lack "Self control" (meaning the Self is not in control!) and have yet to develop the reasoning faculties that will allow them to understand why they should choose to follow the Law. Therefore, for the evolved, the eye through which we must perceive the world (or at least the masses), is the eyes of compassion. It is not that these people are inherently evil, but lack Knowledge of Self, the Knowledge of who they truly are. So just as it would be foolish and nonsensical to get angry, yell, beat an infant for soiling its diaper, crying, hitting, biting, any other thing that infants do, it is equally unwise to take the same approach towards the masses of people. However, effort must be made to enlighten the masses about their divinity.

Auset and the child Heru also signify the relationship of the Sage, and his teaching of the masses. Like Auset nursing the babe, the Sage must give the masses "milk." The teachings must be put into a form that they will be able to understand and benefit from, at their current stage of evolution. Even though the Sage does not (cannot) give them the full depth of the spiritual wisdom, what he/she gives is nutritious enough to further them along in their development.

Auset as nTr.t of wisdom is also identified with "*sSAt Pr mDAt,*" **"Seshat Mistress of the Library" (House of Books)**. In this form she is said to be the scribe to all the nTrw and Nisww, and she writes down all of the deeds of mankind. In this regard, she is definitely a nTr of memory, especially "Genetic Memory," and the "Library" as a storehouse of all the information that has been accumulated throughout time. She is also identified with another nTr.t, though obscure, "*Safekh Aabui,*" who records the names of each person upon the leaves of the Persea tree, along with their lifespan.

In regards to Genetic or Ancestral Memory, her form as *"Hnnwt Pr-MDAt"* or "**Mistress of the Library**," not only speaks to the reservoir of accumulated knowledge and information, but also abilities. This is demonstrated in cases where spiritual "gifts," such as "seeing," may be passed along through the bloodline, especially from mother to daughter. This knowledge and power is contained in the "Library," which is also the "blood" of Auset.

One of the most important (as well as the most powerful) amulets and symbols in the nKmt tradition is called *Tyet*. This symbol is called the "**Buckle**" or "**Knot**" of Auset, and is said to be the "blood" of Auset. In **Prt m hrw**, "**The Chapter of a Tyet of Carnelian**," it is written:

> *" The Blood of Auset, The Hikau of Auset, the Might of Auset, are Wadjet (Protective Amulet) for this Chief, it is a protection from his bwt (taboo)."*

The appendix of the text goes further to say that:

> *"if this chapter is done for him, it becomes the power of Auset to protect him...no path is blocked to him, his hand is to heaven, his hand is to earth..the doors of the nTr Xrtt (dwAt) are open to him...his name shall be like that of the nTrw who are therein..."*

There are two ways of understanding this "buckle" or "knot." On one hand, it is referring to the actual blood of the "Mother" or Woman, the menstrual blood. The power of menstrual blood is very well known amongst practitioners of Afrikan Spiritual Traditions worldwide. It is considered very powerful; so powerful, that it is also dangerous in some cases. Menstrual Blood is so potent, that it has the capacity to annihilate any spiritual forces, magical energies that it comes into contact with. It also has the ability to render any ritual instruments, shrines, and "juju" of any kind obsolete. It is analogous to a "spiritual EMP." It is for this reason that women are asked not to attend shrines or handle ritual objects during their cycle. It has absolutely nothing to do with them being "unclean" or any of that nonsense. It is that during this time they are extremely potent, so potent that they can render anything around them impotent. However, while they are asked not to approach any shrines during this time, any personal rituals that they choose to perform can carry extra shekhem and effectiveness, as it was stated, that the "Blood" "Opens all ways and doors," heaven, earth, and Duat. During this time a woman is "Open," Physically and spiritually, and she is very magnetic.

The Tyet is considered the buckle that a menstruating woman wore to absorb the blood. Therefore, it becomes very useful as a talisman to protect against malefic forces as it has the capacity to destroy them. However, once again, it has the capacity to destroy all forces, positive and negative.

The other side of the Tyet is speaking to the Buckle or knot, as a representation of the lineage or bloodline. As the relationship of Auset with Ancestral Lineage has already been touched upon, the "Blood of Auset" is thus the blood as a symbol of "Lineage," the Buckle or Knot connecting Osir to Heru, or "Yesterday "to Today." What makes the Tyet so powerful is the fact that it connects us to our Ancestors, grants access to their wisdom and power, and this also includes the nTrw, as they are our spiritual Ancestors. As Afrikan people, we trace our lineage all the way back to Ra, back to Nu, Back to Imun! The knowledge of our lineage, and the knowledge of how to "work it," gives us ultimate protection, and opens the way for us. This is why it is stated in the Tyet chapter, that the person that utilizes it, their name "shall be like that of the nTrw," Which means "they" (the nTrw) will recognize the person as one of them, as a relative, a nTr. This is similar to **chapter 125 of the prt m hrw**, in which Anpu states to the nTrw "*He (the initiate/ancestor) knows our paths and our towns. Offerings have been made to me, I smell his smell like one of you,*" acknowledging once again the familiarity (family) of the person.

Auset as a nTr.t of Wisdom gives access to ancestral information, guidance, increases instinctiveness and intuitiveness. She increases "Psychic abilities," especially empath abilities, mediumship, etc. She also increases the ability to receive guidance through dreams, and increases the accuracy and prophetic nature of dreams.

Auset is the nTr.t of women. She is the ideal woman: virtuous, devoted to her family, noble, nurturing, supportive, wise, a healer, spiritually powerful, and a bridge to the spirit world. Traditionally she was what every woman of Kmt aspired to be and embody. She is the archetype of the true Afrikan Queen. She is the nTr.t of women and mothers, while Het Heru is the nTr.t of young women and girls. Auset is the Mature Afrikan Woman, married with a family. As Het-Heru is held to be the wife of Heru, she is associated with the Queenship as well. But just as Every "Heru" shall (or at least should) become Osir, every "Het Heru" shall (or at least should) become Auset, a Queen-mother. As the nTr.t of Womanhood, she is very helpful in healing women mentally, emotionally, and physically. As a nTr.t of Motherhood, she may be worked with when trying to conceive a child, or healing illnesses of the womb, or cultivating the "maternal instinct." She may also be worked with for success in marriage, especially as it pertains to problems with being devoted, exercising patience, gentleness, being accommodating, etc.

Auset also grants the ability to be patient, and passionate, and to allow that passion to nourish and nurture one's goals. Once the idea has been "conceived," With the passion, patience, and devotion of Auset, we can gradually develop our aspirations internally, in the spirit and mind, until it is ready to be born in the world (put into action). Even after it has been "born," she gives the ability to nurture and nourish the objective until it has reached maturity, and a firm foundation has been laid. Like Heru, though he started out as a "seed," he ended up a great and powerful Nisw, seated upon the lap of his mother (The Throne).

While Het-Heru represents what life should be like in this realm and the

410

Duat, Auset represents the ideal characteristics and traits that it will take to achieve such a state. She personifies all of the ideal traits of a spiritual devotee and initiate. She is Maat personified. We are not told much of Osir's personality from the tradition, nor are we taught much about Heru's personality. However, we know that Heru represents the goal of the spiritual aspirant in this realm, and Osir represents the same goal in the Duat. The unifying factor in both cases is Auset. Auset as Maat personified is the key to becoming both (an elevated Ancestor, and an enlightened living individual). This is why she is called "*mwt nTr*," or "**Mother of nTr**" or "**Divine Mother**," for it is she that gives birth to "Divinity" in both realms.

Like any mother, Auset can be a little over protective ☺. There comes a point when she must let go. Heru must be weaned; he's a big boy now. Sutesh must be put down; we know he's your brother, but he has to go! This is represented in the story of the battles between Heru and Sutesh. Sometimes her mercy can be taken too far, causing her to not recognize when a person or situation is incorrigible. In the story she overstepped her bounds, and ended up with the head of a cow! In this form she is called "*Nbt tp-iht*," "**Lady of the Cow's Head**," the "**beheader of the rebel**."

According to the tradition, Heru was about to defeat Sutesh, and Auset stepped in to protect her brother. Heru became furious, and in his rage he beheaded her (two lessons here[14]) . Tehuti replaced Auset's head with that of a cow, as a symbol of surrender, and as a result, she now stands as the force that one must surrender their head to. Though we will not mention her name here, this form of Auset also exists in the dwAt as a protector of the path of Sukari. She is the "limit" and criterion that one must meet in order to pass. She can be seen standing with an imposing presence as a man willfully bows before her beheading himself. This represents, once again, surrendering one's head and the slaying of the ego to become a vessel of the nTr.

---

[14] The Two Lessons here, is that Auset must know her limits, and the limits of mercy, and Heru must know the limits of severity, and not be rash or prone to extremes. Balance is the Key!

Hymns to Auset

iAw n-t Ast wrt

Praise to you Auset the Great

Mwt nTr Nbt Pt

Divine Mother, Lady of Heaven

Hnwt Idyt nTrw

Mistress, Woman of the nTrw

ntt Hmt-Nsw tpt wn nfr

You are the Head royal wife of Un Nefer

Imy-r Imyw-r Nbyw m gsw-prw

The supreme overseer of the golden ones in the temple

sA smsw. tpy n Gbb

The eldest son, first born of Gab

ntt Hmt-nsw tpt n wn Nfr

You are the head royal wife of Un Nefer

kA mAi sxr sbiw-f nb

The Bull, Lion who overthrows all his enemies

Nb HqA Dt

Lord and Ruler for Eternity

ntt stpt tpt n wn-Nfr

You are the first chosen of Un Nefer

Hwn Nfr ir aDt m XAkw-ib n TAwy

Beautiful Youth who hacks up the Rebels in the Two Lands

ntt Hmt-Nsw tpt n wn Nfr

You are the Head Royal Wife of Un Nefer

xw sn-s ir Dsr Hr wrd-ib

Protector of Her Brother, and sets apart (makes sacred) the weary hearted.

ntt Hmt Nsw tpt n wn Nfr

You are the Head Royal Wife of Un Nefer

HH rnpy wtz nHH

Eternal Youth, Holding up Eternity

412

iw t r-Hna-f m snmwt

You are with him in Senmut (Place where he is buried)

Hymn Two

Ast Wrt mwt nTr Nbt iw-arqi

Auset the Great, Divine Mother, Lady of the Limits

Hmt nTr dwA-t nTr Drt nTr

Divine Wife, Divine Adorer, Divine Hands (Hands of nTr)

Mwt nTr Hmt Nsw wrt

Divine Mother and Great Royal Wife (Queen Mother)

skrt Nbt Xkrw aHt

Adornment Lady of Ornaments of the House

Nbt Abw Axxt

Lady of the desired harvest (or refreshing)

imty mH aHt m nfrw-s

Nurse who fills the house with her beauty

idt aHt Hnwt rSwt

Fragrance of the house, mistress of joy

iTyt gst m st-nTryt

who completes her course in the Divine Place

igpt wrx Axt m sxd-s

Rain Cloud that makes green the fields when it descends

Srit bnrt mrwt Hnwt nt Smaw mHw

Maiden, sweet of love, Lady of Upper and Lower Kemet

Irt mdw m-Xnw PsDt

Who issues words (decrees) among the Nine (nTrw)

Sm-tw gr st-r.s

According to whose command one rules

iryt-pat wrt Hswt nbt iAmt

Princess, great of praise, Lady of charm

xnmst xnt-s tftf m antyw wAD

Whose face enjoys the trickling of fresh myrrh

Hymn 3

Ast di.t anx Hr.t-ib iAt wabt stt Hnwt snmwt

Auset, giver of life, residing in the Sacred Mound, Zatit, Lady of Zenemut

Nts sti Hapy

She is the one who floods the Hopi (Nile)

Iri anx Hrw-nb sxpr wADwAD

That makes all people live and green plants grow

Rdit Htpw nTr n nTrw

Who provides divine offering to the nTrw

Prt m xrw n Axw

And voice offerings for the Ancestors

Hr-nty nts nbt pt

Because she is the lady of heaven

TAy-s m nb DwAt

Her man is the Lord of the Duat

sA-s m nb tA

Her son is Lord of the Earth

TAy-s m wab rnpi-f m snmwt r tr-f

Her Man is the pure water, rejuvenating himself at Zenemut at his time

Nts nbt pt tA dwAt

Indeed she is the lady of heaven, earth, and the Duat

Hr sxpr-sn n kmAt-n ib-s m ir.t-n awy-s

Having brought them into existence through what her heart conceived and her hands created.

bA pw nty m niwt nbt

She is the Bai that is in every city

wp-Hr-s Hna sA-s Hr sn-s Wsir

Watching over her son and her brother Osir.

Renu

Ast

414

Ast Rxyt (Auset the Wise Woman/The Knower)

Auset nDt (Auset the Protector/Avenger

Mwt nTr (Mother of nTr/Divine Mother)

Nbt Pt tA dwAt (Lady of Heaven, Earth, and Duat)

Nbt Pt tA dwAt mw Dww nwn mi qd (Lady of Heaven Earth Duat, water, mountains, and the all of Nu)

Irt anx n anxw (Gives life to the living)

Irt anx n psDt (gives life to the psDt nTrw)

Wrt HkAw (Great of Juju)

aprw abA m irt Hrw

nDt sn.s (Avenger of her brother)

nDty wrt (great protector)

sDmt sprw (Listens to Petitions)

Hwt nTr aA (Great House of nTr)

Nbt iAkb (lady of mourning)

StAt wrt (Great Mystery)

MAaT (Maat)

Renenutet

Hnwt m mw idbw nbw (Mistress of water and all riverbanks)

skrt (Sukarit)

tA wrt (Tawarit)

zrqt (Zerqet)

Day
Monday

Number
7

Colors
Blue (Sea), Silver, Red (For Power and Protective forms)

Stones
Moonstone, Quartz, Mother of Pearl, Aquamarine, white Coral

Minerals
Silver

Food
Cereals, Grains, Leafy Greens, Lettuce, Cucumbers, corn, Seaweeds, Watermelon, Melon (Honeydew), Bread

2 bowels of barley grains (A Traditional Offering used to "resurrect" Osir)

Drink
Fresh Water, Milk, Pomegranate Wine, spearmint tea

Herbs
Accacia, Date Palm, Lotus

Totem
Throne, Egg (For Fertility), Phallus (For Fertility), Swallow, Cowries Shells, Coral, Ostrich Feather

Sacred Animal
Sea Swallow (Tern), Cow, Hippo (Protection of Pregnancy), Mother Goose, scorpion, black kite, vulture, Winged Scarab

Nebt Het

Nebt Het is the great great grand-daughter of Nu and Nun.t, great granddaughter of Ra and Rayit, granddaughter of Ishu and Tufnut, daughter of Nut and Gab. She is the second wife of Osir, ex-wife of Sutesh, twin sister of Auset, and sister of Heru War. She is the mother of Anpu by Osir. She is a nTr of the earth/physical plane, the physical body, manifestation, the desert lands (barren lands), limits, death (dying), domestication, nature, construction, labor, physical beauty, illusions, protection, and service. She is mostly known as the devoted, faithful companion, and helper of her sister Auset.

In her highest cosmological form, she represents the universe in its

417

essential and inert state, prior to the coming into being of order. In this regards she is associated with the nTr.t Niyit, with whom she is sometimes identified. It is her intercourse with Osir that serves as the precursor to the creation of the universe and life coming into being.

As Auset represents the "**spirit**" or *kA*," as well as the spiritual plane or "Duat, Nebt Het as her twin sister, represents the physical body and plane: Khat and tA respectively. In this regard, Nebt Het is called "**Nbt XAt**," that is "**lady of the body**." This body is not just the physical body of man, but the physical body of all things.

While it has already been demonstrated that man consists of several bodies that vary according to levels of concentration and density, Nebt Het corresponds to the densest body called "Khat." This is the body that we all are familiar with, and many assume to be the only body we have. This body, the Khat, is a culmination; an end result of a things coming into being through a densification process that begins with the highest spiritual bodies. The Khat is a body of effect, or reaction; the summation following behind the equal sign in the mathematical process of creation. It is totally receptive and dependent. In this regard she is called "*smn.t wD nTrw,*" "**the one who establishes the commands of the nTrw**," or "the one who makes firm (solid) the commands of the nTrw."

This submissive nature is demonstrated in the functions of the nTr.t Nebt Het. Nebt Het is mostly portrayed in a supportive role, as she follows and assists her sister Auset in re-membering the body of Osir; assisting in the rituals, and protecting his corpse. It is as though her purpose, her very reason for being, is to serve Auset and Osir. In fact, when we look at some of her main Renu, they speak to such a notion.

She is called "*sn.t nTr,*" " **Divine Sister**," or "**sister of the nTr**," "*zAw.t sn.s,*" "protector of her brother." All of these epithets describe her in relationship to her siblings. In fact, one could go as far as to say that Nebt Het is defined by her relationship to her siblings, especially Auset. This point is demonstrated by **chapter 30 of the prt m hrw**, in which it is stated "**ntk kA.i imy XAt.i Xnm s.wADA at.i**," that is , "*You are my Khat* *within my body, forming and making my limbs strong.*" Here it is being stated that Auset, the kA exist within the Khat, Nebt Het, and forms (builds) and strengthens her limbs. It has already been touched on how the Duat, which is associated with Auset, exists within tA, which is associated with Nebt Het. They are inseparable, and it is this reason Auset and Nebt Het are inseparable. In fact, be it that the majority of information regarding Nebt Het is mostly in her association with Auset, that in all the countless volumes that have been written on the nKmt tradition, there has been very little commentary on the nTr.t Nebt Het. However, one must not mistake her obscurity for a lack of importance. On the contrary, she is very important. Without Nebt Het there is no physical life; no experience. It is this very fact that is the reason why her coming together with Osir is the event that led to his death, which in the cosmological sense, represents the creation and coming into being of life. Further, it is through Nebt Het that the power of nTr comes to be known; the ability to create, to bring life to something, to give purpose and meaning to a thing. This is symbolized by the fact that Nebt Het was considered barren, yet when nTr (Osir) had intercourse with her, he brought life to the desert lands!

Nebt Het's nature is that of the earth. She is like the humble earth in the hands of an intelligent being, that can be tilled, cultivated, channeled, shaped, molded, and put to use. In the hands of Sutesh she is infertile, but in the hands of nTr she is productive. This is expressed in her name "*Axt,*" meaning "**Useful**."

Nebt Het is the capacity of nTr to show forth its power and glory on earth. Thus her name "*Axt*" is also related (through paronymy) to the term for "**Splendor**' or "**Glory**." Nebt Het makes the "glory" of nTr(w) manifest on earth. This not only speaks to the coming into being of physical existence and new things, and the ability of things from the highest planes to distill and concentrate into the earth, but also "*bAw;*" the manifestation of a nTr or Ancestors presence in the physical world, through the experience of signs, symbols, and omens related to the specific force at work. In this regard, she is a messenger and a guide to those who have initiated eyes and ears. This particular function of the

nTr.t Nebt Het is expressed in her ren "*wn nfr.t,*" which is the feminine rendering of "*wn nfr,*" which is an epithet of Osir, which corresponds to his function as the **bA**, the seat of the Divine Self, Inner Ancestral Spirit, or conscience within man. However, the difference between the "**Wn nfr,**" and "**Wn nfr.t,**" is the fact that "wn nfr" speaks <u>from within the Duat</u> (Spirit), whereas on the other hand "Wn nfr.t" speaks <u>from and through the "powers" of the earth, and all of the creatures on it.</u> Osir is "bA," whereas Nebt Het is "bA.t" or more accurately "bAw." One guides man from within, the other extends that guidance to the external world. This is common knowledge amongst practitioners of Traditional Afrikan Spiritual systems (and really any so-called occult magic systems), that when spiritual agencies are in operation (which is all the time), there is a signature there for the initiate to see, so that they can know how to move accordingly, receive guidance, or maybe a warning. This signature may come in the form of a specific number, colors, animals, time of events, etc.

According to the tradition, Nebt Het was once wedded to the nTr Sutesh. Some may wonder "How could a nTr.t so sweet and helpful ever be with Sutesh, the nTr of Chaos and Confusion?" However, like Sutesh, Nebt Het is not all good, nor is she all bad. She was married to the "Trickster," because she has a few tricks up her sleeves as well.

If one were to recall the events that led up to Osir's intercourse with Nebt Het (which ultimately led to his death), they would find Nebt Het engaging in activities that can easily be considered "trickery." According to one tradition, she intoxicated Osir and disguised herself as her twin sister Auset. As the eye is one of the chief symbols of Osir, the condition of inebriation, along with Nebt Het's disguise, creates a state of impaired awareness. Nebt Het "veils" herself, impairing Osir's awareness through illusion. This is exactly what the physical world does. It veils the spiritual realities (nTrw, Ancestors, Essential Oneness of All) that exists within or beneath the surface of this plane, causing many to fall under the illusion that this physical world is "it;" "this is what's real;" "there is nothing else;" etc. It is this impaired perception that creates theories such as "man is a rational animal," or the belief that there is no "Higher

Purpose," or "Divine Intelligence" present, and in operation in the universe (Atheism). This illusion ultimately leads to all forms and expressions of individualism and materialism. Yes, Nebt Het has a few tricks up her sleeves.

This illusion is created due to the nature of Nebt Het as physical existence. It is the densest expression of reality or matter, the realm of effects. She (Nebt Het) is all that can be physically detected with the naked eye and its instrumentation (microscope, telescope, x-ray, etc). However, as physicists continue to discover (especially Quantum Physics) that there are layers and layers to this thing we call reality, that are far deeper than just what we can see; and the deeper we delve, the more we come to realize that physical existence and the apparent separateness of things is "illusion," and there are realities that exist beyond. This aspect of Nebt Het is spoken to in the **Litany to Ra**, in which it is stated:

"Hknw.n.k Ra qA sxm psd tp.ri imy.t hAt.f Twt is XAt.w Nbt Hwt,"

that

"Praise to you Ra Exalted Shekhem, whose head shines more than the things which are before him. indeed Ra is the bodies of Nebt Het."

The idea of something "shining more than what is before it" means that it will be more visible than the others, yet there are things before it that are not as visible, but still exist. In this case, the things that are "before her," yet she outshines, are the higher spiritual bodies, and the higher planes of reality.

Nebt Het is the "illusion," or at least the illusory nature of the physical world. She is a nTr.t of death and dying. The process of dying and death attests to the illusory nature of physical life. When one is "dying," or

even aging, they are seeing the gradual decay or passing away of their physical body. When one "dies," unless the body is preserved, that body will decay, and all that will be left are bones, leaving no resemblance of the person that lived. To the uninitiated eyes, it appears as though the person is diminishing, and eventually ceases to be. However, anyone that practices an Afrikan Spiritual Tradition knows that though the physical body may cease to exist, the person who inhabited it does not. In reality, the person has not died, only transitioned. A change has taken place.

However, Nebt Het as a nTr.t of dying is not simply speaking to the act of physically dying, but to the process of change, the ever passing away of the moment, and the eventual loss of all physical things one may possess. Similar to Het Heru, she is a nTr.t of beauty, but the kind that gradually fades, and is relative. Nebt Het is also associated with the suffering and mourning that comes as a result of loss and attachment to the things that have passed away, causing difficulty in accepting or adjusting to change. She comforts the mourner, as well as those that are physically dying, escorting them into the West.

Nebt Het's role as a nTr.t of dying and death is two-fold in application, and expression. On one side she is the "spiritual dying" and "spiritual death" that results from attachment to physical things and materialism. When a person is experiencing this side of Nebt Het, they are blind to the spiritual side of life, and don't know their path or destination (Shai). In the tradition this is spoken of as Nebt Het "touching" one's eyes, and being "bound by the hair" of Nebt Het. For instance, in **passage 858 and 859 of the Coffin Text**, one is instructed to *"take possession of the hand of Nebt Het, and keep it from giving it (the eye of Heru) to them,"* them being the "followers" of Sutesh. Also we find in **passage 373** Nebt Het stating *"sStA wAt.w r s.wA tm rf sSp xpr kkw,"* that is, *"Hidden are the paths to those who pass. Light ends and darkness comes into being."* Nebt Het in a way similar to Niyit, serves as somewhat of a veil, that blinds one from seeing the spiritual essence and reality of things. This connects her to her first husband Sutesh, who is noted for being one who "blinds" Heru, either by gouging out the eyes, or by creating a storm (confusion) within it. In this regard she serves as both a "consequence" of a life that is "anti Maat," and also as a "security system" to hide the "paths" of the nTrw, and divine knowledge, from profane eyes.

In **passage 593 of the Pyramid Texts**, one is encouraged to:

"Raise yourself, clear away your dust, and remove the shroud on your face. Loosen your ties: they are not ties; they are the tresses of Nebt Het."

The "tresses" or "hair" of Nebt Het represent the "ties" of the past that holds one back from progressing spiritually. Nebt Het, again, represents that which is passing, and has past. This is the reason why it is her "hair" (which hangs behind her) that has one bound. The "ties" that are spoken of are referring to the linen wraps that are used during the mummification process, which are meant to assist in preserving the body, a form of security. In this passage the individual is informed that what it is that has them bound, is not the ties of linen wraps, but is indeed the "hair of Nebt Het." This implies that the person is mistaking what they're holding onto as something that is for their benefit, providing a sense of security, but is actually a block to their spiritual progression. So they are encouraged to shake off their "dust," and to remove the "shroud" from their face, so that they can see clearly, let go, and move forward. This once again represents one being stuck in the past, as well as being totally wrapped and caught up in the physical world; the illusion, that one is not able to see the truth: the spiritual essence of things, the roads of the nTrw, and the spiritual death, blindness, confusion, and stagnation that takes place as a result living a life of materialism.

However, on the other hand, Nebt Het as a nTr.t of death and dying can assist one in learning to let go; to detach from the physical world and

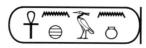

materialism, and learn to accept change. So through Nebt Het, dying on a higher level is the process of gradually withdrawing one's attention and energy that had been previously invested in the physical world and materialism, and over time beginning to yearn for and focus on the spiritual side of things (represented by Nebt Het's yearning for Osir, and joining Auset as a sister-wife). Death through Nebt Het on the highest level, represents death to the "illusion of the physical world," and the experience and realization of the reality of life; death as the experience of "enlightenment."

In further describing Nebt Het's association with illusion, the passage **"for the protection of the tomb"** in the Pyramid Texts, describes Nebt Het in her "bad coming," as a "Substitute (or Imitation) without a womb/vulva." This is speaking to the emptiness of a life without spirituality, a life of materialism but devoid of substance, a life without the knowledge and experience of nTr.

According to the tradition, Nebt Het after having intercourse with Osir, and becoming pregnant with Anpu, began to feel guilty, so guilty, that she abandoned the child Anpu, leaving him in the wilderness to die. Auset, went out and found Anpu, and Nebt Het, and brought them into her home and helped Nebt Het to raise Anpu. The abandonment of Anpu by Nebt Het, represents the condition and vulnerability of the mind of an individual once they are born into the physical world. Being left in the "desert," which is the normal domain of Nebt Het represents the mind being left in a condition where it cannot be nourished. Anpu is the gatekeeper. When we are born Anpu is at the mercy of the world, the door is wide open for any and everything to enter in. Auset coming to Anpu's rescue represents the nurturing of the mind by the spirit. The fact that Auset and Nebt Het raised Anpu together, represent balance being brought to the mind, in which the mind is no longer solely concerned or preoccupied by matters of the physical world, nor at the mercy of it, but now also receives nourishment from the spiritual world. This same principle is spoken of in terms of Auset and Nebt Het being considered the "two mothers" of Heru, or as it is put, "Auset conceived, but Nebt Het gave birth." This represents Heru existing and being "born" in the physical world (Nebt Het), but being "conceived" by the spirit (Auset). Also, Nebt Het is sometimes described as the "wet nurse' of Heru. This speaks of the role that the physical world plays in our spiritual growth and development. She is physical life as a teacher, a lesson, and is said to administer an individual's Shai, also in her name of "*smn.t wD nTrw*" (**she who establishes the commands of the nTrw**)

The highest expression of Nebt Het's path is that of letting go, surrendering, following, and service. She is humble, devoted, and receptive. She cultivates these qualities in her devotees.

Hymns to Nebt Het
inD Hr.T Nbt Hwt
Salute to your face Nebt Het
sn.t-nTr
nTr's sister
mnx.t zAw.t sn.s
excellent protector of her brother
maki Ha.f
protector of his flesh
Axt
Effective one
tm.t Hri r sn.t.s r iri.t zp-nfr n sn.s wsir
who is not far from her sister to make a good time for her brother Osir
smn.t wD nTrw
makes firm the commands of the nTrw

mAat
Maat
sA.t Ra
Daughter of Ra
Hnwt imnt.t
Mistress of the West
Nbt nbi nsrt sbiw nw sn.s

Lady who burns the enemies of her brother with fire

Renu
Nebt Het
Nebt Het mnx.t nTrw nbw (Excellent of all the nTrw)
Sn.t nTr (Divine Sister)
Saw.t HA sn.s (Protects the flesh of her brother)
Nbt XAt (lady of the body)
Axt (Effective)
Wn nfr.T (Good Being)
Nebt Ihy (Lady of Joy)

Day
Saturday

Colors
Black, Dark Blue, Earth Tones. White

Number
12

Stones
Onyx, amethyst

Herb
Everyday kitcthen spices

Cypress (incense and Oil)

Drink

426

Plenty of Beer, Mahewu, Palm Wine, Kombucha

Foods

Pomegranates. Fermented foods (Injera for example), ogi, Akara (Acarajé), Falafel, Yogurt.

Heru Behudet

Heru Behudet is the son of Ra-Herukhuti. He is the nTr of war, protection, justice (vengence), Blacksmiths (Iron, Metallurgy), Masculinity (Manhood), Male Sexuality, and Kingship. He is known as the Great Protector of his father Ra, as Ra travels in his barque. He is fierce, obedient, concise, courageous, relentless, disciplined, militant, and noble. His emblem (Winged Sun) was placed over entry ways of all temples to ward off evil. He is identified with other major warrior nTrw, such as "Inhur," "Munthu," and "Heru War," the son of Nut.

In his supreme form, Heru Behudet is a creator, and is at times identified with his father Ra-Herukhuti, or is considered to be the "Ka" of his father. He is called *"Drti wr pHti pAwti zA pAt-tpit qmA ixt*

428

nbt..." that is "**Hawk, Great of Strength, son of primeval matter, creator of all things.**" These epithets identify Heru Behudet with his father Ra. Also, it is important to note the use of the term "*Drti*' to begin the hymn, which means "**falcon, or hawk,**" instead of the more common term "*bik*." In this context, it is a play on words, in which "*Drti*" is also a homonym of a meaning "**Ancestor**" or "**Ancient One.**" Also, speaking to his identification with Ra, he is called "*Nsw-nTrw,*" or "**King of the nTrw.**" It is said that he "*Xrt tA arf m xfa.f,*"that is, "**carries the earth, holding it together with his grasp.**" It is also said that he "**caused the nTrw to come into being,**" and he is "*nb r Dr HqA psDt pAwtyw tpy xpr m-Hat pAwt SAa tA n pAi.n.f xpr wa pw ir nn r-Aw,*" "**he is lord of all, ruler of the nTrw, the primeaval being who existed before the first time, who first made the land to the one who existed (Nun). He is unique, the one who made all of this.**" However, of all his names, the ones that he is most known by are "*nTr aA nb pt,*" that is "**Great nTr, Lord of Heaven.**"

Herukhuti is a name for the planet Mars in the mdw nTr language. According to the tradition, Ra is the nTr of this planet, which is also called **Heru Desher** (Red/Blood Heru). As Ra-Herukhuti is the father of Heru Behudet, and sometimes Heru Behudet himself, his identification with the planet mars gives us great insight into the essence and nature of Heru Behudet. Historically, Mars has been viewed as a planet associated with war, iron, the color red, masculinity/men, action, and vitality. All of these associations and more are present in the persona of Heru Behudet.

He is called "*Hrw Msn,*" that is "**Heru the Fashioner/Blacksmith,**" and he forges weapons and tools of Iron. He carries knives, sickles, swords, machetes, and big heavy chains to deal with his enemies. He also has an army of "*Msnyw*" or **Blacksmiths (or harpooners)** at his disposal to assist him in conquering all that oppose him. He is mighty, fierce, and relentless. It is important to take note of the fact that as a "Blacksmith," Heru Behudet not only creates weapons, but also tools that may be used to build, speaking again to his role, not only as a nTr of War, but also creation, a craftsman in a way similar to Pitah, Sukari, and Khnum.

Heru Behudet's association, and identification with Ra-Herukhuti, puts his place and role in creation in the nKmt tradition, as the nTr that carries out the actual work of creation, in every tradition, for in his creative form, Heru Behudet is Ra. Also, being a nTr of war, the tradition of Heru Behudet, and his role in creation is very similar to the Orisa Ogun in the Yoruba tradition, also being a warrior according to that tradition, carried out the actual work of creation and making earth a suitable place to live. As Ra is the creator in all major and minor cosmologies (all nTrw being forms of Ra, and come forth as him to create), Heru Behudet as his kA (Persona) is in a way (at least functionally), the creator in every cosmology.

As the son of Ra-Herukhuti, Heru Behudet in his tradition is the chief protector of his father. His task is to keep the forces of Isfet at bay as his father Ra journeys in his boat, to ensure that his journey remains uninhibited. In this particular role, Heru Behudet represents the laws and systems that are meant to preserve life, and that which sustains it, Maat. Ra is life; and Maat, at times referred to as the "food" of Ra, is that which perpetuates, sustains, and optimizes it. Heru Behudet is the great protector of Ra (Life) and the preserver, restorer, and enforcer of Maat (Divine Law and Order). He is the Immune System in the body, as well as spiritual immunity and defense.

According to the tradition, Ra was journeying in his boat, along with the nTr Tehuti, when he noticed that all of his enemies were conspiring against him, and plotting an attack. His enemies were all around him in every direction. Tehuti, serving in the role of advisor to Ra, advised that Ra invoke his son Heru Behudet to come to his defense. Heru Behudet came in the form of the "winged yatin" (Winged Sun). At the command of Ra (via Tehuti), Heru Behudet flew up into the sky and emitted an intense heat. This heat was so intense that it caused the enemies of Ra to lose possession over their faculties. It is said:

"nn mAA m irty.sn nn sDm m anxwy.sn smAw wa

sn.nw.f im.sn m HD At nn tp anx.sn.im,"

that is, they

"neither saw with their eyes neither heard with their ears. Each one slaughters his fellow among them in that harmful moment; there is no head that they live there (in other words they lost their minds)."

From this point on in the story, everywhere Tehuti saw the enemies of Ra, he commanded Heru Behudet to go and deal with them. Heru Behudet did not act without being ordered by Tehuti, and he did not hesitate once commanded. He is disciplined, direct, and precise. As a nTr he gives the ability to act without hesitation or second thought; to be assertive, to seize the moment, and once we know exactly what to do (Tehuti) we act on that knowledge without hesitation.

Heru Behudet is also called *"Hrw DbA"*, that is **"Heru of Retribution"** or **"Vengence."** This particular form of Heru Behudet is the "force of Justice," specifically the force that is responsible for restoring the "balance" once one has violated the laws of Maat. He is the law of Cause and Effect, "Reciprocity," and in the east he is called "Karma." His main role as the protector of Ra, and preserver and restorer of Maat, is to preserve the integrity of life and its progression (evolution). He is the protector of "individuality," assuring each thing its place in the sun, and the survival instinct that kicks in when one thing infringes or imposes upon another, threatening its right to be (a role shared with Sutesh). When this takes place he steps in to enforce Maat, restore order, correct, reestablish the balance, and eradicate any blocks to growth and progress and anything that no longer serves a purpose (redundancy). He is the other aspect of Maat or evolution, known as "Extinction." This term "DbA," also means **"Punish,"** so He is also **"Heru the Punisher."** It is said of him that he *"DbA Dwt m DbAt,"* that is, **"he punishes the evil doer in DbAt"** (Behudet/Edfu).

In the chapter entitled "**Becoming Heru the Elder**," it is stated:

"iw wDa n (N) pn rHwi m sky pt iw Drb (N) sAH m nwty swt (N) pn wDat m pt.tn n Ra iw sSp Dd (N) pn iw knH Dd (N) pn,"

that is,

"...you are Heru War, you have judged between the two fighters (Heru sA Osir sA Auset and Sutesh), the two who would destroy Heaven. You have grasped sAH (Orion) with the two adzes of Sutesh, you have rendered judgment in this sky for Ra, light is at your decree, dark is at your decree."

This passage demonstrates the role of Heru Behudet (Heru War) as justice, in maintaining, and also restoring order in the universe. It is he who decides what is "right" or "wrong." His "judging" between Heru and Sutesh speaks to his role in restoring balance between opposing forces. Without Heru Behudet stepping in to settle this "dispute," the heavens (universe) would be thrown into Chaos, symbolized by the potential for them to 'tear up the sky." Duality is the fundamental constituency of Order. Without it, life, and all that it entails, could not exist. So in this particular instance, the dispute between Heru and Sutesh must be settled, for if any side destroys the other, the universe, and life, would cease to be; all would return to Nu. So it is Heru Behudet's job to ensure that the scales always return to balance, and that they are not allowed to tip to the extreme on either side. It is for this reason it is said, "*light and dark are at your command,*" for in the "grand scheme" of things, it is not about "right or wrong," but the perpetuance of life. It is for this reason, that in many instances Heru and Sutesh are said to reach a stalemate in their battles, or Heru wins sometimes, and

Sutesh wins at other times; and while ultimately Heru must prevail (take precedence) over Sutesh, he is not allowed to annihilate him. This is evidenced by the fact that even when Sustesh is "killed," he ALWAYS comes back.

As a nTr, Heru Behudet gives us the ability to impose justice upon ourselves; to go head to head with our negative qualities and make corrections where needed. He gives the ability for us to force ourselves to live Maat. He is also the power to stop bad habits and make changes in an instant, or as some say "cold turkey." For instance, because I am a son of Heru Behudet, when I decided I was going to stop eating pork, I stopped right then and there. Later when I decided I would stop eating meat, I stopped the very day the decision was made. While some people may find it more of a challenge, and have to implement these types of changes gradually, Heru Behudet allows me to change at the drop of a dime. However, there is also present the urge to rush or force changes that should be implemented gradually, it's a double edged sword, and balance is a necessity, which is why Tehuti must serve as the precursor to action.

The fact that Heru Behudet gives us the ability to impose justice, to correct, and to discipline ourselves is evidence that this is a force within us that can be harnessed and directed. This means that while it is true that justice exists in the universe and will eventually restore all imbalances and correct all wrongs, it is also something we ourselves can enforce. This is important for many of us as Afrikan people have bought into the western and far eastern ideals (two extremes in thought) that we should leave justice up to the "Hrw DbA" in the universe and in the meantime "turn the other cheek" and pray for our transgressors, thinking this keeps us in harmony with Maat and expressing our divinity. However, such ideas are either the result of misunderstanding Maat and what it means to be a "divine being," or it is an illogical excuse for cowardice. nkmt spirituality and Maat are life centered traditions, and as stated before, Maat is that which perpetuates, sustains, and optimizes life. Therefore, being a pacifist, choosing not to defend yourself and your family are not expressions of Maat, nor is it "Divine"

by any means. Choosing not to protect the Life (Ra) you've been given is Isfet. Ra's boat must continue to move uninhibited, otherwise "Chaos" shall ensue, and it is the defense of Heru Behudet that ensures that does not happen.

As Afrikan people, because of what we have been through (colonization, Slavery, Jim Crow, Apartheid, Genocide, etc), and our adherence to the oppressor'fs religions, it has caused us not to seek justice for ourselves. Due to our miseducation, we believe that we should let "god" fight our battles. We believe that a nTr such as Heru Behudet has no place in spirituality, which we think is all about "loving" everybody. We have "loved" everybody to our detriment, to the point where we hate ourselves. The nTrw are the divine forces of nature, and it is through maintaining order and harmony with them that order and harmony is maintained in the universe. We exist in and as the universe and are a part of nature. Therefore, the nTrw are also present within us, and must be brought into order, harmony, and must be nourished, nurtured, and given expression. If the nTrw are not taken care of, and given proper expression, then they will become corrupted and negating. This is what is taking place in the community of Afrikan people. Because we have chosen to turn the other cheek to those that have, and continue to commit the greatest injustices against our people, we find ourselves in a condition where everyone has a free go at taking advantage of us. We think that it is a noble or sacred thing to forgive the murderer of our Ancestors, who today murder our children. It has gotten to the point where we don't even want those that have played a hand in destroying our people to reap what they have sown. As a result of this, the Heru Behudet within us has become negating, in that we have turned his sword inward. We seek retribution only when the transgressor looks like us. We are quick to get violent against our own kind but refuse to even raise a hand to impose justice on others. This is why our communities are filled with bloodshed and violence. It is because we refuse to give Heru Behudet his proper expression. Simply put, if we don't respect the life we've been given enough to defend it, then we don't deserve to keep it. We must stand up for ourselves in Self Defense.

434

While we are not in a condition to compete with the oppressors in terms of arms, we have another "weapon" at our disposal, and that is the weapon of the spirit. Yet some of us won't even seek justice and retribution through our ritual, Ancestors and nTrw. Some of us refuse to use Hika to deal with those that intend to harm us, even at the cost of our own lives. nTr is nature and this line of thinking goes against nature, and therefore goes against nTr. Then there are other's that teach that we should use Hika to uplift those that are slaughtering our seeds. What part of the game is that?

Heru Behudet is the "*nxw it.f*," that is, "**protector of his father**", and is called the "**protector of his ancestors.**" He is called the "**Protector of him who created him.**" This is a principle that we have taken for granted, which other nations hold to the utmost importance. Retribution is a natural part of life and is a common custom in the law of any land. Yet we as Afrikan people take it for granted and have sold out our ancestors to be "one with all" to the point that we've lost ourselves. If in truth our turning the other cheek and praying for our transgressors is in harmony with Maat, then we would be protected. Heru Behudet is the "Great Protector," the divine protection that is given to those that live Maat. The fact that we are not receiving this protection betrays the very logic we use for not seeking retribution.

Heru Behudet is the nTr of vitality, and the sex drive. He is the "alpha man" full of virility. He is called "*HsA-Sna m Haw anx.f*," that is, "**Fierce with his limb of life**" (Phallus), and it is said that "**the nTrw.t rejoice because of his scent (pheromone).**" He is also called "*wsn ir nDmnDm msxA nfrwt Hr mAA.f*," that is, "**Procreator who makes sexual pleasure. Beautiful women rejoice at seeing him.**" As the sex drive or libido, Heru Behudet plays the role of assisting Ra in continuing his journey (life), perpetually, through the urge to reproduce Self by means of sexual intercourse. He is the ideal man: a procreator, protector, warrior, provider, and is able to please his women. He is sexually potent ready to impregnate a woman at any moment. In speaking to his virility and fertility, it is said of him that "*wArxi SmAw m pr.f wtT rmT s.xpr nTrw*" that is, "**blossoms are green from what comes forth from him, begetter**

of men, who causes the nTrw to come into being.

As a warrior and nTr of the hunt (Inhur), Heru Behudet governs Athleticism. He is competitive, and as a martial nTr, he governs sports of every kind. This is significance to Heru Behudet's playing the part of "Protector of Ra," as it is exercise that keeps Ra circulating. If Ra is not circulating this is evidence that Heru Behudet is not getting proper expression, as there is stagnation within the life force which manifests as stress and disease. Exercise assists in maintaining proper circulation, whether it's the blood, the life force, or food and its nutrients. Where there is poor circulation there is stagnation, which can lead to a malnourished Heru Behudet (a weakened immune system) constipation, the buildup of toxins in the body, etc. Exercise, especially during Heru Behudet's time of the day (mid day when the sun and temperature is at its highest) is the optimal time to workout, and one should make the effort to break a sweat. This helps to keep the mind clear; the body detoxify, as well as regulate the body's circadian rhythm. Working out helps to keep the energy and blood moving, which is important for sexual performance and drive. This is a way to express and work this nTr of war, without actually going to war ☺.

Like working out, Heru Behudet "cuts the fat," allowing us to cut away at and disregard the impractical and non essential. He is direct and precise in both thought and deed. This allows us to think and act more efficient and effectively, avoiding wasted time, energy, attention, and motion. He gives us the ability and courage to separate ourselves from ideas, habits, things, and people that no longer serve a purpose in our lives, and are either dead weight, a blockage, or parasitic. Mentally, he is the ability to cut through the fat, the jargon and non-essentials of an issue or idea, to get to the essentials or essence of it. As a Blacksmith, the things that he conceives with his mind and crafts with his hands are practical. In other words, if it does not add on or further progress, it is a non-factor/non-issue.

As a nTr, Heru Behudet should be worked with for courage, assertiveness, discipline, and invoked for protection and justice. He helps to bring out the warrior within.

<u>Renu</u>
Heru Behudet
nTr aA nb pt (Great nTr Lord of Heaven)
Hrw Msn (Heru the Blacksmith/Harpooner)
Hrw DbA (Heru of Retribution)
sA Ra Hrw-Axty (Son of Ra Herukhuti)
kA Ra Hrw-Axty (Ka of Ra Herukhuti)
Maky (Protector)
MnTw (Munthu)
Inhr (Inhur)

<u>Hymn</u>
iAw.n.k BHdt
praise to you Behudet
nb pt
Lord of Heaven
apy Sps
noble Winged Yatin
psD m Axt
shining in the horizon
itn nfr
beautiful sun
sHD snk
who illumines the darkness
sf Sps
noble child
iqH idbw
who illuminates the banks
DfD n wDAt
Pupil of the Wajet
Wbg tAwy m stwt.f
Who lights the two lands with his rays
HA HDDwt.f ndb
His rays illuminate the entire earth

Hr iAbtt

Heru of the East

Hr di-tp.f m nnt

Heru, who shows himself in heaven

wpS tA m stwt itn.f

who sprinkles the land with rays of the sun

iAw m wxA

an old man in darkness

xy rnpy m dwAw

young child in the morning

nTr wa

unique nTr

Hry nTrw nbw

Master of all nTrw

Iwr.tw m.f ra nb Hr nHm.f

He conceived everyday upon his lotus

HD tA

Who brightens the earth

di.f sw m Axt

shows himself in the horizon

wbn m bAXw m-Dt.f ra nb

rising in the east in his body daily

aq mAnw m Xt.f Ra

entering into the west in his body daily

nbi Hr biA.f m Xrt-Hrw

swims upon his sky daily

nmt nnt iwty wrd.n.f

traversing the sky without tiring

psD m dwA imy-tw msktt

one who illuminates in the morning those in the morning boat

bAw iAbtt htt n kA.f

the bAw of the east give jubilation for his kA

Htp m mAnw tp SsAt

Who rests in the west upon the night sky

Ssp sw bAw imntt m Htp

The bAw of the west receive him in peace

apy Sps sHD tAwy m mAw.f di dgt.n Hr nb

Noble winged Yatin who illumines the two lands with his rays and causes all to see

psD m nbw wbx niwwt spAwt

who shines as gold brightening the cities and nomes

dwA.tw r ms.tw.f r-a n ra nb

morning begins in order that he is born at the end of everyday (i.e. sunrise)

wa pw ir nn r-Aw xpr tA m wTs nfrw.f

he is the one who does all this, the land comes into being by the raising of his beauty

Xn-Hrt m wiA.f Xrt-Hrw

Who sails the sky in his boat daily

Xnt pt r-a n ra nb m msktt

Sailing the heavens at every day in his morning boat

sHD wr

Great Illuminator

sHD tAwy m kkw

who illuminates the two lands from darkness

wpS irty m Axty.f

whose two eyes gives light to his horizon

spr m mHnyt.f Hry-tp tAwy.f

who comes forth with his Uraeus, chief of the two lands

sn rxyt tA n bAw Hm.f

the Rekhiyet kiss the earth for the bAw of his Majesty

nswt-bity

Nisy Bity (Ruler of Upper and Lower Kmt)

Hr BHdt

Heru Behudet

nTr aA

Great nTr

nb pt

Lord of Heaven

sAb Swt

dappled plumage

pr m Axt

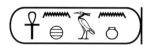

coming forth in the horizon

xnty irty Smaw mHw

Khenti Irty of the South and North

Htp Hr.k nfr n (name)

May your beautiful face be satisfied with (name)

Day

Tuesday

Number

11

Color

Blood Red, Maroon, Purple, Blue and Gold (Military)

Stones

Garnet, Tigers Eye, Fire Agate, Red Coral

Herbs

Pine, Tobacco (Cigar), Cedarwood

Food

Black Beans, Onions, Garlic, Ginger, Peppers (All Kinds), Red Palm Oil, Honey (male fertility)

Drink

Grape Juice with grapes (with seeds) blended. This is a traditional drink. Offered for courage, strength and vitality, invigorates the warrior spirit, protection and assistance. It can also bring joy.

Rum (151) Gin, Vodka, Grape Juice, Red Wine

Animal

Black Boar, Red Dog (for justice)

Sacred Animal

Hawk, Lion, Bull, Baboon (Guerilla)

Totem

Big Knives (Machete, Swords, Sickles, etc), Harpoon/Spear (with iron head), Big Heavy Chain, Hammer (especially blacksmith's hammer)

440

Heru sA Auset sA Osir

Heru sA Auset sA Osir, as the name implies, is the son of Auset and Osir. His parentage makes him the Great Great Grandson of Ra and Rayit, Great Grandson of Ishu and Tufnut, Grandson of Nut and Gab, nephew of Sutesh, Nebt Het, and Heru Behudet (Heru War). He is also

the brother of Babi, and Anpu. He is the nTr of Divine Kingship, and the redemption and continuity of the Divine Ancestral Heritage. As an archetype, Heru is the embodiment and personification of the ultimate goal of the nkmt tradition for the living adherent. In other words, he is a symbol of the fully realized and actualized individual, a person who has come into the fullness of their nTr-hood; the "Living nTr" or "Divine Man/Woman." As a nTr, he governs leaders of all kinds, especially rulers, and nobles. He is the enlightened individual who has totally offered their life to the enrichment of their people specifically, and the world generally. However, his greatest service is the offering of himself as a sacrifice to his father, to serve as his vessel in the world.

In his supreme form, Heru is called *"iTy n pt"* or "**Sovereign of Heaven,**" *"Nsw m pt,"* that is, "**King in Heaven;**" *"wbn m wsrt,'* **who rises in power**; *"wbn m nTrt,"* **rises in divinity**; *psD m sSn,* " **who illuminates from the lotus;**" and *s.HD tAwy,* that he "**Enlightens the Two Lands**." All of these renu identify him with Ra. Also, we should take note of the epithet "he who illuminates from the lotus," which not only identifies Heru with Ra/Itum, but specially the form of Ra that is born from the Lotus which sprang up out of the waters of Nu. This particular form of Ra/Itum is described as a child. This also identifies Heru with the nTr Nefertum.

Heru as a Creator nTr, is *"Heru Pa Khrad,"* "**Heru the child,**" and is associated with the sunrise; Khepri, the idea of "coming into being," birth, and re-birth. Recall the fact that according to tradition, Khepri is the form of Ra that emerges from the Duat (also passing through the waters of Nu), after journeying through that realm from "sunset" to the following "sunrise," from the "west" back to the "east." Midway through the Duat, there is a point where Ra and Osir unite within the egg of Auset, in the domain of Sukari. From this point Ra-Osir continues the journey forward through the Duat until he emerges in the east as Khepri. This emergence is not only the return of Ra and a new creation, but also the return of Osir as Heru Pa Khrad. In this way, Heru is Ra/Osir "wHm anx," or repeating life.

Speaking to the creative forms of Heru, in **passage 326 of the Coffin Texts** entitled "**Becoming Heru**", The *nTrw pAwt*, or "**Primeval nTrw**" (xmnw nTrw of Chaos) state regarding Heru's coming into *being "iw Xnnw m pt mAA.nw mAwt,"* that is "**There is turmoil in Heaven and we see something new**…" it goes further, in speaking of Heru "*psD Ra m nb iAxw*," that is, "**Ra shines as the lord of light**." It further goes to speak of how the psDw nTrw serve him (Heru). Thus it is evident in this text that Heru, in his creative form, is Ra who rises from "Chaos" brings forth a new creation, establishes order, leads the nTrw, etc.

In the "**Litany of Ra**," Heru is said to "**Unite all the members**" and "**Gather the seeds**." This is speaking to Heru, on one hand[15], as the culmination of all of the nTrw, who are considered the "limbs" or "members" of Ra, within himself. He is the capstone and apex of the pyramid, the point at which all of the varying angles converge. This particular quality of Heru is also what associates him with the fully realized man or woman, as man (male and female) contains all of the nTrw within, and when he or she has actualized their divine potential, the nTrw become as their member's or limbs, to be commanded just as one "Wills" their arm to move.

Heru in his fullest capacity is Neb r Jer (Lord of All), and he is "master of the nTrw." It is said of him in the same passage of the **Coffin text 326** that "*dbn (or bdS).f psDw Ra*," that is "**the psDw nTrw of Ra revolve around (or give way to) him (Heru)**." The nTrw "*sDm.sn xrw Ra hwt.f Hr xrw hmhmt wrt*," "**they hear the voice of Ra when he (Heru) shouts with a great roar**." This is to say that when Heru speaks, the nTrw hear the voice of Ra, their father; their Creator. In this same passage Heru proclaims:

---

[15] Heru as one who "Gathers the seeds" also speaks to his being the Archetype of the Nisu Bity, (iterally "of the Sedge Plant and Bee"). This title speaks to the "King" of Kemet, Lord of the Two Lands, as one who has sprouted up from the Land (He's a Native and Royal Stock) and gathers and spreads the "seeds" just as a bee does when during pollination. This is to say that the Nisu is ultimately responsible for the overall prosperity of the Nation (he is called "**SAi n tAwi**" (Destiny or Fortune of the Two Lands), as well as one who is responsible for assisting in extractinting the innate potential of every citizen that "sprouts up" (like the sedge) in the society.

*"iTi.n.i pt psS.i biA sSm wAt xpri Smsw dwAtyw
psD.i mAA.ku m iAbtt pt Htp.i m nHH hny.n.i iTi.n.i
Axt,"*

that is,

*"I have taken possession of heaven, I have divided
the firmament. I shall show the way of Khepri and
the inhabitants of the dwAt follow me. I shine, I am
seen in the eastern sky, I rest in eternity, I am
praised when I take possession of the horizon."*

This particular passage describes Heru's having power and command over all things. He has taken possession over "pt" and "dwAt," and "showing the way of Khepri" and "leading the inhabitants of the dwAt" speaks to him having control over all that comes into being, emerging from the dwAt, and entering into the world. This statement is reiterated in Heru's taking possession of the "Horizon," which essentially represents the "place" where all that manifests in the world (thoughts, events, the moment, actions, etc). This describes Heru as the living "spiritual master," one who has "command over their limbs and faculties," just as texts such as the **prt m hrw**[16] and other Ancestral Ritual texts describe the Ancestors as Osir having mastery over their being, granting them the "power over their own legs," the ability to "eat with their own mouth," etc.

As a nTr, Heru gives us power over our members and faculties, which manifests as "Self Control," and the ability to transcend our base desires, impulses, and emotionalism, which is represented by his defeat of Sutesh. He also gives vigilance and wakefulness, which allows us to spot an infraction immediately, enabling us to maintain order internally as well as externally. Also, he gives us the ability to be direct and precise in

---

[16] Prt m hrw Chapter 26

judgment, and actions.

Heru is our actualized "Divine Potential." This is another meaning of his "gathering the seeds," as a seed represents potential. He gives us the ability to manifest our Highest Self, and sit upon the throne of our lives; chart the course of our destinies. In this regard he is called "*nb SAi*," or **"Lord of Shai (Destiny)."** As a nTr on earth, he grant's man the ability to be a blessing to the world, both spiritual and earthly. As such, he is called "*SAi n bAqt/Kmt*" (Destiny/Fortune of Kemet). He governs leaders, especially those that serve as ideal models, and help to cultivate the potential of others. This in truth is the significance of the title Nisu Bity, for the leader of Kmt, and its symbolism of the Sedge Plant and the Bee, as bees are the exemplary husbandman of the world. Heru as the nTr of the "Divine Kingship," is the archetype for all that fill the position (sits upon the throne), or even more accurately, all that fill the position are identified with Heru. The role of the Nisu Bity is to serve as an example of the ideal individual, and to create and maintain the culture of Maat. He is the leader that creates leaders, and he gives people purpose until they find their own. Above all, Heru is a symbol of the innate potential that resides within each and every individual.

Heru is a symbol, not only of the innate potential that lies within us, but also all that came before him. He is the culminating point of his divine lineage; the bridge between past, present, and future; the present. He is the face and medium of his "father" (The Ancestors/nTr). This is symbolized by his name and role as "*Heru Henu*," the "boat" that carries his father. As Nisu, he is the representative of the nation; the Standard Bearer for his people.

Heru is called "*nD it.f*," that is **"Avenger/Protector of his father."** It is he that goes to war with Sutesh to avenge his father, reclaim his rightful place on the throne, and to reestablish Maat in the land of his Ancestors. As a nTr, it is he that gives us the ability to "*nHm nTr*," or **"save nTr."** Of Heru it is said:

"*abAy pw Hrw zni Hr sAq.n.it.f...ii.n Hrw Hr mw*

445

nw it.f.n.f im Hwa.w"

that is,

"Heru is a commander who has achieved what his father has collected...Heru comes on the waters of his father who is there rotting."

It is also said:

"nHm pw Hrw... HqA.f kmt bAk.n.f nTrw Sdi.f HH.f sanx.f HH m irt.f wa.t nb.s nb r Dr"

that is,

"Heru is the Savior... He rules Kmt, the nTrw serve him, He saves (or educates) millions and causes millions to live with his eye, the one, its master Nebt r Jer."

Heru *"coming on the waters of his father, when his father was rotting"* is speaking to Heru's coming through his father's (who is an Ancestor/Deceased) seed. The description of Osir "rotting," is speaking to, on one hand, Heru's coming through his Ancestral line to clean up the corruption that has found its way in there. On the other hand, this rotting is speaking to the decay of the Divine Potential; the nTr within, the Ba and inner Ancestral Spirit; the Divine Intelligence and Power. Just as it is Heru that redeems his father, it is the Heru within man that will save and redeem his Divinity.

Heru is associated with the Ib or Heart, which corresponds to the "Will" of man. This association is spoken to in the cosmology of Menefer, in which nTr, in this case Pitah, defines and identifies the various aspects of his being. The faculties through which he carries out the work of creation are his "Heart," and "Tongue," Heru being identified with the former. The Heart in this instance is the focused/concentrated intelligence through which the nTr orders, commands, and directs the

446

various forces of its being; the nTrw, who go forward to carry out and manifest as the work of creation. This aspect of Heru grants us the ability to have command of over our spiritual forces and "Will" things into being. In this regard he is associated with "*Hika*," and is a "*Sunwe*," a "**Medicine Man**" who is both a healer and a magician. As Heru Sunwe, his Hika and words are said to "ward off death," restore life, renew and increase lifespan (through invocation of his name), heal/cure disease, liberate one from destiny, and protect (spiritually and physically).

The knowledge of Heru is a combination of what he learned from his mother Auset, and what he "Re-members" from his father Osir (his Ancestors and previous incarnations). In the case of the former we must remember the fact that Auset herself was already, according to the tradition, "*Hika Warit*," that is," **Mighty in Hika**," and this was even before she gained knowledge of the name of Ra, which granted her omnipotence. Then in the case of the knowledge he obtained from Osir, this is speaking to information from his ancestors, as well as what he remembers in life as Osir, (Heru is Osir returned). The latter point is demonstrated in the fact that it is written "Heru, having power over nature (described as serpents), was taught to "Madu," or speak when Osir was still alive." This is to say that Heru has knowledge at his disposal that he learned before he was even born! This aspect of Heru, when realized within man, gives him access to "All knowledge," the information and wisdom acquired in this life (Auset), and that attained in previous incarnations and from one's Ancestors.

Hymns to Heru
i.nD Hr.k nTr sA nTr
Show your face! nTr son of a nTr
i.nD Hr.k iwa sA iwa
Show your face! Heir, son of an Heir
i.nD Hr.k kA sA kA
Show your face! Bull, son of a Bull
ms.n nTrt
born of the nTr.t

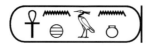

i.nD Hr.k Hr pr m wsir ms.n ist nTrt

Show your face! Heru coming forth from Osir, born of Auset the nTr.t

Dd.n.i m rn.k

I have spoken your name

Sd.n.i m HkA.k

I have recited from your Hika

Dd.n.i m Axt.k

I have spoken with your light

Sn.n.i m mdwt.k

I have conjured with your words

qmA.n ib.k

created by your heart

Hmw-r nb pw pr m r.k

It is all the invocations which come forth from your mouth

wD n.k it.k gb

commanded for you by your father Gab

rdi n.k mwt.k nwt

given to you by your mother Nut

sbA sn.k xnty xm

taught by your brother Khenty Khem

r irt sA.k

to make your protection

r wHm mkt.k

to repeat your protection

r xtm r n Ddft nb imyw pt imyw tA imyw mw

to seal the mouth of every serpent of those in the sky, those on the land, those in the water

448

r sanx rmT
to make people live

r sHtp nTrw
to appease the nTrw

r sAxt ra m snsw.k
to glorify Ra with his adorations

mai n.i As hrw pn
come to me quickly this day

mi ir.n.k Xn n dpt
like you have made the boat to sail

xsf.k n.i mAiw nb Hr mrt
repel for me every lion on the desert slope

msHw nb Hr itrw
every crocodile on the river

r nb psH m tpH.sn
every biting mouth in their hole

ir.k st n.i mi ar n xAst mi sd qrHt m xt
you do it for me like the stone in the desert mountain like the sherd edge in the street

Sd.k n.i tA mtwt nhp ntt m at nb n Xry-ds
You remove for me the posion of the bite which is in every limb of the patient

sAw fiT mdwt.k Hr.s
so that your words are not rejected on account of it

mk nis.tw rn.k m hrw pn

behold your name is called this day

sxpr.k fA Sft.k sqA.n.k m Axw.k

may you create the raising of your renown when you have lifted your light

sanx.k n.i ntt mg

may you cause the sufferer to live for me

di n.k iAw in rxyt

may you be given adoration by the people

dwA mAaty m irw.k

the mAaty are adored in your forms

nis.tw nTrw mitt.k

all nTrw are called in your likeness

mk nis.tw rn.k m hrw pn

behold your name is invoked today

ink Hr Sd

I am Heru the Savior.

Another Hymn to Heru

iw Xnnw m pt mAA.nw mAwt

There is turmoil in Heaven and we see something new

in.sn nTrw pAwt

said the Primordial nTrw

psD Ra m nb iAxw

Ra shines as the lord of light.

s.nhd.n.f nb nrw

He has caused dread in the Lords of Terror

dbn (or bdS).f psDw Ra

psDw nTrw of Ra revolve around (or give way to) him

sDm.sn xrw Ra hwt.f Hr xrw hmhmt wrt

450

they hear the voice of Ra when he (Heru) shouts with a great roar."

iTi.n.i pt psS.i biA sSm wAt xpri Smsw dwAtyw psD.i mAA.ku m iAbtt pt Htp.i m nHH hny.n.i iTi.n.i Axt

I have taken possession of heaven, I have divided the firmament. I shall show the way of Khepri and the inhabitants of the dwAt follow me. I shine, I am seen in the eastern sky, I rest in eternity, I am praised when I take possession of the horizon.

Renu

Heru

Heru pA xrAd (Heru the child)

Heru sA Ast sA Wsir (Heru son of Auset son of Osir)

Heru Sdi (Heru the savior)

Heru NDt it.f (Heru the protector/avenger of his father)

Heru Hnw (Heru the Henu)

Heru swnw (Heru the "Medicine Man")

wHm anx (He who repeats life)

nTr aA (Great nTr)

nTr nfr (Good nTr)

SAi n tAwi (Destiny/Fortune of the Two Lands)

SAi n kmt (Destiny/Fortune of Kemet)

Nb SAi (Lord of Destiny/Fortune)

iTy n pt (Sovereign of Heaven)

nsw m pt (Nisu of Heaven)

wbn m wsrt (Rises in Power)

wbn m nTrt (Rises in Divinity)

Color

Red and White

Number

6

Day

Sunday

Sacred Animals

Hawk, Bull, Lion

Totem

Staffs of Authority, Shekemty (Red and White Crown), Wajet (Eye of Heru) lotus and papyrus

Minerals

Gold, Ruby, Garnet

Bwt

Black Pig

Incense

Frankincense

Oil

Frankincense

Food

Millet, Apple, Oranges, Sunflower Seeds, Black Beans, Red Grapes

Figs and beer (Heru pa Khrad)

Drink

Ginseng, Red Wine, Brandy, Bourbon, Stout

Animal Offering

Pig, Goat, Oxen.

Working with the nTrw 12

The following are purposes, reasons, times, etc, that you would work with certain nTrw:

Peace – Amun, Niyit, Het Heru, Osir Wan Nefir Sukari

Clarity- Tehuti, Osir Wan Nefir, Khnum, Auset Rekhiyet, Osir Khenti Imenityu

Harmony – Het Heru, Ihy, Auset

Compassion, Empathy – Auset, Nebt Het

Courage- Heru Behudet, Heru Sa Auset Sa Osir, Sekhmet

Discipline – Sukari, Heru Sa Auset Sa Osir, Heru Behudet

Patience – Sukari, Khonsu, Pitah, Auset, Het Heru, Nebt Het

Planning – Khonsu, Sukari, Pitah, Tehuti

Judgement/Decisiveness – Heru Behudet, Heru Sa Auset Sa Osir, Anpu

Protection – Heru Behudet, Sekhmet, Anpu, Osir Khenti Imentiyu

Spiritual/Psychic Protection- Anpu, Subik, Khonsu, Heru Behudet, Mafdet (Any nTr in their "Fierce form")

Discernment – Anpu, Auset (Instinctual)

Justice – Tehuti, Anpu, Heru Behudet

Quell Arguing – Het Heru

Receptivity- Auset, Nebt Het, Tufnut

Assertiveness – Heru Behudet, Heru Sa Auset Sa Osir, Ishu

Listening – Auset, Nebt Het, Pitah

Self Control/Command – Heru Sa Auset Sa Osir, Sukari

Memory – Nut, Auset, Anpu

Studies – Anpu, Tehuti, Seshat

Success – Het Heru, Anpu, Osir Khenti Imentiyu

Wealth/Finances - Renenutet, Het Heru

Wisdom- Tehuti, Auset Rekhiyit, Seshat, Khonsu

Remove Negative Influences and things that no longer serve one's evolution – Sukari, Subik, Sekhmet

Warfare- Tehuti, Anpu, Khonsu, Heru Sa Auset Sa Osir, Heru Behudet, Subik, Sutesh, Het Heru, Sekhmet (Must have all of them with them)

Romance – Het Heru, Bastet

Women's Fertility – Auset, Het Heru, Heqet, Khnum

Men's Fertility – Heru Behudet, Khnum, Osir, Min

Work – Heru Behudet, Sukari

Entrepreneurship – Heru Sa Auset Sa Osir, Heru Behudet

Fidelity – Auset

Devotion – Auset

Endurence, perserverence, steadfastness – Sukari, Pitah

Marriage – Auset, Het Heru, Nebt Het, Heru Sa Auset Sa Osir

Husband (To be a good one) – Heru Sa Auset Sa Osir, Het Heru

Wife (To be a good one) – Auset, Nebt Het, Het Heru

Healing – Auset, Het Heru

Direction – Tehuti, Khonsu, Shai, Sukari, Osir Wan Nefir, Osir Khenti Imentiyu

Relaxation – Het Heru, Subik, Auset

Humor – Subik, Bisu (Bes)

Sex – Het Heru, Heru Behudet (for men), Bastet

Atractiveness/Magnetism – Het Heru

Creativity – Het Heru, Pitah, Khnum

Practicality, Usefulness, Resourcefulness – Nebt Het, Sukari

Econimical – Nebt Het, Sukari

Offering to the nTrw   **13**

There are certain offerings amongst the traditional offerings that are considered standard and universal, in that they can and should be offered to all of the nTrw for one reason or another. Examples of these offerings are: water, milk, beer, red wine, incense, myrrh, sistrum (or rattle) etc. Each offering serves a specific purpose for the nTr, and in turn a reciprocal benefit to the donor.

Water (*mw*) is a universal offering, and its libations (*qbHw mw*) should be performed at every shrine. It may be poured into a glass or vase, or a plant, and may also be sprinkled with the hand on to the floor around the shrine and onto the shrine itself. It serves the purpose of giving life to the nTr or ancestor, as well as renewing/rejuvenating and purification. In turn one is given general continued flow of prosperity, life, fertility, as well as the purification of one's self.

Beer (*Hnqt*) is another universal offering. It is prepared carefully, following exact protocols. In this way it is associated with Maat, order, regulation, and exactness. It is offered to establish Maat in the forces it is offered to. It brings balance, as well as joy to the nTrw and Ancestors, and may be offered to certain nTrw, such as Het Heru/Shekhmet to invoke their protection. One receives order, joy, abundance, and protection by making this offering. It is very good to make the beer oneself. However, purchased beer may also be offered.

Wine (*irp, irt Hr wAD*) is another offering that is considered universal

and standard. It like the beer is also carefully prepared, and is offered to bring balance to the forces. Wine is offered to appease/please the nTrw/ancestors, to bring them joy, and to renew/rejuvenate them, as it is associated with the "*wAD.t Hrw*" or "*Eye of Heru,*" that is offered to renew/revive and divinizes the nTr or Ancestor. If you have a palm tree that you have dedicated to your Ancestors, the wine should be poured onto the tree. By offering wine one receives joy (bliss), prosperity, and abundance.

Milk (*irt.t, anx wAs*) is another offering that is universal and standard. It is offered to purify, renew, give life to, and strengthen the nTrw and ancestors. It should be offered to the Osir Khenti Imentiyu every 10 days. I recommend offering milk at every shrine every 10 days. In return, one is given life and prosperity, and strength for making this offering. If you do not drink "dairy" milk, then you may substitute it with Coconut, Almond, Soy, or whatever kind of milk you drink.

Bread is another universal offering. The Ta Wr (Great Bread) is a multigrain bread infused with honey and raisins. It is round in shape and split down the middle. It should be offered hot.

Sa (Shat) bread is a bread offered for victory and protection over one's enemies. It is made from wheat flour, fat, and honey, and shaped in the for an obelisk, or an animal such as a hippopotamus. This is especially offered to nTrw in their warrior forms, and all nTrw of War.

White bread (tA HD) that has been cut in to a triangle shape should be offered with the point up. This should especially be offered to the ancestors

As for incense, Myrrh and Lotus are considered universal/standard offerings in the Kemetic Tradition, and may be offered at any shrine. There is also a Henensu Temple Incense, based upon the traditional *Kapet* incense recipe. Visit our website to purchase.

456

There is also a reciprocal nature to the offerings that should be taken into consideration. In many cases, what is offered to the nTrw varies according to, and depends on the location, and the ecology of the temple/shrine to which the nTr or Ancestor is being venerated. This was especially evident in the case of offerings of produce. In any case, one offered to the nTr what they received from the land that gave them sustenance and brought them prosperity. For instance, if one lived in a corn producing locale, and they heavily relied upon the production of corn, it would be an offering to the nTr of the temple/shrine, the nTr of the town, or the nTr that is responsible for production of the corn in the local. In any case, this offering is made with the understanding that in giving this to the nTr, the nTr would in turn give more corn, and more land to produce more corn, as well as other things that the corn may represent, such as fertility, abundance, fecundity, etc. This same principle should be understood, and applied in this day and time, taking into consideration one's current ecology, and what is provided for their sustenance.

For example, I am from New Orleans, and let's say I worked in the seafood industry. I own a very successful boiled seafood shop famous for its boiled crawfish, crabs, and shrimps. Due to the nature of my business, I would likely have a shrine set up for Subik, and would make offerings to him regularly, as traditionally he is considered "**lord of the swamps and marshes,**" and "**The Great Big Fish.**" While in Kmt Subik manifests as a crocodile, here in New Orleans/Louisiana he is associated and expresses himself in the Gator.

Another example of adapting to one's current ecology can be found in protection rituals, in which papyrus is offered to the nTrwt, in association with Auset's or Het Heru's hiding of the baby Heru in the thickets of papyrus in the Delta. In Louisiana the sedge also grows, however, sugar cane may also be offered in place of the papyrus sedge. The sugar cane and papyrus sedge are close, and even today in Egypt, Papyrus is sometimes made from the Sugarcane. This fact combined with the height in which sugarcane grows makes it a perfect adaptation for the offering of sedge for protection, or for any other ritual purposes in which sedge is offered. However, any tall grass that you ritually and cosmologically associate with the story and offering may be offered.

Auset and Heru 14

Sutesh: An Opposing Force

Sutesh is the force of opposition. But this is not an inherently bad thing. It is this opposing force that facilitates and provides the conditions in which evolution can occur. It is the force that knocks things out of stagnation, gets them moving again. Osir in his cosmic form, is the same as Nun, he is inert. So Sutesh acting upon Osir knocks him out of this inert state of Being, into a state of living, evolving.

Sutesh in his proper context is "the adversary," **or more correctly adversity**. He provides the necessary challenges that will create the conditions that help to facilitate our evolution. "It is said "Sutesh causes Heru." This is to say that Sutesh is the opposing force that creates the friction and heat that will produce the emergence of light. Heru is the Light (enlightenment), but it is Sutesh that creates the conditions that make the light possible. Sutesh is the Darkness. Just as it is from a state of ignorance that knowledge comes into being, to know, there must be a time when one does not know. So this state of darkness, ignorance, confusion, and all of the adversity that it produces creates the conditions that provide the right amount of pressure and friction that forces us to learn, adapt, evolve, and ultimately gives expression to, and awakens, the latent genius that exists within us.

The latter aspect of Sutesh is significant, particularly in regards to his

relationship to the nTr Shai, the nTr of Fate or Destiny. The term Shai, is also the term for "pig' which is one of the "sacred animals" of Sutesh. Shai properly understood, is not only that which causes our coming to earth, but also, the conditions, challenges, and specific tests and lessons we are here to learn and overcome. All of this is represented by Sutesh's role in the Osirian tradition, specifically his role in murdering Osir, which serves as the precursor to Osir's entering into the world as Heru. Sutesh then plays the role of the adversary and challenger to Heru; what he must overcome before he can be elevated to his place on the throne, that is actualize his potential and achieve his Shai.

Each person that enters into the world is brought back to work out some issues carried over from previous incarnations[17]. It is their Shai; their destiny or "life lesson" and challenge that brings them back. This once again is why "Sutesh causes Heru." Heru is the living individual in the world, whereas Osir is the Ancestor in the spirit world. Earth is the place where Osir, through Heru, redeems himself, going to war with Sutesh. Each of us is here to overcome our respective Sutesh, to refine and purify ourselves, and ascend the throne of our lives as Heru. This truth is made evident in a passage from the **prt m hrw**, in which it is stated:

" haa.i r tA Gbb dr.i Dwt-I,"

that is

" I descend to the Earth of Gab, I drive out my evil."

Sutesh as a form of Shai, or destiny, is also a teacher, as Shai, once again, is our life lesson. However, his role as a teacher is also evident in his role and function as a "trickster." We must recall that it was through trickery and deception, that Sutesh was able to get into position to murder Osir. He in essence made Osir believe that he was gaining something to his

---

[17] This is also symbolized by the heavy heart.

460

benefit, a "gift," but in reality it was something to his detriment. We also see the trickster nature of Sutesh in his deceitful actions carried out towards Heru in their contending. Specifically, the case of Sutesh asking for an apparent truce, only to attempt to rape Heru for the purpose of humiliating him before the tribunal, quickly comes to mind, and evokes the understanding of Sutesh as a trickster. He is a nTr of Tricks, deception, and confusion, a mischief maker. He is called "**SAd xrw**," which literally means "**Loud of Voice**," a "screamer," and extends to mean someone who disrupts order and causes trouble.

Finally, speaking to Sutesh as a trickster nTr, we have the **39th chapter of the Prt m Hrw**, which quotes Sutesh concerning himself

" *nwk stS Sdi Xnnw qri m Xnw Axt nt pt mi nbD-ib pw,"*
that is
"I am Sutesh, the robber, bringer of confusion, and storms within the Horizon of Heaven, like the Evil (Twisted) of Heart."

The term "Xnnw" used in the above passage is a term that means confusion, disarray, disorder, irreverent, etc. It is the opposite of mAat, which is order. As this term is also a title or name for Sutesh, it, along with other terms and concepts that include it, are often written with the Sutesh animal as a determinative. This teaches us much about Sutesh, and when he is in operation.

It is in times of "Xnnw," disorder and confusion, that Sutesh is active. He comes into play when our thoughts, words, and deeds are not in sync with mAat, when we, and as a result, things are out of order. One may recall that it was when Osir was out of order, that Sutesh was able to come in and commit his acts. It was when Osir had intercourse with Nebt Het, who was not his wife that elicited Sutesh to come into play. Not only is this misdeed by Osir and Nebt Het considered a literal transgression of mAat or bwt, but on a deeper level it represents things being out of place. The fact that he was inebriated represents the idea that his mind was confused and he was off balance. There was disorder. So Sutesh comes into play to act, and imposes the conditions that would elicit the birth of Heru the Avenger, to come and correct the situation;

reestablish mAat. In this regard, Sutesh is in a way "Teaching Osir a lesson," or creating the conditions in which the lesson may be learned.

Sutesh as a trickster is also present in the West Afrikan traditions of Yoruba/Ifa, and Vodou as the Orisa Esu (Legba). Esu (Pronounced Eishu) is literally Su-tesh in metathesis, the "t," is a phoneme that is known to get lost or is easily dropped over time. While Esu is a major Orisa, being at once the Orisa of the Crossroads, Opener of the Way, mediater between man and the Orisa, heaven and earth, a trickster, and messenger, one may think that it's not likely that he and Sutesh are the same deity. However, in actuality, all of those aspects and functions are present in the nkmt tradition. In the nKmt tradition, the nTrw Sutesh and Ishu (Shu) are actually the same principle/force working on two different planes, and really from two different traditions. Ishu, the son of Ra, is considered the Opener of Heaven, and it is he that creates differentiation in the cosmos that leads to order, which is why he wears the feather of mAat upon his head. He is also the mediator between heaven and earth as it is he that separates Nut and Gab (Heaven and Earth), maintaining his position between them. Sutesh fulfills the same role as the force that creates differentiation within the cosmos in his act of dismembering Osir, who in the cosmological sense is identified with Nu/Nun. Sutesh's dismemberment of Osir is reflective of (and analogous to) Ishu's opening and differentiation of the heavens (separation of Nut and Gab). In fact while Ishu always represent's the force of differentiation on a grand cosmic scale, Sustesh represents the same force on a microcosmic (earthly) scale, pertaining to the differentiation of the individual, the since of individuality, the ego, which may be a reason for the insertion of a "t" in his name, denoting the "earthly" or concrete nature of Sutesh, as opposed to the abstract Ishu. Ishu, like Esu, is also a messenger of the nTr, which is attested to in chapter 75 of the so-called "Coffin Text," in which he states:

> *"I am he who foretells him when he ascends from the horizon... I am he who is among the Chaos-nTrw and who hears the words of the Chaos-gods... I am*

> *he who dispatches the word of the Self-created to the multitudes... I have repeated the words of the ancestral gods and those who came into being after me..."*

Not only does the above passage clearly demonstrate that Ishu is considered the messenger of the Creator (one role of a few that identifies him with Tehuti), but it also further demonstrates his function as an "opener of the way," as it is he that "Foretells" the coming of Ra, a symbol of leading the procession (a function carried out by Anpu in Ritual). Sutesh's role as a messenger is more subtle, and may be hinted at in his role as the one that travels in Ra's boat, and "thunders" from the heavens. However, his role as Opener of the Way and Leader of the procession is symbolized in not only his dismemberment of Osir which "opens" the cosmos, but the fact that it is his actions that serve as prelude to the birth of Heru pA Khrad, an event that is a reflection of the birth of Ra in the morning as Khepri. When one comes to the realization that Ishu and Sutesh are one and the same force, at times in operation on different levels of existence, one can further realize that "they" have survived in West Afrika in the great Orisa Esu.

Man's Spiritual Journey 15

The journey of Auset and Heru in the Osirian tradition, is a symbol of the spiritual journey of Man. We've talked about how Osir's death and dismemberment corresponds to the actual creation of the universe; nTr's coming into being in the ordered, physical, or objective realm. We have also discussed how this creation serves the purpose of providing a vehicle through which nTr can explore, experience, and become acquainted with Self. All of this has been in regards to the cosmological implications of the tradition. But how do these things relate to the spiritual journey of Man? Let's start at the death of Osir; Sutesh's trapping of Osir into a coffin made in his image, and ultimately his dismemberment of Osir. This coffin represents "physical existence," as it relates to man, the "physical body." It is said that Osir suffocated, or in some instances, "drowned" within this coffin. This represents the imposition of limits on nTr that would provide the structure, parameters, and form to allow it to come into manifest. The coffin is then thrown into the Hopi (Nile River) and floats up to Palestine, where a tree sprouts around it, encasing it. This represents the creation process, and how once the process was initiated, nTr had to surrender to the "flow" of the process. As this relates to us, when we are born into this world, in this form, we are born into a process. There are events, plans, a whole scheme already set in motion. We are born into the current, the flow, and initially we are carried along by the flow of the currents against our Will. Then finally we settle, and begin to grow and evolve. This is what the "tree" in the story represents. It represents the evolutionary process, the unfolding of nTr. For us this is our growth and development, our evolution. Next is Osir's dismemberment.

Now on the creative scale, this corresponds to the differentiation of the matter that led to the creation of the ordered universe. For us on a microcosmic scale, this dismemberment also represents the creation of duality, the perception and awareness of it (remember Osir is consciousness) and the fragmentation of awareness. Another way to say this is that this event represents our perception of life and perceiving a host of separate and seemingly unrelated phenomenon (the root of egoism). This is reflective of Ra's eye getting lost in creation following behind Ishu and Tufnut, duality, and as a result Ra is rendered lost and powerless. Osir's body is scattered and lost, and it is up to Auset to find it, each member, and re-member him.

Auset's journey to find Osir, to re-member him is our journey to re-member who we are, to find Self, and to heal. This is something that can be understood from Osir's dismemberment. On a cosmic scale, one could say that this event represents the Big Bang. However, this can also be said in regards to our personal lives. This dismemberment, Big Bang, represents the experiences that leave us broken and injured. This applies mentally, spiritually and physically. Also it represents the various ideas, beliefs and definitions that we've accepted, that go on to shape our awareness, causing us to misinterpret the world, seeing the illusion of separateness, when in reality All is One.

In our spiritual infancy, we are Osir's Coffin. The scope of the nTr's influence is limited to our awareness and the automatic functioning of our physical bodies. Initially Osir's influence does not reach beyond these functionalities. The coffin is nailed shut and nTr is suffocating. At this time, nTr exists within, mainly as a potentiality, a Divine Seed. As we grow, the experiences that we encounter, things that we will learn, will either serve to nurture this seed, or it will further inhibit its expression through hardening the soil, leaving us broken and scarred.

Auset's journey to re-member Osir, put the pieces back together again, and conceive a child, is our own personal journey towards healing and wholeness, and the actualization of our Divine Potential, bringing it to expression. If you will recall all that Auset had to face in this journey, we see that she was willing do anything, go anywhere; whatever she had to do, she was willing to make that sacrifice.

Sutesh trapped Osir in a coffin, nailed the coffin shut, and threw the body into the Hopi where it eventually made its way to Palestine. When Auset became aware of the whereabouts of Osir's body, she made her

way to Palestine. When she got there she learned that it had settled on the banks of the river and a tree grew up around it, encasing it. This tree was then cut down by the king, and placed in his temple as its chief pillar. Becoming aware of this, she made her way to the palace, and was willing to humble herself, and took on the role of a servant. Auset, The Queen Mother of Kemet, became a wet nurse for the Queen of Palestine! All of this was done so she could get into the palace, get closer to Osir. When she was given the body so that she could return to Kemet and perform the proper rituals and burials for her husband, her plans were foiled by Sutesh. Sutesh found the body hiding in the delta marshes. He then proceeds to hack the body into pieces, spreading them throughout the land. Becoming aware of this, Auset then proceeded to search for every single piece of Osir's body, that she might put him back together again. She was not concerned, at all, about how long the journey would take. Osir was her life!

To make matters worse, after all the time that it took to find the missing pieces of Osir, she ends up finding all but one; The Phallus! She then, through the power of her own spirit, according to some traditions, brought forth a phallus, created one from her own being, and placed it upon Osir. According to others, she absorbed his "essence" into her body (or already had it within her), and conceived Heru. After this she gives birth, outside of the comforts of her "queenly status," and lives her life as a refugee; a fugitive going from place to place so that she could protect Heru, that he might grow to avenge his father. This is why she is quoted as saying:

"I am your sister Auset, no nTr or nTr.t has done for you what I have done. I made a man-child, though I am a woman, because of my desire to make your name live upon the earth."

This is to say, that Auset's entire life became a sacrifice to Osir, including the birth of Heru. It was all to "MAKE OSIR'S NAME LIVE IN THE EARTH."

466

Auset became aware of Osir's essence inside her, and once she became aware, she would stop at nothing to make him live again. This is what our lives must look like, once we become aware of the Divine essence within us. We must dedicate the entirety of our existence to its realization, cultivation, and actualization. We must re-member, and heal, that we might give birth to Heru (actualize the seed of the Divine/our Divine potential). And once the body of nTr has been made whole again, we must protect and preserve it.

Auset's life of sacrifice represents the sacrifices we will have to make for the nTr. This does not simply mean ritual sacrifice, though these are included, but generally the things that we will have to let go of, the ways of thinking and ideas, the habits and conditionings, the past, anything that could get in the way of our re-membering; our healing. We must be willing to place it upon the offering table. This is to say that much of our learning to re-member who we are, is a process of un-learning. We must be willing to part with anything that is not Maat. There are ideas that we form about ourselves as we grow up in life, many of which are imposed, or reflective of environment, and the people around us; some good some not so good. As I stated earlier, we are the definition of nTr, but the further we are defined, the further we confine and restrain nTr. So in letting go, sacrificing, and unlearning, we are in essence liberating our nTr; transforming from the coffin of Osir, into Heru Henu (the ship that carries him!).

Heru's birth, on one level, represents that realization, awakening, and manifestation of the Divine in and as our lives. It is when we allow our persons to be a vehicle for the Divine, that it's influence, wisdom, and power flows through our being, out into the world. Heru is Osir incarnate, and he sits upon the throne as a vehicle, a symbol, a totem of his Father. He is the original "Son that is the Father." When we are Heru, we are realized/actualized individuated nTrw. On another level, Heru's birth and maturity represent the birth of the aspect of our being; the Ib, the part through which we consciously and freely make our decisions, and grants us the ability to combat the negative aspects of our being

(Sutesh).

In short, the life of Auset and Heru is a symbol of our spiritual journey. Our search for the Divine Self, the journey to Re-member, the effort to heal, is Auset. The realization of the Divine, going to war with the negative qualities of our Being, and the ultimate actualization of our Divine Potential is Heru. When Osir is liberated, awakened, and elevated to the throne in the Duat, we simultaneously take the throne as Heru in our lives.

Sutesh   16

Sutesh is mainly known as the chief enemy of Osir and all that is righteous. However, to put a period after that statement would be a gross error, misrepresentation, and misunderstanding of who and what Sutesh is. To interpret Sutesh in the same way that many interpret "Satan" or "The Devil" would be very unfortunate. However, it is sad that this is what he has been reduced to by many would be scholars and teachers.

Sutesh as a nTr is the force that is responsible for our individuality. If you will recall in previous chapters, we dealt with the cosmological implications of Sutesh's role in the murder of Osir. Re-member it is said that "Life springs up to us because of Osir's loss of it," This is to say that it is because of what Sutesh did, that we have life. Sutesh is, in some instances, a representation of the Creative force that defines Osir, giving him form and expression, and his (Sutesh's) dismemberment of him creates the multiplicity that makes life possible.

Sutesh as an individuating force is what many refer to as the "ego." This is where he catches a bad rap. Though Sutesh; this individuating force, is very much necessary for life and experience, it should not be allowed to rule, and be "self" serving. This is the entire issue of the tradition regarding Sutesh. Sutesh's place is not upon the throne, yet he always attempts to, and at times succeeds in usurping the throne. This represents when we allow our individuality to take precedence over the

469

whole, and what is in right order. This type of individualism causes us to become a free radical in the body of nTr. We become a cancer to the world.

Sutesh, our individuality, must be placed into service of nTr and the collective. In this way Heru "redeems" Sutesh. In actuality Heru and Sutesh are one in the same as it relates to the force of individualization. When we are self seeking and self serving (all about "me") and are for advancing our desires and aims in spite of the ill effects it may have on the collective, we are allowing Sutesh to rule, and giving him expression. However, when we place our individuality into service of nTr, and live our lives making the effort to be a blessing to the whole, to heal, we are Heru. This is partially the reason why the head of both Heru and Sutesh are sometimes seen joined on the same body (conjoined twins).

However, Sutesh as an individuating force also serves the chief purpose of protecting our individual organism. He is our basic survival and defense mechanism, the "fight and flight" response. He reflects this in his main function as the protector of Ra's boat, keeping the forces of chaos at bay. This "chaos" is the infringement of other individual organisms on our own personal place in time and space. For there to be order, each thing must be allowed it's time and place in the sun, and must be allowed to thrive. Anything that would inhibit our journey, Sutesh is meant to remove it from our path. In this function, Sutesh is the force that is meant to protect the body, the basic animal instinct, the impetus to survive.

This animal instinct is also meant to be of service, and not to rule. When it is on the throne, and not in its proper place, it is chiefly responsible for the animalism, and lack of civility that we see so rampant in the world. In fact, the negative expression of Sutesh, or more accurately the precedence of Sutesh in the world, is the main cause of the condition that the world is in. The fact that individualism is heralded, and militaristic means is the method used to spread its "gospel," is a prime

example of what happens when Sutesh is out of his proper place.

470

Moral Ideal in the nKmt Tradition 17

There is a misunderstanding amongst many in the Afrikan/Conscious community regarding the idea of morality, right and wrong, good and bad, evil, etc, as it relates to nKmt Spirituality, Afrikan spirituality, and indeed spirituality in general. The misunderstanding is the idea that Moral Ideals are concepts that are carried over from the "world of religion" and its indoctrination. However, the truth of the matter is, morality and codes of ethics, are not products of Western Religions carried over to Afrikan Spiritual Traditions, but have always been present with Afrikan people and Afrikan Spiritual Traditions.

The reason why many are turned off by ideas of morality, moral codes, and laws, is because their experience with these ideas in religion has been less then pleasant, and consequentially they run away from, or shun anything that reminds them of that experience. For many, the exit from religion brings the feeling of being released from a prison of oppression and repression, and therefore out of fear of returning to another oppressive system, they dismiss Afrikan Spiritual traditions as just another religion, and in some instances make claims that these spiritual systems have been "westernized' or they are no different from western religion.

The idea of an absence of moral ideals in Afrikan Thought is a lie that has existed within the western world of academia for a very long time, leading people to believe that Philosophy began with Europeans, specifically the Greeks. For the longest Europeans, and many other Non

Afrikan people either believed, or refused to acknowledge that Afrikan people were capable of rational thought, leading to the worst ideas and acts of racism, racial violence, systems of oppression and slavery, and the interpretation, classification, and treatment of Afrikan people as "sub human."

When we as Afrikan people, in our attempt to run away from western worldviews and perspectives, reject the fact that Afrikan People had moral ideals before the European, and that these things already existed within Afrikan Spiritual traditions, to embrace the antithesis of that fact (the absence of Moral Ideals) in actuality, are running from one Western ideology to another, one that is the very foundation and core of Western Racism. The idea that there is no such thing as good, bad, evil, chaos, order, and morality in traditional Afrikan thought is the very foundation of European or western supremacy, and the idea that Afrikans were not capable of "Rational Thought," ultimately led to the erroneous claim that there is no such thing as "Afrikan Philosophy."

Literally speaking, Philosophy means "Love of Wisdom." By extension, it is the act of seeking understanding of oneself, the world (and everything and everyone in it), and one's relationship to the world. It is the study of the nature of knowledge, reality, and existence. It seeks to answer *Metaphysical questions* (ex. Is there a God? What is a person? What is mind? What is cause and effect?), *epistemological questions* (ex. What qualifies as knowledge? How do we know that we know? Do we truly know a thing, or do we simply think, or believe it? *Ethical Questions*: ex. What is good or bad? What makes peoples actions good or bad? What makes people good or bad? Is morality objective or subjective? How should I treat others? And *Logical Questions:* ex. What is correct thinking/reasoning, what is incorrect thinking/reasoning, and how do we know? By definition, we can without a doubt establish that all of these questions/problems are addressed in the nKmt tradition, and are summed up and answered in the concept of Maat. In fact, if one wished to know what to call nKmt 'Philosophy," after careful examination of the tradition, they would reach the conclusion that Maat is the proper nomenclature.

472

Maat is a term in the mdw nTr language that means *"to be true, right, correct, Order, vindicated, justice, righteousness, right doing, real, genuine,* etc. By definition alone, it provides evidence of the fact that these people sought to understand the world around them, and their place in the grand "order" of things. Also, if mAat means to be *"right,"* then they must also have a concept of *'wrong."* If mAat means *"Truth,"* then they must've had a concept of, and a criterion for determining that which is false. If mAat means "real," then they must have also had a notion of that which is not real. If mAat means *to do right*, then they must also have had an idea of what it means to do wrong. The further we examine the subject matter, we to begin see that mAat addresses all of the aforementioned philosophical questions.

To begin, let us note how mAat is determined. Beginning with the meanings *Truth,* and *Real,* let us examine how the truth or reality of a thing is established. To do this, we must look at a term related to mAat (through paronymy?), **"mAA,"** meaning *"to see."* This informs us of how the Ancestors went about determining "truth," and acquiring knowledge, or whether something was considered knowledge, or known. MAA, meaning "to see," is associated with the actual experience of a thing, and more importantly awareness and observation. *"Did you see it for yourself, or is it just hearsay?"* *"Do you know what you're talking about, or are you simply going by what you've heard?'* All matters of philosophy begin and end with experience and awareness, and thus all matters of knowledge rest upon the same. *There can be no knowledge without experience.* This sentiment is expressed by our wise "Philosopher" Pitah Hotep, in his teachings which state:

> *"wHm mdt mA n sDm.n st r-tA rsst mk xft Hr.k rx iqr"*

> *"Repeat a word after seeing, not hearing entirely skewed. Behold, what is before you is excellent knowledge."*

To further demonstrate this point, there is also the term for knowledge "**rx**," which also means *"experience,"* further proving that in the nKmt worldview one cannot have knowledge without experience.

After mAA, there is another term that describes the process in which one arrives at mAat, or *"wpt mAat"* " t*he revelation of truth*," and that is the phrase "*tpy Hsb*."

"**tpy Hsb**" by its simplest definition, means "*to count*," "*to reckon*," "*to calculate*." It extends further to mean "*correct method*," *the standard (of speech and conduct), the norm, etiquette, and rectitude*. As it pertains to the first meanings to count or **to reckon**, it is the nkmt equivalent of what is today called **the Scientific Method**, which is demonstrated beautifully in the "**wsxt n mAati**," or the "**hall of Two Truths**;" in the ceremony known as *"wDa Ddw,"* or *"Weighing the Words."*

During this "ritual," ones "heart (mind)" and "words (theories)" are weighed against a feather, representing mAat, as the "tpy Hsb" or standard. The deceased, **or Initiate** makes certain statements (theories/propositions) before a tribunal, while Anpu and Tehuti test the validity of each statement. *It is a question of what one claims, vs what actually is.* This "judgment scene,' is not simply a religious depiction of "judgment" in the afterlife, but "mental judgment" in this life; the methodology enacted to arrive at a conclusion about a situation. It is "weighing" each situation accordingly, as encountered, to come to the correct conclusion, decision, allowing one's intuition[18] and analytical faculties (Tehuti and Anpu) to examine the situation carefully(holistically when applied to daily life experiences). "Tpy Hsb" meaning "reckon" or *"to conclude after calculation,"* in relationship to mAat, it *represents the thought and reasoning process through which "wpt mAat," or Truth is realized, and Knowledge is acquired.*

---

[18] The intuition is not necessarily included or accepted the Western Scientific Method, but plays a role in the Afrikan's, through the guidance of one's Ba.

Tpy Hsb, in relationship to mAat, speaks to the fact that what is considered "mAat" or "truth, right, correct, etc," is relative to the situation encountered, and therefore each situation must be "weighed." Situations vary, like illnesses, for example, and one "remedy" (approach) will not "cure" all. Likewise, that which is true or correct at one time, may not be true or correct at another time. What is proper for one occasion may be improper for another. The world is full of various types of people and personalities. Events and situations vary as well. Events have "personality," so to speak, and are better suited for people with certain personal qualities than others, certain ways of doing things than others, certain ways of looking at things than others, etc. In a world filled with such diversity, it is important that a **methodology** be set in place that allows us to better know how to interact with life, regardless of the manner in which it presents itself to us. This method is tpy Hsb: the method of observing a situation, carefully weighing (measuring/calculating) the various factors, the "mAaty," or" two truths[19]," i.e "the particular truth" (variable) against the "universal truth" (the standard/control).

An example of this principle at work in the nKmt tradition is in the concept of "**bwt**" or "**taboo**." It is a "Universal Truth" or Maat that one should not commit "bwt," and offer that which is considered bwt (detestable/disagreeable) to a nTr. However, what is considered "bwt" to a nTr, may vary from nTr to nTr. In other words, what is considered bwt for one nTr, may be considered mAat, or "right" for another. Examples of universal "bwt," are the prohibitions found in the "**42 Oaths of Purity**," or so-called "**42 Declarations of mAat**." One example from the 42 Oaths, speaks to the prohibition of slaughtering the sacred animal of a nTr[20]. While the particular animal may vary depending on which nTr one is engaging (and also the city one was in), the prohibition against

---

[19] The "mAaty" or "Two Truths," in the Hall of Judgment can further be broken down: "What one did" "what one should have done (Maat)," and the to "paths," or destinations arrived at depending upon whether what you did and what should be done equate, which represented by the Omomyit and the Shrine of Osir.

[20] Chapter 125 prt m hrw

the slaughter of a sacred animal remains constant and universal. This being the case one would have to employ "tpy Hsb" in order to make the correct decision with offering an animal sacrifice to a nTr, ensuring that the animal meets the specific requirements of the situation at hand. It would not be correct reasoning or tpy Hsb, to say that the slaughter of all animals (and hence animal sacrifice) is bwt, based solely on the universal prohibition, without considering the particulars of one's situation. What is the sacred animal(s) of the particular nTr you are engaging? What is the sacred animal of the town you are in? What does your specific situation require? What is the correct approach and methodology in *this* situation? These are the questions one must ask before making the fallacy of broad generalization. This same methodology (tpy Hsb) must be applied to every aspect of life; that is, first and foremost **treat every situation as unique**, and then **weigh the universals and particulars**; how the situation or "problem" *is similar to*, *equal to*, or *different from* other situations or problems, and judge (conclude), address, or react accordingly.

Another example if the "Universal and Particular" Truths in the nkmt tradition, is in the nTr Shai, which is the nTr of Destiny. Shai is said to be born with each person, and stays with them all the way through to the scales in the Hall of Two Truths. In this way, he can be seen standing there next to the person whose heart is being weighed. Anyway, his being born with each person represents the idea that in the nkmt worldview, each and every person has a Shai. However, no one person's Shai is the same as another. Each person's Shai provides them with different circumstances, difficulties/challenges, lessons, talents, and will ultimately lead them to different destinations and stations in life. This is spoken of in the **Instructions of Imun m Opet** (Amenemope) in which he advises:

"Do not set your heart on riches, none can ignore Shai and Renenutet, do not allow your heart to stray for every man comes to his hour."

476

In other words, the wise Imun m Opet is advising that one stay focused on what is before them, work with what they have, and don't worry for their "hour" (time) will come. This is to say that Shai (and Renenutet) ultimately determine one's state in life, and what happens to and for someone is "time conditioned." While Shai may have one person born into a wealthy family which leaves the individual an inheritance, another person's Shai may have them born with less, even poor. One may be born rich and lose their wealth later in life, while another may be born poor and eventually become wealthy. In each case Shai provides differing sets of circumstances which come with their own unique challenges, and a unique lesson to be learned and applied in the approach to fulfilling one's purpose. However, regardless of the differences in a person's Shai the universal truth here is that each person has a Shai.

Tpy Hsb As Proper Etiquette and Societal Norm

Tpy Hsb is also used as a term to describe what is considered proper etiquette and the societal/collective norm. Again examples are the 42 Oaths of Purity, in which everyone in Kmt was expected to adhere to, but especially the Priesthood (and by extension anyone in a position of Authority as you had to be an initiate to hold a seat of power) for which the "42 Oaths" were actually meant.

We find other examples in the sbAyt (Instructional Texts) or "Wisdom Texts." For instance, in the instructions of Pitah Hotep, he states: *"m sbA xmw r rx r tp-Hsb n mdt nfrt,"* that is, *"...in teaching the ignorant to know According to the standard of Good Speech"*

The term translated "standard" in the above excerpt is "tp-Hsb."
This excerpt is actually taken from an introduction to a section in the text, that pertains two "mdw-nfr," or "Good Speech," which gives instructions on how to properly use speech, i.e. when to speak, when not to speak, and also how not to speak (in terms of content and spirit more so than grammar). For instance, Pitah Hotep advises one not to speak

when in the presence of one "greater" than yourself, until he first speaks to you, or asks you a question, and in doing so one's speech will be pleasing[21]. This not only informs us that the ancestors had a standard of how to conduct one's self in the presence of someone "greater," but this also lets us know that they had a way of determining one's level of "greatness," in comparison to others, and establishing hierarchy amongst men.

The tpy Hsb of "Good Speech" also includes the volume of one's voice. It was considered a violation of tpy Hsb and Maat for a person to raise their voice or yell, so much so, that this prohibition was included amongst the 42 oaths of Purity:

> *i iHy pr m Nw nn qA xrw.i*
>
> *"O Ihy coming forth from Nu, I have not raised my voice."*

We also find the same sentiment being expressed in the Instructions of Ani:

"Do not raise your voice in the house of nTr, He abhors shouting."

Shouting was not prohibited simply on the account of its harshness on the ears, but there was also a scientific/medical reason as well. Thus we find in the Instructions of Pebhor:

"Gentleness in conduct of every kind causes the wise to be praised. Do not make your mouth harsh or speak loudly with your tongue. For a loud voice does damage to the members of a body just like an illness."

---

[21] This same principle is present in the Traditional Afrikan Practice of asking permission of one's elders to speak while in their presence.

This expression of mdw nfr or good speech was so important, that it eventually came to represent the ideal man, whereas those who violate the tpy Hsb of good speech came to represent the individual that no one wanted to be. This point will be expounded upon shortly.

According to Pitah Hotep, a man was also to marry his wife according to her "tpy Hsp." This could imply her standards as in her expectations of you, getting married on her terms (pre-nuptials), dowry, etc. He also gives the standard on how to treat her, respect her, and allow her the freedom to do her thing as it relates to her affairs. The maxims of Ani also speak to this fact, in advising a man:

> *Do not control your wife in her house,*
>
> *When you know she is efficient;*
>
> *Don't say to her: "Where is it? Get it!"*
>
> *When she has put it in the right place*
>
> *Let your eye observe in silence,*
>
> *Then you will recognize her skill...*

The idea of not "controlling" a woman in **her house,** flies in the face of western social order, however, it speaks clearly to the Afrikan social order, especially Kemet as a matrilineal society, and the strong gender roles that were established. Traditionally, the woman was the "nbt pr," "Lordess of the House." It was the "tpy Hsb" for the woman to have free reign over how the house is run and maintained.

tpy IIsb was also used to designate the standard upon which things were to be built, and crafted. This includes everything from the standards for properly building temples, to the correct method for crafting beer. All in all, there was a "tpy Hsb," or right order to and for

everything.

Understanding Maat Cosmologically, and Deducting the tpy Hsb from It's Implications

In order to truly understand what mAat is, we must contemplate her creation. Let us recall the statement made by Ra in his bringing forth Creation, "*I laid a foundation in MAa(t).*" This is the very first thing that is done before Creation can commence (after bringing himself into being). He says "*I found nowhere to stand, so I laid a foundation in mAat.*" This is describing Ra in/as Nu(n). It is from Nu(n) that Ra begins his creation, laying mAat as the foundation. Taking this into consideration, it must be realized that before mAat can be established, there must first be Nu(n), that is to say, rest or peace. In order for our thoughts and actions
to be based in mAat, we must first begin in Nun. *All motion begins from a state of Nun or inertia.*

From Nun, we have infinite potential. We leave room for possibilities, which allow us the ability to observe our environment (internal and external) clearly, and then make our initial motion, be it a thought, word, or deed, we make it efficient, effective, and unbiased; in tpy Hsb. To put it another way, if we are e-motional (moving out) at the offset, then the thoughts and actions coming from that state are not as clear as they can be, and the probability of them being irrational and isfet (chaotic) increases dramatically (pun intended ☺). In beginning from a state of Nu(n) we are actually actively following the motions and creative/thought process of nTr.

Just as important, if not more, than beginning in Nu(n), is the act of Ra "*uttering his own name*" which "*brings him into being,*" This is to say he "establishes" his "*Identity,*" who and what he is, what his function is, which goes on to have the greatest impact on what comes forth from

480

him; what he creates. Traditionally, the "Ren" speaks to the identity of a person, the qualities of that individual, and how they are meant or expected to function in life and society. It informs us as to what kind of "being" a thing is.

In fact, when we contemplate Maat as Law in it's most ambiguous sense, the type of "being" Ra is, or comes forth as, goes on to determine what "laws" (cycles) he sets in motion. This same principle should be taken into consideration in all of our reasoning and planning.

In essence, the tpy Hsb, or "correct method," is the "Divine Method" or the motions of nTr. The best example that we have of this methodology is in the creation account pertaining to Ra. Following this method one can successfully apply the tpy Hsb and "do MAat." This method (Ra's motions) goes as follows:

Nu(n) –Prior to making any decisions or judgments, one should still/center themselves, ensuring that they are at a state of peace, and one's perspective is not clouded by e-motions or preconceived notions. Also it should be realized that from this state of rest one has the infinite potential to go in any direction, be who one wills to be, do what one wills to do. This is a position of possibilities.

Ra/Ren- One should remind themselves of their identity and purpose (universal and particular) and keep the knowledge that they are Ra (nTr) firm in mind as they contemplate their course in life.

Ishu and Tufnut- One should contemplate themselves and their life in relationship to life in general, and their environment before making any decisions, contemplate the individual in relation to the whole. Remember there are always two/dual aspects to every situation: The Self, and the Situation. Make the effort to weigh both sides accordingly.

Het Heru- When contemplating one's Self in relationship to the whole, all efforts should be made to harmonize the Self with the Whole; to produce harmony in one's life, and create a win-win situation (synergy),

in which all parties can be happy (if possible). Harmony is most important to health, wealth, and success. Make Happiness the motivating factor in one's actions (the ends and the means).

Nut and Gab- One should observe and take into consideration the time, and cycles, what is happening in the earth in the heavens. This is speaking to what is taking place within the actual earth, one's external environment, the cosmos (astro-sciences), and also the body, mind/spirit. In taking these things into consideration one can ensure that their actions are in accordance with the time, and also choose the most efficacious time to pursue the potential objective.

Osir- In contemplating and making a decision, one should take the past into consideration for potential lessons and guidance. One should also make the effort to think about their Ancestors, how their decisions may affect them, their legacy and family name. Does this decision elevate ones Ancestors or does it bring disgrace? Lastly, but probably most important, how does one's decision affect the evolution of their bA? Is one able to hear the voice of their bA? What is it saying? This will assist in keeping the individual in line with their soul's progression.

Heru- One should contemplate how their decisions will affect the collective, their family, community, their people, including and especially their children and future generations. Will this decision raise the nation, or will it set us back? After looking to the past, make the effort to follow that which was correct, and correct that which was incorrect.

Sutesh- One should contemplate how this decision will affect them personally as an individual. How does it affect the integrity and security of their individual existence? One must also seek to preserve themselves; Self Preservation.

Auset and Nebt Het- One should contemplate both the spiritual and material resources at their disposal to achieve their objective, where there is lack one should employ the spiritual and physical means (Ritual

482

and Work) to achieve their desired ends. One should also realize that through impregnating their spirits with the seed of their aspirations, they can birth the conditions and/or resources needed to achieve their goal. One should also weigh the pros and cons, the potential gains as well as potential losses and opportunity cost.

In regards to ethical questions, such as determining whether or not a thing is good or bad, it is important to keep the above reasoning method in mind, especially the contemplation of a things purpose and function. Whether a thing is good or not is a question of whether or not it fulfills its purpose and proper function. For instance, a screwdriver is a good screwdriver if it successfully and efficiently tightens and un-tightens screws. Another example is a light bulb, what makes it good or not? It is whether or not it lights up, given that all other factors such as electricity and wiring are good and in place. These things are good or bad depending upon whether or not they fulfill the purpose and function.

Next it should be understood that these things, good and bad, are also time and circumstance dependent, and are not constants. For instance, what happens when the light bulb blows out? Or when the screw driver strips, or rusts and wilts away? It is no longer able to fulfill its purpose, its time has passed. Also the value of a thing is relative, and dependent on the law of form and function relationship. The screw driver is perfect for turning screws, but not fit for properly unlocking a door, or starting a car. That's what a Key is made for. Also certain screw drivers are made for specific screws, while others may be fit for other screws, maybe larger or smaller. This is an easy line of reasoning to understand. However, how does this line of reasoning apply to people? How do we decide whether or not someone is a good or bad person?

This is an easy question to answer when contemplating an individual carrying out a particular role or function, but what about inherently? What makes a person inherently good or bad? To properly answer this, we must contemplate the purpose of man. The purpose of man is dealt with in detail in chapter 6. However, for our purposes here we shall

examine what our Ancestors considered to be the ideal person vs. the unsavory person.

Traditionally, whether or not a person was good or not, depended upon whether or not they "**did mAat**," or "**green things**," that is to say, things that further life, and add on, or "red things, bwt or isfet." The universal standard for determining this are the 42 oaths of purity as already mentioned. Along with this, there are four types of individuals that our Ancestors classified. These are the *GrH mAa*, the *mAa Xrw*, and the *pA Smm* and *SAd xrw*.

The *grH mAa* and the *pA Smm* are described nowhere more eloquently than in the instructions of Imun m Opet. According to the great nKmt Rkhyt Xt or "Knower of Things" (Sage) **Imun m Opet**:

As for the heated man in the temple,

He is like a tree growing indoors;

A moment lasts its growth of shoots,

Its end comes about in the woodshed;

It is floated far from its place,

The flame is its burial shroud.

The truly silent, who keeps apart,

He is like a tree grown in a meadow.

It greens, it doubles its yield,

It stands in front of its lord.

Its fruit is sweet, its shade delightful,

Its end comes in the garden.

The pA Smm or the "Heated Man" is described as a person who lacks any Self control and is thus ruled by his emotions, as opposed to reason or "tpy Hsb." His presence is disruptive, a disturbance to the order of things, and his actions are destructive and divisive. Imun m Opet described this poetically as a "tree grown indoors." The "pA Smm" is unpredictable and undependable, and his path is a Self destructive one. The great Ancestor paints this picture beautifully in describing the pA Smm's end. This type of man is symbolized in the tradition by the negative side of Sutesh. The *grH mAa* or the **"Truly Silent"** man on the other hand, is a man who is civilized. He has distinguished himself by mastering himself. He is a blessing to everything and everyone around him and his actions are fruitful and bring much joy. As the ideal man, the grH mAa is symbolized as Heru in the nKmt tradition, the Divine King who is the symbol of the ideal individual in every traditional society.

mAa xrw is a term that describes the spiritual master, the individual who has purified herself as a result of living mAat, and as a result has been granted access to enter into the shrine of nTr; to behold the deepest "mysteries;" the nTr in its "true form," and is able to wear the clothes of the nTr (become or realize Self as the nTr). This is described in **chapter 125 of the prt m hrw**. The term mAa xrw means **"true of voice,"** or **"true of word."** It speaks to the fact that the individual does what he or she says, specifically in regards to their oath of purity as spoken to in the 42 declarations. Their deeds match their words, and their words become deed.

To be declared mAa xrw, was to say that your "word" or "voice" is True/Truth, Your Word or Voice is Law, Ones Word/Voice is deed. This is some of the deeper significance to the Weighing of the Heart and Words (Judgment Scene). The Weighing of the Ib (Heart), a symbol of the Will and Heru (the King) against the feather of MAat, a symbol of Law and Truth, while the Initiate makes his "Declarations." If his ib was

found "equal" or balanced with MAat he was declared "mAa xrw." From here the deceased/Initiate would unite with Osir (nTr) and would receive the title Osir attached to his ren, followed by the descriptions "mAa xrw." To be declared a nTr was to also be declared mAa xrw. To be a nTr is to be able to create via the Word (as evidenced in many creation accounts the world over). By simply "speaking," making a decree, a nTr causes what he/she wills to come into being; for a nTr's word is deed, truth, a law. This is a fact known by spiritual initiates the world over, regardless of their respective traditions.

Isfet, Bwt, and Bin: The Classification of Thought, Emotions, and Actions in mdw nTr

> *"Beware of entering in impurity (bwt), for nTr loves purity more than millions of offerings, more than hundreds of thousands of electrum, he sates himself with Maat, and his heart is satisfied with great purity."*
>
> *~Temple of Heru Behudet @ Edfu~*

Our Ancestors, through the highly sophisticated construction of the mdw nTr language, were able to classify various types of thoughts, emotions, and behaviors or actions. They did this through the system of determinatives. Determinatives are:

Where one picture represents a category of meaning. Determinatives

help to determine the category of meaning of words pictorially[22].

Determinatives are not voiced, but are there to provide a sense of meaning, and context, and may distinguish between words that may be homophones. This system also performs a great service in allowing us a look into the philosophical mind of the ancestors, and also their psychological and ethical perspectives.

Just as certain thoughts and emotions are classified in Western Psychology, and are broken down in terms of Positive vs. Negative, Psychosis or Psychopathology, etc, likewise the determinative system of mdw nTr does the same.

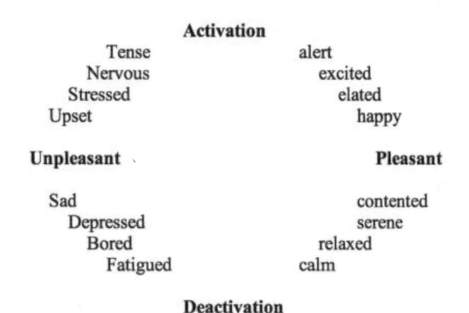

Figure 21: Two Dimensions of Emotion, © Gary Wolf[23]

In the nKmt worldview, all things, all thoughts, words, and deeds

---

[22] Amen, Rkhty The Writing System of Medu Neter: Ancient Egyptian Heiroglyphics, pg. 13 2010.

[23] http://quantifiedself.com/2009/02/measuring-mood-current-resea/

ultimately fall into two categories: *Maat*, or *Isfet*. Maat has already been defined/explained. *Isfet is wrong, wrong doing, falsehood, crime, evil, anything that is not Maat.*

Isfet can further be broken down into two categories, or more correctly two terms that speak to things considered isfet. Those terms are bwt, and bin. *Bwt* is anything, any thought, word, or deed that is considered taboo, or an abomination, abhorrent to the Divine. *Bin* is anything considered bad, or evil.

In the Determinative System, things that fall into the category of bwt are signified by the ⟨glyph⟩ glyph. Things considered bin are signified by the

⟨glyph⟩ glyph. It should also be noted that the determinative for bin, is also used to denote things considered bwt. This should be easy to understand, in that anything that is bin; evil, bad, is contrary to Maat, which automatically makes it bwt.

As an example of how this system works, let us look at the term "nxbdt" which means *malice, envy, wickedness*, etc. This term is written in mdw nTr as so ⟨glyphs⟩. Note the glyph that denotes bin (and bwt) which follows the word, just before the "vertical broken line" (which denotes plurality). This is generally where determinatives are placed, i.e., following the word. This system, and the way that it is organized, gives us an understanding of how our ancestors classified the emotions and thoughts that were considered to be malicious, envious, or wicked; and that classification is that malice, envy, and wickedness is bin/bwt, which would automatically make it Isfet, or anti Maat.

There are other determinatives used, that provide tremendous insight into the depth of philosophical thought our Ancestors engaged in when considering the mind, thinking, and behaviors of man, that also connected these thoughts and behaviors back into their cosmological worldview. These symbols are the Sutesh animal ⟨glyph⟩ , the Subik ⟨glyph⟩ , the enemy ⟨glyph⟩ , and disease ⟨glyph⟩ .

Terms that have the Sutesh animal as it's determinative, informs us that the thought or behavior is associated with the nTr Sutesh, the nTr of chaos, confusion, who himself is called "bwt wr;" "The Great Bwt." An example of such a term is "nSn," meaning "terror, fright, horror, alarm, fury, rage, etc." This term is written ⟨glyph⟩ . The use of the Sutesh animal as the determinative in this term, indicates that these feelings, and also the behaviors that elicit them, are associated with Sutesh, and are thus bin/bwt/isfet. An example of the use of the Subik determinative is the term "Ad," meaning to rage at, to be angry, etc. This term is written so ⟨glyph⟩ . The use of the Subik determinative informs us that rage and anger, especially when expressed or directed, is associated with the nTr Subik, and are likened to the behavioral traits and temperament of a crocodile.

The relating of certain types of thoughts, emotions, and behaviors to specific nTrw is a common motif in the Kemetic tradition, even though the full scope may not be expressed in the current determinative symbol set. However, this does not imply that the determinative set cannot be expanded to include the nTrw in association with their various behavioral, thought, and emotional correlations. For example, the feeling of Joy, pleasure, etc, is easily associated with Het Heru. Wisdom is associated with Tehuti, Seshat, and Auset Rekhiyit. Vengeance and justice is associated with Heru Behudet, etc. The determinative that represents each of these nTrw can easily be utilized in the classification of their corresponding emotion and ways of thinking. This is an example of how our cosmology, along with the mdw nTr language and its determinative system, can be expanded and expounded upon to explore a Kemetic field and study of Psychology, Sociology, and Philosophy, etc, especially in understanding the nTrw as natural forces that constitute reality, and are intrinsic in the mind There are many more fruits to be

born from the study and exploration of this particular subject.

To demonstrate the last two determinatives; the enemy, and disease, let's look at the terms *Ah*, and *magAwt*. The term Ah meaning, pain, grief, trouble, loss, sorrow, poverty, misery, debility, destitution, sadness, ruin, and woe[24] is at times written with both the bin/bwt determinative, and the determinative for "enemy." The term magAwt meaning sadness, grief, and affliction, is written with both the determinatives for disease, and also bin/bwt. This gives us profound insight into the way Ancestors classified things. For instance, grief is not only considered a "diseased" state, but is also bwt and bin, and is associated with the "enemy." It is common knowledge the ill effect extended periods of grief can have on one's health. It like depression, can lead to a state of debility[25]. This last point is relevant when we contemplate why the Ancestors would associate certain thoughts and emotions with the "enemy." As an enemy is ultimately one who stands against you, opposes you, works against you, and attempts to do you harm, any emotion that has a harmful effect on one's mental and physical health could be classified as an enemy. Also, if we were to interpret the journey of Ra in his boat, which must continue perpetually, as the cycling of Energy or the Life Force through one's body, it should be clear that just as it is said that if Ra's boat stops or his journey is inhibited for any reason, the forces of Chaos over take him, likewise when the life-force becomes stagnant, disease manifests. Therefore, an emotion such as grief, which can literally make one sick, and can be debilitating (make a person unable to progress), is not only a disease, but the enemy of Ra, I.e., anti (against) life. It should also be noted that the determinative for enemy actually depicts a man driving an axe or sickle through their own head, i.e., committing suicide, which gives even more insight as to not only what they felt people who made

---

[24] Budge, E.A. Wallis, "Egyptian Hieroglyphic Dictionary Vol 1"

[25] The classification of certain "negative emotions," and ways of thinking and behaving with illness and disease is not an unheard of thing, as this knowledge is found in traditional medicine throughout the world, including Traditional Chinese Medicine and Aryurveda.

490

themselves enemies to "another," were doing (violating the Oneness of Life = Suicide), but also the suicidal nature of allowing our thoughts, words, deeds, and emotions to be other than Maat.

Table 1: Example of the Classification of Thoughts and Emotions based on Mdw nTr determinative system

Emotion	Bin/bwt	Sutesh	Subik	Disease	Enemy
Anger	x	X	x	x	x
anxiety	x				x
deceit	x				
depression	x			x	
envy	x				
fear	x	x	x		
greed	x				x
Grief	x			x	x

It should be clear to the reader that mAat, and tpy Hsb answer all of the philosophical questions, including the metaphysical questions which are dealt with in the greater portion of this work, as it pertains to the nature of "nTr," the constitution, structure and organization of reality, natural forces and their operation in the universe, etc. This provides clear evidence that not only did the Ancestors engage in philosophical thought, but at a level of depth that would rack the brain of the most advanced minds of science. This mode of thinking, the tpy Hsb, if adopted and applied by Afrikan people, will elevate them once again to the level of genius

and civilization that their Ancestors reached, and then beyond, once the pros and cons of that said civilization have been placed on the scales of mAat, and corrections and refinements are made where necessary.

The
"Usekhet n Maati" 18

The *"Usekhet n Maati"* is the place where the "Ib" of an individual is weighed against the feather of Maat. Usekhet n Maati has been translated as the "Hall of Two Truths." What it represents, is the "hall" within the temple that separates the "Outer Sanctuary from the Inner Sanctuary which contained the shrine of the ntr. In the case of the "Weighing of the Heart," the nTr was Osir. In order to enter into the "Holies of Holies," one had to be declared purified through living a life of Maat. To prove their purity, they had to take several oaths. These oaths came to be known as the "Declarations of Innocence" or the so-called "Negative Confessions." As they would make their statements, their "Heart" would be weighed to see if they are "mAa-xrw," or "true of voice;" to determine whether or not their words matched their deeds. After going through this examination, if they were found to be truthful and pure, then they were permitted to go forward into the inner sanctuary and unite with (become) Osir.

This scene has mostly been interpreted as the "Final Judgment" for the deceased. However, this scene and text, just as much of the Kemetic literature, serves various purposes. This scene is not simply the "Judgment" of the deceased, pertaining only to "judgment" after "death," but is the "Judgment Hall" period. What is meant here is that this is the place where "judgment" of/in one's life takes place. If we come to understand that all of the nTrw present are aspects of Self, then we realize that this scene is ultimately depicting something that takes place within us.

The "Usekhet n Maati" is, in essence, the mind; the place where we make our "judgments day" to day; moment to moment. Present within the hall are Tehuti (our intuition, abstract and divine mind, reason) and Anpu (our concrete mind, the intellect, logic). Far off removed is Osir, our Ba or conscience, along with the Maati nTrwt, Auset and Nebt-Het. When we look at the scene from Osir's point of view, we are actually seeing the initial point of reference. When making a judgment we should begin first with Osir, the perspective of the Ba, then Tehuti, looking at the big picture, weighing both sides, for in every situation there are dual components (represented by the dual pans of the scale) i.e. yourself and the situation itself. From here one takes note of how the dual components relate to one another, and takes note of how things measure up. Next, one looks at the situation from the perspective of Anpu. Anpu is normally depicted close, up upon the scales checking the details, making adjustments, whereas Tehuti, stands back, objectively observing, taking notes of the results, and then ultimately renders his judgment. Following this scheme, one gains a holistic perspective of the situation, which can allow them to make the best decision.

The nTrw are present "overseeing" the whole ordeal. Our "Ib" is present representing our Will, our decisions, and is measured against the standard of Maat, represented by the feather. Depending on the choices that we make at any given moment we can go the way of Osir, or we can go the way of the "Ommomyit," which is the way of the "heavy heart[26]" or ego.

---

[26] To do (or not do) things we ultimately will regret, causing us to feel guilt or repression.

Anpu stands at the "plumb bob/plummet," and the crossbeams. This cross beam of the scale represents the "Crossroads[27], " and Anpu as Wapuwat (The Opener of The Way) stands here as the guardian. Every single situation is a "crossroads" situation, in that our decisions at that moment have the potential to take our life in one direction or the other. This "crossroads" also has the same meaning as it does in West Afrikan Spiritual traditions, in that it is the point where the realms cross, the intersection of the "physical" and the "spiritual." The Usekhet n Maati represents this point, which is symbolized by the Outer Sanctuary (the physical) and the Inner Sanctuary or Hwt nTr (House of the nTr) representing the Duat. Anpu is both the guide and examiner through this hall. In his role as "Wapuwat," he plays the same role as Esu in the West Afrikan Traditions (The Yoruba tradition for example). The answers that we give and the statements that we make must be "Maat," otherwise we will not be permitted to pass. This also extends in application and relevance to our rituals, our invocations and hymns. The success of our spiritual work depends on whether or not we are "mAa xrw." This is the only way that we will achieve our goals, represented here as access to Osir's kAri.

Sometimes Shai, Renenutet, and Meshkenet are also present within the hall, to stand either as a defender or a prosecutor of the individual being examined. These are the forces of one's destiny, their name, etc. All of these forces have a say in whether the person lived Maat or not. Did they follow their destiny? Did they live up to their Ren? All of these things should have been factors in their decision making. By following the "Plan" that governs one's life; the Shai, it automatically causes one to live up to their Ren, and places them into sync with Maat.

The Usekheti n Maati is also reflective of the formal initiation ceremony and ritual of the Ancient Kemetic Priesthood. In formal initiation ceremonies, there are certain things that are done in preparation. One is purified prior to entering into the temple. This ritual bath may take

---

[27] In actuality the Usekhet n Maati in it's entirety is analogous to the crossroads.

place within a pool, or within a lake or river. This ritual represents a rebirth, and is the origin of the "Baptism." After the purification, one is accompanied into the temple, and then equipped with information that they will need on their journey. Thus we find it written in **chapter 125 of the "prt m hrw,"** that the Initiate is said to possess certain knowledge that would grant them access. The words *"He is knowledgeable of our paths and our towns."* This kind of language is very familiar in Traditional Afrikans Spirituality, in that Divine forces are called by various names that speak to the varying forms through which a force expresses itself. Each name represents a "path," and is in many cases associated with a specific town. Thus we have for example Het-Heru Nebt Yunut, or Het Heru lady of Yunut (Dendera), and Het Heru Nebt Henensu (Het Heru lady of Henensu). Het-Heru Nebt Yunut is a more festive, fun loving, joyful expression of Het-Heru, whereas Het-Heru lady of Henensu is more of a fierce, aggressive, and violent form of Het-Heru. There is Osir Wan Nefer, and then there is Osir Khenti Imentiyu, the Foremost of the Westerners. One relates to Osir as the conscience (The Ba), the other relates to Osir as the Ancestors. Each of the nTrw have various "paths and towns." We see the same type of organization in the Yoruba tradition. In the book **Fundamentals of the Yoruba Religion (Orisa Worship)** the author states:

> *Religious Oriki...deals with Irunmolem Orisa, their devotees, and the few people who bear special names that Yoruba people believe to be "heavenly given names." Such special names are Aina, Ojo, Ibeji, Dada, Talabi, Salako, Oke, Ige, and others in that line. In addition to this religious Oriki serves as a power house that can be used for various purposes. The oriki can be used to incite the Orisa for action, positive or negative. To charge an Orisa, the part of the Oriki that talks of War, or Warlike actions, can be chanted in addition to other spiritual work. The Oriki can also be used to calm the Orisa if and when the Orisa is so charged. For instance, if Esu,*

496

Osanyin, or any other powerful Orisa in that line becomes too difficult to manage, subtle parts of their oriki can be chanted form calmness. Even though the Irunmole have long ago ascended to heaven, their individual attributes during their sojourn on earth are recorded in their respective orikis. One good purpose that the orikis of these Irunmole serve is that they give concise knowledge of the personalities of the Orisas and their way of life during their existence on earth. In a way, the Oriki says a lot about its subject/s, be it human beings or the Orisa[28].

Examples of Oriki of the Orishas are Esu ota Orisa (Esu, Orisa's Avenger) Alagbara (The Powerful)[29] . Alagbara is one of the Oriki for Esu, and not a separate Orisa in Yorubaland. Esu Odara omokunrin Idolofin (Esu Odara, citizen of Idolofin town). This same type of organization is found in Vodun (West Afrikan and Haitian) and also in India in the Hindu, Vedic, and Tantric traditions, etc.

During a person's Initiation, they are given this information, among other things, its proper usage, as well as the offerings and taboos of each form. They are brought before the Ancestors, the priesthood, and the nTr of path they are being initiated into. There is a series of questions and answers that take place, many times the Initiate being equipped with both the questions and the answers before hand, each answer granting them further access into the ceremony. From here the oath is taken. This is symbolized by the weighing of the heart ceremony and the so-called negative confessions.

One of the "key" things that should be known about mdw nTr is that there is no explicit way in which "Tense" is written or expressed.

---

[28] Fundamentals of Yoruba Religion: (Orisa Worship)

[29] This is the name that has been corrupted into Elegba or Papa Legba

Whether something is present tense, past tense, future tense, etc, is "sensed" from the greater context of the text. With this in mind, the statements that have come to be known as the "Declarations of Innocence" of "Negative Confessions," which have normally been translated to begin with "I have not," can also be read "I do not," or "I will not". For example, "nn iri.i isfet r rmT" which is normally interpreted as "**I have not done isfet (evil) to men**," can also be translated and interpreted "**I don't do evil to men**," or even "**I will not do evil to men**." The latter interpretation allows us to catch a glimpse of the formal initiation ceremony of our Ancestors. These fourty-two statements represent the oaths that one took as they entered into the priesthood, specifically the High Priesthood, who alone could enter into the shrines of the nTrw.

The fact that these statements are oaths of purity is evident in the fact that each statement begins with the invocation of a nTr. For example we find "**I am XAbyt pr m qrnt nn s.mA.i rmT**," which means "**Hail devourer of Shadows, coming forth from Qernet, I have not (or I Will Not) kill a man.**" This is an oath made with the nTr that is invoked in the statement. In this example one is invoking the "Devourer of Shadows" and making an oath not to commit murder. If this oath is broken, then "**am XAbyt**" would exact "punishment" upon the priest, doing more than likely what the name implied. This is the equivalent to the statements today such as "I swear to God." The only difference is, these nTrw **really exist**. These "oaths" granted more power to the priest if they were kept in sincerity. After these declarations, one continued through the temple being asked more questions, and giving answers that would allow them to go further in their journey. I recommend that one studies chapter 125 of the Prt M Hru for more insight as it will prove very helpful in the reconstruction of the tradition of our Kemetic Ancestors, which includes the priesthood initiations.

498

DIVINATION 19

One of the most important universal aspects and pillars of any Afrikan Spiritual Tradition is Divination. The ability to communicate with the Divine and receive insight and guidance into one's life, and advice regarding decisions, is one of the most if not <u>the most</u> invaluable resources afforded to the practitioner of an Afrikan Tradition. This is another part of Afrikan spirituality that completely distinguishes it from western religions, in that one has the ability to not only talk to nTr, but to also have nTr speak back; <u>definitively</u>, right then and there; every time. Indeed, divination grants us the opportunity to engage in a conversation with nTr, to be taught and guided, forewarned, etc. This is a tremendous gift of Afrikan Spirituality.

Divination is a gift in that it allows nTr, via the nTrw and Jertiyu, to speak to us, to guide us. This is very important. There is absolutely no reason for a person who practices an Afrikan tradition to go through life blind; without direction and purpose. They can speak to the one who put them here regarding to their purpose for being here. They can learn exactly where they are meant to go in life and how to safely and efficiently get there. Divination is like spiritual GPS, and nTr is the voice that guides through it. Wouldn't you want a map written by the nTr, the Intelligence that designed the universe, including your life? Better yet, if you had the opportunity for the author of the map to guide you every step of the way wouldn't that be great? Who wouldn't want this? While you contemplate that question, let's look at the nKmt tradition and cosmology for more insight into the subject.

The Journey of Life is represented in a few places in the nKmt tradition;

one of the most important representations is the Journey of Ra as he travels through life and its various phases. Throughout Ra's life, he goes through a few phases; four to be exact. These four phases are Khepri, Ra, Itum, and Iwf respectively. The first three phases Ra goes through from Sunrise to Sunset, and from Sunset to Sunrise he goes through the final phase iwf. Also, there is a boat that he travels in during the day called "*m att*" and a boat that he travels in during the night called "*m sktt*." The Journey of Ra from Sunrise to Sunset represents life in the "East," the Physical Realm or earth, while the Journey from Sunset to next Sunrise represents the journey through Duat, the spirit realm. However, regardless of whether Ra is Khepri, Ra, Itum, Iwf, or whether he is on the Eastside or the Westside, Tehuti is with him every step of the way.

Tehuti and Ra have a very special relationship. In one instance he is called the "**Ib n Ra**" or "**Heart of Ra**," which speaks to him as Ra's "Mind" or "Will," and in another instance he is called the tongue of Ra, and you will remember that he is also considered the tongue of Pitah in the cosmology of mennefer. The heart and tongue of nTr are the creative agencies through which it brings forth creation. It represents the 'Will of nTr," and its Divine Intelligence.

Tehuti is the nTr of wisdom, among other related things in the tradition. This function of Tehuti manifests itself further in the tradition, taking him beyond the personification of Ra's heart or tongue, to being his messenger, herald, scribe, guide, and advisor. Tehuti is so wise that he is called "**nDnD nb waty**," or "**Advisor to the one lord**." That's right even Ra takes advice from Tehuti!

In his role of advisor it is said that as Ra was carrying out the work of Creation, Tehuti along with Maat were at his side advising him, giving him direction. Tehuti continues in this role as Ra sails in his boat, serving as the "**sqdd Ra m wiA**," that is "**navigator of Ra in his boat**." This is very important. While Ra is the captain of the boat, it is Tehuti that advises and guides his course. It is said that he "**di na wiA Ra m Axw nw tp rA.f**" or "**he causes the boat of Ra to sail through the effectiveness of his pronouncements**." This is a very important thing

500

that our ancestors are teaching us here. Imagine sailing without a navigator or navigation technology now days, how easy would it be for one to get lost at sea or even worst shipwrecked? However, through the effectiveness of Tehuti's advice, Ra is able to travel safely to and fro. This principle is further demonstrated in the story of Ra and Heru Behudet.

According to the tradition Ra and Tehuti are traveling through the land when Tehuti alerts him to the fact that his enemies were conspiring against him and plotting to attack. They (the enemy) had completely surrounded them! Tehuti then advised Ra to call on his son, Heru Behudet. Ra taking heed of Tehuti's counsel did as he was advised, and invoked Heru Behudet who quickly laid waste to Ra's enemies. It is said that as they traveled, everywhere Tehuti spotted Ra's enemies he would point them out, in every direction, and he would command Heru Behudet to attack. They did this until none were left, and Ra was able to continue his journey uninhibited.

The above story effectively describes the importance of Tehuti in Ra's life. As the journey of Ra is, in truth, the journey of life itself, it speaks to the importance of Tehuti as an adviser and guide in life, helping us to successfully navigate the worlds; both physical and spiritual planes. When life throws something at us that we weren't expecting, unforeseen difficulties, Tehuti, through divination assists us in overcoming those difficulties just like he did with Ra and his enemies. When we allow Tehuti to guide our actions, we can be as victorious as Heru Behudet, conquering all adversity. However, even more importantly, if we keep Tehuti in place as the navigator of our journey, he can guide us in successfully circumventing many of the problems that we face, most of which are unnecessary. No wise navigator will go into a turbulent situation with foreknowledge, especially if it can be avoided! Tehuti can grant foreknowledge of problems before we reach them, just like he spotted and pointed out the enemies of Ra, alerting him to their presence.

Like Ra on his journey, life is full of all kinds of challenges. Ra encounters all kinds of fiends on his journey, looking to impede his

progress and bring chaos into his world. However, with Tehuti at his side he is as "one well prepared," ready for whatever changes may come his way. This is a critical point. Ra's journey is life, which is motion, which is change; constant change; and just like any pilot or driver, if we are not prepared to face changes in our path our journey will be a difficult one; a potential tragedy. We must be prepared to face change, and we must ourselves be prepared to change: our minds, our plans, our direction, etc, if we wish to be successful in life, rising to the occasion that life's many changes bring our way.

As mentioned in the chapter pertaining to the **Anatomy of Being**, the phases of Ra correspond to the motions of life, the moment, time, and are applicable to everything in existence. It represents change. Everything that exists goes through the four phases of Ra, including ideas or thought. Everything comes into being (**Khepri**), matures and reaches its peak (**Ra**), begins to decline (**Itum**) and passes away (**Iwf**). Everything changes. As these changes or transformations that Ra goes through represent time, the moment, it also represents opportunities, windows of opportunities. It was also mentioned how these phases of Ra correspond as well, to the seasons of the year; and from an agricultural perspective, the seasons represent, once again, window's opportunities, and also time dictated plans and actions.

A wise farmer makes every effort to harmonize with the cycles of the seasons; choosing his crops carefully, and carefully timing when to plant. In other words, each crop has a corresponding season in which it is most conducive to plant that particular crop. Planting out of season will yield a poor harvest, or worst, no harvest at all. So a wise farmer always contemplates the time. <u>Timing is Key</u>.

Divination informs us of the time. It lets us know whether or not what we have in mind to do is in accordance with the time or not. It tells us whether or not the time for a particular decision or goal has come, or whether the time has passed, in which we may have to wait entire cycle of time to pursue that particular course of action. It informs us as to whether or not our plans will be fruitful or futile, as well as what potential challenges we will face in achieving our goals. Divination also advises us on the best course of action, how to think and act in order to make best use of the time.

Tehuti is called **"wHmty n Ra m pt,"** or the **"Herald or Messenger of Ra in Heaven."** He announces the coming or rising of Ra. This is very important. As Ra's rising corresponds to Khepri, this represents the emergence of the moment, that which is coming forth from the dwAt. This role of Tehuti gives a forecast (Prophesy) on what is to come, and how we can prepare, make the necessary changes within ourselves, as well as perform whatever rituals that need to be performed (if any) to be successful in the time to come. Tehuti lets us know the specific form Ra will take in his "rising".

Divination can be performed in various ways, all of which can be referred to by the term "Oracle." An oracle is a medium through which a spiritual agency is able to speak. Oracles might be something as simple as some stones, coins, bones, etc, that when thrown they land in a seemingly random mathematical sequence that allows the Diviner to interpret the information being given by the spirit. An oracle may be a shrine, statue, or even a person that a spirit uses to speak through. All of these forms of oracular divination were present historically in the nKmt tradition. However, when oracles are used in conjunction with, and based on cosmology, a highly sophisticated system of communication is created in which answers to questions, and advise given, is often in depth and profound, while maintaining conciseness and accuracy. In the nKmt tradition, the mdw nTr; both the written and spoken language; especially that of the cosmological texts, provided this highly sophisticated communication system between our Ancestors and the Divine. This is one the reasons why the study of mdw nTr language is critical to the authentic practice of the nKmt tradition. We'll deal with this point more in the next chapter.

Historically oracles played a very important and prominent role in nKmt Society. Every temple had an oracle and a High Priest who was its

keeper and interpreter. Also in some instances the High Priest was considered the oracle of the nTr itself, in that he or she was the medium that the nTr "possessed" to deliver the answer to the querent, and to prophesy. For this reason, the translation of "**Hm nTr**," a term for a High Priest, as "prophet" is appropriate.

The oracle was so important that only the Chief Priest, who was the Nisu Bity, and those priests that had reached the level of High Priest were allowed to use the oracle. People would come to the temple to ask questions pertaining to every aspect of their life, to get the oracle to give them insight regarding the situation, and in many cases assisting them in making decisions. During festivals the priesthood would carry the oracle in a procession or parade, and people from every walk of life would come from miles around to present their situation to the oracle. Everyone in Kmt used the oracle (or at least received consultations), regardless of social class; from the commoner to royalty.

Divination was so intrinsic to the way of life in Ancient Kmt, that it played a role in the selection of governmental official, chiefs, priesthood, and even had a place in the judicial system. In the "courtrooms" and tribunals of Kmt, the oracle was consulted and had the final say in judgment, especially in very complex cases in which reaching a judgment was found difficult. In such cases, two contrasting statements were written on two separate pieces of paper and presented to the oracle. The oracle was then asked to "*wDa*," "*to divide, separate, judge*" between these two. This judgment was rendered either utilizing a method similar to the way in which a pendulum is used today for divining purposes, casting lots, or the answer was given vocally, meaning the nTr would actually speak via the priest. An example of this is found in what's referred to as the **Stele of Sheshonq**. In this particular text, the Oracle of Amun is said to judge some officials that had been accused of fraud and theft, actually stealing the offerings of the nTrw, which is bwt, a transgression of one of the 42 oaths of purity. The oracle was presented with a list of names and he acquitted the innocent, and condemned the guilty. At the end of this account it is said that Amun **<u>actually spoke</u>**, giving blessings to the Nisu and the community.

Another example of an oracle being used to render judgment in judicial matters is found in **papyrus no.10335,** which is found in the British Museum. In this particular text, a question is presented to the oracle of "**Imn nsw nTrw Hr.ib pA xnty;**" "**Amun Nisu of the nTrw in Pa Khenty**," in which a man is accusing some people of stealing five tunics from him. The querent presents the oracle with a list of names, in which it selects one guy, a farmer from the list, condemning him as the thief. The farmer is present when the nTr makes the condemnation (this is actually taking place at a festival of Amun), and it is said that the farmer stated "**in the presence of the nTr,**" "**it is false, I didn't steal them!**" in essence, calling Amun a liar. So the farmer decides to go to another Oracle of Amun and asks the question: "**Did I steal them?**" in which the oracle responded "**Yes!**" This farmer decided he would keep trying until he had asked five different oracles the same question (obviously trying to find one that would lie for him). Needless to say all five oracles condemned him. The last oracle of Amun, a priest **possessed** by the nTr, took the farmer out into the town square and beat him before the townsmen, and then made him take an oath to return what he had stolen. This particular account not only demonstrates the role of oracles in settling legal disputes, but also the role that "spirit possession" played in the tradition, in this case the nTr "himself" via his Priest, handed out the punishment. This is not a farfetched experience for the practitioner of Afrikan traditions, as there are many stories of Afrikan deities possessing individuals during ritual and then delivering justice to the guilty.

As mentioned before, there were several oracles in Ancient Kmt, each temple having its own. However, there are a few of special mention that were considered very powerful and important. Of course there was the Oracles of Amun which were very popular. There was also the Oracle of Khonsu nfr Htp. The Oracle of Wajet was considered one of the most powerful oracles in the known world at that time, and it is rumored that this oracle, or at least two priestesses associated with this oracle were taken to Libya and Greece, and were responsible for establishing the

oracle traditions there[30].

Another very popular oracle was the **Oracle of the Nisu Bity Amen Hotep I**. This oracle is of special interest because it is an example of an oracle dedicated to an elevated Ancestor, Nisu Amenhotep I. This demonstrates the fact that in kmt, oracles were also used to communicate with and receive guidance from enlightened Ancestors.

The final oracle that we would like to deal with at this time, is the **Oracle of Tehuti** found in what is called the "**Hwt iAdyt**" or "**House of the Net**," which was either a name for the temple of Tehuti, or a shrine within the temple of Tehuti. Actually, the *Hwt IAdyt* may have actually been the name of the oracle itself. This oracle is said to have been used by the great Ancestor Imhotep himself.

According to the story of the "**Seven Year Famine**," the Nisu Bity Joser asked his "**tAty**" (Vizier) Imhotep to inform him as to the origins of the Nile River, and who was the nTr that lived there. Imhotep, who is referred to as one of the "Staff of the Ibis," i.e. a Priest of Tehuti, told the Nisu that he would go to the "House of the Net," which was "*designed to support every man's heart and actions*," there he will enter the "**House of Life**," and spread out the "**bAw n Ra**" and be guided by them. After doing this, Imhotep returns with the information that the Nisu Bity needs; the location, the nTr who resides there, and the offerings he must bring, etc. Acting on the information Imhotep received from the House of Net, the Nisu Bity was able to travel to the temple, see the condition it was in, perform the necessary rituals and sacrifices which led to the nTr Khnum ending the flood and allowing prosperity to return to Kmt. This is a very important story as it pertains to divination.

In **Chapter 109b of the prt m hrw**, It is said Tehuti "**gives counsel**" from the "**House of the Net**." Tehuti, from the "House of the Net," through the "bAw n Ra" helped the individual divining to avoid getting caught

---

[30] Herodotus ii 55, and vii 134

up by the forces of the Net (**Chapter 153 prt m hrw**), and in other instances to actually use the net to "catch food" i.e. avoid the negative outcomes and actually use the info to benefit. The *bAw n Ra* are the "**manifestations of the Powers of Ra/nTrw,**" **signatures, omens, etc by which spiritual forces make themselves known and communicate to the initiated**. The bAw n Ra is also associated with the legendary **books of Tehuti**, which also inform man pertaining to the **bAw of the nTrw**, as well as other rituals and protocols.

The *bAw n Ra* were the ways through which the nTr made itself known, manifested it's power, communicated, etc. This happens through a ritual language that only the initiated priest can understand. Through following the bAw, via omens, symbols, signatures, etc, the Priest would be able to divine, foretell or prophesy; determine which spiritual forces were in operation in any given situation. The bAw n Ra were said to serve the one who "**desires to be a sr or srA**" (a prophet) and will allow them to become a "**Hm**" which is a "**craftsman**" or "**expert**," and it is said the "**nb bAw n Ra**," or "**Lord/Master of the bAw of Ra**" is called the "**messenger of Prophecy**." According to the Demotic text called (incorrectly) the **Book of Thoth**, the bAw of Ra used animal omens, (much like the written mdw nTr) to give prophecy. Animals such as dogs, jackals, baboons, and snakes, to name a few, were said to *"prophesy according to their utterances."* This will further elucidate the understanding of the mdw nTr language, of which Tehuti is said to be the creator of the language, as a scientific ritual language for the initiated.

Lastly it must be noted regarding the Oracle of Tehuti, House of the Net, and the bAw n Ra, that this particular oracle differs from the others in a very important way, and seemed to be much more sophisticated. First based on the text, Imhotep is said to have went to the House of the Net to be "guided by the bAw of Ra," and that this particular oracle was designed or put together in a way to *"focus the heart or mind of a man and support him in his actions."* Secondly this particular oracle not only had the ability for Tehuti to speak through it, but Tehuti via this oracle had

the ability to inform the diviner of the particular forces that were at play in the situation, as well as the specific offerings that needed to be made in order to appease the nTrw of the Temple, specifically (in this situation) the nTr Khnum. Whereas other oracles were nTr specific, meaning the nTr that it belonged to spoke through it and it gave answers to questions via a priest through possession, meditation, dreams, or some form of divining used to determine yes or no answers through either a movement, or some form of casting lots. The Oracle of Tehuti in the House of the Net had the ability to give very in depth and specific answers, even pertaining to other nTrw, as well as support the mind and actions of "all men." Also, this oracle was connected to a body of literature and rituals; as it has been attested that the **bAw n Ra** are also associated with the "**Book of Tehuti.**" All of this goes to show that this oracle was a highly developed and sophisticated oracle. Another important thing to note regarding this oracle, is that it was the High Priest of Tehuti (called **wn imA**) that was its keeper, as Imhotep is said to be the **Chief Khari Heb** (Keepers of the sacred texts, also in charge of ritual recitation) of the "Staff of the Ibis." This last point draws a very striking resemblance to another well known Afrikan tradition, namely Ifa (Yoruba), in which it is the **High Priest of Orunmila (Babalawo)**, the Orisa of Wisdom and Messenger of Olodumare (Tehuti is both the nTr of Wisdom and Messenger of Ra!), the Supreme Being, that are the keepers of the Oracle called "Odu Ifa." The Odu Ifa like the Oracle of Tehuti in the House of The Net, is tied to a body of literature (the Odu) which serves the purpose of guiding the thoughts and actions of the community, cultivating good character, and informing the person seeking counsel of the particular Orisa (Deity) that is at play in their situation, and goes on to prescribe rituals and offerings that must be given in order to satisfy that Orisa and bring harmony to their situation. Can someone say the **Continuity and Kinship of Afrikan Spirituality**!

Through the practice of divination, our people can once again be guided by nTr, via Tehuti, which allow our thoughts and actions to be in harmony with the divine once again. All Afrikan communities should have oracles that serve as the center of them, and the leaders of these said communities, elders, priests, priestesses, Queen Mothers, Chiefs, or

508

even Kings, must have Tehuti at their sides to advise them. Without Tehuti, these leaders are like Heru in his "bad coming, " which is blind, on a path to failure, pain, and self destruction, not knowing their friends from their enemies, and as a result, lead their people down the same destructive path. When injury is done to Heru it is Tehuti that heals and restores him. When Sutesh gouged out his eye, it is Tehuti (sometimes in conjunction with Het Heru) that restores his sight. When Sutesh created a storm (confusion) in Heru's eye, it was Tehuti that restored his eye. When Heru was poisoned by Sutesh's scorpion, it was Tehuti that restored him to life. Heru, if he wants to be successful, he must have Tehuti by his side. This principle is evident in the nKmt tradition in that Tehuti is also called "**nDnD n Heru**" (**Advisor of Heru**), and "**TAty n Heru**" or "**Vizier of Heru**," just as Imhotep was to Jozer. The Heru or Nisu Bity may be the executive power on the throne, but Tehuti is there to guide his decisions. Needless to say Tehuti's presence in Heru's life was critical to his ultimate victory against Sutesh. If we wish to succeed we must also allow Tehuti to guide our decisions in life.

mdw nTr

20

Madu nTr is the original and correct name for the language of Ancient Kemet. This term translates to mean "Divine Words" or "nTr Words." This understanding of the language has been translated into the Greek name for the written language, "Hieroglyphics," meaning "Sacred Writings." For the longest, this language was shrouded in mystery until the discovery of the Rosetta Stone, which allowed the language to finally be decoded for the West.

This language Madu nTr was considered a sacred language, given to us by the nTr Tehuti, the "Divine Scribe" and nTr of Wisdom. For this reason, Tehuti is referred to as "**Neb Madu nTr**," that is "**Lord of Madu nTr**." He is also considered to be the "**Tongue of Pitah**" and "**Ib of Ra**" in their role of "Creator." As laid out in the cosmologies, it is said that nTr as Pitah, and Ra "spoke," creation into existence; brought the Divine Forces into existence by uttering their Renu (names). As the "tongue" of nTr, and the "**Neb Madu nTr**," it is being implied that the Madu nTr is in essence, what it's name entails, the "**Language or Words of nTr**," and even more accurately, **nTr Words**, meaning that it is the very language that nTr spoke to bring creation into being, and that the very power of creation is contained within the language. This idea is touched on in the so-called "**Sermon of Aesculapius**," found in the **Corpus Hermeticum**, in which Imhotep is admonishing the King not to allow the wisdom of Kemet to be translated into Greek. According to the text Imhotep says:

"Hermes (Tehuti), my master, in many a conversation, both when alone, and sometimes, too, when That was there, has said, that unto those who

510

come across my books, their composition will seem most simple and [most] clear; but, on the contrary, as 'tis unclear, and has the [inner]meaning of its words concealed, it will be still unclear, when, afterwards, the Greeks will want to turn our tongue into their own,-for this will be a very great distorting and obscuring of [even] what has been [already] written. Turned into our own native tongue, the sermon (logos) keepeth clear the meaning of the words (logoi) [at any rate]. For that its very quality of sound, the [very] power of the Egyptian names, have in themselves the bringing into act of what is said. As far as, then, thou canst, O King-(and thou canst [do] all things) -keep [this] our sermon from translation; in order that such mighty mysteries may not come to the Greeks, and the disdainful speech of Greece, with [all] its looseness, and its surface beauty, so to speak, take all the strength out of the solemn and the strong-the energetic speech of Names. The Greeks, O King, have novel words, energic of "argumentation" [only]; and thus is the philosophizing of the Greeks-the noise of words. But we do not use words; but we use sounds full-filled with deeds."

Based upon Imhotep's statement, not only was the meaning of words more clear in Madu nTr, but the Madu nTr itself contained Power. In the statement *"...For that its very quality of sound, the [very] power of the Egyptian names, have in themselves the bringing into act of what is said.."*It is being stated that the Madu nTr actually possess the power to cause what one is saying to manifest. The reason for this is given in the statement:

> *"...keep [this] our sermon from translation; in order that such mighty mysteries may not come to the Greeks, and the disdainful speech of Greece, with [all] its looseness, and its surface beauty, so to speak, take all the strength out of the solemn and the strong-the energetic speech of Names.... The Greeks, O King, have novel words, energic of "argumentation" [only]; and thus is the philosophizing of the Greeks-the noise of words. But we do not use words; but we use sounds full-filled with deeds."*

This contrast between the "Greek" language and Madu nTr is not simply a "jab" or put down, but a genuine contrast based upon the actual nature of the languages. While it is being stated that the Greek language may sound beautiful, this is only surface level, and is only good for arguing and debate into the meaning of things (Philosophy). On the other hand Madu nTr is said not to consist of words at all, but is a "*speech of names*," or even more interesting "*sounds full filled with deeds*." By this statement, it is being said that Madu nTr is a language of "Names," that has the ability to bring into being the thing to which the name refers. This is the "True Name" of a thing, the very sound that underpins its existence and is responsible for its formation. In this way we come to understand something quite profound about Madu nTr as "Nature Words."

When we look at Madu nTr we find that the written language is a language of symbolism; pictographs. While it is true that all languages are symbolic, in that they use a glyph to represent a sound, the Madu nTr uses symbols that reflect back on Nature; things that exist within the natural world, where many other languages do not. This is because Madu nTr is implying that it is the language of Nature, and that the sounds of the language are the "names" of the things that they represent. These are the very vibrations that constitute its being. These sounds, or vibrations, are the nTrw themselves, which are the forces of Nature that are responsible for everything that manifest in the physical world. **E. A. Wallis Budge in his work Egyptian Magic** states the following on the subject:

> *THE Egyptians, like most Oriental nations, attached very great importance to the knowledge of names, and the knowledge of how to use and to make mention of names which possessed magical powers was a necessity both for the living and the dead. It was believed that if a man knew the name of a god or a devil, and addressed him by it, he was bound to*

answer him and to do whatever he wished...all the "gods" of Egypt were merely personifications of the NAMES Of Râ, and that each god was one of his members, and that a name of a god was the god himself."

As it has been pointed out earlier in this work, and as stated in the tradition, Ra's identity is life. Therefore the nTrw as "**names of Ra**" (this concept can be applied to all Creator nTrw), are the various vibrations/names of life, and the Madu nTr contains within it the nTrw.

 This is not a concept that is exclusive to Madu nTr, but is also present in languages such as Sanskrit, Hebrew, Arabic, etc; this is the idea that the language is a language of "Hikau," or "words of power." For instance In the Tantric tradition of India, the Mantras are made from the 50 Letters of the Sanskrit Alphabet. These 50 Letters are known as the "Garland of Letters," and are symbolized by the "50 decapitated heads or skulls" around the neck of the Devata Kali. These 50 Letters are said to be the "**Matrikas**" or "**Mothers**" out of which all things are produced. This language is a language of Mantra, in which each letter of a word, just as is the case with Madu nTr, carries the **power** or force that goes into creating the thing that the word is referring to, and if carefully constructed, and is a language of Names.

The Madu nTr, like most Afrikan languages, is a language of sounds, vibration and rhythm first, and meaning second; the meaning being derived from the former. According to the illustrious Scholar Professor James Smalls in speaking on this subject in regards to the Haitian Language:

"The Haitian people do not speak French, they speak an Afrikan Language. They may call it Creole or patwa, but you're talking about speaking an Afrikan language using a French vocabulary. But the

grammar construction of the Haitian language is fundamentally African, and many of the words are Afrikan. They have a small amount of Native American vocabulary, but the predominant vocabulary is Afrikan using some French vocabulary, but the grammar structure is solely Afrikan, and your grammar structure is how messages are translated through sound and vibration, which we call language into the human mind, and the vibration of a sound stimulates aspects of the brain as well as other cells in the human body, and carries messages beyond just the mundane definition of the word. You understand, because we're talking about rhythm, we're talking about vibrations."

The sounds or vibration is ultimately responsible for the function and purpose of a thing as well. This understanding was also present in Imhotep's contrast of the Greek and the Madu nTr. Where in Greek one finds themselves arguing over the meaning of things, in Madu nTr this is not the case as the language and words are not primarily words of meaning, but vibration.

The Importance of Learning mdw nTr.

"Egyptian language must be learned technically, because this language is the key to understanding Kmt (Ancient Egypt) from an intrinsic paradigm. Positive discussion about Kmt is no longer sufficient

if our aim is to advance the discipline with sound scholarship. In order for us to have a deep and exciting dialogue with Kmt, it is necessary for us to master the Egyptian language. This requirement is imperative, for without it we have no beginning..." - Dr. Theophile Obenga

One of the most absurd of ideas that is being posited in the Afrocentric Community, is that the study of Madu nTr is unimportant, and that one can practice and understand Kemetic Spirituality and Culture with knowing the language. This has been a major inhibition to the successful reconstruction of the tradition. It is a well established understanding in the world of science and academia, that in order to gain an understanding of a culture, one has to familiarize themselves with the language of the people that live the culture, as the language is not only the "Doorway" to the culture, but contains the culture within it. For example, if one would like to learn about Islam, they could read the Quran. In reading the Quran, the person would gain much more insight and clarity by reading it in Arabic, as opposed to simply reading the "English" translation of it. The same goes for the Bible and Hebrew/Greek, the Bhagatvita and Sanskrit, the Odu Ifa and Yoruba, etc. This general rule is the reason why we have the phrase "**Lost in translation**." Languages are conceptual, and all concepts are cultural. This being the case, many times translators run into difficulties, due to the fact that some terms in the languages they are translating from, have no conceptual equivalent in the language they are translating it to. For this reason, learning the language of Madu nTr (in conjunction with related Afrikan Languages) is critical to the correct understanding and authentic practice of the tradition. Otherwise one runs the risk of following behind the Greeks and calling the nTrw by their "Slave names" ☺, Isis, Horus, etc.

One of the main excuses that is given for teachers not emphasizing the learning of the language, is that the Kemetic Science has been "lost to

time" and destroyed," and the Kemetic Hikau included. This is a major fallacy. The Kemetic Hikau/Words of Power are not lost! LET ME SAY THAT AGAIN! :-) THE KEMITIC HIKAU ARE NOT LOST!!! We know this because <u>the Entire Language, Madu nTr, is a language of Hikau</u>. Also, if all of this information has been lost to time, all of the millions of dollars that are pumped into the field of academia known as "Egyptology," are done so by poor innocent people who have no idea that there is nothing there for them to study and are simply wasting their money; or how about the millions given in research grants for museums to collect all of these artifacts and mummies that don't exists? Further, all of the published materials in <u>peer reviewed journals</u> detailing every observable inch of our Ancestors work, all the way to the inscription on a door knob; all of this is fiction; an invention of the mind of the European Egyptologist? I think you get the point.

There is much of our Ancestors work available, and more being uncovered, literally as we speak. However, what is already available are the essentials that will allow us to successfully and authentically practice the tradition. The discounting of these essentials, ignoring their existence, has lead to people pushing all kinds of doctrines under the guise of a Kemetic costume. Many of the people that are doing this don't even study Kemetic literature. This has also led to the usage of Hebrew and Sanskrit to "invoke" "Kemetic" nTrw, when in actuality what one is actually doing is invoking Hebrew Angels and Vedic/Tantric Devas and Devatas, all the while passing this off as the "Only correct" or "Authentic" way to practice Kemetic Spirituality.

Every Tradition invokes the Divine in its own (native) language. To invoke the nTrw of Kemet, one **calls them by their name in <u>Madu nTr</u>.** The fact that the Kemetic nTrw were invoked by their Kemetic names is evident from both historical accounts, as well as the actual ritual literature that is available to us today, which includes the temple liturgy, and also the Hymns. An example of an historian's account is found in the work of the Roman Historian **Eusebius** in his work "**Praeperatio Evangelica III, 4.9**," he records that:

"...the hymnode (singer of hymns) libates with water and lights the fire at the moment when, standing on the threshold, he awakens the god with sounds of the native Egyptian language."

The fact that the nTrw are/were invoked with "*sounds of the native Egyptian language*" should not come as a surprise, and actually should strike some as common sense. However, what has led to much confusion is that the teachers of the "Kemetic" tradition have attempted to interpret Kemet from a foreign perspective. So due to one's bias in working with Mantras from the Vedic tradition, these teachers seem to look for something identical in the Kemetic tradition, and when they fail to find it (if they looked at all), they then declare, the Kemetic Hikau or words of Power "have been lost to time," and proceed to attempt to use Vedic mantra's to invoke Kemetic nTrw while teaching others to do the same. This would not be a problem if the teacher would make it known that **this is a <u>syncretism</u>**, a teaching and perspective original to himself, as opposed to declaring themselves the "Ultimate Authority on Kemetic spirituality in the world." This practice corrupts and destroys the legacy of the Kemetic Ancestors, and the integrity of the traditions they held dear to for countless thousands of years. Also, for Afrikan people, we haven't seen a civilization yet, that has topped what those great ones have done, and it was their cultures and traditions that allowed them to do so. So the correct thing to do, would be to humble down and salute rank. Show a little respect ☺.

The Madu nTr, has the power to move the forces of nature, and cause things to come into being. This is a higher understanding of the language. The manner in which this was done was through the ritual use of Hymns and litanies, as well as Hesi or chanting the names of nTr(w) in rhythmic manner while in a meditative state. Also, because the Madu nTr has the ability to make things happen, many times the hymns are written in a specific way, in which one states exactly what it is that they want to happen. For example, if one was seeking protection from Anpu, one would begin the hymn by Invoking/Evoking Anpu by name, and then calling him by various other names that relate to his manifesting a protective, guardian type of role, along with "Voice-

517

Offerings" or "praise names," and then ending the hymn with a request of Anpu's protection. Now, this request usually takes on one of two forms: It is written as though the person that is writing and reciting the hymn is speaking, ex. "**di.n.i ankh udja seneb**," that is "**give to me life, prosperity, and health**," or it is written as though it is the nTr(w) that is speaking in regards to itself, and what it intends to do for you, ex. "**iw.i m sA n Aankh Benu**," "**I am the protector of Aankh Benu**." The former is written either as a request or a command, and whether it is one or the other depends upon the "rank and order" of the Priest that is reciting it, and the latter is written as a declaration of intent by a priest that is identifying with the nTr. The latter reflects rank of the highest degree, and is usually found within the inner sanctuary of the Temple, the "**House of the nTr**." However there is something that should be clarified about both expressions, and that is the fact that they are written in a way in which <u>**one is giving Maat to the nTr**</u>; the "laws" that is going to govern the Manifestation of the nTr, and how it is to function. Because of the power of the Madu nTr, one simply has to declare what it is they Will to happen, and the power within the language, the nTr as a result causes it to be. The formula is Knowledge of Self as nTr, command over your limbs/members (nTrw), focused Will, and it's articulation in the Madu nTr. This is the way that our Ancestors did it!

Some people may consider it asinine to learn and speak an "Ancient Language" that is presumed to be dead. However, in the case of Madu nTr, such a presumption would be a mistake. As Afrikan People, especially Afrikans of the Diaspora, most of us have been stripped of our native tongue, and as a result speak the language of our former slave masters and colonizers. Also, due to the fact that many of us don't know where our lineage traces back to in regards to National Origins in the Mother Land, even if we wanted to learn our "Original Language," we wouldn't even know where to begin. As a result of this, many of us take a "Pan-Afrikan Perspective" in ideology, but this is more-so, a political and historical outlook, and not spiritual or linguistic. However, quiet as it is kept, **the Madu nTr is a perfect fit for this Pan-Afrikan Identity we have assumed.**

518

There has been much research carried out by Afrikans from the continent, as well as Afrikans from the Diaspora, showing that the Madu nTr itself is actually a Pan-Afrikan language. In truth the great Ancestor, Dr. Cheikh Anta Diop, was one of the pioneers of the Idea of Ancient Kemet as a Pan Afrikan Nation, and as a reference point for Afrikans worldwide, in this day and time, to use as a compass in reclaiming our rightful place in the world. One of his focuses was on Afrikan Linguistics, detailing the connection between the Madu nTr, and various "modern" Afrikan languages, including his own native tongue, **Wolof**. Dr Diop held the view that all Afrikan languages held a common origin, and could trace their lineages back to Madu nTr. This being the case, many modern Afrikan languages today contain within it cognate terms, that can be found in Madu nTr. The following are just a few of his demonstrations:

Madu nTr	Wolof
Fekh: to go	Feh: to go
Yaba: dance	Yoba: dance
Wat: Route, Way	Wat: Trail
Kem: Black	Kem: Black, to char, charcoal
Desher(t):Red, Blood*	Deret: Blood, Red
User: Strong, Powerful, Rich	Wasar: Countless
Mut: Mother	Muth: Birth

Once again, these were just a few of his findings. Along with Dr. Diop, confirming and adding on are illustrious Scholars such as Theophile Obenga and the Dakara, Banda, Mande, and Nuer languages, Aboubacry Moussa Lam and the Pulaar/Fulani language. Today there are even more esteemed scholars that are making head way, such as Claude Mboli, Mubabinge Bilolo, and Gilbert Ngom in regards to the

Bantu languages. Even major terms such as the names of Divinities, as well as one of the most important concepts, such as Maat, can be found today in modern Afrikan languages. According to the great Kenyan Scholar **Dr. Kipkoeech Sambu**, the nTrt Auset survives to this day among the **Kalenjeen**, who consider themselves to be of the military clan of Ancient Kemet, as the main Kalenjiin deity **Asis**. Also Maat, survives in the language, with much of the meaning intact. Dr. Sambu explains :

> *"Maat plays a role in all the kalenjin spheres of life. Maat governs your behavior towards the other people and what you expect from them. People you expect certain obligations from and they expect obligations from you...that relationship is a Maat relationship, and you call each other Maat...The moment we call each other Maat, we remind each other that we have an obligation, should any one of us be poor for some reason, or run into some misfortune its up to you to help me up and vice versa.*[31]*"*

As described in the Chapter pertaining to Maat, what Dr. Sambu has laid out in regards to the usage of the term Maat amongst the Kalinjiin people, is identical in essence to the meaning of Maat, and what a life of Maat looks like. With the work of the above aforementioned scholars, and numerous others here in the West, including Dr. Rkhty Amen, any efforts to reclaim the Madu nTr as a spoken language shall prove to be quite fruitful.

---

[31] Super Funky Soul Power Hour "Radical Maat: The African Social, Political and Military Order, An Interview with Dr Kipkoeech Sambu **https://soundcloud.com/imixwhatilike/radical-maat-the-african**.

Another perspective is that Ancient Kemet itself was a Pan-Afrikan nation, and the language of Madu nTr was/is a Linga Franka, or an "Umbrella Language" that was constructed to unite several languages and dialects from several diverse tribes of Afrikans. This perspective and the linguistic research supporting it can be found in the works of Dr. Clyde Winters, and Asar Imhotep. According to Dr. Winters in his latest work **Egyptian Language: The Mountains of the Moon, Niger-Congo Speakers and the Origin of Egypt**:

The ancient African nation of Kemet/Egypt confederation of 42 tribes/nomes/states, among them the Mande, Soneke, Haussa, etc." On another occasion Dr Winters has also included Akan and various Bantu goups[32].

This scholarship, combined with the former group allows for Afrikans worldwide to finally learn and adopt a language, Madu nTr, without the burden of feeling as though they are just randomly picking a language which they have no ties to. Also this scholarship opens the way for the eradication of this feeling, and the silencing of Nay-sayers and critics who make the accusation that Afrikans of the Diaspora have no rights to Kemet and the legacy of the Kemetic Spiritual Tradition. The evidence has never been so evident, and what it proves is that Kemet is our Ancestral inheritance, along with the rest of Afrika.

---

[32]   Winters,   Clyde   :   Egypt   and   the   Mountains   of   the   Moon
http://www.youtube.com/watch?v=zZ98RYlt3kQ

HIKA

21

It might have gone unnoticed up unto this point, that I have gone through great length to avoid the usage of the phrase "Kemetic Religion." The reason for this is to avoid the psychological "slips" that can take place as a result of the association of the term "religion" with what has come to be known as religion today, mainly the "three big dogs," Judaism, Christianity, and Islam. Though the term religion itself carries no negative connotations inherently, the institutions that exist under the guise of religion have built up a pretty ugly reputation, due to the demonization of Afrikan people and their culture, the subjugation of women, and the brainwashing of their masses by teaching mythology as actual fact and history. However, this is just the cherry on top of the religious "Sunday," as all three have participated in, and benefited from, participation in the East and West Afrikan Slave trade (Maafa), one as major financiers, the others as the major hands on players. For this reason the name "religion," conjures up bad blood for those Afrikans seeking to return to our Ancestral ways of doing things. Yes, Religion's name has been "made to stink," and this is one of the main reasons why it is not used to describe the Kemetic Spiritual Tradition. However, this is but only one of the reasons for the avoidance of the term.

The other reason why I have opted not to use the term "religion," in pertaining to Kemetic Spirituality, is because the *"Imiw HAt,"* "**those that came before**;" our Ancestors, did not use it, and the reason isn't simply because they didn't speak Greek and Latin. The fact is there is not a word in the Madu nTr that equates with religion. However, there is a term that is used to describe the nature of Kemetic spirituality, the

522

rituals, etc, and that is the term "Hika".

Hika is a term in Madu nTr that has been translated by many scholars as "**Magic.**" However, Hika literally means "*to activate the Ka,*" or "*to strike the Ka,*" In the same way that one would strike a percussive musical instrument, causing the vibration to ascend and project from it. In essence, Hika is the science of acting upon the Ka of a thing, causing its creative elements to come forth to create effects or change in the world (Duat and Ta). The Ka, as stated in the chapter pertaining to the **Anatomy of Being,** is the aspect of a thing that is responsible for giving it its own unique expression of intelligence and power. It is what distinguishes things, as well as unites things on an abstract level. The Ka as pointed out is the manifestation of a nTr within a thing. As this relates back to Hika, Hika then becomes the Science of "Evoking" the Ka, the nTr which exists within a thing. A good analogy is that of Medicines or Herbal Supplements, Vitamins, etc. For example, in the case of Vitamins and Herbal Extracts, one will take some fruit, or some plant, and put it through a process that will extract the essential nutrients from it, causing it to come forth in a more concentrated or potent form. Vitamin C is a very important nutrient that plays a critical role in our general well being and immunity. In this way Vitamin C, can be considered (through analogy) the "Ka" of the Fruit that it was extracted from. When this fruit is eaten it has an effect on the body, boosting our vitality, strengthening our immunity, fiber etc. These are the "powers of the Orange." Likewise, Hika is the science of activating the vital force known as the Ka, which manifests the unique powers of a thing, to utilize it to create change in the world. In this way, Hika is united with, and is an expression of, the oldest spiritual tradition of the world, Traditional Afrikan spirituality, which is known by many names, from Vodou, Ifa, Obeah, Palo, etc, as it is the science of working with the forces of Nature, the nTrw.

Hika is considered to be the very essence and power of the Universe, and was utilized by Ra (Itum) from the beginning. According to "**Coffin Text" 261**, Hika declares:

Nwk.i ir.n nb wa.n xpr.t iSt snwt m tA pn

It is I that the One Lord made when Duality had not come into being in the earth.

m.hAb.f wat mAA.f wn.f wa ii m prt m ra.f

when he sent forth his one eye, when he existed alone, going forth from his own mouth

wnn HH.f n KAw

when existed his millions of Kau

m sa Hnnwt.f

Protection of his women

m mdw.f Hna xpr Hna wsr.f ra.f

when he spoke with Khepri, with him over which he has power

m.Tt.f Hw tp ra.f

when he seized Hu over his speech

nwk wnnt sA pw n msi Itm m msi nn hnnwt mwt.f

It is I who am the son of "who bore Atum," born without a companion as his mother

iw m sa wDt nb wa

I am protected by the Command of the One Lord

Nwk.i s.anx psDwt

It is I who gives life to the Pesejut (nTrw)

Nwk.i mrr.f ir.f

It is I who does as he desires

It nTrw

Father of the nTrw

qA iAt

524

Exalted Standard

s.mnx nTrw xft wDt msi itm
who orders and causes the nTrw to be effective according to the command of "who bore Itum"

m nTr Spsi mdw m ra.f hwn m ra.f
August nTr who speaks and eats with his own mouth

Gr.n.i twA.n.i ii.n.i Tbw
I am silent, I support myself, I have come shod

kAw. Nw pt Hmsi.n.i kAw Nwt m saH.i pw wr n nb kAw
Bulls of Heaven , I seat myself, Bulls of Nut, in this my rank of Great of Lords of Kau

iwa Itm Ra
Heir of Itum Ra

ii.n.i Tt.i nst.i Ssp.i saH.i nnk tm m nn xprt.Tn hA nt.Tn iw pHw

I have come to take possession of my throne, and receive my dignity, for everything belonged to me before you came to be. Get behind me

nwk HkA
I Am Hika

The above chapter, known as **"xpr m HkA,"** or **"Becoming Hika,"** is quite profound and elucidating as it relates to the Nature of Hika. According to the text, Hika states that he existed before the coming into being of Duality. This undifferentiated state of Being has already been classified as Nu/Nun. This means that Hika has existed from the very beginning. He then states, that he is the son of the one "*who bore Itum,*" and that he is "*protected by the command of the One Lord.*" The one who "Bore Itum," according to the text, was his own mouth. "*...when he existed alone, going forth from his own mouth...*" reminds us of the Cosmology of

Inu, in which Ra is said to have brought his own name in to his mouth **as "Hika**," and came into being as a result. So Hika, in this text, is stating that he is the offspring of Itum/Ra's mouth, which is a reference to the "words," the Madu nTr. This is also the reason why he is "protected by the command of the One Lord." So Hika existed prior to the coming into being of Duality, which in the Cosmology of Inu is represented by the coming into being of Ishu and Tufnut, because it is he that is the word that brought them into being. In fact, **Hika is the word that brought Ra himself into being**, which is why he (Hika) declares himself to be the "*Father of the nTrw*," which is a title normally reserved for Ra. In this role, he is said to "*order and cause the nTrw to become effective*." In other words, he "**activates**" them. His title as "**wr n nb kAw**" or "**Greatest of the Lords of KAw**," which in this instance is a play on the word "kA," in reference to Bulls," also serves to confirm his relationship with the kA, as an **engenderer of the KAw**," quickening the Ka within, in the same manner that the seed activates the egg of a woman.

As in most Afrikan traditions, everything that exists is said to have a "spirit," that through certain rituals, can be released and directed toward one's goals and objectives. These "spirits" are in actuality, the forces of Nature known in the Kemetic tradition as nTrw. The nTrw as it has been expounded on in the previous chapters pertaining to them, are the forces that are responsible for everything that we experience in the world, and are the expressions of life itself. It is the nTrw that are manifesting themselves as the "Ka" of a thing. With this understanding, Hika is the science of "releasing, or bringing to the surface and directing, the nTr within. While there are many ways in which this science is applied, one of the chief methods is the "Spoken Word," which is, in a way, the essence of Hika.

The relationship between Hika and the word has been hinted at for years by "Egyptologists," though the depth of the subject hasn't really been understood. As it was pointed out a moment ago, Hika was present from the very beginning, prior to the coming into being of Duality. This means that Hika is related to Nu/Nun. As it has been mentioned in the chapter pertaining to the cosmologies, **Nu**, as the

526

primordial undifferentiated, "ocean" of matter, is the source of everything in existence. Everything that is, consists of the very substance of Nu, and the "ordered universe" sits within Nu in the same manner that an ice cap sits within (and consists of) the sea. However, Nu, this infinite matter was considered "Nun," or inert. Yet, as it has been pointed out, and as Physics has made it clear, "inertia" <u>does not mean no motion,</u> for everything moves. It speaks to a constant state of motion revolving around "self," or motion in place. And of course wherever there is motion, there is vibration or sound. Once again it is for this reason, that Nu is written with $\sim\sim\sim$, which not only represents "water," as has been popularized, but a wave, as it is understood that it is in waves that everything moves, including sound. In this way, Nu also represents sound/vibration as the foundation of all existence. Science is approaching this fact with the String Theory.

It is this "vibrant" Nu that is the origin of the sounds/words that Ra spoke in bringing himself, *as* the universe, into being. This Vibration is the essence of Hika. This is foundational premise for the association of Hika with the "Spoken Word," and has absolutely nothing to do with "spells," as many "Egyptologists" would have us believe. Hika deals with stating one's intention in Madu nTr, in a commanding manner that causes the very vibration of the forces of life to move at a constitutional level. In this way translations of Hika as "**Words of Power,**" "**Incantations**," etc, are acceptable and accurate.

Also serving as a confirmation of Hika's association with the "Word," is the fact that the term is written in Madu nTr with the determinative of a man with his hand to his mouth, which is associated with words and ideas pertaining to actions of the mouth, such as speech, eating, and thinking (one can think out loud; i.e. verbalizing their thoughts, or hear the "Word" within). While there are times in which eating may be a part of the practice of Hika, speech and thought are highly attested for.

It is through Hika as the "Word," that the nTrw are *"ordered and caused to become effective."* This understanding is the foundation of all sacred texts, litanies, hymns, and the renu (names) of the nTrw. It is during

ritual that these things are put into use in evoking these natural forces. These elements are in many cases combined in Hsy (song/chanting), and Yiba (Dance), all of which assist in causing the awakening of these forces. This is something that is present in most Afrikan traditions in the songs and chants, the corresponding dances that serve the purpose of "bringing down the spirits."

The association of Hika with the Word as an agency of Divine Creative Power, unites all aspects of the Kemetic tradition, and allows Hika to serve as a term that can describe the entire Kemetic Tradition. While Scholars make the mistake of separating the so-called religious texts from the "magical texts," and both of these from the medical texts, one will see that there is no such explicit distinctions made between these texts as Hika permeates throughout all of them. This is because in the Kemetic tradition, just as in Afrikan traditions such as Ifa and Vodou, Hika includes working with the divine forces through rituals; in and out of the temple, the use of various herbs and minerals; both in and outside of the temple, and also medicine, as is evident from the various medical papyri also included Hika within it, as illness just as everything else, has its roots in the spirit, with the nTrw. For this reason medical treatments many times included Hika as Hesi or chants, talismans, etc. In many Afrikan traditions, Pharmacology is still a major part of the role of the traditional priest, who serves the role of healer on all levels. Examples of the association of Hika with Medicine can be found as early as the Fifth Dynasty, in which there are several examples of *"Sunuve,"* or *"Doctors"* who also held the titles of *"***Hm nTr HkA***,"* that is "**servant of the nTr Hika**," a title held by a High Priest in the Kemetic tradition. For these reasons, it would be a gross error to assign such distinctions and labels to the literature of Kemet.

One problem with translating the term Hika as "Magic," is the fact that magic like religion, has come to have some negative connotations to it. On one hand, one person hears magic, and the word conjures ideas pertaining to illusions and tricks, such as pulling a rabbit out of a hat, sleight of cards, sawing a half naked white woman in half and then putting her back together again, etc, all of which places magic into the

528

realm of entertainment, but hardly anything to be taken seriously or considered real. On the other hand, there is the other side the coin, that considers magic to be very real, but due to both the misuse of the spiritual science of Hika, as well as the mischaracterization of Afrikan spiritual traditions, many consider magic something very dangerous, and even diabolic or demonic. For these people, the word magic, invokes words such as witchcraft, sorcery, devil worship, etc, and as a result nobody wants anything to do with "Magic" or anyone that practices it. However, none of these things actually reflect what Hika actually is.

Hika is the creative power of the universe. It is the very essence of all things divine and that includes us. Therefore Hika is, in actuality, the science of realizing our connection with nTr; the fact that we in reality are nTr, and applying this knowledge by taking advantage of our connection to these cosmic forces to improve the quality of our lives and the lives of those around us. **Hika is not demonic**; it is our divine right as nTr. It is our ability to create in the same manner in which the universe came into being, through the focus of our minds and power to operate the nTr to cause things to come into being. It is the science of creation.

It is said of Hika in the **Coffin Text 648** that:

> *"it was Hika who came into being of himself, the nTrw rejoice at seeing him, and through the sweet savor of whom the nTrw live, who created the mountain and knitted the firmament (heavens) together.*

This means that Hika is nTr and nTr is Hika, and as nTr is all things, especially Man (Male and Female...let's not forget☺), then it should also be understood that we are Hika...**Yes YOU**!

Another thing that needs to be understood is the fact that Hika is **not**

"supernatural" or "superstitious." **Hika is a natural phenomenon that exists in the universe; it is nature**. The forces that operate in nature, the nTrw are natural forces that exists within the universe and that includes within man. We are talking about the powers of the Mind, our Energy, and the forces of our own being. There is no such thing as "supernatural," as everything that exists, is made up of some form of energy/matter, regardless of how subtle the reality may be. So it should be understood that Hika as expressed in the Kemetic tradition, or vodou, Ifa, Palo, Santeria, Akan/Obosom, etc; all Afrikan Spiritual traditions; all of these operate within a system in which the laws of cause and effect applies. There is a specialized nomenclature and systematic organization of natural forces set in place, and the ability for both causes and effects to be observed in the experiences of those that practice the traditions. This is not to say that those that don't practice the tradition cannot experience the reality of it, as in "you have to be a believer," it just means that they have not been initiated into the tradition and are therefore not privy to the information that will allow them to be aware of the forces at work. It is the same as how someone who doesn't know anything about chemistry wouldn't be able to differentiate between one element and the next. A person's ignorance of physics, or biology and its subject matter does not make these fields any less of a science. It just means that they are not learned in this particular field. With that said, let it be known that **Hika is a science.**

According to Nisu Kheti III, Ra gave us "*Hika as weapons to ward off the blow of events.*" This statement is a reference to the purpose of Hika, as a "Healing" agent; as "medicine." There is a flow to life, a rhythm. In the Kemetic tradition we call this flow Maat. It is cosmic order and harmony. This rhythm of life is personified as the nTrt Het Heru. She is the nTrt of music, joy, rhythm, dance, etc; the great explicit expression of life itself and what it's meant to be. When we are in tune with Het Heru, when we are in harmony with Maat, we are in sync with life, and our experience is one of peace, joy, pleasure, patience, etc. However, when we are not in harmony with Maat, we are off rhythm, dancing like we have two left feet, and we end up stepping on Het-Heru's toes. When

530

that happens, we meet the other side of Het Heru. You remember Shekhemt right, The Destroyer of mankind? Yep that's the one. Well she becomes our experience of life when we are out of sync. We clash with life, we compete with it. We are not on time and not in tune. When this happens it creates the sense as though life "lashes out at us." this is symbolized by Het Heru coming, returning to Ra, and finding that he had another in her place. This means that things were out of sync; out of Maat. Once again we are reminded by the ancestor Khun Anpu in regards to Maat "not to put one thing in the place of another."

Well according to the story, Het Heru lashed out at Ra, and transformed into Sekhemet, and left Ra in a rage. This represents the joy and harmony (Het Heru) leaving our lives (Ra), and replacing it with anger, frustration (Shekhemt), and just like Ra without Het Heru, we find ourselves impotent and depressed. When we find ourselves in this place, something must be done in order to bring things back to balance; back to Maat. In some cases divination may be performed to see exactly what must be done, and is given in the form of Hika as a prescription. This is represented in the story by Ra sending Tehuti, who used stories, song and dance to bring Het Heru back, and is reflected in the renu of Tehuti "*s.Htp nTrw*" (Tehuti who satisfies or brings peace to the nTrw), and "*s.Htp nsrt m snmwt*" (Tehuti who satisfies or brings peace to the fiery one when she rages.) In this way, Hika allows us to work with things; heal things at the root level; to "s.Htp" or bring satisfaction/peace/rest to whichever forces are behind the issues. Through Hika, the homeostasis restored to our lives. This of course is the main purpose of Hika. Hika can also be utilized to optimize our lives, and the lives of others.

Now it would be disingenuous for one to ignore the fact, or pretend as though there aren't those that use Hika for selfish intentions and to cause harm to others. The reality is these things do happen. It is this reality that has been placed under a magnifying glass, and portrayed to the world as the beginning and end of Hika. However, it should be known that the actions of these people do not reflect Hika in the grandest sense, or the mass majority of adherents to traditional Afrikan

spiritual systems. What it is, however, is a reflection of the disease in their hearts. Hika is a tool that allows us to move, manage, and manipulate the nTrw, giving us power over the energy and intelligence of these forces. It's about energy and intelligence. Placed in the hands of one person they will use it to heal themselves and those around them, while placed in the hands of another they will use it to build weapons that will allow them slay their enemies and bring short lived relief to their paranoia. This is the duality of life, and it is present in every aspect of life, including Hika. However, one should not make the effort to utilize these sciences for nefarious purposes. The punishment in Ancient Kemet for the negative use of Hika in many cases was death by execution. While we no longer have a society in which something like this can be tried in the courts, one may think they can get away with such terrible actions, but remember your Ba knows what the Ib has done, and that means so do the nTrw and the Ancestors. One cannot escape from the Self. Also, as it is said "*He who performs negative Hika, it shall enter into him,*[33]" meaning it will come back on him. Let it be known! They can't say Benu didn't warn them ☺.

Hika is also the practice of bringing the power and genius of the nTrw forward in one's own being. Recognizing that the nTrw are responsible for our personalities, characteristics, and talents, Hika is the science of feeding (cultivating) the nTrw within us, that we may express the powers that they give, and have the ability to call these forces forward at any given time. The Kemetic Literature is full of examples of individuals identifying with various nTrw for different reasons, and making declarations that they share in the qualities of these nTrw. For instance in the **Prt m Hru**, there are several chapters in which one transforms into certain nTrw. In the chapter of "**Making a transformation into a Divine Hawk,**" One declares:

"*I am Heru dweller within his Splendor. I have gained the power of his crown, I have gained power of his light rays, I have traveled to the*

---

[33] Papyrus Spiegelberg Col 11/21-22

532

limits of Pet. Heru is upon his throne. Heru is upon his seat. My face is like that of a Divine Hawk...I have risen like a Divine Hawk, Heru has distinguished me like his Ba, to take possession of his things, of Osir in the Duat..."

There are several chapters similar to this one, such as "**Chapter of Transforming into Subik**," The "**Chapter of Transforming into Pitah**," and the "**Chapter of Transforming into the Ba of Itum**." The last two chapters mentioned are of much importance for *they express the highest level of Hika, which is realization of Self as nTr, the Creator.*" For example in "Transforming into Pitah" it is declared:

> *"My head is like Ra, I have gathered myself like Itum (meaning I am complete). The four quarters of Ra are the extent of the earth. I come forth. My tongue is Pitah, my throat is Het Heru...those who are in Inu (the Peseju nTrw) bow their heads to me. I am their Bull, becoming strong moment by moment. I copulate; I have gained power for millions of years."*

In **"Transforming in to the Ba of Itum"** it is declared:

> *"I am Ra coming forth from Nu, my Ba is the Divine Creator of his Members...I have created myself with Nu in my name of Khepri. I come into being in the form of Ra. I am the lord of light...I am Nu, I shall not be overthrown by evil doers. I am the eldest born of Primordial Matter, my Ba is the nTrw...I make darkness in the limits of the sky and if I desire to, I travel to their limits...I am Ba, the Creation of Nu..."*

These passages demonstrate that one has realized or attained Knowledge of Self, the highest level, and end result of the practice of

533

Hika, which is the cultivation and realization of nTr within as the Self. the fact that this is accomplished through Hika, is demonstrated in the chapter "**Transforming into nTr, who gives light in the darkness,**" in which it is declared "**I am the girdle of the Garment of Nu, Shining, projecting light, the Keeper of what is before him, shining light into the darkness, uniting the Rehti (Two Women i.e. Auset and Nebt-Het) who live in my body with the great Hika on my mouth...**" The statement that one has United the "Two Women," within one's body, is speaking to the unification of the dual or opposing forces within one's being, bringing them to equilibrium, which is clarified further in the chapter in the statement "*Maat is in my body,*" which leads to one becoming the "*Enlightened*" or the "*nTr who gives light to the Darkness,*" which in the text is personified as a "Woman," who is the light that shrouds the mystery of the nTr within her, a reference once again to the "nTrt of Light" (remember Imun conceals himself within the light"). At the very end of the chapter one declares themselves to "Hm" or "the Woman," the nTrt of Light which represents the nTr embodied/incarnate. All of this happens by way of the "*Great Hika*" from one's mouth.

The ability to harness the power of the nTrw is very important for life is constantly throwing the proverbial "curve ball" our way. There are various different types of situations, each governed by a particular nTr, each calling for a particular quality and talent from us to be successful in it. The ability to be what one needs to be when the moment calls for it is an expression of Maat, an expression of harmony. Sometimes life will call for Heru Behudet; **the fiery, aggressive, relentless force,** sometimes it may call for the "**watery,**" **cool, devotional, compassionate, gentle,** yet **persistent force** of Auset. Each person has a nTr that they embody more fully than others, and are therefore more likely to thrive in situations that reflect their personality. However, once again, life will not always roll out the red carpet for us. When we are met with a situation that calls for us to "rise to the occasion," we have Hika; the ability to "strike the Ka," just as one strikes a drum, causing the vibration (nTr) to emanate from its depths. With Hika we are, as our Ancestors would say, "**as one well equipped/prepared**" for this journey we call

534

life.

Hika is expressed in various ways such as the spoken Madu nTr, written Madu nTr, song, dance, crafts such as jewelry (amulets and talismans), herbalism/medicine, clothing, statues, totems, etc. All of these are utilized in the life of the Hikai(t)/Sunwe' or Juju Man/Woman. Each expression is rich and deserves deep exploration that is beyond the scope of this present work. However in regards to the written Madu nTr, understand that its use in Hika is very powerful for there is life within it. For this reason it was used by our Ancestors, adorning every aspect of the temple, serving the purpose of blessing, dedicating, and also protection. The talismanic power of the Madu nTr, the images of the nTrw, allowed one to travel to a place where the world of the nTrw, the Duat, and Ta came together. In regards to the other expressions of Hika, it is my intention to devote time to release several works in the future pertaining to them.

22

HERU VS SUTESH

Heru and Sutesh represent the opposing forces within us; the opposing forces of our Being. One, Sutesh is responsible for "earthing" us, while the other is pulling on us to "transcend." Their battle is in actuality, a symbol of our struggle to bring balance into our lives. We spend our lives trying to achieve this balance, and many spiritual traditions hold this balance to be the chief objective of the devotee/aspirant.

There must be balance for life to continue. This is an important thing to understand. It's very rare that Sutesh is killed in the traditions, and even when he is "killed," it is never permanently. This is because he is needed for life to exist. There is no light without darkness, so to speak, and the same goes for all things considered opposites. All opposites are in actuality, compliments that elicit and complete one another. However, one (pole) must take precedence over the other, though at times even these roles fluctuate.

Heru, the force that pulls on us to transcend, is meant to rule. This is demonstrated in the story of the "**Contendings of Heru and Sutesh**." Heru, the son of Osir, is the rightful heir to the throne, but in order to rule he must overcome Sutesh. This is deep on so many levels.

On one level, Heru and Sutesh can be said to represent all opposites. In a way, Heru represents the "present," the "light," while Sutesh can be said to represent "death", the past," and "darkness." Both exist, as forces pulling on us to carry out their bidding. It is the "past" that creates the "present," and the night that gives birth to the day. Yet, every day shall become night, and today will eventually become yesterday. It is a cycle. We will always experience the urge to transcend the past, and take things to new heights, and in doing so, we shall find that the past becomes the greatest challenger to our evolution. This is to say, while Heru is pulling on us to transcend, as he is the "seed of the Divine," which is infinite potential, Sutesh seeks to earth us, is animalistic, a conditional (and conditioning) force, and a creature of habit. So while

538

Heru pushes us to ascend, Sutesh pulls on us to maintain "security," holding on to the ways that we've become settled in or accustomed to.

In this way, every step that we take is a battle between Heru and Sutesh. This is a fundamental law of physics, motion and counter motion, force and counter force. Motion forward is a simultaneous motion backward and vice versa. It is said that "*a tree cannot sprout from the earth without simultaneously shooting its roots down into the ground*," or "*ascending to heaven is a simultaneous descent into Hell.*" In this sense the "followers" of Sutesh are considered "demons."

As we progress in our evolution, we must conquer the "demons" of our past. All of our conditioned and learned negative tendencies; the negative experiences that create a cycle of negative thinking and behavior, and our base animal instinct, must be defeated/overcome. This is the battle of our lives; the penultimate step that we must take to ultimately be victorious on our path to the "throne" (actualizing our Divine potential).

In a way, the battle between Heru and Sutesh is eternal, as these opposing forces become balanced and then come out of balance; one getting the "upper hand" for a time before giving way to the other, is the natural flow of the cosmos, the flow of Khepri (change). We will ascend to a certain level, master it, and then Sutesh will usurp the throne, forcing us to transcend further, and then Heru will usurp the throne. This is another reflection on the reality of the oneness of these forces. They both are usurpers. Sutesh usurps the throne from Osir (Heru) and Heru usurps the throne from Sutesh. When we enter into one phase in life, soon things will change, conditions will manifest that move us out of this phase into another. So the death of one phase is the birth of another, and vice versa. In reality, they are one.

ERECTING A SHRINE

23

One of the most fundamental elements of nKmt spirituality is the erecting, servicing, and maintenance of the Shrine. This element; the Shrine, is something that unites nKmt spirituality, to virtually all Afrikan Spiritual Traditions. The shrine may take the form of a temple, a tomb, a table, a room, or even a tree. Regardless of the form the shrine takes, it is essentially always present. In essence, a shrine is a sacred space, dedicated to honor a deity, or Ancestor.

In the language of mdw nTr, there are a few terms that are used for shrine. For instance, we have the term **kAr**, or **kAri**, which literally means "*Mouth of the Ka*." Then there is the term "**r- pr**" (pronounced ra-par) which literally means "*mouth of the temple*." One can easily notice the similarity in the meanings of these terms. The science behind these names, is the fact that **the shrine was associated with the "mouth**," a place where the nTr or Imi.HAt (Ancestor) could be "fed," as well as speak (feed the person using the shrine guidance). It is a well established fact that the nKmt shrines and their statues also served as oracles (ora- meaning mouth, is in the word!). The shrine was also seen as a portal or door through which interface with the dwAt could take place (both kAr. and r-pr can also mean door of the kA/temple).

It is this understanding of a shrine, that is the reason why the "**r wn r**," or "**chapter/ritual of the "Opening of the Mouth**" was used to dedicate and activate a shrine, as well as the statue's of the nTrw and Jertiyu that would be housed in the shrine. This was performed so that it (the shrine) could serve as a means through which the nTr or Ancestor could be

540

engaged. The kAri/r-pr served as the "House" and new "body" of the nTr or ancestors in this plane (tA). Another term that speaks to this understanding is "**Hwt nTr**," which is a term for the sanctuary, temple and shrine of a nTr, which literally means "*House of the nTr*." This latter term shall somewhat be dealt with a little later.

Setting up, and maintaining the shrines of the nTrw was (is) one of the most important duties of the priesthood. Surely they were not worshipping "idols," neither did they think that these statues that they made themselves were the actual deities. It was a symbol. The preserving of the shrine was symbolic of preserving, purifying, protecting, cultivating, maintaining and sanctifying that corresponding force within themselves and nature. When they cultivated and maintained their Heru shrine, it was symbolic of the detail in attention, and devotion that they had in doing the same for the Heru within them. You find the same practice today in all of the various African and Eastern traditional spiritual practices. On one hand it taught them devotion, discipline and humility, and on the other hand it painted a concrete image of an abstract principal and force in their minds, that provided a means of understanding, identifying, communication with, and manipulation of the said Force.

When setting up a shrine it is important to know the correspondences of the force you are dedicating the space to. The devotee should familiarize themselves with the offerings of the nTrw, as well as those things that are considered bwt (taboo). Heru, for example, should have his shrine set up either in the east (Heru Pa Khrad), or in the South (Heru Sa Osir Sa Auset, and Heru Behudet). His colors are Red and White, his number is 6, his plant is Sunflower (or Lotus), his oils are Frankincense, and Geranium. His totems are staffs of authority, crowns (Shekhemti/Red and White Crown Specifically). His foods are millet, apples, Oranges, sunflower seeds, Black Beans, Grapes, Okra, Blackeye Peas, etc. His drinks are Red Wine, Gin, Stout, Brandy, and natural drinks that energize and increase vitality and virility (like Ginseng tea). His herbs are Frankincense, Bay, etc. His mineral is Gold. His stones are Ruby, Garnet and Fire Agate. His sacred animals are Falcon/Hawks and

Lion. His bwt (Taboo) is the Black Boar, and turtle. This information (and others not included here but are associated with Heru) should be taken into consideration when erecting a shrine, as well as when making offerings.

To make the shrine, you should use a clean cloth(s) (new is best) that consists of the colors of the nTr it is being dedicated to. In the case of Heru, this would be a Red and White Cloth. It should be placed either on a table, or a shelf that has been purified with a good pine oil solution, temple bath, and spring water, and placed in the southern (or eastern) direction of the room. Never place your nkmt shrines directly on the floor. Dirt is a universal Bwt in the nKmt tradition, so placing a shrine on the floor is ill-advised, as it makes it easier to collect dust.

You should adorn the shrine with a mixture of all of the different correspondences of the nTr. For example, seeing that Heru's number is 6, you wouldn't put, or write the number 6 on the shrine, but instead place six candles, 3 Red, 3 white on the shrine. You would put a symbol of authority such as a staff, crown, or throne on the shrine as a totem. You can place the image of the nTr on the shrine; either a picture or a statue. You would place a mineral like a Ruby or some Gold (maybe a Gold ring with a Ruby Stone Placed!) on the shrine. You would place an incense holder/burner with some frankincense on it. You can sit the oils and baths on the shrine, store them there. All minerals should be dipped in the bath made from the herbs, or anointed with his oils[34]. When preparing food for Heru, a plate should be made with some of his foods, or you could fix him a meal like bean soup, or Millet cereal, a spicy Black Bean and Tofu Dish ☺, or Black-eyed Pea Fritters, along with one of his favorite drinks!

Though Heru was used as an example, this is the general scheme for all shrines, the correspondences and thus offerings and items varying depending on the nTr to whom the shrine belongs. Also, the items and

---

[34] Henensu has a particular way in which baths and oils are prepared. See appendix for more info

layout of the shrine may vary depending upon how deep one has traveled into the tradition, or whether or not one is initiated into the priesthood of a specific shrine. There are also cases in which the nTr or Jerti may give the keeper of the shrine specific instructions, or ask for specific offerings. In any case it is good to be a part of a community in which one can share experiences with others that practice the tradition so that they may receive guidance and advice when these special circumstances arise. For instance, if one is not trained in the tradition, and has not taken the time to develop a relationship with the nTrw under close guidance, then there is always the possibility of malefic forces and disingenuous entities fallaciously impersonating the nTr or taking up residence within the shrine. An experienced priest or devotee can alert you to the fact that your shrine has been compromised and that the force occupying it is not a nTr or Ancestor. In all cases, if you are new it is advised that you seek guidance.

A shrine is like a well. Some run very deep and have good "water" and nourishment, while others may have untapped potential, or may even be dry or polluted. Some shrines are like a Great Cauldron in which one cooks a great meal, other shrines are like a rusty or cracked pot where the contents leak out or the pot taints the food. There are several factors that determine the quality of a shrine, as well as its potency. These factors are:

1) The competency of its keeper in terms of knowledge and ritual ability.

2) The Age of the Shrine and whether or not it has been maintained.

3) The Shekhem (Power) of the Keeper as well as the Shekhem that has been invested into the shrine via offerings and sacrifices.

4) The Shekhem of the nTr or Ancestor to whom it belongs (this one is heavily dependent on the preceding factors.

If properly maintained, over time a shrine can become very powerful, a

source of nourishment for the entire community.

The Osirian Ritual Motif in Relationship to the servicing of a Shrine

The Osirian tradition plays a central role in the daily temple rituals and motifs, specifically the trinity of Osir, Auset, and Heru; in regards to the relationship between the nTr or Ancestor, the shrine, and the priest (Keeper of the Shrine). Careful consideration will reveal the fact that the Osirian trinity has symbolic significance and applicability that transcends their own respective traditions and themselves as unique nTrw and their tradition, which is in itself multi-faceted, is greatly integrated into the temple traditions and rituals of all nTrw.

The Osirian tradition is one that mainly pertains to Ancestral Veneration, and is considered by many scholars to be a "funerary tradition." However much of the nKmt tradition and literature serves multiple purposes. This is evidenced by the fact that many of the chapters in the so-called "funerary literature:" gives instructions that are applicable to those that are in the Duat, as well as "those who are on earth." This same multi-faceted" or better yet "multi-dimensional" applicability is present throughout the entirety of the nKmt tradition. An example of this is in the way that the Ancestral Veneration motif of the Osirian tradition, is intricately woven into the fabric of the daily temple rituals. To understand this, it is important that we look at the temple ritual in relationship to the Osirian trinity.

Beginning with Osir, we find that regardless of the nTr to whom the shrine or temple belongs, during the temple ritual, the said nTr is associated with Osir. This being the case, the Osirian themes, such as the death, and resurrection of Osir are present in the temple rituals. However, the most critical element of the temple ritual that confirms for us the underlying Osirian theme is the central role that the "**Eye of Heru**" plays in almost every aspect of the ritual. If one were to examine

544

the Daily Temple Ritual from the Temple of Imun in Waset, it would be seen that from the very beginning of the ritual to the closing, the Eye of Heru's presence and role is prevalent. For instance, to initiate the ritual the very first act that is preformed is the lighting of a candle. In this part of the ritual, the candle is identified with and invoked as the "**ir.t Hrw**," or "**Eye of Heru**," by the words "*ii.tw ii.tw m Htp irt Hrw*," that is *"Come you! Come you in peace Eye of Heru!"* From here the Eye is associated with the act giving an offering, the offering itself being identified with the Eye of Heru. The purpose of the offerings, like the eye which is also called "**wAD.t,** "is to "**s.wAD**" or "**Green**" (Refresh) the nTr, just as the eye plays the central role in refreshing and reviving Osir.   In fact, all of the major "players" in the Osirian tradition play a part in the ritual motif of the temple. For instance, the removal of the bolt of the door from its socket is associated with the removal of the finger of Sutesh from the Eye of Heru, thus allowing one to see the nTr in its "true form." The offering of "the Eye" is to enable the nTr to overcome "Sutesh and his followers." The "High Priest" is identified with Heru the "Nisu." The arms, hands, and fingers of the Priest are identified with Heru, Tehuti, and Anpu respectively. Though this is not mentioned specifically in the recitation (but will be demonstrated shortly), the Shrine/Temple itself is identified with Auset, especially the Hwt nTr or House of the nTr, and the image of the nTr is identified with Nbt Hwt.

Going further, it should be noted that, in actuality, the entire funerary process is played out in the ritual. The nTr is revived by the offerings identified as the "Eye of Heru," the "body" or image of the nTr is washed, anointed with oils and perfumed by the arms, hands, and fingers of the Priest, (Heru, Tehuti, and Anpu). It is then wrapped in cloth, an act associated and identified with the act of mummification. One of the Final acts of the ritual involves the application of an ointment, that is identified with the act of "Opening the Mouth," the ritual that is performed to Awaken and elevate the "spirit" of the Ancestor.

Thus it should be clearly recognized and understood, that the Temple

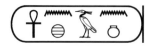

Ritual and Funerary Rituals are reflective of one another, and the Osirian Tradition is the motif that unites them both. The temple/shrine doubles as a tomb and vice versa (the tomb as a shrine). It is the place where the nTr or Ancestor "rests," and is later revived or awakened. Going further in this vein, one will gain a tremendous understanding of not only the rituals, but the nKmt tradition as a whole, by understanding the Osarian Tradition as a ritual motif and "code."

To understand the **Osirian Ritual Code**, we must first come to understand the part that the Osirian Trinity plays as symbols. First we must look at Auset as the personification of the shrine, the medium that unites the dwAt (Osir), and this world (Heru).

Auset is the lineage, the link between the living and their Ancestors. This is the function of the shrine; to serve as a link between the two realms. Auset's name, which is also her chief symbol, "st," means "seat, throne, place." This relationship between the shrine, throne, and lineage is still alive and present today in modern Afrikan traditions, especially West Afrika as in the case of the Asante and the Akan of Ghana. According to David Kumah in his thesis on **Stools in Asante Culture**:

"The stool is also a sacred object when, in association with prestigious persons, it is used in ancestor veneration. Through it, people establish and maintain contact with the ancestors, whose aim is the successful functioning of society...Stools are generally carved or decorated to carry deep symbolic meanings which are powerful vehicles of strong ties with the ancestors, and hence with the spiritual world, as far as the state is concerned...They serve as the occasional abodes of the so-called spirits of the departed ancestors. They serve as ancestral shrines through which ceremonies relating to the ancestors are performed. On special occasions like "Adae", the spirits sunsum of the departed ancestors are invoked to enter into them because it is believed that they have now acquired new and greater power and influence which can be used in the interest of the living."

546

The Relationship between the "throne" and "shrine" of a nTr or Ancestor is also present in the east Afrikan tradition known as *"Zar."* **Zar** is practiced by East Afrikans in "Egypt," Sudan, Eritrea, Ethiopia, and even among the so-called "Hebrew" or "Afrikan Jews" in Israel. It is considered a tradition centered on "Spirit Possession," in which one is initiated into the path of a particular "Deity" or Ancestor. The Initiation is styled like a wedding, in which the Initiate is "wedded" to the force. This is a common motif in Afrikan traditions, including the nKmt tradition in which a priestess is called "**Hamat nTr**" or "**Wife of the nTr**" During the ritual a table is set up as the shrine called "**Al-kursi**" which literally means "**The chair or The Stool**." This Shrine is covered with a white cloth, and decorated with candles, and offerings of dates, nuts, chocolate, sweets, cakes, fruits, milk, sugar, etc are placed on the shrine, after which the deity is invoked[35].

In the nkmt tradition it should be noted that whenever there is a depiction of offerings being made to the nTrw or Ancestors, most of the time the nTr or Ancestor is depicted sitting upon a throne, and sometimes a throne within a shrine.

---

[35] Natvig, Richard "Liminal Rites and Female Symbolism in the Egyptian Zar Possession Cult" Numen, Vol. 35, Fasc. 1 (Jul., 1988), pp. 57-68

The Shrine is literally the "Throne," of a nTr, it's seat/place of power, and also as touched upon in the above mentioned work by Mr. Kumah, it is also the "Abode" of the nTr, a place where it can take up residence as well as be approached or invoked.

There is another part of the nKmt tradition that connects the Throne with shrines and ancestral veneration, and that is what is called by scholars "Block Statues," which our ancestors referred to by the name "*Hsiw*," which means "**Venerated**" or "**Praised Ones.**" These statues were set up in the temple as pillars, to serve as protectors, which is spoken of in the **prt m hrw** in the chapter of "**Entering into the Usekhet Maati**[36]."

---

[36]   The Chapter "r nw aq r wsxt mAaty" Entering into the Hall of MAaty, there is a passage that reads" iw DADAwt nt sbxyt m iAxw" The Judges of the Gatways (Portals created by Pylons) are in the form of Beatified Ones (Ancestors)." Though the term Hsiw is not used in this particular passage, it is the author's position that the Hsiw are the "Keepers of the Pylons" that the passage is referring to. See referenced source in footnote 36.

It is the author's argument that these statues depict the Ancestor, mimicking the form of a throne. These statues are often inscribed with biographical information such as lineage, prayers, hymns, and appeals to those that may pass it by to make offerings to it, and any information that could further persuade them to do so. For instance, according to the **University of Chicago's Oriental Institute** the image of **Basa's** "Block Statue"

"is covered with a record of the names and titles of 26 generations of Basa's paternal family. This lengthy inscription contains valuable

550

information about how the priesthood was passed on in Kmt through the generations. On the front of the statue, Basa is shown adoring the gods Osiris and Isis. A scene of him adoring Osiris appears on each side."

These statues were used for ritual purposes in which the Ancestor to whom the statue belonged would serve as *"intermediaries between worshipers and deities,*[37]*"* which is the main role of Ancestors in traditional Afrikan spiritual systems[38]. What makes Basa's so special, is the fact that it not only lists his ancestral lineage (going back 26 generations by the way!), but has Osir and Auset portrayed upon it, a symbol of his Ancestors and Lineage.

Finally, in regards to the relationship between the nTr Auset and the kAri or shrine, we have a passage from the chapter **"Becoming a nTr Hawk,"** or **"Becoming the nTr Heru,"** it is written:

> *"I come today from the House of the Double Lion, I have come forth from it to the House of Auset, to the secret mysteries, I have been conducted to her hidden secrets, for she caused me to see the birth of the great god. Heru has invested me with his shape in order that I might say what is there..."*

This passage is speaking to one that has gone through Initiation, and has been granted access to travel beyond the entrance into the Inner Sanctuary or shrine, referred to as "House of Auset' which contains the "secret mysteries," in which is the "Form of the nTr," and can now serve as a medium to speak for the nTr Heru, who in the Osirian ritual code

---

[37] Schulz, Regine. (2011). Block Statue. UCLA Encyclopedia of Egyptology, 1(1). UCLA: Department of Near Eastern Languages and Cultures. nelc_uee_7981. Retrieved from: https://escholarship.org/uc/item/3f23c0q9

[38] ibid

context, is a symbol of the Priest, especially the High Priest. By traveling to the "House of Auset" and being initiated, he is now able to communicate with Osir, who in the ritual context represents any nTr, or Ancestor, who looks out from the shrine (Osir in the Ritual context is the "Eye" that looks out from the Throne (Shrine).

In the shrine ritual the participant goes through a few phases of the Osarian tradition; namely the Burial Ritual, the Purification, and Mummification, and the Opening of the Mouth; the latter also being the means by which the "spirit" of the nTr or ancestor is awakened. This being the case, it also serves as the oracle of the **kAri. It is at once the shrine of the nTr, the tomb or place of burial, and the home of the nTr or Ancestor, the place where communication is possible.**

The identification of the priest or keeper of the shrine with Heru is nowhere more evident than in the ritual offering invocation, "**Htp di nsw**," which translates "*An offering the King gives*." Many scholars interpret this as the performer of the ritual declaring that he or she is sanctioned by the Nisu Bity to make the offering on his behalf. However, this is not entirely accurate. From the last chapter of the "**Coffin text**" mentioned above, it is demonstrated clearly that it is Heru (The Nisu) that **makes the Priest into himself**. This is to say, that once the individual is initiated, they are now a "divine hawk," i.e. a Heru. So not only are they declaring that they are sanctioned by the Nisu Bity, but it is the true Nisu, Heru who is making the offering to his "Father," the nTr of the shrine. In that passage Heru speaks to Osir saying:

"*I send to you one of those who dwell in the sunshine. I have made his form as my form, his gait as my gait, that he may go and come to Djedu, being invested with my shape, that he may tell you my affairs. He shall inspire fear of you, he shall create awe of you in the gods of the Netherworld, and the gates shall beware of you.*"

We also have the words of the Initiated Priest saying:

"Heru is upon his seats and his thrones, and I am he who is in his form. My arms are those of a divine falcon, I am one who has acquired (the position of) his lord, and Heru has invested me with his shape."

From these passages it should be clearly understood that the initiated priest was considered a Heru, a "Nisu" in their own right. This goes for both Priest and Priestesses. When they begin the offering, "*Htp di Nsw*" they are themselves the Nisu, as Heru, making the offering.

Dedicating a Shrine

As the relationship between the Temple Ritual and the Funerary Ritual has been demonstrated, along with the Osirian Ritual Motif, we are now ready to deal with the issue of dedicating a Shrine. Recalling to mind the terms for Shrine, such as "**kAr(i)**," and "**pr-r**," and their meanings (**mouth of the kA and Mouth of the Temple respectively**) we are now able to better understand the function of the Shrine, and what rituals and invocations are, and can be utilized to erect it. The kAr(i) or pr-r in its most fundamental function is a "mouth." It is a place where the nTr or Ancestor can be "fed," and also a place where the nTr can speak. Understanding this fact, the passage that we use in Henensu, which is based upon the methods our Ancestors employed to dedicate and activate a shrine/statue of the nTr or Ancestor, is the Chapters of "Offering a Mouth," and "Opening the Mouth.[39]"

After one has washed completely (shower or bath) including the hair, one should put on a white shirt and white pants. Then one should anoint themselves with Frankincense and Myrrh Oil or the Henensu Temple Oil (see appendix), applying it on the forehead, between the

---

[39] M. de Rochemonteix, E. Chassinat, S. Cauville, D. Devauchelle, Le temple d'Edfou III, Institut Francais d'archeologie orientale, Cairo, 1934-1985 p.331

brows, the knape of the neck, the palms of the hands, the knees, and the top of the feet[40]. After washing one should take the structure (to be used for the shrine) that has been cleaned according to the instructions given earlier, and begin to dress it. Take the clean cloth and place it on the table evenly. Next, place the candle(s), incense, bowl, plant in vase, clean glass, and the image of the nTr to whom the shrine is being dedicated (Either a statue or photo). Get a clean white sheet of paper (no lines) and write the following chapter upon it neatly (as neat as possible):

R n rdi r n Wsir (Name of nTr goes in the blank) mAa-xrw.n.f m nTr-xrt

Chapter of Giving a Mouth to Osir (Name), victorious in nTr-xrt (the spirit realm)

Iw.i wbn.kw m swHt imi.t tA StA

I have risen out of the egg within the hidden land

Iw rdi.n.i. r.i Ddw.i im.f m.bAH nTr aA nb dwAt

May be given to me my mouth that I may speak before the Great nTr, Lord of the Duat.

Nn xsf.tw a.i m DADAWT n nTr nb

My hand will not be repelled by any magistrate of any nTr

Nwk.i Wsir nb r-stAw psS Wsir mAa-xrw m nnw nty tp xt

I Am Osir Lord of Restau, Osir True of Voice shares with the being at the top of the steps.

Ii.ni r mrr ib.i m Si nsrty axm.n.i

I have come at the desire of my heart from the pool of fire, I have extinguished it.

inD-Hr.k nb Ssp xny Hwt Hr.t tp kk.w smAw ii.n.i xr.k

---

[40] This is an excellent technique the Author learned from time in the Osir Auset Society

Show your face, Lord of Brightness, Foremost of the Great Sky, within night and darkness. I have come to you.

Ax.kw wAb.kw awy.i HA.k dni.k tpy.a.k

I am glorious, I am purified, my hands are behind you. Your portion is with your Ancestors

rdi.k.ni r.i Ddw.i im.f sm.i ib.i n wnnwt.f nbdt grH

may I be given my mouth that I may speak with it, may I follow my heart at its season of fire and night.

The above hymn should be written and recited before the shrine, and then placed on the shrine. If one has a picture of the nTr in a Frame, it may be placed in the frame behind the picture. This chapter can also be placed underneath the cloth directly on the table. If you are good at carving and feel as though you could carve this chapter in mdw nTr directly into the table, feel free to give it a shot.

After the shrine has been dedicated, it must next be activated. To activate the kAri, the chapter called "**Opening the Mouth**" from the **prt m hrw** is used. The following chapter should also be copied and placed upon the kAri in the same manner as instructed for the previous chapter.

R wn r n Wsir

Chapter of Opening the Mouth of Osir

Wn r.i in Pitah

Be opened my mouth by Pitah

wHa ntw (sp sn) irw r.i in nTr niwt

be unfettered the bonds (repeat 2x) of my mouth by the nTr of my town

Ii irf DHwty mH apr m HkAw

Tehuti comes fully equipped with HiKau

wHa ntw (sp sn) n stS sAw r.i

unfetter the bonds (repeat 2x) of Sutesh which fetter my mouth

xsf tw tm wdn n.f.sn.f sAi st

Itum shoots at them, repulsing those that would fetter me with them

Wn r.i wpw r.i in Sw m mDAt.f twin t biAt n pt

My mouth is open. My mouth is opened by Ishu with the Iron of Heaven

Nty wp r n nTrw im.s

With which he opened the mouth of the nTrw.

Nwk sxmt Hms.i Hr gs im.t-wrt aAt nt pt

I am Shekhmet. I sit with the great starboard of Heaven

Nwk sAH wrt Hr-ib bAw iwnw

I am the Great SaH (Orion) within the bAw of Inu

Ir HkAw nb Ddt nb Ddw r.i swt aHa nTrw r.sn nb

Regarding all Hikaw and all words spoken against me, may the nTrw stand against them,

psDt nTrw dmdyw

the assembled (collective) nTrw.

The very first shrines that should be erected are Anpu, and Osir Khenti Imentiyu. To erect Anpu's shrine follow the above instructions, making the alterations in terms of the correspondences. For instance, for Anpu, instead of using a white cloth for the shrine, use either a yellow (orange/mustard) and white or Black and Gold. Instead of a white candle, use yellow or Orange. If you have the space you may mix the colors of the candles with his number, that is 2 yellow or orange candles

556

and 1 white candle. From here follow the instructions as given above regarding the dedication and activation of the kAri, and give offerings as listed in Anpu's section. **Anpu must be approached, saluted, and offered to first, before you do so to any other kAri, or before performing any ritual/invocation for nTrw or Jertyiu.**

After Anpu's shrine has been dedicated and activated, one should prostrate before the shrine, bringing the head down to floor, forehead making contact for a few moments. As you arise say "*Inej Hr.k Anpu*" "*Show your face Anpu.*" Afterwards light the candle(s), burn the incense, pure water, make offerings, etc. Next take a seat before the kAri either comfortably on the floor, or in a comfortable chair. Take the time to going into a nice meditative state, focusing on your breathing, once you are relaxed, and the mind is calm visualize (with your eyes wide open) Anpu sitting upon a throne in the place where the shrine is standing. The objective is to make the image of him as real and solid as can be. This may take some time to perfect, but do the best that you can. Once the image is firmly in place, begin to recite the Hesi given in Anpu's section, and also the Hymn given. The Hymn may also be written and placed upon the kAri. Sit there for as long as you can in that meditative state or until you feel accomplished, and then kneel and prostrate before the kAri once more. This is the protocol for all kAri, regardless of the nTr. Once should swap out the hymns and Hesi, being appropriate for each nTr, and also visualize the nTr to whom the kAri belongs. In any case remember to take care of Anpu first.

After the Anpu Kari, the Osir Khenti Imentiyu Kari should be the next erected. Follow the above instructions making the appropriate adjustments for Osir. **The Osir Khenti Imentiyu kAri is the Jertiyu (Ancestral) kAri.** In the nKmt tradition all Jertiyu are identified as Osir, and as the hymn for "**Giving a Mouth to Osir**" advised, they should "*share with the being at the top of the steps*" being Osir. These instructions are reiterated in the instructions that follow the chapter, stating that the Jerty shall be given "*cakes, beer, meat, upon the altar of Osir.*" It is for this reason that in Henensu we venerate the collective Ancestors as Osir Khenti Imentiyu.

Once the Osir Khenti Imentiyu kAri has been dedicated and activated, follow the same procedure given regarding Anpu with the proper adjustments. If this kAri is being erected on a different day, then one should make offerings to Anpu prior to dealing with the Osir Khenti Imentiyu kAri. Meditate as mentioned above, visualizing Osir sitting on a throne before you (with your eyes wide open) in the place where the kAri stands. Sit in that state for as long as possible making **"Hsy"** over the renu of Osir, and afterwards recite the Hymn. The Hymn may also be written and placed upon the kAri. After you are finished prostrate before the kAri.

The dedication and activation of the kAri (Giving and Opening the Mouth) only needs to be performed once, unless for some reason the kAri becomes compromised, by someone touching the kAri who has no business doing so, or someone commits a bwt before the kAri, or bwt is offered to the kAri. If this happens, one must purify all of the objects as instructed. In the case of serious offence one should purify the kAri and all objects with pine, cigar smoke, and Asafoetida (Hing/Devil Weed) or the Henensu Purification Blend (for extreme cases).

Imy rn.f (List of Names)

One of the most important elements of the Osir Khenti Imentiyu kAri is the **"imy rn.f,"** or "**list of names.**" These are the names of all of the ancestors that you intend to enshrine. It is recommended that one enshrines their own Jertiyu first, before listing the names of famous people or national heroes. First list your own personal blood relatives, as many as you know. Feel free to take some time and do research on your Ancestral Lineage before completing this ritual. If you don't know much about your family, begin to ask around your family. The more you learn and know about your Ancestors the more effective these rituals will become. Also, just as with the 'living," those that you know will be most

558

likely to assist you than someone who is a stranger to you (ideally). This same principle applies to the relationship we have with the dwAt.

You should list the names of all of your deceased relatives. All of your relatives should be listed, regardless of your personal feelings towards them, relationship with them, whether you think they were 'good" or not. You must find something to honor, even if it's just the fact that they are an expression of nTr on their own personal journey in evolution. This will bring healing to you them and you as well. Disgrace your ancestors and the very blood within your veins will become a curse to you! Eventually you will find, in a way it is all about healing, re-membering the broken body of Osir, so that we can re-establish harmony within ourselves, and evolution can continue.

However, there are some things that disqualify one from being put on that list. For example, if that person was consciously a traitor to the family or Race they should not be added to the imy rn.f. By consciously a traitor, we mean someone who knew better, yet decided to turn on or sell out our people. Treasonous acts include, engaging in interracial relationships after coming into so-called consciousness, integrating Afrikan Sacred Sciences, (initiating non-Afrikans into, or teaching them our sacred traditions), Siding with the enemies of one's people, revealing critical family business or issues to non family, spy, fighting for one's enemy, disrespecting and disregarding one's duties to their people and ancestors, acting as a sexual predator, engaging white sex/dis-sexual acts, or consciously committing "bwt," after being initiated and knowing better. Most of us that are new to the tradition or consciousness in many regards might be the first of our family in a long time to come into Knowledge of Self. Because of this, there is the possibility that some of our unconscious Ancestors may have committed some acts that are not in accordance with Maat. If you know the story fine, use your intuition. If you don't know the details, don't worry about it. Remember that the Osirian tradition is one in which the Ancestor Is remembered, purified, and then elevated and empowered. The procedure of qualifying or disqualifying one from being counted amongst the Ancestors is a meticulous procedure that requires

tremendous insight and specific information. **Don't concern yourself with this**.

To make the list, you need clean sheets of Paper (no lines), white, green, or gold, in color. Write the names of your Ancestors, one by one, placing each in a shinu. By writing one name at a time and immediately placing it in the shinu will allow for you to have room to write the name of the next ancestor in the same manner neatly.

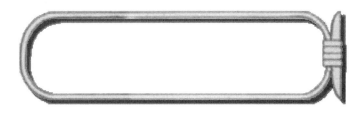

The Ren is placed in a Shinu for protective purposes, as it symbolized protection of the Ren, and thus protection of the Ancestor (or whoever the ren belongs), and also preservation, as the shinu a symbol of eternity. By placing the Ren in the shinu you are willing these things for your ancestors. If you are skilled in engraving or painting and would like to utilize them to do something special such as a plaque etc, feel free as long as it fits on your shrine. I recommend writing their Ren alphabetically (Phonetically) in the mdw nTr, so that you are able to pronounce it correctly when reading it, however, you may also simply write it in English (or whatever language you speak). This should be done in a meditative manner, in a mood of praise, and thanks for your Jertiyu. When your list is complete (for now) you should place it in a frame behind the picture of Osir (if you have one) and keep it on the kAri.

If you ever decide to make a kAri for your Ren (Ren is an actual nTr...treat it as such!) you should also write your ren within the Shinu.

Dedication Ritual (Summarized)

These are the ritual steps: Bathe, wear white. Anoint yourself with oil on your forehead, back of the neck, palms of the hands, kneecaps, top of the feet.

1) Recite the Giving of the Mouth, then place the chapter in the picture frame behind the picture of nTr.

2) Recite the Opening of the Mouth, then place the chapter in the picture frame behind the picture of nTr.

3) Prostrate before the kAri (Visualize the nTr sitting before you in the place where the kAri is sitting, on a Throne. (make the effort to hold that image in mind throughout the ritual).

4) say inD Hr.k (nTr's ren)

5) Say Htp di nsw...Wajet n Hrw (Eye of Heru), light the candle; sanether (incense), light the incense; qwahbihu mu (libations), pour water into the glass. (Offer anything else after the water and call it out ex. Henket (Beer), Jeffa (Food), etc) n kA.k n (Osir Khenti Imentiyu...at his kAri, and Anpu at his kAri)

6) Call out the Renu of your Jertiyu... (Osir..so and so, Osir so and so, etc) going down your list. Once you say the last name (Osir so and so), say "MAa xrw" (true of voice/victorious).

7) Prostrate before the kAri. Let the incense burn, leave the water and offerings, blow out the candle.

*Offerings should be swaped out and refreshed daily.

Iry ikhat ra neb (Daily Rituals) 24

These rituals are organized to flow in harmony with the Four Phases of Ra; the cycles of the day, and are based upon both the traditions of Ra and also the Osirian tradition. There are hymns and meditations spread throughout the day, each placed in the order they are to be carried out. The hymns correspond to the Phases of Ra, and the meditations correspond to Auset, Heru, and Osir respectively. Every day we go through the cycles of these cosmologies and stories. Every morning we are Auset beginning our journey to pick up the pieces and remember who we are (Osir) trying to give birth to Heru (awaken). When Heru comes to the scene he is able to meet life head on and be successful (defeat Sutesh). When we sleep we return to the to unite with Osir (during dream state).

FOLLOWING THESE RITUALS DAILY WILL LEAD TO NEHEST (AWAKENING).

Let us begin first with The "Beginning." The Book of Knowing the Evolutions of Ra and Overthrowing Owapep" just may be one of the most powerful instructions in ritual and practical magic, in spite of the fact that on the surface or to the neophyte it appears to be just plain superstition and mythology. For the Ancient nKmt initiate, the details of this book, and the events that it describes, happens on a daily basis. Every day, Ra/Atum/Osires rose from the waters of Nu ("new") (Chaos or the state before creation...i.e. non existence), giving birth to a new creation. Symbolically, this referred to cycles of waking, and sleeping. It can also be seen in the different modes of sleep in which there is the dream state (the journey through the Duat underworld, spiritual realm; subconscious) and the non dream state of sleep, in which one is not conscious of anything (Chaos/ No-thingness). Conceptually, everyday that one wakes up in the morning or "Prt m hrw" (Comes forth by day);

they are starting over fresh, with a clean slate. As the saying goes, "Today is the first day of the rest of my life." This principle must be kept at the forefront of the initiates mind.

Ritually speaking, just as Ra rose from the "Waters of Nu", likewise when we rise in the morning we should bathe/shower, purifying ourselves from the dirt of the past. Every day we are born again. In fact, this is where the Christians get the concept and ritual of the baptism from, although it has lost its essential meaning and power. It is important that you shower everyday at least twice, once when you wake up in the morning, again before you retire in the evening, if you can get more in great! If you think this is a lot, you should look at our Ancestors; they practiced cleanliness inside and out. They didn't want the filth of ten minutes ago on them. They showered according to some accounts, four to seven times a day. Seven Times! They understood the importance of this ritual. "Negative Vibes" like to house themselves in dirt. Miwt (Malefic spirits) love it!

It is something about the magnetism of water. It has the ability to pull a lot of that bad juju off of you. The Muslims still have that practice today. They are to make "Salaat" at least five times a day, and bathe before every prayer. Now I'm recommending at least two, however, you will find that a shower is very helpful during the day to cleanse the mind, especially if you've been stressed out or upset. While in the shower, it is recommended that you maintain your focus on cleansing yourself of the filth of yesterday, washing yourself in the Waters of Nu/New. You should not sing during the shower. Only focus on cleanliness/purification, renewal, and your Divinity.

There are rituals that can be performed while in the shower. **The magnetism of the water is important...USE IT**! For example, if you've been having money issues, you can use the shower as a ritual to wash the "broke" off of you. Concentrate on the water and soap washing the difficulties away. As the dirty water drains out, see it as the "brokenness" and financial difficulties leaving. The same thing can be done for health, negative emotions, etc. Wash away the old and embrace and emerge from the waters of "Nu." Be "Re-Nu-ed." It is important to make sure that you wash your "crown" regularly. This is especially imperative if you have locs. You'd be surprised at the kind of "stuff" you carry with you. If you are clairaudient, you may even hear "voices" coming from your locs. You should wash your head and anoint it regularly.

Every day after your initial shower, anoint the "**Eight Psychic Centers**[41]". These are "the third eye" (middle of forehead between the eyebrows), the back of the neck at the hair line, the palm of the hands, the knee caps, and the top of the feet. Use Frankincense and Myrrh, or Temple bath/oil. If you don't have any oil, then spring water (only spring water), purified and impregnated with your intention will suffice. Bathe and shower before entering the temple and performing any rituals.

After the shower, you should now purify your mouth. Focus on cleansing it of the filth that it may have spoken in the past. Charge your mouth with the duty of only speaking truth. If you've been arguing, focus on putting out the fire with the coolness of Auset and Het-Heru. Dedicate your mouth to Tehuti, and vow to only speak blessings and kind words to others. This is important because the more mindful and selective in speech you become, the more mAa xrw (True of word and deed) you will become. This means that when you say something it is as good as law, a "Divine Decree," and it will hold greater weight in the spiritual realm. **This is priceless information**, for when this is extended to the use of Hikau, or words of power, understand that those Hikau are the actual deities themselves. In speaking them you are attempting to command nTrw. Who do you think you are? The answer must be nTr! So make your words reflect this truth.

After bathing, and purifying the mouth, the very first thing that you should do is give thanks to nTr! dwA nTr for this wonderful life, this gift! If you don't see it as a gift or wonderful just yet...give it some time,

---

[41] Enkamit, Hehi Metu Ra, "African Names: The Ancient Egyptian Keys to Unlocking Your Power & Destiny," Ser Ap-uat Publishers, 1993 p. 85

you'll come around ☺. Begin your day after your shower/bath, with Libations. Symbolically, it is the act of nTr calling nTrw in to being, the forces of it's being; defining itself.

"After my coming into being many were the things coming forth from my mouth (words of power). Not existed heaven (Nut), not existed earth (Gab), and creeping things in that place. I raised them out of Nu".

So since this is a new beginning for you, a new creation, you begin by "calling your forces into being."

There is a chant that may be sung while performing the libations. If you are alone then sing it for a while before beginning the libations, until you get yourself into the "spirit." If you are performing the libations as a group, then one person should lead the libations while the others continue the chant throughout the duration of libations. The Hsy goes as follows:"**Yahwai nTri.**" This means "Praises/Adorations to nTr." This should be singing slowly and rhythmically

Yawai nTri

Aankh Benu

After (or while) this Hsy has been (or is being) performed, one may begin with their salutations and libations. There is not one set way to perform the libations in the nKmt tradition and libations and salutations may be offered at any kAri individually. However, if you would like to bring it together, begin with the "Pre-Creation nTrw," and then with the creator Ra, and then the psDw nTrw, and then the Jertiyu. If you are a part of a traditional Afrikan community that is organized and structured in a hierarchical manner with government, priesthood, elders, etc, then

566

you should include them in your salutations following behind your Ancestors and parents. This is the Ideal Libations to be performed at the beginning of all public ceremonies, rituals, and events. The salutations should go in the following order:

inD Hr.Tn It mwt nTri
Show your face Father – Mother nTri

xprw m (ex. Imn, ptH, Nw, Nit, any Primordial nTrw of the may be called here)
manifesting as (One of the Aforementioned Primordial nTrw, or any nTr that you work within its <u>supreme form)</u>

Xprw m xmnw nTrw
manifesting as the 8 nTrw

xprw m nw nwn.t
manifesting as Nu and Nun.t

xprw m Ra, Rait
manifesting as Ra and Rait

Xprw m Hwt Hr
Manifesting as Het Heru

Xprw m Dhwty
Manifesting as Tehuti

Xprw m psDw nTrw
Manifesting as the Nine nTrw

Xprw m Sw tfnwt
Manifesting as Ishu and Tufnut

Xprw m Nwt Gbb

Manifesting as Nut and Gab

Xprw m Wsir
Manifesting as Osir

Xprw m swtS
Manifesting as Sutesh

Xprw m Hrw wr (BHdt)
Manifesting as Heru Behudet

Xprw m Ast
Manifesting as Auset

Xprw m nbt Hwt
Manifesting as Nebt Het

Xprw m Inpw
Manifesting as Anpu

Xprw m Hrw sA Ast sA Wsir
Manifesting as Heru Son of Auset and Osir

Xprw m Wsir Xnty Imntt (The Collective Ancestors)
Manifesting as Osir Foremost of the Westerners

Xprw m (begin calling the names of the Jertiyu, Preceded by "Wsir" and followed by "mAa xrw")
Manifestinfg as (Name of Ancestors)

Xprw m Smsw.w (Elders)
Manifesting as the Elders

Xprw m (Government Officials i.e. Nsw BIty, Hmt Nsw Wrt, TAty, imy r mSa)
Manifesting as (Govermental Hierarchy)

568

Xprw m Hm nTr tpy (Chief Priest)
Manifesting as the Chief Priest

Xprw m Hm nTr nbw (All High Priests/ Servants of nTr)
Manifesting as the All of the High Priesthood

Xprw m Xry Hb nbw (All Keepers and Speakers of the Sacred Traditions)
Manifesting as all of the Keepers and speakers of the Sacred Traditions

Xprw m wab.w nbw (All Purified Ones)
Manifesting as the Purificatory Priests

Xprw m bsi.w nbw (All Initiates)
Manifesting as all initiates

Xprw m niwt.nw (Our Community)
Manifesting as our community

Xprw m pA dmd (The Collective)
Manifesting as the collective.

By doing this, one calls all of the forces into agreement, allowing and assisting the community to move forward in harmony to accomplish whatever goals they have collectively. Once again this format is ideal for collective rituals, and events.

For Private Rituals one may begin the day after the morning purification with a **Hymn to Khepri**

<u>**Hymn to Khepri**</u>
iAw.n.k xpr ra nb

Praises to you who comes into being everyday

mss sw tnw dwAyt

who gives birth to yourself every morning

pr m Xt mwt.f nn Abw

who comes forth from the womb of your mother without cessation

iw.n.k itrty m ksw

The two sides (Upper and Lower Kmt, Heaven and Earth, etc) come to you prostrating

di.sn.n.k iAw n wbn.k

They give praise to you at your rising

stHn.n.k tA m iAmw Haw.k

you have made the land to shine through the brilliance of your body

nTr.ti m Sxm imy pt

being divine as the power in Heaven

nTr mnx

beneficent nTr

nsw nHH

Eternal Nisw

nb Ssp

Lord of Light

HqA HDDwt

Ruler of Brightness

Hry nst.f m msktt

Whose seat is in the evening bark

570

aA xaw m manDt

Great in manifestation in the bark of morning

Hwn nTry iwaw nHH

Divine youth, heir of Eternity

Wtt sw

who begot Self

Ms sw Ds.f

Who birth his own Self

dwA tw psDt aAt

The Major Peseju praise you

hnw.n.k psDt nDst

The Minor nTrw jubilate for you

dwA.sn tw m irw.k nfr

they adore you in your many beautiful forms

Immediately after this hymn one may perform "prayer" to their Ib or Heart. This particular hymn is found in the **prt m hrw**[42]. The purpose is to appeal to ones ib, which is a nTr, not to lead one to stray from the tpy Hsb, or Right Order (Maat), causing them to ruin their reputation with the nTrw, Ancestors, and fellow man, consequently losing their heart (will) in the spirit realm. This is a powerful prayer that should be performed while meditating over a green image of Khepri, representing the ability for one to will themselves to become whatever they need to be, in order to be successful in life; the ability to create one's self.

Chapter of Not Allowing a Man's Heart To Be Driven Away
Ib.i n mwt.i, ib.i n mwt.i

---

[42] Prt m hrw chapter 30 a&b

My heart, my mother, my heart, my mother!

HAti.i n xprw.i
My heart of my coming into being

M aHa r.i m mtr
Don't stand against me in testimony

M xsf r.i m DADAwt
Don't be repulsed from me by the Tribunal

M irt rqy.k r.i m.bAH iry mxAt
Don't separate from me before the keeper of the scales

Nt.k kA.i imy XAt.i Xnm s.wADA at.w.i
You are my kA within my body, making whole my limbs

Pr.n.k r bw nfr Hn.nw im
May you go forth to the good place where we advance

M sxnS rn.i n Snyt iryw rmwT m aHa
Don't cause my name to stink to the court that causes men to stand.

As mentioned earlier, libations may be and should be offered at any kAri, as libations are a general offering of water to the nTr of that shrine. However, before one makes an offering to any kAri, be it nTr or Ancestors, one should first approach and offer to Inpw (Anpu), to open the way. As mentioned in step 5 of the dedication summary, one should make offerings in the order of prostratation, candle, incense, water, and then any food offerings and beverage offerings, dwA, and a final prostration. The following is a Hymn that may be offered to inpw as an invocation and offering. One may also salute inpw by his Renu as listed in his section of the nTrw chapter, beginning with "inD Hr.k" and then calling the Ren.

<u>Hymn to Inpw</u>
Inpw tpy dw.f
Inpw on top of his mountain

nTr aA
Great nTr

Nb r.stAw
Lord of R-staw

Nb tA Dsr
Lord of the Sacred Land

di.t n kA inpw nb imy wt
an offering to the kA of Inpw Lord of the house of embalming

xnty sH nTr
Foremost of the nTr's shrine

nb tA
Lord of the Earth

Iw Sm m Xrt-nTr
Coming and going from the Spirit World

Irt xpr m Bnw tw
Making the form of the Benu

inD Hr.k inpw
Show your face Anpu
dwA n wp wAt
Thanks for Opening the way

Immediately after inpw the next kAri that should be served is the **Osir Khenti Imentiyu (Ancestral).** The following hymn may be performed.

The same protocols apply as with Anpu, when approaching the kAri, giving the offerings in the same order. The hymn goes as follows:

<u>Hymn to Osir</u>
dwA wsir wn-nfr
Praise Osir wn-nfr
nTr aA Hr.ib ibdw
Great nTr within ibdw
nsw HH
Eternal Nsw
nb DttA
Lord Everlasting
sbbi HH m aHa.f
traversing millions of years
sA tp n Xt Nwt
first son of the womb of Nwt
wtt n Gbb rpat
begotten of Gab the Chief
nb wrrt
Lord of the wrrt
qA HDt
lofty of Hejet
iTy nTrw rmT
sovereign of nTrw and man

sSp n.f Hq Xw iawt it.w.f
he has received the crook and flail and dignity of his fathers

aw ib.k nty m smt sA.k Hrw mn Hr nst.k
your heart swells with gladness which is in the necropolis for your son Heru is established on your throne

iw.k Xaa.Ti m nb dd.w m Hq imi ibdw
you are crowned as lord of Ddw and ruler in ibdw

wAD.n.k tAwi m mAa.Xrw mbAH a nb r Dr

you make the earth green before the hand of nb r Dr

stA.n.f nty nn xpr m rn.f tA.Hr.stA n.f
he leads in his following that which does not exist yet in his name tA Hr stA n.f

skA.n.f tAwi m mAa.Xrw m rn.f pwi n skr
He drags Two Lands in triumph in his name of Sukari

wsr.f aw aA snd m rn.f pwi n Wsir
He is mighty and great in terror in his name of Osir

wntt.f Hnti HH m rn.f n Wn Nfr
he endures at both sides of time eternally in his name of Wn nfr

inD Hr.k nsw nsw.w
Salute King of Kings

nb nbw
Lord of Lords

Hq Hq.w
Ruler of Rulers

Tt tAwi m Xt Nwt
Possessor of tAwi from the womb of Nut

Hq.n.f tAw.w igrt
He rules the lands and the spirit realm

Dam Hat
Limbs of Fine Gold

Xsbd tp mafkyA Hr.tp awy.f
Head of Lapis Lazuli, Turquois of both arms

In.n HH
Pillar of millions of years

Wsxt Snbt
Wide of chest

Nfr Hr imi tA Dsrt
Beautiful Face within the Holy Land

Rdi.k xw m pt
You give splendor in heaven

Wsr m tA
Might in earth

mAa.Xrw m nTr Xrt
Victory in Xrt-nTr

xd r dd.w m bA anx
sailing down to DdDdw as a living bA

xntiyti r ibdw m Bnw
sailing up to ibdw as a Benu

aq pr nn Sna.tw Hr sbA nb.w n dwAt
coming and going without being repelled at the every door of the dwAt

iw rdi.n.k tAw m pr qbH
you are given loaves of Bread in the house of libations

Htpw m inw
Offerings in Inw

Sxt mn m sxt irw it bdt im.f
An enduring field in the field of reeds with barley and wheat in it

n.kA n Wsir xnti Imntt

for the kA of Osir Khenti Imentiyu

At this point immediately after saying "**for the kA of Osir Khenti Imentiyu,**" one should call out the renu of their Jertiyu... (Osir "so and so," Osir "so and so," etc) going down your list. Once you say the last name...ex Osir so and so... say mAa xrw (true of voice/victorious). This concludes the Ancestral Libations

MIDPOINT BETWEEN SUNRISE AND NOON MEDITATION (9:00AM) AUSET DEVOTION TO NEHEM NTR

Hsy (Chant):

I Ast, mwt nTr, nD.t sn.s nDt wrt

(O Auset, Mother of nTr, Avenger/Protector of her brother, Great Avenger/Protector.)

The purpose of this meditation is to build up the love, passion, and devotion for nTr (the Divine Self). You should focus on expressing those emotions, love and devotion to living in accordance with Maat, and re-membering Osir Focus on your breathing. Recognize that every situation, every person that you encounter during the day is a piece of Osir, and you are on your journey to Re-member. You must put the pieces back together again (become one with these situations). Focus

your passion on Nehem nTr (Saving nTr). Visualize Auset on her journey, yourself as her, willing to sacrifice all to Re-member Osir.

Throughout the day, in every situation you must re-member who you are, and be one with what life brings to you. You must rededicate yourself to your nTr within, your Jertiyu (Ancestors), your family, and your community. The purpose of this meditation is to build up passion/momentum, for you have not yet reached a point of full wakefulness, which makes it easier to allow things (habits, conditionings) to go unchecked. So this is to get the "Water" "boiling." As the day progresses, the body will begin to heat up, which in turn will cause more wakefulness. However, just as the contents of a pot begins to rise to the surface as the water begins to boil, so will the contents of your spirit (positive and negative) begin to surface. This is why it is good to build up the momentum early. This meditation can be as long as you would like. If you don't have much time, five minutes will suffice. Chant the Hsy while visualizing as instructed. The nTrt Auset will assist you in making your vision a reality.

At noon Ra is powerful, confident, and full of life. He shines with brilliance. He is fully equipped to conquer his enemies (overcome adversity) and achieve his goals. Keep these things in mind when reciting the following hymn. At Noon/Midday, we have (should have!) all of the energy and lucidity that we need in order to accomplish whatever tasks we need to, with full confidence and effectiveness. Use this hymn to evoke this sense in thought, feeling, and action.

NOON: INVOCATION OF RA (PERFORM WHILE FACING WEST)

i.nD Hr.k ra m wbn.k itm Hr-Axty
Hail Ra in your rising, Atum Heru-Akhuty
dwA.i tw nfrw.k m irty.i
I worship you, your beauty in my eyes
xpr Axw.k Hr Snbt.i
your light unfurling on my breast.
wDA.k Htp.k m msktt

578

You go, you rest in the evening boat,

ib.k Aw m manDt

your heart is elated in the morning boat

nm.k Hrt m Htp

you travel the sky in peace.

sxr xftyw.k nbw

All your enemies are felled,

hn n.k ixmw-wrd

the untiring stars rejoice for you

dwA tw ixmw-sk

the undying stars worship you,

Htp.k m Axt mAnw

you rest in the horizon of the light-mountain

nfr.ti m Ra ra nb

beautiful as Ra every day

anx.ti Dd.ti m nb.i

alive and stable as my lord

ra mAa xrw

Ra, true of voice

MIDPOINT BETWEEN NOON AND SUNSET MEDITATION (3:00PM) HERU EVOCATION

I Hrw nD.t it.f Hrw SAdi nTr aA nb SAi
O Heru, Avenger of his Father, Heru the Savior, Great nTr Lord of Destiny/Fortune

This meditation is performed after the Hymn of Ra and just when the body reaches its peak in terms of temperature. This will be the period of greatest wakefulness. When we are Nehest (Awake) we are present, lucid, and on top of our game. When we are on top of our game, we are able to check those bad habits and conditionings. We are in charge, the Nsw Heru! Since the morning mediation, Heru has been born and is grown and ready to take the throne! Heru is Present. When we are **Present,** we can rise to the occasion and step out and meet life wherever

579

and however it comes. Heru is the master of his Destiny. This meditation should also be used to reinforce the idea of **nHm nTr,** by living mAat. Chant this Hsy while visualizing yourself as Heru, seated upon the throne with the Shekhem staff in your hand representing power and mastery.

SUNSET: HYMN TO ITM

inD Hr.k itm

Salutations Itum

nwk DHwty wDat rHwy

I am Tehuti Judge of the Two Fighters

iw dr.n.i aHAw.sn

I have ended their fighting

iw sk.n.i iAkbw.sn

I have swept away their mourning

iw mHdw.k adw m nHmw.f

You have seized the adw and carried him away

iw irt.n.k wDt.n.k rf

I have done what you have commanded

sDr.n.i Xnw irt.i

I rest within my eye

nwk Swi m sDb

I am free from restraints

ii.n.i Maat.n.i Xnw Hwt whm.t m wDt.w Dd.t.w iAt.w n Xry sm.w nwk Sriw

I have come that I may be seen within the house of repeating the Ancient Words and decrees that guides. I am the future generation

MIDPOINT MEDITATION BETWEEN SUNSET AND MIDNIGHT (9:00PM) OSIR MEDITATION

580

I Wsir bA wn nfr

O Osir bA Wan nfir

This meditation is done as we prepare to end our day, and make our way back to the Duat; as our consciousness withdraws back into the spirit world. It is in the Duat that Heru/Ra unites with his father Osir, if he is found "mAa xrw" in Judgment. It should be noted that in the "Hymn to Itum" that precedes this meditation, there is a theme centering on laws, decrees, and judgment. One invokes Tehuti, who leads the Judgment or weighing of the heart. The reason this is done is because it is Itum, the Old Ra or 'Setting Sun," that enters into the dwAt to be judged, hopefully to be found pure, thus being allowed to unite with Osir in the dwAt. For this meditation you should begin to visualize Osir sitting on the Throne in front of you in his full garb. Focus solely on his image as you chant the above Hsy. This particular Hsy invokes the bA, which is the conscience (and Inner Ancestral Spirit), that part of us that serves as judge of our actions. As this meditation is performed close to the time one should be getting ready to retire to bed, the objective here is to be able to invoke the bA, the nTr/Ancestor within, to declare that one has lived and kept mAat throughout the day. This meditation strengthens the voice and influence of the bA, and also has the capacity to increase mindfulness, and develop the "Self-Accusing Spirit." In other words, your bA will let you know if you've lived mAat or not. In the case that one's bA has found that they did not keep mAat, or that there are some things that need to be acknowledged and corrected, one should make a note of what is revealed to them, and go back into meditation to correct whatever violations that may have been committed. See yourself behaving and responding in the correct manner. Another powerful visualization is to see yourself giving Anpu your ib (Heart) and he in turn feeds it to the Omomyit, or Subik representing the discarding of one's negative qualities, thoughts, emotions, and behaviors. End the mediation with the words "**dwA n'Ir, iw.i wab.kw** (repeat four times) **wab.i wab bnw pwy aA m Hnnsw**!" **"Thanks to nTr! I am pure (repeat four times) my purity is the purity of the Great Benu in Henensu.** The reason the Benu is invoked here, is

because it purifies and renews itself by burning away and destroying the aspects of itself that no longer serves it, are corrupt, and cannot (should not) be carried into tomorrow. Likewise, we judge ourselves, and willingly kill negative qualities within ourselves that we may go forward free and pure; renewed.

Once you go to sleep your body and spirit go into repair mode. All of the mAat that you consciously willed and lived becomes a little more crystallized, which means that your developing habits that are in accordance with Maat. This will eventually lead to Maat being lived automatically, which is what Osir/Sukari being the "pilot" of Heru who is serving as his Henu or boat, represents.

After this meditation one should make the effort to remember what is dreamt about and take note of it, writing it down in detail, as the nTrw, Jertiyu, and your bA will begin to communicate to you through your dreams. In this way if we are conscious enough we can take heed of the messages being given, and utilize it as a means to assist us in navigating our lives, knowing exactly what is going on within our spirits.

<u>Miscellaneous</u>
Invoking of Jerty (Chapter of Making a man return to his home (kAri) on earth)

Just as the Ka of a nTr can be invoked/evoked, possessed etc, likewise the Ka of a Jerty can be invoked. This particular invocation may be used to invoke the Ka of a specific Ancestor, or Osir Khenti Imentiyu (The Collective Ancestral Spirit) that you have enshrined. If you use it to invoke a specific Ancestor be careful to only invoke an Ancestor that has either made itself known to you and you have personally enshrined, or has been assigned to you by the Nisu Bity[43]. Do NOT abuse this science to bind a spirit to perform nefarious duties for you. Following these

---

[43] This particular instruction is specifically for Henensu

instructions is for your own safety. This is to be used strictly to receive assistance and instruction (Guidance).

With all the protocol out of the way, just think about this: for those of you that have read the nkmt Wisdom texts, such as the Book of Pitah Hotep, Kagemeni, Maxims of Ani etc, and were inspired by the profound wisdom of these great Ancient Sages, you've probably imagined what it would've been like to sit at the feet of these great ones, receiving their wisdom. Can you imagine what it would be like to receive guidance or learn from Imhotep himself? Well, this is the beauty of African Spirituality, this nKmt way of life and science that the Ancestors laid down. You can learn from your Ancestor's Ka, the part of them that housed their experience, the part that made them who they were (personality), directly. This is done through the precise ritual science and Hesi in which the Ren (the Name) of the Ancestor is the Hika through which the Ka is invoked. Just as the Ren of a nTr is the nTr itself (Ka), and performing Hesi of the Ren invokes the said nTr, likewise the Ren of the Ancestor is the Hika (activates/raises the Ka), word of power, that invokes the Ancestor. That is the science. However, to be precise and concise, we will use a specific Invocation that was laid down by our Ancestors, the same one that they used to invoke their Ancestors. This Hymn may be used to invoke the Ancestors, and also call on them for protection.

Nwk rw pr m pd
I am the Lion coming forth striding
Iw stt.n.i
I have shot forth
Iw Dsf.n.i (2x)
I am Restored (2x)
Nwk mAAt Hrw
I am the Eye of Heru
sS n.i Maat Hrw tr.pn
I have opened the Eye of Heru at this time
pH.n.i wDb
I have reached the Riverbank

ma in m Htp Wsir (name)

Behold Wsir (Name) Advances in Peace.

Hymn for Healing

Pr.n.i Inw Hna wrw nw Hwt

I have come forth from Innu with the Great Ones of the Palace

nbw makt

with the Lords of Protection

Hqw nHH nHm

The Eternal Rulers

nHm n.i

I am saved

pr.n.i m saw Hna mwt nTrw

I have come forth from Sais with the Mother of the nTrw

rdi.n.sn.n.i makt.sn

they have given to me their protection

iw Tsw.n.i ir.n nbt r Dr

speeches are for me made by the Nb r Jer

r dr st.a nTr nTrt mt mtt Hmwt r

to dispel the influence of a nTr, nTrt, mt, mtt, and so on

nty tp.i pn

which is in this head of mine

m nHbt.i

in my neck

iptn m qaHw.i

in these shoulders of mine

ipn m iwf.i pn

in this flesh of mine

m at.i

in my limbs

iptn r sswn srxy

to punish these slanderers

Hry s.aqyw Xnnw

584

Chief of those who bring confusion/chaos

m iwf.i pn

in to this flesh of mine

bibi m at.i

dullness in my limbs

iptn m aqt m iwf.i pn

and entering into this flesh of mine

m tp.i pn

this head of mine

qaHw.i

my shoulders

ipn m Ha.i

my body

m at.i iptn

these limbs of mine

ni wi Ra n Dd.f nwk nD sw ma xftaw.f

I belong to Ra. he has said: It is I who will defend him against **his** enemies

smw.f pw DHwty

his guide is Tehuti

iw.f rdi.f mdwt drf

he turns the words in to writing

ir.f dmdt

he makes compilations

rdi.f Ax n rxw xtw n swnw imw xt.f

he gives effectiveness to the wise, to the doctors who are behind him

wHa mrr wi nTr sanx.f sw

to release me from illness, nTr he gives life to him

nwk pw mrr wi nTr s.anx.f wy

I am the one nTr wishes to desires for me to live.

Hymn for Healing #2

wHa wHa in Ast

released is one released by Auset

Ast wHa Hrw in Dwt iryt r.f in sn.f swt m smAm,f it.f wsir

Auset released Heru from the evil done to him by his brother Sutesh when he killed his father Osir

I Ast wrt HkAw

O Auset, Great of Hikau

wHa wi

Release me

sfxt.wi ma xt.nb bin.t Dwt dSrt

deliver me from any thing bad, evil, red (against life)

ma nTr st.a

from the influence of a nTr

nTrt st.a

the influence of a nTrt

ma mt mtt

from a deceased male or deceased female

DAyw DAyit Dat.fy sw im.i mi wHa.t mi sfxt ma sa.T Hrw

From a male opponent, a female opponent who he opposes me just as you were released and separated from your son Heru

Hr ntt aq.n.i m xt

Because I have entered into the fire

pr.n.i m mw

I have come forth from the water

nn hA.i r iabtt xt nt hrw pn

I will not descend into the trap of this day

Dd.n.i x.kw xA.kw wi

I have spoken as a child, when I was a child

I Ra mdw.i Hr Dt.k

O Ra I speak about your body

Wsir sbH Hr pr r im.k

Osir cry out because of what has come out of you

mdw Ra Hr Dt.f

Ra speaks about his body

sbH wsir Hr pr r im.f

Osir cries because of what comes out of him

is.k nHmn.kw ma xt.nb bin.t Dwt dSrt

you have saved me from all things bad, evil, and red

ma nTr st.a

From the influence of a nTr

nTrt st.a

from the influence of a nTrt

ma mt mtt

from the influence of a deceased man or deceased woman.

Hymn to Renenutet for Wealth

Bsi.n.k Hapy

I shall make the Nile burst forth for you

Nn rnpt Ab nn r tA nbw.nw

No more years of thirst and weariness in all the lands

Saw.nbw n kswt xr rwd

Every plant shall bow under the weight of their fruit

wD rnnwtt xnt xt.nbw

Renenutet is within commanding everything

spA xt.nbw m HH

everything flourishes, coming forth by the millions

r.a. mHw hAw.k

I shall let your people fill up

Am.sn Hr nb

Everyone shall embrace you

Sbi gn wAsi Dab m ma XAr.sn

Gone is the weariness, decay, and lack in their storehouses

Iw tA htt r m.st

The land is running because of it

Rwd n wAD.w itr

The river is growing and prosperous

Stp Hr-ib.sn

They advance in there,

Wn Xr Hat

existing as before.

Hymn to the Eight Knowers of Things

in iw wn dy mi Hr-dd.f

Is there anyone here like Hordedef?

in iw ky mi ii-m-Htp

Is there another like Imhotep?

bw xpr hAw n.n mi nfrti

There is no family born for us like Neferty,

Xty pAy.sn tpy

and Khety their leader.

di.i rx.k rn n ptH-m-DHwty

Let me remind you of the name of Pitahemdjehuty

xa-xpr-ra-snb

Khakheperraseneb.

in iw ky mi ptH-Htp

Is there another like Pitahhotep?

kA-ir.s m mitt

Kaires too?

nA n xryt srt iy

Those who knew how to foretell the future,

pr m r.sn xpr

What came from their mouths took place,

gm.tw m Tsw

and may be found in (their) phrasing.

di n.sn msw n ktw

They are given the offspring of others

r iwat mi Xrdw.sn

as heirs as if their (own) children.

imn.st HkAw.sn r tA-tmm

They hid their powers from the whole land,

Sd m sbAyt

to be read in (their) teachings.

st Smt smx rn.sn

They are gone, their names might be forgotten,

m sS r dd.tw sxA.tw.w

but writing lets them be remembered.

Invocation of the bA (Taken from Discourse between a man and his

bA)

This ritual should be performed before the Osir Wan Nefer, Osir Khenti Imentiyu kAri, or Khnum kAri. You should wear white during this ritual.

Dd.i n m min
With whom shall I speak today?
Iw wp.n.i. r.i n bA.i
I opened my mouth to my bA
wSb.i. Ddt.n.f
that I might answer what it said
iw nA wr r.i m min
This is too great for me today
nn mdw bA.i Hna.i
that my bA does not speak with me
iw grt wr r aba
it is too great for exaggeration
iw mi wsf.i
it is like I'm being ignored
im Sm bA.i
may my bA not leave from me
aHa.f n.i. Hr.s
may it attend to me with this
wDa wi DHwti Htp nTrw
may Tehuti the appeaser of the nTrw judge me
xsf xnsw Hr.i sS m-mAat
may Khonsu the Scribe of mAat defend me
sDm Ra mdw.i sgA wiA
may Ra hear my words and stop his Boat!
xsf isds Hr.i m at Dsrt
may isds defend me in the sacred hall
Hr ntt sAr.i wdn.w
For my need is heavy
R fA nf n.i
Too heavy for me

nDm xsf nTrw StAw Xt.i

It is pleasant that the nTrw should eliminate the concealment of my body (What is within me.i.e. on my mind)

Dd.i n m min

With whom shall I speak today?

Purification of the Ba

Using some of the water from the libations offered at the Tehuti, Osir Wan Nefer, Osir Khenti Imentiyu kAri, or Khnum kAri. You should wear white during this ritual. While before the kAri pour some of the water into your hands. Then place both hands upon the crown of your head, rubbing the water into your crown and also on your forehead, and perform the following invocation:

Hymn to Tehuti

nwk Hr irt.f

I am the one who is over his eye

ii.n.i di.i MAat n Ra

I have come to give what is Right (Maat) to Ra

s.Htp n.i stS m nXX n Akrw

I have appeased Sutesh with the spit of Akaru

dSr n imAX n Gbb

and blood from the spine of Gab

This ritual is very powerful. It has a calming effect on the mind, and may be used at anytime when experiencing confusion, or the preoccupation with negative thoughts. Also, though it is prescribed to be performed on Thursdays, it can be performed whenever it is needed. After performing this ritual, one should wrap their heads with a clean white cloth or towel, and wear it for the remainder of the day.

Protection of the Ba
This invocation should be performed after the purification of the Ba, or at any time one feels they are being effected negatively psychically, or under psychic attack.

Hymn to Nut
Nwt pSS Tn Hr sA.T Wsir

Nut spread yourself over your son Osir

sdx sw ma stS xnm sw Nwt

hide him from Sutesh, protect him Nut

iw.n.T sdx sA.T iw.n.T is xnm wr.pn

you have come to hide your son, you have come now to protect this great one

Nwt xr Hr sA.T Wsir

Nut fall upon your son Osir

Xnm sw xnmt wrt wr.pn imi mswt

Protect him great protectress, this great one in the midst of your children.

Performing Divination at the kAri

This same hymn to Tehuti should be used when performing divination at the kAri of the nTrw and Ancestors, just prior to posing your question.

Take four cowry shells that have been cleansed with spring water and incense (temple or cigar), hold them in your left hand while your right hand hovers over them. While doing this recite the aforementioned hymn to Tehuti. This will charge the shells. This method can also be performed with pennies. The hymn should be performed every time that you use the oracle for the first time at a sitting.

When you are ready to perform a reading you should concentrate on your question for a moment while holding the shells in both hands. After this pose your question verbally four times while shaking the shells in your hands. After the fourth time say *"wDa"* (judge), and toss

591

the shells onto the shrine. The answers are rendered as follows:

2 mouths open/ 2 mouths closed (2 heads/2 tails) – Yes
3 mouths open/ 1 mouth closed (3 heads/1 tails) – Yes
4 mouths open (4 heads) – Yes

3 mouths closed/ 1 mouth open (3 tails/ 1 head) – No
*4 mouths closed (4 tails) – No

*If you receive 4 mouths closed, cast again to see if the nTr is trying to convey something more. If you receive a "no" combination again then it should be taken as No. However, if you receive a "yes" combination, then you should either meditate on the question at the shrine, or seek counsel from initiated diviner. This particular system works well, but is best suited for yes or no questions, and it is used in conjunction with the Khepera; the temple oracle of Henensu. After you are finished divining, store the shells on the kAri.

Appendix (Calendar)

nTrw of the Lunar Days
Day 1: Ra-HeruKhuti
Day 2: Itum
DAY 3: ishu
Day 4: Tufnut
Day 5: Gab
DAY 6: Nut
Day 7: Osir
Day 8: Auset
Day 9: Heru sA Auset
Day 10: Nebt Het
Day 11: Het Heru nbt Iunt
Day 12: Heru Behudet
Day 13: tnn.t (associated with Het Heru, Ra.t, msknt, wife of Montu)

Day 14: yonut (Wife of Montu)

Day 15: Tehuti

Day 16: qbH snw.f

Day 17: dwA mwt.f

Day 18: Hapi

Day 19: Imsty

Day20: Heru im pr Aa

Day 21: Nebt Het

Day 22: Auset

Day 23: Heru

DAY 24: Nut

Day 25: Gab

Day 26: Osir

Day 27: Tufnut

Day 28: ishu

Day 29: Itum

Day 30: Tehuti

*Every 6th Day of the Month: Divine at the Osir Khenti Imentiyu kAri to see if your Ancestors need anything.

nTrw of the Days of the week (Planetary)

These days are optimal for making kA offerings to the nTrw, especially during the first 15 days of the month.

Sunday- Heru sA Osir sA Auset

Monday- Auset, mwt, Nyit, Satit, Tufnut

Tuesday- Heru Behudet (War) Montu, inhur, Ishu, Shekhmet, Ra

Wedneday- Anpu, Subik, Sutesh, (Khonsu Nefer Hotep m Waset & Khonsu Pa iri Skher z.Hri Shemau)

Thursday- Tehuti, Renenutet,

Friday- Het Heru, Bast, Osir Khenti Yamentiyu, Khnum, Pitah (artistic forms), Nefertum

Saturday- Sukari, Pitah (funerary). Pitah-Sukari/Pitah Hua, Khonsu Pa Iri Skher & Khonsu Heseb Oho), Nebt Het, Onqit

Henensu Nkmt Spiritual Calendar

April 2015

Sunday	Monday	Tuesday	Wednesday	Thursday	Friday	Saturday
			1 Day 13 tknw Feast Day	**2** Day 14 Hm bA Feast Day	**3** Day 15 smdt (Full Moon) ir-m awAy Feast Day	**4** Day 16 Sdi.f mdw.f Feast Da
5 Day 17 Heru wAD f Feast	**6** Day 18 ioH Feast Day	**7** Day 19 Heru iwn mwt.f Feast Da	**8** Day 20 wpw-wAt Feast Day	**9** Day 21 Anpu Feast Day	**10** Day 22 nai Feast Day	**11** Day 23 nai-wr Feast Day
12 Day 24 Flaming nai Feast	**13** Day 25 Feast of SmA	**14** Day 26 Feast of mAA.it.f	**15** Day 27 Feast of wnt abwy	**16** Day 28 Feast of Khnum	**17** Day 29 Feast of Heru nDt it.f	**18** Day 1 psDntyw (New Moon) Tehuti Feast Day
19 Day 2 Feast of Heru Nej it.f	**20** Day 3 Osir Feast Day	**21** Day 4 Imsety Feast Day	**22** Day 5 Hapi Feast DAY	**23** Day 6 dwA mwt.f Feast DAY	**24** Day 7 Qebehsnuef Feast Day	**25** Day 8 Mas-it.f Feast Day
26 Day 9 ir DnA.f Feast DAY	**27** Day 10 ir.nn.f Ds.f Feast Day	**28** Day 11 nDt.r Feast Day	**29** Day 12 nDt sS Feast Day	**30** Day 13 tknw Feast Day		

Important Reminders

School Calendar Template by Vertex42.com

May 2015

Sunday	Monday	Tuesday	Wednesday	Thursday	Friday	Saturday
					1 Day 14 Hm bA Feast Day	**2** Day 15 smdt (Full Moon) ir-m awAy Feast D
3 Day 16 Sdif mdw.f Feast De	**4** Day 17 Heru wAD.f Feast Day	**5** Day 18 ieH Feast Day	**6** Day 19 Heru iwn mwt.f Feast DA	**7** Day 20 wpw-wAt Feast Day	**8** Day 21 Anpu Feast Day	**9** Day 22 nai Feast Day
10 Day 23 nai-wr Feast Day	**11** Day 24 Flaming nai Feast Day	**12** Day 25 Feast of SmA	**13** Day 26 Feast of mAA.it.f	**14** Day 27 Feast of wnt ebwy	**15** Day 28 Feast of Khnum	**16** Day 29 Feast of witt.tf.f
17 Day 30 Feast of Heru n Dt	**18** Day 1 psDntyw (New Moon) Tehuti Feast Day	**19** Day 2 Feast of Heru Nej it.f	**20** Day 3 Osir Feast Day	**21** Day 4 Imaety Feast Day	**22** Day 5 Hapi Feast DAY	**23** Day 6 dwA mwt.f Feast D
24 Day 7 Qebehsuwef Feast	**25** Day 8 Maa-it.f Feast Day	**26** Day 9 ir.DtA.f Feast DAY	**27** Day 10 ir.nn.f Ds.f Feast Day	**28** Day 11 nDt.r Feast Day	**29** Day 12 nDt sS Feast Day	**30** Day 13 tknw Feast Day
31 Day 14 Hm bA Feast Day		Important Reminders				

Henensu Nkmt Spiritual Calendar

June 2015

Sunday	Monday	Tuesday	Wednesday	Thursday	Friday	Saturday
	1 Day 15 smdt (Full Moon) ir-m awAy Feast Day	**2** Day 16 Sdif mdw.f Feast Day	**3** Day 17 Heru wAD.f Feast Day	**4** Day 18 isH Feast Day	**5** Day 19 Heru iwn mwt.f Feast DAY	**6** Day 20 wpw-wAt Feast Day
7 Day 21 Anpu Feast Day	**8** Day 22 nsi Feast Day	**9** Day 23 nsr-wr Feast Day	**10** Day 24 Flaming nsi Feast Day	**11** Day 25 Feast of SmA	**12** Day 26 Feast of mAA it.f	**13** Day 27 Feast of wnt sbwy
14 Day 28 Feast of Khnum	**15** Day 29 Feast of Heru nDt it.f	**16** Day 1 psDntyw (New Moon) Tehuti Feast Day	**17** Day 2 Feast of Heru Nsj it.f	**18** Day 3 Osir Feast Day	**19** Day 4 Imsety Feast Day	**20** Day 5 Hapi Feast DAY
21 Day 6 dwA mwt.f Feast DAY	**22** Day 7 Qebehsenuef Feast Day	**23** Day 8 Msa-it.f Feast Day	**24** Day 9 ir.Dt&.f Feast DAY	**25** Day 10 ir.m.f Ds.f Feast Day	**26** Day 11 nDt.r Feast Day	**27** Day 12 nDt sS Feast Day
28 Day 13 tknw Feast Day	**29** Day 14 Hm bA Feast Day	**30** Day 15 smdt (Full Moon) ir-m awAy Feast Day				

Important Reminders

School Calendar Template by Vertex42.com

597

Henensu Nkmt Spiritual Calendar

July 2015

Sunday	Monday	Tuesday	Wednesday	Thursday	Friday	Saturday
			1 Day 16 — Sdif mdw.f Feast Day	2 Day 17 — Heru wAD.f Feast Day	3 Day 18 — iaH Feast Day	4 Day 19 — Heru iwn mwt.f Feast
5 Day 20 — wpw-wAt Feast Da	6 Day 21 — Anpu Feast Day	7 Day 22 — nai Feast Day	8 Day 23 — nai-wr Feast Day	9 Day 24 — flaming nai Feast Day	10 Day 25 — Feast of SmA	11 Day 26 — Feast of mAA.it.f
12 Day 27 — Feast of wnt abwy	13 Day 28 — Feast of Khnum	14 Day 29 — Feast of wtt.tf.f	15 Day 30 — Feast of Heru nDt it.f	16 Day 1 — psDntyw (New Moon) / Tehuti Feast Day	17 Day 2 — Feast of Heru Nej it.f	18 Day 3 — Osir Feast Day
19 Day 4 — Imacty Feast Day	20 Day 5 — Hapi Feast DAY	21 Day 6 — dwA mwt.f Feast DAY / Qebehsnuef Feast Da	22 Day 7	23 Day 8 — Maa-it.f Feast Day	24 Day 9 — ir.Dt.f Feast DAY / Rising of spdt (Sirius)	25 Day 10 — ir.rn.f Ds.f Feast D
26 Day 11 — nDt.r Feast Day	27 Day 12 — nDt t5 Feast Day	28 Day 13 — tkhw Feast Day	29 Day 14 — Hm bA Feast Day	30 Day 15 — smdt (Full Moon) / in-m awAy Feast Day	31 Day 16 — Sdif mdw.f Feast Day	
		Important Reminders				

July 25- Heliacal Rising of spdt (Auset is the nTr.t) (mAat Hrw Ast)

August 2015

Henensu Nkmt Spiritual Calendar

Sunday	Monday	Tuesday	Wednesday	Thursday	Friday	Saturday
						1 Day 17 Heru wAD.f Feast
2 Day 18 iaH Feast Day	**3** Day 19 Heru iwn mwt.f Feast DA	**4** Day 20 wpw-wAt Feast Day	**5** Day 21 Anpu Feast Day	**6** Day 22 nai Feast Day	**7** Day 23 nai-wr Feast Day	**8** Day 24 Flaming nai Feast
9 Day 25 Feast of SmA	**10** Day 26 Feast of mAA.it.f	**11** Day 27 Feast of wnt abwy	**12** Day 28 Feast of Khnum	**13** Day 29 Feast of Heru nDt it.f	**14** Day 1 psDntyw (New Moon) Tehuti Feast Day Nkmt New Year	**15** Day 2 Feast of Heru Naj it.f
16 Day 3 Osir Feast Day	**17** Day 4 imsety Feast Day	**18** Day 5 Hapi Feast DAY	**19** Day 6 dwA mwt.f Feast DAY	**20** Day 7 Qebehsnuef Feast Da	**21** Day 8 Maa-it.f Feast Day	**22** Day 9 ir.DtA.f Feast DAY
23 Day 10 ir.m.f Ds.f Feast D	**24** Day 11 nDt.r Feast Day	**25** Day 12 nDt sS Feast Day	**26** Day 13 tknw Feast Day	**27** Day 14 Hm bA Feast Day	**28** Day 15 smdt (Full Moon) ir-m awAy Feast Day	**29** Day 16 Sdi.f mdw.f Feast Da
30 Day 17 Heru wAD.f Feast	**31** Day 18 iaH Feast Day	Important Reminders				

© 2011 Vertex42 LLC. Free to Print.

School Calendar Template by Vertex42.com

August 3rd- Heliacal rising of Stw/ tp.a knmwt (Gab, Hapi-imsty are the nTrw)

August 13th – Heliacal rising of knmt (bA/ Auset is the nTr)

August 23rd – Heliacal rising of Xry Hpd knmt (xnti XAst, Auset, or Sons of Heru are the nTrw)

14th day- New Years

17th Day- Wag Fesitival (Osir Khenti Imentiyu/Ancestor Festival), Tehuti Festival

20th Day- Festival of Drunkeness (Het Heru Festival)

Henensu nKmt Spiritual Calendar

September 2015

Sunday	Monday	Tuesday	Wednesday	Thursday	Friday	Saturday
		1 Day 19 — Heru iwn mwt.f Feast	2 Day 20 — wpw-wAt Feast Day	3 Day 21 — Anpu Feast Day	4 Day 22 — nai Feast Day	5 Day 23 — nai-wr Feast Day
6 Day 24 — Flaming nai Feast	7 Day 25 — Feast of SmA	8 Day 26 — Feast of mAA.it.f	9 Day 27 — Feast of wnt ebwy	10 Day 28 — Feast of Khnum	11 Day 29 — Feast of wtt.tf.f	12 Day 30 — Feast of Heru nDt
13 Day 1 — psDntyw (New Mo... Tehuti Feast Dev	14 Day 2 — Feast of Heru Nej it.f	15 Day 3 — Osir Feast Day	16 Day 4 — imsty Feast Day	17 Day 5 — Hapi Feast DAY	18 Day 6 — dwA mwt.f Feast DAY	19 Day 7 — Qebehsenuef Feast
20 Day 8 — Maa-mk.f Feast Day	21 Day 9 — ir.DtA.f Feast DAY	22 Day 10 — ir.rn.f DA.f Feast Day	23 Day 11 — nDt.r Feast Day	24 Day 12 — nDt sS Feast Day	25 Day 13 — tknw Feast Day	26 Day 14 — Hm bA Feast Day
27 Day 15 — smdt (Full Moon) ir-m swAy Feast D	Day 16 — Sdi.f mdw.f Feast Day Heru wAD.f Feast Day	Day 17	Day 18 — iaH Feast Day			

Important Reminders

© 2013 Vertex42 LLC. Free to Print.   School Calendar Template by Vertex42.com

Spetember 3rd – Heliacal rising of HAT DAt (Auset, sons of Heru are the nTrw)

September 13th – Heliacal rising of pHwy DAt (nbt tpy iht, sons of Heru are the nTrw)

September 23rd – Heliacal rising of TmAt Hrt Xrt (imsty-Hapi, dwA mwt.f are the nTrw)

September 19th – First Day of Opet Festival (27 Days)

600

October 2015

Henensu nKmt Spiritual Calendar

Sunday	Monday	Tuesday	Wednesday	Thursday	Friday	Saturday
				1 Day 19 Heru iwn mwt.f Feast	**2** Day 20 wpw-wAt Feast Day	**3** Day 21 Anpu Feast Day
4 Day 22 nai Feast Day	**5** Day 23 nai-wr Feast Day	**6** Day 24 Flaming nai Feast Day	**7** Day 25 Feast of smA	**8** Day 26 Feast of mAA.it.f	**9** Day 27 Feast of wnt aBwy	**10** Day 28 Feast of Khnum
11 Day 29 Feast of wtt.tf.f	**12** Day 30 Feast of Heru nDt it.f	**13** Day 1 psDntyw (New Moon) Tehuti Feast Day	**14** Day 2 Feast of Heru Nej it.f	**15** Day 3 Osir Feast Day	**16** Day 4 imsety Feast Day	**17** Day 5 Hapi Feast DAY
18 Day 6 dwA mwt.f Feast Day	**19** Day 7 Qebehsnuef Feast Day	**20** Day 8 Maa-it.f Feast Day	**21** Day 9 ir.DtA.f Feast DAY	**22** Day 10 ir.rn.f Ds.f Feast Day	**23** Day 11 nDt.r Feast Day	**24** Day 12 nDt.sS Feast Day
25 Day 13 tknw Feast Day	**26** Day 14 Hm bA Feast Day	**27** Day 15 smdt (Full Moon) ir-m-awAy Feast Day	**28** Day 16 Sdi.f mdw.f Feast Day	**29** Day 17 Heru wAD.f Feast Day	**30** Day 18 isH Feast Day	**31** Day 19 Heru iwn mwt.f Fe
		Important Reminders				

© 2013 Vertex42 LLC. Free to Print.

October 3rd- Heliacal rising of wSAti bkAti/TmAt Xrt (dwA mwt.f, qbH snw.f are the nTrw)

October 13th-Heliacal rising of ipDs/ wSti (dwA mwt.f is the nTr)

October 23rd- Heliacal rising of sbXs sn/bkAti (dwA mwt.f, qbH snw.f, Hapi are the nTrw).

Henensu nKmt Spiritual Calendar

November 2015

Sunday	Monday	Tuesday	Wednesday	Thursday	Friday	Saturday
1 Day 20 — wpw-wAt Feast Day	**2** Day 21 — Anpu Feast Day	**3** Day 22 — nai Feast Day	**4** Day 23 — nai-wr Feast Day	**5** Day 24 — Flaming nai Feast Day	**6** Day 25 — Feast of smA	**7** Day 26 — Feast of mAA.it.f
8 Day 27 — Feast of wnt abwy	**9** Day 28 — Feast of Khnum	**10** Day 29 — Feast of Heru nDt it.f	**11** Day 1 — psDntyw (New Moon) Tehuti Feast Day	**12** Day 2 — Feast of Heru Nej it.f	**13** Day 3 — Osir Feast Day	**14** Day 4 — Imsety Feast Day
15 Day 5 — Hapi Feast DAY	**16** Day 6 — dwA mwt.f Feast DAY	**17** Day 7 — Qebehsnuef Feast Day	**18** Day 8 — Maa-it.f Feast Day	**19** Day 9 — ir.DtA.f Feast DAY	**20** Day 10 — ir.rn.f Ds.f Feast Day	**21** Day 11 — nDt.r Feast Day
22 Day 12 — nDt sS Feast Day	**23** Day 13 — tknw Feast Day	**24** Day 14 — Hm bA Feast Day	**25** Day 15 — smdt (Full Moon) irm awAy Feast Day	**26** Day 16 — Sdi.f mdw.f Feast Day	**27** Day 17 — Heru wAD.f Feast Day	**28** Day 18 — iaH Feast Day
29 Day 19 — Heru iwn mwt.f Fe	**30** Day 20 — wpw-wAt Feast Day					

Important Reminders

School Calendar Template by Vertex42.com

November 1st- Heliacal rising of tpy xntt/ (dwA mwt.f, Hapi are the nTrw)

November 11th- Heliacal rising of Xnnt Hrt (Heru is the nTr)

November 21st- Heliacal rising of Xnnt Xrt (Sutesh is the nTr)

18th Day- Ka Hr Ka Festival (Osir/Sukari)

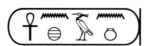

December 2015

Henensu nKmt Spiritual Calendar

Sunday	Monday	Tuesday	Wednesday	Thursday	Friday	Saturday
		1 Day 21 Anpu Feast Day	**2** Day 22 nai Feast Day	**3** Day 23 nai-wr Feast Day	**4** Day 24 Flaming nai Feast Day	**5** Day 25 Feast of smA
6 Day 26 Feast of mAA.it.f	**7** Day 27 Feast of wnt sbwy	**8** Day 28 Feast of Khnum	**9** Day 29 Feast of witt.tf.f	**10** Day 30 Feast of Heru nDt.it.f	**11** Day 1 psDntyw (New Moon) Tehuti Feast Day	**12** Day 2 Feast of Heru Nej
13 Day 3 Osir Feast Day	**14** Day 4 Imsety Feast Day	**15** Day 5 Hapi Feast DAY	**16** Day 6 dwA mwt.f Feast DAY	**17** Day 7 Qebehsnuef Feast Day	**18** Day 8 Msn-it.f Feast Day	**19** Day 9 ir.DtA.f Feast DAY
20 Day 10 ir.rn.f Ds.f Feast D	**21** Day 11 nDt Ds.f Feast Day	**22** Day 12 nDt sS Feast Day	**23** Day 13 tkmw Feast Day	**24** Day 14 Hm bA Feast Day	**25** Day 15 smdt (Full Moon) i~m awAty Feast Day	**26** Day 16 Sdi.f mdw.f Feast
27 Day 17 Heru wAD.f Feast	**28** Day 18 iaH Feast Day	**29** Day 19 Heru iwn mwt.f Feast	**30** Day 20 wpw-wAt Feast Day	**31** Day 21 Anpu Feast Day		
		Important Reminders				

© 2013 Vertex42 LLC. Free to Print.

School Calendar Template by Vertex42.com

December 1st- Heliacal rising of dms n Xntt (Heru is the nTr)

December 11th-Heliacal rising of spty xnwy (Auset-Nbt Hwt is the nTr.t)

December 21st- Heliacal rising of Hry-ib wiA (Sutesh , Heru War are nTrw)

December 31st- Heliacal rising of Ssmw (Heru, Heru war are the nTrw)

Henensu nKmt Spiritual Calendar

January 2016

Sunday	Monday	Tuesday	Wednesday	Thursday	Friday	Saturday
					1 Day 22 — nai Feast Day	**2** Day 23 — nai-wr Feast Day
3 Day 24 — Fleming nai Feast	**4** Day 25 — Feast of smA	**5** Day 26 — Feast of mAA it.f	**6** Day 27 — Feast of wnt abwy	**7** Day 28 — Feast of Khnum	**8** Day 29 — Feast of wtt.tf.f	**9** Day 30 — Feast of Heru nDt
10 Day 1 — psDntyw (New Moon) Tehuti Feast Day	**11** Day 2 — Feast of Heru Nej it.f	**12** Day 3 — Osir Feast Day	**13** Day 4 — Imsety Feast Day	**14** Day 5 — Hapi Feast DAY	**15** Day 6 — dwA mwt.f Feast DAY	**16** Day 7 — Qebehsenuef Feast
17 Day 8 — Maa-it.f Feast Day	**18** Day 9 — ir.DbA.f Feast DAY	**19** Day 10 — ir.rm.f Ds.f Feast Day	**20** Day 11 — nDt.r Feast Day	**21** Day 12 — nDt.tS Feast Day	**22** Day 13 — tknw Feast Day	**23** Day 14 — Hm bA Feast Day
24 Day 15 — smdt (Full Moon) In-m awAy Feast D	**25** Day 16 — Sdi.f mdw.f Feast Day Heru wAD.f Feast Day	**26** Day 17 — Heru wAD.f Feast Day	**27** Day 18 — iaH Feast Day	**28** Day 19 — Heru iwn mwt.f Feast	**29** Day 20 — wpw-wAt Feast Day	**30** Day 21 — Anpu Feast Day
31 Day 22 — nai Feast Day		Important Reminders				

January 10th- Heliacal rising of knmw (sons of Heru are the nTr)

January 20th- Heliacal rising of smdt (Heru is the nTr)

January 30th- Heliacal rising of wSAti bkAti/tpy a smd (Hapi is the nTr).

606

Henensu nKmt Spiritual Calendar

February 2016

Sunday	Monday	Tuesday	Wednesday	Thursday	Friday	Saturday
	1 Day 23 — nai-wr Feast Day	2 Day 24 — Flaming nai Feast Day	3 Day 25 — Feast of smA	4 Day 26 — Feast of mAA.it.f	5 Day 27 — Feast of wnt abww	6 Day 28 — Feast of Khnum
7 Day 25 — Feast of Heru nDt	8 Day 1 — psDntyw (New Moon) Tehuti Feast Day	9 Day 2 — Feast of Heru Nej it.f	10 Day 3 — Osir Feast Day	11 Day 4 — Imsety Feast Day	12 Day 5 — Hapi Feast DAY	13 Day 6 — dwA mwt.f Feast D
14 Day 7 — Qebehsenuef Feast	15 Day 8 — Mesenit Feast Day	16 Day 9 — ir.DtA.f Feast DAY	17 Day 10 — ir.rn.f Da.f Feast Day	18 Day 11 — nDt.r Feast Day	19 Day 12 — nDt sS Feast Day	20 Day 13 — tknw Feast Day
21 Day 14 — Hm bA Feast Day	22 Day 15 — smdt (Full Moon) ir-m awAy Feast Day	23 Day 16 — Sdi.f mdw.f Feast Day	24 Day 17 — Heru wAD.f Feast Day	25 Day 18 — iaH Feast Day	26 Day 19 — Heru iwn mwt.f Feast	27 Day 20 — wpw-wAt Feast Da
28 Day 21 — Anpu Feast Day	29 Day 22 — nai Feast Day					

Important Reminders

© 2013 Vertex42 LLC. Free to Print.

School Calendar Template by Vertex42.com

February 9th- Heliacal rising of srt (Auset is the nTr.t)

February 19- Heliacal rising of sA sA srt (dwA mwt.f, qbH snw.f are the nTrw)

February 29th- Heliacal rising of Xr Xpd srt (qbH snw.f is the nTrw)

Henensu nKmt Spiritual Calendar

March 2016

Sunday	Monday	Tuesday	Wednesday	Thursday	Friday	Saturday
		1 Day 23 nai-wr Feast Day	**2** Day 24 Flaming nai Feast Day	**3** Day 25 Feast of smA	**4** Day 26 Feast of mAA.it.f	**5** Day 27 Feast of wnt abwy
6 Day 28 Feast of Khnum	**7** Day 29 Feast of wtt.tf.f	**8** Day 30 Feast of Heru nDt it.f	**9** Day 1 psDntyw (New Moon) Tehuti Feast Day	**10** Day 2 Feast of Heru Nej it.f	**11** Day 3 Osir Feast Day	**12** Day 4 Imsety Feast Day
13 Day 5 Hapi Feast DAY	**14** Day 6 dwA mwt.f Feast DAY	**15** Day 7 Qebehsenuef Feast Day	**16** Day 8 Msxt.f Feast Day	**17** Day 9 ir Dt.A.F Feast DAY	**18** Day 10 ir.m.f Ds.f Feast Day	**19** Day 11 nDt.r Feast Day
20 Day 12 nDt sS Feast Day	**21** Day 13 tknw Feast Day	**22** Day 14 Hm bA Feast Day	**23** Day 15 smdt (Full Moon) ir-m swAy Feast Day	**24** Day 16 Sdi.f mdw.f Feast Day	**25** Day 17 Heru wAD.f Feast Day	**26** Day 18 inH Feast Day
27 Day 19 Heru iwn mwt.f Fe...	**28** Day 20 wpw-wAt Feast Day	**29** Day 21 Anpu Feast Day	**30** Day 22 nai Feast Day	**31** Day 23 nai-wr Feast Day		

Important Reminders

March 10th – Heliacal rising of tpy a Axwy/ Axwy (sons of Heru?)

March 20th- Heliacal rising of bAwy (dwA mwt.f qbH snw.f are the nTrw)

March 30th- Heliacal rising of tpy bAwy/ xnt Hrw (Imsty, Hapi are the nTrw).

April 2016

Henensu nKmt Spiritual Calendar

Sunday	Monday	Tuesday	Wednesday	Thursday	Friday	Saturday
					1 Day 24 Flaming nai Feast Day	**2** Day 25 Feast of smA
3 Day 26 Feast of mAA.it.f	**4** Day 27 Feast of wnt sbwy	**5** Day 28 Feast of Khnum	**6** Day 29 Feast of Heru nDt it.f	**7** Day 1 psDntyw (New Moon) Tehuti Feast Day	**8** Day 2 Feast of Heru Nej it.f	**9** Day 3 Osir Feast Day
10 Day 4 Imsety Feast Day	**11** Day 5 Hapi Feast DAY	**12** Day 6 dwA mwt.f Feast DAY	**13** Day 7 Qebehsnuef Feast Day	**14** Day 8 Maa-it.f Feast Day	**15** Day 9 ir.Dt.f Feast DAY	**16** Day 10 ir.rn.f Ds.f Feast D
17 Day 11 nDt.r Feast Day	**18** Day 12 nDt s5 Feast Day	**19** Day 13 tknw Feast Day	**20** Day 14 Hm bA Feast Day	**21** Day 15 smdt (Full Moon) ir-m awAy Feast Day	**22** Day 16 Sdi.f mdw.f Feast Day	**23** Day 17 Heru wAD.f Feast
24 Day 18 iaH Feast Day	**25** Day 19 Heru iwn mwt.f Feast	**26** Day 20 wpw-wAt Feast Day	**27** Day 21 Anpu Feast Day	**28** Day 22 nai Feast Day	**29** Day 23 nai-wr Feast Day	**30** Day 24 Flaming nai Feast

Important Reminders

April 9th- Heliacal rising of Xntw Hrw (Heru is the nTr)

April 19th – Heliacal rising of Hr-ib xntw (Heru is the nTr)

April 29th – Heliacal rising of xmt Xrw (Heru is the nTr).

Henensu nKmt Spiritual Calendar

May 2016

Sunday	Monday	Tuesday	Wednesday	Thursday	Friday	Saturday
1 Day 25 Feast of smA	**2** Day 26 Feast of mAA it.f	**3** Day 27 Feast of wnt abwwy	**4** Day 28 Feast of Khnum	**5** Day 29 Feast of Heru nDt it.f	**6** Day 1 psDntyw (New Moon) Tehuti Feast Day	**7** Day 2 Feast of Heru Nej
8 Day 3 Osir Feast Day	**9** Day 4 Imsety Feast Day	**10** Day 5 Hapi Feast DAY	**11** Day 6 dwA mwt.f Feast DAY	**12** Day 7 Qebehsenuef Feast Day	**13** Day 8 Maa-it.f Feast Day	**14** Day 9 ir Dt.f Feast DAY
15 Day 10 ir m.f Dt.f Feast D	**16** Day 11 nDt.r Feast Day	**17** Day 12 nDt sS Feast Day	**18** Day 13 tknw Feast Day	**19** Day 14 Hm bA Feast Day	**20** Day 15 smdt (Full Moon) ir-m awAy Feast Day	**21** Day 16 Sdi.f mdw.f Feast
22 Day 17 Heru wAD.f Feast	**23** Day 18 iaH Feast Day	**24** Day 19 Heru iwn mwt.f Feast	**25** Day 20 wpw-wAt Feast Day	**26** Day 21 Anpu Feast Day	**27** Day 22 nai Feast Day	**28** Day 23 nai-wr Feast Day
29 Day 24 Flaming nai Feast	**30** Day 25 Feast of smA	**31** Day 26 Feast of mAA it.f	Important Reminders			

© 2013 Vertex42 LLC. Free to Print.   School Calendar Template by Vertex42.com

May 9th- qd (st-st Xt swwt mss is the nTr)

May 19th – Heliacal rising of sA sA qd (sons of Heru are the nTrw)

May 29th- Heliacal rising of art (Hapi is the nTr)

Henensu nKmt Spiritual Calendar

June 2016

Sunday	Monday	Tuesday	Wednesday	Thursday	Friday	Saturday
			1 Day 27 Feast of wnt sbwry	**2** Day 28 Feast of Khnum	**3** Day 29 Feast of wtt.tf.f	**4** Day 30 Feast of Heru nDt
5 Day 1 psDntyw (New Moon) Tehuti Feast Day	**6** Day 2 Feast of Heru Nej it.f	**7** Day 3 Osir Feast Day	**8** Day 4 Imsety Feast Day	**9** Day 5 Hapi Feast DAY	**10** Day 6 dwA mwt.f Feast DAY	**11** Day 7 Qebehsnuef Feast
12 Day 8 Mesxt.f Feast Day	**13** Day 9 ir DtA.f Feast DAY	**14** Day 10 ir.rn.f Ds.f Feast Day	**15** Day 11 nDt.r Feast Day	**16** Day 12 nDt tS Feast Day	**17** Day 13 tknw Feast Day	**18** Day 14 Hm bA Feast Day
19 Day 15 smdt (Full Moon) ir-m awAy Feast D	**20** Day 16 Sdi.f mdw.f Feast Day Heru wAD.f Feast Day	**21** Day 17	**22** Day 18 iaH Feast Day	**23** Day 19 Heru iwn mwt.f Feast	**24** Day 20 wpw-wAt Feast Day	**25** Day 21 Anpu Feast Day
26 Day 22 nai Feast Day	**27** Day 23 nai-wr Feast Day	**28** Day 24 Flaming nai Feast Day	**29** Day 25 Feast of smA	**30** Day 26 Feast of mAA it.f		

Important Reminders

© 2013 Vertex42 LLC. Free to Print.

School Calendar Template by Vertex42.com

June 8th- Heliacal rising of xAw/aryt (imsty is the nTr)

June 18th – Heliacal rising of rmn Hrw iwn saH (dwA mwt.f qbH snw.f are the nTrw)

June 28th Heliacal rising of msD saH/Ts arq (mAAt Heru, Heru is the nTr).

July 2016

Henensu nKmt Spiritual Calendar

Sunday	Monday	Tuesday	Wednesday	Thursday	Friday	Saturday
					1 Day 27 — Feast of wnt abwy	**2** Day 28 — Feast of Khnum
3 Day 25 — Feast of Heru nDt	**4** Day 1 — pzDntyw (New Moon) Tehuti Feast Day	**5** Day 2 — Feast of Heru Nej it.f	**6** Day 3 — Osir Feast Day	**7** Day 4 — Imsety Feast Day	**8** Day 5 — Hepi Feast DAY	**9** Day 6 — dwA mwt.f Feast D
10 Day 7 — Qebehsnuef Feast	**11** Day 8 — Msen it.f Feast Day	**12** Day 9 — ir DtA.f Feast DAY	**13** Day 10 — ir.m.f Ds.f Feast Day	**14** Day 11 — nDt.r Feast Day	**15** Day 12 — nDt iS Feast Day	**16** Day 13 — tknw Feast Day
17 Day 14 — Hm bA Feast Day	**18** Day 15 — smdt (Full Moon) ir-m swAy Feast Day	**19** Day 16 — Sdi.f mdw.f Feast Day	**20** Day 17 — Heru wAD.f Feast Day	**21** Day 18 — isH Feast Day	**22** Day 19 — Heru iwn mwt.f Feast Day	**23** Day 20 — wpw-wAt Feast Da
24 Day 21 — Anpu Feast Day	**25** Day 22 — nai Feast Day	**26** Day 23 — nai-wr Feast Day	**27** Day 24 — Flaming nai Feast Day	**28** Day 25 — Feast of smA	**29** Day 26 — Feast of mAA it.f	**30** Day 27 — Feast of wnt abwy
31 Day 28 — Feast of Khnum		Important Reminders				

July 8th- Heliacal rising of rmn Xr saH/waryt (mAAt Heru, Heru is the nTr)

July 18th – Heliacal rising of a saH/tpy a spdt (mAAt Heru, Heru is the nTr)

July 28th (?) –Heliacal rising of spdt (mAAt Heru, Auset is the nTr).

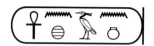

JOURNEY TO KMT

I must admit, prior to visiting Kmt I was under the impression that the place our Ancestors called Kmt no longer existed and the people who are there now were not related to the people that were there in Ancient times. I was completely under the thought that the Kmt no longer existed in that physical location, but what exists there now is the Arab Republic of Egypt, inhabited by people that migrated there during the country's long history of conquest and invasions, by European's and Arab peoples alike. While I always wanted to visit Kmt one day, as a result of the impression I was under, I was not in a hurry to get over there. Little did I know that this impression would soon be challenged.

It was in the month of August that I received a message one morning from my good brother Ra Meri consisting of what seemed like a joke to me. It said simply "Back a bag, we're going to Kmt in August." I thought to myself, "yea right." However, I should've better because he is a very serious guy :-). Anyway after finding out that he was serious, soon plans were made and tickets were bought. So now it went from me kind of wanting to go one day, to "I'm going to kmt..I mean the Arab's Republic of Egypt" in a month's time. All of this coming all of a sudden...seemingly out of the blue...but why?

From practicing the nkmt tradition, I can say that interacting with the nTrw and Jertiyu (Ancestors)

I have learned that nothing is random, coincidence, or just happened. So for this opportunity, this trip of a lifetime to present itself, there had to definitely be a reason. After putting in some work, performing divination, it became clear of a few things, namely that there were something that I needed to see and that there

616

were connections that needed to be made.

Upon arrival in Egypt I was greeted outside of the Airport by a man who would be our guide for our time in Cairo. When I saw this man I must say that I was not surprised because he looked like what I thought all "modern Egyptians" looked, like what many people think expect when encountering someone considered Arab or "Middle Eastern" and I was expecting to most of the people I encountered to resemble him. However, while many of the people that we encountered in Cairo did resemble this man, it is very interesting that none of them that we encountered considered themselves to be Arab, including our Guide in Cairo, and even hinted at some disdain towards Arab people. They considered themselves "Egyptian," and only a few verbally identified as Afrikan and expressing some sense of kinship with the greater Afrikan Continent.

Cairo was crazy! The traffic was hectic, almost lawless. On the way from the Airport it seemed as though the driver was going about a hundred miles per hour. I stole a glimpse at the speedometer and it read 140-150 Kph (Kilometers per hour), which converts to about 80-90 miles per hour. Everybody seemed to be driving this way. We were in a shuttle style bus/van and I was on the edge of my seat thinking to myself "this is different, and these folk are crazy." We appeared as though we would collide with other vehicles several times, but it never happened. People honked their horns but nobody got upset (it was more like look out I'm coming). Everyone seemed to be in a rush. This was the sense of the stay in Cairo, everyone is in a rush.

When we arrived at the hotel I met up with Ra Meri and the owner of the company we were doing the trip and we went over our Itinerary. Of course they hit us for extra money than what we agreed upon. Anyway our journey would begin tomorrow, and I was looking forward to it. I caught a glimpse of the silhouette of the pyramids of Khufu, Khafra, and Menkaura from the interstate, sitting as a commanding yet peaceful backdrop to what was otherwise a very hectic city.

The next morning we traveled to the Saqqara monuments. This was an Old Kingdom ground. As we made our way there we saw a lot of plush looking farm land, Date palms full of fruit everywhere we turned. It was very beautiful, so it came as somewhat of a surprise to hear from our guide that the people here there were very poor. I just don't get it. All of this land, this greenery? How?

When we arrived at the site we stopped at an entrance where there were many dogs gathered. Our guide informed us that whenever he comes he always brings food to those dogs, and I thought to myself, Whoa, Anpu still has these guys making offerings and they don't even know it! I mean here we are at the Entrance to the Saqqara Monuments, and here are the dogs, sacred to Anpu waiting at the gates, just as Anpu sits at the Gates of the Duat, and he must be offered to before one can enter.

Saqqara was once an entire city that served as a burial site. It was literally a "necropolis" or "city of the "dead" The name of the location comes from the nTr that was venerated there, Sukari (Seker) who is the Nisu(King) of the Spirit Realm

(Osir Resurrected) and actually nTr of Death itself. Everywhere we looked, for as far as our eyes could see we could see pyramids. The site was huge.

As we entered we passed through a hall of pylons and we marveled at the level of sophistication and design as this was supposed to be from the early formative years of the nKmt society. After passing through this hall I saw another Dog in the distance giving the impression as though it was there o lead the way. Anpu was very active throughout the entire stay in Kmt, so much so that I had to buy another statue for his shrine. He opened many doors for us, the ones we asked for and the ones we didn't know we wanted.

As we passed through the site, our guide would inform us on who the tombs belonged to. As he would call their names, I would walk slightly behind to pour libations to their kA. I did this throughout the entire trip, sharing the water that I had with the Ancestors, even though it was very hot.

This was my mode for most of the trip. I stayed quiet and a little behind so that I could offer prt xrw (Voice offerings/invocations) and libations to the Ancestors and nTrw.

At one point in the trip, our guide wanted to link with us on Facebook, and then after visiting my page he asked "All of your friends have the names of the Egyptian Gods! Why is that?" I just smiled.

Cairo was very hectic, and also dirty. We were moving so fast it was a little difficult to take things in or have a "moment." Also the hustlers were very aggressive in Cairo, which made it even more difficult to soak it all up. When we traveled to the Great Pyramid, we encountered some brother's, obvious Afrikans, which was exciting, that greeted us saying "Cousins!" I was very happy to see them initially, but then they tried to hustle us, saying that they were giving me some type of headdress as a gift because we are the same (black), but then asking me for some money for it and then when I gave it back they said they couldn't accept it because it was opened! This encounter rubbed me the wrong way.

We were greeted often as brother and cousin by the people we encountered some of them complexion, some of them much lighter. However, I couldn't help but wonder "am I your brother because we're folk or am I your brother because you're broke?" Egypt is doing very badly economic wise as Tourism is a very big pillar of the economy and it has been very slow because people are afraid to travel there since the revolution a few years ago. However, while there was a strong military presence in certain places, our overall experience was trouble free; we did not see any danger or unrest.

The financial difficulty that many of the people were experiencing there as a result of the fear of tourist to travel made me understand somewhat the reason why they were going so hard when they saw us, but for me this was my Hajj, our sacred pilgrimage to our Ancestral holy land and you are killing my vibe. Also, while these things may mean nothing more than economic opportunity to you, to use it is sacred and means the world.

618

Anyway, while in Cairo we visited the Mosque of Saladin, Ben Ezra Temple, and the Coptic Church community. It was very interesting to see that even at these sites, where their religions are totally anti Kmt, they still sold nKmt replica statures of the nTrw and jewelry outside the sites, even at the mosque! Again, am I brother because we folk, or am I brother because your broke?

One thing that I found fascinating at the Coptic Church we visited was that there were shrines around the church where people would light candles and make petitions to the saints that rested there. However, most fascinating was the fact that the actual bones of the saint were encased in the shrines, making the shrine also the tomb. This immediately recalled to my mind how our Ancestor's tombs in Kmt, doubled as their Ancestral Shrine, and how petitions were written in the forms of letters asking for their assistance. Such a practice still exists today throughout Afrika, and even in west, especially in New Orleans as is the case with the tomb of the Great and Famous Vodou Priestess Marie Laveau.

Things got a little intense for me when we visited the Cairo museum, especially in the room that housed the coffins of our ancestors. There was a lot of Shekhem (Power) in that room; it felt like waves were passing through me, I was having hot flashes and feelings of awe, sadness, anger, all at once. It was a little overwhelming, and I could not stay in there very long.

We passed through seeing many of the statues of our Ancestors, including the famous Jet Black Statue of Montu Hotep II. It was told to us by our guide that the reason why the statue was Jet Black, was because the artist was trying to pass it off as a better quality stone than what it actually was (Yea right!). However, later in the trip we would here from another guide in Aswan that Montu Hotep II was a Nubian and that is the reason for the statue's color.

One of the things that we found interesting was that fact that when we asked the guide where did the Ancients come from, his response was "the south." However, we would come to grasp the implications of this once we actually traveled south. Everything was south, we were told. We were interested in purchasing some jewelry and statues of the nTrw, and we were advised to wait until we traveled south.

We continued through the Museum, though we didn't stay too long for our guide seemed to be in a rush, which was the general pace of Cairo. We saw the world famous Exhibit of Tut Ankh Amun which took up the entire second floor. It was amazing. I saw some things there that I'd studied prior to coming to Kmt, things that contained inscriptions that we actually use in Henensu. One thing in particular was a Protection Hymn of Anpu.

There were many interesting statues in the Museum, however none more interesting than that of Akh n Yatin (Akhenaton). Where all of the Nisu Bity had statues that made them look very masculine and athletic, larger than life, Akh n Yatin's statue was the complete opposite, depicting him in a very feminine manner. I'll leave that right there for now.

There was a lot in the Museum and we didn't have enough time. We could've spent the day in the Old and Middle Kingdom exhibits alone. Also we were not allowed to bring our cameras into the Museum which made it even more difficult to bring back info from there to study later. Also the gift shop was closed. We were told that things were this way because of the revolution, in which the museum was ransacked. There was a very strong military presence at the museum, tanks and automatic weapons, armed guards, barbed wire fences, etc

The time was approaching for us to leave Cairo and Travel south to Luxor. However, before we did that we took a ride on the boat called felucca on the Nile. There was a brother from Aswan that took us out on the boat. He was about our complexion and as soon as he saw us he pointed at his arm and then ours to demonstrate kinship. This was the common response in Cairo when we encountered Afrikans that looked like us. However, I was expecting to see more of us once we got to Aswan, which was considered Nubia.

The following morning we caught a domestic flight to Luxor. We had been up the entire night and did not get any sleep because we had to leave for the airport at around 2 am, even though our flight wasn't until around 6 or 7 am. I thought either the traffic was that bad or it's just another example of the rushed vibe of Cairo.

Our flight to Luxor from Cairo was only about 45 minutes. I was able to drift off in that short while, and in that time I was shown a vision of the Temple of Luxor in its original state, with beautiful and brilliant colors, and standing before me with a big smile on her face was the nTr.t Het Heru. Besides the experience at the Museum with the coffins, this was the first "psychic" experience I'd had on the trip. I knew Luxor was going to be different, it was going to be special, and it was.

When we arrived in Luxor we were greeted at the Airport by a brother with a big beautiful smile on his face! We were very happy to see him and he seemed happy to see us. Like before he pointed at his arms to indicate that we were the same. Already the vibe in Luxor was different; there was certain serenity to it. Everyone was chill and laid back, which was a relief from the hustle and bustle we experienced in Cairo.

We arrived at our vehicle and there the driver was waiting for us. It was a brother, a tad darker than myself, and cool than a fan as we say. He kind of reminded me of the guys that played Carlton off of fresh prince.

Ra Meri asked the brother that met us in the airport, what the original "Egyptians" looked like, and his response was, with a smile on his face, "They looked like me," which meant they looked like us. We were loving these guys already, and then we stopped and the guy that picked us up from the airport got out of the car, and a another brother got in the car who would be our guide for the remainder of the trip, from Luxor down to Aswan. This guy was also a brother.

He told us that his mother was from Egypt, but his father was from Saudi Arabia, and he is very dark. I found that very interesting in that this brother here was a tad bit lighter than me, yet his father from Saudi Arabia was very dark, which flies in the facade of what most people believe an Arab person to look like. Later in the trip I would hear this brother say "I'm black and I'm proud."

This guide was very kind and respectful, and he did not rush. We liked his rhythm very much. He always gave us time to do our own thing, to explore the sites and (re)discover things on our own. This allowed us to get great footage and documentation to bring back to the family and study over time.

He (Our Guide) said that he was from Luxor, and that his grandfather's house for a long time was literally in the outer courts of the Luxor Temple. He knew his way around very well, and it appeared as though the people working at the sites all knew and respected him. Yet he was a very humble brother and he quickly recognized and respected our Knowledge.

While in Luxor we visited the Two Gigantic statues of Amen Hotep I (so-called Colossi of Memnon). It is said that these particular statues were once used for divination purposes, as the Great Ancestor Amenhotep I oracle was very famous.

Next we visited the Temple of the Queen Hatshepsut, which was truly magnificent. In its original stat I am convinced that the architecture here would put anything in Washington D.C. to shame. Our guide gave us a brief overview of the history of the site, and then he let us go into the site alone, which we really appreciated because it gave us the time to really soak it all in.

This temple told the story of the Great Ancestor Queen Hatshepsut's divine birth as a daughter of the nTr Imun Ra. Beautiful statues of her were everywhere. Also within the temple are chapels dedicated to Het Heru and Anpu. Anpu's chapel was very special as the color on much of the depictions was still intact. After the temple of Hatshepsut we traveled to the Valley of the Kings. This site was a pivotal moment in our trip as nothing could prepare us for this experience.

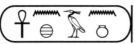

The Valley of the Kings is a site that houses countless tombs of the Nisu Bity, tombs constructed deep into mountains. It was very hot by this time, and this was my very first time entering into a cave. We visited the tombs of Ramses III, Ramses VI, and

As we entered into these tombs, it was though we were entering into an oven. The heat was very thick. Also these tombs were built deep. In some instances it seemed as though some of them pushed 100 meters while others exceeded that. In some cases it was a long journey down and even longer journey back up, but what we witnessed in these tombs made every step of the way worth it.

Within the cave upon the walls was depicted in full vivid color, a text scholars refer to as "The Book of Gates." This text depicts the journey of Ra through the spiritual Realm or Duat, and all of the various forces and spiritual agencies he would encounter along his way. One of the very first things that I noticed quickly as we entered into the tombs was a text called "Litany of Ra," which is a text that we utilize in our daily rituals in Henensu. This was very special as we were able to see something that we learned so much from and had bad become an integral part of our

daily lives. However, what made these tombs even more special was the way in which they were designed.

The integration and interfacing between the spiritual and the physical realms is in my opinion, nowhere more explicit than in the Valley of the Kings. With the Book of Gates depicted upon the walls, with each step you took deeper into the tomb, you were actually traveling deeper into the Duat, witnessing Ra's journey scene by scene, ultimately until you reached the end of the tomb where the coffin of the Ancestor resided. This tomb took you on a journey!

After the Valley of the Kings we visited the Karnak Temple and the Temple of Luxor, both dedicated to the nTr Imun, his wife Mwt, and son Khonsu. These temples were invaluable in understanding the Kemetic Ritual format and motif, and also the festivals that took place annually that people came from far and wide to participate. The depiction of these festivals on the temple walls further bear witness to the Afrikan reality that were the Kemetic people, as this very same ritual and festival format is still practiced today in West Africa among the Yoruba (such as the Osun festival) and the people of Benin and the Vodou Festival. The temples in each city fleshed out this relationship more and more and are very rewarding to the worker in the reconstruction of the Kemetic tradition (Ritual and Festival organization).

An important thing to note is the way in which the Temples were constructed. It is said that the Hwt nTr or House of the nTr (also called holies of holies) was the very first part of the temple constructed, every other part being built around it. In this method of construction, it is my contention; the Ancestors were expressing a most critical aspect of their spiritual worldview.

In the Book of Knowing the Evolutions of Ra and Overthrowing Owapep, Ra states that prior to beginning the work of creation, "he found no place wherein he could stand." This being the case it is said he then "laid a foundation in mAa(t), and created all forms." As the Inner Sanctuary or Hwt nTr is the place where the "Image" of the nTr stood in the temple, as the first part or foundation of the temple, this symbolically represents the very same foundation laid by Ra in which he was able to stand and then "create all forms." As a priest would enter into the temple passing by each layer, they were symbolically penetrating the deepest mysteries, ultimately culminating in reaching the point of beholding the face of nTr.

As it has been said that these temples were also made in a way, to resemble the Human Body, it is also being expressed in its construction, the fact that at the very core or foundation of man's being, the Inner most Sanctuary, stands nTr. Walking deeper into the temple represented the inner journey of the initiate, penetrating the deepest mysteries of the Self which culminates in the realization/revelation of the nTr residing deep within as the Self. Even the organization of the priesthood into classes, in which only certain levels of priests were allowed to enter into the inner most parts of the temple, while priests of a lower rank were not allowed enter to beyond the Outer Sanctuary and Hypostyle Hall, speaks to this reality.

The difference between a wAb and a Hm nTr, is that the wAb was going through a process of purification, which could take an indefinite amount of time, while a Hm nTr has reached the point (after serving as a wAb) in which he or she can be declared "purified" (through "doing mAat"), granting them access to the inner most mysteries of the Divine. In this way, the temple and it's organization not only expresses to us the Ancestor's spiritual worldview regarding the intrinsic reality and presence of nTr, but also how this relates to the person, and the process through which this knowledge and communion could be attained or granted.

After visiting the temples, we traveled by boat across the Nile to visit a place called "Banana Beach." This was not a part of our original Itinerary, but it was an intuitive recommendation made be our guide, which turned out to be a good move. This was a great experience to see some live examples of Self Sustainability which was very important for us as Nation Building is a chief priority of Henensu. The people that live at Banana beach grow their own food; everything from dates, watermelon, hibiscus, Egyptian Mint, mandarin oranges, corn, sugar cane, etc. They built their own homes using Adobe, and generated their own electricity from the Nile. We sat down and talked for a while, sipping on some fresh iced Hibiscus Tea, eating real fresh watermelon, and had a bunch of Bananas.

After this our guide took us to a local bookstore in Luxor. Ra Meri wanted to see if he could find some literature on the Kemetic Tradition written by the locals. However, it was here that I was able to get my hands on a Sistrum which was one of the things that I was determined to acquire during this trip for our Het Heru Shrine, and to use at all of our shrines during rituals. I was also given a booklet that teaches how to use the sistrum as a gift for my purchase. This made Luxor all the more special. However, this was just the icing on an already sweet cake as we encountered nothing but Afrikans in Luxor, and this would be our

630

experience for the remainder of the trip as we took a cruise to travel south.

From Luxor we made our way down the Nile to our next destination, Behudet (Edfu), to visit the temple of Heru Behudet. As we traveled down the Nile, beautiful Afrikan people waved at us from the shores. The scene was so remarkable; I can honestly say that I was completely present.

Another thing that was quite fascinating was the fact that the cities and the people there still expressed the temperament of the nTr that resided there. Luxor for instance, was the domain of Imun, and it definitely reflected the peace and relaxed nature of the nTr. However, we would find no greater example of the bAw of the nTr coming forth from the city and its people, than in Behudet (Edfu). We arrived in Behudet around 11pm, and were scheduled to visit the temple the following morning. However the energy of the city manifested in the people there made itself known immediately. As soon as our ship docked we heard people screaming, music with loud bass pumping, folks riding around the in cars and trucks, hanging out of their cars waving and screaming. Behudet was off the chain! Reminded me of New Orleans, especially around the French Quarter. Like New Orleans, Behudet expressed both the spirit of party and good times, and also the fighting spirit. This is because Behudet is the home of Heru Behudet, and his family which includes the nTr.t Het Heru.

We traveled to the temple by horse and carriage (another very New Orleans French Quarter resemblance), which in spite of my being from New Orleans, this was my first time on a horse and carriage. Also I had on my ritual whites for this particular temple, so I wasn't all the way thrilled about getting on this particular ride. However, it wasn't that bad :-). We made it to the entrance of the temple grounds which had a pretty big market. The people there were more assertive but also friendly, which spoke to the nature of the city. However, I was very focused, as I looked forward to this temple as I am a son of Heru Behudet. Also there was some specific information that I was looking to acquire from the

631

temple walls, things that I had been studying but unable to get in totality. As we passed through the marketplace, some of the brothers who had bazaars asked us to come to see them after we left the temple, and handed us their card. I told them if we had time I would definitely come to see him. On to the temple we went.

The temple of Heru Behudet is argued to be the most well preserved temple in all of Kmt, which is another interesting fact as Heru Behudet is a nTr of protection. This temple was amazing, and it commanded our respect and honor. Unlike other temples, we were able to fully honor Heru Behudet, including a full prostration before his kAri. This was a very powerful experience for both myself and Ra Meri, as he is also a son of Heru Behudet. Nobody bothered us or tried to hustle us here. However, as we left, the heat definitely turned up.

Our ship was leaving for Kom Ombo soon, and I had yet to find the inscriptions I was looking for. So I began to run the entire temple until I found them. I ended up finding them at the very last minute. We then rushed back to the ship and unfortunately did not have time to visit the brother's bazaar. He was less than understanding. In fact he was quite upset, and demanded I give him his card back. The energy of the temple insisted that we get down to business and be mission oriented. Needless to say mission accomplished.

The next temple we visited was the temple of Heru War and Subik at Kom Omobo. This temple was much less preserved than the temple of Heru Behudet. In fact, it was almost completely destroyed. However, the spirit of the nTrw still came through there. It is interesting that this temple was set up as a double Temple, one side dedicated to Heru War, the other side dedicated to Subik. As Subik is one of those nTrw that is both positive and negative, and is sometimes the enemy of Heru War, it was destined to be a conflicting vibration in the temple.

I went into what was left of the kAri of Subik and attempted to pour

libations and apparently out of nowhere there a guy appeared and asked me not to do so. Then he began to watch and follow us around the temple. This of course made it a little difficult for us to honor the nTrw the way we wanted to as we did at Heru Behudet's temple, but we did what we could. Still funny thing is that the Hymns to Subik found in that particular temple speak to Subik in his adversarial or rebellious forms. Also, Subik being ever the trickster, at one point Ra Meri began to praise his camera for taking great shots and lasting so long, and even before he could finish doing so it cut off!!! We laughed because we knew Subik was in the house. Afterwards we went into the Subik museum which housed the mummified crocodiles that had served as the sacred animals of Subik historically. There was a lot of Shekhem in this place, and we were also able to get some great shots there.

After leaving Kom Ombo, we made our way to Aswan, to the Island of Philae to visit the temple of Auset. While in Aswan we also visited the botanical gardens, the High Dam, the unfinished obelisk, and a Nubian Village. Our very first stop was the High Dam. The story behind the High Dam was quite sad, and resonated with me greatly as a native of New Orleans. It is said that the Dam was built in between 1960 and 1970 with the assistance of Russia. Its construction assisted in preventing the temples from being flooded out while there are many points speaking to its benefits and detriments, one of the things that cannot be ignored is the horrific impact it has had on the Nubian people and their civilization. The fact is" The Aswan Dam created a 340-mile long lake which flooded 39 Nubian villages and submerged innumerable priceless artifacts." As our guide expressed it to us, an entire civilization has been lost and the Nubian people are still very upset about it to this day. As a result of this the Nubian people have been displaced and are suffering very badly. This resonated with me tremendously as it recalled the experience of my people in Hurricane Katrina as the city was flooded after the levees broke (or were blown up), and the black communities were flooded out. To this very day, many of the people that were displaced due to this catastrophic event have not returned.

From the High Dam we traveled to the Temple of Auset. This temple

634

was on an island and was actually moved to that island from another island by UNESCO to avoid flooding. This temple was extremely beautiful as it was surrounded by plush greenery, indicating life. This temple was actually dedicated to a form of Auset that was joined with Het Heru, Auset-Het-heru. The vibe there was very peaceful. However, one of the things that stuck out like a sore thumb was the fact that the early Christians vandalized the temple, attempting to strike out the depictions of the nTrw, and even attempted to convert the sanctuary into a Christian chapel. The Muslims would in turn vandalize the Christian imagery. In spite of this, we were able to put in some good work with Auset in her shrines, especially Ra Meri who is a priest of Auset.

After visiting the Temple of Auset, we then went to see the "Unfinished Obelisk," which is the name given to an Obelisk that was broke before it could be completed. The actual site was a stone quarry where our Ancestors gathered the stones that they would use to build their great monuments. This was a particular treat as we got to actually walk up this mountain and place out feet and hands where our Ancestors worked. Also this blows any foolish theory of "Alien" builders of the pyramids out of the water!

We had one last stop to make on our trip, and that was to a Nubian Village. This village was very beautiful. The people there are renowned for their beautiful art, and resourcefulness. The people there were also very pleasant and hospitable. We were invited into the home of a friend our guide. We first entered into a room where our host kept crocodiles. We then entered into a part of the brother's home that he was using as a restaurant. We were given Egyptian tea, Egyptian coffee, Hibiscus, and snacks such as sugar cane syrup and pita and halawa (a candy made from ground sesame) which we were told that the latter is a dish that the women fix for their husbands to "get ready." Needless to say, my wife has fixed this dish several times since my return. :-)

After enjoying the snacks we then went to explore the Village. As we walked we saw several shops full of beautiful and interesting products,

yet the Village itself was mainly empty save use. Because of this the shops were greatly unattended. However, as we continued to walk, we encountered two shops where there were some brothers sitting. Needless to say they were extremely happy to see us and even more eager to make a sell. Who knows the last time "tourists" visited the village. We bought a few things, a purse for the Mrs., a doll for the baby girl, some nTrw statues, etc. We sat and talked with brothers for a minute. Ra Meri took the opportunity to ask the brother who had sold us the statues about the Ancient Kemetic People. The brother got real quiet, and then began to convey to us the fact that they, the Nubians, were the Ancient Kemetic people. His demeanor seemed as if he was divulging a very dangerous secret. However, this was a fact that even our guide in Cairo, as well as our guide current guide expressed to us when asked where the Ancients came from, they all replied "The South." In other words, when we asked the guide in Cairo (which is in Northern Egypt) where the Ancient Kemetic people came from, he replied the south. When we asked our guide in Luxor the same question in response was also "The South." Now mind you, Luxor is already considered Southern (Upper) Egypt! So one of the things we realized is that it is common knowledge among the Egyptian people themselves today, as it pertains to the Afrikan Origins of the Ancients. This fact would further be solidified when we made our way to the airport in Aswan, and the brother that escorted us there, a Nubian Guide, declared to us the sameness of the "Egyptians" and Nubians, as well as the Nubian Origins of the Ancient Kemetic People, going as far as to give exact location of the origin of Nisu Narmer, and also informing us regarding the fact that the oldest mummy found is that of a young Nubian boy. While the information did not surprise us, the confidence and "matter of factness" with which the brother conveyed his knowledge was literally mind blowing. In actuality, he was quite befuddled by the fact that no one else said these things to us outright, specifically the fact that the Nubian and Egyptian people were the same. In other words, the people that live there today are very clear as to who the ancients were, it is Afrikans in the Diaspora that are confused, and White scholars who are either deceptive or in utter denial.

After this trip, we left with a solidified sense of clarity and purpose. We were definitely empowered, and have decided to bring other Afrikans back every year that they may too be inspired. I can honestly say that I when I left for the trip initially, I was expecting to find the Arab Republic of Egypt, but what I found indeed, was Kmt, Afrikan Kmt.

A child who listens is a follower of Heru. It goes well with her when she listens. When she is old and reaches veneration, may she speak likewise to her children, renewing the teaching of her Father. Every man teaches what he does. May she speak to the children, so that they may speak to their children. Set an example, do not give offense. If Maat stands firm, your children live! ~Pitah Hotep~

APPENDIX A

FUNDAMENTALS OF MEDITATION

Many people have tried meditating at some point or another. However, the majority of them felt that they were unsuccessful in their attempt. When asked what the major obstacles they encounter in attempting to meditate are, most people give a unanimous "I couldn't clear my mind." Because of this many people never attempt to meditate again, and dismiss the practice as either too difficult, or it simply does not work. The problem however is not that the person is too stressed out, nor is the problem with meditation itself. The issue lies in the technique that the person is using, whether it is their own or what they've been taught.

It must be known that there is an exact science to successfully meditating. The science is so exact that one can successfully meditate at every single attempt if the proper techniques are followed.

Meditation is a spiritual practice. By spiritual, I don't mean religious but a practice of the Spirit. Spirit is the animating (animal) force, the life force. Etymologically speaking, the word *spirit* derives from the old French term *espirit*, which means "*animating or vital principle in man and animals*", which comes from the Latin *spiritus* meaning "*soul, courage, vigor, breath,*" Which derives from the Greek *spirare* which

means *"to breathe"*. Taking the above into account grants us invaluable insight into the nature of spirit. As the animating or vital principle in man and animals, it is the life force (*espirit*). The life force manifests as soul (spiritus). Soul derives from the Old English term *sawol*, meaning *"the emotional part of a person"*. E-motion literally means to move (motion) out (e). All of the above terms are related and find root in *Spirare* meaning to *breathe* or *breath*. So inherent here is a relationship between the life force, the emotions, and the breath. This is why when the life force is depleted there is a lack of motivation, or desire to move out, emotional instability etc. This is also why emotional instability, especially anger, and excitement, manifests in a change in breathing, and depletion in life force and health. So why does meditation work? Because control of the breath is ultimately control of the life-force, which is control over the emotions. Meditation and deep-breathing exercises have been shown to increase the life force, improve health, stabilize the emotions, calm the mind, and increase intelligence. Look at the relationship between re*spir*ation and in*spir*ation. If you need to be inspired, work on your breathing.

The key to meditation is the breath and the key to the breath is in the posture.

Posture is Key!
Find a comfortable seat that you can sit in with your back straight!

Focal point is the small of your back. Curve the lower back slightly as if you were bending backwards. This should be done very gently; <u>curving forward like the letter C is improper posture and causes the breath to be shallow, which will make you ill.</u> **Always breathe from the lower abdomen, always breathing through the nostrils. <u>Never</u>** breathe from the chest or throat. You will notice that if your posture is correct, the breathing will automatically flow from you lower abs. <u>Always breathe softly; you should not hear your breathing.</u> **On the In-breath (inhale) your stomach should be gently pushed out** as to make a slight pot belly. **On the out-breath (exhale) the stomach should be gently pulled in.**

640

Palms should rest down on the lap.

Head should be slightly bowed, eyes closed. Feet should be flat on the floor.

Shoulders must always be relaxed. Mouth should be closed with tongue resting at the gum line where the teeth meet.

Wait a few hours after meals to assure that your food has properly digested prior to meditation.

If you are adept in meditation and have learned other techniques that work for you, please feel free to use them.

After the posture, the next most important thing that we must focus on is the breathing. As stated in the instructions on posture, we should always breathe from the lower abdomen, and through the nostrils. The breathing should be so soft that you should not hear yourself breathing. There is a specific pattern to the breathing that will facilitate the meditative trance. The breathing should be about 4 seconds on the in breath, 6 seconds on the out breath, and a slight pause or hold for about 1 second afterwards. The count should be natural, and not too fast. It should look something like this:

In 2 3 4…Out 2 3 4 5 6 (short hold 1 sec) and repeat.

Remember that you should be breathing deeply, slowly, and softly. You should not hear yourself breathing (I know I said that already it's important!). Focus on your breath and with each exhale focus on releasing any tension or stress that you may be feeling. After a while you should begin to feel signs of going into meditative trance. The signs can be different from person to person. Your body may begin to feel extremely light, as if you are floating, or you may feel very relaxed and heavy like lead. You may begin to see colors or lights flash. You may begin to feel a warm tingling sensation, or you may not feel anything at all. The most important thing that you must feel is **relaxation**. This relaxation will allow you to focus on your meditation objectives. Sometimes however, it is good to just breathe and relax and focus solely on the peace. This can be done at anytime throughout the day just to calm and balance the spirit.

Once you have entered into trance or a heightened state of relaxation, you should begin to work on your assignment. This can take anywhere from 15 to 30 minutes or even hours. The length of time is totally up to you as long as you feel good. At any time that you begin to feel discomfort please cease from doing the meditation, take time to gather yourself, double check the instructions to make sure that you are following them properly, and make any adjustments that you need to.

If there are any further questions or concerns on the meditation assignments or if you need any assistance, please contact me. ~ Aankh Benu~

nTrw Correspodence With Other

Afrikan Deities

Kemet	Yoruba	Igbo	Fon/Ewe
Nu/Amun/Neith	Olodurmare	Chukwu	Nana Baluku
Ra	Olorun	Anyanwu	Mawu Lisa
Osir/Ptah	Obatala	Chi/Ikenga	Da/Dan
Het Heru	Osun	Ala (Anyanwu as Eye of the Sun)	Ayida-Wedo
Auset	Yemoja	Ala	Mami Wata
Heru Behudet	Ogun	Ogbunabali (?) (Ofo Na Ogu)	Gu
Shu/Sutesh	Esu	Ekwesu	Legba
Tehuti	Orunmila/Ifa	Agwu Nsi	Gbadu/Fa
Heru (Son of Auset)	Shango	Amadioha	Xevioso
Sekhmet	Oya	Oye	Adañe Kuruñe

Kemet	Dogon	Dagara	Akan
Nu/Amun/Neith	Amma	Yielbongura	Nyame
Ra	Nommo Dié	Namwin	Nyankopon
Osir/Ptah	Nommo Semi	Tigen	Awusi
Het Heru	Nommo Sizu		Afi
Auset		Man	Adwoa/Awo
Heru Behudet		Kyere	bena
Heru Son of Auset	Nommo Semi		Yaw
Sutesh	Ogo/Yurugu	Dawera (Hyena)	Awuku/Ananse
Tehuti	**Nommo Titiyayne**	**San**	**Brekyirihunuade**

Kemet	Zulu	Haiti
Nu/Amun/Neith		Bondye
Ra	Unkulunkulu/mvelinchanti	Damballah
Osir	AMADLOZI	Damballah/Ghedi
Het Heru	MBABA MWANA WARESA	Erzuli Freda
Auset	MAMLAMBO	Erzuli Dantor/Erzuli Mapiangue
Heru Behudet	Somandla	Ogou
Heru Sa Auset Sa Osir	Simakadza	
Min	Mlentngamune	

What IS It?

Repat Nation is an organization that promotes and facilitates holistic repatriation to Afrika via the Arts.

By Holistic Repatriation, we mean the spiritual, cultural, political, economic, and physical return of Afrikans (continental and diasporian) to the Mother land

The abandonment of our Ancestral ways for the religious ideologies and culture of foreign colonizers have led to the degeneration of Afrikan Self Confidence and stagnation in Afrikan progression. Therefore spiritual and cultural repatriation to Indigenous Afrikan Traditions is called for to restore a strong sense of Self and Pride in our Afrikan Identity.

Once a strong sense of Self and pride in our Afrikan Identity is restored, there must be political repatriation. As it stands today, the political climate of Afrika as a collective is one in which the agenda and interest of foreign entities takes precedence over the interest and needs of Afrikan people. This has led to corruption; in which governments creates policies and manages resources in a way that benefits the colonizers and their own selfish interest, instead of the collective welfare of Afrikan people. This situation must be reversed, in which the political interest of Afrika and its people comes first.

646

Once a strong sense of Self pride in our Afrikan Identity has been restored and the political climate has been corrected, economic repatriation must follow. As it stands today, Afrikans (continental and diasporian) are operating in a European economic paradigm, resulting in Afrikan economic impotence. Afrika, being the wealthiest continent in natural resources, has become the most dependent continent due to the adoption of the western culture of consumerism and the abandonment of Afrikan self reliance and production. Through economic repatriation, Afrikans can restore the Self sustaining sciences of Agriculture (food and textiles), infrastructure, and essential product manufacture. Furthermore, producing Afrikan, Selling Afrikan, Buying Afrikan, and investing Afrikan will help to empower the Afrikan economy. Finally, through utilizing traditional Afrikan economic models (susu etc) we can move away from inefficient European individualism and capitalism, into an Afrikan communal based economy.

The most efficient and withstanding method of accomplishing the above goals is through the physical repatriation of Afrikans (expatriates and diasporians) back to Afrika. Recently, Afrika has been reaching out and opening its doors to both expatriates as well as Afrikans of the Diaspora to return home and assist in rebuilding the continent through offering incentives such as affordable/free land, business opportunities, dual citizenship, and repatriate readjustment and support programs. Through pooling our respective knowledge bases, skill sets, and perspectives, continental and diasporian Afrikans will be able to fill a void created by colonization and slavery, ultimately healing and strengthening a once crippled people.

The purpose of Repat Nation is to inform and inspire Afrikans to work together to accomplish the above objectives, through the use of Artistic Expression. For Afrikans, art is the creative expression and manifestation of the soul, and historically has served as a storehouse of our culture, as well as a catalyst for change. We intend to inspire Afrikan unity, Afrikan awareness, Afrikan dignity, and Afrikan power. Through visual, literary, musical, and performing arts.

Repat Nation is the Situation!

Now Available

THE BLACK BYBLOS

KHU KHEM

Tune in to Khu Khem Radio
Sundays on Talkshoe.com

Also Available on iTunes

Khu Khem Kemet Tour 2016

"Exploring the Kemetic Tradition in it's Afrikan Context"

Tour Date: July 6th-19th, 2016

<u>12 Days and 12 Nights Tour</u> of our Ancestor's Sacred Sites, and Land, and an Exploration of the Kemetic Spiritual Tradition.

<u>Tour Includes:</u>
- International Roundtrip Airfare from New York

- Domestic Airfare in Egypt (From Cairo to Luxor/ From Aswan to Cairo)

- 2 Nights Stay 5-Star Hotel in Luxor

- 2 Nights Stay 5-Star Hotel in Aswan, Nubia

- 3 Night Stay 5-Star Hotel in Cairo

- 5 Day 5-Star Cruise Down Nile From Luxor to Aswan, Nubia.

- Two Meals Daily (Breakfast and Dinner) Three meals on Cruise

- Ground Transportation

- Admission to All Sites (Temples, Museums, Monuments, etc)

- Experienced Tour Guide

- Live Lectures by Aankh Benu, Asar Imhotep, Ra, and other special guest lecture

<u>Tour Does NOT Include:</u>
- Airfare to and From New York (On the way back)

- Passport

- Tourist Visa (Available at Airport in Egypt for about 25.00 USD)

- Insurance

- Beverages

- Personal Expenses (Spending Money)
- Tips

Itinerary

Day 1-

Evening Departure From New York (U.S. Group Members)

Day 2-

Arrival in Kemet (Egypt) Check in to Hotel in Cairo. Group Orientation and Introduction (Meet and Greet). Dinner

Day 3-

Breakfast. Visit the Saqqara Monuments (Old Kingdom), The Step Pyramid of Nisu Djoser Built by his Vizier, the Great Ancestor Imhotep. Visit Giza, the Great Pyramid of Khufu, the Pyramid of Ka-ef-ra, and The Pyramid of Men-kau-Ra. Visit Heru-m-Akhet (The Sphinx). Visit the Egyptian Museum. Return to Hotel. Dinner.

Day 4-

Early Morning Flight to Luxor Check in to Hotel in Luxor. Breakfast.Visit the Magnificent Temple of Queen Hatshepsut, The Valley of Kings, The Valley of Queens, See the Gigantic Twin Statues of Nisu (King) Amen-Hotep III ("The Colossi of Memnon".)Return to Hotel.

Day 5-

Breakfast.Morning Drive to Abydos and Dendera to visit the Temples of Seti I (The Osirian Temple), and the Temple of Het Heru. Return to Luxor Dinner

Day 6-

Breakfast.Checkout Hotel. Visit the Temple of Luxor and The Temple of Karnak. Both of these Temple are in honor and service of the nTrw Amun-Ra, Mut, and Khonsu, and also contain shrines for several other nTrw.Visit the Luxor Museum. CHECK INTO CRUISE. Dinner

Day 7-

Breakfast.The Banana Beach, Alabaster Shop.Cruise disembarks in the evening for Edfu. Lunch and Dinner on ship

Day 8-

Breakfast.

Visit the Temple of Heru Behudet in Edfu, the Great nTr of War. Return to the Cruise Ship and Continue to Sail South into Nubyit (Kom Ombo)and Visit the Double Temple of Heru War and Sobek. While there we will also Visit the Sobek (Crocodile) Museum, which features the mummified Crocodiles that served as the Sacred Animals of the nTr Sobek. Return to Ship. Dinner. Continue to Sail South into Aswan, Nubia.

Lunch and Dinner

Day 9-

Breakfast. Arrive in Aswan, Nubia. Visit the Nubian Museum, The "Unfinished Obelisk" (Stone Quarry), The Botanical Gardens, Visit (by boat) the Beautiful Temple of Auset at the Island of Philae. Lunch and Dinner on Ship.

Day 10-

Breakfast.Drive South to Abu Simbel, Nubia, to Visit the Temples of Ra-Herukhuti and Het Heru. Built By Nisu Rameses II. The Temple of Het Heru was Built By Rameses in honor of his Great Royal Wife Nefertari, a Nubian Woman. Return to Ship in Aswan

Day 11-

Free Day (Enjoy Beautiful Aswan!)Check into hotel in Nubian Village. Sitdown with Nubian Elder. Dinner at Hotel

Day 12-

Stay at Nubian Village, explore the life and culture of the

Nubians.

Day 13-

Early flight to Cairo. Check into Hotel. Breakfast. Dinner. Prepare to Kemet

Day 14-

Return Home

Total Cost: $3100.00 (All Included)

$2100.00* (Does Not Include Airfare)

Payment Plan Available

*For International Group Members Leaving from Other Than the U.S.

INCENTIVE***

We want to let everyone that intends to go or is interested in going on the Khu Khem Kemet Tour know about our referral/organizer's incentive.

We will give you 10% of the fee amount for each person that you refer (that registers), or bring with you. This money may be used to go towards your trip, or you can put it in your pocket.

For example: If you want your entire trip paid for, you must refer or bring 10 people. If you bring 5 people, half of the cost of your trip is paid for (or the money goes in your pocket). Regardless of how many you refer or bring, we will give you 10%

When signing up the person you referred must put your name on the registration form (there is a field dedicated for this purpose), and then you are good to go!

Please review our packages and registration form for more details.

GLOSSARY OF TERMS

nTr- Nature, the intelligence and Power that is the Universe, reality, and existence itself; the Divine Being.

nTrw- Divine Forces of nature; myriad forces through which the one Divine force manifests itself and carries out its will; the forces that are responsible for all happenings.

Sakhar nTri - Divine Plan, the grand scheme and evolutionary scheme in the universe

Nkmt- Kemetic, Ancient Egyptian

Whm anx- repeating life; the Kemetic equivalent of Reincarnation

Ba- the aspect of our Being that links us as individuals to the All, and consist of Shekhem and Yakhu. However, it is a things own individuated portion of Shekhem and Yakhu; The nTr within; inner ancestral spirit, conscience.

Ka- The Ka is the body that makes each and everything unique as an individual. It is each things unique persona and quality.

Ib-corresponds to the Will, and ones "Conscious Mind." It is the Mental Body through which one manages their attention, their thoughts and their decisions

Sxm- Power; the Essence, source, and energy of existence

Kmtyw- Ancient Egyptians

RmT- Man

Maat- The evolutionary force in the universe; Divine/Cosmic Law; Order, the force that perpetuates, sustains, and optimizes life.

Shai- Destiny; the plan and curriculum for an individual's life that will lead to the further progression of their Ba.

Ren- Name; renu- names.

ABOUT THE AUTHOR

Aankhu Menu Saa Benu (Aankh Benu) is the Chief Priest of Henensu. It was in the hopes of helping African people overcome limitations and achieve their goals via the community that inspired the establishment of the Henensu international community. A gifted teacher, and leader, Aankh Benu was ordained a Priest through the Ancient Kemetic Culture Institute. Today he is an Adept Diviner (Spiritual Reader) author, teacher, Radio Show Host, and lecturer on Afrikan Spirituality (Kemetic), metaphysics, the occult, and divination. He is an advocate for Pan-Africanism and self-sustainability for Afrikan people. Through the application of the teachings of our ancestors, Aankh Benu has helped many achieve harmonious relationships with nTr that balance every individual's needs.

Born and raised in New Orleans, Lousiana. He is the husband of the Hamat Nisu Warit(s) (Great Royal Wives/Queen Mothers) of Henensu; Meri Netert Skherrenut Benu and Warit Rekhiyit Benu and the father of his daughters Khemhlring Benu and Waniset Shukara Benu. This is his second book.

Made in the USA
Middletown, DE
16 August 2023

36304787R10369